Walking in
IRELAND

Sandra Bardwell
Helen Fairbairn
Gareth McCormack

LONELY PLANET PUBLICATIONS
Melbourne • Oakland • London • Paris

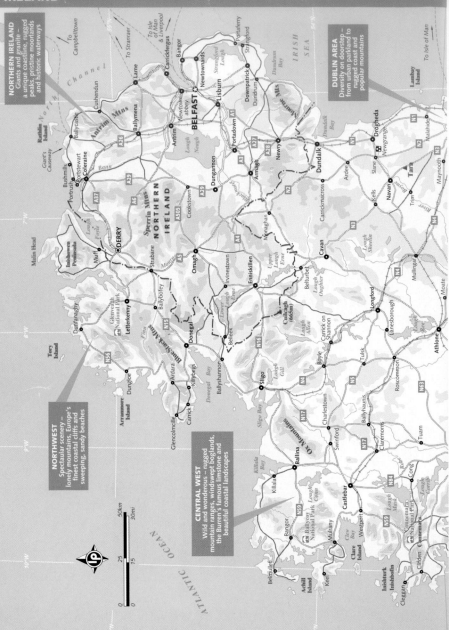

NORTHERN IRELAND
Giants and granite –
a unique coastline, rugged
peaks, pristine moorlands
and historic waterways

DUBLIN AREA
Diversity on doorstep –
from urban parkland to
rugged coast and
popular mountains

NORTHWEST
Spectacular scenery –
lonely mountains, Europe's
finest coastal cliffs and
sweeping, sandy beaches

CENTRAL WEST
Wild and wonderous – rugged
mountain ranges, windswept boglands,
the Burren's famous limestone and
beautiful coastal landscapes

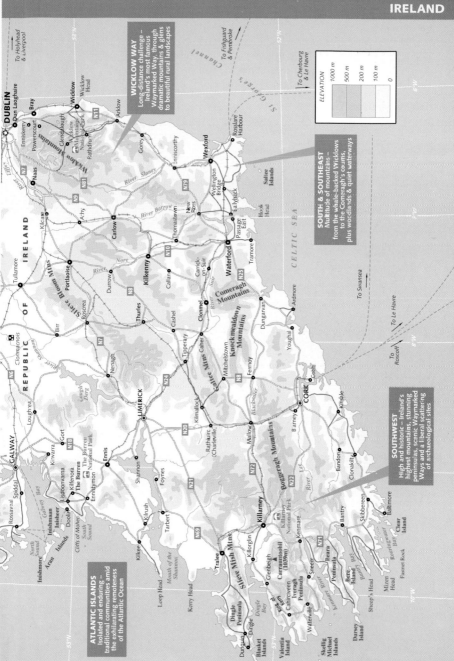

WICKLOW WAY
Long-distance challenge –
Ireland's most famous
Waymarked Way, through
dramatic mountains & glens
to beautiful rural landscapes

SOUTH & SOUTHEAST
Multitude of mountains –
from the whale-backed Wicklows
to the Comeragh's coums,
plus woodlands & quiet waterways

SOUTHWEST
High and historic – Ireland's
highest mountains; stunning
peninsulas; scenic Waymarked
Ways and a liberal scattering
of archaeological sites

ATLANTIC ISLANDS
Isolated and enduring –
traditional communities amid
the exhilarating remoteness
of the Atlantic Ocean

ELEVATION
1000 m
500 m
200 m
100 m
0

To Holyhead
& Liverpool

To Fishguard
& Pembroke

To Cherbourg
& Le Havre

To Swansea

To Le Havre

To Roscoff

St George's Channel

CELTIC SEA

REPUBLIC OF IRELAND

DUBLIN
Dun Laoghaire
Bray
Enniskerry
Powerscourt
Wicklow Mountains
Glendalough
Wicklow Mountains Nat. Park
Rathdrum
Naas
Kilcar
Athy
Carlow
Gorey
Enniscorthy
Wexford
Rosslare Harbour
Wicklow
Arklow
Wicklow Head
Saltee Islands
Hook Head
Wellington Bridge
Ballyhack
Passage East
Waterford
Tramore
New Ross
Thomastown
Kilkenny
Callan
Carrick-on-Suir
Clonmel
Cahir
Comeragh Mountains
Knockmealdown Mountains
Dungarvan
Ardmore
Youghal
Cobh
CORK
Kinsale
Bandon
Clonakilty
Skibbereen
Baltimore
Clear Island
Fastnet Rock
Mizen Head
Sheep's Head
Bantry
Kenmare
Killarney
Killarney National Park
Mallow
Fermoy
Mitchelstown
Kilmallock
Tipperary
Cashel
Thurles
Durrow
Portlaoise
Roscrea
Birr
Tullamore
Clonmacnois
Slieve Bloom Mtns
Nenagh
Lough Derg
LIMERICK
Shannon
Foynes
Tarbert
Ennis
Shannon
GALWAY
Spiddal
Rossaveal
Galway Bay
Kinvarra
Gort
Lisdoonvarna
Doolin
Kilfenora
The Burren
Ennistymon
The Burren National Park
Cliffs of Moher
Kilkee
Kilrush
Loop Head
Kerry Head
Mouth of the Shannon
Tralee
Dingle
Dunquin
Blasket Islands
Dingle Peninsula
Slieve Mish Mtns
Castlemaine
Killorglin
Glenbeigh
Cahirciveen
Valentia Island
Skellig Michael Islands
Waterville
Iveragh Peninsula
Carrauntoohil (1039m)
Sneem
Kenmare River
Beara Peninsula
Castletownbere
Dursey Island
Kenmare Bay
Bantry Bay
Caher Mtns/Galtee Mtns/Galtee Mtns
Knockmealdown Mountains
Boggeragh Mountains
Barna
Charleville
Rathluirc
Inishmore
Inishmaan
Inisheer
Aran Islands
North Sound
South Sound
Inishbofin
River Slaney
River Barrow
Nore
River Suir
River Blackwater
River Lee
River Liffey
River Shannon
River Nore

Walking in Ireland
2nd edition – May 2003
First published – July 1999

Published by
Lonely Planet Publications Pty Ltd ABN 36 005 607 983
90 Maribyrnong St, Footscray, Victoria 3011, Australia

Lonely Planet offices
Australia Locked Bag 1, Footscray, Victoria 3011
USA 150 Linden St, Oakland, CA 94607
UK 10a Spring Place, London NW5 3BH
France 1 rue du Dahomey, 75011 Paris

Photographs
Many of the images in this guide are available for licensing from
Lonely Planet Images.
w www.lonelyplanetimages.com

Main front cover photograph
Keem Strand, Achill Island, County Mayo (Richard Cummins)

Small front cover photograph
Stone marker with the familiar Waymarked Way logo (Tony Wheeler)

ISBN 1 86450 323 8

Printed by SNP SPrint (M) Sdn Bhd
Printed in Malaysia

Contents

TRAVEL FACTS

GLOSSARY

GAZETTEER

INDEX

METRIC CONVERSION

The Walks	Duration	Difficulty	Season
DUBLIN AREA			
Phoenix Park & River Liffey	3½–4 hours	easy	Mar–Oct
Howth Peninsula	4½–5 hours	easy–moderate	Mar–Oct
Bray Head	4–4¼ hours	easy–moderate	Mar–Oct
Great Sugar Loaf	2¼–2½ hours	moderate	Apr–June
Maulin & Djouce	5–5½ hours	moderate	Mar–Oct
WICKLOW WAY			
Wicklow Way	5 days	moderate	Apr–Sept
SOUTH & SOUTH EAST			
Camaderry	4¾–5¼ hours	moderate	Apr–Sept
Mullacor	4–4½ hours	moderate	Apr–Sept
Lugnaquilla	5½–6 hours	moderate	Apr–Sept
Blackstairs Mountain	5¼–5¾ hours	moderate	Mar–Oct
Barrow Way Highlight	5–5½ hours	easy–moderate	Mar–Oct
Knockanaffrin	4–4½ hours	moderate	Mar–Oct
Nire Valley Coums	5–5½ hours	moderate	Mar–Oct
Mahon Valley	4½–5 hours	moderate	Mar–Oct
Seefin Circuit	4½–5 hours	moderate	Mar–Oct
Eastern Knockmealdowns	6½–7 hours	moderate–demanding	Apr–Sept
Western Knockmealdowns	4–4¼ hours	moderate	Apr–Sept
Galtymore via Clydagh Horseshoe	5¾–6¼ hours	moderate–demanding	Apr–Sept
Lough Muskry	4–4½ hours	moderate	Apr–Sept
SOUTHWEST			
Brandon Mountain	8–9 hours	demanding	all year
Dingle Way Highlight	3 days	easy–moderate	all year
Coomloughra Horseshoe	6–7 hours	demanding	May–Oct
Reeks Ridge	6–7 hours	demanding	May–Oct
Purple Mountain & Gap of Dunloe	6–7 hours	moderate–demanding	all year
Muckross	3½–4 hours	easy	all year
Torc Mountain	3½ hours	easy–moderate	all year
Kerry Way Highlight	2 days	moderate	all year
Mullaghanattin	4½–5 hours	moderate–demanding	all year
Derrynane Coastal Circuit	3 hours	easy	all year
Hungry Hill	4–5 hours	moderate–demanding	all year
Eskatarriff	5½–6 hours	moderate–demanding	all year
Beara Way Highlight	2 days	moderate	all year
Gougane Barra	5 hours	moderate–demanding	all year
Sheep's Head Way Highlight	6–7 hours	easy–moderate	all year
Knockomagh Woods & Lough Hyne	3–4 hours	easy	all year
ATLANTIC ISLANDS			
Rathlin Island	4–5 hours	easy	May–July
Tory Island	3½–4 hours	easy	May–Oct
Arranmore Island	5–5½ hours	moderate	all year
Clare Island	5–5½ hours	moderate	May–Sept
Inishmore	6–6½ hours	moderate	Apr–Oct

The Walks *(continued)*	Duration	Difficulty	Season
Inisheer	5 hours	moderate	Apr–Oct
Great Blasket Island	3½ hours	easy–moderate	Apr–Sept
Clear Island	5 hours	easy–moderate	all year
CENTRAL WEST			
Glencar	5 hours	moderate	all year
Glenade	4 hours	moderate	all year
Dún Caocháin Cliffs	5 hours	moderate	all year
Achill Head & Croaghaun	4–4½ hours	moderate–demanding	all year
Slievemore	4 hours	moderate	all year
Corraun Hill	5–5½ hours	moderate	all year
Corranbinna	5½–6 hours	moderate–demanding	all year
Croagh Patrick	4–4½ hours	moderate–demanding	all year
Mweelrea	6½–7 hours	demanding	all year
Killary Harbour	3½–4 hours	easy	all year
Doughruagh & Benchoona	3–3½ hours	moderate	all year
Central Maumturks	5–5½ hours	moderate–demanding	all year
Glencoaghan Horseshoe	7–7½ hours	demanding	all year
Errisbeg	2–3 hours	easy–moderate	all year
Black Head	5 hours	moderate	all year
NORTHWEST			
Crockalough Cliffs	4–4½ hours	easy–moderate	all year
Raghtin More	3½–4 hours	moderate	all year
Binnion	3–4 hours	easy–moderate	all year
Ards	2–2½ hours	easy	all year
Horn Head	5½–6 hours	moderate	all year
Muckish	3–3½ hours	moderate	all year
The Aghlas	4 hours	moderate–demanding	all year
Errigal	3½ hours	moderate	all year
Glenveagh National Park	6½–7 hours	moderate–demanding	all year
Slieve Snaght & the Poisoned Glen	6½–7 hours	demanding	all year
Slieve League & Slievetooey	2 days	moderate–demanding	all year
Blue Stack Circuit	6–7 hours	moderate–demanding	all year
NORTHERN IRELAND			
North Down Coastal Path	4½–5 hours	easy–moderate	Mar–Oct
River Lagan	4¼–4¾ hours	easy	Mar–Oct
Causeway Coast Way Highlight	5–5½ hours	moderate	Apr–Oct
Moyle Way	9–9½ hours	moderate–demanding	May–Sept
Glenariff Forest Park	2¼–2½ hours	easy–moderate	Apr–Oct
Garron Plateau	3¾–4¼ hours	moderate	May–Sept
Newry Canal Way	6½–7 hours	moderate	May–Sept
Mournes Trail	9–10 hours	demanding	May–Sept
Annalong Horseshoe	7–7½ hours	demanding	May–Sept
Slieve Donard	4½–5 hours	moderate	May–Sept
Brandy Pad	5½–6 hours	moderate	May–Sept
Sawel & Dart	5–5½ hours	moderate	May–Sept
Gortin Glen	5½–6 hours	moderate	May–Sept
Florence Court & Cuilcagh	7¼–7¾ hours	moderate–demanding	May–Sept
Cuilcagh Mountain Park	5–5½ hours	moderate	May–Sept

8 Table of Maps

The Maps

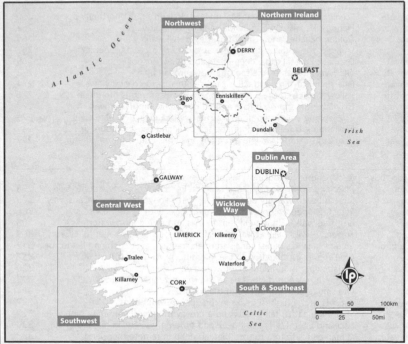

The Authors

Sandra Bardwell

After graduating with a thesis on the history of national parks in Victoria (Australia), Sandra worked as an archivist and then as a historian for the National Parks Service. She has been a dedicated walker since joining a bushwalking club eons ago, and became well known through a Melbourne newspaper column and as the author of several guidebooks on the subject. Since 1989 Sandra and her husband Hal have lived in the Highlands of Scotland, in a village near Loch Ness. For several years she worked as a monument warden for Historic Scotland, until Lonely Planet took over her life. She has walked extensively in Australia and Britain, and for Lonely Planet in Italy, Ireland, France, Scotland and even more extensively in Australia.

Helen Fairbairn

Helen is a writer specialising in adventure travel. Born in Suffolk (England), she now resides in Northern Ireland. Several years spent abroad, an MA in International Development and her current work all feed an ongoing interest in the wider impact of travel. A dedicated outdoor enthusiast, Helen is most at home in wild, mountainous places. This is her fifth walking guide for Lonely Planet.

Gareth McCormack

Gareth is a writer and photographer based in Ireland, and a contributor to several outdoor and adventure travel magazines. He has travelled and climbed extensively in Asia, Australia, New Zealand and North America. Other titles he has co-authored for Lonely Planet include *Walking in Italy*, *Walking in France*, *Walking in Scotland*, *Walking in Australia* and *Hiking in the Rocky Mountains*.

From the Authors

Sandra Bardwell Working with the Lonely Planet team – Sally to start with, then Andrew, Eoin, Jennifer and Karen – has been stimulating and rewarding. It would be hard for an author to find better colleagues than Gareth and Helen.

In Ireland, grateful thanks for the more than usually generous Irish hospitality to Mr and Mrs Farrell in Newry; Frances McDermott, Holywood; Anne McKee, Annalong; Breda Moran, Clogheen; Donal O'Loan, Glenariff and Clare Trouton, Portadown. Special thanks to Brian Roberts at Graiguenamanagh for introducing me to the Blackstairs. Professional advice and information provided by Beatrice Kelly, Heritage Ireland, Jacquetta Megarry, Colum McDaid of Lagan Valley Regional Park and Richard Watson of Marble Arch Caves was much appreciated. And the greatest debt of gratitude of all is owed to Hal, for companionship and unflagging support.

Helen Fairbairn & Gareth McCormack At Lonely Planet, guidance was gratefully received from Sally Dillon and Andrew Bain. Special thanks to Sandra – it was fun to hear about the France disaster first-hand. Cheers to all those who provided company on various routes: Gary and Eadaoin (despite the orange tent), Cait (cover-girl extraordinaire), John (for Rathlin and for Crete), Diane and Dermot (for braving the insults), Dave and Dee (for Slieve League and body board performances), Sarah (great bog acrobatics and midge sufferance) and the Clare Island dog (most faithful mountain companion ever). Finally a big 'well done' to Emily and Tracey who spent the summer of 2002 walking the west coast from Belfast to Cork – your achievement puts ours in perspective.

This Book

Seduced by the Emerald Isle's many charms, the authors responsible for this edition of *Walking in Ireland* bring a wealth of experience and enthusiasm. Coordinating author Sandra Bardwell wrote the introductory, Dublin Area, Wicklow Way, South & Southeast, Northern Ireland and Waymarked Ways chapters. Helen Fairbairn and Gareth McCormack wrote the Southwest, Atlantic Islands, Central West and Northwest chapters. Some material from the 1st edition of *Walking in Ireland*, by Sandra Bardwell, Pat Levy and Gareth McCormack, as well as the 5th edition of Lonely Planet's *Ireland*, was used in this book.

From the Publisher

At Lonely Planet's Melbourne base the coordinating editor was Jennifer Garrett and the coordinating cartographer was Karen Fry. Assisting editors were David Andrew, Nick Tapp, Sally Dillon, William Gourlay, Anne Mulvaney and Nicola Wells. Assisting cartographers were Helen Rowley and Andrew Smith. The colour pages were put together by John Shippick and the layout designer was Sonya Brooke. The cover was designed by Anika Roojun (UK office). Illustrations were selected by Pepi Bluck and the images assembled by LPI. The project was managed through production by Eoin Dunlevy and Bridget Blair, and overseeing the entire process were commissioning editor Andrew Bain and series publishing manager Lindsay Brown. All are now off to the pub for a well-deserved pint.

Thanks

Many thanks to the travellers who used the last edition and wrote to us with helpful hints, advice and interesting anecdotes:

Franck Asselman, Thom Bassett, Betheny Gross, Nancy Harrar, Richard Radcliffe, Sandra Van Tweel

Walk Descriptions

This book contains 51 walk descriptions ranging from day trips to a 30-day walk, plus suggestions for side trips and alternative routes. Each walk description has a brief introduction outlining the natural and cultural features you may encounter, plus information to help you plan your walk – transport options, level of difficulty, time frame and any permits required.

Day walks are often circular and are located in areas of uncommon beauty. Multiday walks include information on camp sites, *refugios* (mountain huts or refuges), hostels or other accommodation and where you can obtain water and supplies.

Times & Distances

These are provided only as a guide. Times are based on actual walking time and do not include stops for snacks, taking photographs, rests or side trips. Be sure to factor these in when planning your walk. Distances are provided but should be read in conjunction with altitudes. Significant elevation changes can make a greater difference to your walking time than lateral distance. In most cases, the daily stages can be varied.

Level of Difficulty

Grading systems are always arbitrary. However, having an indication of the grade may help you choose between walks. Our authors use the following grading guidelines:

Easy – a walk on flat terrain or with minor elevation changes usually over short distances on well-travelled routes with no navigational difficulties.
Moderate – a walk with challenging terrain, often involving longer distances and steep climbs.
Demanding – a walk with long daily distances and difficult terrain with significant elevation changes; may involve challenging route-finding and high-altitude or glacier travel.

True Left & True Right

The terms 'true left' and 'true right', used to describe the bank of a stream or river, sometimes throw readers. The 'true left bank' simply means the left bank as you look downstream.

Maps

Our maps are based on the best available references, often combined with GPS data collected in the field. They are intended to show the general route of the walk and should be used in conjunction with maps suggested in the walk description.

Maps may contain contours or ridge lines in addition to major watercourses, depending on the available information. These features build a three-dimensional picture of the terrain, allowing you to determine when the trail climbs and descends. Altitudes of major peaks and passes complete the picture by providing the actual extent of the elevation changes.

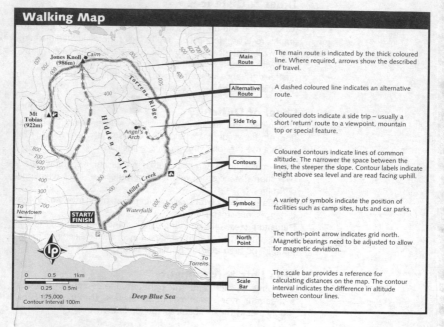

Walking Map

Main Route — The main route is indicated by the thick coloured line. Where required, arrows show the described of travel.

Alternative Route — A dashed coloured line indicates an alternative route.

Side Trip — Coloured dots indicate a side trip – usually a short 'return' route to a viewpoint, mountain top or special feature.

Contours — Coloured contours indicate lines of common altitude. The narrower the space between the lines, the steeper the slope. Contour labels indicate height above sea level and are read facing uphill.

Symbols — A variety of symbols indicate the position of facilities such as camp sites, huts and car parks.

North Point — The north-point arrow indicates grid north. Magnetic bearings need to be adjusted to allow for magnetic deviation.

Scale Bar — The scale bar provides a reference for calculating distances on the map. The contour interval indicates the difference in altitude between contour lines.

Route Finding

While accurate, our maps are not perfect. Inaccuracies in altitudes are commonly caused by air-temperature anomalies. Natural features such as river confluences and mountain peaks are in their true position, but the location of villages and trails may not always be so. This could be because a village is spread over a hillside, or the size of the map does not allow for detail of the trail's twists and turns. However, by using several basic route-finding techniques, you will have few problems following our descriptions:

1. Always be aware of whether the trail should be climbing or descending.
2. Check the north-point arrow on the map and determine the general direction of the trail.
3. Time your progress over a known distance and calculate the speed at which you travel in the given terrain. You can then determine with reasonable accuracy how far you have travelled.
4. Watch the path – look for boot prints and other signs of previous passage.

Map Legend

BOUNDARIES
International
Regional
Disputed

HYDROGRAPHY
Coastline
River, Creek
River Flats
Lake
Glacier
Canal
Spring
Waterfall
Swamp

CAPITAL .... National Capital
CAPITAL .... Regional Capital
CITY .... City
Town .... Town
Village .... Village
Farm .... Settlement

Hut
Camp Site
Lookout
Place to Eat
Point of Interest
Place to Stay
Shelter

ROUTES & TRANSPORT
Freeway
Highway
Main Road
Secondary Road
One-Way Road
Unsealed Major Road
Unsealed Minor Road
4WD Track
Lane
Ferry Route

Tunnel
Train Route & Station
Railway Tunnel
Chair Lift/Ski Lift
Described Walk
Alternative Route
Side Trip
Walking Track
Undefined Track
Walk Number & Direction of Walk (one way; both ways)

AREA FEATURES
Park (Regional Maps)
Park (Walk Maps)
Beach
Urban Area

MAP SYMBOLS
Airport/Airfield
Bridge
Castle
Cathedral/Church
Cave
Cliff or Escarpment
Contour
Gate
Hospital
Lighthouse
Mine
Monument
Mountain or Hill
Museum

National Park
Parking
Pass/Saddle
Petrol or Gas Station
Post Office
Pub
Ruin
Ski Fields
Spot Height
Stately Home
Telephone
Toilet
Tourist Information
Trigonometric Point

Note: not all symbols displayed above appear in this book

Foreword

ABOUT LONELY PLANET GUIDEBOOKS

The story begins with a classic travel adventure: Tony and Maureen Wheeler's 1972 journey across Europe and Asia to Australia. There was no useful information about the overland trail then, so Tony and Maureen published the first Lonely Planet guidebook to meet a growing need.

From a kitchen table, Lonely Planet has grown to become the largest independent travel publisher in the world, with offices in Melbourne (Australia), Oakland (USA), London (UK) and Paris (France).

Today Lonely Planet guidebooks cover the globe. There is an ever-growing list of books and information in a variety of media. Some things haven't changed. The main aim is still to make it possible for adventurous travellers to get out there – to explore and better understand the world.

At Lonely Planet we believe travellers can make a positive contribution to the countries they visit – if they respect their host communities and spend their money wisely. Since 1986 a percentage of the income from each book has been donated to aid projects and human rights campaigns, and, more recently, to wildlife conservation.

Although inclusion in a guidebook usually implies a recommendation we cannot list every good place. Exclusion does not necessarily imply criticism. In fact there are a number of reasons why we might exclude a place – sometimes it is simply inappropriate to encourage an influx of travellers.

UPDATES & READER FEEDBACK

Things change – prices go up, schedules change, good places go bad and bad places go bankrupt. Nothing stays the same. So, if you find things better or worse, recently opened or long-since closed, please tell us and help make the next edition even more accurate and useful.

Lonely Planet thoroughly updates each guidebook as often as possible – usually every two years, although for some destinations the gap can be longer. Between editions, up-to-date information is available in our free, monthly email bulletin *Comet* (ⓦ www.lonelyplanet.com/newsletters). You can also check out the *Thorn Tree* bulletin board and *Postcards* section of our website, which carry unverified, but fascinating, reports from travellers.

Tell us about it! We genuinely value your feedback. A well-travelled team at Lonely Planet reads and acknowledges every email and letter we receive and ensures that every morsel of information finds its way to the relevant authors, editors and cartographers.

Everyone who writes to us will find their name listed in the next edition of the appropriate guidebook. The very best contributions will be rewarded with a free guidebook.

We may edit, reproduce and incorporate your comments in Lonely Planet products such as guidebooks, websites and digital products, so let us know if you don't want your comments reproduced or your name acknowledged.

How to contact Lonely Planet:
Online: ⓔ talk2us@lonelyplanet.com.au, ⓦ www.lonelyplanet.com
Australia: Locked Bag 1, Footscray, Victoria 3011
UK: 10a Spring Place, London NW5 3BH
USA: 150 Linden St, Oakland, CA 94607

Introduction

You have been in Ireland for barely a week and you bump into the first of many people who are visiting the country for the third, fourth or eighth time. If the meeting is during a spell of dire weather, or after you have had your first close encounter with a peat bog, you might wonder, 'What on earth brings these people back for more?' One of the reasons people return again and again is Ireland's astounding diversity.

There is everything from the rolling Wicklow Mountains, the rugged summits of the Mournes and MacGillycuddy's Reeks, and the spiky summits of Connemara, to the sandy beaches of the Dingle Peninsula, the rocky coasts of the Aran Islands and Antrim, the wild peat-bog moorlands, the dry limestone pavements in the Burren and many peaceful waterways.

It's not only the landscape that is varied; Ireland's weather – that unavoidable bane or blessing – often goes through five seasons in one day. However, enduring the elements has its compensations in a welcoming B&B or a warm village pub, rarely far from the end of a walk.

The aim of this guide, which details 85 walks and outlines many more, is to help you explore Ireland's remarkable range of walking areas. The described walks include everything from a few hours to a few days, and are in both Northern Ireland and the Republic.

Ireland's finest treasure is its western coastline, stretching from the southwest peninsulas to north Antrim, with few equals in grandeur and extent in western Europe. The numerous mountains might not be very high (only a dozen or so rise above 900m) but they are extremely scenic, and the panoramic views from their summits convey a great sense of spaciousness in this relatively small island. The Atlantic islands exude a sense of remoteness and timelessness, which is only matched elsewhere in the small, virtually unspoiled national parks. At the opposite end of the scale, bustling Dublin and Belfast and their hinterlands lend themselves to exploration on foot.

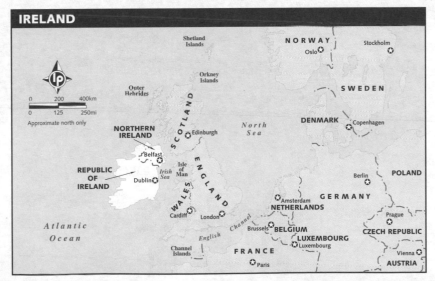

In many places the past is never far away: there are prehistoric tombs and forts, relics from early Christian times when European scholars and pilgrims travelled to Ireland; and the canals in the North and South helped to launch the industrial revolution from the late 18th century.

Thousands of kilometres of Waymarked Ways have been developed across the length and breadth of the island. Some of these walking routes along paths, tracks and minor roads offer extremely attractive and interesting excursions. This book includes highlights from these ways and a complete guide to the Wicklow Way.

This book also takes you to many places that are second to none among their peers – things are rarely done by halves in Ireland. The canals are part of Europe's largest system of inland waterways, Achill Island has Europe's highest sea cliffs, Dublin's Phoenix Park is the largest enclosed urban park in Europe, the Burren has Europe's greatest collection of wildflowers, and the Giant's Causeway is Ireland's first World Heritage site.

Another of the captivating features of walking in Ireland is the way in which it takes you close to the people. The small population and the innate friendliness of the Irish people ensure that some of your most memorable experiences are the chance conversations with locals, which can quickly develop into profound philosophical debates. And then there are walking festivals, an Irish institution and a lively blend of walking, Irish culture and hospitality. Joining in a festival is a sure way of gaining rewarding insights into a society that at times is infuriating and deeply puzzling and at others endearing, but always imbued with infectious enthusiasm and optimism.

Facts about Ireland

HISTORY

If a single word can sum up the history of Ireland, then 'turbulent' is a strong contender. Migration and invasions have both moulded the landscape and people of Ireland. Some knowledge of the country's history can help to illuminate current events and explain how the regions through which you pass came to be as they are, especially areas which have suffered severe depopulation. The following brief outline of significant events can be embellished by a more detailed account in Lonely Planet's *Ireland* and *Dublin* guides.

8000 BC – Ireland's first settlers, Mesolithic hunter-gatherers, arrive

4000 BC – farming begins at the dawn of the Neolithic period

2500 BC – the Bronze Age begins; stone circles are built

500 BC – start of the Iron Age; ring forts are constructed

300 BC – Celtic people begin arriving from eastern Europe

AD 432 – St Patrick begins converting the Irish to Christianity

546 – St Colm Cille (Columba) founds Derry

795 – Vikings land on the east coast and later begin settling Ireland

841 – Dublin founded

1014 – Vikings defeated at Battle of Clontarf; many remain in Ireland

1169 – conquest of Ireland by Normans (from France) begins; Ireland's first castle, Carrickfergus, built on Belfast Lough

1175 – Irish kings submit to English king Henry II under Treaty of Windsor

1297 – first Irish parliament meets in Dublin

1366 – Statutes of Kilkenny passed to protect Anglo-Irish settlers from assimilation

1534 – Henry VIII of England crushes a rebellion; Irish estates given to English settlers

1541 – Irish parliament declares Henry VIII king of Ireland

1557 – English settlers 'planted' in Counties Laois and Offaly, displacing Irish landowners

1571 – Irish language appears in print for the first time

1607 – 'Flight of the Earls', last of the Irish chiefs, from Donegal; their estates taken over by English king

1608 – Bushmills distillery (now the world's oldest) established in Antrim

1610 – Protestants from England and Scotland imported to settle expropriated Irish property, beginning the Plantation of Ulster

1649 – Oliver Cromwell, England's ruler, lays waste throughout Ireland

1652 – population of Ireland stands at about 500,000

1653 – forfeited lands occupied by Cromwell's supporters; Catholic Church suppressed

1689 – Siege of Derry broken by forces sent by Protestant English king William of Orange

1690 – English Protestants led by William of Orange defeat Irish Catholics under James II at Battle of the Boyne

1691 – first harsh anti-Catholic law passed by English rulers

1740 – disastrous famines wreak havoc

1778 – Irish patriots campaign for independence from Britain; Catholics regain some civil rights

1795 – Protestant Orange Society, later renamed Orange Order, founded

1798 – United Irishmen lead rebellion against English rule; English prevail at battles in North and South

1800 – Britain and Ireland merged politically; Irish parliament dissolved; Irish representatives sit in House of Commons; population of Ireland is between 4.5 and five million

1816 & 1822 – famine and typhus devastate the country

1831 – world's first scheme for nationwide primary schooling introduced

1834 – first railway in Ireland opened, from Dublin to Kingstown (Dun Laoghaire)

1841 – population of Ireland stands at around eight million

1845 – potato harvest fails; successive failures until 1851 cause mass starvation (the Great Famine); two million people die or leave Ireland

1851 – population of Ireland down to 6.5 million

1858 – Irish Republican Brotherhood established in Dublin to fight for independence; Fenian Brotherhood formed following year in New York, with same aim

1861 – population declines to 5.7 million

1879 – Irish National Land League formed to win lower rents and better working conditions; economic depression sets in after three years of failed harvests

1881 – population stands at 5.17 million; tenants given fair rents and secure tenure

1885 – anti-independence Ulster Unionist Party founded

1886 – Gladstone's first home rule bill defeated

1893 – Gaelic League formed, partly to campaign for teaching of Irish in schools

1901 – population of Ireland stands at 4.45 million

1907 – Sinn Fein founded, to win political and economic independence

1913 – Ulster Volunteer Force formed to fight against independence; Irish Volunteers established to fight for independence

1914 – WWI breaks out; Home Rule Act, including provision for Ulster counties to be excluded from independent Ireland, suspended for duration of the war

1916 – Easter Rising by Irish Volunteers and Irish Citizens' Army quelled by British forces; upsurge in popular support after 15 leaders executed

1918 – Sinn Fein wins majority of Irish seats in last all-Ireland elections

1919 – Sinn Fein declares Ireland independent and convenes first Dáil Éireann (Irish assembly); Irish Republican Army (IRA) emerges from Irish Volunteers

1920 – Anglo-Irish war breaks out

1921 – Anglo-Irish treaty signed: 26 counties (Irish Free State/Eire/South), option of separation for six mainly Protestant counties in the North

1922 – civil war erupts between pro- and anti-treaty forces in Eire; former prevail the following year

1926 – population stands at 2.97 million (Eire), 1.25 million (North)

1932 – Ireland's first national park, Killarney, established

1937 – new Irish constitution adopted; sovereignty over the six northern counties claimed

1939 – Ireland declares neutrality for duration of WWII

1948 – Eire becomes Republic of Ireland; leaves British Commonwealth the following year and joins new Council of Europe with nine other states

1950 – Ian Paisley forms Free Presbyterian Church in Northern Ireland

1951 – censuses taken: 2.96 million in the Republic, 1.37 million in the North

1955 – Ireland joins the United Nations

1956 – IRA's six-year campaign in the North begins

1957 – measures to boost the economy of Ireland introduced

1969 – riots break out in Derry and Belfast

1971 – decimal currency introduced in North and South

1972 – 'Bloody Sunday' in Derry – civilians shot by paratroopers; Britain imposes direct rule on Northern Ireland; Ireland and UK join European Economic Community

1973 – Northern Ireland Convention elected; dissolved following year

1978 – Irish currency (punt) introduced to replace sterling

1979 – first Irish representatives take seats in European parliament

1980s – intermittent violence on both sides of the border

1990 – Mary Robinson elected first woman president of the Republic

1991 – censuses reveal 3.52 million in the Republic, 1.57 million in the North

1994 – IRA ceasefire begins

1996 – IRA ceasefire ends; worst rioting in 15 years in the North; Irish economy growing at record rate

1997 – IRA resumes ceasefire; 1400th anniversary of death of St Colm Cille celebrated; Mary McAleese elected president

1998 – Good Friday Agreement on constitutional settlement of North's future accepted in referendums in North and South; Irish Constitution amended; new Northern Ireland Assembly meets in September; huge increase in inward investment in the North

1999 – peace process jeopardised by differences about decommissioning of terrorist weapons and release of terrorist prisoners from Northern Ireland gaols

2000 – Northern Ireland Executive suspended for four months; economic problems in the Republic

2001 – outbreak of foot and mouth disease in England causes major disruption throughout Ireland; Republic rejects Nice Treaty regarding enlargement of the EU

2002 – euro replaces punt as Republic's currency; Fianna Fail returns to power in the Republic's elections, in which Sinn Fein and the Greens increase their representation; Northern Ireland struggles to maintain political stability amid sectarian violence and political faction-fighting; Northern Ireland Executive suspended in October

History of Walking

For centuries people have walked through the Irish countryside for reasons many and varied: in search of work, to herd stock, and for supplies and social get-togethers. Pilgrimages to sites of great religious significance, notably Croagh Patrick in County Mayo and Glendalough in the heart of the Wicklow Mountains, have always been made on foot.

Recreational walking is, however, a relatively recent phenomenon, as it has become affordable for more people and as car ownership has become common, bringing once inaccessible areas within easy reach. By the time the Mountaineering Council of Ireland was founded in 1971, several clubs were well established, including the Holiday Fellowship Walking Club (1930), the Irish Mountaineering Club (1948), the Tralee Mountaineering Club (1954) and the North West Mountaineering Club (1955).

Both the 1960s and 1970s were eventful decades: Tiglin (now called the National Adventure Centre), which offers training in outdoor activities such as walking and climbing, was being developed, and the Irish Mountain Rescue Association, covering both North and South, was set up. The appointment of the Long Distance Walking Routes Committee in 1978 was soon followed by the opening of the Wicklow Way, Ireland's first official long-distance walk and the brainchild of one JB Malone. In Northern Ireland, the Ulster Way, long the dream of its founder Wilfred Capper, was inaugurated in 1983. The number of ways has since grown steadily (39 in 2002), the official response to the ever growing popularity of walking.

Ireland's oldest walking festival, Castlebar International, dates from 1967 and anticipated, rather than coincided with, the growth

---

Dolmens & *Dúns*

From prehistoric burial cairns and enigmatic Ogham stones to early Christian chapels, Ireland's rich archaeological heritage dates back to around 3000 BC.

Archaeological sites feature on some walks in this book; two common types are megalithic tombs and forts (described here). Among many others, Peter Harbison's *Guide to the National & Historic Monuments of Ireland* is readable and places the monuments in their wider historical contexts.

Megalithic tombs were burial chambers built of large stones (hence megalithic) with a roof; some were covered by piled-up stones, with a gap for an entrance. Typically, the burial chamber alone survives as a distinctive landscape feature in the form of three to seven upright stones or legs, on which sit one or two massive capstones. Resembling tortoises or mushrooms, they're popularly known as dolmens.

It's been estimated that 30,000 **forts** were built in Ireland, although many have disappeared under the onslaught of settlement. Irish forts go by any one of five names: rath, *lios, dún, cashel* and *caher*.

Usually circular, oval or D-shaped, forts have a stone or earth wall enclosing an area between 15 and 50m across. They were probably ordinary dwellings for a family and its animals, rather than refuges from attack. Shelter was most likely provided by a timber structure inside the walls, possibly roofed and insulated with heather.

Raths and *lios*, earthen round houses or ring forts, have been dated to around AD 1000; some may have been used as late as the 18th century. Stone-built forts are known as *cashels* in the northwest, and *caher* in the west and southwest; they were probably built around 700 BC. *Dúns* are the most substantial forts, usually on hilltops, making use of natural defences. A bank and ditch, or a massive stone wall, or all three encircle the summit. Promontory forts, along the coast and inland, are earth banks or stone walls across the narrowest part of a neck of land and usually date from about 300 BC.

MATT KING

Dolmens, or megalithic tombs, are impressive links to Ireland's past.

of interest in walking. Two other notable events in the Irish walking calendar – the Glover Highland Walk and the Maumturks Walk – were launched during the 1970s.

The Mountaineering Council's magazine, now *Irish Mountain Log*, was first published in 1978. The commercial but equally valuable *Walking World Ireland* is a relative newcomer, first hitting the streets in 1994. By then, local and all-Ireland walking guides had been on the book shelves for a few years, and they're still proliferating.

Many walking clubs were set up in the 1980s and '90s; in 2002 the Mountaineering Council had 103 member clubs and 855 individual members, a total of 7485 people.

GEOGRAPHY

The island of Ireland lies to the west of Britain, across the North Channel, Irish Sea and St George's Channel. It is 486km from north (Malin Head) to south (Mizen Head) and 275km east (Wicklow Head) to west (Dunmore Head).

Political Geography

Ireland is divided into 32 counties. The Republic (or the South) consists of 26 counties

Counties & Provinces

and Northern Ireland (or the North) of six. The island has traditionally been divided into four provinces: Leinster, Ulster, Connaught and Munster. The six counties of Northern Ireland are often loosely referred to as Ulster, but three of the Republic's counties – Donegal, Cavan and Monaghan – were also in the old province of Ulster.

Landscape

Ireland's coastline measures 5631km. In the west, facing the Atlantic Ocean, the coast is dramatically rugged and deeply indented, notably by Donegal, Clew and Galway Bays and the Shannon estuary. The east coast has a comparatively smooth profile, wavering markedly only around wide, shallow Dundalk Bay.

Hundreds of small islands, more than 20 of them inhabited, lie off the west and north coasts. There are also a couple of islets off the east coast near Dublin, and in St George's Channel. Sandy beaches punctuate the cliffs and rocky inlets of the west coast, and there are also a few strands along the south and southeast shores.

The extensive central lowlands, generally no more than 120m above sea level, are interspersed with low hills (up to 300m), ridges, lakes and bogs, and are fringed by coastal hills and mountain groups, except along the central eastern coast. In the North the main mountain areas are the gentle Antrim Mountains, the Mourne Mountains with the North's highest peak, steep-sided Slieve Donard (850m), the rounded Sperrins in County Tyrone and the plateau-like Cuilcagh Mountains mainly in County Fermanagh. The South has Donegal's Blue Stack Mountains, clusters of rugged high ground in Connemara and County Mayo, magnificent MacGillycuddy's Reeks in County Kerry (with Ireland's highest peak, Carrauntoohil, 1039m) the Galtees, Knockmealdowns and Comeraghs in County Tipperary, and the rolling Wicklow Mountains in the southeast.

The Shannon, which rises in the Cuilcagh Mountains, is the longest river (386km) in Ireland, followed by the Barrow, which rises in the Slieve Bloom Mountains and reaches the coast at Waterford Harbour. Lough Neagh, in Northern Ireland, is the largest lake with an area of 388 sq km. Upper and Lower Loughs Erne, in Ireland's northwest corner, dominate an extensive and very picturesque network of smaller lakes and streams.

GEOLOGY

The mountains of Ireland evolved during two main, drawn-out events. About 450 million years ago the quartzite and schist, which predominate in the Connemara area and Counties Donegal, Mayo and Tyrone, were formed when older sedimentary rocks were transformed by great heat and immense pressure. At the same time, vast deposits of sandstone were laid down in Connemara and County Mayo, and later raised to form a plateau through which rivers subsequently carved deep valleys. The granite of County Donegal's Derryveagh Mountains and the Wicklow Mountains emerged from beneath the earth's surface near the end of this era.

There followed a relatively tranquil period when Ireland was part of the European landmass; vast areas of sandstone were laid down and later cover by deposits of limestone – the origin of the Burren area.

The second mountain-building era, between 340 and 280 million years ago, mainly affected the south of the island, where the high, parallel sandstone ridges of the southwestern peninsulas and lower groups of hills, including the Comeraghs, were formed.

Volcanic activity about 60 million years ago gave rise to the Mourne Mountains. Then came ice ages, ending about 10,000 years ago, during which much of Ireland was buried under ice for long periods. The three most obvious features caused by the erosive impact of ice are corries, U-shaped valleys and arêtes (see the boxed text 'Signs of a Glacial Past', p24). Extensive deposits of glacial clay and sand throughout the central lowlands overlie the older limestone and are, in turn, overlain by raised bogs – mounds of peat covered with heather and moss (see boxed text 'Ireland's Peatlands', p35).

Climate

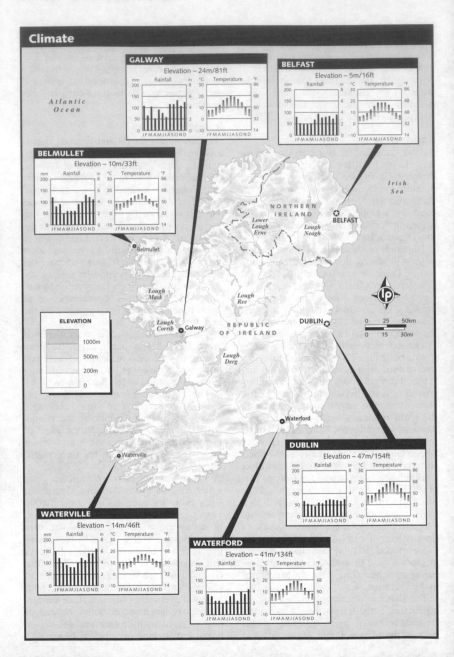

CLIMATE

Ireland has a relatively mild climate with a mean annual temperature of about 10°C and no great variation between the seasons. The main reason for this is the Gulf Stream, a current surging northeast across the Atlantic, carrying warm water from the Caribbean. Consequently the coastal climate is milder than inland areas, especially in winter.

The coldest months are January and February, when daily maxima range between 0° and 4°C in central Ulster and the Donegal highlands, and up to 6° or 7°C on the west coast. Air temperatures don't often linger below 0°C for more than a day. Even the highest mountains in the southwest rarely carry snow for very long. In the northwest, away from the coast, the Derryveagh Mountains can be snowcapped for longer, while the higher Wicklow Mountains and the Mournes can hold snow for several weeks in mid-winter. July and August are the warmest months when the temperature ranges between 16°C and the low 20s°C; it's a rare day if the temperature exceeds 25°C.

From mid-June to mid-August Ireland enjoys an average of about 18 hours of daylight. Sunshine is something else: Ireland only sees an average of five to six hours daily, but up to seven hours in the southeast in May and June; the daily average everywhere is below two hours by December.

Rainfall varies markedly from west to east. The soggiest places in the southwest endure 1500mm or more per year, whereas the driest places in the east have barely half that amount. In the west it can rain on more than 225 days per year, but in the southeast rain falls on fewer than 200 days.

The prevailing winds are from somewhere between south and west, and gales are much more frequent on exposed western coasts than in the east and inland.

The changeability of Ireland's weather is its most annoying *and* its most rewarding characteristic. No sooner have you climbed into all your waterproof gear than the squall ceases and the sun comes out, so it pays to always be prepared for four seasons in one day (see the Clothing and Equipment chapter, p52, and Weather Information, p50).

CONSERVATION & ENVIRONMENT

The emergence of public environmental awareness and the proliferation of groups campaigning on environmental issues came later to Ireland than to some other European countries. Ireland's environmental movement is now very vigorous and committed, even increasing its representation in the Dáil Éireann at the 2002 elections.

The countryside is the manifestation of centuries of agricultural practice and changing land uses. Small-scale farming has been a mainstay of the Irish economy until very recently, but the trend is now towards amalgamation and exodus from farming's relatively low incomes and uncertain future.

Upland farming has never been prosperous but has sustained small communities in remote areas. Government subsidies help maintain sheep flocks on open moorland, but the consequent sheet erosion on sparsely vegetated hillsides is obvious in many walking areas. Although it is now recognised that increased runoff from bare hillsides pollutes water supplies and harms fish breeding grounds, withdrawing stock from the uplands will be a long and very slow process.

Several thousand years ago Ireland was largely covered by forests. Neolithic farmers cleared small areas for crops, and the process of deforestation began and was scarcely interrupted until late in the 20th century. Large areas of native woodland survived until about the mid-16th century, but then the demand for timber for shipbuilding, charcoal, firewood and barrels stripped the country's forests. During the 19th century, tree planting on some large estates, the development of iron-hulled ships and the replacement of charcoal as a fuel saved the forests from extinction. However, the demand for timber during WWI reduced the forest cover to 1% of Ireland's land area.

Planting of conifers began in the late 19th century to try to reverse the decline; later the motive was extracting some return from otherwise unproductive moorland. More than 8% of the country is now under conifer

Signs of a Glacial Past

Many of the world's finest walks are through landscapes that have been substantially shaped by glaciers. As a glacier flows downhill with its great weight of ice and snow it creates a distinctive collection of landforms, many of which are preserved once the ice has retreated or vanished.

The most obvious is the *U-shaped valley* (1), gouged out by the glacier as it moves downhill, often with a bowl-shaped *corrie* (2) at its head. *Corries* are found along high mountain ridges or at mountain passes or *cols* (3). Where an alpine glacier – which flows off the upper slopes and ridges of a mountain range – has joined a deeper, more substantial valley glacier, a dramatic *hanging valley* (4) is often the result. In a post-glacial landscape, hanging valleys and corries commonly shelter hidden alpine lakes or *tarns* (5). The thin ridge which separates adjacent glacial valleys is known as an *arête* (6).

As a glacier grinds its way forward it usually leaves long, *lateral moraine* (7) ridges along its course – mounds of debris either deposited along the flanks of the glacier or left by sub-ice streams within its heart. At the end – or snout – of a glacier is the *terminal moraine* (8), the point where the giant conveyor belt of ice drops its load of rocks and grit. Both high up in the hanging valleys and in the surrounding valleys and plains, *moraine lakes* (9) may form behind a dam of glacial rubble.

The plains which surround a once-glaciated range may feature a confusing variety of moraine ridges, mounds and outwash fans – material left by rivers flowing from the glaciers. Perched here and there may be an *erratic* (10), a rock carried far from its origin by the moving ice and left stranded in a geologically alien environment; for example, a granite boulder sitting in a limestone landscape.

View of area before glacier's retreat

KATE NOLAN

plantations, mainly sitka spruce and lodge-pole pine, and the aim is to increase this to about 17%. Around three-quarters of the plantations are owned and managed by Coillte, the state-owned forest company.

However, not everyone is impressed with the extent of conifer plantations, their rigid, unnatural shapes and the impact of fertilis-ers, which compromise the economic return from the use of infertile land. Reforestation projects using native species, notably oak, are becoming more common, especially in national parks and in private woodlands. Experiments are underway on areas of cut-away peatland, where peat harvesting has finished, to test the viability of conifers and other trees; success would add substantially to the area of the country under trees.

During the 1990s the proliferation of 'wind farms' – clusters of 20 or more wind-driven turbines to generate electricity – became a major issue, as the farms sprang up in scenic parts of the country. While new and often controversial farms continue to appear, the rate of proliferation has slowed as the potential of offshore turbines for elec-tricity generation begins to be exploited.

Ireland has become very good at gener-ating waste; the *Environment in Focus 2002* report revealed a 60% increase in the previ-ous five years. Walkers will see abundant evidence of this problem in derelict vehicles and all kinds of rubbish dumped in the countryside. The report made sobering read-ing – Ireland faces a truly mountainous problem and is struggling to improve its 7.8% rate of recycling household waste, far below the European average of 14.4%.

The economic boom of the 1990s had an-other downside in the so called 'bungalow blitz' – the haphazard, uncontrolled build-ing of single houses in the countryside – all too obvious from vantage points on many walks described in this book. Environmen-tal organisations readily identified reasons for this – lack of strong planning controls and environmental policies – but reining in such highly profitable developments may be difficult.

Access to the countryside is the most pressing issue for walkers in Ireland (see also Responsible Walking, p41). Footpath erosion in the more popular areas such as the Mournes and the Wicklows is causing concern. In the North, the National Trust has carried out extensive path construction and repair using local stone; in the Wicklow Mountains and Connemara National Parks, boardwalks made of railway sleepers con-tinue to be built across eroded and peaty ground.

Conservation Organisations

Many organisations in Ireland are cam-paigning on environmental issues. A good place to start is the national environmental information service, **ENFO** (☎ *1890 200 191, 01-888 2001;* w *www.enfo.ie; 17 St An-drew St, Dublin 2; open 10am-5pm Mon-Sat).* ENFO operates Europe's first dedicated en-vironmental information centre, where you can pick up free information and use the ex-cellent library. The centre's website con-tains full texts of its leaflets and links to other environmental sites.

Other organisations include:

An Taisce (☎ 01-454 1786, w www.antaisce.org) Tailors Hall, Back Lane, Dublin 8. This is Ireland's oldest and most wide-ranging environmental organisation, which strives to conserve and pro-tect the best of Ireland's natural and built heri-tage. It's an outspoken critic of government planning decisions, cares for various nature re-serves and historic buildings, and coordinates the Blue Flag awards for clean beaches.

BirdWatch Ireland (☎ 01-280 4322, w www .birdwatchireland.ie) 8 Longford Place, Monks-town. This organisation claims to be the largest and most active voluntary conservation group in Ireland with more than 6000 members. Bird-Watch works for the conservation of wild birds and their habitats in Ireland, and manages more than 20 reserves.

Dúchas (☎ 1890 321 421, 01-647 3000, w www .ealga.ie) 7 Ely Place, Dublin 2. Ireland's heritage service, Dúchas manages national parks and na-ture reserves, national monuments, produces numerous publications and operates the ranger service in parks and reserves. A separate web-site (w www.heritageireland.ie) has basic infor-mation about the places managed by Dúchas in six languages (including English, French and German).

Environment & Heritage Service (EHS; ☎ 028-9054 6527, Ⓦ www.ehsni.gov.uk) 35 Castle St, Belfast. Covering the North, this agency is responsible for nature reserves, historic monuments and administering access legislation. It publishes an excellent series of guides to the nature reserves.

Irish Peatland Conservation Council (☎ 01-872 2384, Ⓦ www.ipcc.ie) 119 Capel St, Dublin 1. This council runs the 'Save the Bogs' campaign, purchases boglands and manages them as nature reserves, and repairs damaged boglands.

Irish Wildlife Trust (☎ 01-676 8588, Ⓦ www.iwt.ie) 107 Lower Baggot St, Dublin 2. This trust campaigns to protect Ireland's wildlife and its habitats through consciousness-raising activities and active conservation projects.

National Trust (Northern Ireland) (☎ 028-9751 0721, Ⓦ www.nationaltrust.org.uk) Rowallane House, Saintfield, Ballynahinch. This trust is the presence of the English organisation in the North. It cares for more than 20 properties, including the Giant's Causeway and several historic houses.

Waterways Ireland (☎ 028-6632 3004, Ⓦ www.waterwaysireland.org) 20 Darling St, Enniskillen. Established in 1999 as a cross-border organisation, Waterways Ireland is responsible for managing, developing and restoring Ireland's inland waterways for recreation.

NATIONAL PARKS & RESERVES

The Republic has six national parks: Wicklow Mountains (159 sq km), Glenveagh (165 sq km), Killarney (102 sq km), Connemara (29 sq km), the Burren (16 sq km) and Ballycroy (118 sq km).

These areas are managed by the national parks and wildlife division of Dúchas (see Conservation Organisations, p25), the heritage service of the Department of Environment and Local Government. All the land within the parks is owned by the state, having been gifted or purchased from previous owners since the first national park, Killarney, was established in 1932. Although small by international standards, the parks are managed in accordance with the strict guidelines laid down by the International Union for Conservation of Nature (IUCN). The parks are virtually free of development, apart from historical features and public facilities near the park entrances, and the main aim is to protect wildlife and natural habitats.

Dúchas is also responsible for supervising 77 nature reserves, and more than 370 Special Protection Areas for Birds and Special Areas of Conservation (both EU designations). Dúchas' responsibilities also include protecting more than 800 national monuments (archaeological and historic sites), and several historic properties and gardens.

Coillte Teoranta (Irish Forestry Company; ☎ 01-661 5666; Ⓦ www.coillte.ie; Leeson Lane, Dublin) looks after 11 forest parks. Coillte also manages around 370 sq km of commercial conifer plantations and 90 sq km of broad-leaved forests, lakes, bogs and open mountain land. Northern Ireland's **Forest Service** (☎ 028-9052 4480; Ⓦ www.forestserviceni.gov.uk; Upper Newtonards Rd, Belfast) manages six forest parks, all with recreational facilities, and around 34 forests consisting mainly of productive conifers.

In Northern Ireland the Environment and Heritage Service (see Conservation Organisations, p25) protects and conserves 'the natural and built environment' covering various nature reserves and historic sites. At the time of writing there were no national parks in the North, but a study was underway to evaluate the suitability of three areas for declaration as parks – the Glens of Antrim, the Mournes and the Giant's Causeway. These were drawn from the nine Areas of Outstanding Natural Beauty, which together cover 20% of the province. Area of Special Scientific Interest is the designation conferred on sites with the greatest conservation value; there are more than 190 scattered across the province. The 47 National Nature Reserves, though much smaller, are still valuable preserves of natural and seminatural habitats. There are 11 Special Protection Areas for Birds. The heritage service's 'built environment' classification means historic monuments, of which there are around 180, ranging from prehistoric burial tombs to ancient castles, such as Dundrum in the Mournes and Dunluce near the Antrim Coast. The North also has one Mountain Park, a special designation conferred on part of the Cuilcagh mountain area by the local council.

[Continued on page 35]

WATCHING WILDLIFE

Isolated on the Atlantic margin of Europe and with a restricted range of wildlife habitats (lacking heaths, chalk downs, extensive woodlands and high mountain ranges), Ireland is home to relatively few species of animal. The island does, however, host many migratory birds for a few months each year, making it an interesting bird-watching destination.

And, while Ireland's flora is much less diverse than that of other countries in northwestern Europe, it's of enormous scientific importance because of some unusual plant communities. Species found elsewhere only in habitats as diverse as Europe's high mountains, the Mediterranean basin and the colder regions of continental Europe and Asia grow side by side at sea level in parts of Ireland. The Burren has the best example of such unusual associations.

Despite long-term changes in rural land use, Ireland's peat bogs and wetlands are still extensive enough to be of major European significance. However, massive tree felling from the mid-17th century left Ireland the least wooded country in Europe by 1800; even now, only 8% of its area is under forest, and most of that is commercial conifer plantations.

This section provides an introduction to the animal and plant species you're most likely to see on the walks described in this book. Any locally unusual species are noted under Natural History in the respective walk chapters. For anything more than casual observation and identification along the way, you'll need to carry specialised field guides (see Books, p49) and binoculars – and have plenty of patience. ENFO, BirdWatch Ireland and the Irish Wildlife Trust are also fruitful sources of further information (see Conservation Organisations, p25, for contact details).

At present no animal species is endangered in Ireland; only the otter and corn crake are described as vulnerable and therefore could easily become endangered. Go to **w** www.list.org for comprehensive information compiled by the UN-run International Union for the Conservation of Nature (IUCN).

BIRDS

The number of bird species recorded in Ireland totals 424, although only about one-third are resident; these include a handful of distinct Irish subspecies, such as the red grouse and jay.

Seabirds

You're certain to see many birds along coastal cliffs and on sea stacks, where they sometimes congregate in huge colonies.

KATE NOLAN

Red Grouse

27

The most numerous of Ireland's terns, the **common tern** (*greabhróg*) is migratory. It lives and breeds in Ireland from May onwards, migrating to Africa in September. Most likely to be seen on rocky islands off the coast and on mainland dunes, it has a black cap and bright red beak, and can be identified in flight by its long forked tail.

Seen on both inshore and inland waters throughout the year, the **cormorant** (*broigheall*) is glossy black with white patches just above the leg, and on the cheeks and chin. Cormorants have a distinctive habit of standing on rocks to dry their outstretched wings.

The **fulmar** (*fulmaire*) is one of Ireland's most common coastal species. Fulmars are easily identified as they glide and bank near the cliffs, with grey wings stiffly outstretched, then land on tiny ledges.

Gannets (*gainéad*) are among the largest seabirds in Irish waters, congregating in a limited number of breeding colonies, notably off the Kerry coast and on Clare Island. Pure white with a yellow head and black tips to its 1.8m wingspan, at sea it's easily identified as it plunges arrow-like into the water in search of fish.

Guillemots (*éan aille*) congregate in compact bunches in coastal waters close to cliffs, where large numbers lay their eggs on bare rock ledges. Likely to be seen almost anywhere along the coast between March and July, guillemots are completely dark brown with a white breast.

The **herring gull** (*faoileán scadán*) is the most common gull and can be seen anywhere on the coast at any time, although it also ranges widely inland where it has become a rather aggressive scavenger.

The **kittiwake** (*saidhséar*) is a small member of the gull family and takes its name from its characteristic call – a constant 'kitti-ee-wayke'. They're most likely to be seen on coastal cliffs from March to August, mainly in Antrim, Donegal, Clare (the Burren area) and Kerry.

Commonly seen along beaches and rocky coasts, the black-and-white **oystercatcher** (*roilleach*) is easily identified by its long orange-red bill and legs. They're present all year, in greatest numbers along western, northwestern and northeastern coasts.

The endearing **puffin** (*éan giúrainn*), resembles a penguin in its upright stance and black and white uniform, but has an unmistakable, vividly coloured triangular bill and orange feet. Puffins come to Irish coasts in March to breed and stay until August when they return to the Atlantic, anywhere between Newfoundland and the Canary Islands. The best places to see them are on Rathlin Island and along the Donegal, Mayo, Kerry and Cork coasts.

LPP

Puffin

Waterbirds

These include waders, often seen on mudflats or moorland during the breeding season, and the species you first think of in association with lakes and ponds, such as ducks.

The **curlew** *(crotach)* is a common wader with a long, down-curved bill, long legs and variegated brown plumage. Apart from coastal mudflats and farmland, it is also found on moorlands on lower mountain slopes between March and about August. Its name reflects its rather sad 'coor-li' call.

The beautifully camouflaged **golden plover** *(feadóg bhuidhe)* is rather rare and confined mainly to the bogs of Connemara, western Mayo and western Donegal. It is easier to hear than see, with its eerie, mournful cry.

The **lapwing** *(pilbín)* is a common sight on farmland almost everywhere throughout the year, although it moves into marshlands to breed between March and June. This noisy, agile member of the plover family has a trademark black crest, greenish-black back and white underparts.

Almost everything about the **grey heron** *(corr éisc)* is long, including its legs, neck and bill. A common sight throughout the year along canals and rivers almost anywhere in Ireland, it often stands motionless on one leg, or may be seen flying slowly with deep wing beats and its neck pulled in.

With its glossy, dark green head, white collar and dark brown chest, the drake (male) **mallard** *(lacha fhiáin)* is instantly recognisable, whereas the brownish female is well camouflaged. Mallards are widespread across Ireland all year and a common sight along canals and rivers, and in urban ponds.

With dark glossy plumage, a red forehead and red, yellow-tipped bill, the **moorhen** *(cearc uisce)* is easily identified along canals and rivers almost anywhere in Ireland throughout the year. In flight it looks rather ungainly, trailing its long yellowish legs.

Mute swans *(eala bhalbh)* glide about quietly on the margins of lakes, streams and canals, but these large white birds are anything but mute if disturbed on their nests – hissing and snorting at intruders, human, furred or feathered. They have a rather comical habit of upending themselves in shallow waters to feed on vegetation.

Land Birds

The woods, moorlands and fields are home to a great variety of birds, from skulking warblers to birds of prey overhead.

The **blackbird** *(lon)* is the leader of the dawn chorus in urban and rural fringe areas. This very common bird is aptly named, although the female is brown. It is very adaptable and may also be seen in relatively bare areas in the west.

Aristocratic Swans

Mute swans look rather aloof and haughty but, considering their origins in Ireland, perhaps it's no wonder. Brought here by English landlords to decorate their estates, the swans were Crown property until the 18th century, when they were freed from the control of the King's Swan Master and able to roam free.

The **chaffinch** *(bricín beatha)* is probably Ireland's most common bird, and lives in deciduous woodlands and urban parks. The male is easily identified by its grey cap and dull pink chest; the female's plumage is less colourful.

Dippers *(gabha dubh uisge)* can be seen at any time of year darting about on rocks in fast-flowing upland streams, and even feeding underwater while it swims or wades against the current.

Dipper

Kestrels *(seabhac buidhe)* are likely to be seen over most of the country, hovering above fields and open ground or perched on fence posts. This common bird of prey has pointed wings and a wedge-shaped tail; the brick-red male sports a blue-grey head and dark brown markings on its back and wings.

The most common bird on the blanket bog moors throughout the year is the **meadow pipit** *(riabhóg mhóna)*. A small, dappled brown bird, its distinctive thin, whistling call is usually given in flight. Meadow pipits may also be seen in young conifer plantations.

The large, all-black **raven** *(fiach dubh)* has a wide range and typically nests on upland or coastal cliffs. With their glossy plumage, big bill and deep croaking call, ravens are unmistakable companions on mountain tops.

The dark-plumaged **red grouse** *(coileach fraoich)* is a denizen of heather moorland, where it has an unnerving habit of bursting suddenly from cover in a flurry of rapid wingbeats, the male screeching its harsh 'go-bak-go-bak' call. Feeding on heather, its strongholds are in Donegal and the Wicklow Mountains, where it may be seen year-round.

The orange-chested **robin** *(spideóg)* is widespread throughout Ireland all year and most likely seen busying itself in hedgerows or woodlands.

The **skylark** *(fuiseóg)* is usually seen fluttering and hovering above grassland, farmland or moors, filling the air with its trilling song throughout the year.

MAMMALS

Ireland has 25 species of mammal, none of which is endemic, although some have been isolated from Continental forms of the same species long enough to evolve into a distinct Irish subspecies. Most mammals are nocturnal or very nearly so; the best times to see them are early morning or at dusk.

Fallow deer *(fia buí)* are a fairly common sight in Dublin's Phoenix Park and other large wooded parklands. These deer are predominantly deep fawn in colour with dense white spotting on the back. The stags' (males') antlers are flattened at the ends and resemble small hands.

Thanks mainly to a concerted conservation programme, **red deer** *(fia rua)* persist in the wild after centuries of

Red Deer

Hedgerows

These elongated strips of dense vegetation were once planted along property boundaries, and still separate fields and line country roads. Most are 150 to 200 years old, although some date back to the 16th century. This distinctive feature of the Irish countryside now provides immensely valuable wildlife habitat and enhances the rural landscape. Usually from 1.5m to 4m high, the main hedgerow plant species are hawthorn, blackthorn, hazel and holly.

hunting and the destruction of their forest habitat. The only native herds are probably in Kerry; the Glenveagh (Donegal) herd was introduced (see the boxed text 'Glenveagh National Park', p278). During summer the mature stags are a magnificent sight: red-brown in colour, they stand up to 1.4m at the shoulder; their multi-branched antlers are shed after the autumn rut (mating season).

The **fox** *(sionnach)* has survived persecution for eating game and domestic birds, and still ranges widely across the country, although it prefers open ground. Unmistakable with its reddish-brown coat and long bushy tail, it is sometimes seen during the day, although it is mainly nocturnal.

Although mainly nocturnal, **otters** *(dobhrán)* can sometimes be seen early and late in the day around rivers and lakes, and on western rocky shores. About 1.5m long overall, dark brown with a white face, they are very agile in the water. Their tracks, resembling a cat's paw prints, can be traced on bank edges from where they dive into the water.

An avid eater of hazel nuts, the **grey squirrel** *(iora glas)*, was introduced to Ireland in the early 20th century and is now a fairly common sight in mature woodlands, scampering across the ground and straight up tree trunks.

The **Irish hare** *(giorria)* is a living link with fauna resident in Ireland during the last Ice Age. Ireland's hare can be seen throughout the country at all levels, on peatlands, farmland and among sand dunes. It has brown fur, relatively short ears (for a hare) and a white tail and can run at speeds of up to 60km/h.

Half of Europe's population of **grey seals** *(rón glas)* is found along Ireland's north, west and south coasts. The bull is dark grey with black blotches whereas the cow (female) is lighter in colour. Grey seals have been cast as villains by the fishing industry as catches have declined and illegal culling isn't unknown.

Several cetaceans (porpoises, dolphins and whales), including **blue** and **killer whales** (orcas), may be seen off the Irish coast, mainly during their migratory travels. The **porpoise** *(muc mhara)* is the most commonly seen resident cetacean, and most likely to be seen offshore along the south and west coasts from August to October. Porpoises live mainly in small groups (pods), but sometimes congregate in large schools. They have a domed head, flat face and small, triangular dorsal fin.

SHRUBS & FLOWERS

Bell heather is one of three heather species found almost everywhere on moorland and peat bogs. Its deep red-purple flowers are largely responsible for the beautiful purplish carpets that adorn the otherwise rather drab moors during August and September.

Bilberry (*fraochán*) is usually found growing in moorland with heather. This small, deciduous plant has bright green leaves and edible dark purple fruit, which ripen during July and were traditionally harvested for jam-making.

A denizen of pond margins in upland moors and boglands, **bog asphodel** is fairly easy to spot: its long stem, surrounded by slender leaves at the base, is topped by a cluster of tiny yellow, star-shaped flowers during July and August.

Buttercups are shunned by grazing stock as the leaves are poisonous, so are plentiful in fields and farmland generally. They are easily identified by their compact, bright yellow flowers, which bloom from May to July.

The **common butterwort** (*liath uisce*) is one of Ireland's few insectivorous plants. The pale yellow-green leaves at the base of the stem are covered with tiny hairs, which secrete a digestive fluid when an insect lands on them; the leaf curls up to trap the insect. This butterwort grows in boglands of the west and north, its small, purplish flowers blooming in May and June.

The **common spotted-orchid** is found in damp pastures and occasionally in open woodland. The dense spikes of white, pale lilac or pinkish flowers with dark dots on the three-part lower lip appear during June; the distinctive elongated leaves are patterned with dark blotches.

Bringing colour to bogland ponds, the **common cotton grass** is actually a sedge with downy white 'fruiting heads' that look rather like flowers. From June to August, fields of them waving in the breeze are one of the most attractive sights on the moors.

Widespread in woodland and pastures, and on sand dunes, the low-growing **common wild violet** has roundish leaves. Its violet blooms appear twice each year, in March and April, and July and August.

Cross-leaved heath is another of the three heathers found on Irish moors and peatlands, favouring more boggy ground than its two relatives. Its pale pink flowers, grouped on top of the shoots, bloom during August and September.

The white-flowering **daisy** is common throughout sandy areas around the coast, and usually lasts from April to August.

Early purple orchid is a common sight near rocky coasts and in woodlands in April and May, when the deep purple (sometimes pinkish-mauve or white) flowers appear. The leaves are elongated with dark spots.

The tubular pink or purple flowers of the tall **foxglove** (*méaracán dearg*) are a common sight in hedgerows and on roadsides between June and August. It is poisonous, although

Bilberry

Harebell

the leaves have been used to make a drug used in the treatment of heart disease.

Gorse is a vigorous, spiny shrub that grows almost anywhere in Ireland, although it prefers waste ground and rocky areas. During May and June, and on and off at other times, it is covered with masses of aromatic yellow, pea-like flowers.

The pretty, pale blue, bell-shaped flowers of **harebell** (*méaracán gorm*) are found on dry, rather open areas, such as grassland or dunes, mainly near northern and western coasts. Commonly called bluebell, the flowers appear in July and August.

The most common species in hedgerows, **hawthorn** (*sceach gheal*) is a shrub that quickly grows into an impenetrable thicket, particularly in limestone areas. Its loose clusters of white flowers appear in profusion in May and June; the small red berries, produced in September, are inedible.

Heather, or ling, grows on the drier reaches of moors and peatlands throughout Ireland, often in association with the related bell heather. Its pinkish flowers appear during August and September.

A low spreading shrub, **juniper** is a type of conifer with sharp, pointed leaves and fleshy, dark purple-black berries (the consolidated scales of small cones) that appear around September. It grows on rocky outcrops, limestone pavements and cliffs throughout Ireland, although not plentifully.

The first plant to bring some spring colour to the forest floor, pastures and dunes, the **primrose's** pale yellow flowers appear in March and last until May. The leaves are bright green and crinkled.

You will find the white-flowering **sea campion** growing singly, rather than in clumps, along rocky coasts throughout the country. From June to August the flowers are readily identified by the swollen calyx (the outer petals which protect the flower in bud) with a ring of white petals above.

This pretty, yellow-flowering **seaside pansy** looks like a refugee from a domestic garden, and is widespread on sand dunes anywhere along the Irish coast. The flowers can also be purple or yellow and purple, and appear between April and August.

The hardy **thrift** (*nóinín an chladaigh*) is a familiar sight along rocky coasts and on rocky ground in the mountains, where it forms dense clusters in crevices and hollows. Also known as sea pink, its deep purple-pink to pale-pink flowers can last from March to September.

A woodland resident, the **wood anemone** (*nead cailleach*) produces small delicate white flowers, which fold up at night, between March and May. It is fairly widespread in the north but more restricted in distribution in the south.

Traditional Medicine Cabinet

Long before antibiotics and wonder drugs, Irish people learned to use freely available plants to cure – or to try to cure – all manner of ailment.

- bogbean for boils
- chamomile as a remedy for whooping cough and consumption (TB)
- cowslip to treat shattered nerves
- dog rose hips as a source of Vitamin C
- milkwort juice to cure warts
- self-heal to treat strokes
- tormentil for burns

The tall, vivid **yellow iris** *(seilistrom)*, or flag, grows pro-
lifically in wet fields, ditches and along waterside banks, and
blooms from June to August. In the past its stiff, pointed
leaves were occasionally used for roof thatching and even
bedding.

TREES

Trees have had a bad time in Ireland over the centuries; the
surviving areas of deciduous woodland include species resident since the last Ice Age and several which have been introduced since the 18th century.

Alder *(fearnog)* is a tall, fairly open tree that likes to keep
its feet damp: it is always found close to lake shores and along
stream margins. It can be identified by its broad, flat-topped
leaves which turn black, rather than yellow or orange, during
autumn.

A common woodland tree, particularly in limestone areas,
hazel *(coll)* sometimes looks more like a bush – a legacy of
coppicing in earlier times, when it was harvested as a commercial species. Its nuts are much sought-after by grey squirrels and other small mammals.

In late summer and autumn several species of bird feast on
the bunched, bright red berries of the **mountain ash**
(caorthann), also known as rowan. A hardy tree, it is widespread on acid soils, often in association with silver birch, up
to 300m in altitude.

Although once common in Ireland, the **Scots pine** *(peine
albanach)* disappeared around the same time as peatland
became widespread, and had become extinct by about 1200.
Reintroduced to Ireland in the 17th century, this tall conifer is
easily identified by is reddish-brown bark, tall trunk and irregular branches. Although once grown extensively for commercial purposes, its aversion to waterlogged ground has limited
its use in modern plantations.

For centuries **sessile oak** *(dair)* was the dominant tree in
Ireland's deciduous woodlands. The name means 'lacking a
stalk', referring to the acorns which grow straight from the
shoot. Up to 30m high with a trunk several metres across, it
can live for around 400 years. Commercial plantations flour-
ished during the 19th century, when it was used in charcoal
production and shipbuilding. It is still prominent, despite extensive felling, and Glendalough in the Wicklow Mountains is
one of the best places to see oak woodlands.

Silver birch *(beith)* is a graceful, attractive tree that
usually grows in association with oaks. It has drooping
branches and smooth, grey-white banded bark; its small
leaves, bright green during summer, turn yellow and brown
in October.

Superstitions

- It's unlucky to use oak timber
  in house roofs.
- Wisdom and knowledge both
  come from hazel nuts.
- The sacred yew tree was a
  symbol of life everlasting.
- The rowan was believed to
  have protective properties
  and was planted to prevent
  places being bewitched.
- Bad luck will befall anyone
  who brings hawthorn flowers
  into the house.

[Continued from page 26]

POPULATION & PEOPLE

The total population of Ireland is around 5.57 million (2001 censuses), still lower than it was 150 years ago. It is generally accepted that the population was around eight million in 1841, but a decade later the Great Famine's death toll and emigration robbed Ireland of 1.5 million people. Continuing emigration ensured no let-up in the decline.

In the Republic the tide turned only after 1961 and the population increased steadily to 3.884 million in 2001, thanks to natural growth and immigration. Dublin is Ireland's largest city and the capital of the Republic, with 1.12 million people. The Republic's other large cities are Cork (123,400), Galway (65,800), Limerick (58,000) and Waterford (44,600). Overall about 60% of the population live in cities and towns of 1500 or more.

In the North, the census figures show steady but slow growth to 1.69 million in 2001. Belfast (277,000 people) is the capital of the North and overwhelmingly the largest centre, followed by Lisburn (109,000) and Derry (105,400).

Since the early 1990s many Irish people have returned home, and immigrants have arrived from various EU countries and North America, while some African and Eastern European refugees have also been accepted. In the North, the Protestant culture developed by Scottish and English settlers has remained distinct and largely separate from the Catholic community to this day.

RELIGION

The Republic is overwhelmingly Roman Catholic (95%) with about 3% Protestant, 0.1% Jewish, and the rest of the population belonging to other religions, including Islam and Buddhism, or professing no religious belief. In the North about 60% of the population is Protestant and 40% Catholic.

Ireland's Peatlands

Ireland's 220 sq km of peatlands are of international conservation significance, a vastly greater area than in any other European nation. Even so, 81% of Ireland's original peatlands have disappeared.

What is peat? It is a soil formed from partly decomposed plants, mainly sphagnum moss, heathers, grasses and sedges, which have piled up in waterlogged places over thousands of years. The microorganisms that cause plant decay are starved of oxygen, so decomposition is never thorough. Some energy stays locked in the plants, making it a convenient source of fuel.

Peatlands or bogs, with a water content of up to 95%, are simply large accumulations of peat and come in three varieties. You're least likely to see fens or flat bogs, which are found around lake shores. **Raised bogs**, which dominate the central lowlands and are also found in the central North, are domed mounds between 9m and 12m thick, and they sit in basins of old lakes. **Blanket bogs**, extensive carpets of peat 1.2m to 3m deep, differ in character between the lowlands (below 200m) and mountains (above 200m), and are the type with which walkers will become most familiar, mainly in the west.

Peatlands are unique natural archives, and scientific analysis of their contents can reveal much about changes in land use and vegetation. They also preserve buried archaeological sites such as ancient trackways called *toghers* – Ireland's first walking paths perhaps. *Toghers* were wooden roads formed of planks or brush laid across peatlands. They date back 5000 years and some were still in use in the mid-16th century.

The Irish Peatland Conservation Council (see Conservation Organisations, p25) works hard to educate people about the values of peatland, the area protected from exploitation or damage is slowly increasing with the designation of conservation reserves. Special Area of Conservation status for about 84 sq km of bogs should bring an end to peat cutting in the Republic. In the North, 10% of the original resource is conserved by government or nongovernment organisations.

SOCIETY & CONDUCT

The Republic's amazing economic growth since the late 1970s, earning it the nickname the Celtic Tiger, social changes and the resurgence of Irish culture have largely supplanted the old stereotypes of Ireland as a predominantly poor, rural land of quirky folk, from which bright young people were fleeing in droves.

Class distinctions are scarcely recognisable; personal wealth now attracts greater social status than birth or upbringing. Nevertheless, plenty of people aren't riding the Celtic Tiger; the housing estates of Dublin are especially blighted by crime and drugs.

As the hordes of pubs and the proliferation of festivals, especially walking, attest, the Irish are gregarious and sociable folk, although in rural Ireland the process of getting to know people may be relatively gradual and low-key. A quiet approach and readiness to settle down for a friendly chat on almost any topic under the sun is the way to go. It's prudent to tread carefully if politics and religion crop up, at least until you understand other people's views. This is especially so in the North, although surprisingly frank discussions can get going once people have relaxed and overcome a seemingly ingrained concern for your enjoyment of their country.

LANGUAGE

English is the main language of Ireland, but it's spoken with a distinctive Irish lilt. Irish, a Celtic language, is the first language in parts of western and southern Ireland; these areas are collectively called the Gaeltacht.

Officially the Republic is bilingual, and most official documents and road signs are printed in Irish and English. Even in the Gaeltacht heartland, English is the language of communication with visitors, so you won't need a grasp of even survival-level Irish.

Irish Language Signs

English	Irish	Pronunciation
Men	Fir	fear
Women	Mná	me-naw
Toilets	Leithreas	lehrass
Police	Garda	garda
Post Office	Oifig an Phoist	if-ig on pwist
Telephone	Telefón	tay lay foan
Town Centre	An Lár	an laah
Street	Stáid	sroyed
Road	Bóthar	bowher
Town	Baile	bollyeh
City	Cathair	kawher
Bank	An Banc	an bonk
Shop	Siopa	shuppa
Hotel/Hostel	Óstán	oh stahn
Welcome	Céad mhíle fáilte	kade meela fawlcha

However, it's worth learning to recognise common public signs to save confusion and embarrassment (see the boxed text above). The pronunciation guidelines are an anglicised version of the 'standard' form, which is an amalgam of Connaught Irish (County Galway and north County Mayo), Munster Irish (Counties Cork, Kerry and Waterford) and Ulster Irish (County Donegal).

In addition, the Glossary (p355) includes a comprehensive list of Irish terms you're likely to find in public places, on maps and in guide books. Irish and English versions of place names are given in the Getting To/From the Walk sections of the Southwest, Central West, Northwest and Atlantic Islands walks chapters, as well as in the Gazetteer (p358).

Lonely Planet's *Europe phrasebook* devotes a chapter to the Irish language.

Facts for the Walker

SUGGESTED ITINERARIES

Travelling around Ireland can be a time-consuming business, especially by public transport, so it's best to plan conservatively, particularly if your visit can only stretch to a week or two. Then there's the unpredictable weather, which can play havoc with the best laid plans.

One Week

Northern Ireland Scale the Mourne Mountains' Slieve Donard or follow the Brandy Pad. Then head north to Antrim for the Causeway Coast Path. For a complete contrast, go on to a remote corner of County Fermanagh for one of the Cuilcagh walks.

Southwest Corner Warm up on the Torc Mountain walk, then tackle the Coomloughra Horseshoe, and finally relax on the beaches and byways of the Sheep's Head Way highlight.

Two Weeks

Northern Ireland & Northwest Stroll along the North Down Coastal Path or the River Lagan near Belfast, then dash off to the Mourne Mountains for the Annalong Horseshoe walk. Head north for a day on the Causeway Coast Path and a day on Rathlin Island. Beautiful Glenariff Forest Path provides a relaxed contrast before heading to Errigal, County Donegal's highest peak. Have a look at small Tory Island then finish on a high note over Slieve League and Slievetooey.

Dublin, Central South & Southwest Spend a day or two doing Dublin with one of the city walks and Phoenix Park. Head for the Wicklow Mountains for the Camaderry walk and, on a good day, the area's highest peak, Lugnaquilla, is irresistible. Continue to the Comeragh Mountains for the Nire Valley Coums exploration. Then it's west to the Dingle Peninsula for an ascent of Brandon and the Dingle Way highlight.

Highlights

Traditional Pilgrimages
Joining the faithful as they climb Croagh Patrick (p231) on Reek Sunday. Visiting the ancient sites of Glencolmcille on the annual *turas* (pilgrimage) to Slieve League (p281)

Coastal Walks
Exploring Europe's finest stretch of coastal cliffs between Slieve League and Slievetooey (p281). Walking the remote Dún Caocháin sea cliffs (p219). Enjoying beautiful beaches and soaring peaks on the Dingle Peninsula (p140).

River/Canal Walks
Otter-spotting along the tranquil River Barrow (p116). Reliving history beside the Newry Canal (p312) and Belfast's River Lagan (p298).

Bird Walks
Viewing puffins and guillemots at West Lighthouse on Rathlin Island (p188). Keeping an eye out for golden eagles in Glenveagh National Park (p277) and Slieve Snaght (p279).

Natural Wonders
Seeing the extraordinary rock formations of the Giant's Causeway (p303). Gazing at the massive cliffs of Coumshingaun from Mahon Valley (p124). Wandering across karst landscapes at Black Head (p252) and Inisheer (p200).

Archaeological Sites
Finding inspiration at Glendalough's Monastic City on the Mullacor walk (p110) and the Wicklow Way (p84). Exploring stone circles on the Beara Way (p175). Seeing an old lead miners' village on the Camaderry walk (p109).

Authors' Favourites
Enjoying perhaps the finest views in Ireland on a perfect day on Brandon (p142). Scrambling along tremendous, knife-edged ridges to the summits of Ireland's highest mountains on the Coomloughra Horseshoe (p246) and Reeks Ridge (p152). Sharing Lugnaquilla (p111) with no-one else on a calm sunny day.

Walking Festival Calendar

festival	county	contact
March		
Achill	Mayo	Achill Tourism (☎ 098-47353, W www.achilltourism.com)
Ardara	Donegal	Ardara Walking Festival Committee (☎ 087-234 1061, W www.ardara.ie)
April		
Glen of Aherlow	Tipperary	Glen of Aherlow Fáilte Society (☎ 062-56331, W www.tipp.ie/aherlow-failte.htm)
North Leitrim	Leitrim	Glens Centre (☎ 071-985 6217, W www.leitrimtourism.com)
South Sligo	Sligo	Lough Talt Ramblers (☎ 071-918 1291)
West Cork	Cork	West Cork Tourism (☎ 028-22812, W www.westcork.ie)
May		
Ballyhoura International	Limerick	Ballyhoura Country Holidays (☎ 063-91300, W www.ballyhouracountry.com)
North West Mayo	Mayo	NWM Hillwalkers (☎ 097-82967, e nwmhillwalkers@eircom.net)
Slieve Bloom	Offaly	Community Centre Kinnitty (☎ 0509-37299, W www.kinnitty.net)
Wicklow Mountains	Wicklow	Wicklow County Tourism (☎ 0404-20070, W www.wicklow.ie)
June		
Mourne International	Down	Mourne Activity Breaks (☎ 028-4176 9965, W www.mournewalking.com)
Sliabh an Iarainn	Co Leitrim	Sliabh an Iarainn Hillwalking Club (☎ 071-964 1569)
August		
Sperrins	Tyrone	Sperrins Tourism (☎ 028-8674 7700, W www.sperrinstourism.com)
September		
Curlew Walkers	Roscommon	The Curlew Walkers (☎ 071-966 3053)
Hills of Donegal	Donegal	Hills of Donegal Tourism (☎ 086-838 4882, W www.hillsofdonegal.com)
Wee Binnians	Down	Wee Binnian Walkers (☎ 028-3026 7556, W www.mountaineering.ie)
October		
Donegal International	Donegal	North West Walking Guides (☎ 074-973 5967, W www.northwestwalkingguides.com)
Fingal	Dublin	Fingal Tourism (☎ 01-840 0077, W www.fingal-dublin.com)

A Month or More

This might sound like a long time but even so, you couldn't realistically expect to sample all the areas covered in this book.

Northern Ireland, Northwest & Central West

After a day or three around Belfast, including the North Down Coastal Path, head down to the Mourne Mountains, and tackle Slieve Donard and the easier Brandy Pad walk. On the way to the Antrim coast, wander across the Garron Plateau and don't miss the Causeway Coast Way highlight. Head for the Inishowen Peninsula, and the Crockalough Cliffs and Raghtin More walks. Then tackle the dramatic Slieve League and Slievetooey, finishing in the pilgrimage village of Glencolmcille. Explore the wilds of Cuilcagh, then the beautiful Glenade and Glencar walks. Achill Island has a choice of coast and mountain walks, and Clare Island offers that special island experience. Don't miss Mweelrea and the Maumturks.

Dublin, Central South & West Coast

Start with an exploration of Dublin and its neighbourhood. Then head into the Wicklow Mountains via the Maulin and Djouce walk, an excellent introduction to the area. Next stop is the Blackstairs Mountain and a stroll along the River Barrow. Continue generally west to the Galtee Mountains for an ascent of Galtymore and a gentler walk to Lake Musky. Then head to Clear Island, followed by the Hungry Hill and Eskatarriff walks, good warm-ups for the Reeks Ridge. Great Blasket Island is an unforgettable experience. Then head to the Burren, followed by more memorable islands – Inishmore and Inisheer. Try the Glencoaghan Horseshoe in Connemara, followed by the less challenging Doughruagh and Benchoona, or Killary Harbour walks. Further north, Croagh Patrick offers something completely different. Enjoy a final fling over Corranbinna and along Dún Caocháin.

WHEN TO WALK

The driest months are April, May and June, with July not far behind; this is a particularly important consideration in western areas where rainfall is much higher than in the east (see Climate, p23). September can be relatively settled – a tranquil interlude before the autumn gales set in. Many low-level walks (going no higher than about 300m) are suitable for any time of the year; snow at this level is fairly rare but you'd always need to be alert to the possibility of icy patches on sheltered ground. On the other hand, the much shorter hours of daylight between late November and late January rule out longer walks. But each day is different, so a cold clear day in January could make for better walking than a warm but hazy July day.

During the peak tourist season in July and August, accommodation can be elusive in the most popular areas, especially Dingle Peninsula, County Kerry, Antrim Coast and the Wicklow Mountains. Many places stay open all year, but the choice could be severely limited in less visited areas between November and March. Many useful bus services are strictly seasonal, so a visit outside say June to September really means private transport if you want to travel fairly extensively.

In the mountains and on the coast, the potential hazards of difficult route finding and high cliffs make it unwise, if not downright foolhardy, to go out in bad weather and poor visibility. Strong wind and driving rain can turn a straightforward ascent or cliff-top walk into a desperate struggle. Rivers can rise very rapidly – a gentle stream can become a raging, uncrossable monster almost as you watch.

WHAT KIND OF WALK?

Variety is what walking in Ireland is all about; from level, formal canal paths to precipitous, rocky mountain ridges, and from bare, windswept cliff tops to lush riverside paths. There are well-marked paths, trackless routes over remote peaks, quiet and green boreens (country lane or narrow road), firm forest tracks and quaking bogs. The extent of peat bogs in walking areas can make early experiences something of a trial by mud, but there's almost always firmer ground nearby. The numerous Waymarked

Ways, making extensive use of sealed roads, often, but not always, carrying little traffic, provide easier walking through a wide variety of rural landscapes.

Most of the walks described are one-day outings, from short strolls to energetic and challenging mountain traverses; there are also multiday walks, most following the best parts of some of the Waymarked Ways.

Walking Festivals

A typically Irish invention, festivals are a lively mix of organised walks and social events spread over two to four quite challenging days. Since the Castlebar International Walking Festival began in 1968, festivals have sprung up across Ireland – around 30 took place during 2002, many attracting hundreds of walkers. Festivals are anything but local events and people come from several European countries, Japan and the US. They're a great way of meeting Irish walkers and usually offer the opportunity to visit more out-of-the-way places, which may not usually be accessible. An entry fee is charged to help cover organising costs, refreshments en route and a certificate and/or T-shirt at the end of it all. For a chronological list of Ireland's major festivals, see the boxed text 'Walking Festival Calendar', p38.

ORGANISED WALKS

An organised walking holiday can provide a relaxing change of pace during a longer visit, or perhaps an introduction to Ireland before you embark on an independent trip. There are numerous small companies that organise walking holidays in most of Ireland's main walking areas. Some include other activities and/or have a special focus for their walks, such as wildlife or archaeology. Two types of holidays are usually offered: fully guided – with the services of a guide from beginning to end; and self guided – with the company organising all your accommodation and luggage transfer between bases, and providing maps and detailed notes for the walks you'll be doing. All companies are run by people with detailed local knowledge and experience.

Walking World Ireland (see Newspapers & Magazines, p50) is a useful source of contacts, as is the marketing group **Walking Cycling Ireland** (W *www.kerna.ie/wci*).

When making inquiries check whether the price of the holiday includes insurance, transport to and from the place(s) where the walks are based, and whether the leaders have formal mountain leadership qualifications. Brief details of programmes of guided walks in national parks or similar areas, and of organisations offering walks locally are given in the walks chapters. Following is a list of larger companies, both in Ireland and abroad, offering organised walking holidays in Ireland.

Ireland

Croagh Patrick Walking Holidays (☎ 098-26090, W www.walkingguideireland.com) Belclare, Westport, County Mayo. This company concentrates on the Achill Island–Connemara–Burren area and the adjacent islands with a variety of walks.

Footfalls Walking Holidays (☎ 0404-45152, W www.walkinghikingireland.com) Trooperstown, Roundwood, County Wicklow. This group offers several guided tours with around six days' walking, including Glens of Antrim (which includes Rathlin Island) and Donegal and Mayo (with Glenveagh National Park, Slieve League and Croagh Patrick as the highlights).

Go Ireland (☎ 066-976 2094, W www.goactivities .com) Killorglin, County Kerry. Go Ireland runs guided walks in County Kerry (including Mt Brandon, Killarney National Park and the Dingle Peninsula), County Donegal and Northern Ireland (including Antrim Coast & Glens).

Irish Ways Walking Holidays (☎ 055-27479, W www.irishways.com) Ballycanew, Gorey, County Wexford. This company organises guided and independent walking holidays, from easy valley and coastal strolls to more strenuous mountain walks in Counties Antrim and Donegal, Connemara, the Burren, Dingle Peninsula and the Wicklows, and along selected Waymarked Ways.

Michael Gibbon's Walking Ireland (☎ 1850 266 636, 095-21492, W www.walkingireland.com) Market St, Clifden, County Galway. This company runs five-, seven- and 10-day trips that focus on Celtic heritage, including Connemara Highlights, Island Hopping and Sacred Mountains (which includes Brandon and Croagh Patrick among others).

The UK

HF Holidays (☎ 020-8905 9556, W www .hfholidays.co.uk) Imperial House, Edgware Rd, London NW9 5AL. This group operates a West of Ireland tour with five days' walking in Counties Mayo and Galway, including a brief visit to the Aran Islands. The Dingle Way trip comprises five days walking along the Waymarked Way. Both trips use comfortable hotels or guest houses.

Ramblers Holidays (☎ 01707-331 133, W www .ramblersholidays.co.uk) 2 Church Rd, Welwyn Garden, Herts/PO Box 43, Welwyn Garden AL8 6PQ. Ramblers runs Highlights of the Kerry Way, with five days' walking, based in Killarney.

France

Terres d'Aventure (☎ 01 53 73 77 73, W www .terdav.com) 6 rue Saint Victor, 75005 Paris. This company operates a trip to Counties Donegal and Mayo with seven days' walking including Clare Island and Slieve League; another involves 12 days on foot from the Kerry Peninsula to Connemara with three days on boat trips to the Blasket and Aran Islands.

The USA

Backroads (☎ 800-462 2848, 510-527 1555, W www.backroads.com) 801 Cedar St, Berkeley, California 94710-1800. Backroads organises Marvels on Foot in Counties Cork and Kerry, a six-day inn trip taking in Glencar, the Beara Peninsula and the MacGillycuddy's Reeks area.

Cross Country International (☎ 800-828 8768, W www.walkingvacations.com) PO Box 1170, Millbrook, New York 12545. This company has three trips, each involving five days' walking: the Island Walk, taking in Inishbofin and Inishturk and walks near Westport (County Mayo) on the mainland; West Coast, which includes Croagh Patrick and Kylemore Abbey; and Connemara and Burren, with visits to Achill Island, Killary Harbour and, of course, the naturalists' paradise, the Burren, among others.

Wilderness Travel (☎ 1800-368 2794, 510-558 2488, W www.wildernesstravel.com) 1102 Ninth St, Berkeley, California 94710. This group has the 11-day Emerald Isle Adventure visiting, among others, the Aran and Blasket Islands, part of the Kerry Way and the Beara Peninsula.

Australia

Ecotrek (☎ 08-8383 7198, W www.ecotrek .com.au) PO Box 4, Kangarilla, South Australia 5157. Ecotrek organises a Celtic Rambling holiday of 12 days taking in Connemara, the Burren, Aran Islands, Dingle and Beara Peninsulas and MacGillycuddy's Reeks.

Peregrine Adventures (☎ 03-9663 8611, W www .peregrine.net.au) 258 Lonsdale St, Melbourne, Victoria 3000. Peregrine offers two tours, each with five days' walking: the Ring of Kerry tour on the Dingle and Beara Peninsulas; and the Spirit of Ireland, concentrating on the Dingle Peninsula.

RESPONSIBLE WALKING

Walking in the Irish countryside is a privilege, if not necessarily a right, to be respected. Wherever you go you will be walking across land owned by someone, so make sure you stick to the following guidelines and protect that privilege.

Rubbish

- If you've carried it in, you can carry it back – everything, including wrappers, citrus peel, cigarette butts and empty packaging, stowed in a dedicated rubbish bag. Make an effort to pick up rubbish left by others.
- Sanitary napkins, tampons and condoms don't burn or decompose readily, so carry them out, whatever the inconvenience.
- Burying rubbish disturbs soil and ground cover and encourages erosion and weed growth. Buried rubbish takes years to decompose and will probably be dug up by wild animals who may be injured or poisoned by it.
- If you're camping, before you go on your walk remove all surplus food packaging and put small-portion packages in a single container to minimise waste.

Human Waste Disposal

- If a toilet is provided at a campsite, please use it.
- Where there isn't one, bury your waste. Dig a small hole 15cm deep and at least 30m from any stream, 50m from paths and 200m from any buildings. Take a lightweight trowel or large tent peg for the purpose. Cover the waste with a good layer of soil and leaf mould.
- Toilet paper should be burnt, but this is not recommended in a forest, above the tree line or in dry grassland; otherwise, carry it out – burying is a last resort. Ideally, use biodegradable paper.
- Contamination of water sources by human faeces can lead to the transmission of giardia, a human bacterial parasite; gastroenteritis is probably caused by exposed human faecal waste.

Camping

- If camping near a farm or house, seek permission first.
- In remote areas, use a recognised site rather than create a new one. Keep at least 30m from watercourses and paths. Move on after a night or two.

- If your tent is carefully sited away from hollows where water is likely to accumulate, it won't be necessary to dig damaging trenches if it rains heavily.
- Leave your site as you found it – with minimal or no trace of your use.

Washing

- Don't use detergents or toothpaste in or near streams or lakes; even it they are biodegradable they can harm fish and wildlife.
- To wash yourself, use biodegradable soap and a water container at least 50m from the watercourse. Disperse the waste water widely so it filters through the soil before returning to the stream.
- Wash cooking utensils 50m from watercourses using a scourer or gritty sand instead of detergent.

Fires

- Use a safe existing fireplace rather than making a new one. Don't surround it with rocks – they're just another visual scar – but clear away all flammable material for at least 2m. Keep the fire small (under 1 sq m) and use the minimum of dead fallen wood.
- Be absolutely certain the fire is extinguished. Spread the embers and drown them with water. Turn the embers over to check the fire is extinguished throughout. Scatter the charcoal, and cover the fire site with soil and leaves.

Access

- Most of the walks in this book pass through private property – although it may not be obvious at the time – along recognised routes where access is freely permitted. If there seems to be some doubt about this, ask someone nearby if it's OK to walk through – you should not have any problems.
- Leave all farm gates as you find them.
- Keep to paths or Waymarked Ways across farmland; always use stiles or gates on paths.
- Avoid damaging fences, walls and hedges.
- Do not park across farm entrances.
- Go carefully on country roads.
- Avoid interfering with livestock, crops, farm machinery or other property.

ACCOMMODATION
Camping

There are commercial camping grounds close to most major cities and towns, and in or near many smaller places in rural areas, especially popular holiday resorts on the coast. Some are convenient for the walks in this book,

including the Burren and Connemara (Central West) and the Southwest. Many cater mainly for caravans, but most provide plenty of space for pitching tents on lush grass. Washing facilities are always provided, although you occasionally find that the hot showers only work with tokens (around €1 for a good five minutes). Additional facilities can include a laundry, on-site shop and payphone. As a guide, expect to pay about €8.50/£5 to €18/£11 per night for a tent, two people and a car. Many sites are closed between late September and early April.

The **Irish Caravan & Camping Council** *(fax 098-28237;* W *www.camping-ireland.ie; PO Box 4443, Dublin 2)* publishes a detailed annual guide *Caravan & Camping Ireland* (€3), available from the council or from tourist information centres (TICs) in the Republic. It lists more than 140 sites throughout the South, all of which have been graded and registered with Bord Fáilte (Irish Tourist Board). The North Ireland Tourist Board (NITB) publishes a free annual brochure called *Caravanning and Camping in Northern Ireland*, which lists around 40 camping grounds, all inspected and rated according to facilities. Copies are available from Northern Ireland TICs.

Youth Hostels

Hostelling International (HI) or Youth Hostel Association (YHA) hostels date back to 1931 and were established to provide simple, inexpensive accommodation for people exploring the countryside. They've come a long way and the most up-to-date resemble guest houses, complete with en suite bedrooms, although hostels in more remote areas still have dormitories sleeping as many as 10 people.

Facilities always include a kitchen, while an Internet kiosk, laundry, drying room and payphone are fairly common. To stay at a YHA hostel you need to be a member of HI (which you can join in your home country or in Ireland) or pay a supplement. Once you've collected six supplement tokens you become a member. Tariffs range from €11/£9 to €17/£16 in the largest hostels; a high season rate applies in the Republic between

Trying to Keep Ireland Open

Traditionally, walkers in Ireland enjoyed almost unhindered access to the mountains, moors and coasts, based on a genuine respect for the property and livelihood of the people through whose land they passed. However, since the 1990s many successful attempts have been made to curb this freedom. In response, an Ireland-wide organisation, Keep Ireland Open (KIO), was founded in 1994 following a campaign against a proposal to subdivide a large area of commonage in the mountains near Mulrany, not far from Achill Sound, County Mayo, where freedom of access had long been enjoyed. KIO's main aim is to preserve unhindered access for the public to mountains, beaches, lakes, forests and other amenity areas.

The organisation encourages and supports local people seeking to uphold access to walking routes and beaches in particular, and it has had some success in persuading county councils that planning permission is needed to erect fences that enclose previously unfenced land and where public access has been enjoyed for at least 10 years.

Access disputes have blown up right across the country – Cape Clear Island in County Cork, Counties Wicklow and Sligo, and at Ugool Beach at the western foot of Mweelrea – now a *cause cele-bre* after years of campaigning.

One key reason for the fraught access situation in the Republic is the near absence of legally recognised rights of way (as there are in Britain, for example). Access across private land is either granted as traditional practice, such as in the main mountain areas, or by an agreement between the landowner and, for example, the local council. Disputes about mountain access are few, whereas the great majority of problems arise in the lowlands where landowners more readily jettison access agreements.

Contact the secretary, Michael Carroll (☎ 01-494 3221) or look at W www.keepirelandopen.org to find out more about KIO.

June and September. Some hostels close between about 10am and 5pm, others are open all day, although a night-time curfew may be imposed.

An Óige (☎ 01-830 4555; fax 830 5808; W www.irelandyha.org; 61 Mountjoy St, Dublin 7), the Irish Youth Hostel Association, looks after 32 hostels from Donegal to Cape Clear Island; details are set out in a brochure available from the association and in TICs. In Northern Ireland, **Hostelling International Northern Ireland** (HINI; ☎ 028-9031 5435; fax 9043 9699; W www.hini.org.uk; 22/32 Donegall Rd, Belfast BT12 5JN) has eight hostels, some are purpose-built and others are fully refurbished.

Independent Hostels

Ireland's first independent hostel was opened at Glencolmcille, County Donegal, in the early 1970s, in the spirit of traditional hospitality towards travellers. Today, among more than 200 hostels, you can still find accommodation that is an extension of the owner's

home; other hostels are purpose-built and the equivalent of budget hotels. You don't have to belong to an organisation to stay at an independent hostel and curfews are rare.

Self-catering facilities are usually provided; while a laundry, drying room and transport to and from bus and train stations may also be available. Accommodation is almost universally in small dormitories and most have private rooms. Tariffs, highest between June and August, range from €10/£7.50 to €35/£30. There are two umbrella organisations: **Independent Hostel Owners Ireland** (☎ 074-973 0130, fax 30339; W www.holidayhound.com/ihi; Information Office, Dooey Hostel, Glencolmcille, County Donegal) and **Independent Holiday Hostels of Ireland** (☎ 01-836 4700; W www.hostels-ireland.com; 57 Lower Gardiner St, Dublin 1). Both organisations publish a guide to their respective member hostels in the Republic and in Northern Ireland.

Other hostels remain totally independent. There's always the chance they will provide substandard accommodation and/or facilities, but, then again, you may be pleasantly surprised.

B&Bs & Guest Houses

Bed and breakfasts (B&Bs) and guest houses are a major industry in popular towns and villages. The main streets are decked out with a forest of enticing signs, a clear indication that providing hospitality is one of the many things Irish people enjoy doing – and do very well. B&Bs can also be found in surprisingly remote places, far from even a village.

Prices per person, sharing a double or twin room, range from €25/£16 to €40/£30 in towns and country areas, and higher in Dublin, Belfast and other cities. Rates for single rooms tend to be higher; beware the single supplement, charged for sole occupancy of a twin or double room – even if you're the only guest in the house. En suite rooms are almost standard; many establishments in isolated areas also provide evening meals by arrangement.

If you stay in a B&B or guest house registered with Bord Fáilte (displaying a green shamrock symbol) or the NITB you can expect quality facilities, a warm welcome and, if you wish, a very sustaining, cooked breakfast; a lighter, continental-style menu is always on offer. Many B&Bs prefer not to pay the considerable cost of affiliation to these tourist organisations but don't compromise on the quality of hospitality offered.

If you plan to stay in B&Bs and don't want to make all your arrangements before you leave home, it's worth getting hold of the guides printed annually by both bodies. The *Ireland Accommodation Guide* (€4) covers all Bord Fáilte approved B&Bs, guest houses, and restaurants and pubs, which also provide accommodation. The NITB publishes a *B&B Information Guide* and a *Hotels and Guesthouses* guide, both free and available from TICs.

Hotels

The range of hotels in Ireland covers everything from country pubs to stately mansions, as well as city-based, relatively anonymous establishments belonging to the international chains. Generally hotels are more – far more – expensive than B&Bs and belong to the 'special treat' category for most economy-minded visitors. Tariffs may be on a room-only basis or may include breakfast.

FOOD

Ireland and cuisine weren't two words that readily coupled in most people's minds until recent years. The Irish food scene has undergone a radical transformation thanks to growing awareness of the benefits of healthy eating, and promotion of the plentiful and high-quality local produce. The influx of discerning international visitors and the experiences of Irish people returning from sojourns abroad have boosted the transformation, as has the realisation that vegetarians are actually sane. In two countries where agriculture is still economically significant, it's not surprising that beef and lamb are prominent on restaurant menus. Fish is remarkably varied and very popular, and you're also likely to find such exotic delicacies as ostrich and kangaroo. Experimentation with local ingredients can yield extraordinary results – try to imagine mackerel with rhubarb for example.

Bread is an Irish specialty and is still available in great variety, especially wheaten bread, made with buttermilk instead of yeast; it's, well, solid and very filling, and is commonly offered for breakfast.

Small cheese makers produce a wide variety of specialty cheeses, especially blues and soft styles, and numerous variations on the cheddar theme.

If you're captivated with new Irish cuisine, have a look at **w** www.irishfood.com for a raft of interesting recipes, including many traditional ones.

Traditional dishes include:

Boxty Potato griddle cakes consisting of grated raw and mashed potato, flour, milk, egg and seasoning
Carrigeen A type of seaweed
Champ Mashed potatoes made with plenty of spring onions (scallions) steamed in milk and served in a heap with a well of melted butter in the centre

Coddle A casserole of bacon, pork sausages, onions, potatoes and parsley

Colcannon Mashed potato, cabbage and onion fried in butter with milk added

Dulse A dried seaweed that's sold salted and ready to eat, mainly in the North

Irish Stew A ubiquitous item on menus consisting of mutton, potatoes and onions, flavoured with parsley and thyme, and simmered slowly

Where to Eat

It's rare not to find at least one good bistro, café or restaurant in towns and large villages where you can expect to eat well for around €20/£15.

Bar meals (bar suppers, pub grub) are less expensive and can be just as interesting as restaurant fare, with an emphasis on fresh produce and imaginative combinations of flavours. Dishes usually start at €8/£6 and go up to €20/£15 for steaks and salmon.

Most towns have at least one Indian and/or Chinese restaurant, which should be relatively inexpensive and good value; expect to pay around €12/£10 for a substantial meal. In Dublin, Belfast and Cork you'll find a remarkably cosmopolitan range of cuisines.

Fast food places are an almost universal stand-by for traditional fish and chips, or pizzas, kebabs and burgers.

Vegetarians are well catered for, although you may long for a change from broccoli pasta bake and stir-fried vegetables.

Buying Food

Supermarkets are fairly common in Ireland, although resistance to invasion by the major, multinational companies remains strong; small owner-run bakers, grocers, delicatessens, butchers and health food shops are very much part of the shopping scene. In larger towns you can usually find at least one place that specialises in Irish products.

Fruit and vegetables, other than the locally grown staples (potatoes, onions, cabbage and carrots) are expensive. Nevertheless, bargains can still be had if you hunt out small shops – and never miss a street market, if only for the lively atmosphere.

DRINKS
Alcoholic Drinks

Ireland is renowned for its stout or Guinness, the dark, heavy beer brewed in Dublin, and described as 'the devil's buttermilk' by one of Northern Ireland's more notorious figures, Ian Paisley. If you find it's not to your taste, even after a creamy, smooth 'pulled' Guinness straight from the tap in a pub, then try the slightly lighter Murphys, Beamish, Caffreys or Kilkenny versions – or, far better, one of the stouts produced by Ireland's handful of small, independent breweries (see the boxed text 'Not the Guinness Guide', p46).

Lager can be more refreshing; Harp, the best known Irish brew, is passable. Numerous international brands, brewed locally, are also available, including Foster's, Heineken and Budweiser. However, they all pale into insipidity beside the lagers from the small brewers.

In pubs, ask for a Guinness or a Harp and you'll be given a pint (570mL) for around €3.20/£2.80. If this is likely to put you on the floor, ask for a half or a glass (€2/£1.50).

Cider is very popular (lots of apples are grown in Ireland) and several bottled varieties are available. Wine is generally expensive; larger outlets usually stock a good international range.

Whiskey, as distinct from the Scottish whisky, is always ordered by the brand name, such as Bushmills, Jameson or Paddy's; a generous measure in a pub costs around €3/£2.20.

Nonalcoholic Drinks

The Irish are great tea drinkers – you'll often be offered a cup of tea when you arrive at a B&B. It's generally made quite strong, and the milk and sugar are offered separately. Genuine tea aficionados will have to travel far and wide to find tea made with leaves rather than tea bags. Herbal teas are widely available, as an alternative at breakfast and in health food shops and supermarkets.

Coffee bars are now a standard feature along the streets of cities and larger towns, offering a generous range of variations on the theme. Look for places that have proper

Not the Guinness Guide

There is much more to enjoying the fruit of the hop vine in Ireland than the slightly medicinal bitterness of a Guinness or the insipidity of one of the many mass-produced lagers. In the face of the mighty Guinness Brewing Company, around a dozen independent brewers are producing their own traditionally brewed 'real ales'; if the packed bars of three micro-breweries in Dublin are anything to go by, they've won many loyal devotees.

Maguires, the Porterhouse and the Dublin Brewing Co supply only their own premises – sufficient reason alone for visiting the capital. You'll need to search diligently in larger supermarkets and off-licences for 500mL bottles (€ 2.20/3) of the other brews briefly described here. Sláinte!

Carlow Brewing Co (☎ 059-913 4356; W www.carlowbrewing.com; The Goods Store, Station Rd, Carlow) was established in 1998 in a traditional malt and hop growing region. The brewery's beers revive ancient Celtic recipes: Curim Gold is a Celtic wheaten beer 'lightly hopped' according to the label, but nevertheless with a sharp, clear hop flavour on top of a 'hint of fruit' (it's slightly spritzig and very refreshing); Moling's is a traditional Celtic beer that has a splendid dark colour and delicious raisin fruitiness, and while the advertised smoky flavour is elusive, the hops are not (this is a 'real' drink); O'Hara's Celtic Stout is smooth and silky, nowhere near as bitter as better-known stouts (it has won

a top award in the world's most esteemed brewing competition). The website includes information about where you can buy them.

The No 1 Brew from the **Irish Brewing Co** (☎ 045-435 540; Unit 3, Newbridge Industrial Estate, Newbridge, County Kildare) is a natural pilsner lager brewed to that style's exacting standards, with a lovely pale, straw colour and crisp, sharp hops flavour, both refreshing and satisfying.

Celtic Brewing Co (☎ 046-954 1558; Industrial Estate, Enfield, County Meath) produces Finian's Irish red ale, a very malty, faintly fruity ale brewed with pure spring water.

Messrs Maguire (☎ 01-670 5777; W messrsmaguire.ie/brewery; 1-2 Burgh Quay, Dublin) occupies a restored building dating from 1808 and overlooking the River Liffey. Eight beers are made in the on-site cellars and are only available by the glass. These include three lagers (MM Pils, faithfully observing German purity laws; Haus, a pilsner-style lager, and Yankee, a quaffing lager); two stouts (Plain and Extra – a fiendish double Irish stout); Weiss, a wheat beer; MM Draught, a Dublin ale; and Rusty, a superb, fruity red ale with appropriately chestnut colour, a creamy head and a slightly bitter finish. The website has detailed tasting notes among much else.

The Porterhouse (☎ 01-679 8847; W www.porterhousebrewco.com; 16-18 Parliament St, Dublin) has an awesome stock of Irish and international beers. As well as serving lunch and supper, from the Porterhouse cellars emerge three lagers (Hersbrucker and Temple Bräu, both in the pilsner style, and Chiller, a North American lager); three stouts (Oyster, used in one of their supper dishes with sausages, Wrasslers, 'like grandfather used to drink', and the complex and challenging An Brainblásta); and three ales (Red, a fine combination of malt and tangy hops, TSB and Plain).

Dublin Brewing Co (☎ 01-872 8622; W www.dublinbrewing.com; 141-146 King St North, Dublin; open Mon-Fri) has four beers (and one cider). Maeve's Crystal beer is based on a recipe used in Dublin 400 years ago. The company also makes Darcy's Dublin Stout, Revolution Red bitter and Beckett's Dublin lager.

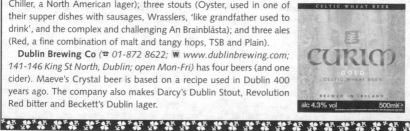

espresso machines to make real cappuccinos, rather than concoctions that emerge all too quickly from imitations.

On the Walk
In general it's safest to regard all stream water as unfit to drink, given the prevalence and intensity of grazing. See Water Purification, p59.

WALKING WITH CHILDREN
It's true that walking with your children is very different from walking as you knew it before they came along. If you can adjust happily to living with children, you'll probably enjoy walking with them.

'Kids – they slow you down', you'll often hear, and that's never truer than when you set out on a walk. There's an age when children go at exactly your pace because you're carrying them all the way (a good backpack built for the purpose is worth its weight in chocolate), but their increasing weight, and a growing determination to get down and do everything for themselves, mean that phase soon passes. Once your first child is too big or too independent for the backpack, you simply have to scale down your expectations of distance and speed.

This is when the fun really starts. No longer another item to be carried – at least, not all the time – a walking child must be factored into your planning at the most basic level. Rather than get partway into a walk and ask yourself in desperation, 'Why are we doing this?', make that the first question you ask. While walking driven by statistics, such as kilometres covered and peaks bagged, isn't likely to work with kids, other important goals can surface: fun, a sense of something accomplished together, and joy in the wonders of the natural world.

Easy and small is a good way to start – you can always try something harder next time. Too hard and what should be fun can become an ordeal for all especially the child.

Don't overlook time for play. A game of hide and seek during lunch might well be the highlight of your child's day on the track. A few simple toys or a favourite book brought along can make a huge difference.

Play can also transform the walking itself; a simple stroll in the bush becomes a bear hunt in an enchanted forest.

For the sake of sanity, or at least increased satisfaction, you may need to plan for some walking *without* children. This is harder to arrange away from home and the regular network of family, friends, babysitters, etc. Child-minding services are often accessible to travellers, although some parents will feel uncomfortable leaving kids with unfamiliar carers.

There's another alternative; if you're desperate to stretch the legs and enjoy some terrain that's simply beyond you as a family, split up for a few hours. Find a short but suitably challenging walk – maybe a peak close to a town or road, or a side trip – and take turns. Consider whether you could take your walking holiday with another young family. This enlarges the pool of both walkers and carers, and gives the kids company their own age.

Among the walks described in this book, the following are suitable for children as young as six or seven years.

Dublin Area Phoenix Park, Bray Head, Howth Peninsula

South & Southeast A part of Barrow Way Highlight

Southwest Muckross, Torc Mountain, Knockomagh Woods & Lough Hyne, Derrynane Coastal Circuit

Atlantic Islands Rathlin Island, Tory Island, Clare Island, Inisheer, Inishmore (shorter route), Great Blasket Island, Clear Island

Central West Killary Harbour, Errisbeg

Northwest Ards, Binnion

Northern Ireland Part or all of the North Down Coastal Path, River Lagan, Causeway Coast Way Highlight, Newry Canal Way, Glenariff Forest Park, Gortin Glen

MAPS
Small-Scale Maps
The four 1:250,000 maps in the Ordnance Survey of Ireland (OSI) *Holiday Map* series – *North, South, East* and *West* – cover the whole island. They're suitable for trip planning and access to walking areas, and cost €6.29/£4.95 each.

The OSI *Complete Road Atlas of Ireland* contains road maps (1:210,000) and large-scale city and town maps. Priced at €10.29/£7.25 it's a good investment for detailed route-finding, often necessary to reach the start of walks in remote areas.

Large-Scale Maps

The whole island is covered by 1:50,000 maps of the OSI *Discovery* and Ordnance Survey of Northern Ireland (OSNI) *Discoverer* series. With a contour interval of 10m and detailed depiction of topographical features, these maps provide very good coverage of walking areas. They're priced at €6.60/£5.20. The relevant OSI or OSNI maps are quoted for each walk described in this book. The OSI also publishes 1:25,000 maps for areas of special interest, including the Aran Islands and Killarney National Park (€5.71), and OSNI has a 1:25,000 *Mourne Country* map (£4.95).

EastWest Mapping (☎/fax 054-77835; W *http://homepage.eircom.net/~eastwest*; *Clonegal, Enniscorthy, County Wexford*) specialises in maps and guides of Waymarked Ways in the Republic. These are excellent maps – clear, accurate and with a great deal of helpful information.

Harvey Maps (☎ 01786 841 202; W *www .harveymaps.co.uk*; *12-22 Main St, Doune, Perthshire FK16 6BJ, Scotland*) has ventured into Ireland with two excellent 1:30,000 maps (£7.95) covering Connemara and the Wicklow Mountains; the maps are printed on waterproof paper.

Details of other locally produced or specialised maps, such as those for national parks, are given with the relevant walks.

Buying Maps

Large-scale OSI and OSNI maps are widely available in bookshops, newsagents and TICs. In Dublin, the **National Map Centre** (☎ 01-476 0487; W *www.irishmaps.ie*; *34 Aungier St*; *open Mon-Fri*) stocks the entire OSI and OSNI ranges; you can purchase maps from the online catalogue. In the North, OSNI (☎ 028-9025 5768; W *www .osni.gov.uk*; *Colby House, Stranmillis Rd, Belfast BT9 5BJ*) has a map shop.

PLACE NAMES

Irish language place names are now shown on both the OSI and OSNI series of maps. The OSI's earlier policy of anglicisation extinguished many original Irish names, thus losing the insights into the appearance or significance of places, and usually obscuring the fact that the Irish name had a distinctive meaning.

Ireland is universally county-conscious and it's fairly common practice to refer initially to the location of places by their county. To confuse things further, the old provinces are also widely used, not least for weather forecasts. See Political Geography (p20) for details of all counties and provinces in Ireland. For a comprehensive list of place names (in English and Irish) and their respective counties and provinces, see the Gazetteer (p356).

USEFUL ORGANISATIONS

Government agencies and public organisations involved in conservation and the environment are listed under Conservation Organisations (p25).

Walking Organisations

Keep Ireland Open (KIO; ☎ 01-494 3221, W www .keepirelandopen.org) The work of this organisation in highlighting public access issues is outlined in the boxed text 'Trying to Keep Ireland Open' (p43).

Mountaineering Council of Ireland (MCI; ☎ 01-450 7376, W www.mountaineering.ie) Longmile Rd, Dublin 12. This council represents the interests of walkers (and climbers) in Ireland. It takes a prominent role in access and safety matters, and is involved in many environmental issues that directly affect walkers, such as forestry, mountain roads and footpath erosion. The council's website is full of useful information and links.

Government Organisation

Geological Survey of Ireland (☎ 01-670 7444, W www.gsi.ie) Beggars Bush, Haddington Rd, Dublin 4. This organisation publishes the excellent *Landscapes from Stone* series of guides to various geologically interesting parts of the country (details are given with the respective walks descriptions).

Youth Organisation

Union of Students in Ireland (usitNOW; ☎ 01-602 1600, **W** www.usitnow.ie) 19-21 Aston Quay, O'Connell Bridge, Dublin 2. This is the Irish youth and student association. It also has offices in Cork, Galway, Limerick and Belfast. Here you can apply for the International Student Identity Card (ISIC), International Youth Card and European Youth Card. The Dublin office has a travel guide shop, bureau de change and Internet café (around €2.50 for 45 minutes). usitNOW also organises cheap fares to Ireland for students.

DIGITAL RESOURCES

Cyberspace is crowded with websites about Ireland, which can tell you far more about the country than you could ever hope to assimilate. The tourist organisations for the North and South both maintain comprehensive sites; those relating to particular regions are mentioned in their respective chapters. See Accommodation (p42), the Travel Facts chapter (p345), Conservation Organisations (p25), and Useful Organisations (p48) for related sites.

Other useful sites include:

Lonely Planet Here you'll find a summary about travelling to the country, postcards from other travellers and the Thorn Tree bulletin board, where you can ask questions before you go or dispense advice when you get back. You can also find travel news and guidebook updates and the subwwway section links you to travel resources elsewhere on the Web.
W www.lonelyplanet.com.au/destinations/europe/ireland
Hill-Walking in Ireland This site has photos and descriptions of long walks and good links to related Irish sites.
W www.simonstewart.ie
Irish Times This is the site of Ireland's leading broadsheet newspaper and is an excellent source of information about current affairs.
W www.ireland.com

CitySync *Dublin* is Lonely Planet's digital city guide for Palm OS handheld devices. With CitySync you can quickly search, sort and bookmark hundreds of Dublin restaurants, hotels, attractions, clubs and more – all pinpointed on scrollable street maps. Sections on activities, transport and local events mean you get the big picture plus all the little details. Purchase or demo CitySync *Dublin* at **W** www.citysync.com.

BOOKS
Lonely Planet

Indispensable companions on a visit to Ireland are Lonely Planet's *Ireland*, *Dublin*, *Dublin Condensed*, *Dublin City Map* and, if you have space, *World Food Ireland*. A title in the Journeys series, *Home with Alice: Journey in Gaelic Ireland*, by Steve Fallon, describes the author's private odyssey to the land of his ancestors.

Travel

A Walk in Ireland, by Michael Fewer (one of Ireland's best known walkers), is a selection of accounts of pedestrian travel during the last 200 years, ranging from John Keats to Paul Theroux. RL Praeger's *The Way that I Went*, first published in 1937, is a detailed record of Ireland's greatest field botanist's exploration of the countryside on foot, when walkers were universally welcome. *Footloose in the West of Ireland*, by Mike Harding, is an account of the author's love affair with the west, lasting more than 30 years and distilled into descriptions of 27 walks.

Natural History

The illustrated pocket guides in the Appletree series provide inexpensive introductions to natural history. The guides include *The Animals of Ireland*, by Gordon D'Arcy, *Irish Wild Flowers*, by Ruth Isabel Ross, and *Irish Trees & Shrubs*, by Peter Wyse-Jackson. Of the many guides for birdwatchers, the *Pocket Guide to the Common Birds of Ireland*, by Eric Dempsey & Michael O'Clery, has good diagrams and descriptions; *Birds of Britain & Ireland*, by Dominic Couzens, is more wide-ranging. Any comprehensive guide to wildflowers and trees of Britain and Northern Europe will serve you well in Ireland. Brendan Lehane's *Wild Ireland* is a guide to '70 wild places' and is very strong on natural history (but not travel information).

Reading the Irish Landscape, by Frank Mitchell & Michael Ryan, covers geology, archaeology, modern history, urban growth, agriculture and afforestation, all against the backdrop of the landscape.

Buying Books

While Ireland is highly geared to electronic communication, books remain an essential part of Irish culture. Bookshops are plentiful and, in larger towns, often have their own coffee shop. Details of shops in individual towns are given in the walks chapters. See also Buying Maps (p48).

NEWSPAPERS & MAGAZINES

Apart from publishing the most authoritative weather forecasts, Ireland's leading broadsheet newspaper, the *Irish Times*, regularly covers environmental issues, often of direct interest to walkers.

Ireland has its own home-grown walkers' magazine, *Walking World Ireland*, which is a lively, well produced and informative publication. It comes out bimonthly and can be found on the shelves of outdoor equipment shops, large bookshops and newsagents. For €3.30, it's excellent value, with articles on environmental issues, equipment and a good quota of walk descriptions (subscription details ☎ 01-496 8344).

WEATHER INFORMATION

The Irish meteorological service, **Met Éireann** (☎ 01-806 4200; W *www.met.ie; Glasnevin Hill, Dublin 9*), provides forecasts for the whole island and the five provinces, plus isobar and other charts. These are available online, in the *Irish Times* or through the Weatherdial service. For Weatherdial phone ☎ 1550-123 followed by the relevant provincial code: Munster (813), Leinster (814), Connaught (815), Ulster (816) and Dublin (817). These forecasts are

---

Taking Photos Outdoors

For walkers, photography can be a vexed issue – all that magnificent scenery but such weight and space restrictions on what photographic equipment you can carry. With a little care and planning it is possible to maximise your chance of taking great photos on the trail.

Light and filters In fine weather, the best light is early and late in the day. In strong sunlight and in mountain and coastal areas where the light is intense, a polarising filter will improve colour saturation and reduce haze. On overcast days the soft light can be great for shooting wildflowers and running water and an 81A warming filter can be useful. If you use slide film, a graduated filter will help balance unevenly lit landscapes.

Equipment If you need to travel light carry a zoom in the 28–70mm range, and if your sole purpose is landscapes consider carrying just a single wide-angle lens (24mm). A tripod is essential for really good images and there are some excellent lightweight models available. Otherwise a trekking pole, pack or even a pile of rocks can be used to improvise.

Camera care Keep your gear dry – a few zip-lock freezer bags can be used to double wrap camera gear and silica-gel sachets (a drying agent) can be used to suck moisture out of equipment. Sturdy cameras will normally work fine in freezing conditions. Take care when bringing a camera from one temperature extreme to another; if moisture condenses on the camera parts make sure it dries thoroughly before going back into the cold, or mechanisms can freeze up. Standard camera batteries fail very quickly in the cold. Remove them from the camera when it's not in use and keep them under your clothing.

For a thorough grounding in photography on the road, read Lonely Planet's *Travel Photography*, by Richard I'Anson, a full-colour guide for happy-snappers and professional photographers alike.

Gareth McCormack

updated three times daily and cost €0.73 per minute. Faxed forecasts are available from ☎ 1570-131 838 (€1.26 per minute).

PHOTOGRAPHY

For landscapes it's worth using 35mm transparency film, which is widely available in Ireland, for the best results. Kodak Elite (€11/£7 for 36 exposures) and Fuji Sensia (€13/£8 processing prepaid) are good, readily available films. Kodak Ektachrome E100 or Fuji Velvia give extra warmth and saturated colours, helping to compensate for overcast conditions.

Print film is widely available in Ireland. Fuji or Kodak 400 ASA film (€5/£4.30 for 36 exposures) is well suited to Irish conditions. For processing a 36-exposure film, expect to pay €10.15/£7.20 (ready in an hour) or €7.60/£5.50 (24 hours).

Restrictions

If you want to take a shot of one of the fortified police stations, army posts or other military installations in the North, ask first to be sure.

Airport Security

The major airports are all equipped with inspection systems that do not damage film or other photographic material carried in hand luggage.

Clothing & Equipment

Irish television weather presenters have an admirable ability to say the same thing, 'It's going to be wet again,' in 50 different ways, and always with a smile. While it is true that rain, drizzle, showers – and rain – do recur with dispiriting regularity, that smile hints at the undeniable fact that it's not always so. Spells of fine, dry, almost warm weather are also regular features of Irish weather, and can occur at any time of the year. Consequently you need to be dressed and equipped for everything from prolonged sunshine to heavy rain.

CLOTHING
Layering
A secret of comfortable walking is to wear several layers of light clothing, which you can easily take off or put on as you warm up or cool down. Most walkers use three main layers: a base layer next to the skin; an insulating layer; and an outer, shell layer for protection from wind, rain and snow.

For the upper body, the base layer is typically a shirt of synthetic material such as polypropylene, with its ability to wick moisture away from the body and reduce chilling. The insulating layer retains heat next to your body, and is often a windproof synthetic fleece or down jacket. The outer shell consists of a waterproof jacket that also protects against cold wind.

For the lower body, the layers generally consist of either shorts or loose-fitting trousers, polypropylene 'long-john' underwear and waterproof overtrousers.

Waterproof Clothing
In addition to the advice given in the boxed text 'Buying Tips' (p56), there are a few other points worth keeping in mind when you're deciding what you'll need to keep dry. A large cape, made of waterproof material, that drapes over you and your pack has much to recommend it. It's less constricting than a jacket, doesn't leak through the seams (a common failing of jackets) and underneath a cape you're less likely to overheat than in a jacket. A cape would be most useful for lower-level walks rather than on exposed, windy ridges and summits. The same goes for an umbrella – not as daft as it sounds if there's little wind, the main advantage being that your all-round vision isn't restricted.

Gaiters
These are absolutely essential for rough, wet walking and, to a considerable extent, can replace overtrousers in all but the wettest, coldest conditions. They postpone the awful moment when water starts to seep into your boots and can help to minimise the discomfort of wading through shallow water.

Windproof Jacket
Given that Irish weather is windy as often as not, especially in western areas, protection against breezes and gales is worth serious consideration. Garments that serve this purpose, that are waterproof except in steady downpours *and* weigh less than conventional rain jackets, are now fairly plentiful in outdoor shops; collectively they're known as soft shell tops.

Footwear
Boots are absolutely essential for most of the walks described in this book – those that involve walking cross-country or only on rough tracks, or where you have to follow paths that are usually wet and muddy. Runners or specialised walking shoes are fine for canal walks, and those following firm, dry paths, such as the near-urban walks in and close to Dublin and Belfast.

You'll be very lucky if you don't finish at least one day with sodden boots; beware the eager B&B host who rushes to grab your boots and dry them in front of the fire. Stuff your boots with newspaper and make sure they are placed in a warm room, well away from any direct heat source such as an open fire.

EQUIPMENT
Stove Fuel

Canned gas and liquid fuels are stocked by the larger outdoor equipment shops (see Buying & Hiring Locally, p56). As a guide to prices, irrespective of brand, expect to pay at least £3/€5.30 for 250ml or £5/€8 for a 500mL gas canister. A 500mL container of Coleman fuel (white gas Shellite, Fuelite) sells for around £4.50/€6.50. Methylated spirits (which is labelled 'mineralised methylated spirits' in Ireland) costs around £2/€2.50 for a 500mL bottle; you may also be able to find this in hardware shops and larger supermarkets.

Sleeping Sheets

The majority of hostels – both the youth and the independent varieties – provide sheets, either for an additional fee or as part of the

Check List

This list is a general guide to the things you might take on a walk. Your list will vary depending on the kind of walking you want to do, whether you're camping or planning on staying in hostels or B&Bs, and on the terrain, weather conditions and time of year.

Clothing

- ☐ boots and spare laces
- ☐ gaiters
- ☐ hat (warm), scarf and gloves
- ☐ jacket (waterproof)
- ☐ overtrousers (waterproof)
- ☐ runners (training shoes), sandals or thongs (flip flops)
- ☐ shorts and trousers or skirt
- ☐ socks and underwear
- ☐ sunhat
- ☐ sweater or fleece jacket
- ☐ thermal underwear
- ☐ T-shirt and shirt (long-sleeved with collar)

Equipment

- ☐ backpack with liner (waterproof)
- ☐ first-aid kit*
- ☐ food or snacks (high-energy), and one day's
- ☐ emergency supplies
- ☐ insect repellent
- ☐ map, compass and guidebook
- ☐ map case or clip-seal plastic bags
- ☐ pocket knife
- ☐ sunglasses
- ☐ sunscreen and lip balm
- ☐ survival bag or blanket
- ☐ toilet paper and trowel
- ☐ torch (flashlight) or headlamp, spare batteries and globe
- ☐ water container
- ☐ whistle (for emergencies)

Overnight Walks

- ☐ cooking, eating and drinking utensils
- ☐ dishwashing items
- ☐ insulating mat
- ☐ matches and lighter
- ☐ sewing/repair kit
- ☐ sleeping bag and bag liner/inner sheet
- ☐ spare cord
- ☐ stove and fuel
- ☐ tent, pegs, poles and guy ropes
- ☐ toiletries
- ☐ towel (small)
- ☐ water purification tablets, iodine or filter

Optional Items

- ☐ altimeter
- ☐ backpack cover (waterproof, slip-on)
- ☐ binoculars
- ☐ camera, film and batteries
- ☐ candle
- ☐ emergency distress beacon
- ☐ GPS receiver
- ☐ groundsheet (lightweight)
- ☐ mobile phone**
- ☐ mosquito net
- ☐ notebook and pen/pencil
- ☐ swimming costume
- ☐ walking poles
- ☐ watch

*see the First-Aid Check List, p59
**see Mobile Phones, p348

NAVIGATION EQUIPMENT

Maps & Compass

You should always carry a good map of the area you are walking in (see Maps, p54), and know how to read it. Before setting off on your walk, ensure that you understand the contours and the map symbols, plus the main ridge and river systems in the area. Also familiarise yourself with the true north-south directions and the general direction in which you are heading. On the trail, try to identify major landforms such as prominent summits and streams, and features such as forests, and locate them on your map. This will give you a better understanding of the region's geography.

Buy a compass and learn how to use it. The attraction of magnetic north varies in different parts of the world, so compasses need to be balanced accordingly. Compass manufacturers have divided the world into five zones. Make sure your compass is balanced for your destination. There are also 'universal' compasses that can be used anywhere in the world.

How to Use a Compass

This is a very basic introduction to using a compass and will only be of assistance if you are proficient in map reading. For simplicity, it doesn't take magnetic variation into account. Before using a compass we recommend you obtain further instruction.

1. Reading a Compass

Hold the compass flat in the palm of your hand. Rotate the **bezel** so the **red end** of the needle points to the **N** on the bezel. The bearing is read from the **dash** under the bezel.

2. Orientating the Map

To orientate the map so that it aligns with the ground, place the compass flat on the map. Rotate the map until the **needle** is parallel with the map's north/south grid lines and the **red end** is pointing to north on the map. You can now identify features around you by aligning them with labelled features on the map.

3. Taking a Bearing from the Map

Draw a line on the map between your starting point and your destination. Place the edge of the compass on this line with the **direction of travel arrow** pointing towards your destination. Rotate the **bezel** until the **meridian lines** are parallel with the north/south grid lines on the map and the **N** points to north on the map. Read the bearing from the **dash**.

4. Following a Bearing

Rotate the **bezel** so that the intended bearing is in line with the **dash**. Place the compass flat in the palm of your hand and rotate the **base plate** until the **red end** points to **N** on the **bezel**. The **direction of travel arrow** will now point in the direction you need to walk.

5. Determining Your Bearing

Rotate the **bezel** so the **red end** points to the **N**. Place the compass flat in the palm of your hand and rotate the **base plate** until the **direction of travel arrow** points in the direction in which you have been tramping. Read your bearing from the **dash**.

1 Base plate
2 Direction of travel arrow
3 Dash
4 Bezel
5 Meridian lines
6 Needle
7 Red end
8 N (north point)

GPS

Originally developed by the US Department of Defence, the Global Positioning System (GPS) is a network of more than 20 earth-orbiting satellites that continually beam encoded signals back to earth. Small computer driven devices (GPS receivers) can decode these signals to give users an extremely accurate reading of their location – to within 30m anywhere on the planet, at any time of day, in almost any weather. The theoretical accuracy of the system increased at least tenfold in 2000, when a deliberate in-built error, intended to fudge the reading for all but US military users, was removed. The cheapest hand-held GPS receivers now cost less than US$100 (although they may have an in-built averaging system that minimises signal errors). Other important factors to consider are weight and battery life.

It should be understood that a GPS receiver is of little use to hikers unless used with an accurate topographical map – the GPS receiver simply gives your position, which you must locate on the local map. GPS receivers only work properly in the open. Directly below high cliffs, near large bodies of water or in dense tree-cover, for example, the signals from a crucial satellite may be blocked (or bounce off the rock or water) and give inaccurate readings. GPS receivers are more vulnerable to breakdowns (including dead batteries) than the humble magnetic compass – a low-tech device that has served navigators faithfully for centuries – so don't rely on them entirely.

Altimeter

Altimeters determine altitude by measuring air pressure. Because pressure is affected by temperature, altimeters are calibrated to take lower temperatures at higher altitudes into account. However, discrepancies can still occur, especially in unsettled weather, so it's wise to take a few precautions when using your altimeter.

1. Reset your altimeter regularly at known elevations such as spot heights and passes. Do not take spot heights from villages where there may be a large difference in elevation from one end of the settlement to another.

2. Use your altimeter in conjunction with other navigation techniques to fix your position. For instance, taking a back bearing to a known peak or river confluence, determining the general direction of the track and obtaining your elevation will usually give you a pretty good fix on your position.

Altimeters are also barometers and are useful for indicating changing weather conditions. If the altimeter shows increasing elevation while you are not climbing, it means the air pressure is dropping and a low-pressure weather system may be approaching.

overnight tariff. In fact in more luxurious ones you might even find your bed made up for you. Even so, if you plan on doing a lot of hostelling, it would be worth taking your own sleeping sheet to save some money.

Buying & Hiring Locally

You'll find outdoor gear shops with helpful staff, and the full range of equipment and clothing, in the two capital cities, and larger towns in the North and South. Those in

Buying Tips

Backpack

For day walks, a day-pack (30L to 40L) will usually suffice, but for multiday walks you will need a backpack of between 45L and 90L capacity. A good backpack should be made of strong fabric such as canvas or Cordura, a lightweight internal or external frame and an adjustable, well-padded harness that evenly distributes weight. Even if the manufacturer claims your pack is waterproof, use heavy-duty liners.

Footwear

Runners or walking shoes are fine over easy terrain but, for more difficult trails and across rocks and scree, the ankle support offered by boots is invaluable. Nonslip soles (such as Vibram) provide the best grip.

Buy boots in warm conditions or go for a walk before trying them on, so that your feet can expand slightly, as they would on a walk.

Most walkers carry a pair of sandals or thongs (flip flops) to wear at night or rest stops. Sandals are also useful when fording waterways.

Gaiters

If you will be walking through snow, deep mud or scratchy vegetation, gaiters will protect your legs and help keep your socks dry. The best are made of strong fabric, with a robust zip protected by a flap, and secure easily around the foot.

Overtrousers

Choose a model with slits for pocket access and long leg zips so that you can pull them on and off over your boots.

Sleeping Bag & Mat

Down fillings are warmer than synthetic for the same weight and bulk but, unlike synthetic fillings, do not retain warmth when wet. Mummy bags are the best shape for weight and warmth. The given figure (-5°C, for instance) is the coldest temperature at which a person should feel

comfortable in the bag (although the ratings are notoriously unreliable).

An inner sheet helps keep your sleeping bag clean, as well as adding an insulating layer. Silk 'inners' are lightest, but they also come in cotton or polypropylene.

Self-inflating sleeping mats work like a thin air cushion between you and the ground; they also insulate from the cold. Foam mats are a low-cost, but less comfortable, alternative.

Socks

Walking socks should be free of ridged seams in the toes and heels.

Stoves

Fuel stoves fall roughly into three categories: multifuel, methylated spirits (ethyl alcohol) and butane gas. Multifuel stoves are small, efficient and ideal for places where a reliable fuel supply is difficult to find. However, they tend to be sooty and require frequent maintenance. Stoves running on methylated spirits are slower and less efficient, but are safe, clean and easy to use. Butane gas stoves are clean and reliable, but can be slow, and the gas canisters can be awkward to carry and a potential litter problem.

Tent

A three-season tent will fulfil the requirements of most walkers. The floor and the outer shell, or fly, should have taped or sealed seams and covered zips to stop leaks. Most walkers find tents of around 2kg to 3kg a comfortable carrying weight. Dome- and tunnel-shaped tents handle windy conditions better than flat-sided tents.

Waterproof Jacket

The ideal specifications are a breathable, waterproof fabric, a hood that is roomy enough to cover headwear but still allows peripheral vision, capacious map pocket, and a heavy-gauge zip protected by a storm flap.

smaller places are listed under the Nearest Town heading for relevant walks.

Prices are competitive, so the merits of purchasing equipment and clothing locally depend largely on the exchange rate with your home currency.

Outdoor gear shops in the larger cities include:

Dublin
Great Outdoors (☎ 01-679 4293) Chatham St, Dublin 2
Lowe Alpine Shop (☎ 01-672 7088) Temple Bar, Dublin 2

Cork
Mahers Outdoor Shop (☎ 021-427 9233) 7–8 Parnell Place

Galway
River Deep Mountain High (☎ 091-563 938) Middle St
Great Outdoors (☎ 091-562 869) Eglinton St

Sligo
Call of the Wild (☎ 071-46905) Rockwood Parade

Belfast
Tiso (☎ 028-9023 1230) 12–14 Cornmarket
Millets (☎ 028-9024 2264) 1 Cornmarket

Derry
Tiso (☎ 028-7137 0056) 2–4 Carlisle Rd

Hiring equipment is completely unknown, so you'll need to come fully equipped or prepared to patronise the local outlets.

Health & Safety

Keeping healthy on your walks and travels depends on your predeparture preparations, your daily health care while travelling and how you handle any medical problems that develop. While the potential problems can seem quite frightening, in reality few travellers experience anything more than an upset stomach. The sections that follow aren't intended to alarm, but they are worth reading before you go.

PREDEPARTURE PLANNING
Medical Cover
Citizens of European Union (EU) countries are covered for emergency medical care upon presentation of an E111 form, which you need to get before you travel. In Britain, you can pick up forms free at post offices. All you need to do is quote your name, address, date of birth and National Insurance number. In other EU countries, obtain information from your doctor or local health service. Although the form will entitle you to free treatment in government clinics and hospitals, you will have to pay for dental treatment, medicines bought from pharmacies, even if a doctor has prescribed them, and also, possibly, tests. Once home, you may be able to recover some or all of these costs from your national health service.

Australian citizens are entitled to subsidised health care in both the Republic (benefits for hospital treatment, but not for private medical services or prescription medicines) and Northern Ireland (some hospital and medical services, and limited ambulance transportation) through their respective national health systems. The entitlements are part of a reciprocal health care arrangement with the Australian government, and you will need to provide your Australian passport and valid Medicare card. For more information contact **Medicare** (W *www.hic.gov.au*).

Health Insurance
It is essential that you have adequate travel health insurance, even if you are eligible for limited medical cover in Ireland. See Travel Insurance (p345).

Physical Preparation
Some of the walks in this book are physically demanding and most require a reasonable level of fitness. Even if you're tackling the easy or easy–moderate walks, it pays to be relatively fit, rather than launch straight into them after months of fairly sedentary living. If you're aiming for the demanding walks, fitness is essential.

Unless you're a regular walker, start your get-fit campaign at least a month before your visit. Take a vigorous walk of about an hour, two or three times per week, and gradually extend the duration of your outings as the departure date nears. If you plan to carry a full backpack on any walk, carry a loaded pack on some of your training jaunts. Walkers with little previous experience should have a medical checkup beforehand.

Immunisations
No immunisations are required for Ireland, but before any trip it's a good idea to make sure you are up to date with routine vaccinations such as diphtheria, polio and tetanus. It's particularly important that your tetanus is up to date.

First Aid
It's a good idea at any time to know the appropriate responses to make in the event of a major accident or illness, and it's especially important if you are intending to walk for some time in a remote area. Consider learning basic first aid on a recognised course before you go, or including a first-aid manual with your first-aid kit. Although detailed first-aid instruction is outside the scope of this book, some basic points are listed under Traumatic Injuries (p62). Prevention of accidents and illness is as important – read Safety on the Walk (p65) for more advice. You should also know how to summon help should a major accident or

illness befall you or someone with you – see Rescue & Evacuation (p66).

Other Preparations

If you have any known medical problems or are concerned about your health in any way, it's a good idea to have a full check up before you go. It's far better to have any problems recognised and treated at home than to find out about them halfway up a mountain. It's also sensible to have a dental check up since toothache on the trail, with solace a couple of days away, can be a miserable experience. If you wear glasses, take a spare pair and your prescription.

If you need a particular medicine, take enough with you to last the trip. Take part of the packaging showing the generic name, rather than the brand, as this will make getting replacements easier. It's also a good idea to have a legible prescription or letter from your doctor to prove that you legally use the medication to avoid any problems at customs.

DIGITAL RESOURCES

The health page of the Lonely Planet website (Ⓦ www.lonelyplanet.com/health) offers extensive travel health information, with links to many other useful sites.

STAYING HEALTHY
Hygiene

To reduce the chances of contracting an illness, you should wash your hands frequently, particularly before handling or eating food.

Water

Many diseases are carried in water in the form of bacteria, protozoa, viruses, worms and insect eggs etc. The number one rule is to be careful of the water. If you don't know for certain that the water is safe, assume the worst.

Water Purification The simplest way of purifying water is to boil it thoroughly. Vigorous boiling should be satisfactory.

If you cannot boil water you can use a chemical agent to purify water. Chlorine and iodine are usually used, in powder, tablet or liquid form, and are available from outdoor

---

First-Aid Check List

Following is a list of items you should consider including in your first-aid kit – consult your pharmacist for brands available in your country.

Essentials
- ☐ adhesive tape
- ☐ bandages and safety pins
- ☐ elasticated support bandage – for knees, ankles etc
- ☐ gauze swabs
- ☐ nonadhesive dressings
- ☐ paper stitches
- ☐ scissors (small)
- ☐ sterile alcohol wipes
- ☐ sticking plasters (Band-Aids, blister plasters)
- ☐ sutures
- ☐ thermometer (note that mercury thermometers are prohibited by airlines)
- ☐ tweezers

Medications
- ☐ antidiarrhoea and antinausea drugs
- ☐ antifungal cream or powder – for fungal skin infections and thrush
- ☐ antihistamines – for allergies, eg, hay fever; to ease the itch from insect bites or stings; and to prevent motion sickness
- ☐ antiseptic (such as povidone-iodine) – for cuts and grazes
- ☐ cold and flu tablets, throat lozenges and nasal decongestant
- ☐ painkillers, eg, aspirin or paracetamol (acetaminophen in the USA) – for pain and fever

Miscellaneous
- ☐ calamine lotion, sting relief spray or aloe vera – to ease irritation from sunburn and insect bites or stings.
- ☐ eye drops – for washing out dust
- ☐ rehydration mixture – to prevent dehydration, eg, due to severe diarrhoea; particularly important when travelling with children.

---

equipment suppliers and pharmacies. Follow recommended dosages and allow the water to stand for the correct length of time. Chlorine tablets will kill many pathogens, but not some parasites like giardia and amoebic cysts. Iodine is more effective in purifying water. Remember that too much iodine can be harmful.

You could also consider purchasing a water filter. There are two main kinds. Total filters (which are often expensive) take out all parasites, bacteria and viruses. Simple filters (which can be a nylon mesh bag) take out dirt and larger foreign bodies, so that chemical solutions work much more effectively; if water is dirty, chemical solutions may not work at all. It's very important when buying a filter to read the specifications, so that you know exactly what it removes and what it doesn't.

Food

The stringent food hygiene regulations imposed by the EU are in force in Ireland, so you can feel confident that the food you buy or eat in pubs and restaurants is safe.

Common Ailments

Blisters This problem can be avoided. Make sure your walking boots or shoes are well worn in before your visit. At the very least, wear them on a few short walks before tackling longer outings. Your boots should fit comfortably with enough room to move your toes; boots that are too big or too small will cause blisters.

Similarly for socks – be sure they fit properly and are specifically made for walkers; even then, check to make sure that there are no seams across the widest part of your foot. Wet and muddy socks can also cause blisters, so even on a day walk, pack a spare pair of socks. Keep your toenails clipped but not too short.

If you do feel a blister coming on, treat it sooner rather then later. Apply a simple sticking plaster, or preferably one of the special blister plasters, which act as a second skin, and follow the maker's instructions for replacement.

Fatigue A simple statistic: more injuries of whatever nature happen towards the end of the day rather than earlier, when you're fresher. Although tiredness can simply be a

nuisance on an easy walk, it can be life-threatening on narrow exposed ridges or in bad weather. You should never set out on a walk that is beyond your capabilities on the day. If you feel below par, have a day off or take a bus.

To reduce the risk, don't push yourself too hard – take rests every hour or two and build in a good half hour's lunch break. Towards the end of the day, take down the pace and increase your concentration. You should also eat properly throughout the day, to replace the energy used up. Things like nuts, dried fruit and chocolate are all good energy-giving snack foods.

Knee Strain Many walkers feel the judder on long steep descents. Although you can't eliminate strain on the knee joints when dropping steeply, you can reduce it by taking shorter steps, which leave your legs slightly bent and ensure that your heel hits the ground before the rest of your foot. Some walkers find that tubular bandages help, while others use hi-tech, strap-on supports. Walking poles are very effective in taking some of the weight off the knees.

MEDICAL PROBLEMS & TREATMENT
Environmental Hazards

Walkers are at more risk than most groups from environmental hazards. However, the risk can be significantly reduced by applying common sense – and reading the following section.

Warning

Self-diagnosis and treatment can be risky, so you should always seek medical help. The local tourist office or your accommodation host can usually recommend a local doctor or clinic.

Although we do give drug advice in this section, it is for emergency use only; correct diagnosis is vital. Note that we have used generic rather than brand names for drugs – check with a pharmacist for locally available brands.

Sun Protection against the sun should always be taken seriously, even in Ireland. Slap on the sunscreen and a barrier cream for your nose and lips, wear a broad-brimmed hat and protect your eyes with good quality sunglasses with UV lenses, particularly when walking near water, sand or snow. If, despite these precautions, you get yourself burnt, calamine lotion, aloe vera or other commercial sunburn relief preparations will soothe.

Cold Too much cold can be just as dangerous as too much heat.

Hypothermia This occurs when the body loses heat faster than it can produce it and the core temperature of the body falls.

It is frighteningly easy to progress from very cold to dangerously cold due to a combination of wind, wet clothing, fatigue and hunger, even if the air temperature is above freezing. If the weather deteriorates, put on extra layers of warm clothing: a wind and/or waterproof jacket, plus wool or fleece hat and gloves are all essential. Have something energy-giving to eat and ensure that everyone in your group is fit, feeling well and alert.

Symptoms of hypothermia are exhaustion, numb skin (particularly toes and fingers), shivering, slurred speech, irrational or violent behaviour, lethargy, stumbling, dizzy spells, muscle cramps and violent bursts of energy. Irrationality may take the form of sufferers claiming they are warm and trying to take off their clothes.

To treat mild hypothermia, first get the person out of the wind and/or rain, remove their clothing if it's wet and replace it with dry, warm garments. Give them hot liquids – not alcohol – and some high-kilojoule, easily digestible food. Do not rub sufferers: instead, allow them to slowly warm themselves. Sitting between others and on a mat, not on the cold ground, are good methods of warming. This should be enough to treat the early stages of hypothermia. The early recognition and treatment of mild hypothermia is the only way to prevent severe hypothermia, which is a critical condition.

Infectious Diseases

Diarrhoea Simple things like a change of water, food or climate can cause a mild bout of diarrhoea, but a few rushed trips to the toilet, with no other symptoms, is not indicative of a major problem. More serious diarrhoea is caused by infectious agents transmitted by faecal contamination of food or water, by using contaminated utensils or directly from one person's hand to another. Paying particular attention to personal hygiene, drinking purified water and taking care of what you eat are important measures to take to avoid getting diarrhoea on your trek or travels.

Dehydration is the main danger with any diarrhoea, particularly in children or the elderly as dehydration can occur quite quickly. _Fluid replacement_ (at least equal to the volume being lost) is the most important thing to remember. Weak black tea with a little sugar, soda water, or soft drinks allowed to go flat and diluted 50% with clean water are all good. With severe diarrhoea a rehydrating solution is preferable to replace minerals and salts lost. Commercially available oral rehydration salts (ORS) are very useful; add them to boiled or bottled water. In an emergency you can make up a solution of six teaspoons of sugar and half a teaspoon of salt to a litre of boiled or bottled water. You need to drink at least the same volume of fluid that you are losing in bowel movements and vomiting. Urine is the best guide to the adequacy of replacement – if you have small amounts of concentrated urine, you need to drink more. Keep drinking small amounts often. Stick to a bland diet as you recover.

Gut-paralysing drugs such as diphenoxylate or loperamide can be used to bring relief from the symptoms, although they don't cure the problem. Only use these drugs if you do not have access to toilets, eg, if you *must* travel. These drugs are not recommended for children under 12 years, or if you have a high fever or are severely dehydrated.

Seek medical advice if you pass blood or mucus, are feverish, or suffer persistent or severe diarrhoea.

Fungal Infections Sweating liberally, probably washing less than usual and going longer without a change of clothes mean that long-distance walkers risk picking up a fungal infection, which, while an unpleasant irritant, presents no danger.

Fungal infections are encouraged by moisture, so wear loose, comfortable clothes, wash when you can and dry yourself thoroughly. Try to expose the infected area to air or sunlight as much as possible and apply an antifungal cream or powder like tolnaftate.

Tetanus This disease is caused by a germ that lives in soil, and in the faeces of horses and other animals. It enters the body via breaks in the skin. The first symptom may be discomfort in swallowing, or stiffening of the jaw and neck; this is followed by painful convulsions of the jaw and whole body. The disease can be fatal. It can be prevented by vaccination, so make sure your shots are up to date before you leave.

Insect-Borne Diseases

Lyme Disease This is a tick-transmitted infection (see Ticks, p64). The illness usually begins with a spreading rash at the site of the tick bite and is accompanied by fever, headache, extreme fatigue, aching joints and muscles and mild neck stiffness. If untreated, these symptoms usually resolve over several weeks but over subsequent weeks or months disorders of the nervous system, heart and joints may develop. Treatment works best early in the illness. Medical help should be sought.

Traumatic Injuries

Sprains Ankle and knee sprains are common injuries among hikers, particularly when crossing rugged terrain. To help prevent ankle sprains, wear boots that have adequate ankle support. If you do suffer a sprain, immobilise the joint with a firm bandage, and, if feasible, immerse the foot in cold water. Distribute the contents of your pack among your companions. Once you reach shelter, relieve pain and swelling by keeping the joint elevated for the first 24 hours and, where possible, by putting ice on the swollen joint. Take simple painkillers to ease the discomfort. If the sprain is mild, you may be able to continue your walk after a couple of days. For more severe sprains, seek medical attention as an X-ray may be needed to find out whether a bone has been broken

Major Accidents Falling or having something fall on you, resulting in head injuries or fractures, is always possible when walking, especially if you are crossing steep slopes or unstable terrain. Following is some basic advice on what to do in the event of a major accident.

If a person suffers a major fall:

1. Make sure you and other people with you are not in danger
2. Assess the injured person's condition
3. Stabilise any injuries, such as bleeding wounds or broken bones
4. Seek medical attention – see Rescue & Evacuation p66 for details

If the person is unconscious, immediately check whether they are breathing – clear their airway if it is blocked – and check whether they have a pulse – feel the side of the neck rather than the wrist. If they are not breathing but have a pulse, you should start mouth-to-mouth resuscitation immediately. In these circumstances it is best to move the person as little as possible in case their neck or back is broken.

Check for wounds and broken bones – ask the person where they have pain if they are conscious, otherwise gently inspect them all over (including their back and the back of the head), moving them as little as possible. Control any bleeding by applying firm pressure to the wound. Bleeding from the nose or ear may indicate a fractured skull. Don't give the person anything by mouth, especially if they are unconscious.

You'll have to manage the person for shock. Raise their legs above heart level (unless their legs are fractured); dress any wounds and immobilise any fractures; loosen tight clothing; keep the person warm by covering them with a blanket or other dry clothing; insulate them from the ground if possible, but don't heat them.

Some general points to bear in mind are:

- Simple fractures take several weeks to heal, so they don't need fixing straight away, but they should be immobilised to protect them from further injury. Compound fractures need urgent treatment.
- If you do have to splint a broken bone, remember to check regularly that the splint is not cutting off the circulation to the hand or foot.
- Most cases of brief unconsciousness are not associated with any serious internal injury to the brain, but as a general rule of thumb in these circumstances, any person who has been knocked unconscious should be watched for deterioration. If they do deteriorate, seek medical attention straight away.

Fractures Indications of a fracture (broken bone) are pain (tenderness of the affected area), swelling and discoloration, loss of function or deformity of a limb. Unless you know what you are doing, you shouldn't try to straighten an obviously displaced broken bone. To protect from further injury, immobilise a nondisplaced fracture by splinting it, usually in the position found, which will probably be the most comfortable position.

Fractures of the thigh bone require urgent treatment as they involve massive blood loss and pain. Seek help and treat the patient for shock. Fractures associated with open wounds (compound fractures) also require more urgent treatment than simple fractures as there is a risk of infection. Dislocations, where the bone has come out of the joint, are very painful, and should be set as soon as possible.

Broken ribs are painful but usually heal by themselves and do not need splinting. If breathing difficulties occur, or the person coughs up blood, medical attention should be sought urgently, as it may indicate a punctured lung.

Internal Injuries These are more difficult to detect, and cannot usually be treated in the field. Watch for shock, which is a specific medical condition associated with a failure to maintain circulating blood volume. Signs include a rapid pulse and cold, clammy extremities. A person in shock requires urgent medical attention.

Cuts & Scratches

Even small cuts and grazes should be washed well and treated with an antiseptic such as povidone-iodine. Dry wounds heal more quickly, so where possible avoid bandages, which can keep wounds wet. Infection in a wound is indicated by the skin margins becoming red, painful and swollen. More serious infection can cause swelling of the whole limb and of the lymph glands. The patient may develop a fever, and will need medical attention.

Burns

Immerse the burnt area in cold water as soon as possible, then cover it with a clean, dry, sterile dressing. Keep this in place with plasters for a day or so in the case of a small mild burn, longer for more extensive injuries. Seek medical help for severe and extensive burns.

Bites & Stings

Bees & Wasps These are usually painful rather than dangerous. However, in people who are allergic to them severe breathing difficulties may occur and urgent medical care is required. Calamine lotion or a commercial sting relief spray will ease discomfort and ice packs will reduce the pain and swelling.

Midges – Walkers' Bane

The midge is a tiny black insect which gathers in dense, dark clouds and descends on humans. The female of the species uses her powerful mouth to break the skin, inject saliva and suck blood through her food tube. The saliva makes the bite itch, and the more you scratch it, the itchier it becomes. Discomfort generally lasts for a few hours, longer if you're allergic to the bite.

Midges usually appear in late May and infest the countryside until the first chilly weather in September. They congregate over damp ground, rushes and sphagnum moss, and are most virulent in the early morning, in hazy sunshine and during the evening. They don't like wind, dry ground, heavy rain or bright sunshine, and rarely venture indoors.

For protection, cover your arms and legs and wear a hat with a fine netting veil, available in most outdoor equipment shops. Liquid insect repellents should keep exposed skin midge-free for a few hours at a time. Some contain DEET, a slightly toxic chemical, others are made from plant oils including citronella and eucalyptus.

Permethrin, an insecticide derived from chrysanthemums, can be applied to clothing and equipment and lasts for a week or two, but only for several minutes on the skin. Read all labels carefully and follow the directions to the letter.

Ticks Always check all over your body if you have been walking through a potentially tick-infested area as ticks can cause skin infections and other, more serious diseases. Ticks are most active from spring to autumn, especially where there are plenty of sheep or deer. They usually lurk in overhanging vegetation, so avoid pushing through tall bushes if possible.

If a tick is found attached to the skin, press down around the tick's head with tweezers, grab the head and gently pull upwards. Avoid pulling the rear of the body as this may squeeze the tick's gut contents through its mouth into your skin, increasing the risk of infection and disease. Smearing chemicals on the tick will not make it let go and is not recommended.

Hay Fever

If you suffer from hay fever, bring your usual treatment. The danger period is from late May to around July, anywhere near land under crop, which is the greater part of the island.

Women's Health

Walking is not particularly hazardous to your health, however, women's health issues can be a bit trickier to cope with when you are on the trail.

Menstruation A change in diet, routine and environment, as well as intensive exercise can all lead to irregularities in the menstrual cycle. This, in itself, is not a huge issue and your cycle should return to normal when you return to a more regular lifestyle. It is particularly important during the menstrual cycle to maintain good personal hygiene, and regularly change sanitary napkins or tampons. (Sanitary napkins and tampons don't burn or decompose readily, so make sure you carry them out in sealed, plastic bags, whatever the inconvenience.) Anti-bacterial hand gel or pre-moistened wipes can be useful if you don't have access to soap and water. You can also use applicator tampons to minimise the risk of contamination, although these are quite bulky. Because of hygiene concerns and for ease while on an extended trip, some women prefer to temporarily stop menstruation. You should discuss your options with a doctor before you go. It is also important to note that failure to menstruate could indicate pregnancy! If concerned about irregularities seek medical advice.

Pregnancy If you are pregnant, see your doctor before you travel. Even normal pregnancies can make a woman feel nauseated and tired. In the third trimester, the size of the baby can make walking difficult.

Thrush (Vaginal Candidiasis) Antibiotic use, synthetic underwear, tight trousers, sweating, contraceptive pills and unprotected sex can each lead to fungal vaginal infections. The most common is thrush (vaginal candidiasis). Symptoms include itching and discomfort in the genital area, often in association with a thick white discharge. The best prevention is to keep the vaginal area cool and dry, and to wear cotton rather than synthetic underwear and loose clothes. Thrush can be treated by clotrimazole pessaries or vaginal cream.

Urinary Tract Infection Dehydration and 'hanging on' can result in urinary tract infection and the symptoms of cystitis, which can be particularly distressing and an inconvenient problem when out on the trail. Symptoms include burning when urinating, and having to urinate frequently and urgently. Blood can sometimes be passed in the urine. Drink plenty of fluids and empty your bladder at regular intervals. If symptoms persist, seek medical attention because a simple infection can spread to the kidneys, causing a more severe illness.

SAFETY ON THE WALK
You can significantly reduce the chance of getting into difficulties by taking a few simple precautions. These are listed in the boxed text 'Walk Safety – Basic Rules' (above).

Crossing Rivers
Sudden downpours are common in the mountains and can speedily turn a gentle stream into a raging torrent. If you're in any doubt about the safety of a crossing, look for a safer passage upstream or wait. If the rain is short-lived, it should subside quickly.

If you decide it's essential to cross (late in the day, for example), look for a wide, relatively shallow stretch of the stream rather than a bend. Take off your trousers and socks, but keep your boots on to prevent injury. Put dry, warm clothes and a towel in a plastic bag near the top of your pack. Before stepping out from the bank, unclip your chest strap and belt buckle. This makes it easier to slip out of your backpack

---

Walk Safety – Basic Rules

• Allow plenty of time to accomplish a walk before dark, particularly when daylight hours are shorter.

• Study the route carefully before setting out, noting the possible escape routes and the point of no return (where it's quicker to continue than to turn back).

• Monitor your progress during the day against the time estimated for the walk, and keep an eye on the weather.

• It's wise not to walk alone. Always leave details of your intended route, number of people in your group, and expected return time with someone responsible before you set off; let that person know when you return.

• Before setting off, make sure you have a relevant map, compass, whistle, and that you know the weather forecast for the area for the next 24 hours.

---

and swim to safety if you lose your balance and are swept downstream. Use a walking pole, grasped in both hands, on the upstream side as a third leg, or go arm in arm with a companion, clasping at the wrist, and cross side-on to the flow, taking short steps.

Dogs
During walks in settled and farming areas, you're likely to encounter barking dogs – tethered or running free. Regard any dog as a potential attacker and be prepared to take evasive action: even just crossing the road can take you out of its territory and into safety. A walking pole may be useful, although use it as a last resort.

Lightning
If a storm brews, avoid exposed areas. Lightning has a penchant for crests, lone trees, small depressions, gullies, caves and cabin entrances, as well as wet ground. If you are caught out in the open, try to curl up as tightly as possible with your feet together and keep a layer of insulation between you and the ground. Place metal objects such as metal-frame backpacks and walking poles away from you.

Rescue & Evacuation

If someone in your group is injured or falls ill and can't move, leave somebody with them while another one or more goes for help. They should take clear written details of the location and condition of the victim, and of helicopter landing conditions. If there are only two of you, leave the injured person with as much warm clothing, food and water as it's sensible to spare, plus the whistle and torch. Mark the position with something conspicuous – an orange bivvy bag, or perhaps a large stone cross on the ground.

Remember, the rescue effort might be slow, perhaps taking more than 24 hours to remove the injured person.

Emergency Communications Dial ☎ 999 or ☎ 118 (the national emergency numbers) and ask for the mountain rescue or contact the nearest garda or police station. Be ready to give information on where the accident occurred, how many people were injured and the injuries sustained. If a helicopter needs to come in, what are the terrain and weather conditions like at the place of the accident? Also provide details on where you're calling from and stay put until someone arrives.

Telephone Mobile phone coverage in the areas most frequented by walkers is patchy, irrespective of which provider you use. It can vary from good to hopeless over an incredibly short distance, so using your mobile is really a matter of luck (see also Mobile Phones, p346).

Distress Signals If you need to signal for help, use these internationally recognised emergency codes. Give six short signals, such as a whistle, a yell or the flash of a light, at 10-second intervals, followed by a minute of rest. Repeat the sequence until you get a response. If the responder knows the signals, this will be three signals at 20-second intervals, followed by a minute's pause and a repetition of the sequence.

Search & Rescue Organisations The **Irish Mountain Rescue Association** (W *imra .ie.eu.org*) is a voluntary organisation. Member groups, which are locally based teams of highly trained, experienced and dedicated people, provide a rescue service to anyone in distress in the mountains. The local team will coordinate the rescue and organise a helicopter for evacuation if necessary.

Helicopter Rescue & Evacuation If a helicopter arrives on the scene, there are a couple of conventions you should be familiar with. Standing face on to the chopper:

• Arms up in the shape of a letter 'V' means 'I/We need help'
• Arms in a straight diagonal line (like one line of a letter X) means 'All OK'

For the helicopter to land, there must be a cleared space of 25m x 25m, with a flat landing pad area of 6m x 6m. The helicopter will fly into the wind when landing. In cases of extreme emergency, where no landing area is available, a person or harness might be lowered. Take extreme care to avoid the rotors when approaching a landed helicopter.

Dublin Area

Standing in the middle of O'Connell St at 5pm on Friday evening, the idea that Dublin could be a walking centre might seem ludicrous: the city itself is rather flat and attractive hills seem remote. Yet Dubliners are fortunate to have a good variety of walks within easy reach.

Within Dublin itself is Phoenix Park, Europe's largest walled urban park, where you can lose yourself for hours on end. Despite the depredations of developers, Ireland's capital still has many fine buildings of considerable architectural interest, many sites associated with famous writers and, of course, an unbelievable number of pubs and bars, all of which provide themes for fascinating city walks.

To the north is Howth Peninsula with its scenic cliff walk, and to the south is the rugged coastline between Bray and Greystones, and the nearby landmark peak of Great Sugar Loaf.

And then there are the Wicklow Mountains, laying claim to being one of Ireland's most popular walking areas, with numerous hill walks and the famous Wicklow Way (p84). In this chapter there is a suggestion for a day's walk along the Way, feasible from Dublin. The Royal and Grand Canals extending west and southwest (respectively) from the city are covered in the Waymarked Ways chapter (p335).

You can base yourself in Dublin for the walks described in this chapter; the quiet coastal suburb of Dún Laoghaire is also an alternative worth considering.

HISTORY

The first residents of Dublin were the Celts, arriving around 700 BC from eastern Europe; Dublin's Irish name, Baile Áth Cliath, meaning 'Town of the Hurdle Ford', comes from an early Celtic settlement on the north bank of the River Liffey. The Vikings set up a trading port on the other side of the Liffey, near a *dubh linn* (black pool, between today's Patrick and South Great George's

Highlights

Howth Peninsula, just out of Dublin, offers excellent cliff and coastal walking

- Exploring the historical and wildlife heritage of Phoenix Park, and strolling along the River Liffey (p72)
- Rambling around the surprisingly unspoiled and scenic coastline of the Howth Peninsula (p75)
- Discovering a spectacular path that is glued to the precipitous slopes of Bray Head (p78)
- Enjoying amazingly wide coast and mountain views from the Great Sugar Loaf (p80)

Sts) early in the 9th century, but they were soon followed by the more enduring Anglo-Normans.

During the next few centuries Dublin had its ups and downs; Trinity College was founded in 1592, initiating a deep and lasting commitment to the highest standards in education. William of Orange's victory at the Battle of the Boyne in 1690 led to the exclusion of Catholics from parliament and denial of their civil rights. Thus, in the 18th century Dublin became an attractive refuge for French Protestant Huguenots, who contributed to the city's rapid growth and booming economy; fine Georgian mansions were built while the Catholic poor languished in the slums. The Irish parliament was abolished in 1801, diminishing the city's status, at least in the eyes of some. Although Dublin escaped the worst effects of the Potato Famine (1845–51), starving people from rural areas descended on the city in huge numbers. From the mid-19th century, the movement to win independence from Britain largely centred on Dublin; the city

Exploring Dublin

Despite the depredations of ill-conceived building developments during the 1960s and 1970s, Dublin is still blessed with a fine architectural heritage, scores of individual buildings associated with famous and notorious people and events, and countless pubs, coffee bars and bistros to which you can retreat to gather strength. Naturally, the best way to explore all this is on foot, steering clear of the traffic-choked streets as far as possible.

Lonely Planet's *Dublin* and *Dublin Condensed* guides together describe seven fascinating city walks (walks mentioned here in italics are described in full in these two books). Dubliners have made their marks at home and abroad in remarkable numbers, although it has to be said that virtually all the names that crop up are those of men. (As a start to achieving some balance, the Phoenix Park & River Liffey walk (p72) passes Áras an Uachtaráin, the president's residence, the present and immediate past occupants being Mary MacAleese and Mary Robinson.) The amazingly varied crew of *Distinguished Dubliners*, on the south side of the city, includes George Bernard Shaw and his museum; Chaim Herzog, President of Israel in 1983; Gay Byrne, Ireland's most famous TV celebrity; John Henry Cardinal Newman, first rector of the Catholic University of Ireland; Edward Carson, founder of Unionism in the North; and playwright Oscar Wilde.

The *Mountjoy Square to St Stephen's Green* walk links two fine Georgian squares on the north and south sides of the city via O'Connell Bridge. On the way you pass memorials to the fallen of the 1916 Uprising, O'Connell Street's statues and some of the capital's finest public buildings, including the National Library and National Museum.

Peramabulating with a Pint challenges you to last the distance of 4km and 15 pubs, starting with Dublin's oldest, the **Brazen Head** in Bridge St and reeling via Temple Bar to finish in Merrion Row at **Doherty & Nesbitt**, which is popular with journalists and politicians. On the way there are **Messrs Maguire's** microbrewery; **Mulligan's**, the home of the best pint of Guinness in Ireland; and **Kehoe's** with its fine Victorian bar.

Dublin Tourism (☎ 01-605 7700; Ⓦ www.visitdublin.com; 2 Suffolk St) has devised three Tourism Trails all starting from their office. *Cultural Heritage* concentrates on the north side of Dublin; *Georgian Heritage* focusses on the south side, and the *Old City Trail* starts at College Green and takes in the markets, Temple Bar and much else. The information-rich notes are available at the office or online.

A guided tour is an ideal way of experiencing the famous Irish gift for storytelling, and discovering something of the city's colourful history and traditions. Dublin Tourism issues a list of several such enterprises, also available online. A great variety is on offer, among them the **1916 Rebellion Walking Tour** (☎ 01-676 2493; Ⓦ www.1916rising.com) and **Historical Walking Tours** (☎ 01-845 021; Ⓦ www.historicalinsights.ie) combining 'history and humour' and led by history graduates of Trinity College. A **Musical Pub Crawl** (☎ 01-478 0193; Ⓦ www.musicalpubcrawl.com), with two professional musicians, has a free songbook thrown in – you have been warned!

was devastated by the ill-fated 1916 Easter Rising and was torn apart again in the struggle following the signing of the Anglo-Irish Treaty in 1921.

Once peace was restored, Dublin slowly settled into its role as a national capital. One of the great achievements was the rehousing of people living in the appalling slums. On the other side of the coin, reckless developments during the 1960s and 1970s robbed the city of many of its fine old buildings until public protests impelled more sensitive policies. It wasn't until the 1990s that the city, carrying much of the country with it, surged into an era of unprecedented economic growth – the famed era of the Celtic Tiger. However, the Tiger has become a slightly lame beast and in the early years of the new millennium Dublin is showing signs of strain. It is struggling on several fronts, notably to cope with modernisation of its archaic road system and to harmoniously assimilate people from around the world, who have been attracted by the city's apparent sympathy towards refugees. The renowned cheerfulness of its citizens is perhaps less obvious, but still there for the finding.

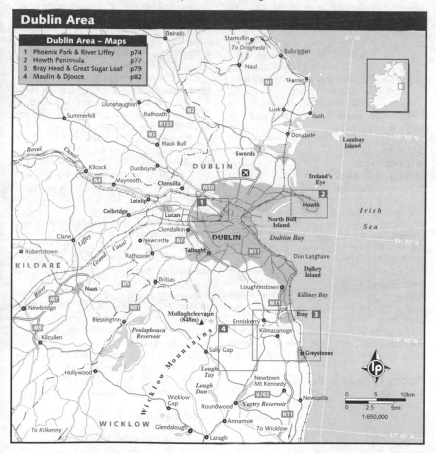

Dublin Area

Dublin Area – Maps
1	Phoenix Park & River Liffey	p74
2	Howth Peninsula	p77
3	Bray Head & Great Sugar Loaf	p79
4	Maulin & Djouce	p82

INFORMATION
Maps
The OSI 1:50,000 *Dublin Motoring Map* (€6.60) is invaluable for navigating the road maze. For finding your way about the city on foot Lonely Planet's *Dublin City Map* is – of course – the best.

Dublin's **National Map Centre** (☎ *01-476 0487;* ⓦ *www.irishmaps.ie; 34 Aungier St; open Mon-Fri)* stocks the entire OSI and OSNI ranges.

Books
Lonely Planet's *Dublin* and *Dublin Condensed* are indispensible guides for exploring the city.

Walking Dublin, by Pat Liddy, describes 24 'original' walks, mostly within the city and in the outer suburbs. *Easy Walks near Dublin*, by Joss Lynam, takes you out into the countryside with descriptions of 40 outings within an hour of the city.

Hodges & Figgis *(Dawson St, Dublin)* is the best place to go for walking guides and Irish titles generally.

DUBLIN
Information
At the busy **Dublin Tourism** (☎ *01-605 7700;* ⓦ *www.visitdublin.com; 2 Suffolk St; open daily July & Aug, Mon-Sat at other times)* office you can pick up maps, guides and information about activities in Dublin. The accommodation booking service at Dublin Tourism is always in demand; alternatively call ☎ 1800 668 668.

Internet cafés are fairly numerous around town. **Planet Cyber** (☎ *01-670 5183; 13 St Andrew St; peak rate €0.10 per minute; open daily, until late Thur & Fri)* is typical of the going rates.

If you need equipment try **Great Outdoors** *(☎ 01-679 4293; Chatham St)* or **Lowe Alpine Shop** *(☎ 01-672 7088; Temple Bar)*.

Places to Stay & Eat
The **Camac Valley Tourist Caravan & Camping Park** *(☎ 01-464 0644, fax 464 0643;* ⓔ *camacmorriscastle@eircom.net; Naas Rd, Clondalkin; camping per person €7, showers €1)* is a well-run site with plenty of grass for tents and good facilities, including a laundry and lockers. The staff are very helpful. Dublin Bus service No 69 stops at the entrance gate on the way to the city (€1.45, 21 services Monday to Saturday and nine on Sunday); a timetable is available at reception.

The large but not impersonal **Avalon House** *(☎ 01-475 0001, fax 475 0303;* ⓦ *www .avalon-house.ie; 55 Aungier St; dorm beds/ twins €20/34)* is a hostel with a range of accommodation from en suite singles to 12-bed dorms, and loads of extra services, including luggage storage and a café.

You are made to feel genuinely welcome at **Harvey's Guest House** (☎ *01-874 8384, fax 874 5510;* ⓦ *www.harveysguesthouse .com; 11 Upper Gardiner St; singles/doubles €50/90)*, a restored Georgian terrace where the rooms are furnished with antiques.

Minimarkets, small **grocers** and **street markets** are scattered throughout the city.

There are scores, probably hundreds, of cafés, bistros and restaurants from one end of Dublin to the other.

The popular **Cornucopia** *(☎ 01-677 7583; 19 Wicklow St; mains €8.25-8.95; open to 8pm Mon-Sat, to 9pm Thur)* is an unlicensed, cafeteria-style vegetarian-vegan oasis offering pasta bakes, quiches, bean stew and many other dishes. There's a wide choice of fruit juices and herbal teas.

The best coffee in Dublin is served at **Dunne & Crescenzi** (☎ *01-677 3815; 4 Frederick St South; mains to €9; open to 7pm Mon-Wed & Sat, to 8pm Thur & Fri)* with authentic Italian ambience; you can also enjoy a snack or light meal.

A big place spread over three floors, **Messrs Maguire** *(☎ 01-670 5777; 1-2 Burgh Quay; mains €8-12)* serves superior pub fare to help soak up some of their eight brewed-on-the-premises beers.

The extremely popular **Pasta Fresca** *(☎ 01-679 8965; 2-4 Chatham St; mains €9.50-21.50)* serves good Italian fare and has some outside tables for those welcome dry nights.

Getting There & Away
For information about international services see Getting There & Away (p350).

Air This is the fastest but most expensive way of travelling between Ireland's major centres. Dublin's international **airport** (☎ 01-814 1111; W www.dublin-airport.com) is 10km north of the city. Dublin Bus' Airport Express (Airlink) service No 747/748 links Busáras (the central bus station) and the airport (€5, 35 minutes, every 20 minutes) via Connolly, Tara St and Heuston train stations, and O'Connell St (near Dublin Bus office). Single fares are given here; return tickets generally cost much less than twice the single or even less than the single itself.

There are regular **Aer Arann** (☎ 01-814 1058; W www.aerarann.ie) flights between Dublin and Cork (€96, 55 minutes, seven Monday to Friday, three Saturday, two Sunday), and Dublin and Galway (€66, 45 minutes, five Monday to Friday, three Saturday and Sunday). **British Airways** (☎ 0845-773 3377 UK, 1800 626 747 Ireland; W www.britishairways.com) links Derry and Dublin (£44.40, 50 minutes, twice daily). There are also **EuroCeltic** (☎ 0818-300 100; W www.euroceltic.com) flights between Dublin and County Donegal's Carrickfinn (€45, 55 minutes, two Monday to Friday, one Saturday and Sunday), and Dublin and Sligo (€45, 50 minutes, two daily).

Bus The Republic's national bus line, **Bus Éireann** (☎ 01-836 6111; W www.buseireann.ie) operates services to and from **Busáras** (Store St), Dublin's central bus station.

Service No 200, run in conjunction with Northern Ireland's **Ulsterbus** (☎ 028 9066 6630), links Dublin and Belfast's Europa bus centre (€16.50, two hours 55 minutes, seven Monday to Saturday and six Sunday).

Bus Éireann operates two direct services between Dublin and Cork's **Parnell Place** (☎ 021-450 8188): No 7 goes via Kilkenny (€19, 6¼ hours, at least two daily) and No 8 is routed through Caher (€19, four hours 25 minutes, six daily). Service No 20 goes to Galway (€12, three hours 40 minutes, 15 daily), arriving at the **Galway Bus Station** (☎ 091-562 000).

Train The Republic's railway network is operated by **Iarnród Éireann** (☎ 01-836 6222; W www.irishrail.ie) out of Dublin's **Connolly** (☎ 01-836 3333) and **Heuston** (☎ 01-836 5421) stations.

The cross-border *Enterprise* service, run in conjunction with **Northern Ireland Railways** (☎ 028-9066 6630) links Dublin Connolly and Belfast Central (€29, two hours five minutes, eight Monday to Saturday and five Sunday). It isn't the fastest of services, but much less stressful and subject to delays than driving.

Iarnród Éireann operates services from Dublin Heuston to Cork (€44.40, around three hours, four daily) and to Galway (€32.50, two hours 55 minutes, four daily).

Car By road the distance between Dublin and Belfast is 167km; the bits and pieces of the M1 are gradually being joined up between Dublin and the border so the route is now dual carriageway as far as Drogheda, but is plagued by delays. The linking major roads in the North are generally better. The road distance between Dublin and Cork is 257km via the N7 and N8; between Dublin and Galway it's 219km via the M4, N4 and N6. The M50 virtually rings Dublin and removes the need to go anywhere near the city on cross-country routes. Late in 2002 it was still incomplete, but the end is somewhere in sight. A toll of €1.30 is charged between junctions 6 (for the N3 to Navan and Cavan) and 7 (for the N4 to Mullingar).

Getting Around

Given the motorised madness that is driving around Dublin, public transport is a very convenient, inexpensive alternative. Indeed, for all but one of the walks in this chapter, public transport is the preferred option.

Dublin Bus (☎ 01-873 4222; W www.dublinbus.ie; 59 O'Connell St; open Mon-Sat) blankets the metropolitan areas with its services. **DART** (Dublin Area Rapid Transport; ☎ 01-836 6222; W www.irishrail.ie; Connolly Station) trains run along the coast, and four suburban rail lines reach further north and south and into the hinterland. In 2003 the first of three city routes opened on the **Luas** (☎ 1800 67 6464; W www.luas.ie), a light rail system.

Bus-only and combined bus-rail tickets are available at the Dublin Bus office. Rail-only and combined tickets can be bought from the **Rail Travel Centre** (☎ *01-836 6222; 35 Abbey St Lower*).

The short-hop zone reaches north to Balbriggan, south to Kilcoole and west to Maynooth. The following tickets are intended for visitors; no ID is required.

duration	transport	cost
one day	rail only	€6
one day	rail & bus	€7.20
three days	rail & bus	€13.30
seven days	rail & bus	€24

Another option is the Rambler bus ticket, which provides unlimited travel on consecutive days on all Dublin Bus scheduled services, including Airlink. This covers access to the Howth Peninsula, Bray and Phoenix Park walks. Tickets are issued for one, three, five and seven days and cost €4.50, €8.80, €13.90 and €16.50 respectively.

Phoenix Park & River Liffey

Duration	3½–4 hours
Distance	12.7km
Difficulty	easy
Start/Finish	Parkgate St entrance
Transport	bus

Summary Europe's largest enclosed urban park, home to herds of fallow deer and Ireland's president, has a variety of monuments and an excellent visitor centre.

Phoenix Park is a miracle; a 300-plus-year-old park that, at 708ha (the size of thousands of suburban housing blocks), is still intact. Occupying an oval-shaped tract of open fields and woodlands, it lies above the north bank of the River Liffey and is surrounded by busy roads and Dublin's mid-western suburbs. Its name is believed to be an anglicised version of the Irish *fionn uisce*, referring to the stream which trickles through the park. Originally set aside in

1662 (see the boxed text 'Phoenix Park at a Glance', p73), it has witnessed deer hunting, all manner of sporting events, murders, a Papal mass and the invasion then partial banishing of motor vehicles. The unifying threads throughout its history are the countless Dubliners and visitors doing nothing more adventurous than walking, jogging or cycling and enjoying its open spaces, relative peace and naturalness.

Fields and the extensive web of paths make possible a great variety of walks within its boundaries. The roughly circular route described here concentrates on the eastern half of the park, takes in a diversion to the surprisingly quiet south bank of the River Liffey, and returns to the park for a final triumphal stroll past the towering Wellington Monument.

PLANNING

The best time to visit the park depends on whether you want to enjoy its open spaces unhindered during the week, or join the crowds to watch a football or hurling match, or perhaps even a polo chukka, during the weekend.

There's no need to bring food or drink – you'll pass a kiosk and restaurant on the walk, and a couple of shops and a pub en route to the River Liffey.

Maps

The OSI 1:50,000 map No 50 *Dublin City and District* shows the park but not all the paths. More useful is the OSI 1:20,000 *Dublin Street Map*, which covers the area within the M50 motorway.

GETTING TO/FROM THE WALK

Iarnród Éireann's (☎ *01-836 6222*) Heuston station, the terminus of the Arrow suburban line (to Kildare), is only 10 minutes' walk from the park via St John's Rd West and Parkgate St.

Numerous **Dublin Bus** (☎ *01-873 4222*) services pass the Parkgate St entrance, including Nos 25, 25A, 26, 66 and 67 from Wellington Quay; Nos 68 and 69 from Aston Quay; and No 51 from Emmet St. The single fare is €1.05.

THE WALK

Just beyond the impressive pillars at the Parkgate St entrance, turn right into the **People's Garden**, the only formal part of the park. Shortly bear left at a junction, then right along paths between colourful flower beds, past a pond on your right and then a statue of **Sean Heuston** (a leader of the 1916 Rising) on the left. Cross a road and continue down a path; a 19th-century bandstand sits in **Band Hollow** on your right and soon you reach **Phoenix Park Tea Rooms** (*light meals €2.50-5.30; open 10.30am to around 5pm daily*) in a well-preserved 19th-century timber building.

Cross the road on the far side of the building and follow a path bending right beside the fence of **Dublin Zoo** (☎ *01-677 1125*; **W** *www.dublinzoo.ie*; *admission €10.10; open daily*), which is one of Europe's oldest zoos, then paralleling a road leading north with a polo field on the left. At a road junction turn left; behind the gates on the right is **Áras an Uachtaráin**, the Irish president's residence. Walk along the road, past the **All-Ireland Polo Club** building, and shortly, from the end of the road, follow a grassed path beside the wall on your right; look out for a gap in the hedge opening up a fine view of the imposing presidential quarters.

With the **Phoenix Monument** on your left, cross another road leading to the presidential home and head towards the visitor centre, as a sign indicates, along a narrow road. Beyond the centre's car park you come to **Ashtown Castle**, which dates from the 17th century. The oaks at the castle entrance are as old as the building itself. Next to the **restaurant** (*light meals to €6.50; open for lunch daily*) are the only public toilets you'll easily find in the park.

Next door is the **visitor centre** (☎ *01-677 0095*; *adult €2.50; open daily*). Allow at least an hour to watch the excellent video on the park's long and varied history, and to absorb the informative display about its natural and cultural heritage.

To resume your exploration of the park, walk back down the road to Chesterfield Ave, cross the road and pass the entrance to the **US Ambassador's Residence**. Follow a

Phoenix Park at a Glance

Here is a quick reference list of key dates in the history of the park, and of people who have been associated with it in some way.

1662 – Royal Deer Park set aside by order of King Charles II; later populated with English fallow deer
1684 – park reaches its present size
1735 – Magazine Fort built
1747 – park opens to the public; Phoenix Monument unveiled by Lord Chesterfield, who also planted thousands of trees in the park
1751 – work starts on Vice-Regal Lodge, now *Áras an Uachtaráin* (residence of Ireland's president)
1764 – Royal Hibernian Military School opens, now St Mary's Hospital
1776 – Deerfield Park built to house British chief secretary for Ireland
1817–61 – Wellington Monument built to commemorate the achievements of Arthur Wellesley, the famous Duke and a Dubliner
1831 – Dublin Zoo founded
1864 – People's Garden opens
1875 – demonstrations in favour of Sunday closing of pubs
1882 – British Chief Secretary, Frederick Cavendish, and Under Secretary, Thomas Burke, murdered in the park
1903 – 3000 trees damaged by fierce storm
1927 – US Embassy opens in the former Deerfield Park
1932 – 31st Eucharistic Congress conducted in the park
1979 – 1.25 million people attend Mass celebrated by Pope John Paul II
1980's – Dutch elm disease finishes off trees planted in 18th century; extensive replanting program begins
1986 – Phoenix Park declared a National Historic Park

path south beside the road to a car park and the nearby **Papal Cross**, erected in 1979. From the car park go on to the nearby road and continue to the right for a short distance then left along the road ahead (Kyber Rd), which is closed to vehicles. Continue down through a wide, shallow valley to a car park below **Magazine Fort** – worth a diversion for the view of Dublin. Continue to a road junction and turn right, passing below the fort; bear right up to a narrow path beside football fields and go on to Acres Rd. Bear left, cross a road close to the gate of **St Mary's Hospital**, then descend the steps to a road and turn right. Continue down to a wider road and turn right again. Opposite the entrance to Cheshire Home, a respite care facility, is a roadside plaque describing the nearby **Knockmaree cromlech**, a prehistoric burial chamber. With luck you might find it in the long grass at the top of the hill behind you (as you read the plaque), on the left beside the railings around the lodge.

Continue on to the next plaque, featuring **Chapelizod Gate**, and walk down a bitumen path, through that gate and along Park Lane to meet Martin's Row and turn left into **Chapelizod village** (this strange-sounding name is thought to be a corruption of Chapel of Isolde). There's a small **shop** here and, a

few steps to the left, **Kelly's grocery** in a 400 year-old building. Continue to traffic lights, cross the River Liffey bridge ahead and turn left beside the **Bridge Inn** along St Laurence Rd. About 700m further on, go through a gateway between stone pillars to the river bank. A bitumen path makes for easy walking downstream beside the remarkably peaceful river, through a couple of gates into the **Irish National War Memorial Park**, the main features of which are some distance from the river. At the eastern end of the park, bear right along a minor road and left again to cross the Liffey and then Conyngham Rd to the **Turnstile Gates** and back into Phoenix Park. Go up steps and bear right to a roadside path for about 250m and on to the 67m-high **Wellington Monument**. In its day this was the world's tallest obelisk; the bronze bas-reliefs, made from captured cannons, depict Wellington's battlefield victories. Cross the grass to Chesterfield Ave and turn right to the Parkgate St exit.

Phoenix Park & River Liffey

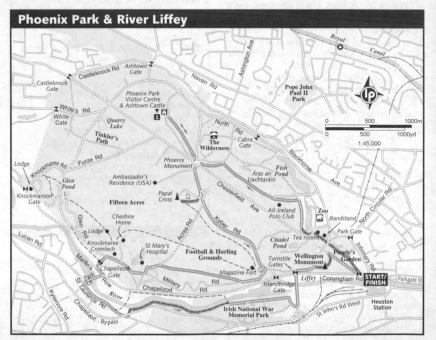

Howth Peninsula

Duration	4½–5 hours
Distance	15km
Difficulty	easy–moderate
Start/Finish	Howth (p76)
Transport	train, bus

Summary Seemingly remote from Dublin, ramble across a heathy hill and along the cliffs of the Howth Peninsula overlooking Dublin Harbour, with seabirds and seals for company.

The Howth Peninsula forms the northern shore of Dublin Bay. Despite the relentless march of suburbia elsewhere around the capital, the peninsula has managed to retain a sizable tract of open space around the Ben of Howth (171m) and stretches of quite rugged coastline.

A web of paths, some clear, some obscure, on the open heathland, and the well-maintained path along the southern and eastern coastlines, are linked in the walk described here. It's an extremely scenic excursion for, on a really good day, you can see both the Mourne Mountains and the Wicklows. At different times of the year, these vistas are framed by bright yellow gorse, and the vivid pinks and mauves of heath and ling heather.

Surprisingly perhaps, given Dublin's proximity, the Howth Peninsula is home to the largest seabird colony on Ireland's east coast. Thousands of birds, including fulmars, kittiwakes and guillemots, nest on the steep quartzite cliffs between Balscadden Bay and the Baily lighthouse. What's more, the southern shore is an internationally important wintering ground for waders and wildfowl, such as redshank and brent geese.

The name Howth perpetuates the Viking visitation here centuries ago and is derived from the Norse word *höfuth*, meaning 'head'. In the early 19th century the British government built defensive Martello towers along the east coast, three of which survive in and near Howth – one on the southwest coast and two above the western shore of Balscadden Bay (see the boxed

Martello Towers

Still a fairly common feature along Ireland's coast, these elegant structures are part of the scene on the Howth Peninsula and Bray Head walks; there are also two near Dún Laoghaire.

They date from colonial times, when 27 were built along the east coast (about one-third of the total planned for the whole country) between 1804 and 1814. The intention was to defend the coast from French invasion – an indignity already endured twice during the 1790s and perceived as a real threat with Napoleon in power. Ironically based on a prototype from Napoleon's birthplace, Corsica, they were three storeys high, had 2.5m-thick walls, sported huge, rail-mounted cannons on the roof and could house a small band of troops.

They've endured remarkably well and now often serve the harmless purposes of restaurants and residences.

There's one about 1.5km west of Dún Laoghaire near the Seapoint DART station, but of much greater interest is the one at Sandycove Point, the same distance east of the town. It houses the **James Joyce Museum** (☎ *01-280 9265; admission €5.50; open daily Apr-Oct)* where you can see letters, photographs, first editions of Joyce's work, and perhaps relive some of the events in his famous work *Ulysses*.

text 'Martello Towers', above). The harbour dates from 1812, when the village became the main port for passengers and mail arriving from England, but it soon silted up and traffic moved south to Dún Laoghaire. Nowadays the harbour is crammed with sailing craft and on fine weekends the village is usually invaded by beach-starved Dubliners seeking a day by the sea – but most likely spending half their time in a traffic jam.

The moral is, of course, use public transport, so the following walk starts and finishes at Howth's DART station.

PLANNING

There are no easily reached places for a snack along the way, so come self-sufficient.

Maps

The OSI 1:50,000 map No 50 *Dublin City and District* covers the walk, although it doesn't show the fine detail of paths around the Ben of Howth.

NEAREST TOWN
Howth

Despite its proximity to Dublin, Howth feels like a large seaside village and, with excellent transport to the city it's a popular alternative base from which to explore the capital. There's an ATM diagonally opposite the DART station. The nearest TIC is in Dublin.

Places to Stay & Eat The nearest camping ground is the **North Beach Caravan & Camping Park** (*☎/fax 01-843 7131; Rush; camping per person €6*) reached either by suburban train to Rush and Lusk on the Dublin–Dundalk line or Dublin Bus service No 33 from Eden Quay.

For a welcoming, older style B&B head to **Highfield** (*☎/fax 01-832 3936; Thormanby Rd; singles/doubles €30/50*), which has decent-sized, homely and mostly en suite rooms; the hosts will pick you up from the station (about 20 minutes' walk uphill) by arrangement.

All the superbly decorated rooms in **King Sitric Hotel** (*☎ 01-832 5235, fax 839 2442; ⓦ www.kingsitric.ie; East Pier; en suite rooms €57-95*) enjoy sea views. The name recalls Sitryggr, a Norse King of Dublin in the 11th century. The **restaurant** (*mains to €30*) is renowned for its amazing array of fish dishes and includes a couple of vegetarian choices.

There are a **supermarket** and a small **grocer** in Harbour Rd.

Seafood is also prominent at the popular **Wheelhouse Restaurant** (*☎ 01-839 0555; Harbour Rd; mains €15-22*), although poultry and some vegetarian dishes also feature. Cheaper bar meals are served downstairs in the Waterside Lounge.

Getting There & Away Howth is at the northern end of the **DART** (*☎ 01-703 3504*) train line out of Dublin Connolly (single/return €1.45/2.75, 14 minutes). **Dublin Bus** (*☎ 01-873 4222*) service No 31B goes from Lower Abbey St, Dublin, to Howth DART station (€1.45, at least 12 daily). By road, Howth is 17km from Dublin; follow the M50, N32 and R105.

THE WALK

At Howth's DART station, cross the main road and go through a gap in the wall (beside the bus stop) and walk up a ramp through woodland, soon with houses on the left. Cross a small park to a suburban road and turn right. About 120m along turn right up a bitumen path to a road and go right again for about 50m up to a flight of steps. Climb them to a cul-de-sac. Again it's right, to the road end, then go through a narrow gap in a wall between two houses to grassland, leaving the houses behind. Bear left here to follow a narrow path up through Scots pine woodland and a gorse thicket; then follow a grassy path, past a playing field on the left, with the Ben of Howth, topped by a mast, now visible ahead.

At a fork go left, up through bracken to a wider track. Make a right turn, then shortly it's left at another junction. This broad track takes you up through heather to a rough bitumen road. Turn right and go up to the summit of **Ben of Howth** (about 45 minutes to an hour from the start). The wide view, which takes in Great Sugar Loaf, Bray Head, the northern Wicklows and Dublin Harbour to the south, and Ireland's Eye and Lambay Island to the north, makes it easy enough to ignore the communications mast and other assorted rubbish that defile the summit.

Retrace your steps down the road to a wide path on the left and descend it to a track; turn left for about 50m then right to reach rocky **Dun Hill**. You'll find a small prehistoric burial chamber here, possibly once covered by a large cairn. In the early 19th century a semaphore station stood on the hill, from which messages were relayed between the local Martello towers and ships in Dublin Bay. The excellent view takes in the Howth Peninsula and North Bull Island.

Return along the path to a junction and bear right. About 130m further on, go right again to an intersection. Keep to the right and the track soon merges with another from the left, bends left and descends to a gate and a gap in a wall. Turn right at the bitumen road (Windgate Rd) here. Follow roads down, past palatial mansions in vast grounds, turning right at successive junctions to a three-way junction where a sign says you've come down **Old Carrickbrack Rd**; the main road is the R105 (Ceanchor Rd goes down to the left). Turn right along a path on the north side of the R105; after about 300m cross to an iron gate in a stone wall behind which is a sign, 'Warning: Dangerous Cliffs'. Descend through trees and bracken, and bear right near a farm building on the left, continue along a grassed path and down to the cliff path (about 1½ hours

from Ben of Howth), a few hundred metres east of a **Martello tower**; see the boxed text 'Martello Towers' (p75).

The path wanders up and down along the coast, at first beside an unusual wall made of compacted shells studded with small rocks. Soon you cross a short stretch of shingle beach; look out for seals around here – a large, lazy grey seal was spotted around here when the walk was surveyed. Around Drumleck Point and into **Doldrum Bay**, Baily lighthouse, built in 1814, comes into view. When you reach the lighthouse road, cross it diagonally to the left and continue along a path. About 500m further on, a long flight of steps climbs the hillside – an optional detour to the lookout at **the Summit** (145m). At the Nose of Howth the path changes direction, now heading westwards, and soon ends at a large car park. Walk along Balscadden Rd then Harbour Rd, back to Howth DART station (2½ hours from the start of the cliff path).

Howth Peninsula

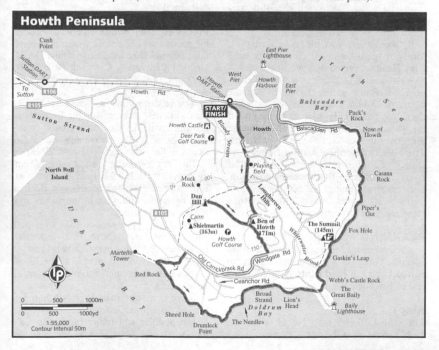

Bray Head

Duration	4–4¼ hours
Distance	10km
Difficulty	easy–moderate
Start	Greystones
Finish	Bray
Nearest Town	Dún Laoghaire (p78)
Transport	train

Summary A dramatic walk above coastal cliffs separating two popular seaside towns; far-reaching vistas from Bray Head's summit.

The southern seaside suburbs of Greystones and Bray, fast spreading inland towards the foothills of the Wicklow Mountains, are still recognisable as the traditional seaside resorts to which Dubliners have escaped on holidays. They remain extremely popular on weekends, sunny or not – places where fun parlours have not (yet) been ousted by computer games; kids play happily in the sand and water; shops sell dreadful souvenirs; and people can enjoy ice cream parlours and simply strolling.

Between these two places is a marvellously rugged stretch of coastline around Bray Head, traversed by a well-used path – so well-used, in fact, that on a Sunday afternoon it feels almost like O'Connell St in the centre of Dublin. Don't miss the ascent to the summit of Bray Head towards the end of the walk – it's well worth the effort for the view over the scene of the day's exertions. The walk is described starting from Greystones and finishing in Bray; it can of course be done in the opposite direction, but remember that there are many more trains back towards Dublin from Bray than there are from Greystones.

PLANNING

For refreshments, there are small **grocers** opposite Greystones station, and **ice cream parlours** and **fast food joints** at the southern end of Bray beach.

Maps

The OSI 1:50,000 map No 56 *Wicklow, Dublin, Kildare* is the one to carry.

NEAREST TOWN
Dún Laoghaire

Although only 7km separate this town and Dublin, it could easily be 107km. While Dún Laoghaire (pronounced 'doon-lair-ah') is refreshed by sea breezes, Dublin steams. Dún Laoghaire is far quieter and more relaxed, and prices are generally lower without sacrificing quality. The DART takes you to and fro speedily and inexpensively.

Information There is a **Dublin Tourism office** (☎ 1800 668 668, 01-605 7700; open Mon-Sat) in the ferry terminal opposite the DART station. It provides all the usual TIC services and has an excellent range of maps and guides.

Easons bookshop (Upper Georges St) is good if you are looking for local and Dublin background titles. There are three ATMs located in the same street. For Internet access, **Net House** (☎ 01-230 3085; 20 Upper Georges St; 15 minutes for €1.50) is open daily until late.

Places to Stay & Eat The nearest camping ground is at Shankill, which is five stations beyond Dún Laoghaire on the DART: **Shankill Caravan & Camping Park** (☎ 01-282 0011, fax 282 0108; camping per person with car €14).

A variety of rooms from single to family, plus a kitchen and comfortable living areas are offered at **Marina House Hostel** (☎ 01-284 1524; W www.marinahouse.com; 7 Old Dunleary Rd; dorm beds/singles €18/25.50).

The very comfortable and hospitable **Annesgrove** (☎ 01-280 9801; 28 Rosmeen Gardens; singles/doubles €50/64) is a B&B in an older-style, suburban home and is situated in a quiet street.

As well as a pleasant outlook over park and sea, the **Ferry House** (☎ 01-280 8301, fax 284 6530; e ferry_house@hotmail.com; 15 Clarinda Park North; singles/doubles €38/64) is conveniently located and offers large, en suite rooms.

There is a **supermarket** in Northumberland St off Upper Georges St.

The popular and rather loud **Mao Cafe Bar** (☎ 01-670 4899; Unit 3, The Pavillion;

mains €12.50-18) faces the sea, and offers a varied Asian menu and a good range of Asian beers.

The menu at **Walter's Restaurant & Bar** (☎ 01-280 7442; 68 Upper Georges St; mains €15-24), an upstairs restaurant with a cool, contemporary look, is more interesting than usual, and includes Moroccan-style lamb, salads and pasta.

Getting There & Away Dún Laoghaire is on the **DART** (☎ 01-836 6222) line with frequent services from Dublin's Connolly (€1.65, 23 minutes).

Dublin Bus (☎ 01-873 4222) services Nos 7 and 7A from O'Connell St (€1.45, frequent) and No 46A from Fleet St near Trinity College (€1.65, frequent) link Dublin and the town.

By road, coming from the south, turn off the N11 along the R118; from the north take the clearly signposted N31 from the N11. Dún Laoghaire is 7km from Dublin.

GETTING TO/FROM THE WALK
Greystones is at the southern end of the **DART** (☎ 01-703 3504) line with frequent services from Dún Laoghaire (€1.65, 28 minutes). **Dublin Bus** (☎ 01-873 4222) service No 84 from Dublin's Eden Quay stops near Greystones station (€2.95, one hour 20 minutes, at least 12 daily).

Bray is also on the DART (€1.65, 18 minutes to Dún Laoghaire). Dublin Bus service No 46 from Bray station returns to Eden Quay (€1.65, every 20 minutes daily). Service No 45A from Bray station goes to Crofton Rd in Dún Laoghaire (€1.45, at least 15 daily).

THE WALK
From Greystones station exit turn right for about 200m then take the first left, a nameless lane; cross a footbridge over the railway and go on to the promenade beside the rocky shore. Beyond the small harbour follow a cul-de-sac between houses, past the

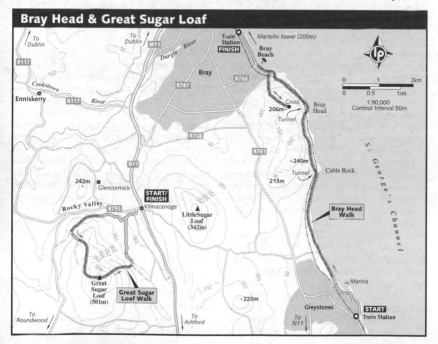

Bray Head & Great Sugar Loaf

Greystones Sailing Club, through an informal parking area – and the walk really gets going, along a wide gravel track. From here you have a good view of conical Great Sugar Loaf (see the walk description this page) to the west and Bray Head fills the prospect northwards.

Now on a path, pass a playing field, and soon dip left to bypass a washed away bridge. The path gradually rises, past **Cable Rock** below, along the low cliff top, through several hundred metres of woodland and tall scrub then across the precipitous, open slopes of Bray Head. In places you look straight down to the railway line, perched rather precariously on a wide ledge.

Eventually you round a bend: Dalkey Hill and its adjacent island come into view, and the gradual descent towards Bray beach soon starts. Well down towards the strand you come to a gap in the stone wall on the left and a flight of steps (two to 2¼ hours from Greystones). This is where you can diverge to climb to the top of Bray Head.

The concrete steps soon end so continue on a steep, rough path up through woodland, keeping more or less straight ahead, ignoring paths diverging right and left. From a crude rubbish tip in the trees, trend left, keeping to the widest path. Soon you emerge from the trees and the path winds around, up through gorse, heather and rocks, to the **summit** (206m) and a large cross. The wide view takes in the Howth Peninsula and Dublin to the north, and Great Sugar Loaf to the southwest.

Return to the wide path more or less at sea level (having taken about 1¼ hours for the ascent and descent) and stroll along the promenade, or take to the beach if the tide is out. Bray's **Martello tower**, now a private home, is partly hidden among houses a short distance inland from the marina (see the boxed text 'Martello Towers', p75). About 250m short of the harbour breakwater and marina at the northern end of Bray beach, turn left along a side street; there are two pubs here – the **Hibernia** and the **Katie Gallaghers**. Cross the railway and the station is a short distance to the left (another 45 minutes after returning to the wide path).

Great Sugar Loaf

Duration	2¼–2½ hours
Distance	6.5km
Difficulty	moderate
Start/Finish	Kilmacanoge
Nearest Town	Enniskerry (p80)
Transport	bus

Summary A steep ascent to the breezy summit of an unmistakable landmark between the coast and the Wicklow foothills.

A perfect cone from most angles, Great Sugar Loaf (501m) is always there in the views during the first day of the Wicklow Way (p84), and from Dublin's southern beachside suburbs. It stands proud as an outlier of the Wicklows between Djouce Mountain and the coastal town of Greystones. Quartzite boulders and scree spill over the summit and well down the steep slopes; in late summer, magenta-coloured bell heather between the grey rocks, and the ubiquitous bright green bracken make the mountain very colourful.

PLANNING

The best time for this walk is during spring (April to early June) before the bracken reaches its full towering height. At any time, it's advisable to wear gaiters and/or long trousers as protection against lurking gorse bushes. Although the walk is of relatively short duration, bus journeys to and fro on top of this make a full day of it.

There are **shops** in the two service stations at Kilmacanoge, on either side of the N11; the nearby **Glencormac Inn** (☎ 01-286 2996) serves lunches and sandwiches.

Maps

The OSI 1:50,000 map No 56 *Wicklow, Dublin, Kildare* covers the walk, although it doesn't show all the paths or the subtleties of the mountain's contours.

NEAREST TOWN
Enniskerry

This small village is fast becoming a trendy commuter village for people working in

Dublin, but services are still limited. Enniskerry has **supermarket**, post office and a couple of pubs.

Places to Stay & Eat As well as offering good-sized rooms, **Cherbury** (☎ 01-282 8679; Monastery; singles/doubles €38/65) is a very walker-friendly B&B where breakfast is well matched to the needs of walkers, and a pick-up and drop-off service is available by arrangement.

The **Powerscourt Arms Hotel** (☎ 01-282 8903, fax 286 4909; singles/doubles €51/90) is a traditional pub with comfortable en suite rooms. The menu of standard pub fare offers good value.

The informal **Wingfields Bistro** (☎ 01-204 2354; Church Hill; mains €17-26, early bird menu mains €14) offers beautifully cooked dishes with Asian and Italian influences.

Getting There & Away There are two **Dublin Bus** (☎ 01-873 4222) services from Enniskerry: No 44C to Townsend St in the city (€1.65, minimum 24 daily) and No 185 to Bray DART station (€1.30, minimum 16 daily), from where you can catch a train to Dublin Connolly (€1.65, 42 minutes).

GETTING TO/FROM THE WALK

Bus Éireann (☎ 01-836 6111) service No 133 from Dublin's Busáras stops in Kilmacanoge (€2.75, one hour 25 minutes, minimum six daily). On the outward journey the bus stops at the service station about 250m north of the start of the walk, so cross the N11 on a footbridge and turn left. For the return, the stop is beside the other service station, just up from the N11-R755 junction.

At the time of writing there was nowhere safe or sensible to park a car in the village amid the chaos of roadworks on the N11. Parking at the Glencormac Inn is strictly for patrons only.

THE WALK (see map p79)

Set out along the R755 past Glencormac Inn; 30m beyond the entrance to the adjacent Church of St Mochonog turn left along a minor road and then almost immediately right to continue along a narrower road.

Further on, you'll come to a junction opposite an impressive two-storey house on the left, set back from the road; turn right here. This vehicle track winds up across moorland and on to meet a gravel road – turn left. A short distance along go through a gate into a lane enclosed by stone walls and you soon pass a house entrance on the right. Another gate leads to a slightly overgrown path through gorse. The path crosses a shallow saddle and rises, with the busy R755 snaking through Rocky Valley below. Press on through more gorse, crossing a small stream; the path bends left and widens to parallel a fence and an old stone wall on the right. A wall on your left ends a few minutes further on; continue on a wide, clear track for about 250m to an oblique junction on the left and head uphill.

Soon you should see the unmistakable tip of Great Sugar Loaf ahead as you follow the grassy track. Beyond a rock-strewn hill on the left, the track swings east to cross the foot of another, bigger rocky hill on the right. What is by now a path rises towards the eastern flank of Great Sugar Loaf itself at a prominent junction; go right here. Continue up and southwards then cross the mountain's northern ridge to its western flank and go south for approximately 175m. Bear left up a scree slope, trending right for a safer, more stable route to the small flat **summit**, unadorned by trig pillar or cairn (about 1¼ to 1½ hours from Kilmacanoge). Among the multifarious features in the view are Howth Peninsula and Dublin to the north, Bray Head and Greystones to the east, and Djouce Mountain among the northern Wicklows to the west.

Start the descent northeastwards, going carefully over the boulders; there isn't a consistent path. Generally aim for the southern corner of the woodland far below and keep fairly close to the gully on the left. After a while you should be able to make out the line of a path roughly parallel to the gully; head for it and with luck you'll emerge unscathed on a track close to the corner of the deciduous woodland; turn left and it's no more than 20 minutes back to the start along a gravel track then bitumen (an hour from the summit).

DUBLIN AREA

Maulin & Djouce

Duration	5–5½ hours
Distance	15.5km
Difficulty	moderate
Start/Finish	Glencree
Nearest Town	Enniskerry (p80)
Transport	private

Summary A pair of easy-to-reach, not too challenging mountains in the northern Wicklows with fine coast and mountain views.

Maulin (570m) and Djouce Mountain (725m, pronounced 'jowss') are the first really substantial chunks of high ground encountered as you delve into the Wicklow Mountains from Dublin, and they offer the best mountain walking close to the city. Overlooking the source of the Dargle River in wild and lonely Glensoulan, both summits are close to the Wicklow Way. However, most Way walkers (including the author) have their minds set on chasing waymarkers and the prospect of adding to the day's ascent total is, most likely, a step or two too far. Besides, these two fine hills are well worth doing in their own right, one at a time or together.

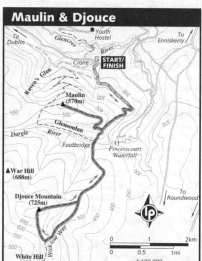

The route to Maulin is a basic out and back one; for this alone allow three hours. It is possible to vary the described walk in two ways. By descending southwest from a point about 400m west of the summit into Glensoulan and following the youthful Dargle River down to a footbridge and path; from there you can continue to Djouce or return to the start (allow about four hours for the latter). Alternatively, you could continue west from the summit then descend northeastwards and generally north on paths and forest tracks (shown on the OSI map) to meet a forest road; the car park is almost 1km east along the road.

PLANNING
Maps
Carry the OSI 1:50,000 map No 56 *Wicklow, Dublin, Kildare* or the Harvey 1:30,000 map *Wicklow Mountains*.

GETTING TO/FROM THE WALK
From Enniskerry, drive south along the R760 for 3km to a junction on the right; follow the minor road down, across the Dargle River and northwest to the clearly signposted 'Crone Wood' car park. Here a sign indicates that the gate is closed at 6pm.

THE WALK
From the car park, put 2km behind you along forest roads, south and southeastwards, then ascend steeply above the valley of the Dargle River. Suddenly you emerge into the **open** (one to 1¼ hours from the start), to a spectacular view of Powerscourt waterfall. At 119m this is the highest waterfall in Ireland and drops in silvery streams down sheer cliffs to the wide valley below. A narrow path snakes across the precipitous flank of the valley, then veers away into the adjacent conifer plantation. No more than 20m along, and at the point where the path starts to descend, bear right along a path between the conifers to a gap in the forest fence, a few metres beyond which is a wide track; turn right and head uphill. Memorise this access into the forest for the return leg. The ascent track soon becomes a path across heather moor and up to the summit

Miraculous Escape on Djouce

On 12 August 1946 mist and low cloud enveloped Djouce Mountain and much of the eastern half of the country – nothing unusual, but at the same time, a severe storm triggered flash floods and unroofed houses.

Around noon a plane crossed the coast just south of Dublin at an altitude of about 600m, heading straight for the Wicklows, which are higher by 100m or more. On board were more than 20 French Girl Guides, en route to an international camp. The inevitable happened and the plan collided with Djouce's southern ridge, bounced off and thumped down on the far side. Miraculously, the fuselage was intact and a fire did not break out.

Two of the leaders extricated themselves from the wreckage and headed for help, in opposite directions. One, accompanied by the pilot, eventually reached a farm in Glencree after just missing the Powerscourt waterfall cliffs; the other made it to Luggala Lodge by Lough Tay. After heroic efforts by rescuers the entire party and crew were brought down and, despite some serious injuries, all survived.

of **Maulin** (about 45 minutes from the waterfall view). The superb view embraces the Howth Peninsula and Dublin Bay to the north, Great Sugar Loaf to the east and beyond, to the northeast, Bray and Bray Head.

Retrace your steps, continuing past the turnoff into the forest, and go right and down to cross the **Dargle River footbridge** (about 45 minutes from Maulin). Go up the wide path beside the plantation to a stile over a stone wall from where a moorland path rises across the northeastern flank of Djouce. Pass a much-trodden path junction east of the summit. The path leads on across the steep slope and up to a shallow saddle between Djouce and White Hill to the south. Turn north and follow the path up to the summit of **Djouce** with its rock outcrops and trig pillar (1¼ hours from the Dargle River). Predictably, the magnificent view takes in far more mountainous country than that seen from the lower Maulin, and of course the south coast.

Descend generally east down the wide path to meet the path you followed on the outward journey and retrace steps, down to the Dargle River and back to the start (1¼ to 1½ hours from Djouce).

WICKLOW WAY

The 132km-long Wicklow Way passes through some of Ireland's finest mountain landscape. The Way crosses wild, breezy moorlands, and wanders through beautiful, deciduous woodlands, as well as several marvellous glens – from the rugged magnificence of Glendalough to the pastoral tranquillity of Glencullen and Glencree. The Way's timeless and distinctive Irish rural scenery of hedgerows, stone walls and copses is not commonly seen elsewhere these days. Plentiful vantage points with superb views offer a seductive sense of progress through the countryside and historic sites feature along the Way most days. But, surprisingly, the Way doesn't pass through any villages or towns and consequently it has a remote feel to it.

Conceived by one of Ireland's best-known walkers, JB Malone, the Wicklow Way, between Marlay Park on the southern outskirts of Dublin and Clonegall in County Carlow, was opened in 1982. Two decades later, it's still immensely popular and attracts walkers from many countries.

Left: Wicklow Way signage with Great Sugar Loaf in the background.

EMMA MILLER

Wicklow Way 🚶

Duration	5 days
Distance	132km
Difficulty	moderate
Start	Marlay Park
Finish	Clonegall
Nearest Town	Dublin (p70), Clonegall (p88), Bunclody (p89)
Transport	bus

Summary Ireland's most famous long-distance walk: from Dublin's suburbs, through the dramatic Wicklow Mountains to the tranquil beauty of their southern foothills.

The Wicklow Way is well waymarked with black posts bearing a yellow walking figure and arrow indicating the direction of travel on opposite sides. You'll also find finger board signs at road and track junctions indicating direction, and in some cases distance, to the next village or significant landmark. However, experience proves that these distances are inaccurate, to put it politely, and are best ignored. Posts and signs can disappear overnight and not be replaced for some time. In July 2002, only one junction was not marked in any shape or form; lines of posts through some conifer plantations were too widely spaced for relaxed walking. Most signs bear the Way's Irish name Slí Cualann Nua. Cuala is an old name for the area embracing much of southern County Dublin and northern County Wicklow. One of the roads linking this area to Tara, Ireland's pre-Christian seat of political power and pagan worship, was known as Slí Cualann. Thus Slí Cualann Nua is the New Cualann Way.

The Way's one shortcoming is the character of the walking. You'll follow true walkers paths across moorland and through some forests, but you'll become all too familiar with forest tracks and roads through conifer plantations. True, they're convenient, but where they're surrounded by tall, dense forest they're not particularly interesting. And then there are the roads: most are quiet, country roads, but they are still thoroughfares you have to share with vehicles and farm machinery.

Despite this, a shortcoming which the Way shares with virtually all other Irish Waymarked Ways, the Wicklow Way does offer a wonderful opportunity to discover a beautiful part of Ireland and to meet many very friendly and hospitable people.

PLANNING
When to Walk

May and September are the most settled months in Ireland and also enjoy reasonably long hours of daylight; June is the next best bet with even more daylight. Before May and after September you can expect cooler, wetter and windier weather, and less daylight. Although fine, clear days certainly aren't unknown during the darkest months, dire weather is more likely and less accommodation available. Conversely,

July and August are usually very busy and it's highly advisable to book accommodation ahead. Such a commitment can be a comforting thought at the start of the day, but an embarrassment if something goes wrong and can shackle an impulse decision if you happen upon an inviting B&B.

What to Bring

Waterproofing your pack, and water-tight plastic bags or specialist cases for maps are particularly important along the Way. Reckon on carrying all the money you'll need; at the time of writing the only ATM within easy reach along the Way was at Tinahely. Credit cards will see you fed at night, but many B&Bs accept only cash. A mobile phone is very useful for contacting B&B hosts who provide a pick-up service, although reception in the mountains is patchy.

Accommodation

The only commercial camping ground near the Way is at Roundwood and entails 5km to 6km extra walking. The opportunities for camping on unenclosed ground are limited; camping is prohibited in Wicklow Mountains National Park. Elsewhere, finding fresh water in country heavily and extensively grazed by sheep and cattle would be difficult. It's *always* far better to ask for permission to camp (and it's likely to be given), but there's the problem of finding someone to ask; access is a fraught issue in Ireland these days. You'll see plenty of forest clearings, seemingly far from the nearest sheep, but don't forget that midges love these still, damp places at any time of the day and especially in the mornings and evenings.

It's no longer possible to stay in hostels for most of the Way and there are no independent hostels within easy reach. So that leaves B&Bs, guest houses and hotels. The only settlements (not even villages) right on the Way are Glendalough and Glenmalure, where the choice is limited. But there are several isolated establishments, far from a village, on or within 2km of the Way; basic details of several are provided in the walk description. Otherwise, as much as 7km separates the Way and accommodation providers. Many B&B proprietors provide a pick-up and drop-off service, but you must arrange this in advance, being realistic about the time of arrival at the agreed rendezvous. A cash fee will most likely be charged for the service.

Itineraries

This description of the Way follows convention, starting in the north. Some commercial guided walk operators, and more than a few independent walkers, do it in reverse, starting in the less attractive country south of the Wicklows and leaving the finest mountain scenery to the closing stages. However, there is nothing particularly inspiring about Dublin's urban sprawl becoming ever clearer and more audible on the last half-day's walking. It is also worth considering that the most strenuous days are in the northern half of the walk; the whole Way involves around 3530m ascent, almost half of which lies ahead – or behind – at Glendalough. Many north–south walkers finish the Way at Tinahely, from where there's a limited bus service. In the opposite direction Enniskerry, better served by buses, is a possible finishing point.

When planning your itinerary, keep in mind that the daily distances (see the table below) are those between the two places specified, and do *not* include extra distances to accommodation. The five-day trip described here verges on the heroic (but the author proved it's possible). Six days is the usual minimum, with Roundwood as the intermediate point between Enniskerry and Iron Bridge. Between Iron Bridge and Clonegall there are various choices for spreading the two described days over three. Yet another consideration is the scope for day walks from the Way, including the Glendalough area (see Camaderry, p109, and Mullacor, p110) and Lugnaquilla (p111), so you could easily turn the trip into a 10-day Wicklow Odyssey.

day	from	to	distance
1	Marley Park	Knockree Youth Hostel	20km
2	Knockree Youth Hostel	Laragh	28km
3	Laragh	Iron Bridge	32km
4	Iron Bridge	Derry River	20km
5	Derry River	Clonegall	32km

If you haven't the time to do the whole Way but would still like to sample it – which section should you choose? Faced with a choice, the author (and probably many Way walkers) would vote for part or all of the section between Knockree and Glenmalure, a good 44km. However, this is much too far for a day walk, and Glenmalure isn't on a bus route anyway. Laragh, only 28km from Knockree is a feasible destination – if you're fairly fit. Alternatively, finish the day at Roundwood, a distance of just 20km; there's a daily bus service through here (from Laragh) to Dublin. One possible itinerary would entail staying in Enniskerry overnight (accessible by bus from Dublin), arranging a lift to the start of the walk, and reaching Roundwood or Laragh in time to return to Dublin on the evening bus.

Maps & Books

The Way is not well served by reliable maps at a scale suitable for accurate route finding. The four relevant OSI 1:50,000 maps, Nos 50 *Dublin City and District*, 56 *Wicklow, Dublin, Kildare*, 61 *Carlow, Kildare, Kilkenny, Laois, Wicklow* and 62 *Carlow, Wexford, Wicklow*, are to some extent out of date, although satisfactory enough in conjunction with a set of notes. The Harvey 1:30,000 map *Wicklow Mountains* is ideal between Crone Wood (Glencree) and Glenmalure.

The OSI guide *The Wicklow Way*, with 1:25,000 maps, is very good for background information and for maps, although there have been a few route changes since it was published. The same applies to the EastWest Mapping publication *The Wicklow Way Map Guide*, which has maps at 1:50,000. Rucksack Readers innovative guide, with 1:100,000 strip maps, is more up to date. EastWest Mapping's guide to *Wicklow Way Walks* describes 26 varied walks close to the Way.

Information Sources

For accommodation along the Way, contact **East Coast & Midlands Tourism** (☎ 044-48761; Ⓦ *www.ecoast-midlands.travel.ie; Dublin Rd, Mullingar)* for places in County Wicklow and **South East Tourism** (☎ 051-875 832; Ⓦ *www.southeastireland.com; 41 The Quay, Waterford)* for the Bunclody area (County Wexford).

An Oige (☎ 01-830 4555; Ⓦ *www.irelandyha.org; 61 Mountjoy St, Dublin 7),* the Irish Youth Hostel Association, is the best source of information about hostels en route.

At the time of writing, there was no single agency or organisation with overall responsibility for practical management of the Way. The **National Waymarked Ways Advisory Committee** (☎ 01-240 7727; Ⓦ *www.walkireland.ie; 21 Fitzwilliam Sq, Dublin 2)* promotes the Ways' development, and establishes and maintains standards; it has to be said that its website is not much help.

Guided Walks

Having a local expert organise all your accommodation and transfer your baggage from one night's B&B to the next certainly simplifies things and ensures you don't finish the day with aching shoulders. The tariff normally includes at least B&B accommodation, luggage transfer, maps and a route description, as well as a list of recommended restaurants. Transport to and from the start and finish is often also included. Two reputable Irish companies offering such services for the Wicklow Way are:

Footfalls (☎/fax 0404-45152, Ⓦ www.walkinghikingireland.com) Trooperstown, Roundwood. This company offers a self-guided holiday of five days starting in Tinahely and finishing in Enniskerry for €379. A guided tour, which includes all accommodation, meals and transport, starting in Dublin and finishing in Tinahely, with five days of walking on the Way costs €722.

South West Walks Ireland (☎ 066-712 8733, Ⓦ www.southwestwalksireland .com) 40 Ashe St, Tralee. This company offers an eight-day, self-guided walking holiday finishing in Tinahely, for €430.

NEAREST TOWNS

See Dublin (p70).

Clonegall

This very pretty village has a handful of **pubs**, three multi-purpose **shops** and little else. There is just one B&B in the area. **Raheengraney House** (☎ 055-29455; Ⓔ *jillian@iol.ie; Bunclody; en suite rooms per person €65)* is about 1km east of Wicklow Bridge, which is about 3km northeast of Clonegall.

Bunclody

About 5km south of Clonegall by the most direct route, Bunclody is the nearest town with a choice of accommodation and places to eat, and a good bus service to Dublin. There are ATMs on the Enniscorthy road (N80) near a crossroads, and in Main St, where you'll also find a **supermarket**.

Places to Stay & Eat There are comfortable en suite rooms at **Meadowside** (☎ 054-77459, fax 76226; Ryland St; singles/doubles €38/64), a welcoming B&B in the centre of town on the main road. Set in spacious grounds, **Moss Cottage** (☎ 054-77828; e mosscottage@ eircom.net; singles/doubles €38/64) is a grand Victorian home, with comfortable rooms, close to the town centre.

The choice of places to eat is scarcely inspiring. For burgers, steak and chicken try **American Style Diner** (☎ 054-77606; The Square; mains €7-12), a dressed-up fast food joint. Chips come with everything at **The Mall** (meals €5-9.50), a traditional Irish café in Main St that closes at 7pm. Those craving Chinese take-away should head for **Canton House** (☎ 054-76967; Ryland St; meals to €8; open till midnight).

There are several **pubs** along Main St ready to serve you a celebratory pint or two.

Getting There & Away The **Bus Éireann** (☎ 01-836 6111) service No 7 to Dublin (€9, two hours, two Monday to Saturday and three Sunday) stops outside Finn's newsagency in Main St.

GETTING TO/FROM THE WALK

To get to Marlay Park and the start of the Way, catch the **Dublin Bus** (☎ 01-873 4222; w www.dublinbus.ie) service No 16 from O'Connell St (outside Clery's) in central Dublin (€1.45, 40 minutes, every 20 minutes). Alight at the Marley Grange stop opposite the park entrance.

Right: Monastic City with round tower and churches - Wicklow Mountains National Park, County Wicklow

SANDRA BARDWELL

Marlay Park

The rather elegant estate house and the surrounding parklands were the work of David La Touche, a Huguenot by birth who made his fortune running a successful banking business in Dublin. He purchased the estate in 1768 and over the years poured vast sums of money into reconstructing the early-18th-century building and landscaping the extensive grounds. Waterfalls and ponds were created by impounding the waters of the Little Dargle River, and large numbers of trees and shrubs were planted. The house and the estate were named after La Touche's wife, Elizabeth Marlay.

La Touche's descendants sold the estate in 1872 and it was broken up by developers. A century later Dublin County Council acquired the house and surviving 86 hectares, and established a regional park in 1975. The house was rescued from semi-dereliction by a major refurbishment scheme between 1992 and 2000, which involved numerous people on training schemes reviving traditional crafts.

At the southern end, in the absence of a bus service through Clonegall, you have to get on foot to Bunclody, 5km to the south. Cross the bridge over the Derry River and walk east up to a crossroads. From here continue straight along a quiet road, which goes up and over a lowish ridge and down to meet the R746. Turn right and right again about 1km further on; this roads leads right into Bunclody.

THE WALK
Day 1: Marlay Park to Knockree Youth Hostel
5½–6 hours, 20km, 630m ascent

You get off to a good start through the woods of Marlay Park and soon leave all thought of the city behind as you tackle the Wicklow foothills. Reaching Knockree at the end of the day, the big hills loom ahead. The Way follows quiet roads, forest tracks and paths where boggy places are few.

Inside Marlay Park gates bear left towards the signposted craft centre and keep the main buildings, including the estate house, on the right to reach the first waymarker, near a car park on the left. The route along wide paths through the beautifully wooded grounds is well waymarked and essentially follows the Little Dargle River upstream. At a T-junction turn right along a path parallel to the M50 motorway. Soon, cross a car park and turn right out of the park along a path and go down to a junction. Pass under the motorway and bear left up a minor road, soon gaining height quickly. Fork left into **Kilmashogue Wood** (1¼ hours from Marlay Park); keeping left along a forest track, you soon catch sight of Dublin Harbour and the Howth Peninsula to the north. Bear left at the top of a small zigzag (about 2km from the wood entrance) then, about 300m further on, turn right up a rocky path to the forest edge. Go left here and almost immediately you're in open

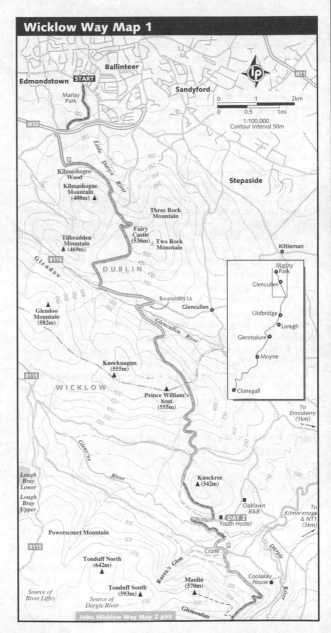

Wicklow Way Map 1

Edmondstown

Ballinteer

START

Marlay Park

Sandyford

N11

M50

Little Dargle River

0   1   2km
0   0.5   1mi
1:100,000
Contour Interval 50m

Stepaside

Kilmashogue Wood
Kilmashogue Mountain (408m) ▲

Three Rock Mountain

Fairy Castle (536m)

Two Rock Mountain

Kiltiernan

Tibradden Mountain ▲ (469m)

Glendoo

R116

DUBLIN

Marlay Park

Glencullen

Bohallaalry La

Glencullen

Oldbridge

Laragh

Glendoo Mountain (582m)

Glencullen River

Glenmalure

R115

Knocknagun (555m)

WICKLOW

Prince William's Seat (555m)

Moyne

Clonegall

To Enniskerry (1km)

Glencree River

Knockree ▲ (342m)

Lough Bray Lower

Lough Bray Upper

Oaklawn B&B

To Kilmaranoge & N11 (3km)

DAY 2 Youth Hostel

Powerscourt Mountain

R115

Crone

Dargle River

Tonduff North (642m) ▲

Raven's Glen

Maulin (570m) ▲

Coolakay House

Source of River Liffey

Tonduff South (593m) ▲

Source of Dargle River

Glensoulan

River

Joins Wicklow Way Map 2 p93

moorland. The next change of direction is right at a T-junction (a left turn would take you to the top of 536m Fairy Castle; 1km return). Then a steep descent lands you at a bitumen road (R116) in the vale of **Glencullen** (1½ hours from Kilmashogue Wood entrance); turn left.

It takes about 30 minutes to cover the distance along the fairly busy road to Boranaraltry Lane on the right. Follow this down, across the Glencullen River and up the side of the glen; about 200m into the forest, turn right at a fork. The forest road winds about up to moorland, about 600m northeast of the summit of Prince William's Seat (555m). A potentially boggy path then leads to another forest track; continue with forest on the left for about 200m then take to a narrow path into the trees. Descend, steeply at first, through boulders then trend to the right, keeping an eye on the waymarkers, only just in line of sight here, down to a forest track. The descent is sustained, although relieved by the first view of peaceful Glencree, across track junctions to a road (two hours from Glencullen). If you are staying in Enniskerry (p80), this would be a convenient place for a rendezvous if you can arrange a lift by your accommodation host; otherwise it is about a 4km walk along the road to the village.

To continue to Knockree walk south along the road for about 200m to a junction and bear left along a narrow lane for about 800m. Then follow a path diverging southeastwards to skirt **Knockree** hill and drop down to a minor road near the youth hostel (45 minutes from the Enniskerry road).

Only a few metres from the Way, **Knockree Youth Hostel** (☎ 01-286 4036, fax 276 2722; Lackan House, Knockree; dorm beds €11) is in an old farmhouse; you'll need to bring your own supplies as meals are not provided but there are cooking facilities.

Just 1km east of the Way along a minor road, **Oaklawn B&B** (☎ 01-286 0493; Glaskenny, Enniskerry; singles/doubles €38/65) is a large two-storey home that can provide transport into Enniskerry for an evening meal.

Day 2: Knockree Youth Hostel to Laragh
7½–8 hours, 28km, 935m ascent

This day offers much of the best walking along the Way, with a long stretch across open moorland with excellent views; there is only one significant road walk. Keep in mind historic Monastic City at Glendalough – one of the unmissables if you're interested in local history (see the boxed text 'A Park, a Monk and a Mine', p107). You could also include ascents of Maulin and Djouce (p82), two fine mountains close to the Way.

Rejoin the Way and cross the road to follow a forest track then a path on the left down to Glencree River. A mostly grassy riverbank path gives delightful walking downstream for about 1km to a footbridge; cross and walk up a path then a forest track to a road. Go left for about 250m to the entrance to Crone Wood and a car park. **Coolakay House** (☎ 01-286 2423, fax 276 1001; Enniskerry; singles

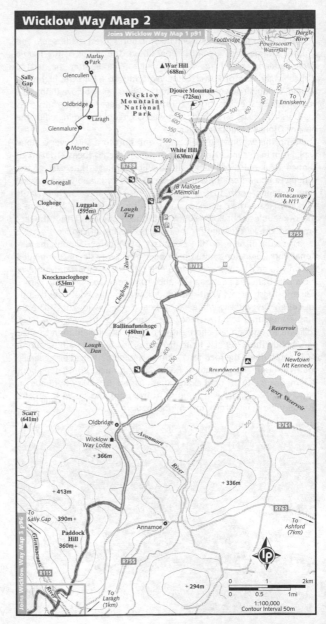

Wicklow Way Map 2

Joins Wicklow Way Map 1 p91

Dargle River

Footbridge

Powerscourt Waterfall

▲ War Hill (688m)

Djouce Mountain (725m)

To Enniskerry

Marlay Park

Glencullen

Wicklow Mountains National Park

Sally Gap

Oldbridge

White Hill (630m)

Laragh

Glenmalure

JB Malone Memorial

R759

To Kilmacanoge & N11

Moyne

Cloghoge

Luggala (595m) ▲

Lough Tay

R755

Clonegall

R759

Knocknacloghoge (534m) ▲

Cloghoge River

Reservoir

Ballinafunshoge (480m) ▲

Lough Dan

450

400

350

300

250

To Newtown Mt Kennedy

Roundwood

Vartry Reservoir

Scarr (641m) ▲

Oldbridge

Wicklow Way Lodge
+ 366m

Avonmore River

+ 336m

R761

+ 413m

To Sally Gap

390m +

Paddock Hill
360m +

Annamoe

+ 294m

To Ashford (7km)

R763

R755

Glenmacnass

R115

Joins Wicklow Way Map 3 p96

To Laragh (1km)

0   1   2km
0   0.5   1mi

1:100,000
Contour Interval 50m

€33) is about 1.5km further southeast along the road; evening meals are available.

From the car park, put 2km behind you along forest roads, south and southeastwards, then ascend steeply above the valley of the Dargle River. Suddenly you emerge into the open (1¼ hours from the start) to a spectacular view of **Powerscourt Waterfall**, at 119m the highest in Ireland, dropping down sheer cliffs to the wide valley below. Paths take you on above the cliffs, briefly through the forest then down to cross the Dargle River on a footbridge, in wild **Glensoulan** dominated by the bulk of **Djouce Mountain** ahead.

Go up the wide path beside the plantation to a stile over a stone wall. From here a moorland path rises across the northeastern flank of Djouce to a much-trodden path junction almost 1km east of the summit (an hour from the waterfall view). The remarkably wide coastal view extends north to the Howth Peninsula and south towards Wicklow Head. The path leads on across the steep slope and up to a shallow saddle about 800m south of Djouce's summit. This is the recommended take-off point for the walk to the top of Djouce.

Just south of here, on the boundary of **Wicklow Mountains National Park**, join a long raised path built of railway sleepers; intended not only to give walkers a bog-free ride but, more importantly, to give the much-trampled peat bog a chance to regenerate. The path carries you effortlessly across **White Hill** and down to a lookout over beautiful **Lough Tay** with its white sandy beach. At this lookout there's a simple **memorial** to JB Malone, the founder of the Wicklow Way. Follow a forest path left and right through a small plantation to a car park beside the R759 (1¼ hours from the first Djouce path junction). Walk south down the road for 1.4km to a wide path leading generally south through the plantation. Follow forest tracks south for about 3.3km; diverge to the right along a path for about 300m. Continue on a forest track, which bends around to the right and down to a gate, then along a vehicle track to a minor road.

Left: Trackside memorial to JB Malone, 'father' of the classic Wicklow Way, near Lough Tay, County Wicklow

If you intend to spend the night in **Roundwood**, 2km from here, turn left then take the first right to reach the centre of the village. It has a good **supermarket**, post office and **Wicklow Web Centre** (☎ 01-201 2988; W www.wwc.ie, Main St; 15 minutes for €2; open Mon-Sat). At the northern end of the village you'll find the **Roundwood Caravan & Camping Park** (☎/fax 01-281 8163; Roundwood; camping per person €12.70). **The Coach House** (☎ 01-281 8157, fax 281-8449; W www.thecoachhouse.ie; singles/doubles with breakfast €65/80) has large, comfortable rooms and an excellent **restaurant** (mains €11.20-20.50). with a varied menu. Although small, **Woodside** (☎ 01-281 8195; singles/doubles €32/54) is a walker-friendly B&B.

To continue southwards on the Way, bear right at the junction. A good 4km of road walking carries you southwest through attractive, partly wooded countryside with fine views of **Scarr**, a big sprawling, dappled hill to the west. You descend through fine oak woodland to cross the **Avonmore River** and reach the hamlet of **Oldbridge** (1½ hours from the R759). The road rises steeply southwards, soon passing **Wicklow Way Lodge** (☎/fax 01-281 8489; e wicklowwaylodge@eircom.net; singles/doubles €47/70), a very welcoming, large architect-designed place with beautiful big rooms and lovely views from the deck.

About 400m south of a small stream, turn right along a vehicle track which leads up to two stiles and a path southwards beside a plantation. Beyond a short moorland path follow a forest track with a plantation on your left across **Paddock Hill** and soon Laragh village comes encouragingly into view below to the south. A fairly rapid descent on paths lands you on the R115. Turn left for about 200m then head right down a wide path to a footbridge across the **Glenmacnass River**. A short distance further on you come to a junction (1¾ hours from Oldbridge). Follow the path left through conifers to a forest road; cross over and pursue a narrow path through trees and a bramble thicket to a minor road. At a car park beside the parish church bear left to reach the centre of **Laragh** (p108).

Day 3: Laragh to Iron Bridge
6¾–7¼ hours, 32km, 1035m ascent
This day takes you through some of the more remote parts of the Wicklow Mountains and down into the southeastern foothills. There's relatively little road walking but the greater part of the day is through conifer plantations.

Return to the path junction above the Glenmacnass River and bear left for Glendalough, along a path that leads to a forest road. This soon takes you out into the open, via a left turn at a junction, and, with luck, a magnificent view of Glendalough's **Lower** and **Upper Lakes**. Then it's down to a gate from where you follow a forest road briefly. Make a left turn onto a path that winds down to a cluster of four stiles. Descend, cross a road and continue down to a minor road opposite Glendalough Hotel (45 minutes from the Laragh path junction), which is next to a small TIC. See Glendalough (p108) for information and accommodation details.

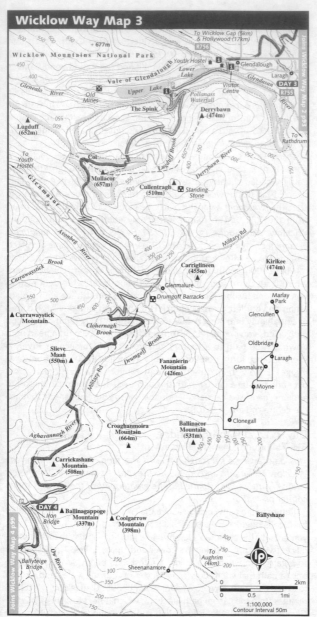

Wicklow Way Map 3

Head left for the Glendalough visitor centre; walk through the grounds and cross a footbridge to 'Green Road' and turn right towards Upper Lake. This wide track leads up the valley through beautiful oak woodland; after 1.5km and shortly beyond the small **Wicklow Mountains National Park visitor centre**, turn left and ascend beside Lugduff Brook and **Pollanass Waterfall**. Veer left when you meet a forest track then left again at a junction and cross two bridges. The Way leads northeast for about 600m then, from a tight right bend, heads almost directly southwards (via a series of clearly marked junctions), up through the conifer plantations, across Lugduff Brook again and beside a tributary, to open ground on the saddle between **Mullacor** (p110) and **Lugduff** (1¾ hours from Glendalough). From here on a good day, massive Lugnaquilla (p111) sprawls across the view to the southwest; in the opposite direction is Camaderry's (p109) long ridge above Glendalough, framed against the bulk of Tonelagee (p134). Follow the raised boardwalk down, contour above a plantation then drop into it where a steep muddy and rocky path descends to a forest road; turn left.

If you're planning to stay at Glenmalure Youth Hostel, rather than go all the way down to the crossroads in Glenmalure, follow the Way from the left turn for about 1km southwards. At an oblique junction where the Way turns southeast, bear left in a westerly direction and descend steeply to the road in Glenmalur. The hostel is about 2km northwest.

Military Strongholds in the Mountains

You'll probably notice the title 'Military Road' along the minor road south from Glenmalure, and you can't miss the gaunt, empty building near the Avonbeg River bridge. Both hark back to more turbulent times at the end of the 18th century.

Thoroughly discomforted by the 1798 rebellion (see the boxed text 'Rebellion in the Mountains', p113), the British government soon moved to strengthen its hold on the country. Even after decisive government victories in that year, rebels continued to wage guerrilla warfare in the mountains, not least in the Wicklows. The government needed to be able to move its troops about more quickly so the 'Military Road' was built between 1800 and 1809 from Rathfarnham on the outskirts of Dublin, across Glencree, on to the Glendasan valley, up and over to Glenmalure and south to Aghavannagh, a distance of 70km. The original alignment is virtually unaltered though the surface has been improved.

Troops needed shelter, so starting in about 1803, barracks were built at Laragh, Drumgoff (Glenmalure) and Aghavannagh; the first is now a private residence. Drumgoff was sold to the Mining Company of Ireland and used to house miners working in Glenmalur but is now derelict. Aghavannagh was used as a youth hostel by An Oige for many years, but spiralling maintenance costs have unfortunately forced its closure.

To continue straight on along the Way from the left turn, follow forest roads south then southeast for 1.6km to a wide zigzag above open ground, then contour the steep slope, swing northeast and drop down to a minor road beside two bridges. Continue down to an intersection and Glenmalure (p112); about 1¼ hours from the saddle.

The Way presses straight on (south) through the crossroads for 500m, across the Avonbeg River and past silent **Drumgoff Barracks** (see the boxed text 'Military Strongholds in the Mountains', p97) then right along a forest track. Keep left past a ruined cottage and start to gain height in two fairly long reaches; go through two left turns then it's down and across a stream. About 800m further on, turn right along a path to start the long ascent almost to the top of **Slieve Maan** (550m) via four track junctions, maintaining a southwest to south-southwesterly direction. Back on a forest track, the Way turns left (southeast) close to unforested ground to the west. With a few more convoluted turns, you're out of the trees and on a path between the plantation and the road (mapped as the Military Rd). The Way eventually meets the latter beside a small tributary of the Aghavannagh River (two hours from Glenmalure).

Walk down the road for about 250m then turn off left along a forest track, shortly bearing left to gain height steadily on a wide path over **Carrickashane Mountain** (508m). Descend steeply to a wide forest road and continue down for about 1km. Bear right to reach a minor road and turn right. Leave the road 500m further on and drop down to another road – Iron Bridge is just to the right (an hour from Military Rd).

Aughrim

This small, pretty village is 8km southeast of the Way. From Iron Bridge, walk 150m up to a road and turn left; follow this road down the valley of the Ow River for 7.5km to a junction – the village is to the left, another 500m. Aughrim has limited facilities; **Byrne's mini market & deli** is on the Rathdrum road.

You'll go a long way to find a more helpful and friendly B&B than **Butler's Byrne** (☎/fax 0402-36644; Rednagh Hill; singles €28). A transport service from/to the Way is provided and breakfast is a major event. A large, popular establishment in the centre of the village, **Lawless's Hotel** (☎ 0402-36146, fax 36384; W www.lawlesshotel.com; singles/ doubles €65/110) dates back to the 18th century and offers comfortable, modern rooms but basic, cafeteria-style bar meals (€9-10.50).

Day 4: Iron Bridge to Derry River
4¾–5¼ hours, 20km, 400m ascent

On this relatively undemanding day forest tracks and minor roads take you right out of the mountains and into pleasant pastoral foothills. The highlight comes during the later stages in superlative walking on a classic green boreen (lane).

From Iron Bridge walk up to a road and turn left; 600m further on bear right along a forest track, which soon bends right to a minor road.

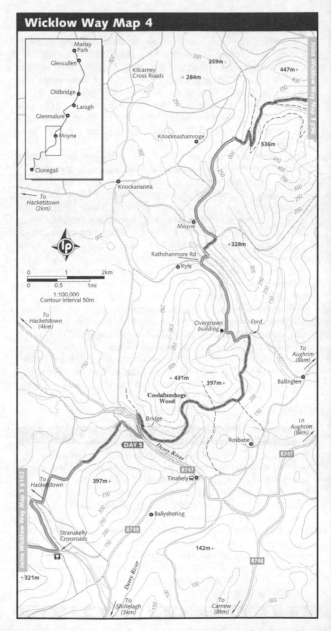

Wicklow Way Map 4

Marlay Park
Glencullen
Oldbridge
Laragh
Glenmalure
Moyne
Clonegall

To Hacketstown (2km)

1:100,000
Contour Interval 50m

To Hacketstown (4km)

Kilcarney Cross Roads
+ 284m
359m
447m +
536m
Knocknashamroge
Knockananna
Moyne
+328m
Rathshanmore Rd
Kyle
Overgrown building
Ford
To Aughrim (8km)
+ 431m
397m +
Ballinglen
Coolafunshoge Wood
Bridge
To Aughrim (8km)
DAY 5
Derry River
Rosbane
R747
To Hacketstown
397m +
R747
Tinahely
Ballyshonog
R749
142m +
R748
Stranakelly Crossroads
+321m
Derry River
To Shillelagh (3km)
To Carnew (8km)

Joins Wicklow Way Map 3 p96

Joins Wicklow Way Map 5 p102

Continue along it to **Ballyteige Bridge**, from where you follow a forest road west and up beside a stream. Go through a crossroads then left at a T-junction. The forest road turns almost south and soon descends to a minor road. Follow this south through tranquil countryside.

If you take the second road to the right (to Moyne), you'll come to hospitable **Jigsaw Cottage** (☎/fax 0508-71071; ⓦ www.wickloway .com; singles/doubles €40/70; evening meal €27.50).

Continue along the road to a T-junction and turn right. This lane takes you down to another minor road; turn left then shortly right down Rathshanmore Road. Cross a bridge to a junction (2½ hours from Iron Bridge).

From here **Kyle Farmhouse** (☎ 0508-71341; ⓦ www.kylefarm.com; singles/doubles €33/51; evening meal €20) is 500m to the right.

Turning left at the junction, the narrow road meanders along the side of a small valley with lovely, ever-widening rural views. At a junction near an overgrown stone building, bear left and go down to a ford. Head south and uphill on what soon becomes a delightful grassy boreen (45 minutes from the Kyle junction), contouring the uplands to the west. About 1.6km from the ford, fork right uphill and, a little further on, continue uphill at a track junction.

From the junction it's a 2km walk along minor roads (to the left) to accommodation at **Rosbane Farmhouse** (☎ 0402-38100; singles/ doubles €32/54; evening meals €19).

A short steep rise gives ever more expansive views over the Derry valley; keep on generally westwards into a wide glen and down through the beautiful beeches of **Coolafunshoge Wood** (which was partly saved from felling by a determined campaign). The track swings around the hillside and Tinahely materialises below, but then recedes, and you have to deal with numerous gates in the course of almost 2km before reaching a narrow lane. Turn left and go down and across the Derry River bridge to the fairly busy R747 (1½ hours from the boreen).

What's In a Name?

There is a true story behind the intriguing name of the marvellous old pub popularly known as 'The Dying Cow'. It's as atmospheric as they come with the absolute minimum of concessions to modern pub decor – no fancy lighting and comfortable seating here.

Apparently, the present (in 2002) owner's grandmother ran a pub of sorts as an offshoot of her farm. One evening, long after closing time, as she was catering for the unquenchable thirst of a group of locals, the local constable bowled up. Clearly a man not to be trifled with, he threatened to haul her into court for breaking the law.

She admonished him: 'Sure and would you summons a poor widow woman to court, just for repaying the kindness of neighbours who'd helped her with her dying cow?'

Tinahely

This small, slightly dour village, 2.2km southeast of the Derry River bridge, has an ATM, Syme's small **grocery** and a good **greengrocer**.

Places to Stay & Eat The first place you'll come to is **Sunindale House** (☎/fax 0402-38170; singles/doubles €32/56; evening meals by arrangement €21), a large, modern home right by the road. The friendly and relaxed **Orchard House** (☎ 0402-38264; e appletree@ eircom.net; singles €30) is a B&B with large rooms and a packet-free breakfast.

For traditional fare in informal surroundings head for **Madeline's** (☎ 0402-38166; mains to €17; open Wed-Sat). Part of Murphys Hotel, **Manna Restaurant** (☎ 0402-38109; mains €8-14) offers excellent pizzas and old favourites such as beef Guinness stew.

Getting There & Away Heading to Dublin Busáras, the **Bus Éireann** (☎ 01-836 6111) service No 132 leaves Tinahely (€10.20, one hour 50 minutes) early on Thursday morning and returns early evening; on Sunday a bus departs Dublin at noon and returns from Tinahely early evening.

Day 5: Derry River to Clonegall
7½–8 hours, 32km, 530m ascent

The greater part of this section is along bitumen roads; most of the rest is along forest tracks through very attractive countryside to the pleasant village of Clonegall.

The Way continues from the R747, 300m southeast of the Derry River bridge; walk up a lane and turn left where it starts to descend. Head up a narrow path between trees, then bear left up a vehicle track. Go through a gate and bear right at a three-way junction along a lane that contours the hill that lies to the southeast. Descend through a gate and turn left at an intersection, and further on join a wider forest track that goes down to a narrow road; turn left. Go downhill some more to a T-junction; bear right for a short distance to a crossroads. Go straight ahead (towards Hacketstown) briefly, then left past stone-built houses, across a bridge and around to the left.

In time you come to Stranakelly Crossroads (1½ hours from the start); the place opposite, bearing the name **'Tallons'** is a pub, better known as **The Dying Cow**. It's anything but moribund on regular Irish music nights when the place is packed to the rafters (see the boxed text 'What's In a Name?', p100).

For most of the ascent generally westwards across a pair of hills you're enclosed between high hedges; then comes a more open descent to a crossroads near the hamlet of Kilquiggan, where you turn left. About 1km on, turn right at the busy R725 then left up a minor road. Then it's left again at a T-junction. This narrow road wanders southeast; leave it to the right after 1.3km and descend to cross a small stream. The road wanders up and down with a youngish plantation on

WICKLOW WAY

Wicklow Way Map 5

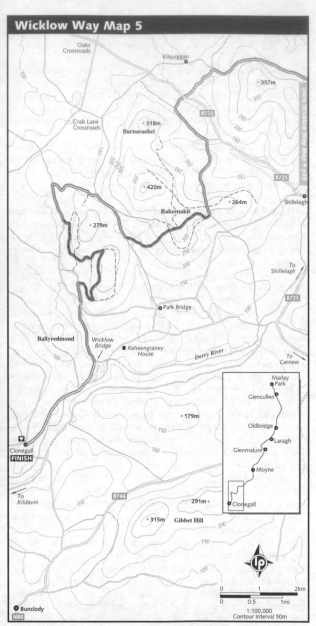

Oaks Crossroads

Kilquiggan

+357m

R725

R725

Crab Lane Crossroads

+318m

Barnacashel

150

R725

+420m

+264m

Shillelagh

Raheenakit

+279m

To Shillelagh

R725

Park Bridge

Ballyredmond

Wicklow Bridge

Raheengraney House

Derry River

To Carnew

100

+179m

Marlay Park

Glencullen

Clonegall

FINISH

Oldbridge

Laragh

Glenmalure

To Kildavin

R746

Moyne

291m+

Clonegall

+315m Gibbet Hill

150

100

Bunclody

N80

0 ———— 1 ———— 2km
0 — 0.5 — 1mi
1:100,000
Contour Interval 50m

the right. Take the forest track on the right at Raheenakit and you're off the bitumen at last (two hours from The Dying Cow).

If you're heading for Shillelagh, continue south down the road to an intersection where you turn left; the village is about 2km further on. Here you'll find **Park Lodge** (☎ 055-29140; *singles €33*), a comfortable B&B in a Georgian farmhouse; evening meals are available.

The Way follows a generally westerly route through the plantation via a well-waymarked series of junctions. After about 2km you come to a corner of the plantation on your left; go left over a stile and drop down with the forest on the right to a track junction. Turn right and continue to a minor road and right again. After about 1km, turn left; this road wiggles about to another junction – turn left. About 1km southwards, bear left at a gate into a plantation (1¾ hours from Raheenakit).

The route winds about south and eastwards through a few junctions and rises to an intersection, from where you can clearly see where you were more than an hour ago, but just across the valley below. Turn right and continue south for 1.2km to a junction; turn right. Go left at the next one – back to the bitumen. Turn left, then right and on down to a Y-junction at **Wicklow Bridge**. The final turn is to the right; nearly 3km further on you reach the centre of **Clonegall** (2¼ hours from the plantation gate). There's nothing obvious to welcome you, nor indeed to send northbound walkers on their way. But, if you look around you will find JB Malone's (the Way's founder) map on a notice board in a small, flower-filled park just left of the wide intersection you inevitably reach. So there's only one thing to do – head for **Osbourne's** – a fine old pub down the road on the right.

South & Southeast

The south and southeast corner of Ireland, which extends from Dublin's fringes south through County Wicklow and southwest as far as the Tipperary–Cork county border, is perhaps the most beautiful part of the country. True, it lacks the rugged grandeur and wildness of the west, but its patchwork of farmland, villages and woodlands – from which rise several fine mountains ranges – has a captivating, gentle charm. Among these mountains are one of the country's best known and most popular walking areas, and some of its better-kept secrets.

This chapter describes some of the best walks in the Wicklows, including the highest peak, Lugnaquilla; much less crowded and equally scenic are the Comeragh, Knockmealdown and Galtee Mountains, and Blackstairs Mountain, deservedly well known among Irish walkers; and the peaceful River Barrow provides a completely different experience. This varied collection of walks follows paths and forest tracks, some of which can offer quite an adventure, especially in poor weather. The area is generally accessible, although some walks are beyond the reach of public transport.

Snow isn't unknown on the highest peaks in the region in winter (December to February), but this season can also bring magnificent cold, clear days – ideal for brisk days out.

INFORMATION
Maps & Books

The OSI 1:250,000 Holiday map *East* is best for general planning. Details of larger scale topographical maps are included in each walk description.

Walk Guide: East of Ireland, by Jean Boydell, David Herman & Miriam Joyce McCarthy, describes 67 walks and has interesting background information.

Information Sources

For general travel information, there are two umbrella organisations that are useful first

Highlights

New Ross Town at sunset seen across the River Barrow, County Wexford

RICHARD CUMMINS

- Glendalough's awesome cliffs and lakes, and beautiful oak woods in the Wicklow Mountains (p106)
- Easy walking along the historic and scenic River Barrow (p116), a haunt of the playful otter
- Spectacular glacial lakes, dramatic waterfalls and wide views in the Comeragh Mountains (p119)
- Scaling a 900m-plus peak in the Galtee Mountains (p130), above secluded mountain lakes and long, sweeping ridges

points of contact. Covering the Wicklow Mountains is **East Coast & Midlands Tourism** (☎ 044-48761; ⓦ *www.ecoast-midlands.travel .ie; Dublin Rd, Mullingar*). The rest of the area is covered by **South East Tourism** (☎ 051-875 823; ⓦ *www.southeastireland.com; 41 the Quay, Waterford*).

GATEWAYS
Dublin (p70) is the logical gateway to the area from the northeast, while Cork (p138) offers the best approach from the southwest.

Kilkenny
A large, busy town with an intriguing medieval centre, Kilkenny is an absorbing destination in its own right, en route to the mountain areas beyond.

Information Kilkenny's **TIC** (☎ 056-775 1500; Shee Alms House; open daily) is very helpful and efficient, and sells OSI maps.

Other sources of maps and books in town are **The OK House** (64 High St), which also sells phonecards; and the **Kilkenny Book Centre** (10 High St), which also has its own café if you are looking for a coffee, snacks or lunch.

There are ATMs in High St and Parliament St. For Internet access, head to **Kilkenny e-centre** (☎ 056-776 0093; e ecentrekilkenny@ hotmail.com; 26 Rose Inn St, €3.50 for 20-30 minutes)

Padmore & Barnes (☎ 056-772 1037; Wolf Tone St; open Mon-Sat) sells camping gas canisters and outdoor gear.

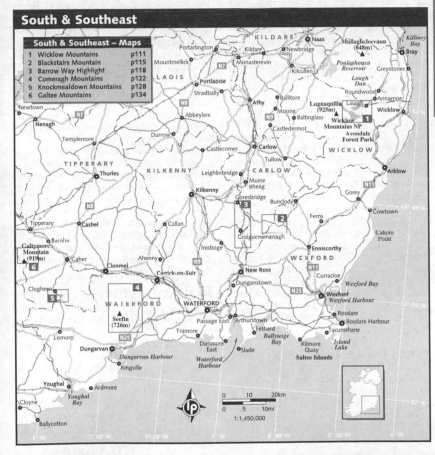

Places to Stay & Eat The nearest camping ground with plenty of space for tents is **Nore Valley Caravan & Camping Park** (☎ 056-772 7229, fax 772 7748; ⓦ http://norevalleypark.tripod.com; camping per tent/person €7/2; open Mar-Oct), 11km south of Kilkenny, which has excellent facilities and its own café. The site is clearly signposted from the town of Bennettsbridge.

Right in the town centre is **Kilkenny Tourist Hostel** (☎ 056-776 3541, fax 772 3397; ⓔ kilkennyhostel@eircom.net; 35 Parliament St; dorm beds/twins €13-15/33); facilities include a laundry. The **Celtic House** (☎/fax 056-776 2249; 18 Michael St; singles/doubles €38/64) is a B&B with comfortable en suite rooms. The art of hospitality is finely honed by the hosts at **Dunromin** (☎ 056-776 1387, fax 777 0736; ⓔ valtom@oceanfree.net; Dublin Rd; singles/doubles €32/64); rooms at the back have a rural view. Another B&B, **Riverside** (☎ 056-772 2863; Riverside Dve; singles/doubles €35/46) is conveniently located in a quiet street and serves a good breakfast.

For self-catering supplies there are two **supermarkets** (St Kieran's St & Market Cross Centre, High St); both are open Monday to Saturday. Don't miss **The Gourmet Store** (High St) for Irish cheeses; and at **The Wine Centre** (15 John St, open daily) you can find Irish, Scottish and English real ales. The **Italian Connection** (☎ 056-776 4225; 38 Parliament St; mains €8.50-21) does very good pizzas. Offering rather classy dining, **Lautrec Brasserie** (☎ 056-776 2720; 10 The Parade; mains €18-25) specialises in fish, but does good pizzas and pasta dishes. A shortish walk from the town centre, **Shimla** (☎ 056-772 3788; 6 Dean St; mains €8.50-18; set menu for two €47) offers North Indian and Bangladeshi dishes, and Indian beer.

Getting There & Away There are at least three daily **Iarnród Éireann** (☎ 1850 366 222) trains from Dublin Heuston to Kilkenny (€21.50, two hours). Change at Kildare for trains to Cork, Killarney and Tralee.

Bus Éireann (☎ 01-836 6111) has services from Dublin's Busáras to Kilkenny railway station or Patrick St (€9, two hours, at least five daily) and from Cork (Parnell Place) to Kilkenny (€15.20, three hours, at least two daily).

By road, Kilkenny is 117km from Dublin and 148km from Cork.

Wicklow Mountains

Right on Dublin's southern doorstep, the Wicklows are one of the most popular walking areas in Ireland, with many easily accessible summits and the famous Wicklow Way (p85), Ireland's first official Waymarked Way. There is plenty of variety: waterfalls, lakes and tarns; mountains of all shapes and sizes; woodlands; forests and open moors. But the cost of the region's popularity is theft from parked cars (see the boxed text 'Beware Thieves', p108) and chaotic traffic on most weekends along the narrow, substandard roads.

There are strong pluses, of course: the scenery, especially around Glendalough, is very fine indeed; it's not difficult to escape the crowds; and you can do several walks from one base, thus avoiding long drives. The big, rounded hills and deep valleys have a unique character, and even the most travelled of walkers will find much to enjoy here. Three mountain walks are described in this section: to Camaderry and Mullacor, on the northern and southern sides of Glendalough, respectively; and over Lugnaquilla, the Wicklows' highest.

NATURAL HISTORY

The geology of the Wicklows is at once simple and intricate. Essentially the mountains have a granite core surrounded by metamorphic rock, mainly schist; complex chemical processes in the contact zone produced outcrops of lead, silver and zinc. The schists originally blanketed the granite, but over millennia they have been eroded to leave broad, undulating mountain uplands.

During the last Ice Age glaciers filled the Wicklows' upper reaches and carved deep, steep-sided valleys, notably Glendalough.

A Park, a Monk and a Mine

Wicklow Mountains National Park is a patchwork of two large and several small upland areas which together cover 15.9 sq km owned by the state. Established in 1991, the Park extends from Glencree generally southwest to the southeastern slopes of Lugnaquilla (925m). Although the summit is just outside the park, several other major summits are not, including Mullaghcleevaun (849m), Tonelagee (817m) and Conavalla (734m); spectacular Glendalough is undoubtedly the showpiece. Several roads cross the parklands and traditional sheep grazing continues, but there are no settlements of any size within its boundaries. The Glendalough Visitor Centre (see Glendalough, p108) is the best place to find out more about the park; there's also a small park information office (see The Walk, p110) near Upper Lake.

Nearby Monastic City is focussed on the monastery founded by St Kevin in AD 570. It graced Glendalough until the dissolution of Irish monasteries in 1537. In its heyday, the monastery was a centre of learning and a magnet for pilgrimages (see St Kevin's Way, p134), which continued until well into the 19th century, particularly on 3 June, St Kevin's feast day. The monastic settlement comprises a splendid, 30m-high round tower, the substantial remains of a cathedral, priests' house and three churches.

During the 19th century as many as 2000 miners worked in the Wicklows; activity centered on the galena or lead-ore deposits in the western end of Glendalough, in Glendasan and in Glenmalur. Lead, extracted from the ore at a smelter in south Dublin, was used in the city's rapidly expanding plumbing system. Mining left its mark on the landscape not only in white spoil heaps and adits (mine entrances) at the foot of cliffs, but also in the Scots pines along the northern shore of Upper Lake, planted by the Mining Company of Ireland in 1856 and 1857 to provide pit props. However, mining ceased in 1890 before the trees were ready; a revival was launched in 1919 but yields were unprofitable and the mines closed in 1950.

After the glaciers had vanished a single lake filled the glen, but Lugduff Brook dumped vast amounts of mud, sand and gravel on the valley floor. The resulting barrier (or alluvial fan) created two lakes, now known as Upper Lake and Lower Lake (see the boxed text 'Signs of a Glacial Past', p24).

Much of the higher ground in the Wicklows is covered with blanket bog, but the steeper and drier ground supports mats of ling, bell heather and bilberry. In the valley woodlands sessile oaks and their natural companions – birch, rowan, holly, hazel and ash – have staged a recovery from near extinction. Plentiful 1000 or more years ago, the forests were decimated from the 17th century onwards to provide building materials, and charcoal to fuel iron ore smelters. Although the woodlands were coppiced (periodically cut down to near ground level to promote regular regrowth) rather than felled, the frequency of coppicing was excessive. More enlightened practices since the establishment of state forests in the 1930s have encouraged the expansion of oak woods; Glendalough Woods Nature Reserve protects one of the few oak woods left in Ireland. There is also a fine stand of Scots pines on the northern side of Glendalough.

Hybrid red and sika deer are now plentiful in the area, and with luck you may see some. Red squirrels live in the conifers beside Upper Lake; and on a quiet day you may see foxes and hares on the higher ground, and smell, if not see, feral goats. The moors are also home to birds typical of such areas: red grouse, skylarks, meadow pipits and the more elusive kestrel and peregrine falcon (see Watching Wildlife, p27).

PLANNING
Maps & Books
The OSI 1:50,000 map No 56 covers all the walks described in the area. However, the Harvey 1:30,000 *Wicklow Mountains* map is better for detailed route finding, as are the

Beware Thieves

Sadly, it's necessary to warn visitors to the Wicklow Mountains to lock cars and not to leave *any* valuables – in fact, preferably nothing at all – in your car, wherever it's parked. Thefts from vehicles are rife and the perpetrators will smash windows in search of plunder.

1:25,000 map *Glendalough. Glenmalur*, published by Pat Healy and available locally, and Dúchas' 1:25,000 map *Glendalough*, which also has a plan of Monastic City.

David Herman's *Hill Walkers' Wicklow* describes 30 day walks in the area. *The Monastic City of Glendalough*, by Kenneth MacGowan, is an informative guide to the site and available at the Glendalough TIC. Dúchas publishes a useful booklet called *Exploring Glendalough*, which covers the natural and mining heritage of the area.

ACCESS TOWNS
Laragh

This busy village is at the eastern end of the Vale of Glendalough and has plenty of B&Bs but a limited choice of restaurants. The nearest TIC is in the hamlet of Glendalough, 2km westwards; the nearest ATM is in Rathdrum, 10km south.

Places to Stay & Eat The nearest camping is 7km north of Laragh at **Roundwood Caravan and Camping Park** (☎/fax 01-281 8163; camping per person €12.70).

Although Annamoe is about 4km north of Laragh, **Carmel's B&B** (☎/fax 0404-45297; e carmelsbandb@eircom.net; singles/doubles €30/50) is worth mentioning; the operators are exceptionally friendly and helpful, and breakfast is first rate. In Laragh, **Dunroamin House** (☎ 0404-45487; singles/doubles €40/60) has large en suite rooms and breakfast is rarely bettered. A short distance from the main road, **Oakview** (☎/fax 0404-45453; singles/doubles €35/60) is a B&B with smallish rooms, although most are en suite.

There are two shops: **McCoy's** (Glendalough Rd), which also sells petrol; and **Glendalough Stores** (Sally Gap Rd).

Although it's more expensive than the competition, **Lynham's Hotel** (☎ 0404-45345; mains in bar/restaurant €10-13/15-22) offers a skillfully prepared menu featuring pasta, trout, salmon and steaks. The varied menu at family-friendly **Wicklow Heather Restaurant** (☎ 0404-45157; mains €11-21) is good value, and includes venison, Wicklow lamb and vegetarian choices.

Getting There & Away Departing Dublin from in front of 119 St Stephens Green, **St Kevin's Bus Service** (☎ 01-281 8119; w www.glendaloughbus.com) travels via Bray and Roundwood to Laragh (€9, 1½ hours, two daily) and on to Glendalough Visitor Centre.

By road, Laragh is 57km from Dublin and 107km from Kilkenny.

Glendalough

Although strictly speaking Glendalough (pronounced 'glen-da-lock') refers to the whole glen, here it refers to the locality near Lower Lake, 2km west of Laragh.

Glendalough Visitor Centre (☎ 0404-45425; admission €2.50; open daily) houses excellent displays on the environment and history of Glendalough, and screens a most interesting video, *Ireland of the Monasteries*. The adjacent car park is free, but from June to September the gates close at 6pm (earlier during the rest of the year). Guided walks are organised from the centre on Sunday afternoons; booking is essential. Talks about the area are given on Thursdays during summer in the **Education Centre**, on the northern side of Upper Lake about 200m from the car park.

A small **TIC** (☎ 0404-45688; open Mon-Sat May-Sept), next to the Glendalough Hotel, provides the usual services, and has a good selection of maps and guides.

Places to Stay & Eat The large, modern **Glendaloch Youth Hostel** (☎ 0404-45342; fax 45690; e glendaloughhy@ireland.com; dorm beds €19.50; evening meals €9.50, breakfasts €4.50-6.50) is popular but big enough to separate groups from quiet-loving individuals; all rooms are en suite and there's a kitchen, drying room and Internet access.

The large **Glendalough Hotel** (☎ 0404-45135, fax 45142; e info@glendaloughhotel.ie; singles/doubles €67/100) dates back to the 19th century, but the en suite rooms are right up-to-date. Bar suppers (€9.50–17.75) are served in the lively atmosphere of the Tavern.

Getting There & Away Departing Dublin from outside 119 St Stephens Green, **St Kevin's Bus Service** (☎ 01-281 8119) goes via Bray, Roundwood and Laragh to Glendalough Visitor Centre (€9, one hour 35 minutes, at least two daily). By road, the visitor centre is 59km from Dublin.

Camaderry

Duration	4¾–5¼ hours
Distance	14km
Difficulty	moderate
Start/Finish	Upper Lake car park
Nearest Town	Glendalough (p108)
Transport	bus

Summary Experience the isolation of Glendalough's mining village then the wide open spaces of a beautiful ridge high above the valley.

Overlooking Glendalough from the north, Camaderry (698m) is the highest point on a long, sloping ridge that is high enough to give good all-round views. The route described takes in some cross-country walking between the Glenealo River and Turlough Hill, but it is at least free of peat hags (exposed areas of peat). Otherwise you're on tracks and paths all the way.

The remains of the miners' village above Upper Lake stand in stark contrast to the wild and relatively natural environment up on Camaderry. At the peak of activity in the mid-19th century, there were at least four dwellings and a large building housing the water-driven ore crusher. Lead, zinc, copper and silver were most abundant.

PLANNING
Maps
The best map for this walk is either the Harvey 1:30,000 map *Wicklow Mountains* or Pat Healy's 1:25,000 map *Glendalough Glenmalur*. The OSI 1:50,000 map No 56 is an acceptable alternative.

GETTING TO/FROM THE WALK
The Upper Lake car park is about 1.5km west of Glendalough Visitor Centre. The parking fee is €1 per car.

The walk can also start at the Glendalough Visitor Centre, from where you can reach Upper Lake via Green Road (see The Walk, p110, for Mullacor); at the National Park Information Office turn right to the car park. Here you'll find toilets and the Lakeside Take-away.

THE WALK (see map p111)
The walk starts easily, along a gravel road leading west from the car park entrance, just above the lake shore and through Scots pines. Soon you can glimpse **Kevin's Bed** – the remains of a tiny cottage that is the reputed resting place of St Kevin – on a small grassed shelf across the lake. Near the western end of the lake you emerge into the open and reach the site of the old mines. Drop to the remains of the stone buildings of the miners' village and make your way through, crossing and recrossing small streams. A clear track picks up from a long, low stone wall, then zigzags up beside the tumbling Glenealo River. The track becomes a path by the upper cascades and generally keeps close to the stream. Pass an outlying mine near the top of the cascades. Ignore a solid footbridge across the river and follow a narrow path westwards beside the stream into the wide glen.

By keeping a watercourse on your left, you soon turn northwestwards by a major tributary of the Glenealo River. Soon you should catch sight of an unnaturally flat-topped, elongated mound that is Turlough Hill (near the reservoir up there). Head for the hill, crossing some minor streams and fairly rough heathery ground. There is a narrow path lurking among the heather, but it's exact location is impossible to pinpoint so it's a matter of luck as to whether you hit upon it. Make you way up the glen and almost to the base of Turlough Hill, where you should come upon a wide track leading southeast and down to a saddle. It's easy to follow this dry, well-trodden track through a maze of peat hags then up through boulders to the spread-eagled summit plateau of **Camaderry** (about three hours from the start). The highest point (698m) is unmarked by a cairn, but is distinguished by fine views of Lugnaquilla to the southwest, Mullacor to the south and the massive bulk of Tonelagee to the north.

Continue southeastwards then almost east on a good track along the ridge and over the point '677', marked by a small cairn. Descend steadily on a clear path through the northern end of a line of old conifers, then follow a grassed path through an ocean of bracken and into mixed woodland with Scots pine, larch and a few oaks. The track zigzags down to a minor junction. Turn left here to join a narrow path through the bracken then a boardwalk and steps of railway sleepers (ties) into forest. Descend northwestwards to a forest road beside the Glendasan River. Turn right and follow it to the Glendalough road (nearly two hours from Camaderry); the visitor centre is 250m left, the youth hostel and Upper Lake car park 250m and 1.25km respectively to the right.

Mullacor

Duration	4–4½ hours
Distance	14km
Difficulty	moderate
Start/Finish	Glendalough (p108)
Transport	bus

Summary An exceptionally scenic ridge walk high above Glendalough's lakes, starting and finishing through beautiful oak woodlands

Mullacor (657m) is the highest point on the south side of Glendalough and a deservedly popular destination. This walk makes a circuit of Lugduff Brook via the Spink – an airy, scenic ridge – Mullacor and Derrybawn Mountain (474m). You follow wide, firm forest tracks, steep walkers paths and a long boardwalk, built by Dúcahs out of

old railway sleepers. Before the walk, a wander through the Glendalough Visitor Centre is highly recommended.

PLANNING
Maps

The best map is the Harvey 1:30,000 map *Wicklow Mountains* or Pat Healy's 1:25,000 map *Glendalough Glenmalur*; the OSI 1:50,000 map No 56 also covers the walk.

THE WALK (see map p111)

From the visitor centre car park, cross the Glenealo River footbridge and follow a broad path signposted 'Green Road' towards Upper Lake. About 1.5km along you come to the **Wicklow Mountains National Park Information Office** (*open daily May-Aug, weekends at other times*), which houses informative displays about the parks natural and cultural heritage. Take time to stroll across to the shore of **Upper Lake** for the beautiful views, especially of the awesome cliffs above which you'll soon be walking.

Just 50m beyond the centre, turn left up a wide path towards **Pollanass Waterfall**, spelt 'Poulanass' on the sign. A long flight of steps beside Lugduff Brook and the falls takes you to a T-junction; turn right, walk down and round a bend for about 100m and climb a stile on the left. Follow a narrow path steeply up through oakwoods then beside conifers to open ground. Here you meet the sleeper path, which makes relatively easy, bog-free work of the long ascent of the **Spink**; the views of the Upper Lake and the old mine workings at the head of Glendalough are magnificent. Eventually bear left at a fork; a few metres on from the end of the sleepers continue on a path by the forest edge. After another short sleeper path you're back on natural ground and a wide path leading directly towards the Lugduff–Mullacor ridge ahead (southwest). Contour south and southeast across the slope to the crest of the ridge and down to the col along more sleepers. Here you briefly meet the **Wicklow Way** (p85) crossing the col, where there are excellent views south across Glenmalur to Lugnaquilla. Head up the wide path, which is peaty but not too soft, to the

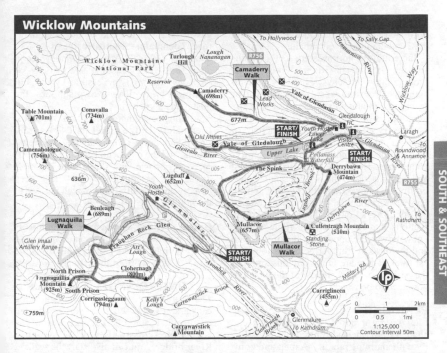

Wicklow Mountains

amorphous summit of **Mullacor** (2¼ hours from the start).

From there a wide path descends generally east to a broad saddle where you'll find a stile over a fence on the left, about 200m south of the forest corner. Cross the stile, turn left and descend beside the fence to the top corner of the forest and turn diagonally right on a narrow path. This crosses the wide glen below Cullentragh; cross a forest track and follow a clear path along the narrow rocky ridge to **Derrybawn Mountain** (45 minutes from Mullacor). Continue along the ridge for a short distance on a worn path then drop down to the left to a small col; keep left to descend an eroded path to a stile over the forest fence. Press on downhill through conifers; cross a forest road and keep descending on a narrow path to another forest road – turn left, rejoining the Wicklow Way. Shortly, cross two bridges and turn right with the Way towards the signposted 'car park'. Go down beside Lugduff

Brook, turn right and continue back to the Glendalough Visitor Centre (an hour from Derrybawn Mountain).

Lugnaquilla

Duration	5½–6 hours
Distance	15km
Difficulty	moderate
Start/Finish	Glenmalur car park
Nearest Town	Glenmalure (p112)
Transport	private
Summary Lug your pack up to the Wicklows' highest mountain for huge views from its vast summit.	

At 925m Lugnaquilla (popularly known as 'Lug' or 'The Lug') stands more than 100m higher than the next highest peak in the Wicklows, and is one of Ireland's 12 Munros (see the boxed text 'The Irish Munros', p152).

It's a massive mountain with generously proportioned spurs reaching north, south and east, and dominating Glenmalur.

Incredibly, its northwestern sector lies inside the Glen Imaal Artillery Range, so although there are days when it's safe to approach from the west, the very idea of reaching a mountain summit through a firing range is disturbing.

The very scenic route described here from upper Glenmalur is not without blemish either, in the very untidy felling of conifer plantations. However, this is soon passed and surpassed by the wildness of upper Fraughan Rock Glen, the ever-widening views across the Wicklows and the secluded beauty of Art's Lough. There are two tricky sections that require a little route-finding know-how – the upper reaches of the glen and the descent from Art's Lough to a forest track. There are fairly obvious signs of the passage of walkers most of the way, but you need to be watchful.

PLANNING

Lug is very exposed, and conditions can change from fine and sunny to zero visibility with alarming rapidity. A map and compass are essential to ensure you don't stumble into the firing range or over the ominously named corries, North Prison and South Prison. For information about firing days in Glen Imaal, contact the **Army Advice and Information Centre** (☎ 045-404 653); the Mountaineering Council of Ireland's website (W www.mountaineering.ie) is also worthwhile.

Maps

Harvey's 1:30,000 map *Wicklow Mountains* map and Pat Healy's 1:25,000 map *Glendalough Glenmalur* cover the walk, as does the OSI 1:50,000 map No 56.

NEAREST TOWN
Glenmalure

Scattered around a crossroads near the Avonbeg River bridge, Glenmalure (the local spelling) has an isolated feel compared with busy Laragh (p108), where you'll find the nearest shop and post office.

Places to Stay & Eat Set in a historic, gas-lit house at the end of the Glenmalur road, **Glenmalure Youth Hostel** (☎ 01-830 4555, fax 830 5808; W www.irelandyha.org; dorm beds €12; open 24 June-31 Aug & Sat night year-round) is accessible by car, but you must bring all your own supplies; the hostel has a kitchen.

Although extremely popular on weekends, **Glenmalure Lodge Hotel** (☎ 0404-46188; singles/doubles €32/64) has unexceptional rooms, and the bar menu (mains €7–14.50) offers very basic fare. **Coolalingo** (☎ 0404-46583; singles/doubles €25/44) is a very homely and friendly B&B, which is close to the hotels.

Getting There & Away Glenmalure is 14km southwest of Laragh via a minor road (the 'Military Road') diverging from the R755, 1.4km south of the village.

GETTING TO/FROM THE WALK

The best place to start in Glenmalur is the car park at GR 079929; it's not signposted on site and is about 2.7km northwest of the Glenmalure crossroads near the Avonbeg River bridge. You can also start the walk at the larger car park, beside a ford, 1.2km further west along the road or at the youth hostel.

THE WALK (see map p111)

Walk up the Glenmalur road, cross the ford (or a bridge about 60m upstream) and continue, past Glenmalure Youth Hostel, to a T-junction. Here turn left and let the forest road take you deep into magnificent **Fraughan Rock Glen**, below the fractured cliffs of its northwestern rim. About 45 minutes from the T-junction, the road – now a rough track – forks; bear left for about 20m then left again down a path to cross a stream, an easy matter unless it's in spate.

Gain height through bracken and boulders close to the stream for a couple of hundred metres; a discernible path then swings away from the stream and continues up to rejoin it close to the lip of a wide hanging valley. Generally stay near the stream, still on your right; hop across some wettish

Rebellion in the Mountains

It was a long way from the riotous streets of Paris in 1789 to the wilds of Glenmalur, but there was once a strong connection.

The ideals of the French Revolution –'Liberty, Equality and Fraternity' – inspired many Irish people to seek a truly national government and Catholic emancipation. The United Irishmen, an organisation with these aims, was founded in 1791 but was forced underground when war broke out between Britain and France two years later. French support for the Irish cause was readily forthcoming, but a French-led invasion in 1796 foundered. In the aftermath, the British launched an indiscriminately brutal search for United Irishmen and captured many of their leaders.

With nothing to lose, the survivors hit back, unleashing the 1798 Uprising. Fighting was largely confined to the southeast (and Antrim and Down in the North), most famously in Wexford, but also, as local memorials reveal, in Glenmalur and elsewhere (see Blackstairs Mountain, p114). A Battle of Glenmalure raged briefly; according to a commemorative plaque near the end of the road there, more than a score of people died. The rebels were soon crushed; the Act of Union with Britain came into force on New Year's Day 1801.

Many rebels eluded capture for a few years, including a group from Glenmalure and neighbouring Glen of Imaal led by Michael Dwyer and John Mernagh, who grew up at the foot of Lugnaquilla. They were eventually transported to Botany Bay (Australia) in 1805 and given land to start farming. Dwyer, seemingly a rumbustious character, died in 1825, a week before his Irish children arrived in Sydney; Mernagh lived on until 1857.

ground and start to ascend again, crossing two streams coming down from the left. Make straight for the head of the valley, trending left up to the base of some vertical rock slabs. Continue south up through scattered boulders for a few hundred metres to a steep gully on the right. This provides a relatively straightforward route to more open, broken ground. Keep heading south, perhaps a little southwest, up a slight spur to the broad eastern spur of Lug. From here it's easy, across mostly firm, sheep-cropped turf, west then southwest, past **North Prison's** cliffs to **Lugnaquilla's summit** with its trig pillar nesting on a sprawling cairn (about three hours from the start). There's an almost overwhelming sense of space on this vast summit with excellent views, including most of the Wicklow Mountains and, to the west, Mt Leinster with its tall mast. A direction finder nearby identifies any and every feature you can see.

To start the descent, retrace steps northeast and east; along here you get the best views of the rugged cliffs of **South Prison**. Continue east along the mainly grassy spur (taking care in poor visibility not to charge off to the southeast towards Carrawaystick Mountain) to the slight summit of **Clohernagh** (800m), where a cairn stands just east of the summit. Follow the well-worn path eastwards and down from here for no more than 200m. You should then pick up a path leading northeast then north down an increasingly well-defined spur, bypassing steep fractured cliffs overlooking beautiful **Art's Lough**, framed by the Fraughan Rock Glen cliffs. With the lough (lake) clearly in view, swing northwest with the lake in sight. The rough path doesn't go up to the rocky shore, although on a hot day it would be worth wading through the heather to cool off in its limpid waters.

Then cross a stile near the corner of the fence parallel to the lough and turn left. A soggy, well-used path leads on beside the fence, swings left at a corner and descends, gradually trending away from the fence on the left to drop steeply and muddily to a conifer plantation. Continue descending for a few hundred metres, now more gently northeastwards, with trees on your left. The path here isn't particularly clear; it bears left across a wide tree-free area within the plantation to a rough forest track which soon becomes well defined. About 15 minutes' walking brings you to a T-junction; turn left and descend through a series of zigzags to the Glenmalur road and the car park (about 2½ hours from the summit).

Blackstairs & Barrow

Blackstairs Mountain and the River Barrow are a marriage of opposites – a rugged, relatively wild peak and a tranquil river, once thronged with boats carrying people and cargo between Dublin and the south coast. The Mountain forms an eastern boundary of the river's catchment and an impressive backdrop to the patchwork of woodlands, fields and villages in the broad valley. The historic small town of Graiguenamanagh is a pleasant base from which to explore the area on foot – and don't overlook Brandon Hill (p135), south of the town, from where you can contemplate both mountain and river and their beautiful setting.

PLANNING
Maps
Both walks in this section are covered by OSI 1:50,000 map No 68.

ACCESS TOWN
Graiguenamanagh
The town grew up around Duiske, a Cistercian abbey that was founded in 1204, where the farmer-monks ran an estate of nearly 1000 hectares. Graiguenamanagh prospered even after the abbey was forcibly closed in 1536; the abbey was rebuilt and restored in the 19th century, and is still used as a place of worship.

There's an ATM in Main St Upper; the nearest TIC is in Kilkenny.

Places to Stay & Eat For details of the nearest camping ground and hostel see Kilkenny (p105).

Closer to St Mullin's than Graiguenamanagh (6km southeast), **Brandon View**

(☎/fax 059-972 4625; *Ballying Lower; singles/doubles €25/46*) is nonetheless a hospitable, contemporary B&B that couldn't be better named.

The **Waterside Guest House** (☎ *059-972 4246, fax 972 4733;* e *info@waterside.iol.ie; singles/doubles €60/90*), a restored cornstore, welcomes walkers (no singles at weekends); the big rooms have river views, and local OSI maps and guidebooks are available. The menu in Waterside's excellent **restaurant** (*mains €17-20*) always features a vegetarian option.

For supplies, you'll find two **supermarkets** in Main St Lower.

The **Duiske Inn** (☎ *059-972 4445; Main St Lower; mains €12-16*) is a down-to-earth pub that serves quality bar meals.

Getting There & Away The noon **Kilbride's** (☎ *051-423 633*) bus from Kilkenny (single/return €3.30/6), via Goresbridge, arrives at 12.55pm and the evening run gets in at 6.25pm. For the return, buses leave Graiguenamanagh at 7.45am and 2pm.

Graiguenamanagh is on the R703, 15km southeast of Kilkenny.

Blackstairs Mountain

Duration	5¼–5¾ hours
Distance	18km
Difficulty	moderate
Start/Finish	Sculloge Gap
Nearest Town	Graiguenamanagh (p114)
Transport	private
Summary Exceptionally far-ranging vistas on a superb ridge walk east of the Barrow valley, returning along an ancient track.	

From the west Blackstairs Mountain looks like a huge humpback whale basking on the skyline, its long spine, with a few bristly tors, rising gracefully to the rocky summit plateau. During the last Ice Age the tops of some peaks poking through the ice were severely eroded and the underlying rock was exposed as elongated columns of hard granite – the tors. The long ridge affords magnificent views, including the three ranges covered later in this chapter: the Comeraghs, Knockmealdowns and Galtees.

The route described follows firstly forest roads and tracks, then a rough stretch over heather with a few wettish spots leads to a good walkers path across the mountain. The return is along a hill track, long ago the main road to Wexford. The final leg of the walk is along very quiet country roads back to the start. You can't avoid this by using two cars because there are no parking places near where you meet the road.

The walk picks up two other reminders of the area's turbulent past. In the small car park at the start is a memorial 'To the men and women who gave their lives for liberty, equality and fraternity', unveiled in 1998 to commemorate the bicentenary of the 1798 Uprising (see the boxed text 'Rebellion in the Mountains', p113). And Caher Roe's Den, a cluster of tors on the ridge, was the hiding place of one Cathaoir na gCapall.

PLANNING
Maps
The OSI 1:50,000 map No 68 is needed for this walk.

GETTING TO/FROM THE WALK
The walk starts and finishes at a small car park (GR 827477) on the south side of a minor road through Sculloge Gap, at its junction with the R702 between Ballymurphy and Kiltealy. From Graiguenamanagh, follow the R703 (signposted to Borris) to a T-junction at the western end of the village of Ballymurphy. Continue on the R702 (towards Enniscorthy) to the car park.

THE WALK
Walk east along the R702 for 200m and turn right along a narrow road, keep left round a bend then take the second turn on the right, going through a gate and along a forest track. Pass through another gate at the forest boundary; about 300m further on turn

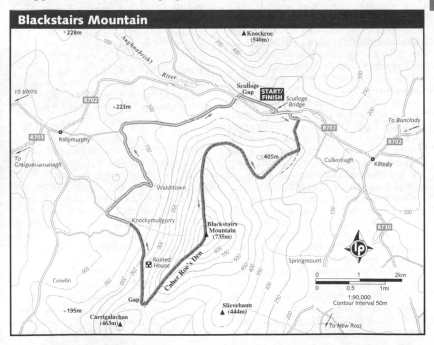
Blackstairs Mountain

right along a rough track through a gap between the trees. Go up this track to open ground and follow it round to the left and right bends. About 70m beyond the latter, turn sharp left (south) along a track, gaining height close to the forest edge. The track swings west and widens the distance from the forest edge and levels out as it skirts the hill mapped simply as '405'. At a distinct corner of the plantation, the track starts to drop noticeably southwards; diverge along a rough track on the right. Unfortunately this soon fades; simply head west, over heather wherever possible for the driest going, to the ridge crest on the skyline.

Once on the western side of the ridge you should be able to see the dark line of a path through heather ahead – this is the next objective. It proves to be a well-used path, and takes you all the way up the ridge to the small summit plateau where the top of **Blackstairs Mountain** (735m, two hours from the start) is marked by a cairn perched on a peat hag; there's also a small cross marked 'R.I.P.' nearby. The magnificent view encompasses Mt Leinster, the Galtee Mountains with a pointed peak in the middle, Slievenamon, the Knockmealdowns, the Comeraghs and the south coast.

Descend steeply over rocky ground, past **Caher Roe's Den**, the spiky tors on the western rim of the ridge that was Cathaoir na gCapall's hiding place. After his family lands in County Laois were forfeited to the Crown in the 18th century, he took to horse trading and set up a network of horse thieves who sold their haul at country fairs. The law eventually caught up with him and he was hanged in Portlaoise in 1735.

Continue down to a prominent gap (45 minutes from the top). Turn right along an old track, known locally as the Wexford road – which it once was: its wide course, marked by stone walls, is still evident across the lower slopes of the mountain except where water gathers in shallow hollows. It bends right after about 200m and loses height; it's generally easy to follow, mostly with a stone wall on one or both sides. It has become overgrown across a few patches of marshy ground, but just keep

heading northwestwards; in one place, the wall of a ruined building, punctuated with a window, serves as a useful objective. Eventually you come to a dense gorse thicket; swing left down over wet ground to a stonewalled field. Turn right beside the wall, bend left to a gate and a bitumen road at Knockymullgurry (a handful of farm buildings). Turn right (45 minutes from the gap) and take the first right after about seven minutes; this road leads northeast and uphill, then swings northwest at Washtown and wanders up and down to a T-junction (GR 790473). Turn right; cross the northern shoulder to an intersection on the R702. Cross diagonally right, go up a short narrow road to a T-junction and bear right; it's only a few hundred metres, over Sculloge Bridge, back to the start (1¾ hours from the gate).

Barrow Way Highlight

Duration	5–5½ hours
Distance	21km
Difficulty	easy–moderate
Start	Goresbridge (p118)
Finish	St Mullin's (p118)
Transport	bus

Summary A tranquil, easy-going walk along the bank of an historic waterway, passing through medieval Graiguenamanagh; otter sightings are likely.

The River Barrow, Ireland's second longest river, rises in the Slieve Bloom Mountains in County Offaly, right in the middle of Ireland, and flows eastwards to the town of Monasterevin in County Kildare. There it turns south and reaches the sea at Waterford Harbour, joined on the way by the River Nore at New Ross and the River Suir at Waterford. In the late 18th and early 19th centuries the Barrow was linked to the Grand Canal at Robertstown by a system of canals, opening up a navigable waterway from Dublin to Waterford. The Barrow section was known as a 'navigation', rather than a canal, as it comprised long stretches of navigable river and comparatively short sections of cuts, or canals, that bypassed the rapids or rough water.

The Barrow Way extends 109km from Robertstown to St Mullin's, the limit of navigation for most boats. The southern section, from Goresbridge to St Mullin's, is easily the most beautiful and is described here. The towpath you follow is grassed almost the whole way, and makes a pleasant change from watching for waymarkers at track junctions or from following a map and compass across misty, trackless moors. Nearly all this section is well away from roads; the views change constantly as the river wends its way through farmland, woodland and, near Graiguenamanagh, through a cliff-lined valley. The granite from these cliffs was used in the construction of the bridges, weirs and locks on the canals. The old locks are still in use so it's not difficult to imagine how busy the river was in its heyday as a major transport artery in southeastern Ireland.

You should see graceful mute swans, mallards, shy grey herons, black moorhens and coots, robins and chaffinches in the hedgerows, skylarks above the fields and perhaps a kestrel or two. When this walk was surveyed, the author was rewarded with a wonderfully agile display by a lively otter, who seemed at least as interested in her as she was in it.

HISTORY

The River Barrow has a long history as a watery highway, which is scarcely surprising since St Mullin's was settled from about the 7th century and Graiguenamanagh was well established by the mid-13th century. Not only was this town a major farming centre, but the area was also a rich source of timber. *Clarauns*, flat-bottomed boats of up to five tonnes, were pulled along by rope from the river bank or punted with a long pole.

In 1761 the Barrow Navigation Company started work above St Mullin's, the limit of navigation on the tide upstream from New Ross. Huge sums were spent building short canals (or cuts) with locks to bypass shallow reaches, so that the boats could reach Graiguenamanagh. At each lock a keeper, who lived nearby, worked the lock gates and collected tolls. Weirs were also built across the river nearby to control the flow through the canals, but the river usually had the last word when it fell to inconveniently low levels in summer and winter.

By 1801 work was complete: 23 locks over a distance of 67km upstream to Athy, from where a link to Robertstown took off. Barges up to 20m long, pulled by two horses plodding along the tow path, carried grain and flour to and from mills beside the river. Supplies for local shops, corn, timber, manure and, of course, Guinness kept the barges busy. A passenger boat plied the river in the early years; even though hotels for travellers were built at Graiguenamanagh and Carlow, the service never caught on and closed in 1809. Engines replaced horses around 1911, but railways and then motor vehicles eventually put the canal out of business in 1959. The barges' place has been taken by cruise boats, canoeists, cyclists and walkers.

Without the benefit of private transport, the local bus service connecting Kilkenny, Goresbridge and Graiguenamanagh can be used to do a through walk, at least as far as Graiguenamanagh. Otherwise, it's no hardship to do out-and-back excursions from Goresbridge and Graiguenamanagh. The whole experience on the return legs, particularly the views and lighting, is completely different.

PLANNING
Maps & Books

The walk is covered by OSI 1:50,000 map No 68. The EastWest Mapping *South Leinster Way Map Guide* covers the Barrow between Ballyteigelea Bridge and Graiguenamanagh, and has some interesting background information. *Guide to the Barrow Navigation of Ireland*, published by Dúchas, is aimed at boat travellers and has plenty of detailed descriptions. *Goodly Barrow*, by TF O'Sullivan, covers the river's history and personality, and has a chapter on the Barrow Navigation; it's available at the Kilkenny Book Centre.

SOUTH & SOUTHEAST

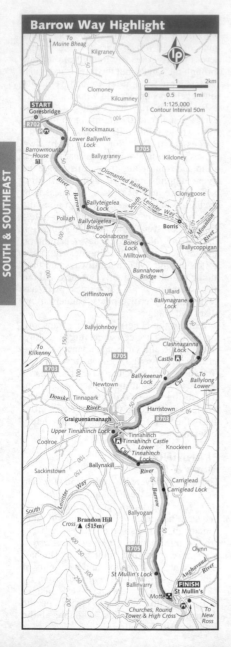

Barrow Way Highlight

START
Goresbridge
R702

To
Muine Bheag
Kilgraney
Clomoney
Kilcumney
Knockmanus
Lower Ballyellin
Lock
Barrowmount
House
Ballygraney
River Barrow
Dismantled Railway
South Leinster Way
Ballyteigelea
Lock
Pollagh
Ballyteigelea
Bridge
Coolnabrone
Borris
Lock
Milltown
Bunnahown
Bridge
Griffinstown
Ballyjohnboy
To
Kilkenny
R703
R705
Newtown
Douske Tinnapark
River
Graiguenamanagh
Upper Tinnahinch Lock
Coolroe
Tinnahinch
Tinnahinch Castle
Lower
Tinnahinch
Lock
Knockeen
Sackinstown
Ballynakill
River
South
Leinster Way
Brandon Hill
Cross ▲ (515m)
Ballyogan
R705
St Mullin's Lock
Ballinvarry
FINISH
St Mullin's
Motte
Churches, Round
Tower & High Cross
To
New
Ross

Kilcloney
Clonygoose
Borris
Mount
Leinster River
Ballycoppigan
Ullard
Ballynagrane
Lock
Clashnaganna
Lock
Castle
To
Ballylong
Lower
Cut
Ballykeenan
Lock
Harristown
R703
Carriglead
Carriglead Lock
Glynn
Aughavaud
River

0   1   2km
0   0.5   1mi
1:125,000
Contour Interval 50m

NEAREST TOWNS
Goresbridge
This small village is the most convenient base for this walk, although facilities are limited. For details of the nearest TIC, camping ground and hostel, see Kilkenny (p105).

Places to Stay & Eat Just west of the village centre, **The Alamo** (☎ 059-977 5467; singles/doubles €30/60) is a very friendly farmhouse B&B that serves an excellent breakfast. The welcoming **Pauline's B&B** (☎ 059-977 5581; Main St; singles/doubles €22/44) is in the centre of the village; evening meals are available by arrangement.

There's a small **supermarket** in Main St.

Although **Pauline's Coffee Dock** does sandwiches, toasties and salads, none of the pubs in Goresbridge serves meals and the nearest restaurant is the **Green Drake Inn** (☎ 059-977 3116) in Borris, 7km to the southeast.

Getting There & Away From Kilkenny, **Kilbride's** (☎ 051-423 633) bus service leaves The Parade (near the castle) at noon and 5.30pm Monday to Saturday for Goresbridge (single/return €3/5, 30 minutes). Departures from Goresbridge for Kilkenny are at 8.10am and 2.25pm.

Goresbridge is on the R702 about 6km east of its junction with the N9 at Gowran, and 19km from Kilkenny.

St Mullin's
This peaceful hamlet, scattered about the hinterland of the river, is only convenient if you have a car.

Places to Stay & Eat If you're looking for a B&B, **Mulvarra House** (☎/fax 051-424 936; ⍵ www.mulvarra.com; singles/doubles €35/60; evening meal €18) has a superb location overlooking the river and luxurious en suite rooms.

The **River Valley House** (☎/fax 059-972 4055; ⊜ river.valley.house@indigo.ie; Bahana, St Mullin's; singles/doubles €37.50/60; evening meal €19) is a restored farmhouse with a lovely outlook across the Barrow valley.

Getting There & Away St Mullin's is 11km by road from Graiguenamanagh, via the R703 east to a T-junction then south along R729 to the hamlet of Glynn where you turn right to St Mullin's.

THE WALK

From the car park and picnic area beside the river at Goresbridge, cross the nine-arched bridge and skirt an old building to reach the towpath. During the first hour you pass two locks that, like all on the waterway, are manually operated. The first is **Lower Ballyellin**, its adjacent lock keeper's cottage painted an incongruous bright pink. **Barrowmount House**, standing mute and unlived-in across the river, was the residence of the Gore family, whose name lives on in the nearby village. Brandon Hill (515m) to the south soon makes the first of many appearances during the walk; the prominent feature on the summit is a mission cross. Next comes **Ballyteigelea Lock**; 1km or so further on, Ballyteigelea bridge carrying the R705 across the river intrudes, but tranquillity soon returns.

The South Leinster Way (p337) meets the towpath at the bridge (and follows it down to Graiguenamanagh). Next, there's a very long weir leading to **Borris Lock**. Dense, mature woodlands lining the eastern side of the river are part of the Borris demesne, once held by the Kavanagh family. In the midst of this, the Barrow is joined by Mountain River, spanned by the stone-built **Bunnahown Bridge**. From **Ballynagrane Lock**, about 30 minutes further on, the river glides through more open countryside of fields and scattered woodlands, and soon you reach **Clashaganna Lock**. Now the river is pushed away from its southward course by spurs reaching out from the nearby hills, and heads southwest then southeast. **Ballykeenan Lock**, unique on the waterway in being a double lock, soon marks the end of an unusually long cut. Another half hour of walking and around a bend you'll find civilisation in the shape of the small town of **Graiguenamanagh** (about three to 3¼ hours from Goresbridge), which is well worth exploring.

Back on the riverside path, which has a bitumen surface for a while, pass a broad weir and the tall remains of **Tinnahinch Castle**, built by the Butler family before the 16th century, and **Upper Tinnahinch Lock**. The bitumen gives way to grass beside a long cut bypassing river rapids; opposite, Brandon Hill rises steeply to its domed moorland summit. A few hundred metres beyond **Lower Tinnahinch Lock** the river bends southwards into a wooded, steep-sided valley. Well beyond the next lock, **Carriglead**, the valley widens and you come to **St Mullin's Lock**, the end of the navigable river for most boats.

A broad track leads into St Mullin's; the tall buildings by the river were once a mill, one of many along the river which used water power to grind grain. Just beyond a small stream is a grassy riverside picnic area. The hamlet of **St Mullin's**, up the hill via the more westerly of the two roads leading away from the river, originated as a monastic settlement about 1300 years ago. Its historic buildings and the remains of a motte (a large, flat-topped green mound, on top of which a timber tower once stood) are well presented.

Comeragh Mountains

The larger part of this mountain group is more a plateau with a few upstanding bumps, than a range of individual peaks separated by gaps. The one exception is at the northern end where distinctive Knockanaffrin stands apart, rising steeply from the Gap below the main plateau. The OSI maps use two separate names for the group – Comeragh (the northern half) and Monavullagh (the southern section); for simplicity, the single name Comeraghs – as the area is known among Irish walkers – is used here.

With the River Suir and its tributaries to the north and northeast, and various streams flowing into the Atlantic elsewhere, the Comeraghs rise steeply from the surrounding fertile plains and river valleys. The main rock in the mountains is Old Red Sandstone, laid down when Ireland was part of the European landmass and a desert-type climate prevailed. The tough sandstone survives in the long ridge and central plateau structure of the range, although on the ridges and plateau you are more likely to see a dark, pebbly conglomerate.

There are two obvious impacts of later glaciation. Most spectacular are precipitous corries carved by lingering ice bodies, some of which now cradle lakes. The finest example, Coumshingaun Lough, with a 500m-high headwall, is a highlight of one of the walks described here. There are also lakes dammed by moraine, the debris left behind as the ice melted (see the boxed text 'Signs of a Glacial Past', p24).

Four walks are described in this section, taking in almost all the outstanding features in the Comeraghs: the isolated ridge of Knockanaffrin; the superb corries on the western face of the mountains; Seefin, a fine vantage point at the southern end; and a jaunt taking in Mahon Falls, an awesome view of Coumshingaun and the highest point in the Comeraghs.

PLANNING
Maps & Books

OSI 1:50,000 map No 75 covers all the Comeragh walks covered in this section. The 1:25,000 *Comeragh Mountains: Nire Valley* map, published by Eileen Ryan & Pat Healy in 1992, is still entirely reliable for its topographical information. You should find a copy at the Clonmel TIC.

Barry Keane's *The Galty, Knockmealdown and Comeragh Mountains* has several walks (and scrambles) in the area.

ACCESS TOWNS
Ballymacarbry

This village is the ideal base for the Comeraghs, provided you're content deep in the countryside, far from town. The nearest TIC and ATMs are in Clonmel (p121). There is one **shop-service station**, a couple of bars and a post office in the village.

For accommodation, the walker-friendly **Clonanav Farm Guesthouse** (☎ 052-36141,

fax 36294; ⓦ www.clonanav.com; singles/doubles €70/100) has comfortable en suite rooms and does a great breakfast.

Ballymacarbry is on the R671 Clonmel–Dungarvan road, 16km south of Clonmel. The village is not served by public transport.

Carrick-on-Suir

A busy, no nonsense town, Carrick suffers from being on the chaotic Cork–Waterford road, but is the most convenient base for the eastern side of the Comeraghs. There are two ATMs in Main St, between the N24 and the River Suir (pronounced 'shooer'); the nearest official TIC is located in Clonmel (p121).

Places to Stay & Eat The nearest hostel is a few kilometres south of Caher (p131).

The small but well-kept **Carrick-on-Suir Caravan & Camping Park** (☎ 051-640 461; Kilkenny Rd; camping per person & car €4.50) has adequate facilities and a useful shop for basic supplies. Centrally-located **Fatima House** (☎ 051-640 298; ⓔ fatimahouse@eircom.net; John St; singles/doubles €28/56) is a very welcoming B&B.

There are two **supermarkets** (open daily), one on the N27 at the traffic lights, and another in Greystone St, the western extension of Main St.

Several pubs serve bar meals, but two stand out. The extensive menu at **Galleway's Bistro** (☎ 051-641 604; Main St; mains €7.95-14.50) in the Carraig Hotel includes steaks, seafood and a couple of vegetarian dishes. The **Park Inn** (☎ 051-640 156; 1 New St; mains €10.50-21.50) offers more imaginative fare, including River Suir salmon.

Getting There & Away Carrick is well served by buses and a few trains. **Bus Éireann** (☎ 01-836 6111) operates service No 7 from Dublin's Busáras to Cork, via Carrick (€11.50, two hours 50 minutes, four daily Monday to Saturday and six Sunday). There is also a train service between Dublin's Heuston and Carrick (€36.50, 3½ hours, two daily Monday to Saturday). Carrick is on the N24, 40km south of Kilkenny and 20km east of Clonmel.

SOUTH & SOUTHEAST

Clonmel

With an attractive riverside setting, many reminders of its long history and innumerable small shops, Clonmel is an interesting place to look around.

The **TIC** (☎ 052-22960; Sarsfield St; open Mon-Sat May-Sept, Mon-Fri rest of the year) sells maps and walks guides.

Internet access is free at **Clonmel Library** (☎ 052-24524; Emmet St; open at least 10am-5pm Mon-Sat) but bookings are virtually essential. Three banks in O'Connell St have ATMs. For OSI maps, guidebooks and Irish titles, drop in to **Eason's** (19-20 Gladstone St) or **The Book Centre** (O'Connell St).

Places to Stay & Eat The nearest hostel is not far south of Caher (p131).

With lush grass surrounded by a thriving orchard, **The Apple Camping & Caravan Park** (☎ 052-41459; Moorstown; camping per person €5) is a lovely place to pitch a tent.

On the western side of town, **Hillcourt** (☎ 052-21020; e jmorrissey@hotmail.com; Marlfield; singles/doubles €37/46) is a comfortable B&B with en suite rooms; breakfast is excellent. Across the river on the eastern side of town, **Knockainey** (☎ 052-23148; Coleville Rd; singles/doubles €35/60) has a peaceful setting and good-sized rooms.

Clonmel has two **supermarkets**: in Gladstone St and in Market Place, off Emmett St.

The restaurant at Buttermarket Steakhouse is called **La Scala** (☎ 052-24147; Market St; mains €9-21; closed Sun) and, apart from steaks, offers Irish stew and pasta. The subterranean **Catalpa** (☎ 052-26821; 5 Sarsfield St; mains €6.30-18; closed Mon) is good value if you go for steak or fish, and has tasty pizzas. The best pub in town is **Sean Tierney's** (☎ 052-24467; O'Connell St; mains €11-24), with a popular restaurant upstairs; servings are generous.

Getting There & Away You can reach Clonmel by bus or train. **Bus Éireann** (☎ 01-836 6111) operates service No 7 from Dublin's Busáras to Cork, via Clonmel (€11.50, three hours 15 minutes, four daily Monday to Saturday and six on Sunday). There is also a train service between Dublin's

Heuston and Clonmel (€40, three hours 50 minutes, two daily Monday to Saturday).

By road, Clonmel is 50km from Kilkenny and 17km from Caher.

Knockanaffrin

Duration	4–4½ hours
Distance	10.5km
Difficulty	moderate
Start/Finish	Nire Valley car park
Nearest Town	Ballymacarbry (p120)
Transport	private

Summary Magnificent panoramic views on a very scenic traverse of a ridge dotted with extraordinary knobbly tors.

The 755m summit of Knockanaffrin crowns this rock-strewn ridge in the northern Comeraghs. Among the highest summits in the range, it commands wonderful panoramic views and has the great attraction of being blessed with less boggy ground than the Comeragh plateau to the south. The ridge rises quite steeply from the Nire Valley; the Clodiagh River drains the eastern slopes where two open corries cradle small tarns at the base of rugged cliffs. The route described follows minor roads, rough farm tracks, open mountain slopes and walkers paths.

The mountain's Irish name 'Cnoc an Aiffrin' means 'hill of the mass', perhaps recalling the harsh laws of an earlier time when the Roman Catholic mass was banned but continued to be celebrated in isolated places in the open air.

GETTING TO/FROM THE WALK

From Ballymacarbry on the R671 Clonmel–Dungarvan road, turn left along the Nire Valley Scenic Drive at a junction opposite Melody's Bar. At a junction 5.2km further on, keep right and follow the road for 4.2km to its end at a large car park (GR 276128).

THE WALK (see map p122)

Walk northwest and west down the road from the car park (GR 276128) for about 2km to a bitumen road on the right and follow it

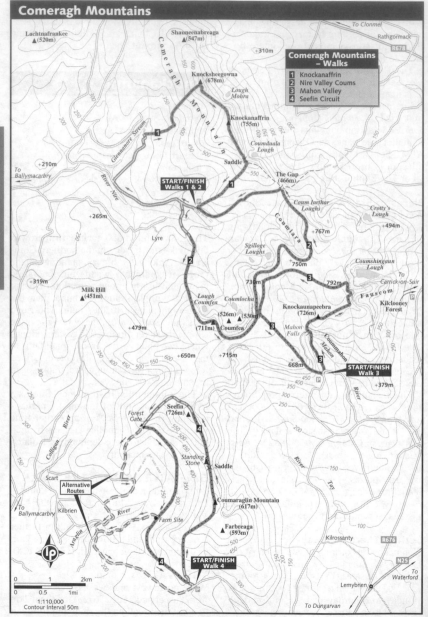

Comeragh Mountains

Comeragh Mountains – Walks
1 Knockanaffrin
2 Nire Valley Coums
3 Mahon Valley
4 Seefin Circuit

To Clonmel
Rathgormack
R678

Lachtnafrankee (520m)
Shauneenabreaga (547m)
+310m
Knocksheegowna (678m)
Lough Mohra
Knockanaffrin (755m)
Coumduala Lough
Saddle
The Gap (466m)
START/FINISH Walks 1 & 2
Coum Iarthar Loughs
Crotty's Lough
+494m
+265m
Coumlara
+767m
Lyre
Sgilloge Loughs
+750m
792m
Coumshingaun Lough
To Carrick-on-Suir
+319m
730m
Kilclooney Forest
Milk Hill (451m)
Lough Coumfea
Coumlochu
Knockaunapeebra (726m)
Fauscom
(526m) (530m)
+479m
(711m) Coumfea
Mahon Falls
+650m
+715m
Coumnahon
START/FINISH Walk 3
668m
+379m
Forest Gate
Seefin (726m)
Standing Stone
Saddle
Coumaraglin Mountain (617m)
River Tay
Alternative Routes
Scart
Farbreaga (593m)
Kilrossanty
R676
Kilbrien
To Ballymacarbry
Farm Site
To Waterford
N25
START/FINISH Walk 4
Lemybrien
Colligan River
To Ballymacarbry
River Nire
Glennamore Stream
Comeragh Mountain

0   1   2km
0   0.5   1mi
1:110,000
Contour Interval 50m

To Dungarvan

northeastwards, steadily uphill for about 1km. From an old farm house and numerous derelict farm buildings continue on a farm track, passing a track, a stone building and gate all on the left. The track becomes a rocky path between stone walls and trees, and brings you to a gate. Beyond it cross a fence, then a stream and follow a rough track northwards for a few hundred metres to a rivulet flowing eastwards (this is a tributary of Glennanore Stream).

Bear right and walk upstream beside this ever-deepening gully for about 500m. Cross a steep-sided northwest-southeast gully, then a larger gully; follow the latter up for a few metres to a fence and stone wall on the left. Walk beside them for about 120m then cross a larger stream and head northeast to ascend the broad, rather shapeless spur trending northeast. The very steep going is mostly over smooth or tussocky grass and some broken ground, all the way to the summit of **Knocksheegowna** (678m, two hours from the start). The view from the summit is fabulous, taking in the Galtee and Knockmealdown Mountains, Coumfea and the Comeragh plateau, the south coast and, a little closer, Lough Mohra below to the east.

Continue down the rocky ridge to a flat saddle then tackle the steep ascent, keeping west of a large heap of boulders high up, to gain the summit ridge. **Knockanaffrin's summit** (755m, 45 minutes from Knocksheegowna) is distinguished by a tiny cairn on top of the highest tor among the grey pebbly boulders. The view is unsurpassed, especially of the Comeragh plateau and its corries, and the rural landscape of small green fields separated by hedgerows right across the east and southeast.

Continue south along the ridge, shortly crossing a simple stile over a fence. Descending, keep on the east side of some tors then lose height seriously, following a well-trodden path down to a narrow gap high above **Coumduala Lough**. Go up a little to an east-west fence; don't cross it but follow it down westwards on a clear path through heather with only the occasional innocuous boggy bit. As soon as you can see the Nire

Valley car park, the path swings right (west) and joins a grassy track, sunken at first, which leads to a widely spaced line of white posts. At the last of these, bear left and drop down to the car park, following sheep paths through the heather (about 1¼ hours from Knockanaffrin).

Nire Valley Coums

Duration	5–5½hours
Distance	18km
Difficulty	moderate
Start/Finish	Nire Valley car park
Nearest Town	Ballymacarbry (p120)
Transport	private

Summary A spectacular outing high above the coums hollowed out of the rugged western face of the Comeraghs.

Glacial coums or corries and lakes are the glories of the Comeraghs – all 10 of them. The eastern side of the mountains is graced by magnificent Coumshingaun Lough and a few others, and the western flanks also have their fair share, although they are generally less enclosed and more accessible. They're best appreciated from the high ground above: you can view them in their rugged setting and clearly make out the jumbled contours of the small moraine hummocks nearby, with the beautiful Nire Valley as a backdrop.

This walk takes you right along the western rim; surprisingly perhaps, given the vast expanses of bogland covering the Comeragh plateau, the going is mostly dry and peat-free. For this we may have to thank sheep (an unusual debt perhaps), which have worn down narrow paths along the edge. The only rough going is on the upper part of the descent from the plateau rim towards the Gap, from where an old track, along which the one boggy patch is avoidable, leads back to the start.

GETTING TO/FROM THE WALK
See Getting to/from the Walk (p121) for Knockanaffrin.

THE WALK (see map p122)

From the car park walk northwest down the road for about 500m and go through a gate on the left; follow a vehicle track down to a bridge over the River Nire. Go up a vehicle track, rising above the river, for several hundred metres to a gate giving onto open moorland. Head south; cross the stream above a small gorge then make your way generally south up a broad spur towards Coumfea's domed heights. Keep on the eastern side of the spur higher up for the best views of **Lough Coumfea** and **Coumalocha**, sparkling blue on a sunny day, set in green hummocky moraine and nearly enclosed by steeply tiered cliffs (1¼ hours from the start).

Next, you're treated to remarkably easy going along the plateau rim, mostly on firm dry grass with spectacular views of the pastoral Nire Valley, and the Knockmealdown and Galtee Mountains beyond. It's a bit rougher as you turn north beyond Coumfea to reach the rim above **Sgilloge Loughs** (an hour from Coumalocha). Cross the stream tumbling into the lough then contour the steep spur northwards on clear sheep paths to overlook **Coumlara** and its slender waterfall. Heading southeast, you need to keep above the broken cliffs on the western side of the coum; cross the stream well above the falls. Work your way generally north from there, part way up the steep-sided spur. Eventually you reach a prominent outcrop of **conglomerate boulders** perched above the Gap.

To reach the Gap comfortably, start the descent in a northwesterly direction, bypassing precipitous crags and weaving through conglomerate boulders, then head back towards a fence on your right (east) and generally follow it to **the Gap** (1½ hours from Sgilloge Loughs). The line of the old track from the Gap is marked with white-painted posts. After a dry start it becomes wet and disjointed across lower lying ground, but improves after a while and provides fine views of most of where you've been. With the Nire Valley car park in sight, the posts come to an end. Bear left and go down to the car park (45 minutes from the Gap), following heathery sheep paths.

Mahon Valley

Duration	4½–5 hours
Distance	10km
Difficulty	moderate
Start/Finish	Mahon Falls car park
Nearest Town	Carrick-on-Suir (p120)
Transport	private

Summary A magnificent waterfall, an awesome glacial corrie and the highest point in the Comeraghs – all on an energetic tour around the Mahon Valley.

Mahon Falls, spilling over the southeastern corner of the Comeraghs, and Coumshingaun Lough, midway along the eastern flank, are the mountains' two most popular tourist attractions – they deserve to be and they're easily accessible. The falls, flanked by the towering, broken cliffs of a wide amphitheatre, drop in an almost unbroken 150m-long stream through a succession of narrow rock shutes. While Coumshingaun can be reached at lake level (see Coumshingaun Lough, p135), its awesome ruggedness is best appreciated from the top of the soaring headwall – the next highlight of this walk. After that, the highest point in the Comeraghs is a bit of an anticlimax but an achievement nonetheless. The walk continues with a rough slog around the wild, lonely upper reaches of the Mahon River valley, and finishes with a scenic descent overlooking the falls.

If the roughest part of the walk doesn't appeal, you could return to Knockaunapeebra from above Coumshingaun, cross the Mahon River and go up to a cluster of boulders to meet the path leading to the final descent, saving a couple of hours and a few kilometres.

GETTING TO/FROM THE WALK

From Carrick-on-Suir drive south on the R676 Dungarvan road for about 18km. At Mahon River bridge turn right to signposted Mahon Falls and almost immediately right again. Nearly 2km along this narrow road, bear right towards the falls. The car park (GR 314081) is 2km further on.

THE WALK (see map p122)
This walk starts easily, along the wide path leading to the foot of **Mahon Falls**. Cross the river and ascend steeply on dual-purpose sheep paths, between boulders and beside the falls – this is not as hair-raising as it looks from below. From the top of the falls you should be able to see the coast to the south. Continue ascending, now east, up the steep slope of **Knockaunapeebra** (726m), topped with a pair of cairns and giving an excellent view of Dungarvan Harbour. Press on northeastwards across a shallow gap then contour northeastwards below the feature mapped as '792' and soon what looks like an edge above nothingness looms ahead. Cross fairly innocuous peat hags and gullies to reach the plateau rim above **Fauscoum**; continue generally north along the rim, soon above awesome bluffs and tiers of red sandstone in **Coumshingaun Lough** to the highest point on the rim (two hours from the start).

The next leg of the walk takes you a few hundred metres southwest to the undistinguished highest point in the Comeraghs (792m) and marked only by a modest cairn. Nonetheless it provides a fine panoramic view of coast and mountains. Then set a course northwest across tussock grass and clumps of heather to the watery gap at the head of the Mahon River. Go westwards up the steep slope to the crest of the ridge forming the western side of the Mahon Valley, thus bypassing the swamps and peat hags below. Stay on the ridge, over a couple of tops, almost intersecting with part of the Nire Valley Coums walk (p123). Once the ridge starts to turn southwestwards and, as intimidating peat hags loom and the cliffs of Coummahon beckon, head southeast, aiming for prominent rock outcrops above the coum (1¾ hours from Coumshingaun Lough).

Among these warty conglomerate boulders, pick up a path leading southeast along Coummahon's rim; continuing to the top of a steep drop. Here you'll find a fence and a much-used path. Keep your eye on the car park and, rather than follow the fence all the way to the road, head straight for the cars where the fence veers off the direct line. It takes 45 minutes to reach the car park.

Seefin Circuit

Duration	4½–5 hours
Distance	14.5km
Difficulty	moderate
Start/Finish	car park at GR 276018
Nearest Town	Ballymacarbry (p120)
Transport	private

Summary An almost bog-free tour over a shapely peak in the southwestern Comeraghs, with a choice between tracks and roads or cross-country for the return.

Seefin (726m) is the highest point on a long ridge rising from the lovely Colligan River valley in the southwest corner of the Comeraghs, and rejoices in an almost complete absence of peat hags and soggy ground. Although the mountain lacks the spectacular corries found elsewhere in the Comeraghs, the eastern face is very steep and corrie-like. Much of the return leg of the route described is mixed cross-country walking; alternatives following tracks and minor roads, and avoiding the roughest ground (but involving more ascent) are described after the main route.

GETTING TO/FROM THE WALK
From Ballymacarbry; head south on the R671 for 4.8km to a junction and go left towards Dungarvan on the R672. Take the first left past a service station at an intersection 6.5km further on. Continue to a T-junction and turn right then fork first left; go on to a T-junction and turn right towards 'Dungarvan'. At a junction where there's a bridge immediately on the right, continue ahead, now on 'Comeragh Drive'. At an oblique junction where the drive goes left, turn right; the car park at the start of the walk is 4km further on.

THE WALK (see map p122)
Walk southwest up the road for about 60m then head north up a rough track through heather and bracken; it soon fades, so continue northwest to a low ridge. Here you should find a track of sorts; head north then northeast, going steeply in places up the

long spur leading past a communications installation to **Coumaraglin Mountain** (617m, 1¼ hours from the start). The best view is from the eastern edge, taking in the south coast and much of the Comeragh plateau. Follow a fence northwards down into a broad saddle in which is a 2m-high **standing stone**, possibly of prehistoric origin, and nearby, the remains of a stone-walled enclosure. Then, the lower half of the ascent, steep in places, is over heather and grass; higher up the grass is more tussocky. **Seefin's summit** (726m; 1¼ hours from Coumaraglin Mountain) is blighted by a small ugly building, but there's a cluster of conglomerate boulders nearby among which the trig pillar lies forlornly on its side. Here you can comfortably contemplate the panoramic coast and mountain view.

Walk down the vehicle track leading northwest then southwest for almost 2km to a gate and track junction. This is the parting of the ways for the main route and the first Alternative Route (from Forest Gate, this page). Cross the fence on the left of the gate and go down the narrow path through the plantation to its eastern boundary; cross a fence and a small stream to open grassy moorland. Head generally south, across the lower slopes of Seefin, keeping well to the east of the fields lower down (by at least 150m and more further on), and above a clump of trees sheltering a red-roofed building. Beyond there, aim for the western edge of a one-time farm enclosed by tall old trees. From this site (GR 265038), the second Alternative Route (from Farm Site, this page) diverges westwards along a vehicle track. The track shown on the OSI map leading generally south from here no longer exists. Nevertheless, if you're determined to avoid road walking altogether head south, but keep well to the east of the low saddle ahead to avoid the bracken jungle on the spur of Coumaraglin Mountain. Then turn generally east and make your way up to the head of a shallow valley – the only wet part of the route. The last stretch is then southeastwards across the broad spur and back down to the car park (two hours from Seefin's summit).

Alternative Route: from Forest Gate

2–2½ hours, 8km, 100m ascent

Continue down the forest track from the gate to a minor road and turn left (at GR 255049). Descend to a T-junction and make another left turn. Cross the Araglin River and soon turn left. Pass a track on the left and almost immediately bear left at a fork and continue up to the car park (two hours from Seefin).

Alternative Route: from Farm Site

1½–2 hours, 6km, 90m ascent

From the walled farm site, follow the vehicle track west and southwest to a T-junction and turn left, then almost immediately fork left and walk up to the car park (two hours from Seefin).

Knockmealdown Mountains

Western neighbours of the Comeraghs, the Knockmealdown Mountains have a similar geological history, but differ markedly in their form and landscape. A 25km-long, east-west aligned range, the Knockmealdowns lie between the River Tar (a tributary of the River Suir) to the north and the beautiful Blackwater River to the south. They're a proper mountain range with at least 15 distinct summits, the highest being Knockmealdown (794m).

Signs of the work of glaciers are few; apart from the Gap, which sharply divides the range, there is Bay Lough, a corrie lake dammed by moraine, and the corrie on the northeastern side of Knockmealdown.

The Irish name for the main peak, 'Cnoc Maol Donn' meaning 'bare, brown mountain', accurately describes the appearance of the uplands. However, jarringly straight-edged conifer plantations on the northern and southern slopes belie this to some extent, as does the spread of another exotic species, rhododendron. You'll go a long way to see a more striking example of the rhododendron's invasiveness than in the glen cradling Bay Lough (see the boxed text 'Scourge of the Rhododendron', p269).

Two walks are described in this section: a long traverse of the eastern half of the range, with a shorter alternative concentrating on Knockmealdown itself, and a shorter walk on the lower, gentler western part of the range.

ACCESS TOWN

Caher (p131) could well serve as a base for doing the Knockmealdowns, but Clogheen is right on the doorstep.

Clogheen

This village, close to the Knockmealdowns and the justly famous road through there via the Vee, has very limited facilities. The nearest TIC and ATM are in Caher.

Spacious, family-oriented **Parson's Green Caravan and Camping Park** (☎ 052-65290, fax 65504; @ kathleennoonan@oceanfree .net; camping per person €7.60-9.10) is just north of the village, and has simple facilities, a coffee shop, take-away food place and laundry.

The superbly restored **Ballyboy House** (☎ 052-65297; W www.tipp.ie/ballyboy-house .htm; singles/doubles €34/56) is nearly 400 years old, and offers a warm welcome, large en suite rooms and a big breakfast. Evening meals can also be provided at Ballyboy by arrangement.

In the village are a **supermarket**, **greengrocer**, **butcher** and several **pubs**. If you've forgotten to bring a map, you'll need to go to Caher to buy one.

The only place recommended for a meal in the area is the **Village Inn** (☎ 052-41705; mains €9-14) in Ballylooby, 5km to the north along the R668.

Getting There & Away There is a **Bus Éireann** (☎ 01-836 6111) service (No 7) from Kilkenny to Cork, via Clogheen (€17, one hour 50 minutes, two daily Monday to Saturday and one on Sunday). Clogheen is around the intersection of the R668 and R665, 13km south of Caher and 24km southwest of Clonmel.

Eastern Knockmealdowns

Duration	6½–7 hours
Distance	21km
Difficulty	moderate–demanding
Start/Finish	The Vee car park
Nearest Town	Clogheen (p127)
Transport	private

Summary Over the high points of the eastern half of the range with plenty of walking on amazingly bog-free, clear paths.

The long, sharply undulating eastern half of the Knockmealdown range just begs for an extended traverse, taking in as many as possible of the summits; an invitation made all the more attractive by the comparatively dry ground and the ease of access from the road carving through the mountains. Although conifer plantations do little to enhance the landscape of the northern slopes of the range, the network of roads through the trees does serve walkers well, making for a relatively easy return from the high ground.

If the prospect of this rather long walk is too daunting, try the shorter alternative, which takes in Knockmealdown alone. It involves one short section of heather-hopping, but is otherwise on good paths and tracks.

PLANNING

Although the well-worn path and the stone walls flanking most of the route make for easy route finding, you should still carry a compass and map because the mountains are prone to sudden onsets of cloud and rain.

Maps

OSI 1:50,000 map No 74 is the one to carry.

GETTING TO/FROM THE WALK

The walk starts and finishes at a roadside car park on the R668 close to the Vee, about 6km south of Clogheen.

THE WALK (see map p128)

Follow the well-trodden path which leads up to **Grubb's monument** commemorating one Samuel Grubb; he was a local property

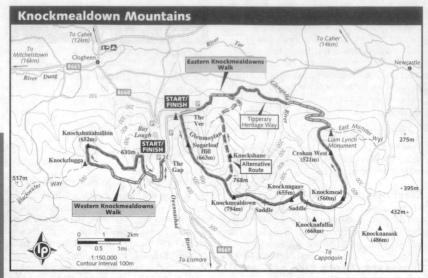

Knockmealdown Mountains

owner who was buried overlooking his domain. Continue up the heathery hillside on the clear path to the broad, cairn-strewn summit of **Sugarloaf Hill** (663m, an hour from the start). From here the route to Knockmealdown is perfectly straightforward: simply follow the very wide, undulating path beside or, in places, on top of an old stone wall, over peat-free ground, to the trig pillar standing alone on **Knockmealdown** summit (794m, an hour from Sugarloaf Hill). Among much else, Dungarvan Harbour and the wide ribbon of the River Blackwater to the south are prominent in the wide vista.

It's a steep descent east and southeastwards to a broad saddle where the stone wall peters out, but it reasserts itself on the way up to the double summit of **Knocknagauv** (655m, an hour from Knockmealdown). Continue northeastwards with the wall for a few hundred metres to a slight knoll. Then, rather than crossing the wide col and going up to Knocknafallia (unless you really want to), keep on with the low wall to contour the northern slope of Knocknafallia to a forest road in the gap between it and Knockmeal. Turn left and about 50m along on a bend,

continue up the slope on a narrow path beside a well-camouflaged wall to **Knockmeal's** summit plateau, passing about 60m west of the small summit cairn. The way onwards is now more northwards as you descend to a shallow gap, go over a bump and down some more on a narrow path. It's fairly rough going on the ascent to the final summit – **Crohan West** (521m, 1¾ hours from Knocknagauv), which is topped by a large cairn. The view from here is as good as from any of the higher summits, taking in the Galtee Mountains and the vast patchwork of the vale of the River Suir.

Drop down towards the forest, following a line of old posts to a fence corner; bear left for 20m to a narrow clearing between the trees and descend, soon swinging right to reach the impressive **Liam Lynch monument** (see the boxed text 'Liam Lynch – Revolutionary', p129), 30 minutes from Crohan West. A short path takes you to a forest road; turn left along the well waymarked East Munster Way (p337). About 3.5km further on, shortly before a bridge over the Glengalla River, the Tipperary Heritage Way (p337) joins the East Munster Way and the two continue in tandem from there to the

Evening over Avonbeg River, Glenmalure, County Wicklow

Doldrum Bay's Baily lighthouse, close to the route of the Howth Peninsula walk

Mahon Falls, Mahon Valley, Comeragh Mountains

On the Spink, above Upper Lake, Glendalough

Exploring the Comeragh Mountains, County Waterford

end of the walk. The route is partly through conifer plantations but more in the open. Close to the deeply entrenched Glenmoylan River, be on the lookout for a left turn, up the eastern side of the river to a left bend in the forest track. Continue ahead through bracken to a stile; cross a footbridge from which a path winds steeply up to the Vee (2¼ hours from the monument).

Alternative Route: via Knockshane
1½ hours, 5km

Follow the route described to the summit of Knockmealdown. Retrace your steps down the final ascent to the summit, cross a slight dip and, as you start to gain a little height, diverge northeast to a prominent cairn on a rounded hill ('768' on the map, two hours from the start).

Head generally north down a broad spur, mapped as Knockshane, to another cairn,

fringed with stones. Continue down; as the gradient steepens, keep slightly to the western side of the spur through deep heather to meet a track beside the forest fence. Turn right and follow it into the forest and down to a T-junction; turn left. This forest track soon meets the Tipperary Heritage Way at a bend (1½ hours from '768'). Follow the directions for the main walk from here up to the Vee.

Western Knockmealdowns

Duration	4–4½ hours
Distance	10.5km
Difficulty	moderate
Start/Finish	The Gap car park
Nearest Town	Clogheen (p127)
Transport	private
Summary	A relatively gentle ramble over two modest, unassuming summits with lovely views far and wide.

The gentler, more rounded hills west of the Gap are much less frequented than their higher, steeper associates to the east. The Blackwater Way crosses the upper southern slopes and simplifies access and route finding – although you wouldn't want to be caught on the high ground, beyond its reach, in mist. Forest tracks and a waymarked path take you to about the half-way mark, from where the route is cross-country to Knockshanahullion and eastwards to a high point above the Gap. The last stretch is on more open ground, heading down to rejoin the outward route.

PLANNING
Maps
Make sure you have the OSI 1:50,000 map No 74 for this walk.

GETTING TO/FROM THE WALK
From Clogheen drive south along the R668 towards Lismore, over the Vee, to a car park (GR 031100) on the western side of the road in the Gap.

Liam Lynch – Revolutionary

The wording on the plaques of the impressive monument in the forest north of Crohan West is, understandably perhaps, entirely in Irish. Here is a brief explanation.

Liam Lynch was born at Barnaguraha just north near the small town of Angleshorough at the western end of the Galtee Mountains in 1893. His early passion for Irish history and the Irish language almost inevitably led him to determined opposition to British rule. As a member of the Irish Republican Army (IRA) he fought in the War of Independence and became the IRA's Chief of Staff. A fierce opponent of the Anglo-Irish Treaty, he advocated carrying on the fight – against the new Irish government. Early on 10 April 1923 he was shot dead, apparently by former comrades, in the Knockmealdowns. Among his dying words were '... I am glad I am going from it all, poor Ireland ...' His successor declared a cease-fire soon after. The memorial was unveiled in 1935 at a ceremony attended by about 15,000 people.

THE WALK (see map p128)

From the car park follow a track up past the white statue of **Our Lady of Knock** and a nearby domed shelter, across the hillside to a wide rocky track. Go up beside it to a much more amenable track on the left leading towards a small plantation. Follow this track, the route of the Blackwater Way (p338), past the plantation; just as it starts to drop into a deep valley, turn right along a track leading west into a valley. At its head cross a stile beside a gate and continue along the track, paralleling the forest on the left, to a T-junction and turn right. The directions are the same at the next junction; shortly there's another stile to cross beside a gate. The track bends sharp left and leads onto one more stile at the forest boundary fence. From here, posts adorned with fluorescent strips mark the route of the Blackwater Way, a steep, well-used path up the moorland hillside. Leave the Way as soon as the path starts to level, at the first bare ground you encounter, just short of the crest. Head north across bare ground and you should pick up a narrow path through the heather and grass up the broad spur to the trig pillar on the summit of **Knockshanahullion** (652m, two hours from the start). A huge pile of stones nearby looks for all the world like a prehistoric burial cairn. The excellent panorama takes in the eastern Knockmealdowns and the Comeragh Mountains beyond.

Descend southeastwards, steeply at first over springy heather, aiming for the corner of a fence below. Follow a rough path beside the fence heading generally eastwards over intermittently wet ground. Having gained some height, the direction changes to southeast, still uphill and with a fence on the right. More or less on a crest, turn north with the fence and continue up to the flat summit of **'630'** for a great view of Sugarloaf Hill and Knockmealdown across the Gap (an hour from Knockshanahullion). Drop down slightly eastwards to a north-south fence and follow it down, southwards, to a gate at a bend in the forest track and rejoin the Blackwater Way. Retrace your steps to the start (an hour from '630').

Galtee Mountains

The Galtee Mountains stand slightly aloof from the other mountain groups in the south; they rise comparatively gradually from the sprawling 'Tipperary Plain' and much more steeply from beautiful Glen of Aherlow to the north. The range extends west from Caher for 23km, the highest peak is Galtymore Mountain (919m), which towers over at least 12 other distinct summits. Valleys bite deep into the main ridge, composed of Old Red Sandstone, so that the Galtees (pronounced with a short 'a' as in 'fact') are characterised by long spurs reaching out from the relatively narrow main ridge. Tors, created by frost-shattering during the last Ice Age, are scattered along the ridge, and notably form a heap of conglomerate boulders known as O'Loughnan's Castle. The north face of the range is punctuated by corries, relics of the Ice Age that hide Lough Muskry and Bohreen Lough, impounded by massed moraine. A third small lake, Lough Curra, is a hollow predating glaciation and later blocked off by moraine. The uplands of the range are largely covered with blanket bog and conifer plantations are widespread across the lower slopes.

There are several good walks in the range and two of the best are described in this section: a fine horseshoe route over Galtymore, and a less strenuous excursion to Lough Muskry. Other Walks (p134) includes notes about alternative routes up Galtymore from both sides of the range and a walk to Lough Curra.

PLANNING
Maps & Books

The OSI 1:50,000 map No 74 is the one to carry for both Galtee walks described here. *The Galty, Knockmealdown and Comeragh Mountains*, by Barry Keane, describes several walks in the area. Four leaflets published by the Glen of Aherlow Fáilte Society and titled *Galty Mountains Walks* describe low-level waymarked walks to Glencush, Lake Muskry, Slievenamuck and another in the Galbally area; the waymarking is sparse in moorland areas. Each leaflet has descriptive notes and shows the route on a topographical map at 1:10,000 or 1:20,000. The leaflets are available from the Society's office in Glen of Aherlow (this page).

While browsing in bookshops look out for *The Galtees Anthology*, edited by John Gallahane, a collection of writings about places, people and events.

ACCESS TOWNS
Caher
At the eastern foot of the Galtees, Caher (pronounced 'care') is a small heritage town dominated by its massive medieval castle.

Information The **TIC** (☎ 052-41453; *Castle St; open daily July & Aug, Mon-Sat at other times*) is the best place for maps, and walking and general guide books.

There's an Internet café in the **Caher Development Business & Training Centre** (☎ 052-42616; *Market Yard; €3.81 for 30 minutes; open Mon-Fri*) off Church St. A bank in Castle St has an ATM.

Places to Stay & Eat See Clonmel (p121) for information about camping.

The nearest hostel, **Lisakyle Hostel** (☎ 052-41963; *Lisakyle, Caher; dorm beds €12, twins or doubles €28; open Mar-Oct*), is about 2.4km south of Caher along the R670 to Ardfinnan. For something different, **Carrigeen Castle** (☎/fax 052-41370; e carrigeencastle@yahoo.co.uk; *singles/doubles €40/60*) is an impressive old building overlooking the town; some rooms are en suite. Right in the centre of town, **Tinsley House** (☎/fax 052-41947; *the Square; singles/doubles €38/51*) is a convenient B&B with comfortable en suite rooms.

There is a **supermarket** in Bridge St that is open daily.

The standard bar supper offered at **Caher House Hotel** (☎ 052-42727; *the Square; mains €15-19*) includes local salmon and a vegetarian dish. The **Galtee Inn** (☎ 052-41247; *the Square; mains €9.50-22*) is a traditional pub which takes pride in its grills, and also offers wild salmon and some vegetarian temptations.

Getting There & Away There is a **Bus Éireann** (☎ 01-836 6111) service (No 7) from Dublin's Busáras to Caher (€17, three hours 45 minutes, one daily). There is also a train service between Dublin's Heuston and Caher (€36.50, 3½ hours, two daily Monday to Saturday).

Caher is on the N24 close to its intersection with the N8 and 17km from Clonmel, 77km from Cork.

Glen of Aherlow
Fringing the northern side of the mountains, this beautiful glen is home to a community of scattered small villages and isolated farms, and is a very convenient base from which to explore the Galtees.

Glen of Aherlow Fáilte Society (☎ 062-56331; W www.tipp.ie/aherlow-failte.htm; *Coach Rd, Aherlow; open daily June-Oct*) has a 'tourist information point' at Newtown, at the R663 and R664 junction, that provides local walks and accommodation information. The Caher TIC is the nearest full-scale office for reservations; the nearest ATM is in Caher. There are public telephones at the hamlets of Lisvarrinane and Rossadrehid.

Places to Stay & Eat As well as an incomparable view of Galtymore, **Glen of Aherlow Caravan & Camping Park** (☎ 062-56555; W www.tipperarycamping.com; *camping per person/tent & car €2/10*) is well grassed, has friendly, helpful hosts and excellent facilities, including a basic campers kitchen.

The Galtees are rarely out of sight at **Ballinacourty House** (☎ 062-56000, fax 56230; e info@ballinacourtyhse.com; *Glen of Aherlow; singles/doubles €36/51*), which has large rooms in 18th-century stables. The adjacent **campsite** (*camping per person/tent €1.50/11.50*) is a spacious, sheltered area with good facilities. Self-catering cottages are also available, and there's a **restaurant** (☎ 056-775 6224; *set menu €27*) that emphasises Irish produce.

In the heart of Aherlow, the **Glen Hotel** (☎ 062-56146, fax 56152; *singles/doubles €50/80; dinner, bed & breakfast €68*) is an older style hotel with comfortable en suite rooms. Its **restaurant** *(meals about €30)* is open to all comers; request vegetarian meals in advance. **Bar meals** *(mains €11.50-17.50)* are served in the lounge.

There are small **shops** in Bansha, Newtown, Lisvarrinane and Rossadrehid.

Getting There & Away There are no bus services in the glen. From the east the R663, the main road through the glen, branches from the N24 at Bansha, about 14/10km from Caher/Tipperary. From Tipperary the north, the R664 leads to Newtown on the R663 in the glen.

Galtymore

Duration	5¾–6¼ hours
Distance	12km
Difficulty	moderate–demanding
Start/Finish	Clydagh valley car park
Nearest Towns	Glen of Aherlow (p131), Caher (p131)
Transport	private

Summary A classic horseshoe route over the highest peak in the Galtees with magnificent panoramic views and awesome corries below.

Galtymore (919m) is one of the 12 munros in Ireland (see the boxed text 'The Irish Munros', p152). It stands proud of the rest of the range by almost 100m and is a prominent landmark far and wide. The route described, which includes 1020m of ascent, is the most scenic and satisfying among several; surprisingly perhaps, it's over virtually trackless ground, boggy in places but not excessively so. Along the spine of the main ridge you're treated to thrilling views of each of the tarns in the corries far below. A shorter, more direct route from Glencush, and another from the southern side of the range are both outlined in Other Walks (p134).

PLANNING

It can be warm and sunny down in the glen but bitterly cold and windy on the tops – never take the Galtees lightly, and don't forget your compass.

GETTING TO/FROM THE WALK

To reach the start, drive along the minor road on the south side of Glen of Aherlow (known as Glen of Aherlow Scenic Drive) to a junction about 100m east of Clydagh Bridge (at GR 874280). Drive south along the narrow road into the Clydagh River valley for about 300m to an informal car park at a junction with a forest track on the right.

THE WALK (see map p134)

Walk south along the bitumen road from the car park; immediately beyond the forest edge climb concrete steps on the left then a stile. Go up a rough vehicle track beside a fence and cross a stile onto open moorland. Steer a southeasterly course up the generally steep spur of Cush (there's no consistent path through the turfy, sheep-grazed grass) to the unadorned summit of **Cush** (639m, 1¼ hours from the start). The views are lovely: patchwork plains and hills merging with the northern horizon and, in contrast, the rugged cliffs above nearby cirques.

Descend steeply southwards following a low turfed wall to a soggy col. Then there's nothing for it but to tackle the ascent to Galtybeg, with little relief from exceeding steepness but good views of teardrop-shaped **Borheen Lough**. **Galtybeg's** small summit, like that on Cush, lacks a crowning cairn (799m, 1½ hours from Cush). Next, descend sharply southwestwards to the col above **Lough Dineen**. The driest route through the maze of peat hags is on the south side, below the crest; the scenic route along the rim above the lough is very soft in places. Happily most of the ascent to **Galtymore** is relatively firm and dry; the cairn on the highest point beside the broken trig pillar is about 30m east of a **memorial cross** (45 minutes from Galtybeg). To the southeast the Comeragh and Knockmealdown Mountains are prominent, and to the northwest the Shannon estuary is visible on a clear day.

Drop down southwestwards to meet a curving stone wall and follow it, through some peaty places and past a breathtaking view of **Lough Curra** far below, to a corner just east of **Slievecushnabinnia** (766m). This wall dates back to about 1880 and marked the boundary between the estates of two local families.

Head north across this heathery-grassy dome and soon start to lose height north-northeastwards. After a while, aim for a tall cairn on the broad spur of Knocknanuss. Continue down from it and when the slope on the right eases, change course to north-eastwards, eventually crossing a prominent grassy knoll. Continue down more towards the east, aiming for an east-west trending stone wall. Cross a stile over a forest fence and follow a path between the wall and some conifers to a forest track; turn left. A circuitous 1.5km further on, at a track junction by the remains of an old chimney, turn left and follow the track through the plantation and back to the start (2¼ hours from Galtymore).

Lough Muskry

Duration	4–4½ hours
Distance	13km
Difficulty	moderate
Start/Finish	track junction at GR 917283
Nearest Towns	Glen of Aherlow (p131), Caher (p131)
Transport	private

Summary A fine circular walk above a spectacular glacial lake on the northern face of the Galtees.

Lough Muskry is the largest of the glacial lakes in the Galtees, sitting at the foot of narrow tiers of dark Old Red Sandstone cliffs and steep green slopes. You'd scarcely guess that the lough now contributes to the local water supply. This tour takes you up past the lake to Greenane (802m), the highest summit east of Galtymore. You'll also pass O'Loughnan's Castle, which is not a ruin but a squat pile of flat, angular conglomerate boulders amid a clutter of pebbly rocks – more of a cottage than a castle. Beyond the plantation at the start of the walk the route crosses open moorland; inevitably there are some peat hags to plough through but nothing too horrendous.

GETTING TO/FROM THE WALK

Reach the hamlet of Rossadrehid (at GR 927292) at a crossroads on the south side of the glen. Drive south from here along a narrow bitumen road signposted 'Lake Muskry', then west for 400m and park at a minor junction on the left. There are a few other places where you can safely park along the east–west road and on the forest track, southeast from the start of the walk.

THE WALK (see map p134)

Set off southeast along the forest road (following the route of an unidentified way-marked walk and soon turning into a long valley). After about 2km you come to a stile beside a gate at the plantation boundary, well up the valley. The forest road continues, although it's not shown doing so on the OSI map, rising steeply across the eastern slopes of **Knockastackeen**, over a stream and up to a point above tranquil and secluded **Lough Muskry** (an hour from the start). To reach the crest of the ridge high above the lake, start from the end of the track and keep high above the lake to ascend the very steep grassed slope well to the west of the cliffs tumbling into the lake. Eventually you emerge on the ridge, probably around the unnamed top '785'; turn east and drop down to the broad, rather peaty col between 785 and Greenane. Here you'll find not merely a 'cairn' as the OSI map has it, but **O'Loughnan's Castle**. Continue eastwards up to the trig pillar on the summit of **Greenane** (802m, 1½ hours from Lough Muskry).

The next objective is **Farbreaga**, 1.5km northeast down a fairly well defined spur; it's marked by a spread-eagled mass of stones on a slight mound. Here, with a bit of imagination, you can make out the shape of a small one-time dwelling, possibly a booley hut (see the boxed text 'Booleying Summer in the Mountains', p224). Head generally north for no more than 200m then turn decisively northwest and descend into the valley below, eventually aiming for the forest boundary you crossed earlier in the day. You will have to ford the anonymous stream that flows through the glen – an

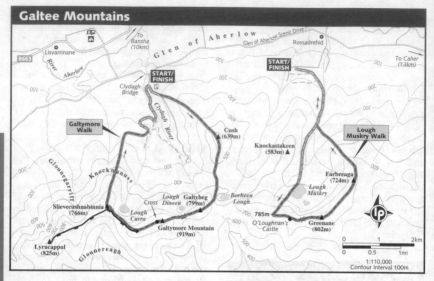

Galtee Mountains

interesting but not impossible proposition even after heavy rain. Return to the start down the forest road (about 1½ hours from Greenane).

Other Walks

WAYMARKED WAYS

There are four official Waymarked Ways in this area: South Leinster (Kildavin to Carrick-on-Suir), East Munster, Tipperary Heritage and Blackwater Ways. For more information see the Waymarked Ways chapter (p335).

WICKLOW MOUNTAINS
St Kevin's Way

This is one of five Pilgrim Paths developed by the Dúchas, several other agencies and local committees as a heritage awareness-raising, sustainable-tourism project. This one, 26km long, links the village of Hollywood on the northwestern edge of the Wicklows and Monastic City in Glendalough via Wicklow Gap and Glendasan (see the boxed text 'A Park, a Monk and a Mine', p107). It follows the possible and probable route of the monk Kevin (who became a saintly hermit) and later pilgrims. Small parts of a primitive road, possibly built for him, have been identified; examples can be seen at Wicklow Gap. About half the way is

along bitumen roads, including a perilous section near the western end. Much of the rest follows forest tracks and paths, some very wet. The route is generally well waymarked.

There is no public transport to Hollywood itself; **St Kevin's bus service** (☎ 01-281 8119) serves Glendalough (p108). B&B accommodation is available in Hollywood, contact **East Coast & Midlands Tourism** (☎ 0404-45688; W www.ecoast-midlands.travel.ie). The excellent guide to the Way may be available at the Glendalough Visitor Centre, alternatively it can be purchased online from EastWest Mapping. Part of the route is shown on the Harvey 1:30,000 map *Wicklow Mountains*; two OSI 1:50,000 maps, Nos 55 and 56, cover the area but don't show the Way.

Tonelagee & Brockagh Mountain

Tonelagee (817m) is the third-highest summit in the Wicklows, rising steeply from Wicklow Gap to the south and less so from Glenmacnass to the northeast; it can be ascended directly from the roads through both places. A longer and more scenic approach is via Brockagh Mountain on the long southeastern ridge, starting with the Wicklow Way near Laragh. The simplest return route is merely to retrace steps. Allow 5½ to six hours for this 19km walk, with 800m ascent. The map to carry for ths walk is the Harvey 1:30,000 *Wicklow Mountains*.

BLACKSTAIRS & BARROW
Brandon Hill

This broad hill (515m) comes and goes in the outlook from the Barrow Way (p116) and gives marvellous panoramic views west to the Galtees, Knockmealdowns and Comeraghs, and south to Waterford Harbour. From Graiguenamanagh follow the South Leinster Way for about 4km; the Brandon Way, waymarked with granite stones inscribed 'B.W.' and an arrow, loops around the eastern half of the mountain on minor roads, forests tracks and a moorland path. The waymarker stones assume a clockwise course but the reverse direction gives better views. Allow 4¼ to five hours for this 12km walk involving 600m ascent. Use the OSI 1:50,000 map No 68.

COMERAGH MOUNTAINS
Coumshingaun Lough

Described as 'the finest example of an ice age corrie in Europe', this truly spectacular lake and its 500m-deep corrie featured in the Mahon Valley walk (p124). You can appreciate its awesomeness with much less effort on a lower level walk to the lake shore. Drive to Kilclooney Forest car park (GR 341102) on the R676 Lemybrien–Clonmel road. Follow a well-used path through conifers to a forest road; turn right to a path which rises steeply, generally westwards, and leads to the lake. Allow 1½ hours for the return, the walk involves about 5km and 220m ascent. Take OSI 1:50,000 map No 75.

GALTEE MOUNTAINS
Lough Curra

This is the most secluded and scenically dramatic of the small lakes on the Galtees' northern flanks. Follow a blue-waymarked route from Clydagh Valley car park (see Galtymore walk, p132) to the 'Lough Curra stile' over a forest fence. Waymarkers are sparse from there so head west for 500m and pick up an old track, shown on the OSI map contouring the hillside southwards. Follow it to the shore of the lough. Allow three to 3½ hours for this 9.4km walk involving 450m ascent. Carry OSI 1:50,000 map No 74.

Galtymore Direct

If time is short you can tackle Galtymore head on, leaving the longer Galtymore walk (p132) for another day. Start from the Clydagh Valley car park and follow blue waymarkers and signs to a stile over a forest fence. From there go up beside a burn then southwest to a skyline spur. Ascend steeply to the ridge, reaching it near the summit. Return by the same route. Allow 3½ to four hours for this 10km walk involving 770m ascent; carry the OSI 1:50,000 map No 74.

Galtymore from Mountain Lodge Youth Hostel

The southern side of the range is more forested and feels less remote than the Aherlow side, not least because it rises directly from the busy N8 between Caher and Mitchelstown. A circuit from Burncourt River valley taking in Galtybeg and Greenane involves five to 5½ hours walking, 14.5km and 940m ascent, partly on tracks and with much cross-country walking over wet ground.

To reach the start, turn off the N8 about 12km southwest of Caher along a narrow road signed to Mountain Lodge Youth Hostel and Glengarra Wood. There are car parks about 150m and almost 1km along on the right. Use the OSI 1:50,000 map No 74. The route takes you north through the Glengarra Wood, passing the youth hostel en route, across the Burncourt River, up to the saddle north of Knockeenatoung and on to the foot of Galtybeg; climb Galtymore from the saddle between it and Galtybeg. Then retrace your steps across Galtybeg, continue east past O'Loughlan's Castle, then down a spur into Burncourt River valley and back through the forest.

Deep in Glengarra Wood, the gas-lit **Mountain Lodge Youth Hostel** (☎ 052-67277; dorm beds €12), harks back to earlier hostelling times, but the lack of electricity has become a liability, so check with **An Óige** (☎ 01-830 4555) that it's still open if you're contemplating a visit.

SOUTH & SOUTHEAST

Southwest

Southwest Ireland is a region of superlatives. It boasts the country's highest peaks, receives its greatest volume of international visitors, and offers months of walking to challenge enthusiasts of all persuasions. Encompassing Counties Cork and Kerry, the region is split into a series of peninsulas, each very different in character. The Sheep's Head in County Cork is the most remote and untouched by tourism, and is a place where solitude is still possible. The Beara Peninsula, on the border between Cork and Kerry, has a wild, craggy landscape juxtaposed with colourful and picturesque villages. The Iveragh Peninsula has the highest and most challenging mountain range in Ireland. Meanwhile, walkers are drawn to the Dingle Peninsula in the hope of a clear day on majestic Brandon Mountain and to experience an iconic coastal landscape that has starred in several Hollywood films. Each peninsula has its own Waymarked Way, giving excellent long-distance paths as well as a wide selection of shorter, easier walks.

Besides the stunning scenery, the main attraction of the region is the opportunity to experience Irish culture both past and present. From the numerous standing stones, *clochains* (beehive-shaped, dry-stone huts) and other historical relics, to the friendly pubs that so often provide the focal point for celebrations after a good day's activity, the southwest can be difficult to beat.

HISTORY

The landscape of the southwest is littered with evidence of its early history. Numerous promontory forts, stone circles, stone rows, mounds and cairns can be dated as far back as 5000 years.

By the 8th century the Vikings had arrived on the peninsulas, raided them and settled in Smerwick Harbour near Dingle. Four hundred years later it was the turn of the Normans to settle in the area, intermarry with locals and adopt the language. Soon after this time, the recorded history of the area

Highlights

Sampling the best of the Dingle Way – looking at Dunmore Head from Slea Head

- Discovering the wonderfully serrated coastline around Slea Head on the Dingle Way (p143)
- Climbing Carrauntoohil, the highest mountain in Ireland, on the Coomloughra Horseshoe (p151)
- Challenging yourself with scrambles along the knife-edged ridges of the MacGillycuddy's Reeks (p152)
- Exploring the tip of the Sheep's Head (p179), the most isolated peninsula in the southwest

becomes a series of battles against the English. In 1601 the Irish and Spanish fought the English at Kinsale, and O'Sullivan Beare's stronghold at Castletownbere, County Cork, was besieged.

The English forces were victorious, and a harsh regime of penal laws was put in place by 1695. Many Catholics were forced into the hills to worship; the many 'mass paths' in the region testify to this period in Ireland's history. It wasn't until the 19th century that a Kerryman, Daniel O'Connell, changed the course of Irish history when he successfully campaigned Catholics to be emancipated. O'Connell died in 1847 in the middle the Great Famine. His ancestral home in Derrynane is featured on one of the walks in this chapter (see Derrynane Coastal Circuit, p164). Other legacies of this traumatic period appear in the form of famine roads, mass graves and deserted villages.

During the early 20th century the countryside was further depopulated as young men and women emigrated abroad. More recently this displacement has been offset by a gradual influx of European settlers, and by a newfound affluence that owes much to the steady stream of tourists.

NATURAL HISTORY
Southwest Ireland consists largely of Old Red Sandstone, laid down 400 million years ago when the country lay beneath a shallow ocean. As marine life developed, the surface of this rock was overlaid with deposits of

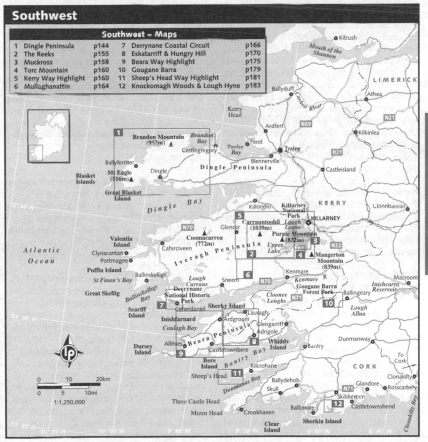

Southwest

limestone and then coal. Tectonic movements 300 million years ago then threw these layers into tangled folds. Much of this folding is still evident on the glaciated flanks of the higher mountains. Weathering and the scouring effect of glaciers during successive ice ages eroded the limestone from the tops of the mountains but preserved it in the valleys. Glaciers also created corries (small, high, cup-shaped valleys) on the sides of the hills, and left the area strewn with high passes such as the Connor Pass on the Dingle Peninsula.

After the ice retreated Ireland entered a period during which the mild climate encouraged forests to grow. When humans first settled in County Kerry the region was covered in Scots pine, oak, yew, elm, juniper, birch and hazel. Today there are very few deciduous woods left, the most notable examples being the woods around Killarney and Glengarriff. Unfortunately rhododendrons, an introduced species, are endangering the remaining woodlands (see the boxed text 'Scourge of the Rhododendron', p269). In some parts of the southwest eradication programmes are under way.

The area is also well known for its abundance of Lusitanian plants, a group of species specific to the mild, moist, western coasts of Portugal, Spain, Britain and Ireland. Some of the Irish Lusitanian plants are not found in Britain and theories abound as to their origins. One is that the plants spread along land links with southern Europe after the link with mainland Britain had disappeared.

INFORMATION
Maps & Books
The best map for overall planning is the OSI 1:250,000 map No 4 *South*.

Seán Ó'Suilleabháin's *New Irish Walk Guide: South West* describes routes on most of the major mountains in the region.

Information Sources
Cork Kerry Tourism (☎ 021-425 5100; W *www .corkkerry.ie; Aras Failte, Grand Parade, Cork*) is the regional tourism authority for southwest Ireland. Its website is a good source of general information, and there are links to accommodation listings and walking sites. The website W www.kerrygems.ie offers a good introduction to Kerry.

Place Names
Several parts of the region – particularly on the Beara and Dingle Peninsulas – are designated Gaeltacht areas, where Irish is the first language written and spoken. In these places road signs and place names are often written in Irish only, without the usual English translation. To help navigate through these areas, Irish names have been given in the relevant places in the text.

GATEWAYS
Cork
The Republic's second largest city, Cork is a popular arrival point. The **TIC** (☎ 021-425 5100; Grand Parade; open year-round) has a large selection of walking maps and books and offers accommodation information for the whole county. **Mahers Outdoor Shop** (☎ 021-427 9233; 7-8 Parnell Place) is a large store and should be able to satisfy most equipment needs. **Waterstones Bookshop** (69 Patrick St) has extensive travel and Irish interest sections.

Places to Stay & Eat There are several hostels in Cork. **Kinlay House** (☎ 021-450 8966; Bob and Joan's Walk, Shandon; dorm beds/doubles from €14/44) includes a continental breakfast in the price. **Aaron House Tourist Hostel** (☎ 021-455 2477; Glanmire Rd Lower; dorm beds/doubles €11/26) is simple but cheap.

B&Bs abound: **Tara House** (☎ 021-450 0294; 52 Glanmire Rd Lower; singles/doubles €39/56) is one of the cheaper options, while **Acorn House** (☎ 021-450 2474; 14 St Patrick's Hill; singles/doubles €52/80) is central. Alternatively, **Isaac's Hotel** (☎ 021-450 0011; 48 MacCurtain St; singles/doubles €80/110) is just one of a good selection of hotels.

Cork also has a wide range of cafés, pubs and restaurants. **Greene's Restaurant** (☎ 021-455 2279), at Isaac's Hotel, has a great menu, while **Valparaiso** (☎ 021-427 5488; 115 Oliver Plunkett St) is a Spanish restaurant with an excellent atmosphere.

Getting There & Away There are direct Iarnrod Éireann (☎ 021-450 6766) train services to/from Dublin (€44.40, two hours 50 minutes, six daily). There are also connections to other Irish towns and cities. Within the southwest, destinations include Killarney (€17.70, 1¼ hours, five daily) and Tralee (€22.80, two hours, five daily). Cork railway station is on Glanmire Rd Lower.

Bus Éireann (021-450 8188) has regular bus services to Dublin (€19, four hours 25 minutes, six daily), and links to most other Irish towns and cities. Major destinations in the southwest include Killarney (€11.90, one hour 35 minutes, at least 11 daily) and Tralee (€12.70, 2½ hours, at least 11 daily). Cork bus station is on the corner of Merchant's Quay and Parnell St.

The ferry terminal is at Ringaskiddy, 18km southeast of the city centre. Several buses a day travel to the terminal from the bus station. Buses also travel at 30-minute intervals to/from **Cork Airport** (☎ 021-431 3131; w www.corkairport.ie), which is 8km south of the city on the N27. For details of international plane and ferry services see Getting There & Away, p348.

Tralee

Despite having plenty of facilities, Tralee remains a working town rather than a tourist destination. The **TIC** (☎ 066-712 1288; Denny St) is behind the Ashe Memorial Hall. The **Walk Information Centre** (☎ 066-712 8733; 40 Ashe St) is the headquarters of Southwest Walks Ireland, a commercial walking tour operator. The centre stocks a good collection of walking maps and guidebooks.

Places to Stay & Eat At the budget end, Tralee has a surprisingly limited selection of accommodation. **Bayview Caravan & Camping Park** (☎ 066-712 6140; Killeen; tent sites €12.70; open May-Oct), 1.5km out of town on the R556, is the closest camping ground.

Finnegan's Holiday Hostel (☎ 066-712 7755; 17 Denny St; singles/doubles €25/40) is the cheapest place to stay in Tralee. The rooms of the hostel are located above **The Imperial Hotel** (☎ 066-712 7755; singles/doubles €55/90). Of the many B&Bs in the

town, **Conn Oriel** (☎ 066-712 5359; 6 Pembroke Square; singles/doubles €33/58) is good value and central.

Of the numerous restaurants, **Finnegan's Basement** (☎ 066-718 1400), beneath The Imperial Hotel, has a varied menu. Alternatively, **The Skillet** (☎ 066-712 4561; Barrack Lane) is good value and serves meals from breakfast to dinner.

Getting There & Away You can catch a direct Iarnrod Éireann (☎ 066-712 3522) service to/from Dublin (€46.90, four hours, four daily). The company also has connections to other Irish towns and cities. Within the southwest, destinations include Killarney (€6.60, 45 minutes, five daily) and Cork (€22.80, two hours, five daily). Tralee train station is on John Joe Sheehy Rd.

Bus Éireann (☎ 066-712 3566) has regular services to Dublin (€19, five hours 10 minutes, six daily), and links to most other Irish towns and cities. Major destinations in southwest Ireland include Killarney (€5.55, 40 minutes, at least 11 daily) and Cork (€12.70, 2¼ hours, at least 11 daily). Tralee bus station is next to the train station.

Killarney

A bustling place at any time of the year, Killarney sometimes seems ready to burst at the seams in summer. The **TIC** (☎ 064-31633; Beech Rd; open year-round) can be a hectic place; it sells OSI maps and provides details of tourist services in the area. **Trailways** (☎ 064-39929; College St) is probably the best outdoor shop in Killarney; it stocks a good range of gear, maps and books.

Places to Stay & Eat Killarney has a wide choice of accommodation, although you would be advised to book ahead. **Flesk Muckross Caravan & Camping Park** (☎ 064-31704; Muckross Rd; camping per person/car €6.50/3.50; open Easter-Sept) is the closest camping ground, around 1.5km from the town centre along the N71 to Kenmare.

Hostels include the large and sometimes noisy **Killarney Railway Hostel** (☎ 064-35299; Park Rd; dorm beds/doubles €11.50/35), and the central **Neptune's Town Hostel**

(☎ 064-35255; New St; dorm beds/doubles €11/34). **Sugan Hostel** (☎ 064-33104; Lewis Rd; dorm beds/doubles €12/28) is an unusual and intimate place, and is also central.

Killarney has literally thousands of B&B and hotel rooms – unless you are booking well in advance you could save time by letting staff at the TIC book a place for you. **Fairview Guesthouse** (☎ 064-34164; Lewis Rd; singles/doubles €63/76) is just one of the well-run B&Bs, while **Ross Hotel** (☎ 064-31855; Kenmare Place; singles/doubles €80/110) is well located in the town centre.

There is also plenty of choice when it comes to places to eat. **Sceilig** (☎ 064-33062; High St) is reasonably cheap and cosy, and, nearby, **Gaby's** (☎ 064-32519; High St) has a good reputation and specialises in seafood.

Getting There & Away A direct Iarnrod Éireann (☎ 064-31067) service goes to/from Dublin (€46.90, three hours 20 minutes, four daily). There are also connections to most other major Irish cities. Within the southwest, destinations include Tralee (€6.90, 45 minutes, five daily) and Cork (€17.70, 1¼ hours, five daily). Killarney train station is on Park Rd.

Bus Éireann (☎ 064-30011) has regular services to Dublin (€19, five hours 10 minutes, five daily), and links to most other Irish cities. Major destinations in southwest Ireland include Tralee (€5.55, 40 minutes, at least 11 daily) and Cork (€11.90, one hour 35 minutes, at least 11 daily). Killarney bus station is next to the train station.

The Dingle Peninsula

Characterised by long sandy beaches, scattered villages and rounded, heather-covered mountains, the Dingle Peninsula is fast becoming one of the most popular tourist destinations in Ireland. Thankfully the north and west extremities of the peninsula have escaped the worst of the tour-bus invasion. Instead, the influx of independent visitors has turned Dingle town into a surprisingly cosmopolitan place. The buzz that pervades the capital town doesn't extend far; while the rest of the peninsula couldn't quite be described as remote, it at least retains its feeling of space and low-key authenticity.

From the point of view of walking, the peninsula has much to offer. Its greatest attractions are probably the two described here: Brandon Mountain, Ireland's highest summit outside the Iveragh Peninsula; and the Dingle Way, one of the country's most scenic long-distance routes. However, there is plenty of scope for further exploration. The combination of challenging mountain terrain, spectacular coastline and relatively well-developed tourist infrastructure makes the Dingle Peninsula a perfect base for a week's walking holiday.

HISTORY
The first evidence of human habitation on the peninsula dates back to the Mesolithic period; shell middens have been discovered on the beaches at Inch Strand and the Magharees Peninsula. Ancient field systems have also been uncovered during turf cutting, indicating that they predate the spread of the bogs somewhere between 2000 and 4000 years ago. Megaliths, so common in other areas of Kerry, are rare on the Dingle Peninsula. More common are the beehive-shaped huts, ring forts and Ogham stones of the Bronze Age.

The Dingle Peninsula was hard hit during the Great Famine of the 19th century, and the Connor Pass and Slea Head roads were built as part of relief efforts. The irony was that the soup the workers were given as part of their payment had fewer calories than they burned each day, so they actually died more quickly than they would have without working for food rations.

In the early 20th century, the Dingle Peninsula declined further as young people left to work abroad. Few newcomers settled in the area and the trappings of modern society arrived late. However, this meant that the Irish language and associated traditions have survived on the peninsula. For years, Irish people from other regions have been coming to Dingle to relearn their language. Today the area is a Gaeltacht stronghold, and you will no doubt hear Irish spoken in shops and pubs.

NATURAL HISTORY

Dingle is particularly rich in plants that are not native to Ireland. Fuchsia is one example of this. Lanes throughout the peninsula are bordered by the plant with its striking red flowers, but fuchsia is actually an import from New Zealand that only arrived in Dingle about 65 years ago. It survives Irish winters well but, although it may look beautiful, it is useless to wild Irish bees, which cannot reach its nectar. New Zealand flax is another naturalised plant. Flax was brought to Dingle in the early 20th century by Lord Ventry, who planned to use the plant to produce linen. While that plan failed it has become a useful windbreak plant and can now be seen growing in great swathes along Ballydavid Head.

The shallow sea around the Dingle Peninsula provides easy food for diving seabirds, as well as good shore fishing for humans. Behind the tombolo at Inch is a vast area of shallow water that is home to many wading birds, including Brent Geese, which feed on the plentiful eelgrass. Ringed plovers and turnstones feed off the debris at the sea's edge. Lough Gill, at Castlegregory, is a breeding ground for rare natterjack toads. You may also see the small, black Kerry cow, which is now extremely rare. One of the few herds in existence is transported to the slopes of Brandon Mountain for summer pasture.

PLANNING
Books

David Herman's *Hill Walker's Kerry* describes many of the mountain routes on the peninsula. Kevin Corcoran's *Kerry Walks* also has a selection of alternative routes that keep away from the most popular summits. *The Dingle Peninsula: 16 Walks Through its Heritage*, by Maurice Sheehy, details a selection of historical walks in the area.

Information Sources

The main source of local information is **Dingle TIC** (☎ 066-915 1188; W www.dingle -peninsula.ie). Its website includes accommodation information.

ACCESS TOWNS
Dingle

In recent years, Dingle town (An Daingean) has developed into a bustling cluster of restaurants, pubs and accommodation, but it manages to retain its character thanks to a working harbour and a fishing industry. It is the largest settlement on the Dingle Peninsula and most visitors will pass through even if they chose to stay somewhere a little quieter.

The **TIC** (☎ 066-915 1188; Strand St; open year-round) is on the waterfront. Several banks with ATMs are on Main St, and walking maps are available in numerous outlets, including the TIC. Several **outdoor shops** along Main St stock walking gear, although the selection is limited.

Places to Stay & Eat Dingle has a host of accommodation options at all levels, but you are advised to book ahead during July and August. The **Ballintaggart Hostel** (☎ 066-915 1454; dorm beds/doubles from €12.50/40; camping per person €5.50) is 1.5km east of town on the N86, in a spacious early-18th-century house. It offers the closest camping to Dingle and has a free shuttle bus service into town; however, the hostel is a regular stopover for several backpacker tour companies and can be very noisy. Alternatively, **Grapevine Hostel** (☎ 066-915 1434; Dykegate Lane; dorm beds from €12), in a 100-year-old townhouse, is homely and central, but you usually need to book in advance.

Dingle also has numerous B&Bs including the **Townhouse** (☎ 066-915 1147; Main St; singles/doubles €35/70), which is friendly and very central. **Ocean View B&B** (☎ 066-915 1659; 133 The Wood; singles/doubles €20/40) is one of the cheapest in town.

There is a large **supermarket** near the quay, and there are many restaurants, pubs and cafés. **Armarda** (☎ 066-915 1505; Strand St) and **The Old Smokehouse** (☎ 066-915 1061; Main St) are just two of the places offering good food.

Getting There & Away Scheduled **Bus Éireann** (☎ 066-712 3566) services go from Dingle to Tralee (€7.85, 1¼ hours) and Killarney (€9.75, 2¼ hours). There are four services Monday to Saturday and three services on Sunday, year-round, to each destination, with additional services from June to September.

Cloghane

A good base for walkers climbing Brandon, Cloghane (An Clochán) is a picturesque village and a pleasant stopover on the Dingle Way. The village's small **TIC** (☎ 066-713 8277; open June-Aug) is opposite the church. It sells OSI maps and walking guides, and the staff can provide local walking and accommodation advice.

Mt Brandon Hostel (☎ 066-713 8299; dorm beds/twins €14/33) is an attractive new hostel with modern facilities and its own **café** at the front. The village also has several B&Bs, including the **Abhainn Mhór** (☎ 066-713 8211; singles/doubles €26/52). **O'Connor's Guesthouse** (☎ 066-713 8113; singles/doubles €32/56) offers evening meals and packed lunches, and has a luggage transport service.

The village has a small **grocery shop** and both **pubs** serve bar food.

Bus Éireann (☎ 066-712 3566) runs two bus services between Cloghane and Tralee (€5.90, one hour) on Friday only. By car Cloghane is 13km north of Dingle via the Connor Pass.

Brandon Mountain

Duration	8–9 hours
Distance	20km
Difficulty	demanding
Start/Finish	Cloghane (p142)
Transport	bus

Summary A steep climb through a lake-studded corrie leads to magnificent coastal views. A challenging but highly rewarding route – one of the true classic Irish mountain walks.

At 952m, Brandon Mountain is Ireland's eighth-highest peak, and the highest outside of the MacGillycuddy's Reeks on the Iveragh Peninsula. The route's dramatic terrain and magnificent summit views are unforgetable,

and the sheer charisma of the peak makes it an inevitable favourite with walkers. The route described explores the entire Brandon massif, climbing Brandon Mountain and then continuing across a cliff-lined ridge to the southern summits of Brandon Peak (840m) and Gearhane (803m).

A path between Cloghane and Brandon Mountain makes route-finding relatively straightforward along this section, and a wall acts as a guide over most of the rest of the ridge. Nonetheless, it's essential you know how to use a compass. With 1150m of ascent there is no denying that the trip is a strenuous one, but the scenery is wonderful throughout – given a little luck with the weather you should feel well rewarded for your effort!

A shorter route option is to follow the path described to the summit of Brandon Mountain and then retrace your steps to Cloghane instead of continuing over the rest of the massif. This option is still a wonderful walk; it's around 11km long and takes about six hours.

If you have two vehicles at your disposal, the road walking can be avoided by leaving one vehicle at Faha at the start of the route, and the other at the end of the road at the top of the Cloghane River valley. This will shave around 8.5km and 150m of ascent off the day's walk.

PLANNING
When to Walk

The coastal location of the Brandon massif means that it is notorious for bad weather; it is well worth taking the time to make your trip coincide with clear conditions if at all possible. Wet or icy rock will also make the route more challenging. The length of the route means that the shorter, out-and back option might be a better choice on short winter days.

What to Bring

The weather on the mountain can change very quickly and you must carry full mountain clothing, even on apparently sunny days.

Maps

Use the OSI 1:50,000 map No 70.

THE WALK (see walk p144)

The first 2km north of Cloghane follows the Dingle Way – look for the waymarking posts as they indicate a left turn off the road around 300m north of the pub and café in the centre of Cloghane. The posts lead up a track and past a ruined church, then divert through fields to the right and out onto another lane. Leave the Dingle Way here and turn left along the lane, climbing to the road end at Faha.

An arrow painted on the rock then directs walkers left, through a gate and out onto the open mountainside. Another sign indicates the ascent route up a stony path marked by a series of white poles. The trail passes a well-tended grotto before beginning to steadily climb the shoulder and around the ridge ahead. Here the landscape that makes Brandon so special is revealed. Hollowed out above Loch Cruite lies a deep rock **corrie**, with a network of small loughs (lakes or inlets) filling the depressions on the basin floor. The dark walls of the corrie are sheer and imposing, and it is difficult to see how the route might escape. It is a dramatic scene and the atmosphere of the place is powerful.

The path contours down to the corrie floor and picks through the rocky maze, crossing streams and passing small loughs. It gradually makes its way to the back left corner of the basin, where it steepens and begins to zigzag up the headwall. This is perhaps the most challenging terrain of the route; you'll need to use your hands for support in places and some sections can be slippery in the wet. The climb is absorbing, and it is a shock to suddenly find yourself exiting the corrie and atop a ridge, with the coastline of the Dingle Peninsula in all its glory below.

A signpost at this point marks the descent if you chose to return via the same route to Faha. The summit of **Brandon Mountain** is still a 100m ascent along the ridge to the south (three to 3½ hours from the start). A large metal cross and a stone oratory dedicated to St Brendan mark the peak, which boasts a 360-degree panorama sweeping from the MacGillycuddy's Reeks to the Blasket Islands.

From the summit, head southeast around the top of the corrie and pick up the ridge that leads towards Brandon Peak. A fence and then a stone wall follows the ridge a safe distance from the sheer edge, and are good navigation guides in poor visibility. The ridge undulates before climbing to the summit of **Brandon Peak**. Cross the stone wall to make the final climb to the summit cairn. The top provides fine views towards the Iveragh Peninsula across the waters of Dingle Bay to the southeast.

From Brandon Peak the route veers southwest, and the **ridge** narrows to a blunt knife-edge finale just before reaching Gearhane (803m). Pass through a gate at the summit of Gearhane and follow the southwest shoulder of the mountain over Fallaghnamara and down to the Mullaghveal col below. The waymarked Pilgrim's Route passes through this col on a bog track, and offers the easiest line of descent. Turn left along the track and follow it down to the Cloghane valley road. If you have left a vehicle here this will mark the end of the route; otherwise it is a 6km walk along the quiet road back to Cloghane.

Dingle Way Highlight 🏃

Duration	3 days
Distance	67km
Difficulty	easy–moderate
Start	Dingle (p141)
Finish	Cloghane (p142)
Transport	bus

Summary Long sandy beaches, ancient ruins and a mountain crossing on one of the best stretches of Waymarked Way in Ireland.

The Dingle Way is an eight-day, 153km-long route that circumnavigates the Dingle Peninsula, starting and finishing at Tralee. Without a doubt one of the most scenic Waymarked Ways in the country, the three days described here represent the best part of the route. If you are walking the entire Way, these stages will provide the fourth, fifth and sixth days respectively.

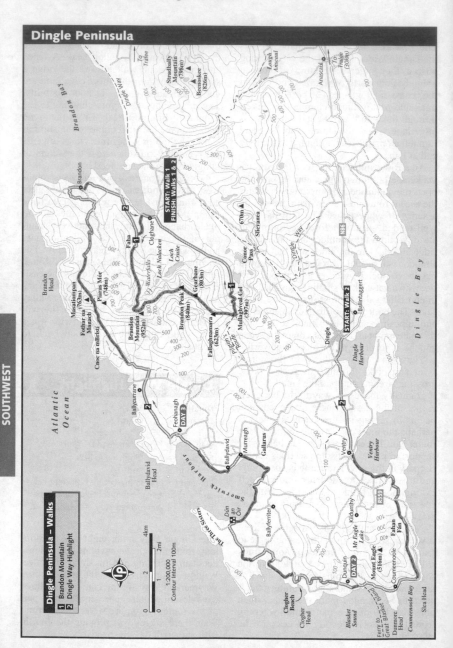

Dingle Peninsula

Dingle Peninsula – Walks

1 Brandon Mountain
2 Dingle Way Highlight

1:200,000
Contour interval 100m

The route described here follows country roads, sandy beaches and open mountainside as it explores the very tip of the Dingle Peninsula. While the terrain is generally relatively flat or undulating, the third day entails a climb to 610m on the northern slopes of Mt Brandon; for many walkers this is the metaphysical as well as the physical high point of the route. The wild terrain of this section is frequently cloud-covered and can prove challenging for anybody unused to mountain walking.

The first day begins rather uninspiringly with 5km of road walking to Ventry, albeit along a relatively minor road, which can be avoided by catching a bus (see Getting to/from the Walk, this page).

The daily sections are long enough to leave even the most experienced walker grateful to reach their accommodation at the end of the day, and you'll be forgiven for shortening the stages, taking your time, and spending longer exploring the scattered villages and intricate coastline of the area. For the energetic, possible side trips include Great Blasket Island (203) and Brandon Mountain (142).

PLANNING
What to Bring
The villages at the end of each day have small shops or accommodation outlets that can supply food, so there is no need to carry more than one day's food or water with you. The route is waymarked, but it is still advisable to carry a map and compass. The third day – from Feohanagh to Cloghane – crosses mountainous terrain, so bring all the appropriate clothing.

Maps & Books
The route described here is covered by the OSI 1:50,000 map No 70, although you will need No 71 as well if you intend to undertake the entire eight-day route. Note that these maps contain routing inaccuracies – the path has been amended since they were published. Our description notes the deviations from the OSI map at the time of writing. In general, trust waymarking posts over map routings.

For those interested in attempting the entire Way, a good account of the route, its history and natural history is *The Dingle Way Companion*, by Tony O'Callaghan. The route is also described in Michael Fewer's *Waymarked Trails of Ireland*, although parts of the routing detailed in this book have now changed. However, it still provides lots of colourful background information.

Guided Walks
Several organisations offer guided walks along the Dingle Way, or arrange self-guided trips with back-up support (providing services such as luggage transport and accommodation booking). Companies include: **Go Ireland** (☎ 066-796 2094; W *www.goactivities .com; Old Orchard House, Killorglin, County Kerry*), **Southwest Walks Ireland** (☎ 066-712 8733; W *www.southwestwalksireland.com; 40 Ashe St, Tralee, County Kerry*) and **Tailor-Made Tours** (☎ 066-976 6007; W *www.tailor -madetours.com; Ferry Rd, Keel, Castlemaine, County Kerry*).

GETTING TO/FROM THE WALK
To avoid 5km of road walking at the start, take the **Bus Éireann** (☎ 066-712 3566) service from Dingle to Ventry (€1.10, 10 minutes, one to four buses daily Monday to Saturday from June to September, two services daily on Monday and Thursday during the rest of the year) and start the route there.

Bus Éireann also runs scheduled bus services between Dingle and the towns at the end of Days 1 and 2, Dunquin (€5.10, 40 minutes, one to four buses daily Monday to Saturday from June to September, and three services daily on Monday and Thursday during the rest of the year) and Feohanagh (€3.50, 30 minutes, Tuesday and Friday) respectively.

Unfortunately there is no public transport between Cloghane, at the end of the route, and Dingle. Without private transport, options for returning to Dingle include taking the Friday bus via Tralee, looking for a lift over the Connor Pass or adding a fourth day's walking to your itinerary.

To return to Dingle by foot, the easiest route is to follow the waymarked Pilgrim's

Route (marked on the OSI map). Follow the minor road that leads southwest from Cloghane, continuing up a track where the road ends to cross Mullaghveal col at 397m. Descend along the track to Dingle-Ballycurrane road, turn left, and continue along the road to Dingle town. This final walk is 15km long and involves around 400m of ascent.

THE WALK (see map p144)
Day 1: Dingle to Dunquin
7 hours, 21km, 300m ascent

The first day's walk begins modestly but improves all the way to Slea Head, by which time the scenery is nothing short of spectacular.

From Dingle, pick up waymarking posts at the roundabout at the western end of town. Follow them west, crossing the Milltown Bridge and continuing along the Slea Head road for 300m before turning right onto a minor road. The surrounding fields are littered with prehistoric standing stones, some decorated with patterns.

The OSI map indicates the route turning right after about 4km to loop around to the north; ignore the map here as this loop has now been cut from the route. Instead, follow the marker posts as they lead you straight along the minor road and directly into Ventry, where there are several **shops** and **pubs**.

Cross straight over the main road in Ventry and onto the **beach**, where the route turns right and continues along the sand for almost 3km. Along the way you will cross two streams; the second may need a 'boots off' approach depending on the tide and water levels. Almost at the end of the beach a short track leads inland past a red brick bungalow and onto a road. Watch carefully for this turn, as it may not be signed. Waymarks then direct you swiftly left, right, and right again, and onto a narrow paved road.

The road terminates at a farm, but the Dingle Way continues to the right along a single-file path. This is a charming section that weaves between high hedges, though it can be muddy. Before long the path broadens into a track and rejoins the main road. Turn left onto the road and continue for

100m until painted arrows on a rock direct you up a *boreen* (old country lane) to the right. Look behind you for great views of Ventry, Dingle Harbour, and beyond to the Iveragh Peninsula.

The *boreen* soon peters out, and a line of stone walls provides most of the guidance between here and Slea Head, 3km away. Sheep are likely to be in attendance as the route contours around the rock-studded slopes of Mt Eagle (516m). On the seaward side of the route are several clusters of **clochains** (they lie on private land, but good views are available from the path). These are known as the Fahan group (Fahan Fán) and there are around 500 ruins in all; it is thought that they are the remains of a late pagan/early Christian village. The various dwellings range from simple shelters to quite complex multi-roomed houses.

After crossing a stream and passing a particularly splendid clochain, the path begins to round **Slea Head** and great views of Dunmore Head and the Blaskets open up before you. It is a wonderful panorama, and one to treasure before you descend back to the main road. Turn right along the road and you'll soon pass a **café** and **Slea Head Farm B&B** (☎ 066-915 6120; singles/doubles €39/58). Follow the road for a little over 2km before a marker post directs you to the left, past the departure point for the Blasket Island ferry. Cross a small stream to reach the Blasket Centre and Dunquin.

Dunquin

A scattered collection of houses, Dunquin (Dún Chaoin) lacks any real focal point. However, its unusual pier is the departure point for ferries to Great Blasket Island and the village is home to the new, informative (but architecturally controversial) **Blasket Centre** (☎ 066-915 6444; adult/child €3.10/ 1.20; open daily Mar-Oct).

The cheapest place to stay is the An Óige **Dunquin Hostel** (☎ 066-915 6121; dorm beds €12), which is conveniently located near the Blasket Centre, has family rooms and serves meals. B&B options in the village include **Kruger's** (☎ 066-915 6127; singles/ doubles €25/50), the village pub, which also offers a wealth of information about the local area, and can provide evening meals and packed lunches. Recommended by several readers, **An Portan B&B** (☎ 066-915 6212; singles/doubles €30/59) has good views and an on-site restaurant. **Dunquin Pottery and Café** also offers sandwiches and snacks.

Day 2: Dunquin to Feohanagh
7 hours, 20km, 200m ascent

The second day of the route is spent exploring the coastline along the tip of the Dingle Peninsula. Continue north from the Blasket Centre, cross the main road and climb a hill past Dunquin Hostel. The route then turns left onto a wide gravel track. Ahead you can see Clogher Beach. The route returns to the main road, turns right and follows it for almost 1km before turning left down a minor road and onto a small path running around the back of **Clogher Beach**. You might want to take some time to explore the western end of the beach, where the cliffs are full of fossils of ancient sea plants and tiny, shelled creatures.

Walk through the car park and follow the marker posts back to the main road, turn left, and after 100m bear left again down a lane. After 500m, the track turns northeast and travels along the shore. Cross a stream and follow the coast: after about 1km of coastal walking a marker sends you right, over a boggy field and through a gate towards some houses and a gravel road. Four and a half kilometres of road now separate you from the next stretch of sand at Smerwick Harbour.

Turn left at the first road junction and pass a group of holiday bungalows and a hotel with a **coffee shop**. At the end of the road turn right and then quickly left again, following a lane up the eastern side of a golf course. The road crosses a windswept plain, through reed-filled marshes that are dotted with irises, mallows and blackberries. Ahead, the land rises to the sudden cliffs of the Three Sisters. The route makes two more right turns before reaching scenic **Smerwick Strand**. A short detour to the left just before the beach leads to **Dún an Óir**

Ogham Script

Ogham writing is thought to be pre-Christian in origin, and most of the 316 examples found in Ireland are concentrated in Cork and Kerry, particularly on the Dingle Peninsula. Ogham was the written language of the Celts and lasted until the 10th century AD, when it was supplanted by other scripts introduced by missionaries. Other examples of the text have been found in Wales and on the Isle of Man.

The writing system is extremely primitive and took archaeologists a long time to decipher. It consists of a series of strokes made across the corner of a piece of stone (you can see how it might have been difficult to make a shopping list to take to the market!). The strokes correspond to 19 of the characters of the Roman alphabet, plus the sound 'ng'. What is most interesting about Ogham writing is that it contains two consonants that are not present in Gaelic – 'h' and 'z' – suggesting that it did not originate in Ireland.

Most examples of the writing are found on standing stones representing boundaries or graves. Words that have been translated usually turn out to be a name and the patronymic. Some stones are also engraved with crosses, but these are generally thought to be later additions. Some of the Ogham stones on the Dingle Peninsula have another set of markings, thought to be a later addition to the alphabet. At Ballintaggart, just outside Dingle, is a series of Ogham stones in an ancient burial site. Some of these bear only Ogham script, while others are carved with crosses, suggesting that the burial ground was used during the transitional phase between paganism and Christianity. In some areas, later groups have endowed these stones with their own spiritual significance, and are now part of Christian holy sites. One such stone is at Coachford in County Cork, where a nearby holy well and boulder have become included in the site.

promontory fort. It was here in 1580 that Elizabeth I's troops laid siege to Spanish and Irish rebels.

Continue along the beach to the far end. The route leaves the beach briefly at an un-official **camping ground**, and rounds a set of holiday cottages where there's a small **shop**. You are then directed back down onto the sand, where you'll need to ford a stream. Follow the beach to Ballydavid, joining the road at the southern end of the village. Turn left and pass through the village, and then turn left again to rejoin the coast beside a seafront **pub**. For the next couple of kilo-metres the route follows a footpath around a headland accompanied by extensive views. The Way joins the road again for the final 1.5km to Feohanagh.

Feohanagh

One of the most remote villages on the peninsula, Feohanagh is little more than a disparate scattering of houses. Convenient B&Bs include **An Riasc** (☎ 066-915 5446; singles/doubles €50/60) and **Coill an Rois** (☎ 066-915 5475; singles/doubles €27/54). Four kilometres east of Feohanagh at Bal-lycurrane (further along the route of the Dingle Way) is another good option: **An Bóthar Pub** (☎ 066-915 5342; singles/doubles €32/64) can also organise packed lunches and provice advice on walks in the area. The pub's restaurant is a good option for evening meals.

Day 3: Feohanagh to Cloghane

8 hours, 26km, 750m ascent

This is a long day involving a strenuous climb, and walkers will be forgiven for short-cutting some of the final, circuitous road sections; doing this will cut 4.5km off the total distance. The first 6km of the day is also on roads.

From Feohanagh, a 4km stretch of road leads northeast beneath Ballydavid Head. Continue through a crossroads (An Bóthar pub is a short distance to the right here) and turn left at the end of the road. Brandon Mountain looms ever closer and the road soon begins to climb to meet it, winding be-tween farm buildings to a large car park.

A farm track continues ahead and to the left, while a fence stretches away from the top right corner of the parking area. Avoid the temptation to follow the track to its end, and instead veer right after 50m or so and cross open ground towards the fence. The point where the route leaves the track is rather badly marked, and many walkers miss it. Once at the fence things becomes sim-pler; the route follows the fence up the slope to a momentary break in the climb be-side the knoll of Cnoc na mBristi. Here the fence turns away to the left (west). If it is a clear day, you could leave the waymarked route for a few minutes and follow the fence to a junction with a wall. Here you can peer to the west at the system of ancient walls below known as **Fothar na Manach** (Fields of the Monks), where a community of monks once lived and farmed.

Back on the Dingle Way, the remaining ascent to the col between Brandon and Ma-satiompan (763m) will be obvious if the weather is good; in poor visibility it will be lost beneath a blanket of cloud. There are xtra markers to guide walkers in mist, but you still need to take care in bad weather.

At the **col** (610m), walkers lucky with the weather will be rewarded by wonderful views. Cross a fence via a stile and pass an **Ogham stone** (see the boxed text 'Ogham Script', p147). Now pick your way down the steep, and occasionally boggy, slope to the northeast. Yellow paint splashes on the rocks mark the way. On cloud-free days great views will open up across Brandon Bay, the Magharees and the Slieve Mish Mountains as you descend.

The descent soon becomes gentler, cross-ing open moorland and bringing you to the end of a track. Turn right and follow this for around 2.5km to a paved road. After 1km on the road you will come to a junction and the route is indicated to the left (ignore the waymarking posts and turn right here if you wish to save yourself 3km of largely road walking and descend directly to Cloghane). The official route turns left again after 200m and loops through the scattered houses of Farran to Brandon village, passing a **pub** on the way.

The route passes briefly around the back of Brandon Strand before rejoining the road and heading inland. Around 2.5km later, turn right onto a more minor road (again, continue straight ahead here for a more direct route to Cloghane). Cross a stile on the left after 2km and head across a field towards a forestry plantation, turning left again after 500m to head back towards the coast. Turn right once you meet the road; you can either walk along the road or the beach for the final 300m into Cloghane.

The Iveragh Peninsula

If there is one place in Ireland that can be considered a mecca for walkers, the Iveragh Peninsula is it. The mountains of MacGillycuddy's Reeks dominate the region, and boast no less than nine out of the country's 10 highest peaks (see the boxed text 'The Irish Munros', p152). Granted such superlative terrain, it is little wonder that the area is a magnet for mountain enthusiasts.

However, the high ground of the Reeks is not a place for the uninitiated. Ridges are steep and exposure can be extreme, and the mountains claim human lives on an annual basis.

Thankfully Iveragh has much more to offer walkers than these demanding peaks. Lower summits offer comparable views and as great a sense of achievement, without the degree of danger. The long-distance Kerry Way also provides almost 200km of walking through Iveragh's remote valleys and along its varied coastline.

The peninsula also has plenty to offer walkers who prefer an even more leisurely approach. Killarney National Park is certainly not a place to seek solitude, but its gardens and lakeside nature trails are undeniably popular.

The number of visitors to the region also means that tourist infrastructure is more developed here than in other parts of Ireland, and operators have many years of experience when it comes to catering to walkers'

needs. If you are somebody who likes to walk without the hassle of preparing your own sandwiches or carrying your own luggage, this is the place for you!

HISTORY

The many ancient remains you will see on your walks in Iveragh are testament to the long history of human habitation on the peninsula. Most obvious are the stone forts, many of which are believed to date from the Bronze Age or earlier (see the boxed text Dolmens & *Dúns*, p19). The best example is Staigue Fort, near Derrynane. These structures are a stone version of the more common ring fort and were probably inhabited by the very wealthy. Stairs and alcoves can generally be found within the dry-stone walls, which can be up to 4m thick.

The Normans never really conquered Iveragh and the local clans held the land well after Queen Elizabeth I's invasions of the Dingle and Beara Peninsulas. It was against this background that Daniel O'Connell (an inhabitant of Iveragh who would become known as the 'Great Liberator') led the first mass movement of Irish people in support of Catholic emancipation. However, by the 18th century Killarney had become a popular tourist spot, and a foreign invasion of a different kind had begun.

Iveragh is also famous for its role in the development of communication technology. Valentia Island was the site chosen for the first transatlantic cable station, which was regarded as a scientific wonder in its day. When the connection was made in 1858, the village of Cahirciveen was put in direct contact with New York – even though there was no through-connection beyond the region.

NATURAL HISTORY

Made up of great chunks of Old Red Sandstone, Iveragh is home to some curious plant life, including many Lusitanian plants.

Pick up any stone on your travels and you may also encounter another unusual creature, the Kerry slug. This large (it grows up to 10cm long), spotted slug is becoming increasingly difficult to find because it's natural habitat is slowly being destroyed by forestry activities.

The mild climate of the peninsula has encouraged several subtropical gardens, most notably the garden of the Knight of Kerry on Valentia Island, which is now open to the public. Yucca, datura, New Zealand flax, several species of bamboo and the ugly gunnera (a native of South America) are also quite common in local gardens. The introduced montbretia, which flowers in August, covers hedgerows and colonises waste ground, while fuchsia, another introduced plant, creates many of the peninsula's windbreaks.

Killarney boasts one of the country's largest tracts of ancient native forest, which contains species of oak, holly, birch and beech that are up 800 years old. Unfortunately rhododendrons are also everywhere (see the boxed text 'Scourge of the Rhododendron', p269). Secreted in the grounds of Cahernane National Park is the endangered Kerry lily, which grows only in this area.

PLANNING
Books
David Herman's book *Hill Walker's Kerry* describes routes up most of the popular mountains on the peninsula. Kevin Corcoran's *Kerry Walks* also has a selection of routes that are largely shorter, low-level circuits.

ACCESS TOWNS
Killorglin
This pretty town spanning the River Laune is a much less hectic place than Killarney and has plenty of amenities, but is short on budget accommodation.

Places to Stay & Eat Friendly but slightly run-down, the **Laune Valley Farm Hostel** (☎ 066-976 1488; *dorm beds/doubles €12/28, tent sites €5*) is 1.8km out of Killorglin and signed off the Tralee road. If you don't mind being woken by roosters crowing then you'll enjoy the pastoral setting and good views of the Reeks; cooked breakfasts are available. Camping is also available at **West's Holiday Park** (☎ 066-976 1240; *Killarney Rd; tent sites & 2 adults €15*).

In town, the more luxurious accommodation provided at **River's Edge B&B** (☎ 066-976 1750; *singles/doubles €40/60*) comes highly recommended.

Killorglin has a good **supermarket** on the main street. It also has plenty of eateries, which range from greasy takeaway joints to gourmet restaurants. **Bianconi Inn** (☎ 066-976 1146; *Annadale Rd*) and **Nick's Restaurant** (☎ 066-976 1216; *Lower Bridge St*) both have good reputations and offer fare with seafood themes.

Getting There & Away Regular **Bus Éireann** (☎ 064-30011) services run to/from Tralee (€5.05, 40 minutes, seven daily) and Killarney (€4.25, 30 minutes, twice daily Monday to Saturday).

Killorglin is situated at the junction of the N70 and the N72, around 20km west of Killarney.

Glencar & Lough Acoose
More of a geographic area than a village, many of Glencar's houses are a kilometre or more apart.

The one focal point is **the Climbers Inn** (☎ 066-976 0101; *dorm beds €19, singles/doubles €48/70*), a walking centre that also offers guided walks in the area, luggage transfer, a drying room, packed lunches and information. There is an adjacent post office and a **pub** serving bar meals.

The other most convenient accommodation options are situated about 3.5km northeast of the Climbers Inn, where the Kerry Way joins the main road on the northeastern shore of Lough Acoose; this is also where the Coomloughra Horseshoe starts.

Lake View Farmhouse (☎ 066-976 0136; *singles/doubles €30/50*) also has a **camping ground** (*camping per person €5*) with views of Carrauntoohil. Next door, **Lough Acoose B&B** (☎ 066-976 0105; *singles/doubles €35/55*) can provide evening meals.

There are no public transport options to/from Glencar and Lough Acoose. By car, Glencar and Lough Acoose are around 15km and 11.5km south of Killorglin respectively; follow the signs to Glencar from Killorglin's main street.

Coomloughra Horseshoe

Duration	6–7 hours
Distance	11km
Difficulty	demanding
Start/Finish	Lough Acoose
Nearest Towns	Killorglin (p150), Glencar & Lough Acoose (p150)
Transport	private

Summary This spectacular and challenging mountain circuit crosses the three highest peaks in Ireland and features tremendous views and an exciting, narrow rock ridge.

This is arguably the finest circular walk in the country and probably the best way to climb Ireland's highest mountain Carrauntoohil (1039m). It crosses narrow ridges as it passes over Carrauntoohil, and the second and third highest peaks in Ireland: Beenkeragh (1010m) and Caher (1001m). Along with the MacGillycuddy's Reeks Ridge (p152), this route provides the highest-level walking in the country, with around 5km at an altitude in excess of 800m. Given the nature of the terrain, it is little wonder that the route involves a challenging 1128m of ascent.

In fine weather this route is strenuous but straightforward, with the exception of the rocky, knife-edge ridge linking Beenkeragh and Carrauntoohil, where you might need to use your hands for support (see 'Warning', this page). A highly recommended and immensely rewarding route, it is worth waiting for a fine day to fully appreciate the views from the roof of Ireland.

PLANNING
Maps
The OSI 1:50,000 map No 78 covers the described route.

GETTING TO/FROM THE WALK
Lough Acoose marks the start and finish of the route, 12km south of Killorglin and 24km west of Killarney. Follow signs for Glencar and keep your OSI map handy to navigate the many junctions. On reaching the northern shores of the lake turn left at a junction marked by an information board about the

mountains of the area. There is parking just a short distance down this minor road.

THE WALK (see map p155)
From Lough Acoose, a steady climb of just over 1.5km brings you past rock outcrops and over heathery ground into the Coomloughra corrie (one hour). Lough Eighter, in the centre of the corrie, is a good spot to stop for a drink and admire the ring of mountains that encloses Coomloughra.

Cross the outlet stream of the lough and immediately begin to climb steep slopes to the north, ascending to the shattered crest of Skregmore (848m). Faint tracks lead through the heather and springy turf, though these give way to boulders and shattered rock slabs near the top. The slopes converge to a spiky crest at the summit, and there are expansive views across Dingle Bay to the west. To the north, a patchwork of flat green fields leads across Kerry's rich dairy country.

The ridge now leads southeast for 1km, crossing a couple of unnamed summits to the foot of a broad, boulder-strewn ridge leading to the summit of **Beenkeragh** (three hours from the start). A path twists and turns through the outcrops and leads to the small cairn marking Ireland's second-highest summit. To the east, the ground suddenly falls away into Lough Gouragh, and a dizzying space leads the eye across to the cliffs on Carrauntoohil's northern face. Some walkers might find the sight of the ridge spanning this gap a little intimidating.

Warning

This walk features a section along a narrow and exposed ridge. The ridge should be avoided in windy conditions and will not suit walkers who don't have a head for heights. In poor weather, or when there is snow and ice on the summits, the entire route is a serious undertaking. In winter, if there is a chance of encountering significant snow or ice, then an ice axe and perhaps other mountaineering equipment should be carried, and the route should only be attempted by those with winter mountaineering experience.

SOUTHWEST

Although it does require care in places, generally it is not as difficult as it looks.

Follow a path that descends steeply onto the ridge and, after picking your way along the crest for a stretch, follow it onto the right-hand (west) side of the arête. At about half distance, the path crosses to the steeper left-hand side for 100m (care should be taken here), before returning to the right again. Most of the difficulties are now over and it is a short, steep climb from the end of the ridge to the broad summit of **Carrauntoohil** (1039m; 45 minutes to one hour from Beenkeragh), the highest point in Ireland. New views open up from the summit, especially to the east along the saw-toothed MacGillycuddy's Reeks ridge. The summit

cross was erected in 1977 and originally featured a windmill that powered light bulbs on the cross.

Descend southwest to a col; a short, steep ascent where the ridge becomes narrow again leads to the summit of **Caher** (1001m). A small cairn marks the top and another, slightly lower, summit (975m) comes into view just to the west. Pass over this and start the long descent back to the start. After a bouldery section, a small path leads down the shoulder of Caher on springy turf. The descent to Lough Eighter is quite pleasant, and from here you might take a final look back into Coomloughra before heading back down to Lough Acoose.

The Irish Munros

The term 'munro' is an import from Scotland, and has come to indicate a mountain that is more than 3000ft (900m) in height. The name was coined in memory of Sir Hugh Munro, who completed a survey of all the Scottish peaks and, in 1891, published the first comprehensive list of Scottish mountain tops over 3000ft.

The list of Scottish munros has been revised several times, with current accounts detailing 284 summits. The task of listing Irish munros is somewhat easier, thanks to the lower elevation of the country's high ground. It is generally accepted that there are just 12 munro peaks and tops in Ireland, though the list can vary depending on the definition of a mountain 'top'.

The Irish munros are located in four regions of the country. The MacGillycuddy's Reeks, on the Iveragh Peninsula (County Kerry), contain nine of the 12. Brandon Mountain, on the Dingle Peninsula (County Kerry), is the country's eighth-highest summit. Lugnaquillia, in the Wicklow Mountains (County Wicklow), and Galtymore (County Tipperary), just slip in as Ireland's 11th and 12th munros respectively. Routes over all of these summits are detailed in this book; the small number of peaks means that experienced mountain enthusiasts should be able to 'bag' all the Irish munros within a single visit.

Reeks Ridge

Duration	6–7 hours
Distance	13km
Difficulty	demanding
Start/Finish	Hags Glen
Nearest Towns	Killarney (p139), Killorglin (p150)
Transport	private

Summary   The longest and most sustained ridge walk in Ireland, this requires a good head for heights and confidence over steep ground; the rewards are tremendous views.

Suitable for experienced walkers only, this is one of the finest ridge walks in the country and scales six summits over 900m (3000ft). Among these are Knocknapeasta (988m) and Maolán Buí (973m), the fourth- and fifth-highest summits in Ireland respectively. The total ascent for the walk is 1050m. The initial section of ridge between Cruach Mór and Knocknapeasta is a rocky knife-edge, and requires both a good head for heights and solid route-finding skills. You'll need to use your hands for support over this section, and basic scrambling manoeuvres are also required (see 'Warning', p153). Thereafter, the ridge broadens and you can relax and enjoy the wide-ranging views. If you're not sure whether the ridge will be suited to your abilities it is worth walking at least as far as the summit of Knocknapeasta. From here you'll get a good appreciation of the difficulties involved, and views that are more than worth the effort, even if you decide to go back down the way you came.

PLANNING
Maps
Use the OSI 1:50,000 map No 78.

GETTING TO/FROM THE WALK
The walk starts and finishes at Hags Glen, at the end of a minor road about 18km west of Killarney. At Beaufort, turn south off the Killarney–Killorglin road (the N72) and follow signs initially for the Gap of Dunloe and then for Carrauntoohil. At a crossroads beside Kissane's store you should slow down; take the next left turn onto a narrow road that ends at a farm after 3km. Parking is available here, sometimes for a small charge.

THE WALK (see map p155)
From the farm at Hags Glen pass through a gate on the right side of the yard. Follow a grass track along the side of a field, across a stile and onto a stony track that climbs gently above the Gaddagh River. Leave the track where it crosses a tributary of the Gaddagh and head southeast across open ground, climbing the increasingly steep slopes towards the conspicuous summit of **Cruach Mór** (932m). Aim slightly to the east of the summit to find easier ground. The top is marked by a stone grotto, and has impressive views south across the Iveragh Peninsula (1½ to two hours from the start).

However, more than the views your attention is likely to be drawn by the sight of the rock ridge running south towards the Big Gun (939m). Huge blocks of rock (gendarmes) adorn the crest of the ridge, making the job of keeping to the top very difficult at first. Follow informal paths below and to the west of the ridge, being careful not to lose too much height. Scramble back up to the ridge at a notch, and then climb – with care – directly along the exciting rocky arête to reach the Big Gun. The ridge now swings southwest towards Knocknapeasta. Stick to the crest as you descend

to a col, but where the ridge becomes difficult again you can drop to the left (south) of the arête before rejoining it just beneath the summit of **Knocknapeasta** (988m; around one hour from Cruach Mór).

The views from the highest point on the walk are tremendous, taking in Ireland's three highest summits to the west and the serrated ridge you have just traversed to the east. To the north, wild cliffs fall away into the dark waters of Lough Cummeenapeasta, and beyond that the patchwork fields of north Kerry stretch to the horizon. To the south the mountain falls away to Black Valley, and ridge after ridge of mountains extend towards the Atlantic.

Walk south from Knocknapeasta along a broad, stony ridge, and then bear southwest as you drop to a col and climb a short distance to the summit of **Maolán Buí**. Cross an unnamed top at 926m to reach Cnoc an Chuillin (958m), the last major peak on the ridge. Now descend to a col and climb onto another unnamed summit. It is best to descend directly into Hags Glen from here, keeping to the west of steep ground. Many

Warning

This walk features sustained sections along a narrow and exposed ridge. It should be avoided in windy conditions and is not suited to walkers who suffer from vertigo. In poor weather, or when there is snow and ice on the summits, the entire route is a serious undertaking.

In winter, if there is a chance of encountering significant snow or ice, then an ice axe and perhaps other mountaineering equipment should be carried, and the route should only be attempted by those with winter mountaineering experience.

It is also best to avoid the Devil's Ladder, a loose and eroded gully that has traditionally provided the main route between Hags Glen and the Reeks. Numerous accidents – sometimes fatal – have occurred here over the years, often caused by people carelessly dislodging rocks. Use one of the two descents in the walk description instead.

SOUTHWEST

walkers still use the Devil's Ladder further to the west but this is best avoided (see 'Warning', p153). Once in Hags Glen, simply follow the stony track for 4km to the finish (one to 1½ hours).

Alternative Route: Reeks Ridge & Carrauntoohil
8–10 hours, 15km, 1450m ascent
To really make this a route to remember, very fit walkers may want to consider extending the route west across Ireland's two highest peaks – Carrauntoohil and Beenkeragh – before descending back to Hags Glen.

From the col at the top of the Devil's Ladder, climb steadily northwest to the summit of Carrauntoohil. Then reverse the narrow ridge walk between Carrauntoohil and Beenkeragh described for the Coomloughra Horseshoe (p151). Continue over Beenkeragh before making a long, steep descent northeast, over Knockbrinnea (854m), to the Gaddagh River. This descent is initially over boulders, but eases to heather and grass on the lower slopes.

Purple Mountain & Gap of Dunloe

Duration	6–7 hours
Distance	14.5km
Difficulty	moderate–demanding
Start/Finish	Kate Kearney's Cottage
Nearest Town	Killarney (p139), Gap of Dunloe (p154)
Transport	private

Summary Enjoy stunning views of Ireland's highest mountains from this airy, conical summit. The Gap of Dunloe approach is impressive if you can dodge the crowds.

In summer, the Gap of Dunloe is one of Ireland's biggest natural tourist attractions, comparable to the Cliffs of Moher in terms of visitor numbers and overcrowding. If you must walk between June and August, make an early start to avoid the crowds.

Fortunately the sheer-sided valley, gouged by glacial action aeons ago, manages to retain its imposing character. Purple Mountain rises steeply to the east of the gap, and derives its name from the distinct, purple-tinged sweeps of sandstone talus near its top. The summit offers superlative views across the Reeks to the west. An informal path has formed along stretches of the route, easing progress and aiding navigation. The total ascent for the walk is 890m.

If you can manage the logistics, then an alternative start can be made at the Head of Gap (at the top of the Gap of Dunloe), which will save around 6km of walking. See Getting to/from the Walk (p156) for details.

PLANNING
Maps
The OSI 1:50,000 map No 78 covers the route, although the extra detail given by the OSI 1:25,000 *Killarney National Park* might be preferable.

NEAREST TOWNS & FACILITIES
See Killarney (p139).

Gap of Dunloe
While there is no village as such at the Gap of Dunloe, there is some accommodation in the area.

Five kilometres east of Kate Kearney's, the pub at the entrance to the gap, is **Mountain Rest Hostel & Camping** *(☎ 064-44272; dorm beds €12; camping per person €6)*. The hostel is new but the facilities for campers are rather dirty.

A few B&Bs are scattered around the Gap's south entrance. **Wayside B&B** *(☎ 064-44284; singles/doubles €38/50)* is 1km south of Kate Kearney's Cottage. A kilometre further east in the direction of Killarney is **the Purple Heather** *(☎ 064-44266; singles/doubles €38/48)*, where evening meals are also available. Two kilometres west of Kate Kearney's is **the Mountain Lodge** *(☎ 064-44181; dorm beds/doubles €30/80)*, a luxurious facility run for walkers and climbers. Breakfast is included in the price and the lodge has a drying room and library.

Kate Kearney's Cottage *(☎ 064-44146)* offers bar food as well as more formal evening meals, though prices are steep.

The Reeks

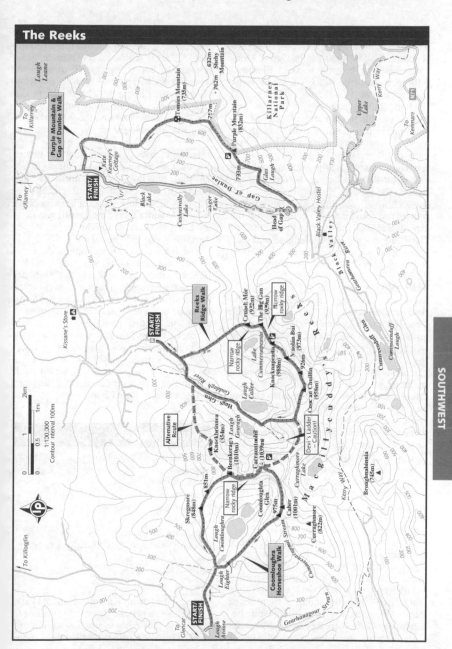

GETTING TO/FROM THE WALK

The start of the walk is 12km southwest of Killarney. Follow signs for the Gap of Dunloe south from Beaufort, on the Killarney–Killorglin road (the N72). There is a large parking area at Kate Kearney's Cottage, at the bottom of the gap.

It is possible to start at the Head of Gap. The surface of the minor road through the gap is seriously broken in places, but it does carry traffic and there is space to park at the top. Unfortunately it is all but impossible to take a car through during the day in summer, as the road is blocked by a crawling procession of jaunting cars (ponies and traps). You could always decide to join the crowds and take one of these to the Head of Gap. Services are led by demand and cars transport a maximum of four people; expect to pay up to €45 for a one-way trip.

THE WALK (see map p155)

From Kate Kearney's Cottage follow the road heading south into the Gap and climb steadily through hairpin bends to the northern shores of Black Lake. On calm days, a wonderful reflection of the valley appears in the reedy waters of the lake. The road is then essentially flat for the next 1.5km, passing a tearoom before climbing again above Auger Lake, where imposing cliffs begin to close in on either side. Pass over a narrow bridge and climb steeply to Black Lake, where the gradient eases and the valley opens out again. A final ascent then brings you to the Head of Gap (1½ to two hours from the start).

Now you must leave the road and climb east towards the steep, cliff-girt slopes that seem to bar progress. You should soon pick up traces of a path running along some old fencing. This will lead you steadily up and northeast beneath the crags to Glas Lough, which appears quite suddenly, hidden in a small hollow in the mountain. There are great views from here out across the Gap to the many peaks and valleys of central Iveragh.

Follow a path around the lough and then climb steeply onto the southern shoulder of Purple Mountain. There is a brief respite before the gradient increases once more, taking you across stunted heather and patches

of talus to a small subsidiary summit at 793m. The actual summit of **Purple Mountain** (832m) is reached a few minutes later (1½ to two hours from the Head of Gap), where you can rest and take in the lofty views in all directions. The Reeks to the west demand most attention, but the Killarney Lakes to the east and the patchwork of farmland stretching north also catch the eye.

Descend along a pleasantly narrow ridge to the northeast and cross a small col before climbing to an unnamed summit at 757m. The route now doglegs to the north (be careful in mist), dropping into another saddle before making the final climb to the summit of **Tomies Mountain** (735m). Beside the summit cairn is a conspicuous sprawl of stones marking a Neolithic burial site.

The initial descent from Tomies Mountain is quite steep, leading to a flat shoulder. Contour around a slight rise and then descend steeply again, making a beeline for the small ridge above Kate Kearney's. As the angle of descent eases, bracken begins to appear and a small path winds through this to reach a track. Turn left onto this, but only for a few metres. Cross the gate on your left and follow a rough track down through a series of gates giving access to a sealed road. Follow this for a short distance and then turn left to return to Kate Kearney's.

Muckross

Duration	3½–4 hours
Distance	11.5km
Difficulty	easy
Start/Finish	Muckross Park entrance
Nearest Town	Killarney (p139)
Transport	bus

Summary This popular lakeside walk through Killarney National Park features interesting geology, ancient ruins and tracts of precious native woodland.

Forming the core of Killarney National Park, Muckross is a popular day trip for visitors to Killarney. This route is a casual stroll along marked routes; it passes labelled trees and is generally shared with lots of other walkers. However, on some of the more remote paths, such as the one through the yew wood, you may find enough solitude to spot deer and other wildlife; binoculars and books for identifying wildflowers and birds will add extra interest to the route. Also keep an eye out for the small, black Kerry cow. One of the few herds in existence grazes at Muckross.

It is possible to spend some time visiting Muckross House, which portrays the elegant lifestyle of the 19th-century landowning class and is surrounded by lavish gardens. The adjacent Muckross Traditional Farms, where traditional farming methods are on display, are also worth a visit.

HISTORY

The area once belonged to the McCarthy Mór clan, which owned the land from the time of the Norman invasion till the 18th century. In 1448, the family founded Muckross Priory and the ruins (it was destroyed by Cromwell's troops in 1652) still stand in the grounds . The estate then passed to the Herbert family, who built Muckross House between 1840 and 1843. After less than a century the Herberts ran out of cash and sold to Lord Ardilaun, of the Guinness family. The estate changed hands again in 1910 when WB Borne, a wealthy American, bought it as a wedding gift for his daughter. It was this family that donated it to the state.

PLANNING
Maps

The OSI 1:50,000 map No 78 covers the route, though the extra detail given by the OSI 1:25,000 *Killarney National Park* is preferable. Killarney TIC sells maps of Muckross in the series *Simple Pocket Maps for Walkers & Cyclists*.

Geology & Ecology of Muckross

The main feature that makes Muckross such an interesting place to walk is its unusual geology and ecology. Underneath the park two types of rock sit side by side, and clear differences can be seen in the kind of vegetation that favours each one. In general, the area immediately next to the lake has limestone foundations, while surrounding this are patches of sandstone. In places the limestone has metamorphosed into marble, and Muckross once held a marble quarry.

The limestone at the lakeshore dissolves easily, and over the years networks of small tunnels have been carved by the water, providing a perfect habitat for otters. These endearing mammals leave signs of their presence in the form of spraints (droppings). Alder trees are common in the woodlands around these areas. This is a species that is native to Ireland and can survive in damp conditions because it forms a symbiotic relationship with small bacteria, which help the trees to absorb nitrogen from the soil. Although deciduous, Alder fruit takes the form of tiny cones.

Of all the habitats in the park, the oak wood is perhaps the most celebrated. Though all of Killarney was once dense woodland – so dense that Cromwell's enemies were able to hide within it – only remnants of the original forest now remain. Though relatively small, the Muckross wood supports an enormous range of bird life, from tits and jays to robins, fly catchers, siskins, wrens, treecreepers and wood pigeons. Few plants survive in the deep shade of the trees, though woodrush builds up great tufts, needing little light.

In another part of the park, Reenadinna Wood consists largely of Irish yew, and is the largest such forest in Europe. The yews manage to find sustenance from a tiny layer of soil covering the limestone, though their roots burrow into the rock for stability. Birds such as coal tits, blue tits, chaffinches and fieldfare thrive on the yew berries. Of other trees in the park, the low-growing arbutus stands out. Commonly known as strawberry trees, arbutus have strawberry-sized (and flavoured) berries which ripen in autumn.

Mammals also thrive in the park's protected habitat. Three species of bat, pygmy shrews, stoats, red squirrels, badgers and red deer all call Muckross home.

SOUTHWEST

GETTING TO/FROM THE WALK

The walk starts at the main pedestrian entrance to Muckross, 3km south of Killarney town centre on the road to Kenmare (N71). There is a large car park directly opposite the entrance (this is the first car park on the left that you come to when approaching from Killarney).

O'Connor's Tours (☎ 064-30200) runs a bus service between O'Connor's pub, on Killarney's High St, and Muckross House (€8), leaving at 1.45pm and then returning at 5.15pm daily. The **Bus Éireann** (☎ 064-30011) Killarney–Kenmare service (up to three daily June to September and once daily Monday to Saturday the rest of the year) will also drop you off if you ask the driver.

THE WALK

Pass through the entrance and walk west along the main driveway towards the house. At an iron bridge, leave the path and walk north to the shady **woodland** on the shore of the lake. The shore is dotted with damploving wildflowers such as marsh woundwort, purple loosestrife, wood anemones, bluebells and celandines. Water mint also flourishes where the water level changes.

Keeping to the shore, you soon leave the parkland behind and enter native **oak forest**, which has survived the deprivations of two centuries of felling for fuel for iron ore smelters, for charcoal or for export. Further along the shore, the rock base turns to limestone; you'll recognise the change when you see the dull, whitish rock and eroded formations standing up out of the water. At a wall go left, following a tarred road, turning away from Muckross House, and signs for Dinish Cottage and the meeting of the waters.

A right fork (still heading west) takes you into **Reenadinna Wood**, the largest yew forest in Europe. You are now on the Arthur Young Nature Trail; if you follow it to the east, you will pass the marble quarry and its attendant arbutus trees. Follow the nature

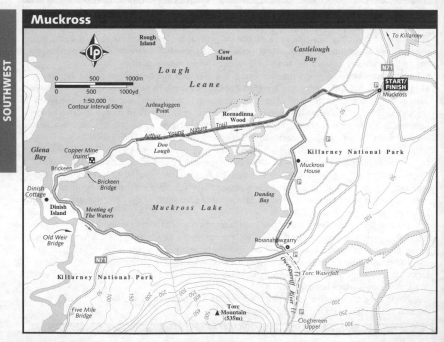

Muckross

trail until you are back on sandstone again, where the oaks and rhododendrons return.

At the end of this peninsula, near Brickeen Bridge, are the remains of a **copper mine**. It is thought Bronze Age people were the first to mine copper here, although it was mainly extracted from 1749. From here you can follow the road to **Dinish Cottage**, set in unusual gardens of eucalyptus, magnolias, azaleas and camellias. From the garden take a look at the Old Weir Bridge, where tourist boats navigate the rushing waters at the Upper Lake flows into Muckross Lake.

Now follow a road skirting the southern shore of the lake, exiting onto the busy N71. Turn left and walk towards Killarney for about 1.5km along this road (take great care), to a park entrance with waymarkers for the Kerry Way. Follow the signs to **Muckross House** (☎ 064-31440; w www .muckross-house.ie; admission €5; open 9am-5.30pm daily Sept-June, 9am-6pm daily July-Aug) and the adjacent **Muckross Traditional Farms** (☎ 064-35571; admission €5, open 10am-7pm daily June-Sept, 1pm-6pm daily May, 1pm-6pm Sat & Sun Mar, Apr & Oct); there is also a combined ticket (€7.50) for the house and farms. Pedestrian entry to the estate grounds is permitted at all times.

To finish the walk, follow more signs back to the car park where you started.

Torc Mountain

Duration	3½ hours
Distance	8km
Difficulty	easy–moderate
Start/Finish	Torc Waterfall car park
Nearest Town	Killarney (p139)
Transport	bus

Summary For a perfect introduction to Irish hillwalking do this relatively easy climb up a mountain path to superlative views over the Killarney Lakes and surrounding peaks.

Torc Mountain (535m) has a compact summit providing what are arguably the best views available over the Killarney Lakes and the backdrop of mountains to their south and west. At the same time, the route to the top involves very little of the difficult ground that is normally associated with mountain walks in Ireland. The Kerry Way provides a solid walking surface for the first half of the route and then a clear, if more rugged, path ascends the remaining distance to the top, climbing 490m in all. This makes it a great option for those who want to experience the pleasure of standing atop a peak, but who are normally put off by the effort demanded to get there. The route is not quite a walk in the park – it crosses open mountain terrain and walkers unfamiliar with compass navigation should avoid walking in poor visibility. You will need to bring all of the bad-weather equipment associated with mountain walking.

Walkers who don't mind missing Torc Waterfall (an impressive cascade that is worth visiting at least once) can make an alternative start at the top of the falls; see Getting to/from the Walk. Starting and finishing here will save you 1.5km and 110m of ascent. The walk can also be completed as a side trip from the Kerry Way (p160).

PLANNING
Maps
The OSI 1:50,000 map No 78 covers the route, though the extra detail given by the OSI 1:25,000 map *Killarney National Park* may be preferable.

GETTING TO/FROM THE WALK
Torc Waterfall car park is 5.5km south of Killarney on the N71; **Bus Éireann's** (☎ 064-30011) Killarney–Kenmare service (up to three daily June to September and once daily Monday to Saturday the rest of the year) will drop you off if you ask the driver.

To start at the top of the falls take the minor road that leads south from the N71, 1km north of the waterfall car park. Follow this for 1.5km to a car park at the end of the road.

THE WALK
From the car park, follow a wide path through natural broad-leaved woodland to a viewpoint beneath the 12m-high **Torc Waterfall**. A flight of steps then leads to the left, climbing

SOUTHWEST

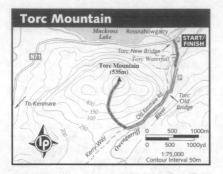

Torc Mountain

it zigzags up the grassy southwestern slopes to the **summit** (two to 2½ hours from the start). Hopefully the weather will be clear and you can appreciate the fabulous panorama across the Killarney Lakes and the MacGillycuddy's Reeks to the west. The sprawl of Killarney is plainly visible north of Muckross.

Return by reversing the inward route.

Kerry Way Highlight

Duration	2 days
Distance	41km
Difficulty	moderate
Start	Killarney, (p139)
Finish	Glencar (p150)
Transport	train, bus, boat

Summary A highly rewarding distillation of Ireland's most popular Waymarked Way, with waterfalls, forests, lakes and a section in the shadow of Ireland's highest mountain range.

steeply through the trees to the top of the falls. Follow signs for the Kerry Way towards Kenmare and turn left at an old stone bridge, and then right at a paved road (passing the car park that is the alternative start/finish – see Getting to/from the Walk, p159). The road soon dwindles to a track, crosses the river, and exits the woodland.

Around 300m after the last trees, just as you begin to descend slightly, watch out for a mound of gravel beside the track on the right. The path up Torc Mountain branches off here and climbs to the right of the stripped tree trunk on the horizon. Follow the path as

The Kerry Way is a nine-day, 214km-long Waymarked Way that starts and finishes in Killarney and circumnavigates the Iveragh Peninsula. The two days described here are

SOUTHWEST

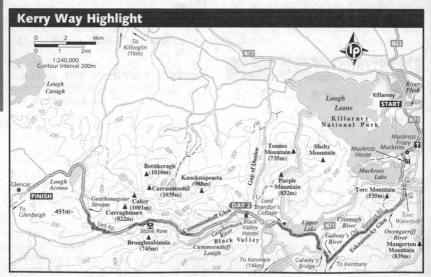

Kerry Way Highlight

Remote Black Valley at the southern foot of MacGillycuddy's Reeks

Approaching Gearhane, Brandon Mountain

Limestone landscape of the Burren near Fanore

Little remains of the promontory fort of Dún Balair, Tory Island

Dry-stone walls of Dún Dúchathair on Inishmore, Aran Islands

probably the wildest, most beautiful consecutive stages on the route, and together they offer some of the finest mountain scenery to be found on any low-level walk in Ireland. For walkers taking on the entire long-distance path, this section will form either the first or last two days of the trip.

The majority of the walking is along tracks and informal paths, with most of the road sections encountered at the beginning and end of each day. The first section of the walk out of Killarney is particularly urban and a better start might be made at Torc Waterfall, leaving Muckross for another day's walk (see the Muckross walk, p156). Starting at the waterfall will cut 5.5km from the first day's total. You can also finish at Lough Acoose, dispensing with the last bit of road walking. The route is well furnished with waymarking posts, stiles and lengths of duckboard across boggy sections, easing your progress and making it relatively straightforward to navigate.

Unfortunately there is no public transport from Glencar, at the end of the second day, back to the start. If you can't arrange your own transport, consider walking only the first day of the route and then returning to Killarney on the afternoon water taxi (see Getting to/from the Walk, this page).

Accommodation and meal options are very limited en route, so it is advisable to book ahead.

PLANNING
Maps & Books
The OSI 1:50,000 map No 78 covers the route. In addition, OSI 1:25,000 *Killarney National Park* shows the first day to Black Valley. Other maps of the entire Waymarked Way include Cork Kerry Tourism's rather simple strip map *Kerry Way Map Guide*, and a more detailed strip map by EastWest Mapping.

Slightly dated descriptions of the complete long-distance route can be found in a number of guide books, notably Michael Fewer's *Way-marked Trails of Ireland*, *The New Irish Walk Guide South West*, by Seán Ó'Suilleabháin, and *The National Trails of Ireland*, by Paddy Dillon.

Guided Walks
Several organisations offer guided walks along the Kerry Way, or arrange self-guided trips with back-up support (providing services such as luggage transport and accommodation booking). Companies include: **Go Ireland** (☎ 066-796 2094; **w** *www.goactivities .com*; Old Orchard House, Killorglin, County Kerry), **Southwest Walks Ireland** (☎ 066-712 8733; **w** *www.southwestwalksireland.com*; 40 Ashe St, Tralee, County Kerry) and **Tailor-Made Tours** (☎ 066-976 6007; **w** *www.tailor -madetours.com*; Ferry Rd, Keel, Castlemaine, County Kerry).

GETTING TO/FROM THE WALK
To start the walk at Torc Waterfall head to the fall's car park, which is 5.5km south of Killarney along the N71; the **Bus Éireann** (☎ 064-30011) Killarney–Kenmare service (up to three daily June to September and once daily Monday to Saturday the rest of the year) will drop you off if you ask the driver.

If you're ending the walk at Black Valley the only public transport is provided by **Tangney's Boating Tours** (☎ 064-34730), which runs a daily water taxi over the Killarney Lakes to Killarney (€12, March to November only). The boat departs at 11am from Ross Castle, 2km southwest of Killarney town centre, returning from the pier near Lord Brandon's Tearooms on the Upper Lake at 2.15pm. The trip can be popular with tour groups in summer, but nonetheless is a great experience.

THE WALK
Day 1: Killarney to Black Valley
6 hours, 21km, 375m ascent
Begin at the bridge over the River Flesk and follow the N71 south for 3km to Muckross House. Pass through the gates. At the turn-off to Rossnahowgarry, turn left and follow the waymarkers back across the main road to the car park for **Torc Waterfall** (an alternative starting point).

The way passes through natural broad-leaved woodland to a viewpoint beneath the 12m-high waterfall. It then climbs steeply through the trees to the top of the falls, ascending flights of steps through a tunnel of

SOUTHWEST

vegetation before veering left at a stone bridge (the route marked on the OSI map is out of date here). The path joins a track and the route is signed to the right, following the first of many sections along the old road to Kenmare. Cross Torc Old Bridge and the woodland soon ends. The track crosses out onto open mountain terrain, and passes between the peaks of Mangerton Mountain to the left and Torc Mountain to the right. Torc Mountain is a possible side trip from the path – see Torc Mountain walk (p159).

You soon leave the Owengarriff River behind and cross the Crinnah River in a low, wet valley, where the remains of the old road have long since sunken out of sight into the bog. Fortunately, a long section of wire-covered duckboard offers easy passage for walkers. The way rejoins the old road once it reaches firmer ground, and passes through the rocky ravine of **Esknamucky Glen**. It then descends to Galway's River and meets a paved track and a junction of alternate routes. The Kerry Way to Kenmare turns left here; you should turn right for Black Valley (four to 4½ hours from the start).

Pass Derricunnihy church and cross the N71 by Galway's Bridge and you will soon re-enter natural oak forest. The path cuts a wide trail through abundant woodland before crossing grasslands around the south-western shores of **Upper Lake**. A large metal stile then gives access to the grounds around Lord Brandon's Cottage, with its adjacent **tearooms**. This is a good place for lunch and is the departure point for boats back to Killarney; it is likely to be a busy spot at midday in summer.

From the cottage follow a minor road alongside the picturesque **Gearhameen River** and exit Killarney National Park. Three and a half kilometres of road then runs from the east end of Black Valley to the west; how far you need travel depends on your chosen accommodation – options are well spaced along the way.

Black Valley

This valley can feel remote after the bustle of Killarney; the hostel's tiny **shop** is the only place for fresh supplies. Accommodation

options are also limited, so you should book this part of your trip in advance.

The An Óige **Black Valley Youth Hostel** (☎ 064-34712; dorm beds €13) is in the valley centre, just east of the Gap of Dunloe. It has a drying room, and can prepare evening meals and packed lunches. **Hillcrest Farmhouse B&B** (☎ 064-34702; singles/doubles €42/60; open Mar-Nov) is a short detour from the Kerry Way at the eastern end of the valley. Evening meals, luggage transport and a drying room are available if required. **Shamrock Farm House B&B** (☎ 064-34714; singles/doubles €23/46), alongside the route at the western end of the valley, can provide evening meals.

Day 2: Black Valley to Glencar
7 hours, 20km, 500m ascent

Continue along the minor road towards the western end of Black Valley; ahead and to the right are the massive southern flanks of the MacGillycuddy's Reeks. The road runs out at a farm and you follow tracks into a small forest before setting off across open slopes with great views across Cummeenduff Lough and Broaghnabinnia. Follow waymarks up and right along a lovely *boreen* lined with stone walls and gnarled holly. Pass a new bungalow and continue ahead onto a green road, passing the stark remains of an old farm framed by the slopes of Caher (1001m), Ireland's third-highest summit. The road ends at a couple of bungalows. Follow waymarks around these and up over open ground to the boulder-strewn **pass** between Broaghnabinnia and Curraghmore. Off to the left is a Neolithic stone arrangement (visible against the skyline on the ascent) which indicates that this pass has been important to people long before the days of waymarks.

From the pass descend steeply to reach a farmyard, looking carefully for waymarks and arrows painted on rocks. Walk along the paved road for a little over 1km to a set of prominent signs; these direct you over steep grass slopes to the **Lack Road**, an old droving route that is now being reassimilated into the mountain. The steep climb zigzags up to the pass (at almost 400m) between the brooding

Curraghmore (822m) to the east and the smaller, unnamed peak (451m) to the west. From here there are fabulous views across the interior of Iveragh before you begin the steep descent towards Lough Acoose

At the bottom of this descent the Way meets the Gearhanagour Stream and traces its bank to a track. Follow this to a farm and onto a minor road (note the change of route from that shown on the OSI map), which you follow for almost 3km to the north end of Lough Acoose. At a junction with the main road, turn left (there are two **B&Bs** just to the right here – see Glencar & Lough Acoose, p150) and continue for 4km to Glencar.

Mullaghanattin

Duration	4½–5 hours
Distance	10.5km
Difficulty	moderate–demanding
Start/Finish	Tooreennahone
Nearest Towns	Killarney (p139), Glencar & Lough Acoose (p150)
Transport	private

Summary Indulge in fine ridge-top walking and wonderful 360-degree views on this compact circuit of remote mountain summits.

The Mullaghanattin horseshoe is a compact yet challenging walk, which is tough enough to give a real sense of achievement but short enough to fit into a summer's afternoon. The circular ridge is well defined and numerous streams tumble down the into the horseshoe in waterfalls hundreds of metres high, joining at the bottom to form the source of the River Blackwater. 'The Pocket', a sheer-sided corrie providing the centrepiece of the horseshoe, is clear evidence of the glacial sculpting that defined the landscape of Ireland during the last Ice Age (see the boxed text 'Signs of a Glacial Past', p24). The layers of Old Red Sandstone that have been exposed around the corrie are so folded that they give the impression of having been moulded like putty.

Mullaghanattin (773m) provides the high point of the circuit, but with at least six other summits along the ridge and height losses of up to 150m between some peaks, the total ascent of the day adds up to an impressive 950m. While the area is isolated and impractical for those without a car, it also guarantees a degree of solitude that can be rare on the Iveragh Peninsula.

PLANNING
When to Walk
Much of the terrain of this circuit is steep and care is required in places, especially in wet conditions. Ice will further complicate the route; in winter conditions it should only be attempted by experienced walkers. Also note that in poor visibility a navigational error could have serious consequences.

Maps
OSI 1:50,000 map No 78 covers the walk.

GETTING TO/FROM THE WALK
Arriving at the start and finish of the walk necessitates navigating through a warren of country roads and for this part of the day alone an OSI map is essential. The destination is a fork in the road just north of the buildings at Tooreennahone, in the centre of the Mullaghanattin horseshoe. There are limited parking spaces along the roads near this junction.

If you are approaching from Killarney, follow the N71 south for 20km and turn right onto the R568, passing over Moll's Gap. Take the second right after 11km (signed for the Ballaghbeama Gap) and continue straight over a crossroads to reach Tooreennahone. From Glencar, follow signs for the Ballaghbeama Gap and once over the pass turn right at the first crossroads to arrive at Tooreennahone.

THE WALK
From the road junction just north of Tooreennahone walk for around 50m along the road leading north. Cross a fence to the right of the road and immediately begin climbing; a steep ascent takes you straight up the shoulder ahead, or less acute slopes can be found by looping around slightly further east. About two thirds of the way up the

mountain the cone-shaped profile of Mullaghanattin comes into view, with the ridgeline that you are about to follow clearly visible. Cross a fence and continue climbing over easier ground to the first summit cairn.

From here the route is fairly straightforward: follow the ridgeline as it dips into cols and climbs over peaks for the duration of the horseshoe. The ridge is distinct throughout and navigation poses little problem in good visibility. For the eastern arm of the circuit the most compelling views are to the northeast, over the peaks of the MacGillycuddy's Reeks – the highest mountains in Ireland.

From the summit of the unnamed peak in the northeastern corner of the horseshoe, the ground becomes steeper. The profile of Mullaghanattin is formidable from this angle. Cross a fence in the col before Mullaghanattin and then follow another fence almost to the top, crossing this to climb the final metres to the **summit** and trig point (three hours from the start). The views are wonderful, but you need to take care on the descent: there are precipitous drops to the north. A plaque in the next col pays respect to Noel Lynch, who died here in 1973, and highlights the dangers associated with mountain walking.

The route climbs a further two peaks in the northwestern corner of the horseshoe, with views to the northwest encompassing Brandon Bay and even Brandon Mountain on a clear day. At this stage the route is rounding 'The Pocket' itself and the fenced **ridge** is narrow. From the summit of the last peak a final vista spreads before the eye: the intricate coastline of the Iveragh and Beara Peninsulas. Descend southeast from the ridge, aiming for the end of a rough track. The track brings you onto a paved road, which leads back to the junction where you started.

Derrynane Coastal Circuit

Duration	3 hours
Distance	8km
Difficulty	easy
Start/Finish	Derrynane House car park
Nearest Town	Caherdaniel (p165)
Transport	bus

Summary This varied, low-level circuit explores sandy beaches, old mass paths and Derrynane National Historic Park.

This relatively short circuit, with a total ascent of 180m, passes through a wide range of different habitats and various points of interest in the southwestern corner of the Iveragh Peninsula. A long sandy beach, a rocky mass path, country lanes and the Kerry Way all provide passage along various sections of the route. Highlights include wonderful views over the islands and islets that litter the coastal waters in these parts, with the sharp outlines of the Skellig Islands prominent among them.

Dating from the 10th century and linked to St Finian, a ruined abbey sits on the northeastern shore of Abbey Island. A wander around the building and adjacent graveyard is well worthwhile. The mass path that is followed to the west of the ruins has provided locals with access to the abbey for centuries. The route starts and finishes in the grounds of Derrynane National Historic Park; a visit to Derrynane House is another possibility at the end of the walk. The house

Mullaghanattin

Derrynane National Historic Park

Derrynane National Historic Park was opened in 1975 to preserve the ancestral home of the 'Great Liberator', Daniel O'Connell. Daniel was one of a long line of O'Connells who fought against English oppression. The family had governed Ballycarbery Castle, near Cahirciveen, from the Middle Ages until the 17th century when, like most Irish landowners, they became involved in wars against Oliver Cromwell's forces. Like many of their peers, they destroyed their castle rather than give it up to the English, and the family fled to Waterford.

Connections with Kerry were maintained and the family were soon quietly reacquiring land in the area, despite anti-Catholic laws prohibiting them from doing so. In 1702 **Derrynane House** (☎ 066-947 5113; admission €2.50; open daily Apr-Oct, Sat-Sun only Nov-Mar) was built, then just a large farmhouse. Around a century later, Hunting Cap O'Connell adopted his nephew Daniel and brought him to live at the house. Daniel was educated in London and Dublin, and went on to become a lawyer. He extended the house and transformed it into the mansion that stands today.

Daniel O'Connell is significant in Irish history because he mobilised the Irish people into their first mass movement. He demanded the state's anti-Catholic laws be removed, including the ban on Catholics becoming members of parliament. In this way, he is responsible for beginning the process by which Ireland gained its independence, though he was not a nationalist and sat in the British parliament. O'Connell's efforts eventually earned him a prison sentence, and one of the exhibits on display in the house is the ornate 'triumphal chariot' that was brought by his supporters to the prison gates to collect him on his release. O'Connell died in 1847 and his death bed can also be seen in Derrynane House. The village of Caherdaniel is now named in his honour.

is open to visitors, and it is recommend that you wander through the gardens even if you choose not to enter the house itself (see the boxed text 'Derrynane National Historic Park', above).

Maps & Books
The OSI 1:50,000 map No 84 covers the described walk. The visitor centre at Derrynane House sells two pamphlets that give more background to the area: *Derrynane Dunes* lists points of natural interest along the nature trail; while *Derrynane National Historic Park* offers a comprehensive history of the O'Connell family, the house and its surrounds.

NEAREST TOWN
Caherdaniel
A small coastal village, Caherdaniel has become used to receiving visitors thanks to its location on the Ring of Kerry. Despite its diminutive size it has plenty of facilities, including a small shop that sells OSI maps, a petrol station, a bakery, several cafés and pubs, and a range of accommodation.

Places to Stay & Eat There are several camping grounds around the village, including **Wave Crest Caravan Park** (☎ 066-947 5188; camping with car per tent/person €10/2, without car per person €5; open Easter-Sept), 1.5km east of the village along the main road. It has a wide choice of flat, scenic sites and great facilities; the on-site **shop** has a better selection of groceries than the one in the village centre, and stocks OSI maps.

On the main road in the centre of the village, **Traveller's Rest Hostel** (☎ 066-947 5175; dorm beds/doubles €12/30) offers breakfast. Local B&Bs include **O'Sullivan's Country Home** (☎ 066-947 5124; singles/ doubles €26/48), at the west end of the village, and **The Old Forge** (☎ 066-947 5110; singles/doubles €25/50), 1km to the east.

There is a good choice of eating places in Caherdaniel, most of which are clustered around the crossroads in the centre of the village. **The Blind Piper** (☎ 066-947 5126) has both a restaurant and a bar menu, and **Freddie's Bar** (☎ 066-947 5125) serves bar meals. **The Courthouse** has cheaper fare, with chips and burgers a mainstay of the menu.

SOUTHWEST

Getting There & Away A twice-daily **Bus Éireann** (☎ 066-712 3566) service, which stops at Caherdaniel, operates around the Ring of Kerry. The service runs from June to mid-September only. Towns on the route include Tralee (€12.10, three hours) and Killarney (€11.90, two hours 20 minutes). There is no public transport at other times of the year.

GETTING TO/FROM THE WALK

The walk starts and finishes at the car park for 'Derrynane Dunes Nature Trail', a couple of hundred metres east of the main car park for Derrynane House. From Caherdaniel, take the minor road west from the village centre, following signs for Derrynane House. Veer left at a junction after 1.5km, then turn immediately left again into the car park.

If you don't have your own transport, it is possible to start and finish this walk in the village of Caherdaniel; allow an extra hour and add 3km to the total distance. To access the car park at the start of the route, follow the minor road west from the centre of the village towards Derrynane House. Either return along the same road or continue back to Caherdaniel along the Kerry Way.

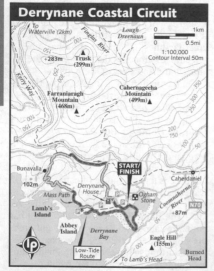

THE WALK

From the car park follow the footpath that leads south, signed to 'Derrynane Dunes Nature Trail'. Turn left at the following junction and continue to the edge of expansive sand flats that adorn the Coomnahorna River estuary. Wading birds can often be seen picking over the spoils offered by the shallow water, and the slopes of Eagle Hill rise across the river.

Turn right and trace the river bank to the back of the dunes, and then continue through the dunes along a smaller footpath. Join the **beach**, turn right (northwest), and begin to walk along the wide, firm expanse of sand. The beach stretches for more than a kilometre; follow it to the end, passing several rock outcrops with painted current warnings along the way.

The route at the end of the beach depends on the tide. If the tide is out you will be able to continue along the sand to the car park and pier just north of Abbey Island. If the tide is in you will be forced off the beach soon after a yellow lifeguard hut, and should cross over the back of the beach to another parking area (where drinking water and toilets are available). Follow the minor road out of this parking area, turn left at a junction (signed to 'Abbey Island') and pass in front of **Keating's Bar** (☎ 066-947 5115), where snacks and limited **camping** facilities are available. Continue to the end of the road and you will arrive at Abbey Island car park and pier, where walkers on the low-tide route leave the beach.

A waymarking post and steps in a stone wall indicate the start of the **mass path**. Follow this around the back of a building and you will soon find yourself weaving between seams of rock and climbing flights of stone steps through a wonderfully wild coastal landscape. Descend to a stony cove and ignore two right turns off the path, continuing to trace the coastline till the path crosses a stile and joins a track. Follow this track around the back of another small beach to a pier, where a minor road leads uphill to the right.

Follow the fuchsia-lined lane for around 1.5km to the corner of a sharp left-hand switchback. Prominent waymarking posts at the corner indicate the route of the Kerry Way. Turn right (east) along a gravel road and follow the marker posts for the next 1.5km. Watch for a left turn off the track soon after a metal gate and stile, and a footpath then leads across open ground and over a low spur of Farraniaragh Mountain. Descend through woodland on the other side of the spur to a minor road. The Kerry Way crosses the lane and continues to Caherdaniel; turn right along the road to return to the start of this circuit.

Descend for 1km and continue straight ahead at a junction, following signs for 'Derrynane Harbour'. Within 200m the white gateposts of **Derrynane House** appear on the left. Pass through these and follow the driveway to the house itself. Cross in front of the house and continue ahead to a wooden gate that gives access to the back of the dunes. Turn left on the other side of the gate and follow a grassy path back to the car park at the start of the route.

The Beara Peninsula

The Beara Peninsula is characterised by rugged terrain interspersed with sudden sea views. The fringes of the peninsula provide its only flat ground and all of the settlements in the area are located along the coast. The interior rises abruptly to a mountainous mass of wild, rocky uplands with the sandstone erupting like broken bones through the skin of bog. Beara is quieter than its northern neighbour, and has thus far escaped the massive seasonal influx of tourists that can sometimes make Iveragh feel oppressive. Though they offer plenty of facilities for visitors, the small villages of this peninsula retain much of their traditional atmosphere and in many cases are still working communities.

Walking on Beara is generally split into two categories. On one hand, there are high mountain excursions with wonderful views; the Eskatarriff horseshoe and Hungry Hill

are two such routes described here. On the other hand, there are low-level walks that explore the peninsula's narrow lanes, colourful villages and numerous prehistoric sites. The eight-day Beara Way is the long-distance showpiece of these routes, and a two-day highlight of this route is described in this section. However, for those who really want to explore further in this area the possibilities are numerous. Besides the routes mentioned here, there are two small islands (see Dursey Island, p208, and Bere Island, p208) and many other walks around the hills.

HISTORY
Ancient standing stones, dolmens (prehistoric tombs), ring forts, stone circles and Ogham stones are liberally scattered around the Beara Peninsula and are testimony to its long history of human habitation. Many of these relics can be seen from the walks described in this section.

More recent human history in the area can be traced from the 11th century, when the peninsula was dominated by the O'Sullivan Beare clan, which had its stronghold at Dunboy castle just outside Castletownbere. They ruled the area for five centuries, until 1601, when a Gaelic rebellion against the English failed and English troops drove the family out. After Cromwell's attacks later in the century large tracts of the Beara were given to Sir William Petty. By the 18th century three Anglo-Irish families largely owned the area: the Whites owned most of Glengarriff, the Puxleys owned the lands confiscated from O'Sullivan Beare and the descendants of Petty owned much of the remainder. Castletownbere, with its mining and fishing industries, became established as the major centre of the region during this time.

Today, after 50 years or so in the economic doldrums, Beara positively bursts with Ireland's new wealth, and little craft shops and other tourist initiatives are testament to this revival right across the peninsula.

NATURAL HISTORY
Until the 18th century the Beara Peninsula was largely covered in dense native oak woods. These were felled to fuel the steam

SOUTHWEST

engines used in local mines. Nowadays, ugly forestry plantations are the chief source of trees except at Glengarriff, where replanted oak woods flourish, and at Lauragh, where the Dereen Gardens are home to many exotic plants.

Land on the peninsula is mainly divided by stone walls, but in many places hedgerows flourish as little highways of wildlife. Besides native plant life, several unusual species can be seen in Beara. These include the New Zealand tree ferns at Dereen, and Gunnera, a gigantic rhubarb-like plant that flourishes in the moist air here. Rhododendron (see the boxed text 'Scourge of the Rhododendron', p269) has become widespread around the peninsula, but thankfully has not proved as destructive here as it is has in the woods around Killarney.

PLANNING
Information Sources
The website w www.bearatourism.com offers valuable information.

ACCESS TOWN
Castletownbere
A bustling little town and a working port, Castletownbere (Baile Chais Bhéara) is by far the Beara Peninsula's largest settlement. The TIC (☎ 027-70344; the Square; open year-round) provides information covering the whole peninsula and also offers Internet access.

The town has a bank with an ATM machine and several shops selling local walking maps and guides, including **The Shell** bookshop on the main street.

Places to Stay & Eat Behind the supermarket, **Harbour Lodge Hostel** (☎ 027-71043; dorm beds or singles/twins €13/26; camping per person €4) is in a large former convent building. Showers are available to nonguests for €4. **Old Bank Restaurant** (☎ 027-70252; singles/doubles €22.50/49.50) is right in the centre of the town and offers B&B as well as a good seafood menu in the restaurant downstairs. The **Knockanror House** (☎ 027-70029; singles/doubles €25/50) is also on the main street. Behind the harbour at the east

end of town is **Cametringane Hotel** (☎ 027-70379; singles/doubles €50/90).

The town has a large **supermarket** and a good selection of **pubs**. There is a wide choice of restaurants along Main St, including **Murphy's Restaurant** (☎ 027-70244) and Niki's (☎ 027-70625). For lighter snacks, **The Bakery Café**, at the west end of Main St, is recommended.

Getting There & Away Services with **Bus Éireann** (☎ 021-450 8188) go via Bantry to Cork (€13.90, 3¼ hours, once daily July and August, Monday, Wednesday, Friday and Sunday only during the rest of the year). In addition, **Harrington's** (☎ 027-74003) and **O'Sullivan's** (☎ 027-74168) are local companies that provide minibus services twice daily between Castletownbere and Cork.

During July and August only **Bus Éireann** (☎ 064-30011) also runs services through the villages on the north coast of the Beara Peninsula to Kenmare (€7.35, one hour 20 minutes, twice daily Monday to Saturday) and Killarney (€11.60, 2¼ hours, once daily Monday to Saturday).

Hungry Hill

Duration	4–5 hours
Distance	9km
Difficulty	moderate–demanding
Start/Finish	Coomgira
Nearest Town	Adrigole (p169)
Transport	bus

Summary This complex climb up the highest peak on the peninsula includes a scramble across great blocks of sandstone to a pair of hidden mountain loughs, and amazing views over Cork and Kerry.

Hungry Hill (685m) is the highest point on the Beara Peninsula and it has a fascinating topography that makes it both compelling and difficult to climb. The sandstone that creates the mountain has been gouged by glacial action on its east side into a complex system of cliffs and corries. These contain two hidden lakes, one of which feeds a waterfall that is arguably the highest in Ireland, plunging more than 200m over slabs and cliffs into the Coomgira valley. The route described here is the pick of several possible approaches, and is really only worth doing in good visibility because of the difficulty of route finding and the constant proximity of steep and dangerous ground. Total ascent for the walk is 710m.

PLANNING
Maps
Use the OSI 1:50,000 map No 84, but bear in mind that the contours don't illustrate the complexity of some of the slopes, nor do they indicate the profusion of small cliffs.

NEAREST TOWN
Adrigole
At the southern end of the Healy Pass, Adrigole is a disparate collection of scattered buildings rather than a village with a definite centre. However, it does offer enough amenities to make it a viable base for Hungry Hill (and for walkers on the Beara Way).

Hungry Hill Lodge (☎ 027-60228; dorm beds/doubles €11/28; camping per person €5) is one of the best reasons to base yourself here. The hostel sits just west of the Healy Pass road, offers cooked breakfasts, and has a take-away menu in the evenings (also available to nonguests). Modern facilities include a fully equipped kitchen for hostel guests and campers. B&Bs in the area include **Ocean View** (☎ 027-60069; singles/doubles €22/44), which is signed off the R572 Glengarriff-Castletownbere road just east of the junction with the Healy Pass road.

Boat House Café & Bistro (☎ 027-60132), at the sailing centre, signed off the R572, 2km east of the junction with the Healy Pass road, offers lunches, snacks and evening meals. **Peg's Shop**, near the junction of the R572 and the Healy Pass road, sells groceries and local walking maps, while the **supermarket** 2km east along the R572 has a larger range of goods.

All of the bus services between Castletownbere, Bantry and Cork stop in Adrigole;

see Getting There & Away (p168) under Castletownbere for details of these services. By car, Adrigole is around 14km east of Castletownbere or 16km west of Glengarriff along the R527.

GETTING TO/FROM THE WALK
To reach the start, turn west from the R572 at Reen Bridge, 1.5km southwest of Adrigole. If approaching from Adrigole, cross the bridge before turning onto the narrow road lined with high fuchsia hedgerows. Follow this for 2km to a clearing on the left where several cars can be parked (GR 780493).

The R572 is used by buses travelling between Castletownbere, Bantry and Cork, and drivers will deposit/collect you at Reen Bridge if requested (see Getting There & Away, p168, for Castletownbere for details of these bus services).

It is not unusual for guests at the Hungry Hill Lodge in Adrigole to make the return trip up the mountain from there; add 1½ hours and 7km of easy road walking to the route. Alternatively, walkers with their own transport could start and finish at the top of the Healy Pass (already at 300m), and follow an undulating ridge southwest for more than 5km to reach the summit.

THE WALK (see map p170)
Cross the stile at the back of the parking area and climb the slopes to the south, heading towards an obvious broken shoulder. A 20- to 30-minute climb should bring you onto the shoulder, which has a fence running along the top. Follow the fence west to a small stile; cross this to continue across rough ground to the base of Hungry Hill's southeast ridge, which rises steeply in a series of sweeping rock slabs.

The route ahead looks more difficult than it actually is. By following a line of least resistance to the right (north) or through the middle, a series of grassy ramps and easy scrambles leads to a vertical cliff. The easiest route leads around to the left (southwest) of this, but you can also find a slightly more adventurous route to the right. Either route will take you onto easier ground, where the way is now indicated by small

SOUTHWEST

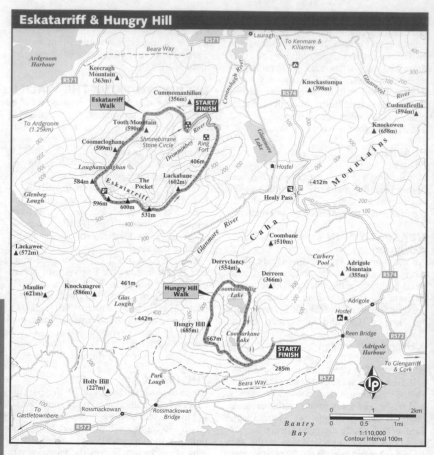

Eskatarriff & Hungry Hill

stone cairns, and brings you in 10 to 15 minutes to a large cairn marking Hungry Hill's south summit (667m).

The trig pillar marking the actual summit of **Hungry Hill** is just a few hundred metres north across boggy ground. At this point in clear weather the marvellous views you've been enjoying to the south across Bantry Bay will be joined by those to the west across the rest of Beara and Dursey Island, and those to the north across Eskatarriff to the mountains of Iveragh.

The descent begins gently, but soon steepens as eruptions of sandstone run at 45° to

your angle of travel. Use the turf between these outcrops as ramps and zigzag down to the east side of the col between Hungry Hill and Derryclancy. You should now be able to see the lake in Coomadavallig. Don't descend to the lake but contour around and then walk down to the outlet, which can be easily crossed.

Climb across a spur to Coomarkane, where another lake lies beneath tremendous rock walls. Descend to the outlet, cross it, and drop diagonally across wet ground back to the parking area (20 to 30 minutes from the outlet stream of Lough Coomarkane).

Eskatarriff

Duration	5½–6 hours
Distance	12km
Difficulty	moderate–demanding
Start/Finish	Shronebirrane
Nearest Town	Lauragh (p171)
Transport	private

Summary Probably the most scenic mountain circuit on the Beara Peninsula, there are great views and an enjoyable descent. The overall quality of the walk is ample reward for some rough terrain.

While it barely rises to 600m in height, Eskatarriff and its surrounding summits provide one of the most scenic mountain circuits in the southwest outside of the Iveragh and Dingle Peninsulas. Past glaciers have hollowed out a mighty corrie known as 'the Pocket', which forms the centrepiece of the walk. The peaks loom over it, creating an air of challenge and foreboding, especially on an overcast day. Over the second half of the walk, in particular, the ridges offer pleasant walking with great views.

However, there is also 750m of ascent and some rugged terrain to negotiate, which means you'll probably travel more slowly than you'd normally expect. You need to pay careful attention for route finding, even in clear weather, as there are only a few safe routes of ascent and descent. Think twice before starting the circuit if there is a chance of the cloud coming down.

PLANNING
Maps
The OSI 1:50,000 map No 84 covers the described route.

NEAREST TOWN & FACILITIES
Lauragh
The houses and facilities at Lauragh (Láith Reach) are even more spread out than most villages on the Beara Peninsula. The only identifiable centre is the road junction where the road from the Healy Pass joins the R571. The nearest shops are in Ardgroom (p173), 10km west.

Creeven Lodge Caravan & Camping Park (☎ 064-83131; camping with car per tent/person €9/1.50, without car per person €4.75; open Easter-Oct) is 1.5km south along the Healy Pass road. It has grassy sites and a common room with basic cooking facilities. Alternatively, the An Óige **Glanmore Lake Hostel** (☎ 064-83181; dorm beds €12; open June-Sept) is in an old schoolhouse beside the remote but beautiful Glanmore Lake, 4km south of Lauragh.

The **Mountain View B&B** (☎ 064-83143; singles/doubles €26/52) can provide evening meals, and is around 800m south of the crossroads along the road to the Healy Pass.

An Sibin is the only pub in the village; it is just south of the crossroad and offers bar snacks.

Lauragh is served by public transport in July and August only. For these months, **Bus Éireann** (☎ 064-30011) links the village to Castletownbere (€4.70, 30 minutes, twice daily Monday to Saturday) in the southwest, and via Kenmare to Killarney (€8.90, one hour 35 minutes, once daily Monday to Saturday) in the northeast.

GETTING TO/FROM THE WALK
The start of the walk is along minor roads just south of Lauragh. From Lauragh, follow the R571 west for around 1km and look out for a left turn signed for the Rabach Way. Follow this road for a little less than 1km and turn right onto a very narrow road with patches of grass in the middle. Follow this for around 2km until the impressive rock walls of the valley come into view and the road draws alongside the Drimminboy River. A track leads to the left, crossing the river on an old concrete bridge that is gated in the middle. The descent route off the mountain comes out here. Park the car at one of several small grass verges further along the minor road taking care not to block gates or entries.

THE WALK (see map p170)
From your parking spot walk southwest along the minor road to within sight of the final house in the valley. Set incongruously in the garden of this house are the largely untouched stones of Shronebirrane Stone

Circle, probably dating to the Bronze Age. You may want to wander down for a closer look, but the route onto the mountain heads up the faint spur to the right, heading towards a huge boulder set into the grassy slope. Cross the fence (with care) and climb past the boulder, continuing up steep slopes towards a band of rock outcrops. Move left and pick your way over some awkward terrain to the right of the cascading Shronebirrane stream to reach easier ground above. The views into the valley are already superb.

Follow the stream as it veers to the west, heading towards a steep grass gully just north of the intimidating rock terraces of Tooth Mountain (590m). Sheep tracks make for easy progress up the gully and lead you to a broad col just below 500m (one hour from the start). From the col, cross the fence and follow it south, climbing over some rough ground to reach a broad shoulder southwest of Tooth Mountain, where there are fine views over Lackabane and across the Kenmare River to Scariff Island. Descend gently southwest into a col and then climb again to the trig point at the summit of Coomacloghane (599m).

Now you have to descend, keeping left around jagged rock outcrops before climbing gently across grassy slopes east of a flat summit (584m) to reach a small cairn on the west top of Eskatarriff (596m; two to three hours from the start). Progress to the main summit of **Eskatarriff** (600m) is hindered by rock terraces and peat hags set perpendicular to the direction you need to walk. The terrain remains difficult as you descend southeast from the summit towards a curious pyramidal summit at 531m, though views across the wild expanse of the Glanmore Valley to Hungry Hill are impressive. Either climb over or contour around the small summit and then veer northeast, climbing over easier ground to **Lackabane** (602m), the highest summit on the route. From here, tremendous views open out across Kenmare Harbour towards the distant peaks of the Iveragh Peninsula.

Do not attempt to descend directly from Lackabane, but head northeast along an airy ridge across a small unnamed summit at 406m. From here you can descend north across grassy slopes, aiming for a gate and track. At first this may not be very obvious but you may be able to make out the green outline of an old ring fort. The gate is a few hundred metres northeast of here, and should become apparent as you pick your way over some awkward ground near the valley floor. Be careful not to stray too far north on your descent, where the ground steepens into cliffs. Turn left along the track and follow it for 500m to the bridge and gate beside the minor road. Turn left at the road to return to your starting point.

Beara Way Highlight 🚶

Duration	2 days
Distance	37.5km
Difficulty	moderate
Start	Castletownbere (p168)
Finish	Ardgroom (p173)
Transport	bus

Summary This superbly varied waymarked route explores the colourful villages, rocky coastline and archaeological sites of the Beara Peninsula.

The Beara Way is an eight-day, 196km-long Waymarked Way that starts and finishes in Glengarriff, at the eastern end of the Beara Peninsula. The route circumnavigates the peninsula and includes side trips to both Bere Island (p208) and Dursey Island (p208), as well as several other 'spurs' which, if walked, can add several days to the route.

The walk described here is a short highlight of the longer route. It can either be walked in three reasonably short days (finishing the second day at Eyeries), which would warrant a grade of easy–moderate, or in a combination of one short day followed by a fairly long day. Accommodation is plentiful, so how long you take depends purely on how quickly (or slowly) you want to travel. All the villages passed have shops or restaurants, so there is no need to carry more than one day's food or water with you.

Wonderful coastal and mountain views, quiet and colourful villages and a liberal sprinkling of ancient archaeological sites all go to make the route a memorable one. Terrain covered is a mixture of minor roads, farm tracks and open moorland, and the waymarking posts and stiles that furnish the route make navigation relatively straightforward. Note that the markers are occasionally placed on telegraph poles.

PLANNING
Maps & Books

The route described here is covered by the OSI 1:50,000 map No 84; you will also need map No 85 if you are walking the entire route. EastWest Mapping and Cork-Kerry Tourism both produce less detailed strip maps for the entire route, entitled *The Beara Way*. Use all maps with discretion; the way is changed slightly every year. Where there is a contradiction, you should normally rely on marker posts rather than the map.

A slightly dated description of the complete Way can be found in Michael Fewer's *Way-marked Trails of Ireland*.

Guided Walks

Several organisations offer guided walks along the Beara Way, or arrange self-guided trips with back-up support (providing services such as luggage transport and accommodation booking). Companies include: **Go Ireland** (☎ 066-796 2094; **w** www.goactivities.com; Old Orchard House, Killorglin, County Kerry), **Southwest Walks Ireland** (☎ 066-712 8733; **w** www.southwestwalksireland.com; 40 Ashe St, Tralee, County Kerry) and **Tailor-Made Tours** (☎ 066-976 6007; **w** www.tailor-madetours.com; Ferry Rd, Keel, Castlemaine, County Kerry).

NEAREST TOWNS

See Castletownbere (p168).

Ardgroom

Another small village, Ardgroom has a **shop**, a petrol station and several pubs. B&Bs in the centre of the village include **O'Brien's** (☎ 027-74019; *singles/doubles €20/40*) and the **Kingdom House** (☎ 027-74403; *singles/doubles €24/48*). The **Canfie House** (☎ 027-74105; *singles/doubles €25/44*) is 1km east of the village along the main road (along the route of the continuing Beara Way). **The Village Inn** bar and restaurant on the main street is the best place for evening meals.

Ardgroom is served by public transport in July and August only. For these months, **Bus Éireann** (☎ 064-30011) links the village via Eyeries to Castletownbere (€2.95, 25 minutes, twice daily Monday to Saturday) in the southwest, and via Kenmare to Killarney (€9.95, one hour 50 minutes, once daily Monday to Saturday) in the northeast.

THE WALK
Day 1: Castletownbere to Allihies

5 hours, 13.5km, 340m ascent

Highlights of this day are archaeological sites and fine views during the climb over a shoulder of Knockgour Mountain.

From the centre of Castletownbere, head to the west end of the main street and take a right turn in front of the Bakery Café, following a sign for the stone circle. About 1.5km along the minor road a gate leads into a field on the right and provides access to the **Derreena Taggart Stone Circle**, a well-preserved, compact ring of 12 rock slabs.

After a further 1.5km waymarkers indicate a right turn onto an old turf road heading towards Miskish Mountain. The track climbs gently past old turf cutting areas; look behind for views over Castletownbere and Bere Island. After a short distance the route turns left off the turf road, passes a great, rusting hulk of a machine, and heads across open moorland to the west. The markers along this section are well placed and the path is fairly clear as a worn line through the grassy expanse.

The path soon joins a road. Turn right and follow the road for a little over 2km – a departure from the route marked on the OSI map. Despite the hard surface underfoot, this section is a delight; the verges are covered with flowers in summer and vehicles are a rarity. After 500m a gate gives access to the roadside Teernahilane Ring Fort (now more recognisable as a raised circular mound) and, 1km further along from the ring fort, you pass a cluster of deserted stone buildings.

The road section ends at a T-junction where the lane turns sharply left and the Beara Way is waymarked onto a forestry track to the right (around three hours from the start). The steepest ascent of the day can now be seen stretching up though the pine plantation ahead. Climb steadily straight up the track until, 2km after leaving the road, the terrain levels out and becomes a pleasant green road crossing a spur of **Knockgour Mountain**. The dense forest is replaced by wonderful views across the entire western tip of the peninsula, and the coastline around Allihies lies spread out ahead.

The track meets a minor road alongside another prehistoric site, this time a stone row. Follow the road down the hill, and a signed left turn and then two right turns will bring you into the centre of Allihies.

Allihies

A small village set above a sandy beach, Allihies has a remarkably wide range of accommodation options.

The Village Hostel (☎ 027-73107; dorm beds €12.50, singles/doubles €18/36) is at the northern end of the village. Alternatively the An Óige **Allihies Hostel** (☎ 027-73014; dorm beds €12.50; open June-Sept) is signed off the Beara Way, 750m before you arrive at the village. B&Bs in the centre of Allihies include **Veronica's** (☎ 027-73072; singles/doubles €18/36), which serves breakfasts and snacks in its café, and **Sea View Guesthouse** (☎ 027-73004; singles/doubles €35/50).

There is a reasonable-sized **supermarket** in the main street, and a water tap opposite **Jimmy's** pub, which serves lunches. **O'Neill's Bar & Restaurant**, next door to the Village Hostel, is the best place for evening meals.

There is no public transport access to/from Allihies.

Day 2: Allihies to Ardgroom
7 hours, 24km, 338m ascent
This fairly long and arduous day can be split into two with an overnight stop in the attractive little village of Eyries.

At the north end of Allihies waymarkers direct you onto a beautiful old *boreen* that takes you in a direct line towards the smelter of the now-disused **Bearhaven Copper Mine**.

The Puxleys

So much like the plot of a romantic novel is the history of this family that Daphne Du Maurier turned it into one in her novel *Hungry Hill*. The Puxleys were originally from Wales, but had already established a base in Galway. In the 18th century the first Puxley settled near Castletownbere, buying land that had been confiscated from the O'Sullivan clan after the Battle of Kinsale. The area at this time was well known for its smuggling: wool and timber were exchanged for French wines and spirits.

The Puxleys at first took an active part in the smuggling, but in 1740 Henry Puxley was made Commissioner of the Peace and given a frigate and troops, so changed his allegiances. This caused a good deal of resentment among the local people, many of whom were the descendants of the O'Sullivan Beares and felt that they had a claim on the land. Tension grew as local O'Sullivans planned to enlist French privateers in an uprising against the English. In 1757 Henry, who went everywhere armed with a pistol, was shot and killed on his way to church.

Undeterred, the Puxleys continued to live and prosper in the area and in the early 19th century discovered a vast seam of copper ore on land that they owned at Allihies. The mine opened in 1811 and the family was soon reaping the rewards, demonstrating their new-found wealth by beginning to build the fabulously extravagant grand mansion that can still be seen in the grounds of Dunboy Castle. However, they never finished building the house and it lay unoccupied for most of the time while the Puxleys lived in Cornwall.

The mines began to fail in the early 20th century, just as things were hotting up on the political front. By 1920 the IRA was using the grounds of Puxley Manor to train recruits. In 1921, the IRA burned down the house rather than have it used as an English army base.

Just beneath this building, ringed with fences and signs warning of old mineshafts, the Way joins a small road, which it follows steeply uphill through rugged outcrops of sandstone to a broad col at almost 300m (45 minutes to one hour from Allihies). The excellent views southwest, across the furthest extremities of the Beara Peninsula, include the humped profile of Dursey Island.

These views are soon surpassed as the road becomes a gravel track, and you begin a long gradual descent. A great panorama opens out across the Kenmare River to the Iveragh Peninsula, with the MacGillycuddy's Reeks,

the highest mountains in Ireland, serrating the skyline. After a descent of little more than 3km, the track becomes a sealed road again and you soon reach a waymark directing you up a narrow, fuchsia-lined *boreen*. You can cut almost 2km from the day's total by continuing straight ahead here. Otherwise, head off on a higher but unremarkable routing on the lower slopes of Miskish Mountain.

The remaining distance into Eyeries (4km) is along sometimes-busy roads. You could shorten this by navigating, using the OSI map, down to Pallas Strand and across the Abha na gCaolinse where you will rejoin

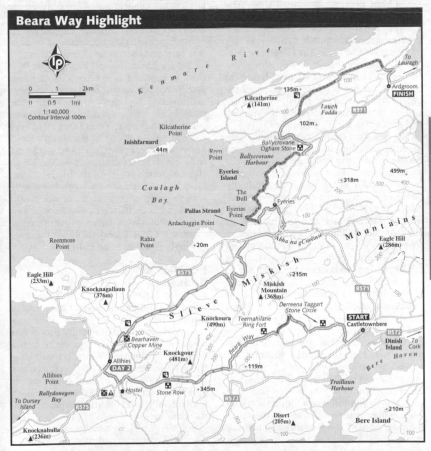

Beara Way Highlight

1:140,000
Contour Interval 100m

SOUTHWEST

the Beara Way and either turn right towards Eyries (1.5km) or left to continue along the coast for Ardgroom.

Eyeries would be a solid contender in the 'brightest village in the world' contest, and its rainbow array of colourful buildings make it a popular visitor attraction. Accommodation is limited to B&Bs, including **Coulagh Bay House** (☎ 027-74013; singles/doubles €28/46), on the main road (and the Beara Way) opposite the turn-off into Eyeries. Alternatively, **Shamrock Farmhouse** (☎ 027-74058; Strand Road; singles/doubles €20/40) is 50m along the Beara Way to the west of the village. Eyeries has a small **supermarket** with petrol pumps. **O'Neill's Bar** and **Causkey's Bar** both serve evening meals. Eyeries is served by public transport in July and August only, when **Bus Éireann** (☎ 064-30011) links the village to Castletownbere (€1.40, 10 minutes, twice daily Monday to Saturday) in the southwest, and via Ardgroom and Kenmare to Killarney (€11.50, two hours five minutes, once daily Monday to Saturday) in the northeast.

The first 4km out of Eyeries winds along a scenic coastline of rock headlands and boulder-clad storm beaches. You cross numerous stiles; take care using the slightly rickety wooden stiles, which are gradually being replaced with aluminium versions. Also take care when walking across the sections of storm beach and the mounds of ankle-turning boulders. The routing differs from the OSI map close to the end of this coastal section, as the waymarks take you inland from an old boat shed and slipway to cross reed-filled meadows. Roads then lead around Ballycrovane Harbour, and just right of **Ballycrovane Ogham Stone**, at 5.3m-high the tallest Ogham stone in Europe – see the boxed text 'Ogham Script', p147.

The road ends at Lough Fadda, and waymarks lead across rough and sometimes wet ground to reach an old *boreen*, with wide-ranging views of the mountainous spine of the Beara Peninsula. The *boreen* ends at a road, which you follow east for a short distance before setting off once more across rough ground. Clever routing makes the most of rock terraces and an informal path

has formed underfoot. Cross a small gully and then descend to meet the final road at Cappul bridge. Ardgroom is slightly more than 1km south (right) along this road.

West Cork

Although Cork is a large county, many of its best walking routes are clustered in the west; the landscape here tends to be wilder, less populated and more rugged. Outside of the Beara Peninsula (see the previous section), which is regarded as being in West Cork, it has few mountain ranges that can rival those of neighbouring Kerry. However, West Cork does contain several peaks that are worthy of note, including the horseshoe of summits that surround the lake at Gougane Barra.

But for many the real character of West Cork is captured in quieter, less imposing places. With its warren of tiny country lanes enclosing lush pockets of natural habitat, many of the routes in the area are walks of a contemplative nature. One of the best of these can be found at the tip of the Sheep's Head, the most isolated peninsula of the southwest, and a haven for the discerning walker. Lough Hyne, Europe's only seawater lake, is another route that is popular with locals but a well-kept secret from most of the outside world. The area has an intricate coastline with several offshore islands that are worth exploring, including Clear Island (p205) – the most southerly populated land in Ireland.

PLANNING
Books

Kevin Corcoran's *West Cork Walks*, with detailed descriptions of several easy routes, makes it one of the best guides to the area. An environmental biologist by profession, the author's delightful background information on the habitats of West Cork will be of particular interest to wildlife enthusiasts. Also look for a series of local guides written by Damien Enright, who provides meticulously detailed and informative descriptions for walks in several parts of Cork. Sean Higgisson's *Hillwalker's Guide to County Cork* details 12 mountain and coastal routes.

Information Sources

Bantry TIC (☎ 027-50229; the Square) can provide useful information on accommodation and transport links in West Cork.

Gougane Barra

Duration	5 hours
Distance	10km
Difficulty	moderate–demanding
Start/Finish	Gougane Barra Hotel
Nearest Towns	Gougane Barra (p178), Ballingeary (p178)
Transport	bus

Summary This mid-level mountain circuit around beautiful Gougane Barra lake crosses some rough ground but provides fine views over West Cork.

This is probably the most rewarding hillwalk in West Cork outside of the Beara Peninsula. The route gains 550m in height to soar in a great horseshoe around and above the beautiful lake of Gougane Barra. There is only a little bit of navigating to distract you from great open tracts of mountain scenery.

Although the route starts and finishes along tracks and paved lanes, most of it is over great tufts of mountain grass and heather. When you spot sedges, rushes and coarser, thicker-looking grasses, the ground will be wetter and becomes 'quaking bog' (you might find it hard to work out whether that refers to the ground beneath you or your leg muscles as you try to balance across!). The broad shoulders and virtually flat plateaus of similarly cloaked terrain give an impressive sense of space, but could make navigation difficult if you stray off route in mist. There are few signs of passing feet over most of the open ground, and a compass bearing or two will offer extra confidence even on a clear day.

HISTORY

Gougane Barra has a long and curious history for what is, after all, just a lake with some cliffs around it. St Finbar established a monastery on the island in the lake during the 6th century before moving on to found Cork city. On the last Sunday in September people still make the pilgrimage to Gougane Barra to commemorate St Finbar.

As Gougane Barra is an out-of-the-way spot, a Catholic church was tolerated even when the penal laws were at their strictest. People from all around the area travelled to Gougane Barra to attend services, arriving via routes into the valley known as 'mass paths'. Although there is little sign of these historic routes on the ground today, two of the paths are encountered on this route. The Kerry Path, along which you will travel at the end of the walk, is situated at the northeastern end of the valley, while a mass path, known as the Poll, climbs over the mountains via a col in the western corner of the horseshoe described. These routes were used for religious ceremonies of all kinds – when you are up on the mountain, spare a thought for the processions of villagers who struggled over the Poll with a coffin during funerals.

The Poll also played a role in the War of Independence, when nationalist troops led by local hero Tom Barry were trapped by English forces in the Coomhola-Borlin valley, southwest of Gougane Barra. Local men led the Irish over Conigar Mountain and down to Gougane Barra via the Poll. Without guides and with the route invisible from the ridge tops, the English were unable to follow and the Irish escaped.

NATURAL HISTORY

The Gougane Barra basin was created by a glacier around 200,000 years ago; the ice accumulated in the corrie at the western end of the valley and, as it ebbed and flowed, carved the valley out of the red sandstone rock. The lake that fills the basin today is relatively shallow and the island on which the church is built is a moraine, where the soils carried by the glacier were dumped as the ice retreated.

PLANNING
Maps

Use the OSI 1:50,000 map No 85.

NEAREST TOWNS & FACILITIES
Gougane Barra

The only place to stay at Gougane Barra is **Gougane Barra Hotel** (☎ 026-47069; singles/ doubles from €69/100; open Apr-Sept). The hotel offers lunches and dinners to guests and nonguests alike. Next door, **Cronin's pub** also serves bar food.

Bus Éireann (☎ 021-450 8188) has one service in each direction, on Saturday only, between Gougane Barra and Bantry (€5.80, 40 minutes) in the south, and via Ballingeary to Macroom (€5.55, one hour) in the north. However, the bus schedule means that a day trip is only possible from Ballingeary or Macroom; you'd have to stay in Gougane Barra for a week if you were relying on the bus services from Bantry. Macroom is situated on Bus Éireann's Cork–Killarney route; there are at least 11 services daily in each direction. Bantry is on Bus Éireann's Cork–Castletownbere route; there are at least seven services daily in each direction, with four services on Sundays.

By car, Gougane Barra is well signed off the R584 road that links Macroom in the north to the N71 in the south.

Ballingeary

The closest real settlement to Gougane Barra, Ballingeary is a large village 5km east along the R584. It has several **pubs**, **cafés**, petrol pumps and **supermarkets**, but little accommodation. The most convenient option is **Tig Barra House** (☎ 026-47016; Tooreenduve, Ballingeary; singles/doubles €24/48), which is the nearest B&B to Gougane Barra. The house is 1km west of Ballingeary along the R584. It can provide evening meals and has a **café** attached to the back.

See information under Gougane Barra (above) for getting to/from Ballingeary.

THE WALK

Before you begin the walk stand in front of the Gougane Barra Hotel and look across the lake. To the north, you can see an outcrop of rock known as Sron: the 'Nose'. To the right of it, a track – the 'Kerry Path' – winds its way behind the cliffs; on your descent, this is the route you are looking for.

Starting from the hotel car park, turn left and approach the public toilets about 70m along the road. Pass through the farm gate behind the toilets and follow a track as it zigzags past farm buildings towards open mountain terrain. A long straight section of track leads to a sharp left and right turn; pass these and leave the track at the next left-hand hairpin, at the corner of a forestry plantation. A metal gate in the stone wall just off the track is a clear sign that you are in the right spot.

Pass through the gate and climb up the broken slope to the southwest. You will find yourself negotiating a route up broad, marshy gullies separated by pinnacles of rock. There are good views over the lake as you climb, but take care to leave a wide berth between yourself and steep cliffs to the right. Continue climbing until you reach the summit of **Foilastookeen** (500m), from where there are good views over Bantry town, Bantry Bay and Whiddy Island.

Continue southwest from the summit, looking for a sheep fence on the horizon. Once you meet the fence turn right (west) and walk along it, keeping it close to your left. A faint path indicates that other walkers have used this navigation guide. Follow the fence until it runs into Lough Fadda, around 1km further on. Veer northwest at this point and climb a short distance to the smaller Lough Glas.

Trace the shore of Lough Glas to its northwest extremity and begin to descend the broad slope beyond. A tiny lough will soon come into view in the col ahead. Before making your way down to this, look north to Bealick, with its small summit cairn. This is your next destination, but it goes out of sight once you start descending through the tall grasses and boggy depressions ahead.

At the col you cross the Poll path that ascends from the Coomhola–Borlin valley to the southwest. A stile to the east of the little lough allows passage over the first of two sheep fences, though the second must be negotiated without help. Head north for almost 1km to avoid the cliff edge, then veer northeast towards **Bealick** (537m; three

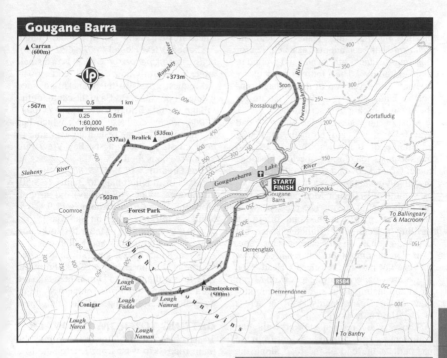

Gougane Barra

to 3½ hours from the start). On a clear day, fine views from the summit cairn extend across much of West Cork and all the way to the MacGillycuddy's Reeks in the west.

Descend Bealick, still heading northeast towards another small lough set amid an expanse of wet, grassy ground. Pass the lough and continue along the flat, marshy plateau to the northeast. When a band of rock-studded cliffs begins to loom ahead, veer eastward and pass in front of these, descending behind the Nose. If you can see the hotel as you descend, you have not gone far enough northeast; backtrack to avoid steep cliffs ahead. The descent follows a stream down slopes covered with long grass, then passes under the outcrop of the Nose and crosses a sheep fence to join the wide track of the Kerry Path.

Follow the path down through a couple of gated fields to a paved lane. Turn right past a wonderful old stone bridge, continuing back to the main road and the hotel.

Sheep's Head Way Highlight

Duration	6–7 hours
Distance	16km
Difficulty	easy–moderate
Start/Finish	Letter West
Nearest Town	Kilcrohane (p180)
Transport	private

Summary A high-quality coastal circuit, this walk explores wild scenery at the tip of the southwest's most remote peninsula. A shorter loop walk is an option.

The Sheep's Head is the least well known of all the peninsulas in southwest Ireland, yet it boasts wonderful views of the western seaboard and possesses a quiet, rural beauty in its interior. This route explores the last, wild stretch of land before the Sheep's Head Peninsula finally concedes to the sea. The entire headland is circumnavigated by the four-day, 88km-long Sheep's Head Way. The closing line of Seamus Heaney's poem *The Peninsula* has been adopted as an epithet for this long-distance path: 'water and ground in their extremity'. The motto is particularly relevant to the very tip of this isolated outpost of land, which provides the terrain for the one-day highlight described here.

Most of our walk uses the Sheep's Head Way, following obvious footpaths and taking advantage of the stiles, footbridges and marker posts that furnish the long-distance route. Ground covered is generally undulating, involving 380m of ascent, with the modest summit of Ballyroon Mountain providing the high-point at 239m. The route passes a series of steep cliffs at one point, offering a thrilling impression of height and space, but demanding that you take care near the edge. Complete the circuit on 3km of narrow lanes that are not part of the Sheep's Head Way. Views are wonderful throughout, with Mizen Head dominating to the south and the mountains of the Beara Peninsula rising across Bantry Bay to the north.

Those who prefer a shorter walk can complete a 4km alternative circuit from the car park at the end of the road along the headland. This route is fully waymarked (it is one of the shorter loop walks that have been set up to complement the Sheep's Head Way) and takes in what is arguably the most impressive section of the longer route. Allow two hours for this option.

PLANNING
Maps & Books
The OSI 1:50,000 map No 88 covers this route. For a description of the entire Sheep's Head Way, the locally produced *Guide to the Sheep's Head Way* is available from shops around the peninsula.

NEAREST TOWN
Kilcrohane
A small, quiet village, Kilcrohane still has enough facilities to make it a viable base for the walk around the tip of the Sheep's Head. There is one old-fashioned **grocery shop**, with a post office counter, petrol pumps and a café; the shop sells the *Guide to the Sheep's*

Head Way, but does not stock OSI maps. There are no banking facilities in the village.

Carbery View Hostel (☎ 027-67035; dorm beds/camping per person €10/5) is in a small annex to a family house. The friendly owners request guests to telephone in advance wherever possible. B&Bs in the centre of the village include **Bridge View House** (☎ 027-67086; singles/doubles €34/56), which has evening meals in the restaurant available to both guests and nonguests. **Bay View Pub** also serves bar food.

Bus Éireann (☎ 021-450 8188) has limited services from Kilcrohane to Bantry (€5.50, 40 minutes, twice on Saturday) and through Gougane Barra to Macroom (€11.95, two hours 25 minutes, once on Saturday). Frequent buses connect Bantry to Cork, and Macroom to both Cork and Killarney.

By car Kilcrohane is generally approached via the N71 from Bantry or Cork. From the N71 follow the R591 to Durrus then take the road that leads along the southern shore of the peninsula, following signs to Kilcrohane.

GETTING TO/FROM THE WALK
To reach the start of the walk follow the main road 4km west from Kilcrohane to a junction where a road branches to the right (the junction is marked by a signpost reading 'The Black Gate'). One hundred metres further west is a roadside parking area, with space for eight to 10 vehicles.

THE WALK
From the parking area walk west along the main road for around 400m. A prominent waymarking stone directs you right, over a stone stile and across a small field. Cross a second stile and walk between several farm buildings to a gate on the left. Negotiate this and you are out onto open terrain.

The path is well marked as it contours the hillside. Marshy patches of ground need to be negotiated from time to time; pick the easiest-looking route around the edge of these. The route crosses a couple more stiles and passes close to two small loughs before descending onto a road. Turn left along this for just 20m before veering up a lane to the right. Pass between three houses and the road dwindles to a grassy *boreen* and then a path as you ascend Ballyroon Mountain.

The climb up the boulder-studded hillside is steady but rarely steep. The path joins the **summit ridge** near a jumble of rocks that is actually a ruined 17th-century signal tower; the tower was standing until 1990 when it was blown down in a gale. Continue along the ridge to the trig point that marks the top of the hill at 239m (2½ hours from the start); views encompass the Beara and Iveragh Peninsulas to the north, and Mizen Head to the south.

A short descent leads past a building (a WWII lookout) to the parking area at the end of the Sheep's Head road. If you are lucky the **mobile café** in the car park will be open. This car park is the start/finish point for the shorter loop option outlined in the introduction to this walk.

The path is now well-trodden all the way to the lighthouse. At the end of Lough Akeen a wooden bridge offers passage over a marshy ditch, and a final short climb leads to a helicopter landing pad encircled with white stones. The **lighthouse** is down a flight of concrete steps to the right (one hour from Ballyroon Mountain).

Return to the helicopter pad and veer left to join the return path along the north side of the peninsula. Several marshy hollows lie alongside the first section of this route; skirt around them to their immediate left or climb a little way up the ridge further to the left to avoid them. The path then passes along the top of sheer cliffs. The scenery is impressive, but care is needed near the steep drops.

Climb gently up a wide hollow; the short loop option back to the car park will soon be signed off to the right. Continue ahead for the longer route, where the landscape becomes more pastoral and less rugged. Intricate coastal scenery begins to take centre stage as the path descends past a beautiful sea inlet.

Continue over grassy undulations until the scattering of houses of Eskraha comes into sight. Cross a stile beside a gate and follow a narrow lane past these buildings, ignoring subsequent waymarking posts. Turn right and then right again at the following road junctions, climbing towards the ridge of the peninsula. Turn left at two subsequent junctions to reach the main road along the south coast. Turn right here and within 100m you will return to the start point.

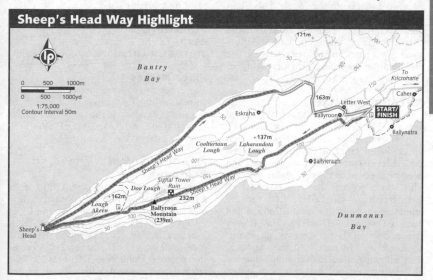

Sheep's Head Way Highlight

Knockomagh Woods & Lough Hyne

Duration	3–4 hours
Distance	9km
Difficulty	easy
Start/Finish	Lough Hyne car park
Nearest Town	Baltimore (p182)
Transport	private

Summary Pleasant woodland trails lead to a summit viewpoint, then country lanes head to the lakeshore, where you can scramble across rough slopes to view an impressive tidal race.

A peaceful stretch of water, Lough Hyne is overlooked by the modest but scenic Knock-omagh (197m). The walk up the wooded slopes of the hill to the summit viewpoint is a beautiful and popular excursion, and views from the top are excellent. A well-benched path provides easy travel up and down; the total ascent is 200m. From the woods to Barloge Pier, at the southern tip of Lough Hyne, the route follows a quiet country lane. From here a different option awaits the adventurous, who can scramble over rough ground to a viewpoint over tidal rapids at the seaward entrance to the lough. This short section traverses steep coastline and can be quite overgrown. Whether or not you choose to do this stretch, the rest of the walk offers a scenic yet peaceful half-day's activity. The pier and the lakeshore provide plenty of good spots for a picnic.

NATURAL HISTORY

This walk explores two areas of unusual ecology. The first is Lough Hyne, Europe's only seawater lake. About 4000 years ago the gradual warming of the climate (and rising sea levels) meant that this hillside lough became exposed to the encroaching ocean. This was a process that was repeated all over Ireland – the valleys between the mountain ranges to the north flooded and became Dingle Bay, Dunmanus Bay, Bantry Bay and so on. Here, however, an almost complete wall of rock held the sea back, only allowing it access through a narrow channel between the two bodies of water.

Consequently, at high tide seawater flows into the lake, and at low tide the lake's waters flow out

When the difference in height between low and high tide is about 1cm on the seashore, the water level on the lough side changes by about 30cm. This means that although the lough has an area of less than 100 hectares, it can be 40m deep in places. The consequence of this phenomenon is that the lough is able to support sea creatures more common in much warmer waters such as the Mediterranean. Coral survives in the lough as well as sea squirts, sponges, fan worms and the distinctive red-mouthed goby fish.

The other special habitat explored on this walk is Knockomagh Woods, one of Ireland's few remaining native oak woods. The trees are direct descendants of those that recolonised the area after the ice sheets retreated during the last Ice Age. Beech, whitethorn, hazel, holly and several species of conifers also now grow in the woods. The spindle tree has also made a home here, which is unusual as it generally prefers growing on lime foundations. This species is most noticeable in the autumn when its coral pink berries stand out.

PLANNING
Maps
The OSI 1:50,000 map No 89 covers the area.

Place Names
There seems to be some controversy over the correct spelling for the lough at the centre of this route; signposts in the area indicate both 'Lough Hyne' and 'Lough Ine'. Follow both signs to arrive at the same lough.

NEAREST TOWN
Baltimore
A picturesque seaside village, Baltimore is a popular summer holiday destination. It is also the departure point for ferries to Clear Island (p205). It has plenty of tourist facilities and the post office sells OSI maps and local walking guides. The nearest information centre is **Skibbereen TIC** (☎ 028-21766; *North St; Skibbereen*), which has a display

dedicated to Lough Hyne and offers lots of background information about the lake and its surrounds. Banking facilities can also be found in Skibbereen.

Places to Stay & Eat Follow the signs for 1km to **Rolf's Holiday Hostel** (☎ 028-20289; dorm beds/doubles €11.45/34.30), which is above the village and away from the late-night revelry that can make the village rather noisy. The hostel is in a recently renovated complex with modern facilities; breakfasts are available and the attached bar and **Café Art Restaurant** are popular with guests and nonguests alike. Of the numerous B&Bs in Baltimore, **The Posthouse** (☎ 028-20155; singles/doubles €28/56) is central, while the **Abbey View** (☎ 028-20255; doubles €60) is slightly quieter, but is still only 500m from the main street.

There is a small **supermarket** in the village centre, as well as a good selection of pubs and good-quality restaurants. **La Jolie Brise** specialises in breakfast and pizza, while **Chez Youen** (☎ 028-20600; 3-course set menus from €30) is a seafood specialist with a great reputation.

Getting There & Away Regular **Bus Éireann** (☎ 021-450 8188) services travel between Baltimore and Skibbereen (€2.75, 20 minutes, three daily Monday to Saturday). From Skibbereen frequent services connect with both Cork and Killarney.

Baltimore is on the R595, around 12km south of Skibbereen and the N71.

GETTING TO/FROM THE WALK
Lough Hyne is 6km northeast of Baltimore: head north along the R595 for 2km and turn right, following signs for the lough. There are several sizeable parking areas along the north shore of the lough. There is no public transport to the area.

THE WALK
From the car park on the north shore of the lough walk west along the road to a junction. Cross the main road and join a forestry path heading to the right. Within 20m, turn right onto a path that climbs into the woods.

The route is obvious as the wide path climbs gradually; several series of steps provide easy travel over steep ground and two signposts indicate the way at path junctions (follow directions to the 'hill top'). At the ruin of a building the path goes around the back and continues to climb.

You travel through beautiful shaded woodland, passing moss-cloaked trunks and lots of understorey vegetation. Rush, bluebells, herb robert, honeysuckle and pennywort are abundant and you'll see many different types of ferns. Occasionally, the view opens to splendid vistas of the lough and seashore below. At the **summit viewpoint** (45 minutes from the start) the trees clear and you walk out to an open space of gorse, heather and rock outcrops. This clearing is situated just beneath the summit proper; conifer plantations surrounding the knoll obscure views from elsewhere. From this high point, however, the vista over Baltimore, Clear Island, Skibbereen and the lough are superb.

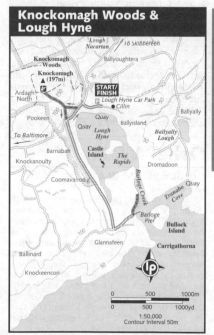

Knockomagh Woods & Lough Hyne

SOUTHWEST

Backtrack down the path and at the second signpost, near the ruined building, turn right. This will lead quickly to the main road; cross this and continue straight ahead following the narrow road along the western shore of the lough. This minor road is overhung with deciduous trees; in the woodland alongside grow vast tracts of woodrush and irises. You can make your way down to the shore and peer into the lough to look for the unique creatures living there.

At a T-junction 1.5km from the corner, turn left and follow the road down to Barloge Pier and Creek. The water here is strange and still. Bullock Island, in its centre, almost rejoins the mainland at low tide. Herons stand in the shallow water among more sea plants. If you choose to scramble towards the tidal rapids, climb onto the rocks from the northern end of the pier, and carefully make your way around the shoreline. Lots of small paths run through the bracken and furze above the cliffs but gradually come together into a single, rugged path. Cross a ruined stone wall ahead of you and the path soon peters out amid thick vegetation. The tidal race is visible from here. At the point where the levels of the incoming tide and the out-flowing stream are exactly the same, the river seems to stand still for a few minutes and then starts to flow in the opposite direction.

Make your way back to the pier and retrace your steps to the car park.

Other Walks

DINGLE PENINSULA
Mt Eagle

Several walks are possible around Mt Eagle (516m), on the tip of the Dingle Peninsula. Starting from Kildurrihy village, a moderate 14km, six-hour route climbs the mountain, skirting Mt Eagle Lake before reaching the summit. From there the route crosses a subsidiary summit, Beenacouma, to the southwest, and then descends to meet the Dingle Way, which it follows back to Kildurrihy. There isn't any public transport to Kildurrihy but it is possible to get off the Dingle–Dunquin bus about 2km west of Ventry (see Getting to/from the Walk, p145). For this walk use the OSI 1:50,000 map No 70.

Stradbally & Beenoskee

The twin summits of Stradbally (798m) and Beenoskee (826m) dominate the centre of the Dingle Peninsula. From a start at the parking area beside Lough Anscaul, 4km north of Anascaul village, you can follow a good track up past waterfalls to a col at almost 400m. From there turn northeast and make the long climb to the summit of Beenoskee, from where there are superb views over the Dingle Peninsula. Walkers can opt to continue for another kilometre to the slightly lower top of Stradbally before retracing the outward route to Lough Anscaul. Total distance including Stradbally is 13km, with 770m of ascent, and a grading of moderate–demanding. Use the OSI 1:50,000 map No 70.

IVERAGH PENINSULA
Mangerton Mountain

Mangerton Mountain (839m), south of Killarney, has two sides to its character; the summit plateau and southern slopes are rounded and wet, while to the north steep cliffs and sharp arêtes enclose the dramatically-named Devil's Punchbowl. The moderate-grade route to the top starts and finishes at a car park at the end of a minor road at GR 983848; take the N71 south from Killarney and turn left where a sign indicates Mangerton (just south of Muckross Hotel) and then turn right 1.5km later. Follow a path alongside the Finoulagh River to the lough that fills the Devil's Punchbowl, and climb the ridge to the east. The small summit cairn is 400m south of the edge of the plateau. The ridge to the west of the lough can be followed on the descent. The route is 10km long, involves 690m of ascent, and takes around four hours. Use the OSI 1:50,000 map No 78. Seán Ó'Suilleabháin describes this and several other routes up the mountain in *New Irish Walk Guide: South West*.

BEARA PENINSULA
Glanrastel

A mountain circuit on the north of the Beara Peninsula, this route starts and finishes at the end of a minor road 2km east of Lauragh (p171). Follow a track along the southern bank of Glanrastel River and then pick a way up beside the stream to the eastern end of the valley. Veer south past Caha Lakes and trace the cliff line west over Cushnaficulla (594m) and Knockowen (658m) before descending to the start. The moderate–demanding route is 10km long, involves 700m of ascent, and should take four to five hours. Use the OSI 1:50,000 map No 84.

Glengarriff Woods

Glengarriff Nature Reserve is a public park set within ancient oak woods and pine forests at the southeastern extent of the Beara Peninsula. The reserve's network of paths are popular with casual walkers, but can also be used to form routes up to 6km long. A left turn 300m after the main entrance leads to Lady Bantry's Lookout, which gives a panoramic view over Glengarriff Harbour. Paths leading from the entrance to Poolin Waterfall, just beyond the northwestern boundary of the reserve, are also worth following. OSI 1:50,000 map No 85 covers the area, though **Glengarriff TIC** (☎ 027-63084) has smaller-scale maps that are more useful. The park entrance is 1.5km north of Glengarriff village along the N71 to Kenmare. Glengarriff has plenty of visitor amenities and is well served by Bus Éireann services between Cork and Killarney.

WAYMARKED WAYS

Additional Waymarked Ways in southwest Ireland include the Ballyhoura Way (p338) in Counties Tipperary and Limerick, the Slieve Felim Way (p339) in County Limerick, the Blackwater Way (p338) in Counties Cork and Tipperary, and the North Kerry Way (p339) in County Kerry.

Atlantic Islands

Ireland's wonderfully fragmented Atlantic coast provides countless opportunities for walkers. Perhaps the most engaging and adventurous of these can be found on the country's many islands. Contrast the ruins of Great Blasket Island, melancholy and redolent of hardship, loss and emigration, with the vibrancy of the Aran Islands, given new life by tourism, Internet-assisted business and an influx of people eager to live on a far-flung fringe of Europe.

The islands have long and often turbulent histories, intertwined with fascinating and unusual cultures. The people are resilient and pragmatic, qualities derived from the need to survive in a wild and ultimately unforgiving environment (see the boxed text 'Struggles & Joys of Island Life', p203). The natural world seems closer out here: cars are few, meadows grow uncut, and relinquished lands provide a haven for a huge diversity of insect and plant life. Birds in particular thrive on the islands; there are more whales than you would imagine cruising by in the deep, offshore waters; dolphins and porpoises hunt in the quiet bays; and seals rest on rocky headlands. Of course walkers benefit too, able to travel in peace along narrow roads and grassy *boreens* (country lanes), with the restless ocean a constant companion.

HISTORY

There were Neolithic communities on Clare Island from as early as the third millennium BC, and the *dúns* (prehistoric stone forts) of the Aran Islands have provided evidence of an established population on those islands from the Bronze Age (see the boxed text 'Dúns of the Aran Islands', p197).

In the early centuries AD and through to the early part of the last millennium, monks found the natural isolation of the islands well suited to their needs. Monasteries were built, most notably on Inishmore and Clare, and *clochains* (beehive-shaped stone dwellings) were built on the smaller and more remote islands.

Highlights

Meandering through the bracken on the way to Croaghmore, Great Blasket Island

- Visiting Tory Island (p190) with its mythical promontory fort Dún Balair and colonies of puffins
- Climbing Knockmore on Clare Island (p194) for panoramic views over the Mayo and Connemara coasts
- Exploring prehistoric forts, wild limestone pavements and stone-walled fields on the Aran Islands (p196)
- Wandering among the melancholy ruins of Great Blasket Island (p203)

During the last few centuries, the Aran Islands – and also to some extent Tory and Clare – became the focus of struggles for control over strategic trading routes, and witnessed bloody conflicts and massacres. Rathlin Island was caught up in struggles for control of Ulster and Scotland.

Many islands escaped the worst deprivations of the Great Famine but emigration gradually depopulated smaller outposts like Great Blasket to the point where communities were no longer viable. Maintaining viable populations is still an issue on the larger islands, although tourism and government support have brought a better standard of living for many.

INFORMATION
Place Names

On many of the islands, Irish is the first language written and spoken. Places, road signs and place names are often written in Irish only, without the usual English translation.

Ferry Delays

Heavy swells and rough seas can halt ferry sailings at any time of the year. If you are planning a visit to the islands, try to wait for settled conditions, or allow an extra day or two in case you have to wait out the weather. Visitors staying overnight on the islands are not guaranteed return passage the following day if the weather turns bad. Outside the summer months, sailings to the more remote islands like Tory can be disrupted for weeks on end.

Atlantic Islands

Atlantic Islands – Maps

ATLANTIC ISLANDS

To facilitate navigation through these areas, some Irish names have been given in this chapter. See also the Gazetteer (p358).

Rathlin Island

Duration	4–5 hours
Distance	14.5km
Difficulty	easy
Start/Finish	Rathlin ferry pier
Nearest Towns	Rathlin (p189), Ballycastle (p301)
Transport	boat

Summary Enjoy pleasant coastal panoramas on the way to West Lighthouse to view puffins and guillemots, and spectacular sea stacks.

L-shaped Rathlin lies 7km northeast of Ballycastle and the Antrim Coast. The main focus for visitors are the cliffs and stacks at West Lighthouse, which support Northern Ireland's largest seabird colony. There is an excellent Royal Society for the Protection of Birds (RSPB) viewing platform at the lighthouse, and spotting scopes to give you a better view of the burrow-dwelling puffins and the crowds of guillemots crammed onto the rock ledges.

This walk focuses on West Lighthouse and the cliffs, and the wetland area of surrounding Kebble National Nature Reserve. It is an easy route that largely follows country roads and involves little ascent. You can shorten the walk by using the minibus service

Calling Rathlin Island

If calling Northern Ireland, including Rathlin, from within the North, you only have to dial the eight digit number supplied in this section.

If calling Northern Ireland from outside the province, you have to use the ☎ 028 area code, followed by the eight digit number.

However, if calling Northern Ireland from the Republic, there is a cheaper option; you can use the special area code of ☎ 048, followed by the eight digit number.

from Church Bay in either direction (see Getting to/from the Walk, p190). Although a return trip along the rugged terrain of the north coast looks tempting, the route encroaches on private land.

Other walk possibilities on the island include the easy trip out to Ushet Lough and Rue Point (8km return), and the short National Trust waymarked trails around Ballyconagan and the Coastguard Lookout, a hut built in 1941 to keep watch over the bustling shipping lanes to the north of the island.

HISTORY

For a relatively small island, Rathlin has been the location of a remarkable number of events of historical note.

Robert the Bruce retreated to the island after his defeat by Edward I in 1306 and hid in a cave on the northeastern cliffs (Bruce's Cave). Watching a spider's resoluteness in repeatedly trying to spin a web in the cave is said to have given him the courage to have another go at the English, whom he went on to defeat at Bannockburn.

Rathlin's strategic position in the turbulent waters between Scotland and Ireland has left a legacy of massacres and conflict. In both 1575 and 1642 the island's population was decimated, first by the forces of the English Earl of Essex and then by the Scottish Campbell clan.

In 1898 Marconi made the world's first radio communication from Rathlin, contacting Ballycastle on the mainland from the East Lighthouse. The concrete base for the apparatus, inscribed with the Lloyds of London name, can still be seen. In the 1990s Virgin tycoon Richard Branson ended up on Rathlin after crash-landing in the sea a few miles to the north, the culmination of his transatlantic balloon flight.

Rathlin – Its Island Story, by Wallace Clark, is good for a more detailed history.

NATURAL HISTORY

Wildlife is everywhere on this island. The main seabird colony at West Lighthouse supports over 90,000 guillemots, as well as thousands of fulmars, kittiwakes, razorbills and puffins. Lapwings are common, as are stonechats, wheatears and eider ducks. Seals can often be seen resting on the rocks around Church and Mill Bays.

In early summer pink swathes of heath-spotted orchids are prominent, while large patches of flag iris fill the waterlogged hollows with their yellow flowers.

PLANNING
Make sure you contact the **RSPB warden** (☎ 2076 3948) prior to your visit to West Lighthouse as the viewing platform is only accessible under supervision.

When to Walk
You should visit between May and July to view seabirds. Outside this time, the breeding season, the birds are well out at sea.

Maps
Use OSNI 1:50,000 map No 5.

NEAREST TOWNS
See Ballycastle (p301).

Rathlin
The main settlement on the island is clustered around the harbour at Church Bay.

The Boathouse Centre (☎ 2076 3951) sells books and brochures and details the history, culture and ecology of the island.

Places to Stay & Eat You can **camp** for free on the eastern side of Church Bay, in a field not far from the harbour. **Soerneog View Hostel** (☎ 2076 3954; dorm beds £8) is around 800m from the harbour along the road towards Rue Point. The hostel is small, but very clean and comfortable. It is recommended that you book and then you'll be met off the ferry. Towels and linen are included in the price. **Kinramer Cottage** (☎ 2076 3948; South Cleggan; dorm beds £5) is a 'camping barn' but resembles hostel accommodation. It is an attractive and well-finished place, located in a peaceful setting 4km west of the main village, en route to West Lighthouse. You'll need your own sleeping bag. B&Bs include **Rathlin Guest House** (☎ 2076 3917; The Quay; singles/doubles £18/36), right next to the pier. Nearby is **Manor House** (☎ 2076 3964; e uravfm@smtp.ntrust.org.uk; singles/doubles £21/42), which also offers evening meals by arrangement. Manor House's **tearoom** is open 11am to 4pm, and serves snacks and light meals. **McCuaigs Bar & Restaurant**,

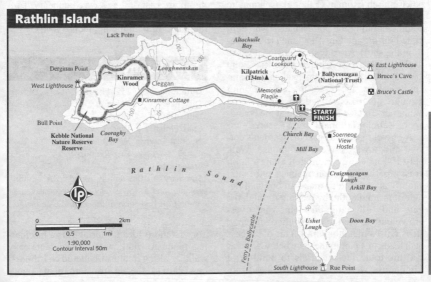

Rathlin Island

Lack Point
Alluchuile Bay
Coastguard Lookout
Derginan Point
Loughnanxkan
Kilpatrick (134m)▲
West Lighthouse ⚲
Kinramer Wood
Cleggan
■ Kinramer Cottage
Memorial Plaque
Ballyconagan (National Trust)
East Lighthouse
Bruce's Cave
Bruce's Castle
Bull Point
Kebble National Nature Reserve Reserve
Cooraghy Bay
Harbour
START/ FINISH
Church Bay
Mill Bay
Soerneog View Hostel
R a t h l i n   S o u n d
Craigmacagan Lough
Arkill Bay
Ushet Lough
Doon Bay
0   1   2km
0   0.5   1mi
1:90,000
Contour Interval 50m
Ferry to Ballycastle
South Lighthouse ⚲ Rue Point

on the eastern side of the harbour, also serves inexpensive meals. There is a small **shop** close to the harbour.

Getting There & Away A daily ferry service from Ballycastle is operated by **Caledonian MacBrayne** (☎ 2076 9299; ⓦ www .calmac.co.uk). From June to September there are four crossings each way (£8.40 return, 45 minutes). Boats leave Ballycastle at 10am, noon, 4.30pm and 6.30pm (7pm on Friday). Boats leave Rathlin at 8.30am and 11am, and 3.30pm and 5.30pm. The winter schedule has boats leaving Ballycastle twice daily at 10.30am and 4pm (4.30pm on Friday).

GETTING TO/FROM THE WALK
Although the walk starts and finishes from the harbour, you can shorten the walk by using the **minibus service** (☎ 2076 3451, 077-4058 6898), which operates on demand between the harbour and West Lighthouse.

THE WALK
Walk left (west) from the harbour, past the shop, and turn right at a church (Church of Ireland). Climb steeply along a narrow road and turn left at a junction, passing the island's other church (Roman Catholic). Continue to climb steeply to reach a **memorial plaque** commemorating the 500 islanders who emigrated during the Great Famine (10 minutes from the start). Already there are great views to the south across Church Bay, Rue Point and out to the cliffs of Fair Head on the mainland. Follow the road for another hour through quiet countryside before passing Kinramer Cottage and arriving at the boundary of **Kebble National Nature Reserve**.

A gravel road leads past the warden's cottage and towards West Lighthouse. Walk only 100m before turning left along a faint, grassy path. You soon reach a red metal gate. It is possible to make an optional detour of around 800m by passing through the gate and following the somewhat overgrown path to the top of a flight of concrete steps with a metal handrail. This old access path leads to a pier in the cove below – it was via this route the materials to build West Lighthouse were brought to the headland.

The path winds steeply and impressively beneath the cliff face, although vertigo sufferers will not appreciate the views. Follow it for as long as you want to before retracing your steps back to the red gate.

Walk west across a field to a wooden gate, from where the cliff line can be followed to the lighthouse. Hexagonal basalt columns and wildflowers line the coast, although care should be taken along the cliffs. Seabirds circling below become more numerous as you progress, and sea stacks break the swells beyond the foot of the cliffs. The way is undulating and stiles provide crossing points over fences as you near the lighthouse.

To access **West Lighthouse** and the viewing platform, follow the obvious concrete path down through a series of gates, which will be locked unless an RSPB official is in attendance. Once you've visited West Lighthouse you can continue northeast along the cliff tops, past Derginan Point and down past a small waterfall to the fringe of Kinramer Wood. Continue along the cliffs to a fence on the eastern boundary of Kinramer Wood, where there are good views across Loughnanskan and Lack Point. Follow the fence south to reach the lighthouse road almost a kilometre east of the reserve boundary. Turn left and return to Church Bay (one hour from the junction with the lighthouse road).

Tory Island

Duration	3½–4 hours
Distance	11km
Difficulty	easy
Start/Finish	West Town
Nearest Towns	West Town (p191), East Town (p192)
Transport	boat

Summary A 10th-century round tower, puffin colonies and a wonderfully rugged coastline are among the highlights of this remote-island walk.

Tory Island (Oileán Thóriagh) is a fascinating place to visit, with some great, easy walking along its storm-battered coastline. It lies 12km off the northwestern tip of County

Donegal and, because ferry services can be affected by winds from every direction, it is often difficult to get to (and leave!). This and its size – Tory is only 5km long and rarely more than 1km wide – contribute to a palpable feeling of remoteness. Standing on the highest point of Dún Balair on a stormy day is quite an experience, especially as you look out across the cliffs of the north coast with spray blowing across the entire island.

This route has two distinct loops that can be readily split into two very short walks. The first loop (5km) explores the low-lying western half of the island and visits the lighthouse. The second loop (6km), takes in Dún Balair and the magnificent cliffs at Tory's eastern tip. The total ascent of the route is around 100m. The walk is feasible as a day trip depending on the ferry schedule, but an overnight visit adds to the experience. Early summer is the best time to visit if you are interested in birds.

HISTORY

Evidence of a Neolithic community has been found on Tory, but the earliest visible signs of habitation are the round tower and Tau Cross. Both are a legacy of the monastery founded here in the 7th century by St Columba (St Colmcille) – the tower is one of the most prominent buildings on the island and dates from the 10th century, while the Tau Cross is one of only two T-shaped crosses in Ireland. Despite the Christian influence, gods of pre-Celtic myth crop up frequently in local folklore, particularly Balor, the one-eyed chief of the Fomorians, after whom Dún Balair is named.

Throughout the centuries, physical isolation (it has been known for the island to be cut off for as long as six weeks by storms) has engendered a resourcefulness and resilience in the islanders that has led to peculiar but necessary customs. For example, it was common until a few decades ago for couples to continue to live in their respective family homes after marriage, such was the shortage of land. Isolation also had its blessings – the potato blight that devastated crops throughout Ireland during the Great Famine did not reach Tory. However, emigration has affected Tory

as much as other islands, and in recent times the population has been in decline.

NATURAL HISTORY

Much of Tory's desolate appearance stems from the fact that islanders have long since stripped every morsel of peat from the island to use as fuel. However, the island's shallow lakes and neglected fields provide habitat for a variety of species. Birds are the main attraction for wildlife fans. Puffins breed on the northern cliffs in early summer, along with razorbills, guillemots, fulmars and great black-backed gulls. Tory is also a stronghold of the endangered corncrake, whose distinctive cry (like two sticks rubbing together) can be heard in early summer.

PLANNING
Maps

Use OSI 1:50,000 map No 1. Note that many of the small tracks on the west side of the island are not shown on this map.

NEAREST TOWNS
West Town

Tory's main settlement, West Town (Baile Thiar) is also the focal point of activity. Ferries dock at the pier in the village centre.

Places to Stay & Eat A modern hotel overlooking the harbour, **Óstán Thóraig** (☎ 074-913 5920; singles/doubles €65/100) has a restaurant specialising in seafood, and the bar also serves food. **Bru Thórai** (☎ 074-916 5145; dorm beds €12; open May-Sept) is a hostel tucked away on the west side of town. **Caife an Cheagháin** serves snacks and meals (mostly of the 'with chips' variety). There is also a small **shop** on the island, but you should take most supplies with you.

Getting There & Away Ferry services to West Town are operated by **Donegal Coastal Cruises** (Turasmara; ☎ 074-953 5061) from Bunbeg (€22, one hour 30 minutes) and Magheraroarty (€22, 50 minutes). Magheraroarty is often on road signs in the Irish: Machaire Uí Rabhartaigh. During July and August the first daily sailing leaves Bunbeg at 9am. The remaining three sailings depart

Magheraroarty at 11.30am, and 1.30pm and 5pm. During June and September there are three sailings daily (the first from Bunbeg and the remaining two from Magheraroarty), in October there is one daily sailing (from Bunbeg), and between November and May five weekly sailings (from Bunbeg).

Lough Swilly Bus Co (☎ *074-912 2863*) has regular services connecting Letterkenny (p259) to both Bunbeg (€6.50, three hours, twice daily Monday to Saturday) and Magheraroarty (19km beyond Bunbeg), passing through Dunfanaghy (p266), Falcarragh (p274) and Dunlewy (p267). There are also connections south, through Burtonport (p193), to Dunglow (€4, one hour 10 minutes, twice daily Monday to Saturday).

East Town

A 20-minute walk from the harbour and little more than a scattering of bungalows, East Town (Baile Thoir) is even quieter (if that is possible) than West Town. There is a good B&B, **Grace Duffy's** (☎ *074-913 5136; singles/doubles €27/43; open Apr-Oct*), which provides evening meals (€12.70) prepared with organically grown produce.

THE WALK

From the pier walk up past the Tau Cross onto the main road running through West Town. Turn left, walk past the **round tower**, and at the edge of the town turn left at a fork, following a narrow road out past Loch Ó Dheas to the **lighthouse**. A high wall encloses the lighthouse but you can walk around this to reach the most westerly point

on Tory. A small stone enclosure acts as a graveyard for eight bodies recovered from HMS *Wasp*, which sank close to Tory in 1884. The navy vessel was on its way to Tory to collect overdue rents; since then, no rents have been paid on the island.

Continue along a track to the ruins of a Lloyds signal station and turn left, following another track up to a small house, which the acclaimed landscape and portrait artist Derek Hill used on his visits to Tory. Follow a faint footpath along the eastern shore of the small peninsular to return to the main track. Turn left along this and follow it back down into West Town (1½ hours from the start).

Walk through the town and head east across a gentle rise to reach East Town. Turn left at a junction and follow the road out to Port Doon. Continue straight ahead where the main road swings right, following the minor road to where it ends on a thin neck of grassy land, giving access to the wonderful cliff-ringed eastern promontory. Walk out across the open ground, climbing steadily past stone cairns to **Dún Balair** (one to 1¼ hours from West Town). At 83m, this is the modest highpoint of the island. Although a promontory fort once graced this spot, little evidence is visible today. Instead panoramic views predominate. To the south the mountainous north coast of County Donegal is spread out along the horizon, with the summits of Muckish, the Aghlas and Errigal prominent. To the east, a 500m-long, knife-edged fin of rock, some 50m high, thrusts out into the ocean. A couple of small stone cairns on the furthest point proves that some brave souls have ventured that far. The eye is also led west across the rest of the island by the sweep of dizzying granite cliffs that protect Tory's northern shores.

Descend back to the road and then trace the cliffs west along the north coast, passing some amazingly jagged sea-stacks, to a large hole set back from the cliffs. This is actually a collapsed cave, and it is possible to scramble down into the grassy depression to get a better look at the natural tunnel that still connects it to a cliff-ringed inlet. Now descend back onto the road, turn right and continue back into West Town.

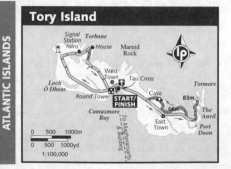

Tory Island map

Arranmore Island

Duration	5–5½ hours
Distance	14.5km
Difficulty	moderate
Start/Finish	Leabgarrow
Nearest Towns	Leabgarrow (p193), Burtonport (p193)
Transport	boat

Summary An outstandingly scenic circuit on one of Donegal's more accessible islands, featuring precipitous cliffs, rocky islets and sea caves.

On Arranmore Island (Árainn Mhór) you can make up your own walk according to the weather and time available. The walk described is an anticlockwise circuit taking in both the impressive sea cliffs on the north coast and the highest point (227m), near Cluidaniller (226m), in the boggy centre. The total ascent is 320m. The walk starts and finishes on narrow roads, although you are unlikely to be bothered by traffic. Elsewhere much of the ground is heavily grazed grassland, which is generally easy walking.

Other route possibilities on the island are provided by the Arranmore Way (Siúloid Árainn Mhór), which comprises three linked, waymarked walks along roads and tracks. Route I (red arrows), the longest, follows an anticlockwise course northwest to the lighthouse and across moorlands in the southwest to meet the end of the public road at Rannagh. Routes II (green) and III (blue-black) are shorter, and concentrated in the settled southeast of the island. Substantial signboards with directional arrows and place names indicate crucial junctions; there aren't any intermediate waymarkers. The way starts at the craft shop about 250m south of the ferry pier.

PLANNING
Maps
Use the OSI 1:50,000 map No 1. Arranmore Way is not marked, nor is the lighthouse.

NEAREST TOWNS
Leabgarrow
This is the main settlement on the island. **Arranmore Hostel** (☎ 074-952 0015; dorm beds/doubles €12/28) is at the back of the sandy beach. Several B&Bs are scattered about the island's southeastern corner, including **Bonner's** (☎ 074-952 0532; singles/doubles €32/60) near the ferry pier, where you'll also find the **Ferryboat Restaurant** serving chips and burgers. **Glen Hotel** (☎ 074-952 0505; singles/doubles €30/60; open Apr-Oct), just west of the ferry pier, serves bar meals. The hotel is at the eastern end of the road that crosses the island. There is also a small, well-stocked **shop** beside **Phil Ban's Bar** at the back of the long, sandy beach.

Getting There & Away A small vehicle ferry, operated by **Arranmore Island Ferries Service** (☎ 074-952 0532), runs from Burtonport to Leabgarrow (€9 return, 30 minutes). There are as many as eight sailings a day in July and August, with the first boat leaving Burtonport at 8.30am and the last leaving Leabgarrow at 8pm. During the rest of the year there are at least five sailings Monday to Saturday and three on Sunday.

Burtonport
Most visitors to Arranmore simply pass through Burtonport. If you need to stay, try **Campbells Pier Guesthouse** (☎ 074-954 2017; singles/doubles €33/56) close to the pier, or **Teac Hughie Ban** (☎ 074-954 2104; singles/doubles €29/46), which is further up the hill back from the sea. However, it is worth stopping for a meal at **Kipper's Tavern** or the **Lobster Pot**, both of which serve decent bar meals with fish specialities. There is also **The Cope**, a fairly large supermarket.

Getting There & Away There are regular **Lough Swilly Bus Co** (☎ 074-912 2863) services between Burtonport and Letterkenny (€7, 2¾ hours, one daily Monday to Saturday), via the north Donegal towns of Dunfanaghy (p266) and Falcarragh (p274). There are connections from Letterkenny to Derry, Sligo, Galway and Dublin.

THE WALK
From the ferry pier follow the road around in front of Bonner's and bear right over a bridge. Turn left onto the road that crosses

the island to the lighthouse. Walk uphill for about 400m, passing Glen Hotel, and take the first road on the right. Turn left after 1km and, 500m later, take a right, following red waymarkers for the Arranmore Way. Turn left onto a vehicle track of yellow stone and follow it gently uphill for 1km, turning right onto a smaller bog track opposite a marker for the Arranmore Way.

The track turns into a peaty path, soon dwindling to nothing as you head out across open slopes of heather and tussock grass towards a line of fence posts running along the top of the ridge ahead. The fence marks the edge of the cliffs at **Torneady Point** (two hours from the start), and a sudden, dizzying view is now revealed across the cliffs of the north coast. The cliffs, which reach 150m in height, sweep around in a horseshoe for over 1km towards Rinrawros Point. The bay is littered with the debris of millions of years of erosion – huge, sheer-sided islands, stacks and pinnacles still defying the pounding swells.

Follow the cliffs first southwest and then west, descending across short grass to the **lighthouse** and its keepers' residences at Rinrawros Point. Built at the end of the 19th century, this was the first lighthouse in County Donegal, and its beam is the most powerful of any lighthouse in Ireland.

Now walk southeast along the obvious road, passing an old coastguard station (used during World War I and later burnt by the IRA during the civil war). Climb steadily towards the island's interior; Lough Shore (30 to 45 minutes from the lighthouse), which you pass on the right, is famous for its stock of rainbow trout. Turn right onto a track shortly before a concrete filtering plant, now following waymarks for the Arranmore Way. The track leads up onto the boggy centre and allows you to make a short detour (a few minutes return) to the southeast to take in the top of **Cluidaniller** (226m). The views from here, particularly of the Donegal mountains to the east are superb. The track then swings around to the southeast (at this point you can detour to the southwest to visit the island's unnamed highpoint at 227m, 10 to 15 minutes return, where the views of Slievetooey to the southwest are good) and begins to descend steadily down to a road along the Owenballintra River. Follow the paved road down to its junction with the island's main road. Turn left to reach Leabgarrow and the ferry pier in 20 to 25 minutes.

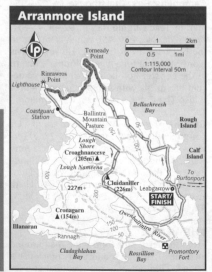

Clare Island

Duration	5–5½ hours
Distance	15km
Difficulty	moderate
Start/Finish	Fawnglass
Nearest Towns	Fawnglass (p195), Westport (p218)
Transport	boat

Summary An impressive walk along the high sea cliffs of an island rich in history and wildlife. The stiff climb to Knockmore is rewarded with great views of the mainland coast.

At the mouth of Clew Bay, Clare Island is the most mountainous of the Atlantic Islands. It boasts tremendous walking packed into 10 sq km of rugged, cliff-fringed terrain. Many short, easy walks are possible along the roads and tracks of the eastern and southern areas, but to get the best from Clare Island you really need to visit the cliffs on the northwest shores. If the weather is fine, the climb to the summit of Knockmore will reward you with panoramic views, although 600m of ascent means this is one of the toughest island walks described in this book.

Walkers looking for an easier variation of the described walk can follow the route to the lighthouse, then proceed a couple of kilometres along the cliffs before heading back inland towards Fawnglass along any one of several tracks. Such circuits are around 11km long and avoid the steepest climbs – allow four to 4½ hours.

HISTORY

Ancient field boundaries, numerous *fulachta fiadh* (horseshoe-shaped mounds of burnt stone – perhaps cooking sites) and a megalithic tomb are ample evidence of Neolithic communities on Clare Island from perhaps 3000 BC. Cistercian monks arrived on the island in the 13th century AD and a small abbey still exists.

One of the island's most infamous former inhabitants was Grace O'Malley (1530–1603), whose much-modified castle still overlooks the harbour. This 'pirate queen' controlled much of Connacht and was a thorn in the side of the English and their allies as she plundered their ships in Clew Bay.

NATURAL HISTORY

Clare Island is a Special Area of Conservation. The celebrated Irish naturalist Robert Lloyd Praeger (1865–1953) organised the Clare Island Survey of 1909–11, which was the world's first area-specific biological survey. Of the flora surveyed on Clare, 585 species were new to Ireland, 55 new to the British Isles and 11 new to science. The cliffs of the northwest provide nesting sites for birds – most prominently fulmars, but also choughs, an increasingly rare bird, which looks like a small raven but has a red bill.

PLANNING
Maps
Use OSI 1:50,000 map No 30.

NEAREST TOWNS
See Westport (p218)

Fawnglass
The townland of Fawnglass includes the harbour and most of Clare Island's amenities.

Places to Stay & Eat At the back of the beach there is a small, enclosed grass area for **camping** *(camping per person €4)*. **Bay View Hotel** *(☎ 098-26307; singles/doubles €40/70)* serves bar food and has an adjacent hostel that was undergoing refurbishment at the time of writing. Among the several B&Bs you could try **Granuaile House** *(☎ 098-26250; singles/doubles €25/50)*, which is close to the pier and serves evening meals on request. There is a small **shop** on Church Rd. For snacks, lunches and evening meals, **Wavecrest Restaurant** *(☎ 098-26546)* is 2.3km from Fawnglass along Church Rd.

Getting There & Away Two companies, **Clare Island Ferries** *(☎ 098-28288)* and **O'Malley's Ferries** *(☎ 098-25045)*, operate between Roonagh Quay and Clare Island (€15 return, 25 minutes). Both companies have up to eight sailings daily during July and August, and fierce competition means that cheap fares are sometimes available. There are three sailings daily during May, June and September. Call the operators for winter schedules.

Roonagh Quay is around 28km west of Westport via Louisburgh.

THE WALK
Turn right (north) from the pier and follow a small road around the back of the beach. Continue uphill past the community centre, following signs for the lighthouse. The road winds inland and climbs across a modest spur, before descending gently towards the coast. At a junction, turn right and climb steadily in a northerly direction to reach the **lighthouse**, impressively perched on the cliff edge, one to 1½ hours from the pier.

Follow the cliff edge southwest, staying on the landward side of a fence. Several

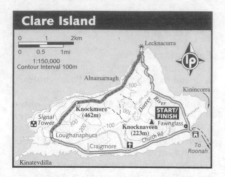

Clare Island

0   1   2km
0   0.5   1mi
1:150,000
Contour Interval 100m

gravity-defying stone walls. Some of the distance you will cover will be along quiet roads, but there are still considerable stretches of green lanes or *boreens* that wind between the stone walls. On Inisheer in particular you can also wander along the wild rocky shores, free from the confines of roads or tracks. Many of the tiny, walled fields and much of the limestone pavement is richly endowed with wildflowers during spring and early summer. On all three islands there are numerous archaeological features including huge forts and early Christian chapels.

steep climbs and descents follow, but the close-cropped turf is generally firm underfoot and the tremendous views of Knockmore and the cliffs are worth the effort. The route swings around to the west as you progress onto the east ridge of Knockmore, climbing unrelentingly to the summit trig (1½ to two hours from the lighthouse). From **Knockmore** (462m) views encompass numerous islands to the south, including Inishturk and Inishbofin, the mountains of Connemara and County Mayo, Croagh Patrick and Achill Island.

Continue along the broad summit ridge for 500m, passing a large stone cairn. Descend steeply to the southwest, following a shoulder towards the prominent track and bungalows below. Out to the west you can see the ruins of a Napoleonic Signal Tower. Once on the road, turn left and begin the walk back to Fawnglass. The 5.5km of paved road will take 1½ to two hours, depending on your pace, and is enlivened by good views of the County Mayo coastline and a chance to visit the Cistercian abbey. The abbey contains some unusual wall paintings of medieval origin, and a canopy tomb that is believed to be the burial place of Grace O'Malley.

The Aran Islands

The three Aran Islands of Inishmore, Inishmaan and Inisheer offer easy walks through fascinating landscapes clad with limestone pavement and patterned with mosaics of

HISTORY

According to folklore, the Fir Bolg people fled to the islands from the mainland and built the great forts as refuges. However, there isn't any concrete evidence for this belief, and the forts were almost certainly built from around 200 BC by Celtic peoples.

St Enda built a monastery on Inishmore at Killeany, at the western end of An Trá Mhór, in AD 490. One of the most important churches on the islands is Inishmore's Teampall Chiaráin (St Ciarán's Church), dedicated to a disciple of Enda and the founder of Clonmacnoise, which is in County Offaly and is possibly Ireland's supreme monastery. Part of the solidly built Teampall Chiaráin, which is still standing, dates from the 8th or 9th century.

In secular matters, the Aran Islands were ruled by the powerful O'Brien family until the late 16th century, when the O'Flahertys prevailed. Their rule was short-lived however, and came to an end when the English government annexed the islands because of their strategic importance.

During the Cromwellian occupation of the 1650s, the islands were garrisoned and eventually handed over to a pro-Cromwell landlord. Until well into the 19th century the islands were neglected by absentee landlords who were only interested in the extortionate rents they could exacted from the tenants.

By about 1920, almost all of the island's families owned their land, thanks to legislation and the work of various government

Dúns of the Aran Islands

The *dúns* on the Aran Islands are among the most impressive archaeological sites in Ireland. These forts, dominating the skyline or perched unnervingly on cliff edges, are thought to date from about 200 BC.

The typically massive walls are, in fact, double walls filled with rubble. These can be 6m or more high, and taper from a base 6m thick to a top of 2m. Within the walls, a tight cluster of stone huts would have provided shelter for people and probably stock. The best examples of these, having been restored, are Dún Dúchathair on Inishmore and Dún Chonchúir on Inishmaan.

The most convincing explanation of the origins of the seven forts on the Aran Islands is that they were built by powerful, well-to-do farming people to demonstrate their wealth and influence, to house cattle and to provide shelter from occasional raiders. Excavations at Dún Aonghasa on Inishmore have uncovered the remains of huts, the bones of a tiny child and some moulds used to cast artefacts in bronze, suggesting to archaeologists that the land was occupied between 500 and 800 BC, before the fort was built.

Dún Aonghasa (or Aengus), on the rim of a 200m-high cliff on the island's southern coast, encloses an area of nearly 6 hectares. The fort proper is protected on the landward side by an intimidating jumble of sharp-edged stones, up to 1.8m high, that stand on end. It has four, roughly crescent-shaped walls, three of them with each end on the cliff edge; the outer wall is 400m long and was probably built with defence in mind.

---

agencies. However, the emigration-induced population decline has seen the number of people living on the islands drop from 3300 in 1851 to 1281 in 2002.

NATURAL HISTORY

The geological make-up of the Aran Islands is almost identical to that of the Burren – see the boxed text 'Karst Wonders of the Burren' (p251). However, the sandy northern coasts of the Aran Islands set them apart from the Burren because of the presence of machair, a low-profile, slender strip of sand. This consists mainly of glacial debris originally blown ashore from a shallow, offshore platform after the last Ice Age, mixed with varying quantities of crushed shells. In many places this sandy landscape is covered with a hardy community of sedges, grasses and wildflowers. In the past it was used for grazing and growing crops such as potatoes. Machair, common on the west coast of Scotland's Western Isles, reaches its southern limit on the Aran Islands.

Maps & Books

The OSI 1:25,000 map *Oileáin Árann* covers the islands and marks archaeological and historic features; the islands are also featured on OSI 1:50,000 map No 51.

Tim Robinson/Folding Landscapes also produces a 1:28,160 *Oileáin Árann* map, which shows all place names in Irish, indicates a wealth of archaeological and historical features, and also has a larger-scale map of the main settlement on each island. Accompanying the map is a companion booklet that explains marked features in lots of detail.

The Book of the Aran Islands, published by Tír Eolas with contributions by nearly two score authors, is hard to beat, although Tim Robinson's superbly written *Stones of Aran: Labyrinth* and *Stones of Aran: Pilgrimage* are also almost mandatory reading for a serious study of the islands. Of several earlier writers, JM Synge's *The Aran Islands* is available in paperback and Inishmore-born Liam O'Flaherty has written several books about life on the islands.

Michael Fewer's *Way-marked Trails of Ireland* describes the ways on all three Aran Islands.

ACCESS TOWNS

See Galway (p210) and Doolin (p251).

GETTING THERE & AROUND

It is possible to fly to each of the islands. **Aer Arann Islands** (☎ 091-593034; W *www .aerarannislands.ie*) has flights year-round from Galway airport to Inishmore (€44 return, eight minutes) and Inisheer (€44 return, eight minutes). Also keep an eye out for the various discount deals available, where you can combine air and rail or bus travel with your accommodation.

However, the ferry is the better way to really become attuned to these remote outposts. The shortest journey to Inishmore is by **Island Ferries** (☎ 091-568903; W *www .aranislandferries.com*) from Rossaveal (€19 return, 35 minutes), at the western end of Galway Bay. The company runs a connecting bus between Rossaveal and Galway (€5 return), departing from its office on Foster St, Galway, one hour before the scheduled ferry. Between April and October there are three sailings daily, with additional sailings during June, July and August. During the rest of the year there are two sailings daily. Island Ferries also operates two services daily year-round to Inisheer (€19 return, one hour) and Inishmaan (€19 return, 50 minutes).

O'Brien Shipping (☎ 091-567676; W *www .doolinferries.com*), which maintains an office in Galway TIC during the summer, operates to all three islands from Galway Docks, calling first at Inishmore (€10/15 one way/return, one hour 30 minutes), then Inishmaan (€10/15 one way/return, one hour 45 minutes) and Inisheer (€10/15 one way/return, two hours). The service runs daily at 10.30am, June to September (three times weekly the rest of the year).

Doolin Ferries (☎ 065-707 4455; W *www .doolinferries.com*) offers the quickest route to Inisheer (€25 return, 30 minutes). There are several sailings daily from Doolin pier from mid-April to September. There are also less frequent daily sailings to Inishmaan (€28 return, one hour) and Inishmore (€32 return, one hour 30 minutes).

Air and ferry services are entirely subject to weather conditions; delays, sometimes for several days, are not unknown – even during summer.

Inishmore

Duration	6–6½ hours
Distance	22km
Difficulty	moderate
Start/Finish	Kilronan (p199)
Transport	boat, plane

Summary This circuit uses green lanes and quiet roads, taking in two prehistoric forts, dramatic cliffs, beaches and plenty of wildflowers.

Inishmore (Inis Mór) is the largest of the three Aran islands – it is 13km long and up to 3km wide – and by far the most developed and populous. As you contend with the tour operators hustling for business, you begin to appreciate why many locals are wondering whether perhaps mass tourism is not a mixed blessing. Nevertheless, it is possible to get away from it all on the quiet roads and lanes. Inishmore has most of the finest archaeological sites, the highest coastal cliffs and the greatest number of sandy beaches of the three islands, and is best explored by a combination of walking and cycling.

The waymarked Inis Mór Way wanders all over the island, making much use of roads, as well as *boreens*. It is marked fairly consistently with yellow arrows and 'walking person' symbols discreetly painted on stones. The walk described here is based on part of the Inis Mór Way and involves 230m of ascent. Only about 10km of the described route follows roads; a considerable proportion of the green roads (8km) are surfaced with walker-unfriendly coarse gravel. The rest of the distance is along grass and gravel paths, and across limestone pavement. If this means less than ideal walking conditions there are compensations: fine, wide-ranging views; opportunities for exploring fascinating limestone pavement; and many archaeological and historic features.

Although the summer schedule for the ferry from Rossaveal (see Getting There & Around, this page) makes it possible for fast walkers to complete the described walk on a day trip, to make the most of a visit an overnight stay is recommended. You could then consider hiring a bike to cover some of the road distance and thus explore more of the many green lanes, especially those leading to the cliffs in the northwest.

PLANNING
Maps & Books

In addition to the Aran Islands maps and books (p197), the leaflet *Inis Mór Way* has a handy map and descriptive notes; it is available locally.

Kevin Corcoran's description of a walk on the island in *West of Ireland Walks* is also useful.

NEAREST TOWN
Kilronan

This is the main settlement on Inishmore. The small **Kilronan TIC** (☎ 099-61263; open Apr–mid-Sept) sells a good range of maps and books. Also at Kilronan is the islands' Heritage Centre (Ionad Árann; ☎ 099-61355; open Apr–Oct), which houses a major display, including historic photographs. An audio-visual presentation introduces the islands' history, flora and fauna, culture and traditions. There is an adjacent bookshop and **coffee shop**. There are several bike hire outlets near the ferry pier, including **Aran Bicycle Hire** (☎ 099-61132; €10 per day). There is a post office with an exchange bureau, but no other banking facilities. For details on how to get to Kilronan see Getting There & Around (p198).

Places to Stay & Eat The **camping ground** (☎ 099-61185; camping per person €4) is in a walled field a few kilometres northwest of Kilronan. Facilities are confined to shower and toilet.

There are several hostels to choose from. In Kilronan there is the prominent **Kilronan Hostel** (☎ 099-61255; dorm beds €13). **Mainistir House Hostel** (☎ 099-61169; dorm beds/doubles €12/20) is 1.5km west of the ferry pier. Breakfast and linen are included, and vegetarian evening meals are also available.

There is a great **supermarket** for self-catering supplies. There are also plenty of places to eat. Apart from the various pubs that offer bar meals there is **Dun Aonghasa & Aran Fisherman Restaurant** (☎ 099-61104), just south of the village centre. The **Bay Café** is a good spot for coffee, lunches and snacks.

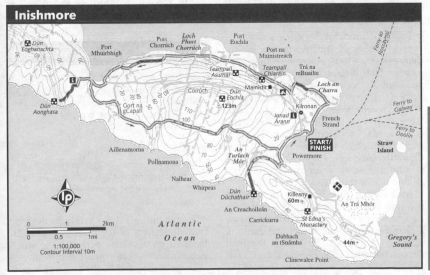

THE WALK

From the pier head northeast along a sealed road. After almost 1km, turn left along a green lane that skirts Loch an Charra. Take the second track on the right and follow it down to the sands of Trá na mBuailte. At the other end of the beach, leave the shore along a green lane, follow this up to a road and turn right.

Opposite the next shingle-fringed bay, Port na Mainistreach (Port of the Monastery), a signed path leads to **Teampall Chiaráin** – the site of the first church on the island (see History, p196). Continue northwest along the road; after another 400m you come to the signed path to the tiny **Teampall Asurnaí**, perched on a ledge against a low cliff and dedicated to a female saint, Soarney.

Continue past Loch Phort Chorrúch for about 1km, passing the remains of a seaweed processing factory that once produced fertiliser and iodine, and leave the road along a green lane, waymarked with a 'walking person' symbol. The lane rises gently southwards; after about 250m go through a gap in the wall on your right and follow a very pleasant, grassy path along the top of an escarpment. This path develops into a wider lane and soon leads on to a road; turn left and then continue around the sands of Port Mhuirbhigh.

Follow the road past waiting horses and carts to the small **Dún Aonghasa Visitor Centre** (☎ 099-61008; admission €1.20; open daily), which houses informative displays and controls access to the gravelled path leading to **Dún Aonghasa** (three hours from the pier; see the boxed text '*Dúns* of the Aran Islands', p197). Beside the visitor centre is **An Sunda Caoch coffee shop**. The best angle from which to appreciate the fort is the northwest, where slightly higher ground also offers fine views of the vertical cliffs on this side of the island.

Back on the road, return to the junction opposite Port Mhuirbhigh and head south along a waymarked green lane. This passes a clump of limestone bluffs and meets a sealed road – turn right. Follow the road through the small village of Gort na gCapall and climb steeply, with good views of the surrounding mosaic of walled fields opening up. The road becomes a track once you've gained the highest ground, where grassland with clumps of heather replaces the limestone pavement. After about 1km – ignore all cross tracks unless you decide to explore the coastline – the track starts its steep descent and the grass gives way to limestone and hazel scrub. Continue to the road by the shore and head right for 300m before turning right again along a narrow road signed to Dún Dúchathair.

Climb steeply to a T-junction and follow a sign to the *dún*; the narrow road soon yields to coarse gravel. The track passes above the bright green vegetation of An Turlach Mór, a turlough, and climbs onto limestone pavement. Leave the track where a low wall crosses it and head southeast, in the direction of a *dún* sign, across the pavement. Breaks in the low stone walls and strips of grass between the clints make for fairly easy walking to the fort, perched on the edge of the cliff. Unburdened by official signs and in a more remote setting, **Dún Dúchathair** is more atmospheric than the larger, better known Dún Aonghasa.

Return to the main road, from where it's a little more than 1km back to the start at Kilronan.

Inisheer

Duration	5 hours
Distance	12km
Difficulty	moderate
Start/Finish	Inisheer ferry pier
Nearest Towns	Inisheer (p201), Doolin (p251)
Transport	boat, plane

Summary A varied circuit of a fascinating stormswept island, following quiet lanes and rock platforms beside the Atlantic Ocean.

Although Inisheer (Inis Oírr) lacks the great prehistoric forts of the other two Aran Islands, it encapsulates perfectly the windswept limestone landscape, the intricate web of stone-walled fields, the amazing wealth of wildflowers and the beguiling, on-the-edge-of-the-world experience. There is also a wealth of other sites with historic and prehistoric significance, several of which can be visited during the described walk. This is the smallest of the three Aran Islands, and can be explored during the summer on a day trip from Doolin.

The route described virtually circumnavigates the island and takes you through the settled northern fringe, past the stone-walled fields in the centre and south, and around the wild and rocky south coast. For all but 2km along the southern shore, the walk follows quiet lanes. The total ascent of this route is around 100m. You'll come across yellow waymarks on some sections of the walk. These mark the route of the Inis Oírr Way, which confines itself to the northern two-thirds of the island.

NEAREST TOWNS
See Doolin (p251)

Inisheer
All inhabited buildings on Inisheer are clustered around the northern shore. In general, the island achieves the delicate balance of providing enough facilities for visitors without losing the natural atmosphere of the locality. There is a post office and a good choice of accommodation. For details on how to get to Inisheer see Getting There & Around (p198).

Places to Stay & Eat There is a **camping ground** (☎ 099-75008; camping per person €5) on a windswept sandy area behind the white sands of An Trá.

The only hostel on the island is **Brú Radharc na Mara** (☎ 099-75024; dorm beds/doubles €12/32). The hostel overlooks the harbour and breakfast is also available. Of the several B&Bs on the island, **Ard Mhuire** (☎ 099-75005; singles/doubles €25/50) is especially well presented, and is located just in front of the pier. **Tigh Ruairí** (☎ 099-75002; singles/doubles €35/70) is adjacent to the **shop** and **pub** of the same name.

Most of the pubs offer bar meals: **Tigh Ruairí** and **O'Flaherty's Ostan Inis Oírr**

(☎ 099-75020) have comprehensive menus. For something more elaborate try **Fisherman's Cottage Bistro** (☎ 099-75073), which is a few hundred metres west of the pier. The bistro specialises in fish and also has a selection of vegetarian dishes. Alternatively there is always the **chip van** located at the top of the pier.

THE WALK
From the ferry pier walk west along the narrow road parallel to the shore and continue past Fisherman's Cottage Bistro. Ignore the waymarker pointing left at the next junction and go on to the small fishing pier at the northwest corner of the island. Continue along the road, now with a gravel surface, past another acute-angled junction on the left (where the waymarkers reappear). Here the shingle shore is on one side and the dense mosaic of fields, enclosed by remarkably intact stone walls, is on the other.

About 1km from the acute junction, turn left with the painted sign, and about 100m along the paved lane is **Tobhar Eínne**, which is an old holy well situated within a walled enclosure.

Return to the coast road and continue southwest as it becomes a rough track. After about 600m, head roughly south across the limestone pavement and strips of grass to the shore. Follow the gently sloping rock platform around the southwestern headland (Ceann na Faochnaí) and east to the **lighthouse** near Fardurris Point (two hours from the ferry pier).

Walk around the wall enclosing the lighthouse and use a stile to cross another wall by the entrance gate. Now back on a level surface, follow the road generally northeast as it climbs gradually. Access to **Cill na Seacht Niníon** (the Church of the Seven Daughters) is from a point 1.5km from the lighthouse, almost opposite two metal-roofed sheds on the right; a pillar next to a gate bears the chapel's name and an arrow points vaguely in its direction. Use stiles to cross three fields to a rusty gate in the ivy-clad walls around the chapel site. In the largest stone enclosure are five grave slabs, one of which still has a faint, incised cross.

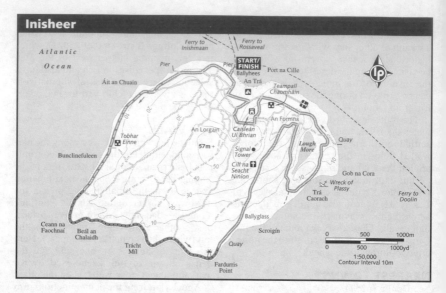

Back on the road, continue northeast to the village of An Formna. Take the right fork then turn right again at a T-junction and head south along the road above Lough More. Keep left at a track junction and continue to the Atlantic shore with the wreck of the *Plassy* just ahead (one hour from the lighthouse). This coastal freighter and one-time armed trawler was driven onto the rocks in March 1960. Local lifeboat crews, helped by about 60 islanders, brought the 11 crew members safely ashore (the bar of Tigh Ned, near the harbour, has a collection of photographs and documents detailing the rescue).

Follow the track north. This track then becomes a sealed road at the northern end of Lough More. Continue to follow the road along the northern shore of the island, past the airstrip.

Here you can diverge, if you wish, to the sandy hummock that shelters the ancient **Teampall Chaomháin** (the church of St Keevaun's. This small, cross-shaped church, which is dedicated to the island's patron saint, is remarkably intact considering it was buried under the sand until the 19th century, when it was rediscovered.

A little further along the road, turn left to reach the 15th-century **Caisleán Uí Bhrian** (O'Brien's Castle), which is the most prominent structure on the island. From the castle follow the narrow road northwest, turn right at a T-junction and then make your way through the maze of lanes back to the pier.

Southwest Islands

The mountainous and fragmented southwest coast of Ireland features numerous small islands – most of which are uninhabited. Two of the more significant of these islands, from a walker's point of view, are Clear and Great Blasket. These two islands provide different insights into the various challenges of island life – contrast the small but vibrant community on Clear Island with the stark ruins of the abandoned village on Great Blasket.

Although Great Blasket Island has the edge in terms of dramatic scenery, walkers on Clear Island have the chance to see tremendous numbers of seabirds, depending on the time of year.

Great Blasket Island

Duration	3½ hours
Distance	8km
Difficulty	easy–moderate
Start/Finish	Great Blasket ferry landing
Nearest Towns	Dunquin (p146), Great Blasket (p204)
Transport	boat

Summary Exploring perhaps the most evocative of the Atlantic islands, this walk features a ruined village and excellent coastal views.

If you are lucky enough to get a day when the boats are running to Great Blasket, grab it. The island is hilly and has a natural, remote character; there are no paved roads and the only buildings are a small cluster of largely ruined stone cottages on the eastern shore. The island's location off the dramatic southwestern tip of the Dingle Peninsula also ensures stunning coastal views.

Great Blasket is an extension of the mountain range that runs down the centre of the Dingle Peninsula, and is the largest of the six isles of the Blasket group. However, at only 6km by 1.2km in size, you can't forget that you're on a tiny island, surrounded by, and at the mercy of, the elements. Despite this, some 208 species of plant have been identified on the island, and most visitors will be rewarded with sightings of seabirds, rabbits and seals. The island's hilly terrain means the route involves 300m of ascent.

For those catching the ferry from Dunquin, it is well worth combining a trip to the island with a visit to the **Blasket Centre** (☎ 066-915 6444; adult/child €3.10/1.20; open daily Mar-Oct), a short distance from Dunquin pier.

HISTORY

Great Blasket Island has been inhabited since the Iron Age – Doon promontory fort (of which little is now visible) is thought to date back to around 800 BC. When parish records

Struggles & Joys of Island Life

Tomas O'Crohan (1856–1937) lived on Great Blasket Island all his life. Raised – as all islanders were – speaking only Irish, he spent the latter years of his life teaching his language to scholars seeking to document the Gaelic vernacular. His novel, *The Islandman*, is an entertaining, autobiographical work that describes his childhood and adult life on Great Blasket. Thanks to a sensitive translation into English by Robin Flower, the book also conveys a sense of the lyrical phraseology and creative expression that is at the heart of the Irish language.

The novel provides a wonderful insight into island life at the turn of the 20th century. Like many of the island children, O'Crohan kept a pet 'gully' when he was young; a seabird that he had risked his life to snatch from a cliff edge. He also had a dog, one of the best 'rabbiters' on the island, who would be sent into warrens to fetch the rabbits from inside. Returning to the village after a day's rabbiting with eight fat animals slung over his shoulder was ample reward for a hard day's work on the hills.

The back-breaking toil of turf cutting, constructing his own house with no help from others and braving the dangerous waters around the island on fishing trips were all normal aspects of island life. Other anecdotes are more revealing – O'Crohan once had a chunk taken out of his leg by a huge seal that he was trying to bring home for the cooking pot. With the closest medical assistance on the mainland, such incidents could be fatal. According to O'Crohan, islanders managed to prevent infection by strapping a raw chunk of the offending seal to the wound!

The Islandman also has a poignant note; O'Crohan's wife died young and several of his children were killed before adulthood. The population of Great Blasket was sliding into irreversible decline, and O'Crohan was acutely aware that his life's experiences would soon be lost forever. The incident that finally pushed the islanders to desert their home was to come after his death. One of the young men on the island became ill, but was prevented from seeing a doctor by a week-long storm. The man died; had he lived on the mainland he would probably have been saved.

began in 1821, the island had 128 inhabitants. Each family had a potato garden and kept sheep on the hills. Their food was supplemented by wild rabbits, seals, seabirds, fish and shellfish. Thanks to this varied diet, the islanders suffered less than people on the mainland during the Great Famine.

A school was built in the early 20th century and a post office with a telephone was built in the 1930s. Unfortunately, it was probably this progress into the modern world that ended the viability of life on the island. With a dwindling population, the school became redundant. Hospitals, priests, and markets for produce were all on the mainland, a short but dangerous journey away. In 1953, the last remaining families were rehoused on the mainland.

Given the number of visitors that now arrive at the island during the summer, it is easy to wonder whether tourism could have offered a lifeline for a viable island existence had the community just managed to hold on for another generation. It is a question that will never be answered, however, and today it is the inhabitants of Dunquin and Dingle who benefit from activities on Great Blasket.

PLANNING
When to Walk
Good weather is a prerequisite for this walk, both because boats don't run in adverse conditions and because the island has limited shelter (you will be waiting in the open for the return boat).

Maps & Books
The OSI 1:50,000 map No 70 covers Great Blasket Island. To get yourself into the mood, you might like to read some of the books written by islanders about life on Great Blasket. Thomas O'Crohan's *The Islandman* is guaranteed to add to your experience (see the boxed text 'Struggles and Joys of Island Life', p203). Written in Irish, *Peig*, by Peig Sayers, has long been a text for Irish school children. *An Old Woman's Reflections*, also by Peig Sayers, has an English translation. Kevin Corcoran describes a walk on the island in *Kerry Walks*.

NEAREST TOWNS & FACILITIES
See Dunquin (p146)

Great Blasket
Currently **camping** is permitted free of charge on the island, although at the time of writing there were plans to build an official site. Fresh water is available from tanks at the top of the village, though there are no other amenities. Simple accommodation is available at the **Great Blasket Island Hostel** (☎ 086-848 6687; dorm beds €18; open Apr-Sept) in several restored buildings. Dinner and breakfast can be provided for guests for €16. The island also has a small **café**, which is open daily and serves cakes and drinks.

Getting There & Away Ferry services to Great Blasket are frequently disrupted by bad weather and can be rather chaotic at other times, especially if there are large groups that want to make the journey to the island. Inhospitable terrain and awkward landing sites mean that trips will involve at least one shuttle by inflatable dingy between boat and shore – in fact the boat trip across can be almost as much fun as time spent on the island.

Most visitors approach the Great Blasket from Dunquin. **Islandman Ferries** (☎ 066-915 6422) has frequent daily sailings from Easter to September (€20 return; 20 minutes). Times vary according to demand, but boats generally leave Dunquin on the hour from 10am to 3pm, and return from Great Blasket on the half hour.

It is also possible to take a boat directly from Dingle to Great Blasket. The **Peig Sayers** (☎ 066-915 1344) holds only 12 passengers, and leaves Dingle marina every two hours daily from Easter to September (€30 return; 40 minutes).

THE WALK
From the ferry landing follow the main green path up through the **ruined stone cottages** towards the top right corner of the village. Here you join a grassy track that makes a circuit around Tur Comhartha (231m). Turn left (southeast) and begin to climb around the slopes of this hill. After an initial steep climb

the track levels out and offers easy walking as you begin heading southwest with fine views over the Iveragh Peninsula and the distant Skellig Islands.

At the western end of Tur Comhartha, the track veers back towards the northeast and a narrow footpath continues west. Follow this footpath through bracken and climb past rock-studded viewpoints to the rounded summit of **Slievedonagh** (281m), one to 1½ hours from the start).

The island now narrows to a blunt **ridge** with a steep, rocky drop to the north and more gentle grass slopes to the south. The arête is enjoyably narrow without really being dangerous. Continue along the footpath, dropping down to a col before making the final ascent to **Croaghmore**, the highest point on the island at 292m. From the trig point at the summit there are great views across the remainder of Great Blasket to the isles of Inishvickillane and Inishnabro. A small circle of stones, perhaps the remains of an ancient *clochain*, is clearly visible below.

It is possible to continue to the end of the island, although most people turn around and begin their return journey at Croaghmore. Retrace your steps over Slievedonagh to the track, turning left to return via the island's north shore. Wonderful views of the mainland open up as you reach the village. The white sand cove and turquoise waters of **An Traigh Bhan** are ahead, although the track emerges near the **café** and this might claim your attention first. Return to the ferry landing in good time for your boat.

Clear Island (Oileán Chléire) lies 12km off the coast of west Cork and 6km north of the Fastnet Rock. Also known as Cape Clear, it is 5km long and up to 2km wide, narrowing to a few hundred metres in the centre where the island is almost cut in two by the inlets of North Harbour and South Harbour. This route explores most of the island and involves 300m of ascent.

Clear Island is a popular destination not only for its status as the most southerly point in Ireland (discounting Fastnet Rock), but also because of the vast number of seabirds that nest here or pass overhead on migratory journeys. Clear has a more vibrant atmosphere than many of the other Atlantic islands, reflected in the fact that it is one of the few islands to have a growing population. The 150 permanent residents earn a living from a variety of sources. There is a goat farm, a holistic medicine centre, sailing and diving schools, and courses in Irish language, together with the traditional fishing and dairy farming economies.

HISTORY
The earliest signs of human habitation are Neolithic boulder burial sites, perhaps 5000 years old. In the northeast corner of the island is a pair of marriage stones that are probably about 2000 years old; one stone has a hole in it and is considered to be the female. Couples were thought to have clasped hands through the stones in marriage ceremonies. Stones such as this are fairly rare in Ireland.

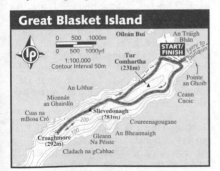

Great Blasket Island

Oileán Buí · An Tráigh Bhán · START/FINISH · Tur Comhartha (231m) · Pointe an Ghoib · An Lóthar · Ceann Cnoic · Mionnán an Ghairdín · Cuas na mBosa Cró · Slievedonagh (281m) · Coureenagougane · An Bheannaigh · Croaghmore (292m) · Gleann Na Péiste · Cladach na gCabhac

0 500 1000m
0 500 1000yd
1:100,000
Contour Interval 50m

In about the 4th century AD, St Ciaran was born on the island and is thought to have established a monastic order at the ruined church at North Harbour. In the 14th century, the O'Driscoll clan – whose descendants still inhabit the island – built Dún an Óir.

In more modern times, a signal tower was built at Carriglure as part of the chain of watchtowers designed to give an early warning of French invasion. Beside it is a lighthouse, built in 1818 and superseded in 1854 by the Fastnet Rock lighthouse, which is also visible from the island.

NATURAL HISTORY

The island is home to about one-third of Ireland's plant species, including some rare plants such as the hairy bird's-foot trefoil and pale butterwort. Wild thyme, wood sage and chamomile line the roads alongside the more common plants of the area. But the real treat on Clear Island are the seabirds. Nesting species include choughs, black guillemots, rock doves and great black-backed gulls, while a long list of rare and sometimes quite exotic species have been recorded during the spring and autumn migrations. May and June are the best months to view nesting birds, while July through to October is the best time to spot migratory species. Towards the end of July numbers of passing shearwaters can reach 10,000 in a single hour!

The island is also one of the foremost recording sites in Europe for cetaceans (whales and dolphins), with killer whales and Risso's dolphins regularly spotted.

The route described here leads itself to being divided into smaller circuits depending on time and energy. The section around the west side of the island covers perhaps the most difficult terrain.

PLANNING
Maps & Books

OSI 1:50,000 map No 88 covers the island. *Walkers Guide to Cape Clear Island* is a local map guide that suggests further walks. *Cape Clear Island: Its People and Landscape*, by Eamon Lankford, is an illustrated book on the history, culture and landscape of the island.

Information Sources

The excellent site w www.oilean-chleire.ie has plenty of useful background and planning information, as well as news of events and festivals.

NEAREST TOWNS & FACILITIES
See Baltimore (p182).

Clear Island

Despite the fact the most visitors to Clear Island are day-trippers, there are enough facilities on the island to make an overnight stay quite viable. The small TIC (☎ 028-39100), at North Harbour, sells natural history books for the area but does not stock OSI maps. The island's Heritage Centre (☎ 028-39119; €2.50; open June-Aug), 2km northeast of North Harbour along the road to the marriage stones, has displays illustrating local life.

Places to Stay & Eat The Clear Island camping ground (☎ 028-39119; camping per person €5; open May-Sept) is located along the road on the west side of South Harbour. The An Óige's Clear Island Youth Hostel (☎ 028-39198; dorm beds €13; open Mar-Oct) has family rooms but closes during the day. There are also several B&Bs on the island, including Ard na Gaoithe (☎ 028-39160; singles/doubles €28/56), which is along the road towards the signal tower and can provide evening meals. Ciarán Danny Mike's (☎ 028-39172; singles/doubles €25/50), between North Harbour and South Harbour, offers B&B beside the pub of the same name. Lunches and evening meals are also available in the bar.

Although there is a small grocery shop, An Siopa Beag, at North Harbour, self-caterers should bring most supplies with them. Snacks and meals can be found at the chip van that is located beside North Harbour during the summer, and at Cotters Bar, which serves good coffee.

Getting There & Away The Naomh Ciarán II (☎ 028-39135) makes regular crossings between Clear Island and Baltimore (€11.50 return, 40 minutes). Ferries run three or four times daily during July and August, and twice daily during the rest of the year.

Karycraft (☎ 028-28278) also operates a ferry to the island from Skull (€12 return; 45 minutes). There are three crossings daily during July and August, one daily in June, and a demand-led service in May and September.

THE WALK

Turn left at the end of the ferry pier at North Harbour and head south, climbing over the island to South Harbour. Pass in front of the youth hostel and turn left, following the lane towards the old **signal tower** and **lighthouse**. The road turns to a track as it reaches the buildings, and a sign prohibits entry to the site itself.

Turn off the road to the left just before the enclosure, following a faint path around the back of the structure. The path then leads northeast across a small depression, to open terrain beyond. The trail is well-defined in places and less distinct in others as it forges a passage through heather and gorse. Keep to the ridge and pass through gaps in several ruined stone walls, heading in the direction of the wind turbines that crown the summit of Quarantine Hill, Clear Island's highest point. However, the route only goes as far as the small **summit** before Quarantine Hill, which is topped by a wall and offers fine views northeast across wild, undulating ground to the cliffs of Sherkin Island.

Cross the wall and descend west through thick grass (bushwhacking skills may be called on for 30m or so) to fields below. Cross the first field to the top right corner, where there is access to another field. Cross this to the left and negotiate a final stone wall, and you will find yourself back on a paved lane. Turn right and within 500m you come to a crossroads; turn right here onto the 'main' road along the island and follow it northeast. Take the fourth left turn after the crossroads and follow a small road down towards the **marriage stones** (see History,

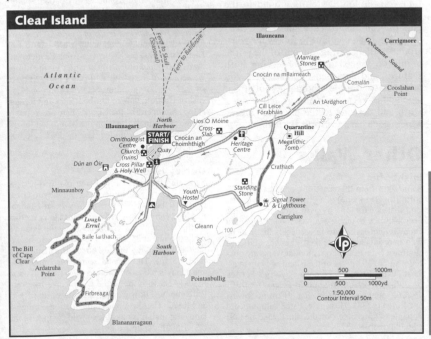

ATLANTIC ISLANDS

p205). A stile and path at the end of the road allows access to the stones themselves.

Return to the main road and turn left to **Gascanane Sound**, where you can take a break on the rocks and enjoy more fine views of the cliffs of Sherkin Island to the northeast. Backtrack to the crossroads, where you should continue straight ahead. The church and then the Heritage Centre are passed before the road climbs across a small **ridge**. There are great views across the western end of the island from here, with the distinctive silhouette of Fastnet Rock in the distance.

Descend back to North Harbour and head south at the road junction. Take the first right at the top of the steep rise and follow a minor road for 200m. Look for a gate on the right (be careful if there is livestock in the field) and follow a track uphill and across a small ridge. Rough slopes lead down to **Dún an Óir**. The views along this section of the walk are quite wonderful, with the Mizen Head Peninsula laid out before you. Follow the cliffs around to the southwest, passing Lough Errul before negotiating an electrified fence. Pass Ardatruha Point and continue to follow the coast around to **Blananarragaun**, one of the prime points on the island for observing both seabirds and cetaceans. In October, you might have trouble finding a spot to sit among the keen birdwatchers. Now walk north and descend to the obvious *boreen*, which leads back to North Harbour.

Other Walks

Inishbofin

Some 9km from the coast of Connemara, Inishbofin (Inis Bo Finne) is a generally low-lying island that is 6km long by 3km wide. It has some fine sheltered beaches, a ruined monastery and a Cromwellian fort. Rare bird species that can be seen here include corncrakes, choughs and corn buntings. Numerous short, circular walks are possible, and a full circuit of the island adds up to almost 20km. Two ferry companies, **King's Ferries** (☎ 095-44642) and **Inishbofin Ferries** (☎ 095-45806), operate from Cleggan, 16km northwest of Clifden (p238). There is a hostel, camping and a couple of good hotels on the island. Use the OSI 1:50,000 map No 37.

ARAN ISLANDS
Inishmaan

Inishmaan (Inis Meáin) is the middle of the Aran Islands and is probably the most natural of the three – visitors are left much more to their own devices than on the other two islands. A waymarked route keeps to the central lanes, but tracks are few in the wild and rocky southern half of the island. A full day can easily be spent completing a coastal circuit, with plenty of off-track walking along the limestone pavements. One place not to miss is Dún Chonchúir, regarded as Ireland's finest hill fort, near the highest point of the island. See Getting There & Around (p198) for details of air and ferry connections to Inishmaan. The island is covered by OSI 1:50,000 map No 51 and OSI 1:25,000 map *Oileáin Árann*.

SOUTHWEST ISLANDS
Bere Island

Just 1km off the coast of the Beara Peninsula, Bere Island is about as convenient as islands get. Poor weather rarely affects ferry crossings and there are tremendous views of the Beara mountains from the high ground. A waymarked spur of the Beara Way makes a 21km figure-of-eight loop around the island, and is described in Michael Fewer's *Way-marked Trails of Ireland*. The entire route takes around seven hours. **Bere Island Car Ferry** (☎ 027-75009) leaves from Castletownbere (p168) and drops you at a pier on the northwestern tip of the island. **Murphy's Ferry Service** (☎ 027-75014) also runs between Pontoon (4km east of Castletownbere on the R572) and Rerrin, at the eastern end of the island. There are a couple of pubs and small shops on the island, but tourist accommodation is limited. Use the OSI 1:50,000 map No 84.

Dursey Island

Separated from the Beara Peninsula by a narrow channel, Dursey is similar in topography to Great Blasket Island. However, Dursey is still inhabited, and can be explored on a 10km-long section of the Beara Way, which takes in the island's highest point at 252m. This route can also be extended by walking out to Dursey Head and back (add 4.5km). The coastal scenery is impressive and many species of bird frequent the cliffs and fields. Access to the island is via cable car from Ballaghboy, 11km west of Allihies on the R575 and R572. There is no accommodation on the island, although it is possible to wild camp. Use the OSI 1:50,000 map No 84.

Central West

The Central West of Ireland stretches from the Burren in County Clare north through Connemara, County Mayo and the hills of County Sligo. It is a region encapsulated by themes of both unity and contrast. The Atlantic Ocean is a constant presence, and the landscape is wild and rugged. At the same time, variety is everywhere, and distinct areas are readily identified according to their unique character. From the amazing limestone formations of the Burren to the sharp, crag-bound peaks of the Twelve Bens; from the country's most holy mountain, Croagh Patrick, to the dramatic cliffs of north Mayo; from the serene beauty of Sligo's waterfalls to the crumbling escarpments that guard its flat-topped hills. There is little in terms of Irish topography that is not represented within this region.

In these stimulating settings, walkers are presented with different opportunities from one area to the next: exploring the finest gathering of wildflowers in the country; challenging themselves over long, strenuous mountain massifs; getting intimate with rolling peat bogland; and, almost everywhere, seeing fine views of mountains, glens and coastlines. It would take years to fully explore a region that offers so much – all most people can do is take their time, open their senses and enjoy!

INFORMATION
Maps & Books
The OSI 1:250,000 map *West*, in the Holiday Map series, neatly covers the region and is useful for general trip planning.

Several books include details of other walks in Connemara and County Mayo. *West of Ireland Walks*, by Kevin Corcoran, has plenty of fascinating natural history and environmental information. *Hill Walkers Connemara and Mayo*, by David Herman, reliably describes 34 routes in a friendly style, while Michael Fewer's *Irish Waterside Walks* includes four walks focused around inland waters in the area. *Walk Guide West of*

Highlights

GARETH McCORMACK

The fascinating limestone landscape, like a vast rock desert, of the Burren near Fanore

- Walking the escarpments of Glencar (p213) and Glenade (p216): towering pinnacles, waterfalls and rare wildflowers
- Exploring some of Ireland's finest coastal cliff walking in remote and peaceful Dún Caocháin (p219)
- Climbing Mweelrea (p234), Mayo's highest peak and a sprawling giant of a mountain full of rugged character
- Wandering across vast limestone pavements in the Burren (p249)

Ireland, by Patrick Simms & Tony Whilde, has succinct descriptions of 30 varied walks.

Information Sources
Ireland West Tourism Authority (☎ 091-563 081; W *www.irelandwest.ie; Forster St, Galway*) covers Counties Galway and Mayo. You'll find planning and accommodation information on the website.

Place Names

Several parts of the region – particularly in the Burren, Connemara and County Mayo – are designated as Gaeltacht areas, where Irish is the first language written and spoken. In these places, road signs and place names are often written in Irish only, without the usual English translation. To facilitate navigation through these areas, Irish names are given in relevant places in the text. See also the Gazetteer (p358).

GATEWAYS
Galway

This large city is a natural gateway to the Burren and Connemara. **Galway TIC** (☎ 091-563 081; W www.irelandwest.ie; Forster St; open year-round) is useful for booking accommodation during busy periods. Outdoor equipment suppliers include **River Deep Mountain High** (☎ 091-563 938; Middle St) and **Great Outdoors** (☎ 091-562 869; Eglinton St), both of which stock a good range of gear, maps and guidebooks.

Places to Stay & Eat The closest camping to the city is at **Ballyloughane Camping & Caravan Park** (☎ 091-755 338; camping per person €8), 5km east of Galway on the N6.

There are plenty of hostels. **Galway Hostel** (☎ 091-566 959; Frenchville Lane; dorm beds/doubles €15/40) is in an old, cramped building, but is clean, close to the station and provides free breakfasts. **Kinlay House** (☎ 091-565 244; Merchant's Rd; dorm beds/doubles €14.50/43) is a modern and well-equipped hostel with spacious rooms, and also offers free breakfasts. If you have a Hostelling International (HI) card then you might want to use the An Óige **Galway International Youth Hostel** (☎ 091-527 411; St Mary's College, St Mary's Rd; dorm beds €9.50; open late-June–late-Aug).

Among the many B&Bs within walking distance of the city centre is the recommended **Mrs Ester Daly** (☎ 091-581 431; 6 Beach Court, Lower Salthill; singles/doubles €29/58). For hotel accommodation you could try **Jury's Galway Inn** (☎ 091-566 444; singles/doubles €94/188) or the **Spanish Arch Hotel** (☎ 091-569 600; singles/doubles €146/228), both of which are centrally located on Quay St.

The best selection of restaurants is on Quay St. **Aideen's Brasserie Eleven** (☎ 091-561 610) is an Italian-style brasserie that caters for vegetarians and people with special dietary requirements. The **Druid Lane Restaurant** (☎ 091-563 015) serves well-presented dishes from an imaginative menu.

Getting There & Away There are **Aer Arann** (☎ 091-593 034; W www.aerarann.ie) flights to Dublin (€70, 45 minutes, six daily and four Sunday) and London Luton (€207, two hours, once daily) from Galway **airport** (☎ 091-755 569; W www.galwayairport.com), which is 6km east of the city. A Bus Éireann service operates between the airport and the city (€3.50, 15 minutes, once daily), departing the airport at 1.40pm. There is a **Budget** (☎ 091-564 570) car hire desk in the arrivals hall.

The **Bus Éireann travel centre** (☎ 091-562 000) is at Cearnt station, adjacent to Eyre Square. As well as connections to just about every town in Ireland there are regular services to Dublin (€12, three hours 40 minutes, 12 daily), Sligo (€11.40, two hours 30 minutes, five daily), Cork (€15.80, four hours 15 minutes, 14 daily) and Killarney (€17.10, four hours 35 minutes, four daily) via Limerick.

Iarnród Éireann (☎ 091-564 222) operates trains between Galway and Dublin's Heuston station (€22, two hours 45 minutes, four daily and three on Sunday).

Sligo

This is the largest town in the north of the region and is a good base for the northern parts of Counties Mayo and Sligo. **Northwest Tourism** (☎ 071-916 1201; Temple St; open year-round) offers general information and accommodation bookings for the area. **Call of the Wild** (☎ 071-914 6905; Rockwood Parade) is the best place in town to pick up outdoor supplies, walking maps and guidebooks.

Places to Stay & Eat The closest camping is **Gateway Camping and Caravan Park**

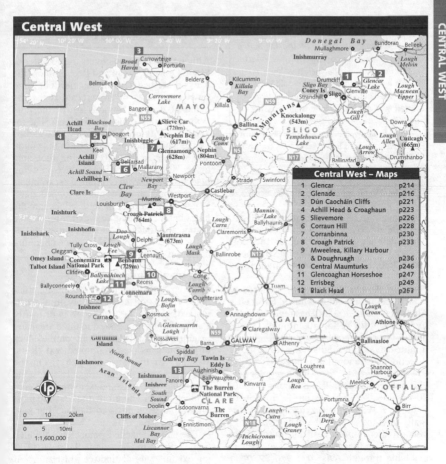

Central West

(☎ 071-914 5618; camping per person €7), a 15-minute walk from Sligo on the N16 towards Manorhamilton.

There are several hostels in Sligo. **Harbour House** (☎ 071-917 1547; Finisklin Rd; dorm beds/doubles from €14/34), 1km northwest of the city centre, is a modern hostel and can provide meals. **Eden Hill Holiday Hostel** (☎ 071-914 4113; Pearse Rd; dorm beds/doubles €11/28) is a 10-minute walk southeast of the city centre and has cosy rooms. The **White House Hostel** (☎ 071-914 5160; Markievicz Rd; dorm beds €10) is centrally located by the river, and the **Yeats Country Hostel** (☎ 071-914 6876; 12 Lord Edward St; dorm beds €12) is beside the bus and train stations.

There are plenty of B&Bs and hotels. The cheaper options are on the edge of town. **Lissadell B&B** (☎ 071-916 1937; Mail Coach Rd; singles/doubles €38.50/59), a 10-minute walk southeast of the centre, is a nonsmoking place. **Sligo Park Hotel** (☎ 071-916 0291; Pearse Rd; singles/doubles €77/140), a 20-minute walk south of town on the N4, is quite modern and has a good restaurant.

Sligo has a good selection of places to eat, including plenty of **fast-food outlets**.

Gleniff Off Limits

A quick glance at a map of the Benbulbin plateau reveals the possibility of a wonderful circular walk round the Gleniff valley.

It is a fantastic circuit and would certainly be included in this book, if the valley were not suffering from a particularly embittered access problem.

Unfortunately, the area – especially around the lower slopes of Ben Whiskin – is currently off limits and if you do decide to walk there it is unlikely that you will be welcome.

For something more substantial, try **Bistro Bianconi** (☎ *071-914 1744; O'Connell St*), which has an Italian theme, or **the Loft** (☎ *071-914 6770; Lord Edward St)*, above Carr's Pub, which offers Mexican dishes.

Getting There & Away If you really want to get in and out in a hurry, **Euroceltic Airways** (☎ *0818-300 100)* has regular flights to/from Dublin (€45, 50 minutes, twice daily). The **airport** (☎ *071-916 8280)* is a 10-minute drive from Sligo on the R292 in the direction of Strandhill. **Bus Éireann** (☎ *071-916 0066; Lord Edward St)* has a regular service between Strandhill and the city (€2.50, 20 minutes, seven times daily Monday to Saturday). While this service doesn't normally pass the airport, the driver will drop you off there on request and can collect you there by prearrangement. Car hire is available through **Avis** *(071-916 8280)* at the airport.

Sligo is well connected by bus and rail to the rest of Ireland.

Bus Éireann has frequent services to Dublin (€12.40, four hours, four daily), Belfast (€22, four hours, three daily and twice on Sunday), Galway (€11.40, two hours 30 minutes, six daily and four on Sunday) and Donegal Town (€9.20, one hour 20 minutes, six daily and three on Sunday).

Iarnród Éireann (☎ *071-916 9888)* operates train services between Sligo station and Dublin's Heuston station (€20, three hours, three daily).

Yeats Country

Although this section covers the counties of Sligo, Leitrim, Cavan and Roscommon, the walks described here are just north of Sligo town in an area often referred to by the name of its most famous son – the poet William Butler Yeats (1865–1939). The romantic quality of Yeats' poetry was fuelled by the landscapes he explored in his youth, and walkers can easily imbibe the same heady draughts of inspiration. Sprawling plateaus fall away in crumbling escarpments and sweeping slopes of close-cropped grass. Waterfalls pour over the cliff edges into the lakes below, lending an air of mini-Alpine grandeur to the area. And, of course, the Atlantic Ocean provides an ever-changing backdrop of light and mood.

NATURAL HISTORY

The area is dominated by flat-topped mountains, which fall away steeply into a network of glens. The local rock is primarily Carboniferous limestone and there are many examples of karst topography on the edges of the plateaus (see the boxed text 'Karst Wonders of the Burren', p251). On the plateaus a layer of impermeable sandstone covers the limestone and is, in turn, covered in blanket bog. Therefore, the best and most interesting walking is to be found around the edges.

The large, detached pinnacles, of which Eagle's Rock in Glenade is the most striking example, are distinctive illustrations of the processes that have also created the steep hills and ridges beneath the cliffs. At the end of the last Ice Age, both Glenade and Glencar were filled with the glacial ice that gouged the U-shaped profiles of the valleys. As the temperature rose, the ice retreated and left the steep, unstable cliffs unsupported. Much material has long since fallen from the cliffs, leaving abrupt cliff lines like those that border the Swiss Valley, while more recent, gradual slippage has left the pinnacles of Glenade detached and in danger of toppling over. (See also the boxed text 'Signs of a Glacial Past', p24.)

For botanists, the Benbulbin plateau is one of the most interesting upland areas of Ireland. Unfortunately, many of the more unusual species cling to rockfaces and are difficult to see. Fringed sandwort is found nowhere else in the British Isles, while the clustered alpine saxifrage and chickweed-leaved willowherb are found nowhere else in Ireland. More common and easier to find are mountain avens, cushion pink and mountain saxifrage.

PLANNING
Maps & Books
Both walks in this section are covered by OSI 1:50,000 map No 16. A good general guide to the area is *North Leitrim Glens*, by David Herman. The guide describes a variety of day walks, and includes notes on local history and geology, accompanied by quotes from Yeats.

ACCESS TOWN
Bundoran
Ireland's consummate tacky holiday town, Bundoran has plenty of facilities. There are several banks, an ATM and a supermarket.

Places to Stay & Eat Dominated by caravans, **Dartry View** (*☎ 071-984 1794; camping per person €8)* also has tent pitches available. **Homefield Hostel** (*☎ 071-984 1288; Bayview Ave; dorm beds/doubles €16/32)* provides a free continental breakfast. Of the numerous B&Bs and hotels, try **Gillaroo Lodge** (*☎ 071-984 2357; West End; singles/doubles €33/46)* or **Grand Central Hotel** (*☎ 071-984 2722; singles/doubles €55/110)*, which is on the main street in the centre of town and has a restaurant. The bar also serves meals.

La Sabbia (*☎ 071-984 2253)*, adjacent to Homefield Hostel and operated by the same people, is a popular and vibrant restaurant with a good selection of mains. Some of the best bar food in town can be found in the **Old Bridge Bar** *(Main St)*, with the bean burger a real surprise given normal standards of vegetarian food in Irish bars.

Getting There & Away There are **Bus Éireann** (*☎ 071-916 0066)* services via Donegal Town and Letterkenny to Derry (€12, two hours, seven daily Monday to Saturday and three on Sunday). There are plenty of buses to Sligo (€6.35, 40 minutes, five daily Monday to Saturday and three on Sunday) and Galway (€13.90, four daily Monday to Saturday and one on Sunday). There are also connecting routes to Belfast and Dublin.

Glencar

Duration	5 hours
Distance	13km
Difficulty	moderate
Start/Finish	Glenvale B&B
Nearest Towns	Sligo (p210), Glencar (p214)
Transport	private

Summary A very scenic walk along a steep and rocky gully to a long and varied cliff line with superb views and some picturesque waterfalls.

This walk and the next (Glenade, p216) explore the edges and adjoining glens of the vast, high plateau sometimes called Benbulbin after that most distinctive of Irish mountains, which forms a promontory on its western end. Glencar is often called Ireland's 'Swiss Valley'; indeed there is such a place and the walk visits it, but it is only a small part of Glencar itself. The valley has huge, limestone cliffs and is one of the best examples of a U-shaped, glacial valley in Ireland. Several waterfalls streak the walls before running into Glencar Lough. Throw in a few conifer plantations and the Alpine imitation is quite effective.

This walk takes in the impressive northern cliffs of Glencar. The approach to the plateau is through an intimidating gully: negotiating this is much easier than it looks, given a little care. The total ascent is 600m. The route can also be extended to include a trip to the summit of Benbulbin (see Side Trip: Benbulbin, p215).

PLANNING
Maps
Use the OSI 1:50,000 map No 16.

NEAREST TOWNS & FACILITIES
See Sligo (p210).

Glencar
A tiny collection of houses in a very beautiful setting, the valley of Glencar (Ghleann an Chairthe) has limited facilities of use to walkers. However, for those who prefer to stay close to the walk rather than in the large town of Sligo, 10km away, the **Glenvale B&B** (☎ 071-916 1706; singles/doubles €25/50) is conveniently situated beside the start/finish of the route. The nearest place for an evening meal is the **Yeats Tavern** (☎ 071-916 3117), a popular pub and restaurant on the N15 at the northern edge of Drumcliff, 4.5km west.

Getting There & Away The only public transport option to Glencar also involves some walking. **Bus Éireann** (☎ 071-916 0066) operates a Sligo–Manorhamilton service three times daily that passes close to

Glencar on the N16. Ask to be dropped off near the exit for Glencar closest to Sligo. It is then a 2km walk to Glenvale B&B and the start of the route. If you are coming from further away, the joint Bus Éireann/Ulsterbus service between Belfast and Sligo could also be used to get to the walk, although you need to check that the driver will stop near Glencar.

If you are approaching by car, take any of the minor roads off the N16 signed for Glencar. At the western end of Glencar Lough, watch for a signpost for Glenvale B&B. Head west along this road to reach the B&B.

THE WALK
Immediately to the left of Glenvale B&B is a gate. Go through this and follow a muddy track for a few hundred metres, past an old ruin and through fields of rushes, until you reach a boundary wall separating enclosed fields from the open mountainside. Here you can opt for a slightly longer but easier

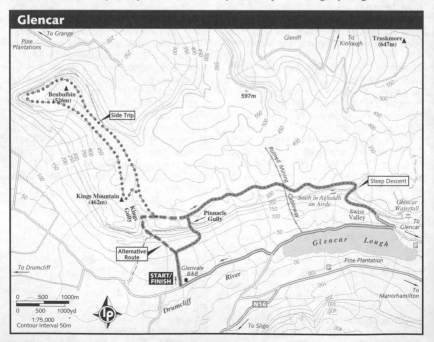

alternative (see Alternative Route: via Kings Gully, this page). Otherwise, turn right and follow the wall until you reach a prominent stone chute coming down from the mouth of **Pinnacle Gully** – the great gash in the cliff line above.

Cross the fence at the bottom of the gully. Climb over boulders and go through the gap between a pinnacle and the main wall. Negotiate another section of bouldery ground to emerge at the top of the gully, where you can begin to take in the full aspect of Glencar, and especially the cliffs and pinnacles on the southern side (one to 1½ hours from the start). From here you can head west, incorporating a side trip to Benbulbin (this page). To continue along the main route head east for about 4km, following the cliff line. However, the edge is not continuously defined. In places, a sheer edge gives way to steep ground, often with cliffs some way further down. In some places the cliffs have two tiers. In poor visibility navigation could be tricky, but bear in mind that steep ground should always be on your right side.

Descend a little and pass a ruin before climbing over a ridge into a narrow valley. Climb out of this and pass under an old **aerial cable**, which used to carry loads of baryte ore (currently used as a lubricant for drills) from an open mine above Gleniff down into Glencar. Mining ceased in 1979. Soon you'll reach a broad, flat **promontory** with an abrupt cliff line. The views from here are worth pausing for. To the west are the broken cliffs and gullies that you have just traversed. To the east are much steeper, clean-cut walls dropping into pine trees. The cliff beneath you drops sheer for about 40m to a long, wide shelf, after which there is another cliff. The shelf makes a good spot for lunch, with interesting shattered boulders strewn across the ground. To reach it, continue east to the end of the promontory where you can walk around to the shelf on steep, grassy slopes.

To continue along the main route, follow the cliffs in an easterly direction, crossing a stream that has the beautiful Irish name Stuth in Aghaidh an Airde (the Stream against the Height). In strong winds the water from this stream is often blown right back onto the plateau. After this, climb a slope to reach another stream (1½ to two hours from the top of Pinnacle Gully). This stream drops steeply into Swiss Valley, which you can see below. There is a rough path descending with the water. Follow this path which, although it zigzags, makes a general tangent to the right, away from the stream. Once on the valley floor follow the path as it turns sharply left leading over a gate and into **Swiss Valley**. At the end of the valley, amid pine trees, you'll reach a track ('Private Property' signs do not apply to the track). Follow this to reach a minor road which can then be followed down to the road running along the scenic lakeside.

Turning left will bring you to **Glencar Waterfall**; if you have the energy, this is well worth the 20-minute return trip. Otherwise, turn right to return to the start, which is 4km away.

Alternative Route: via Kings Gully
1 hour, 2km, 300m ascent
Although Pinnacle Gully presents no real difficulties, it may not be to everyone's taste. If you want easier (but slightly longer) access to the cliff tops, turn left rather than right at the boundary wall and climb to the northwest, where you will find a track leading up through the wide chasm of Kings Gully to the top of Pinnacle Gully. This option adds 1km to the overall distance.

Side Trip: Benbulbin
2 hours, 6km, 100m ascent
By walking west from the top of Kings Gully or Pinnacle Gully, you can walk out onto the spear-like promontory of Benbulbin (Binn Ghulbain, 526m). The walk around its cliffs is not as spectacular as the mountain looks from below; however, the airy views across the coastal plains are excellent.

Simply follow the cliff line via Kings Mountain out to the end of Benbulbin, and return either along the same route or along a routing roughly parallel to your outward journey, taking in the views across the impressive cliffs to the northeast of Benbulbin. There is a good deal of heather and boggy ground in places, so walking conditions are not ideal.

Glenade

Duration	4 hours
Distance	10.5km
Difficulty	moderate
Start/Finish	cottage at GR 786487
Nearest Towns	Bundoran (p213), Sligo (p210)
Transport	private

Summary A spectacular route exploring Eagle's Rock – a huge limestone pinnacle. This is followed by a steep climb onto a plateau and a walk along a cliff line with fine views.

Like Glencar (p213), Glenade (Gleann Éada) is a U-shaped glacial valley with high limestone walls bordering a large lake. This walk focuses on the higher cliffs on the western side of the Glenade valley, and in particular on a group of massive, limestone pinnacles that have detached from the cliffs. The cliffs are more atmospheric than their counterparts in Glencar, and receive much less attention from walkers. Much of the route crosses open, trackless country and there is some bouldery and fairly rugged ground near Eagle's Rock. The total ascent is 420m.

It is possible to complete a shorter circuit of the described route, still taking in the dramatic terrain around Eagle's Rock but avoiding the walk along the plateau. The Alternative Route (p217) outlines this easy–moderate option.

PLANNING
Maps
Use OSI 1:50,000 map No 16 for this walk.

GETTING TO/FROM THE WALK
From Bundoran follow the R280 (signed for Kinlough) through Kinlough, and then east and south for a further 5km. Turn right onto a minor road (beside a wide gravel lay-by and a few hundred metres south of a small post office) and follow this for about 3km to a prominent white cottage with space to park close by.

THE WALK
From the right-hand side of the cottage, pass behind a ruined stone building to a gate. There is a stile on the right. Cross this and continue through the field, keeping the fence on your right and heading directly towards the prominent gap in the cliff wall ahead.

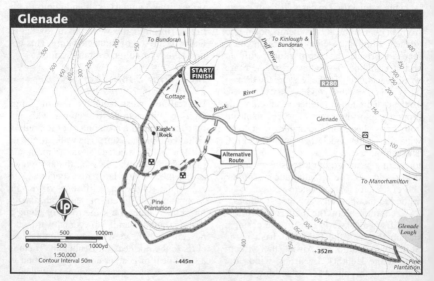

Glenade

Cross the fence at the top of the field and climb steeply into a gully. Walk to the right of the hillock in the centre of the gully. Cross another fence, negotiate the boulder field in the middle of the gully and follow a sheep track along the left-hand side to a **bouldery ridge** (one hour from the start). Sheer rock walls now tower above you on either side, with **Eagle's Rock** to the left, and the main cliffs to the right. There are impressive views back down through the huge defile, while all around rockfaces, jumbles of fallen boulders and looming pinnacles make a powerful impression. Look out for small fossils in the rock slabs – the limestone here was formed from the sediments, marine creatures and coral of a prehistoric tropical sea.

Continue ahead (south) from the ridge, descending steeply into another gully and aim for a small ruin below. Cross a stone wall at the ruin and continue down an extension of the gully, past some trees on the left, until you reach an old stone sheep pen. Here you can head east for a shorter route back to the start (see Alternative Route, below) or continue west. If continuing you should be able to pick out a faint, grassy path leading up the slopes to the right. Turn onto this and follow it as it climbs diagonally up the steep slopes to the plateau above.

Once at the top, turn left and follow the edge of the undulating plateau for 4.5km, taking care to stay back from the cliff edge. There are some great views from the **edge of the plateau**, especially over Glenade Lough. Just before you reach a forestry plantation, cut down to the left and pick up a small path, which leads diagonally down to a minor road. Turn left, and keep left for 4km until you return to the white cottage at the start.

Alternative Route
20 minutes, 1.5km
At the old stone sheep pen turn left (east) onto a grassy path. This is largely defined by a row of gnarled and twisted trees at first, but a gateway in a stone wall soon gives access to a more definite track. Follow this past a collection of ruined cottages

and continue through a charming tunnel of fuchsia until you reach a minor road and the main route. Turn left and walk less than 1km back to the cottage at the start.

Mayo

Mayo is a county of great geographical contrasts, offering walkers a generous variety of walks with the ocean as an ever-present backdrop. The cliffs of the north coast and on the western edge of Achill Island provide some of the country's finest coastal walking. The lonely Nephin Beg Range is a world apart from very public, very rocky Croagh Patrick just across Clew Bay. Then there is Mweelrea, the highest peak in this chapter and a classic route for any serious walker.

HISTORY
The county was created in the 16th century and given the name Maigh Eo, meaning 'plain of the yew trees'. The area has been settled for over five millennia, as illustrated by the discovery of the Ceide Fields on Mayo's north coast. Under the layers of blanket bog archaeologists discovered the stone walls of an extensive farming community, now recognised as the oldest enclosed landscape in Europe and the largest Stone Age monument in the world. Much more commonly encountered by walkers are the forts (*dúns* or *raths*), dating from perhaps 800 BC to about AD 1000, which enclose the summits of isolated hillocks or promontories on the coast. Monastic settlements sprang up in many places from the 6th century, inspired by the work of St Patrick.

Mayo experienced the effects of Cromwell's plantation of settlers during the 17th century, but the tide turned when Mayo became a centre for active opposition to the eviction of tenants; one of the founders of the Irish Land League, established in 1879, was Michael Davitt, who was a Mayo man. The bridge across Achill Sound, linking Achill Island to the mainland, is named in his honour.

Although Mayo was little affected by the civil war in the early 1920s, it suffered from a continuing population drain as people left behind the meagre and uncertain income of farming, the area's mainstay, for a more secure life elsewhere. It was only during the 1990s that the population actually increased as the economy diversified, with tourism playing a significant part.

NATURAL HISTORY

Although the geology of Mayo is quite complex, some key events and processes set the scene. The silts, sands and grits laid down in the ocean about 500 million years ago were transformed into hard, white quartzite, the principal building block of the mountains in the area. The mountains were then subjected to erosion and to the effects of the mountain-building process known as the Caledonian orogeny. The Ice Age resulted in their burial under ice, and the subsequent advance and retreat of glaciers carved out and deepened valleys, and gouged corries in the mountainsides (see the boxed text 'Signs of a Glacial Past', p24).

Mainly in the north, blanket bog covers large tracts of low-lying ground; further south peat bog occupies almost any place that is relatively flat and poorly drained, especially at higher altitudes. The combination of thin, poor soils, exposure to wind and high rainfall, and the ravages of grazing by sheep, yields a limited range of vegetation in the mountains and along the coast. Heather or grass moorland is widespread and the variety of wildflowers is limited. Woodlands are confined to sheltered, usually deliberately cultivated sites, while conifer plantations of lodgepole pine and sitka spruce occupy many of the glens and hillsides.

Due to this scarcity of trees and shrubs, the range of wildlife is also limited. Apart from sheep and more sheep, Irish hares and foxes are the species you are most likely to see. Birds are more numerous and diverse. On the coast, fulmars, great black-backed gulls, common gulls, guillemots and cormorants are plentiful. Skylarks and meadow pipits are the tuneful moorland denizens, together with the occasional grouse. There are also kestrels and the ever-present black ravens.

PLANNING
Information Sources

The Internet is a good source of information about the area; try ⓦ www.mayo-ireland .ie/motm.htm for links to walking information, accommodation and local history.

ACCESS TOWN
Westport

This is a thriving little town with lots of character and plenty of amenities, and has long been a popular place with visitors. **Westport TIC** (☎ 098-25711; James St; open year-round) is a good source of general information for the area. Several places in the town centre sell OSI maps, and **Hewetson Bros** (☎ 098-26018; Bridge St) also stocks outdoor clothing, walking guides and basic camping equipment.

Places to Stay & Eat Westport has a good choice of accommodation options. Camping is available at **Club Atlantic Holiday Hostel** (☎ 098-26644; Altamount St; camping per person/dorm beds/twins €6/12/30). **Old Mill Holiday Hostel** (☎ 098-27045; Barrack Yard, James St; dorm beds €12) is centrally located in an old and large stone building; bikes are also available for hire. B&Bs include **Altamount House** (☎ 098-25226; Altamount St; singles/doubles €27/54). **Wyatt Hotel** (☎ 098-25027; the Octagon; singles/ doubles €95/140) is just one of several good, centrally located hotels.

There is a large **supermarket** in the town centre and there are plenty of places for a meal. **O'Malleys** (☎ 098-25101; Bridge St) is a popular pub with a varied menu, while **McCormack's** (Bridge St) is a bright, friendly place offering café-style snacks and meals.

Getting There & Away There are bus connections between Westport and most other major towns in Ireland. Direct **Bus Éireann** (☎ 096-71800) services include Dublin (€13.30, five hours, three to five daily Monday to Saturday and two on Sunday), Sligo (€12.70, one hour 45 minutes, three daily Monday to Saturday and one on Sunday) and Galway (€11.40, one hour 50 minutes, three or four daily).

Iarnród Éireann (☎ 098-25253) also operates direct trains between Westport and Dublin's Heuston station (€22, four hours, three daily).

Westport is situated at the intersection of the N59 and the N60, at the eastern end of Clew Bay.

Dún Caocháin Cliffs

Duration	5 hours
Distance	9.5km
Difficulty	moderate
Start	Priósúin
Finish	Porturlin
Nearest Towns	Belmullet (p220), Pollatomish (p220)
Transport	private

Summary This route takes you past a profusion of precipitous cliffs, crags, caves, chasms and islands along the remote north Mayo coast.

The remote and rugged north coast of Mayo is one of Ireland's best-kept secrets. The cliffs reach just half the height of Slieve League in Donegal but are far more extensive; they continue almost without interruption for about 30km. This gives rise to at least three great days of walking through dramatic coastal scenery. The walk described is a one-day route (starting at the picturesque bay of Priósúin and ending in the tiny, seaside village of Porturlin) that takes in what is probably the best of the coastline.

The terrain covered is a mixture of short, firm turf and longer grass interspersed with some marshy patches. Several fences have to be negotiated and depending on the length of your legs, it is usually possible to find a low point or some conveniently placed large stones to enable an easy crossing. The total ascent is 470m.

The only drawback of this route is that inevitably associated with a linear walk: transport at either end. If only one car is available, the route can be completed as a shorter circuit, starting and finishing in the village of Carrowteige (Ceathrú Thaidhg) – see Alternative Route: Carrowteige Circuit (p222).

With more time and suitable transport arrangements, the entire 30km stretch of coast from south of Carrowteige to Belderg is also well worth exploring, either in a series of day walks or as a three-day backpacking trip, camping en route.

HISTORY

The Irish name for this area perpetuates Caocháin, a mythical, one-eyed giant; his *dún* on the coast has long since tumbled into the sea. People have lived here since Neolithic times, although the promontory fort that can be seen on this route (little more than a rough stone wall across the neck of the promontory) dates from the Iron Age (about 400 BC to AD 600).

There is little, if any, evidence of events or settlement from the next several centuries. In the later 17th century Irish people ejected from Ulster spread throughout the area. Supporters of Cromwell took up lands confiscated from their Irish owners and strengthened their position by fostering the settlement of Protestant families. While these landowners built roads, they also exacted onerous rents from their tenants.

At the beginning of the 19th century the English authorities, alarmed by the threat of French invasion, built signal towers in line-of-sight along the coast. Late in the 19th century the Congested Districts Board tried to improve the lot of people in remote areas by building piers and boathouses for fishing communities – the pier at Porturlin is on the site of one such landing slip built in 1886.

Following independence, the Irish Land Commission purchased the large, English-owned estate in the area and former tenants became owners of the land they occupied. As a result, the old rundale system based on the communal use of unenclosed grazing land was largely replaced and the land was parcelled out in narrow strips, which were enclosed by stone walls or fences. Both patterns of land use can still be seen in the area.

NATURAL HISTORY

The Dún Caocháin cliffs consist of ancient Precambrian schist and quartzite derived from sandy sediments about 600 million years old. The five offshore rock stacks, the Stags of Broadhaven, are even more ancient, dating back some 1.6 billion years.

Blanket bog covers the flat country inland; along the cliff edges the low vegetation is comprised mainly of bell heather and bilberry with drifts of fluffy, white bog cotton on the most poorly drained ground. You may catch sight of a fox along the way, although the Irish hare, with its characteristic upright stance and long legs, is a more likely sighting. Among the large population of seabirds on the cliffs, fulmars and great black-backed gulls are the most common; guillemots, kittiwakes and cormorants also live here.

PLANNING
Maps
The walk is covered by two OSI 1:50,000 maps, Nos 22 and 23. An excellent, locally produced guide in English and Irish, *Dún Caocháin Walks*, by Uinsionn MacGraith & Treasa Ní Ghearraigh, contains plenty of background information and good walk descriptions; it is available from the TIC in Belmullet.

NEAREST TOWNS
Belmullet
Northwest Mayo is a remote region and one of the least visited areas of Ireland. Belmullet (Béal an Mhuirthead), a small town located 17km southwest of Carrowteige, is the largest settlement in the area. The TIC (☎ 097-81500; *open Easter-Sept)* is small but friendly, and can help with most inquiries. There are also two banks with ATMs in the town centre.

Places to stay include **Mill House B&B** (☎ 097-81181; *American St; singles/doubles €26/52)* and **Western Strands Hotel** (☎ 097-81096; *Main St; singles/doubles €32/52)*, which also offers bar food in the pub below. **Square Meal Restaurant** (☎ 097-20984; *Carter Square)* provides good evening meals. There is a reasonable-sized **supermarket** in the town centre.

Bus Éireann (☎ 096-71800) has regular services between Belmullet and Ballina (€9.25, one hour 20 minutes, twice daily Monday to Saturday and one on Sunday).

Warning
Grass grows right to the *very* edge of these cliffs. Take care when walking in the area – it's all too easy to find yourself teetering on the brink as you line up a photo.

By car, Belmullet is generally accessed either along the R314, or along the R313 and N59 from Ballina.

Pollatomish
Sometimes spelled Pullathomas, Pollatomish (Poll an Tómais) is a small village with a sandy beach. The main reason for basing yourself here is the two hostels, situated just 500m apart. The **Kilcommon Lodge Hostel** (☎ 097-84621; *camping per person/dorm beds/doubles €5/9.50/22)* also offers breakfasts and four-course evening meals. Alternatively, try **The Old Rectory Holiday Hostel** (☎ 097-84115; *dorm beds/doubles €10/30)*. There is a small **shop** in the village, and of the two pubs, **McGrath's** can also provide bar food.

Pollatomish is located around 16km east of Belmullet and 20km southwest of Carrowteige, and is signed from the R314. There is no public transport to the village, although the Belmullet–Ballina bus passes along the R314, 5km to the south.

GETTING TO/FROM THE WALK
To reach the start of the walk at Priósúin, drive generally west from Carrowteige for 2km. At a junction, turn right onto a road that soon becomes a track. There is space for parking about 1km further along. At the other end of the walk, parking is available in Porturlin near the pier.

If you are starting and finishing in Carrowteige, park beside the road between the church and shop (An Siopa) in the centre of the village.

Carrowteige, Portacloy and Porturlin are all accessed via minor roads that lead north from the R314, 2km west of Glenamoy post office. Although all three are signed, your OSI map will still be useful for this bit of road navigation.

THE WALK

From the end of the rough road at Priósúin, head northeast up across the grassy slope, keeping close to the rim of the cliffs. A fairly steady climb, spread over about 2km, takes you to the crowning height of **Benwee Head** (255m). The Irish name for the headland, An Bhinn Bhui or Yellow Peak, describes the colour of the soaring, quartzite cliffs. The wide-ranging view takes in Slieve League to the north and the peaks on Achill Island to the south.

Continue across a fence near the summit and keep to the rim while walking in a generally northeasterly direction, with views of Hag Island and its dense population of fulmars and gulls. Descend across the deep and wide indentation of Doonvinalla, where there are huge slabs of stratified rock partly separated from the cliff and tilting towards the sea. The promontory fort that graces the next peninsula is defined by a ruinous line of boulders across the narrow ridge separating this inaccessible site from the main cliff. A little further on, near the end of a second long finger of land that protects the western side of Portacloy Bay, are two relics from World War II: a small, derelict lookout building and the letters 'EIRE'. The letters are about 10m long and formed of flat stones on the ground, and are within a flat-stone rectangle – a fairly common feature along the coast that reminded wartime pilots they were about to cross neutral Ireland.

You reach **Portacloy beach** (two hours from the start) by descending steadily south across the hillside, crossing a stream and passing through a gate. Then bear left and skirt around the end of a fence to a rough road – the pier is 100m further on. From here you can head southwest to Carrowteige (see Alternative Route: Carrowteige Circuit, p222). To continue to Porturlin, cross the sandy beach and climb the steep slope to the east, and soon you are back above stunning vertical cliffs where fulmars sit unconcernedly on tiny ledges. Much of the remaining section consists of crossing an elevated plateau; the terrain is flatter, and probably wetter, than previously. However, views over **Pig Island**, with its dramatic central arch, and the continuing cliff line and sea stacks to the west provide plenty of distraction.

Several collections of peat hags will need to be negotiated before you descend and then

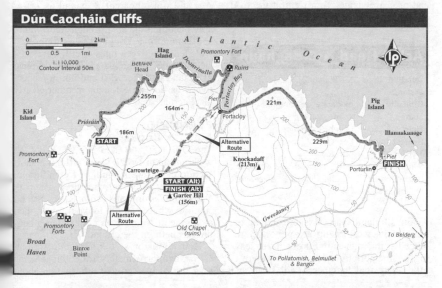

Dún Caocháin Cliffs

climb again across a second rounded mound (229m). Traverse across the remaining boggy slopes to the east, and return to the cliffs before you begin the steep, grassy descent to Porturlin. Head towards a pair of gates in a fence, about 75m south of the cliff edge; go through the right-hand gate to a fenced path (a right of way), which leads to a makeshift gate at the far end. Cross the field between two houses, pass through another gate, and join the end of a road that leads down to the small pier just a short distance to the right.

Alternative Route: Carrowteige Circuit
5–5½ hours, 11.5km, 340m ascent
The circuit from Carrowteige begins with 3km of walking along quiet roads and tracks; follow the directions given in Getting To/From the Walk (p220). The described route is then followed as far as Portacloy.

To return to Carrowteige from Portacloy, follow the road south from the pier and then take the first right turn. Keep left at a fork, and head southwest on the rough road for about 600m to where it swings west. Leave the road here and continue southwest across open, rough ground to the road at the eastern end of Carrowteige. Turn right at the road and continue back to the church and shop.

Achill Head & Croaghaun

Duration	4–4½ hours
Distance	14km
Difficulty	moderate–demanding
Start	Keem Strand
Finish	Lough Acorrymore
Nearest Town	Keel (p223)
Transport	private

Summary A truly spectacular walk above Ireland's highest coastal cliffs with sweeping mountain and sea views.

Achill is Ireland's largest island and the sea cliffs at its western tip are generally regarded as the highest in Europe. Even leaving such superlatives to one side, there is little doubt that together Achill Head and

Croaghaun (688m) make one of the most dramatic coastal walks in western Ireland.

Depending on the weather, however, Achill Island can be either one of the most beautiful or bleakest places in the west; persistent low cloud and mist can be a drawback of the area. It is worth waiting a day or two for fine weather. In general the going underfoot is good, consisting largely of well-grazed grass and low heather on the steep ascent, although a relatively short stretch of moorland is crossed on the descent. The total ascent is 760m.

It is also possible to make a circuit out of this route, starting and finishing at Keem Strand. To avoid the road walk between Lough Acorrymore and Keem Strand, head south from above Bunnafreva Lough West, pass above Lough Acorrymore, and cross Croaghaun's broad spur before descending back to Keem Strand. Allow at least five hours for this circuit.

NATURAL HISTORY
Quartzite and some schist are the main rocks of Croaghaun and, indeed, the rest of Achill Island. Although the ice sheets that covered most of Ireland during the last Ice Age did not, apparently, extend as far as Achill, some small, outlying glaciers probably occupied the area. Lough Acorrymore and Bunnafreva Lough West, sitting on a wide ledge between lines of cliffs, are classic examples of the glacial features typical of Ireland and face east and north, respectively, as do corrie loughs in other clearly glaciated areas.

PLANNING
Maps & Books
The OSI 1:50,000 map No 30 covers the walk and map No 22 shows all but a short section of the walk south of Keem Strand, where a map isn't really required. The path shown on both maps from Keem Strand south to what is an old lookout tower, then along the cliff top, does not exist as a continuous path on the ground.

Bob Kingston's *Achill Island Map & Guide*, at approximately 1:33,000, contains a wealth of background information about

Achill. The exhaustive reference for the island is *Achill Island*, by Theresa McDonald.

NEAREST TOWN
Keel

An open-plan village, Keel (An Caol) thrives during the summer. There is Internet access at Achill IT centre, and plenty of accommodation options, although the nearest banking facilities are 13km east in Achill Sound (p227).

Places to Stay & Eat At the back of Keel Strand, **Sandybanks Caravan & Camping Park** (☎ 094-903 2054; *camping per person €8; open late-May–early-Sept*) has some flat pitches with great views, right beside the beach. It is, however, very exposed to the wind. **The Wayfarer Hostel** (☎ 098-43266; *dorm beds/doubles €9.50/22*) is at the east end of the village, while **Rich View Hostel** (☎ 098-43426; *dorm beds/doubles €10/26*) is at the top of a small hill at the western end. Of the numerous B&Bs and hotels in the area, the **Bervie Guesthouse** (☎ 098-43114; *singles/doubles €45/80*) has direct access to Keel Strand.

There is a small **supermarket** and a choice of **pubs** in the village. **Calvey's Restaurant** (☎ 098-43158) specialises in local produce and has its own butchery. **The Village Inn** (☎ 098-43214) serves bar food and restaurant meals, and is an economical alternative.

Getting There & Away There is a **Bus Éireann** (☎ 096-71800) service that connects Keel to Westport (€9, one hour 35 minutes, twice daily Monday to Saturday and one on Sunday). This service also stops at most of the other main settlements on the island. By car, Keel is situated on the R319, 13km west of Achill Sound.

GETTING TO/FROM THE WALK

The walk starts at Keem Strand, 7km west of Keel. There are two large parking areas (and toilet facilities), above and beside the strand.

To reach the end of the route at Lough Acorrymore, turn north from the main road 2km west of Dooagh and continue for 1.7km along a road signed 'Lough Acorrymore Water Treatment Works'. There is ample parking by the lough.

The closest it is possible to get to the walk without your own transport is Dooagh, 2km west of Keel; add around 9km of (scenic)

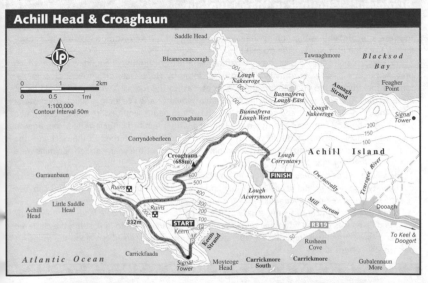

Achill Head & Croaghaun

road walking to your day's itinerary if you use this village as your start/finish point.

THE WALK

Climb the grassy slope rising steeply above Keem Strand to the cliff edge, taking in the signal tower perched high above Moyteoge Head if you want. From here it is simply a matter of walking northwest along the cliff top, either contouring below the rim to avoid a series of undulations, or keeping to the high ground and taking them in your stride. The rises include a high point at 332m, where there isn't much between the knob, the edge of the cliff and the sea far below. The wide views extend from the hills above the Dún Caocháin cliffs in the northeast to Croagh Patrick and beyond to the southeast.

After about 1½ hours you come to a point where the headland narrows to a relatively low but very exposed cliff. If you have the skill and confidence to negotiate this airy stretch, it is possible to continue a short distance towards the long, reptilian spine of **Achill Head** – retrace your steps when the ridge becomes too demanding.

From the exposed cliff, walk back towards Keem Strand for about 800m then head down to the wide, flat col, aiming to reach it just northwest of some small tarns. On the way, you pass the remains of a cluster of booley huts (see the boxed text 'Booleying – Summer in the Mountains', below) along the stream below to the northeast. To the right is another unusual historical link – the site of stone buildings associated with the notorious Captain Charles Boycott. The Captain came to Achill in the late 1850s, living at Corrymore House between Dooagh and Keem Strand. The stone buildings were the estate's stables and stores. By 1880, the Captain had moved to the mainland (near Lough Mask, southeast of Westport) and developed a reputation as an uncompromising land agent. Eventually his tenants refused to work for him in protest and his name was added to the English language (boycott – to shun).

The best way to climb the almost impossibly steep hillside to Croaghaun is to go east-northeast across the slope, changing tack to northwards once the broad southeastern spur comes into view. An effort of

Booleying – Summer in the Mountains

Transhumance is the rather impersonal term for the age-old practice of taking stock, usually cattle, to graze in mountain pastures during the summer. In Ireland it is known more colourfully as booleying, from the Irish word *buaile* (to milk).

This seasonal nomadism was an essential part of the farming year under the rundale system, which prevailed before fields were formally divided or enclosed by stone walls or fences. Each summer, families took their cattle up to the mountains, or at least to the foothills, where they could be let loose on the lush grass. Several members of the family would go and live there in simple, oval, stone huts. The cows were milked and some huts may have included a semi-underground storage area where milk could be kept cool and stored until needed. Other family members visited from time to time with supplies of fresh food. In the autumn, people and cattle returned to the clachan – the cluster of houses and farm buildings that was home for the rest of the year – and the animals were put out on the harvested fields.

The village of Doogort beneath Slievemore on Achill Island is a good example of an old, clustered, clachan-style settlement. Between Achill Head and the western ridge of Croaghaun you can also see the relatively well-preserved remains of the booley village of Bunowna.

From the early 19th century until as late as the 1920s and 1930s, rundale lands were reorganised: good land was divided into square fields and the poorer uplands into long strips; the clustered settlements were gradually replaced by separate houses, or villages spread out along the roads – a pattern still evident today.

about 45 minutes brings you to the crest of the summit ridge, where there is a well-trodden path.

On your left is a vertiginous drop to a wide, grassy basin perched on top of a lower line of cliffs; the path leads northeast along the arête to the **summit** (688m) and its modest cairn. Nearby Saddle Head points its cliff-fringed arm northwards towards the low Belmullet Peninsula, while the crags of Achill Head make an impressive spectacle to the west.

Continue along the rim northeast, then eastwards above the beautiful, pear-shaped **Bunnafreva Lough West**, its shore tidily lined with stones. From here, follow a southeasterly course to skirt the cliffs above Lough Acorrymore and descend steeply towards the northern side of tiny Lough Corryntawy. From here, it's barely 500m to the retaining wall and footbridge across the outlet from Lough Acorrymore; and the car park and road head are on the opposite side.

Slievemore

Duration	4 hours
Distance	10.5km
Difficulty	moderate
Start/Finish	Doogort (p226)
Transport	bus

Summary Strenuous walking on the steep ridges of Achill's second-highest peak is rewarded with tremendous views and a descent into the deserted village of Slievemore.

Slievemore (An Sliabh Mor or Big Mountain) is, at 671m, the second-highest peak on Achill Island. It consists of a great keel of quartzite rising above Doogort on the north coast, and dominates the Achill landscape. A steep and engaging eastern ridge, a cliff-fringed northeastern corrie, and summit views to rival those of Achill Head and Croaghaun (p222) are all part of the mountain's charms. With the added interest of the deserted village of Slievemore, the traverse of the mountain provides a great half-day walk with a total ascent of 750m. Although

the ascent is steep and strenuous, the otherwise straightforward nature of the route lends it an easier grading than the longer route on Achill Head and Croaghaun. It is possible to avoid the road walk back to Doogort by having a car at Slievemore (GR 640072); park beside the cemetery.

HISTORY

The abandoned village of Slievemore on the southwestern slopes of Slievemore mountain provides a haunting reminder of the depopulation of rural Ireland during the 19th and early 20th centuries. Roughly 100 houses are strung out in linear fashion along an old *boreen* (country lane), and most are now ruined and overgrown. Take a peek inside the ruins and you'll see fascinating relics of former lifestyles: the metal rings on the walls were used to tether the animals that were brought in at night for both security and warmth; stone slabs were covered with heather and rushes to make simple beds.

The exact reason for Slievemore's abandonment is not known but it was most likely a combination of the Great Famine and the evictions of the Achill Mission. The Mission was an evangelical-Protestant endeavour that used the threat of rent increases as an aid to proselytising. It is almost certain that mass evictions took place at Slievemore but probably not enough to depopulate the entire settlement. The rest of the population eventually moved to their summer booley village (see the boxed text 'Booleying – Summer in the Mountains', p224) at Dooagh, which was probably closer to their most reliable source of food – fish. Slievemore was then used as a booley village and later abandoned to the ghosts. A small guide to Slievemore village, by Bob Kingston, is available in some local shops.

PLANNING
Maps

Use OSI 1:50,000 maps No 22 or No 30.

Bob Kingston's *Achill Island Map & Guide*, at approximately 1:33,000, contains a wealth of background information about Achill. The exhaustive reference for the island is *Achill Island*, by Theresa McDonald.

NEAREST TOWN
Doogort

Sometimes spelled Dugort, this is a small collection of buildings gathered at the back of a beautiful sandy cove and on the lower slopes of Slievemore. Facilities are limited to a very small **shop** (with sporadic opening hours) and a post office.

The **Seal Caves Camping & Caravan Park** (☎ 098-43262; camping per person €8.70; open Apr-Sept) has flat, grassy pitches; book in at the shop. **Valley House Hostel** (☎ 098-47204; The Valley; dorm beds/doubles €10/28), 3km east of Doogort, is the closest hostel, and has the advantage of an attached bar. At the back of Doogort beach, **the Strand Hotel** (☎ 098-43241; singles/doubles €35/70) offers bar food or restaurant meals to guests and nonguests alike.

There are regular **Bus Éireann** (☎ 096-71800) services connecting Doogort and Westport (€7.85, one hour 45 minutes, once daily Monday to Saturday), as well as other settlements on the island. By car, Doogort is 4km north of the R319 Achill Sound–Keel road; there is a signed turn-off to the village about 3km northwest of Cashel.

THE WALK

From Doogort strand, take the minor road that leads northwest and passes in front of The Strand Hotel. Access to the mountain is opposite a wide, grass verge (where you can park), about 200m from the main road. A faint path, just to the left of a prominent bungalow, leads up onto the mountain, winding between boulders to reach open ground above Doogort. The ground soon steepens and a long, strenuous ascent begins, although some judicious zigzagging will ease the strain of the gradient. Climb steeply for 30 to 40 minutes to reach an even steeper section (thankfully short-lived), which brings you out onto a fairly level shoulder beside the rocky pinnacle so conspicuous from the bottom of the mountain. Take in the superb view back down along the ridge to Doogort and the bays beyond. The beaches at Barnynagappul and Porteen are obvious, and further out across the islands of Blacksod Bay, the wild emptiness of north Mayo stretches out to the Nephin Beg Range. There are also fine views to the south, looking across Keel and the Menawn Cliffs.

From this point, about halfway to the summit, the climb becomes more interesting. On the right the ridge falls away in steep cliffs into the northeastern corrie and to the left the slopes curve away out of sight revealing more airy views across Keel. A rough, mucky path becomes evident, winding up through the boulders that litter the ridge crest. In places many walkers will choose to descend slightly off the crest to the left to avoid some rocky outcrops that overlook the corrie. Braver souls will scramble over these, enjoying the exposure on the right. The ridge steepens once more close to the top before levelling out onto a flat summit only a short distance east of the summit proper. Descend slightly before climbing gently up to the trig point marking the summit of **Slievemore** (671m, two to 2½ hours from the start).

On a clear day there are fine views in all directions. To the north and east the views across Mayo extend all the way across Belmullet to the sea cliffs of north Mayo around Portacloy and Porturlin, although the cliffs themselves are not visible. To the south and southeast many of the summits of south Mayo and north Galway can often be seen – Croagh Patrick, the Sheefry Hills and Mweelrea. To the west the dome of Croaghaun broods over Lough Acorrymore. Descend gently from the summit along a broad ridge, heading in a generally westerly

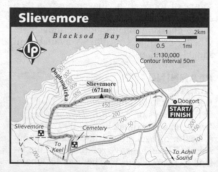

Slievemore

Blacksod Bay

0   1   2km
0   0.5   1mi
1:130,000
Contour Interval 50m

Croaghmaoltrán

Slievemore
(671m) ▲

Doogort

**START/
FINISH**

Slievemore

Cemetery

To
Keel

To Achill
Sound

direction. Cross a flat, boggy area and then descend steeply onto a shoulder. At the end of this shoulder a steep outcrop of rock must either be skirted or descended directly with care, using grassy slopes that wind between the rocks. At this point walkers with the energy might want to view Ooghnadirka, an impressive gully running steeply down to the ocean from close to the ridge top. You'll need to descend a little to the north to fully appreciate this feature, which has been attributed to the weathering of a fault zone. Climb back onto the ridge to continue the route.

From the bottom of the outcrop turn to the south and begin to descend steeply towards Slievemore village. If the cloud isn't down you'll see the remains of the old linear settlement strung out along the southeastern foot of Slievemore. Old boundary walls, animal pens and many stone-built dwellings are visible, and as you reach the lower fields, lazy-beds are also obvious. Your choice of descent is governed by where you'd like to begin exploring the village. The shortest option is to aim for the cluster of ruins just a couple of hundred metres west of the cemetery.

Follow a minor road south from the cemetery and turn left at a T-junction. Walk along this road all the way back to Doogort, some 4km away.

Corraun Hill

Duration	5–5½ hours
Distance	11.5km
Difficulty	moderate
Start/Finish	Belfarsad bridge
Nearest Town	Achill Sound (p227)
Transport	private

Summary A great, rarely walked mountain circuit, featuring steep ridges, deep corries and fantastic coastal views.

The Corraun Peninsula tends to be a place that is registered simply as the last stretch of mainland before Achill Island. However, this does the area an injustice; the walk up Corraun Hill (An Corran or the Sickle) boasts characteristics that rival many of the better-known mountain routes in the country. Although the southern flanks of the mountain drop to the sea in a rather uniform fashion, the cliffs of the northern slopes offer the perfect juxtaposition. Here deep-sided corries are adorned with small loughs and separated by the bony fingers of sharp ridges. It is unusual to find these features on a mountain of such modest height. Corraun Hill has two main summits, with the highest reaching just 541m. Nonetheless, the views over Achill Island, Clew Bay and the west Mayo coast are outstanding, and provide the other major attraction of the route.

A blanket of thick heather covers the lower slopes of the mountain, while the summit plateau is strewn with a mixture of white quartzite and the pink-tinged rock that is characteristic of the area. A 1km-long section of bog towards the end of the route can be very wet, so gaiters are strongly recommended. The route also involves fording the outlet stream of a small lough, so avoid walking immediately after heavy rain. The total ascent is 640m.

In clear weather the well-defined topography of the mountain makes route finding fairly straightforward for those with good map reading skills, but care must be taken in poor visibility to avoid descending via the wrong ridge.

PLANNING
Maps
OSI 1:50,000 map No 30 covers the route.

NEAREST TOWN
Achill Sound
The town of Achill Sound (Ghob a'Choire) spans the access bridge for Achill Island and has a wide range of visitor facilities, including a large **supermarket**, which sells local walking maps, and an ATM.

Accommodation options include the somewhat desolate-looking and spartan **Railway Hostel** (☎ 098-45187; dorm beds €10), on the east side of the bridge (inquire in Lovell's shop over the bridge). A more homely option is **Wild Haven Hostel** (☎ 098-45392; dorm beds/doubles €13/34), behind the church to the west of the bridge. The town also has numerous B&Bs and hotels: **Ostan Ghob a'Choire** (☎ 098-45245; singles/doubles €36/ 60), opposite the supermarket, is one of the cheaper hotels.

Almost all of the town's bars and hotels serve food.

Bus Éireann (☎ 096-71800) connects Achill Sound to Westport (€7.35, one hour 15 minutes, twice daily Monday to Saturday and one on Sunday). This service also continues to most of the other main settlements on Achill Island.

GETTING TO/FROM THE WALK
From Achill Sound it is an easy 2.5km walk to Belfarsad bridge at the start of this circuit; cross the beach to the east of the town and then head south along the road towards Corraun village.

By car approach the area on the N59 and turn west onto the R319 (signed for Achill Sound), 1km west of Mallaranny. Follow this road round the north of Corraun Peninsula and, after around 9km, turn left towards Corraun village. Belfarsad bridge

(GR 748985) is 3km along this road. Park either just south of the bridge or in front of the wooden church 100m further on.

THE WALK
From the bridge over the Belfarsad River, walk north along the road for around 20m and then turn right onto a stone track. The track climbs gently as it leads southeast onto the open bog north of Corraun Hill; follow this track for around 1.5km until you come to a prominent white stone located in the centre of a fork. Veer right here; the track peters out within a few metres, but it sets you in the right direction for the ascent of Corraun.

Continue southeast, across the broken ground, descending briefly to cross a small depression, before reaching the bottom of the prominent shoulder. The ascent up the shoulder is steep, but eases off as it narrows into a more defined **ridge** with steep drops and great views on either side. The ridge is enjoyably narrow without being dangerous, and the heather gives way to rock as you gain height.

The ridge broadens out for a spell and then a final steep climb leads up onto the

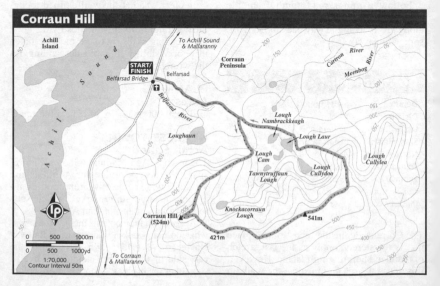

Corraun Hill

summit plateau. Veer southwest and pick a way over the quartzite to reach the cairn and concrete trig point that mark the **west summit** of the mountain (two to 2½ hours from the start). At 524m this peak is 17m lower than the eastern summit, but the views from this point are arguably better. The great mountains and ridges of Achill Island rise to the west, Clare Island lies beyond sandy shores and the mouth of Clew Bay to the south, and the intricate coastline of west Mayo stretches north. It is a wonderful viewpoint and certainly makes the climb worthwhile.

Continue east and then southeast from the summit, descending across a col before climbing more gently up broad slopes towards the east summit. A series of prominent cairns keeps you on the right track as you cross the rather featureless terrain. Be wary of steep cliffs to the north in poor visibility. The cairn marking the **east summit** (541m, 45 minutes to one hour from the west summit) rises amid pink-tinged sandstone rocks, and it is the view across the islands of Clew Bay to Croagh Patrick in the south that is most engaging here.

From this summit another prominent cairn is visible on the far eastern edge of the plateau. Continue in this direction for 500m before veering north onto the ridge that provides the descent route (take care here to avoid descending the even steeper ridge immediately north of the east summit). Bear northwest as you lose height, heading towards the corner of a forestry plantation and a network of small loughs below.

The ground at the bottom of this ridge can be so wet that it glistens from above and acrobatic skills are sometimes called on to avoid wet feet. Follow the fence of the forestry plantation as it skirts the eastern shore of Lough Laur and cross the outlet stream on stepping stones. Continue northwest from the stream, climbing a small mound ahead. The track that you followed at the start of the route should soon become visible; retrace your initial steps back to the road and turn left to return to Belfarsad bridge.

Corranbinna

Duration	5½–6 hours
Distance	14km
Difficulty	moderate–demanding
Start/Finish	Carheenbrack
Nearest Town	Westport (p218)
Transport	bus

Summary A fine circuit over three summits on the western side of the Nephin Beg Range, including splendid views and a short, exciting scramble.

Few ranges in Ireland are as remote as the Nephin Begs, extending as they do into the vastness of the north Mayo boglands. Although the horseshoe-walk described here, around the Glendahurk valley, does not cover the highest of the Nephins (to the northeast), it has the advantages of reasonably easy access and, by Nephin standards, a modest quota of peat bogs. Apart from short sections along a vehicle track at the start and finish, the walk crosses rough, trackless country over Bengorm (582m) to the high point of Corranbinna (716m), with the most broken ground on the long descent from Corranbinna South (681m). Between the two Corranbinnas, the ridge narrows for a few hundred metres to a rocky arête. It's an easy scramble along the crest or you can traverse below to the south. The total ascent is a challenging 1020m.

Enthusiasts for these hills could add a visit to the outlier peak of Glennamong (628m), about 3.5km north-northeast of Corranbinna, entailing 370m of extra ascent.

NATURAL HISTORY
The Nephin Beg Range is an inverted Y-shaped group of quartzite hills, north and northeast of Newport Bay, intersected by numerous streams flowing from its broad, generally steep slopes. Lough Feeagh, between the two arms of the range, was carved out by ice sheets many thousands of years ago; the corries facing north and northeast from the peaks covered in this walk are also of Ice Age origin – see the boxed text 'Signs of a Glacial Past' (p24). The highest point

in the range, an unnamed summit of 721m, broods over the flat boglands to the north. However, to the east, the solitary massif of Nephin, at 806m, is the second-highest peak in Counties Mayo and Galway.

PLANNING
Maps
You will need two OSI 1:50,000 maps, Nos 30 and 31, for this walk.

GETTING TO/FROM THE WALK
Bus Éireann (☎ 096-71800) services on the Westport–Achill Island route pass along the N59, about 1.5km south of the start of the walk (twice daily Monday to Saturday and one on Sunday). Arrange with the driver in advance to be dropped off here.

By car, follow the N59 north from Westport and then west from Newport. About 7.5km from Newport, turn north along a minor road marked by a very modest sign to 'Carheenbrack' (most easily spotted approaching from the east). There is space for two or three cars by deserted farm buildings (GR 913978), about 1.5km along this rough road.

THE WALK
From the deserted farm buildings walk northwest along the road for about 200m and, just before the bridge over the Owengarve River, pass through a gate on the right into open country. Head upstream fairly close to the river; a couple of narrow footbridges cross small tributaries and a ditch or two must be negotiated. After about 500m, as a low spur takes shape ahead, change course and climb eastwards up the long, grassy slope of Bengorm's broad south spur. The banks of the tributary stream of the Glendahurk River, grazed by the ubiquitous sheep, provide the least soggy going up to the spur. The west bank of a stream, which unconventionally flows down the spur's crest, provides reasonably firm footing for the long haul up the spur. A rocky stretch leads to the small summit of **Bengorm** (1½ hours from the start), crowned .with a cairn. Variety is the essence of the panoramic view: Bellacorrick power station and the nearby wind farm in the north; Achill Island's peaks to the west; and to the south Clew Bay, with its flotilla of islets overlooked by vigilant Croagh Patrick.

Descend steeply northwest to a small col and press on over two broad bumps on the spur, keeping left at the second one, well clear of the slabs to the right. For the final pull to Corranbinna, steer clear of the steepest of the boulder fields to the left. From **Corranbinna's survey pillar** (1½ hours from Bengorm), you have an excellent coast-and-mountain view, with the Nephin Begs added to the catalogue of sights from Bengorm.

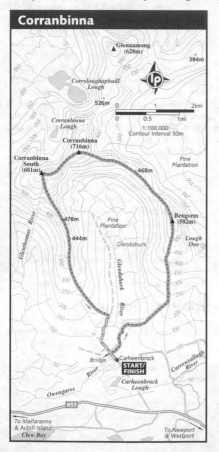

Corranbinna

Glennamong (628m)

Corryloughaphuill Lough

526m

Corranbinna Lough

Corranbinna (716m)

Corranbinna South (681m)

468m

Pine Plantation

478m

Pine Plantation

444m

Glendahurk

Bengorm (582m)

Lough Doo

Glenthomas River

Glendahurk River

Bridge

Carheenbrack
START/ FINISH

Owengarve River

Carheenbrack Lough

Carrowsallagh River

N59

To Mallaranny & Achill Island
Clew Bay

To Newport & Westport

1:100,000
Contour Interval 50m

0   1   2km
0   0.5   1mi

384m

A short descent takes you to the arête leading to Corranbinna South. Either bear left for a steeply angled traverse or scramble along its crest, the only real problem being that of seeing ahead to the next move. **Corranbinna South** is a broad, grassy plateau falling steeply north to the elongated Corranbinna Lough. The long descent begins over wet ground; some rocks intervene and peat hags intrude around the intermediate bumps. The spur becomes more dissected and badly eroded as it broadens; keep to the crest until you can see the southern end of the forestry plantation below in Glendahurk. Head down to that point to meet a forestry track, which emerges from the plantation. Follow it south, then turn left at a T-junction and head back to the start of the walk (2½ hours from Corranbinna).

Croagh Patrick

Duration	4–4½ hours
Distance	10km
Difficulty	moderate–demanding
Start	Belclare bridge
Finish	GR 875808
Nearest Towns	Murrisk (p232), Westport (p218)
Transport	bus

Summary A scenic traverse of Ireland's most climbed peak and most important pilgrimage mountain, which also offers wonderful views over Clew Bay.

Croagh Patrick (764m) occupies a special place in Irish tradition as the country's most hallowed place of pilgrimage and attracts tens of thousands of pilgrims to its summit every year. The most frequently travelled route to the top is the Pilgrims' Path, a track that is as wide as a country road in some places and can be seen scarring the mountainside for miles around. However, the mountain has much more to offer walkers than this well-trodden route. An east-to-west traverse of the entire mountain ridge, including Croagh Patrick, makes a very fine walk, and incorporates a short section along

the Western Way (p340). Generally over firm ground, with only a few peaty patches at the western end, this route also affords superb views. The amount of ascent demanded (960m over the course of the walk) considerably exceeds the height of Croagh Patrick, mainly because of two relatively deep cols on the ridge either side of the main summit.

The route of the western section of the traverse, from Roilig Muire, is marked with large, widely spaced cairns and there is a rough path as well. On the eastern approach you are more on your own, although each of the minor summits on the ridge is topped with a cairn. Inevitably, an A-to-B route such as this depends on your ability to arrange transport at each end – a cooperative driver or more than one vehicle is required. Without such transport, consider a straight out-and-back ascent via the Pilgrims' Path. However, this path could never be described as subtle – it climbs directly up the northern face of the mountain and, bar one relatively gentle section just below the crest of the final ridge, continues steeply all the way to the summit. The terrain is largely rocky and the path is often busy. Allow around three hours for the 8km slog.

Bear in mind that the national day of pilgrimage is the last Sunday in July (Reek Sunday), when thousands of the faithful of all ages (many in bare feet) climb Croagh Patrick from Murrisk – see the boxed text 'Ireland's Holy Mountain' (p232). The mountain will also be particularly busy during the main summer season, from late-June to early September.

NATURAL HISTORY

Croagh Patrick has a distinctive volcanic profile, but its origins are anything but volcanic; it is composed largely of white quartzite, derived from sedimentary rocks laid down hundreds of millions of years ago and later completely transformed by upheavals of the earth's crust. The quartzite has been fractured and shattered into the whitish mantle of scree that gives the mountain its beautiful, Fuji-like outline and makes the rock-strewn climb less than comfortable. While 'The Reek', as it is known locally, bears slight evidence of

Ireland's Holy Mountain

The history of Ireland's best known mountain is a classic blend of myth, ancient tradition and archaeological evidence.

The mountain's ancient name (Cruchán Aigli or Aigle's Peak) suggests that it was linked with the founder of the harvest-time Festival of Lughnasa. The ancient custom of sun worship may well have centred on the mountain. It is believed that early kings of the province of Connaught built a road from Ballintubber (about 20km to the east) to the summit. The line of the road is at least partly followed by the stone wall stretching across Croagh Patrick's southern slopes, which features on the walk described here. Archaeological excavations have also uncovered evidence of a sizable prehistoric settlement on the summit dating from at least 300 BC, consisting of the remains of a substantial enclosure and numerous circular huts.

However, it is the mountain's association with Patrick, the best known of Ireland's three patron saints, that is most enduring. It is believed that the saint fasted for 40 days and 40 nights on the mountain, emulating the biblical accounts of Moses and Christ. The mountain was crucial to his campaign to convert the Celtic people to Christianity, in which he successfully adopted the strategy of simply performing Christian rituals at long-established sacred Celtic sites. Legend also has it that Patrick evicted snakes from Ireland during his time on the mountain.

Historic records of pilgrimages to the mountain date back to the 12th century. Today, the principal or national day of pilgrimage is the last Sunday in July, when services are conducted on the summit, as they are on the last Friday in July (Garland Friday) and on 15 August (the Feast of the Assumption). For many years, the national pilgrimage was made at night, although this practice was stopped during the 1970s.

An integral feature of the pilgrimage is the traditional performance of penance at designated stations along the way. There are three stations in all: Leacht Benain, commemorating Benignus, a disciple of Patrick; three separate substations on the summit; and Roilig Muire (the virgins' cemetery) on the western slope, possibly a pre-Christian burial site. At each of these stations thousands of pilgrims each year repeat key religious texts a prescribed number of times while walking round one or more large cairns.

The chapel on the summit of Croagh Patrick is Ireland's highest church, and was built in 1905 on the site of the remains of the first Christian chapel there, dated between AD 430 and 890.

For more information about the mountain or to make a 'virtual pilgrimage', see Ⓦ www.anu.ie/reek.

the impact of the Ice Age, the bay above which it rises is a textbook study of what happened when a glacier retreated. As it melted, the debris accumulated within the ice was left behind in a cluster of hills, called drumlins. Over time, some have disappeared and the survivors have been worn down, their west-facing slopes carved by wind and the sea into steep cliffs, while the protected slopes to the east are relatively unchanged.

PLANNING
Maps & Books

Croagh Patrick is on the corners of four OSI 1:50,000 maps: Nos 30 and 31 are the most important, covering the northern approaches and the main ridge; No 37 shows the descent to Roilig Muire and part of the climb towards Ben Goram; and No 38, covering the approach to the mountain from the southeast, is not strictly necessary.

An illustrated brochure, *Croagh Patrick – Ireland's Holy Mountain*, is available from local TICs, and contains information about the history and traditions of the mountain.

NEAREST TOWNS & FACILITIES
See Westport (p218)

Murrisk

This is the village at the base of the Pilgrims' Path up Croagh Patrick and offers some facilities. The **TIC** (☎ 098-64114; open Mar-Oct) is located at the start of the path. The centre sells local maps and guidebooks, has a café, and also offers shower facilities (€2.50). There is plenty of car parking space available.

The nearest camping ground to the walk is **Leckanvy Camping and Caravan Park** (☎ 098-64860; camping per person €10), which is 3km west of Murrisk along the R335. In Murrisk, B&Bs located along the N59 include the **Highgrove** (☎ 098-64819; singles/doubles €25/53) and the **Beal-an-Saile** (☎ 098-64012; singles/doubles €30/60), which has sea views.

The Tavern pub and restaurant, which is also along the N59, is a good place for evening meals.

Regular **Bus Éireann** (☎ 096-71800) services connect Murrisk to Westport (€2.35, 20 minutes, two or three daily Monday to Saturday).

By car, Murrisk is located on the N59, around 8km west of Westport. It is also possible to cycle between Murrisk and Westport; bicycles can be hired at Westport's **Old Mill Holiday Hostel** (☎ 098-27045; Barrack Yard, James St).

GETTING TO/FROM THE WALK

The walk starts at Belclare bridge on the R335, 5km west of Westport, and finishes at the end of a minor road about 2.5km from the R335. **Bus Éireann** (☎ 096-71800) services on the Westport–Louisburgh route ply the R335 two or three times daily Monday to Saturday. Check current timetables and make advance arrangements with the driver to be dropped off or picked up near the start or finish of the route.

To get to the start by car, follow signs to Louisburgh and Croagh Patrick from the N59 on the southwestern edge of Westport. There is very limited parking space just west of the bridge, and more about 75m east of the bridge. Alternatively, two cars only can park at the end of the public road on the route of the walk. To access this point, drive 1km south from Belclare bridge along a minor road, then bear right at a fork. Park beside a ruined stone building around 1km along this road.

To reach the western end of the walk, turn south off the R335 1.5km west of Leckanvy and 4.5km west of Murrisk, along a road with a sign reading 'Rapid Signs'. Take the first left after 1km and park beside the road

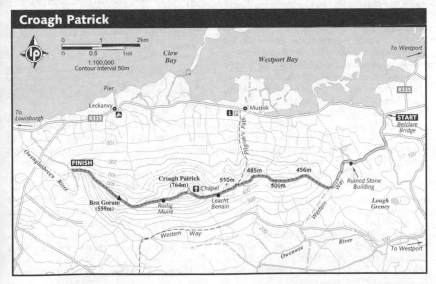

Croagh Patrick

on the left, about 200m below a group of houses (GR 875808).

THE WALK

The walk starts quietly from the main road, heading south along a narrow, leafy lane. After about 500m, where the lane bends sharply left, you meet the Western Way; continue ahead, now following the Way, and bear right at a fork about 400m further on. After about 1km the road bends sharply right and a rough vehicle track, marked by a way-marking post, continues ahead. Go through the gate and climb steadily along the track. The aim is to reach the open moorland on the broad ridge to the west, and about 600m further along a metal gate in the fence parallel-ing the track allows access to this.

Climb the hill to the west, keeping north of another fence leading uphill beside you. You will soon come to an old stone wall; fortunately, gaps have developed in its other-wise sound structure, and it's not difficult to cross and continue up to the crest of the heathery ridge. Several mounds and hillocks then need to be crossed between you and the prominent slopes of Croagh Patrick ahead. Pass over these rises, crossing a peaty col with the remains of another stone wall, and then descend to join the eroded scar of the **Pilgrims' Path** (1½ hours from the start). The col where you meet this motorway of Irish paths contains what could be described as an open-air autograph book: the names and initials of pilgrims and walkers are writ-ten in stones on the ground. A toilet block, complete with flushing water, can also be found slightly further along the track.

The wide path is covered with stones, and doesn't make for particularly easy progress; one can only wonder at the hardiness of pil-grims who make the ascent unshod. Wonder may well turn to bemusement or admiration, depending on your beliefs, as you pass the pilgrims' first station (Leacht Benain) and read the plaque with the prescribed ritual.

About half an hour's steady plodding up the steep, stony highway brings you to the **summit**, which can be crowded at almost any time of the year. Here you will find a chapel, a survey pillar, an offerings box,

several shelters, a second station cairn (with a plaque laying down an even more chal-lenging procedure for pilgrims) and even more toilets. Thankfully the views over Clew Bay to the north are adequate com-pensation for any lack of tranquillity that might result from such a well-visited place.

Continue west from the summit along a narrower stone path and begin a zigzagging descent to the third and last station, Roilig Muire. From here a modest path continues west down to a narrow col. Climb northwest to Ben Goram, a small plateau, and continue in the same direction, soon beginning to lose height. Two large cairns mark the start of the final, steep descent. Keep heading northwest at least until you meet a prominent, pillar-like cairn, to avoid precipitous crags on the western flank of the ridge. As the gradient eases, bear left and head down to the road, where transport should be waiting (1¼ hours from the summit of Croagh Patrick).

Mweelrea

Duration	6½–7 hours
Distance	12km
Difficulty	demanding
Start/Finish	Doo Lough
Nearest Town	Leenaun (p239)
Transport	private

Summary The highest peak in the province of Connaught, this challenging mountain has great character, spectacular corries and fine panoramic views.

Mweelrea (814m) can be climbed by sev-eral routes, all of which entail a good deal of steep ground. The mountain's allure lies not only in its sheer size, but also in its wonderfully contrasting setting. The steep southern flanks soar dramatically above the shores of Killary Harbour. To the east, a deep pass separates the mountain from the sprawling Sheefry Hills and the Ben Gorm massif. Northwards, Mweelrea overlooks low-lying pastoral lands fringing the shores of Clew Bay. At the mountain's western feet, superb sandy beaches face the Atlantic.

Although Mweelrea's Irish name, Cnoc Maol Réidh, translates as Grey, Bald Mountain, the upper reaches are generally grassy – at least where the sheep haven't stripped the protective cover from the stony ground.

The approach described here, via the impressive cliff-lined corrie of Coum Dubh to the northeast, is probably the most spectacular option. This leads to Ben Bury on the northern rim of the broad, central arc of the massif, still a good 2km from the Mweelrea summit. After walking out and back to the summit of Mweelrea you can enjoy another 2km of superb ridge walking around the rim of Coum Dubh to the top of Ben Lugmore and back. The total ascent is 1150m.

An alternative to the out-and-back route is, after visiting the summit of Mweelrea, continue across Ben Lugmore and descend via the mountain's southeastern spur to Delphi Adventure Centre (see Alternative Finish: Delphi, p237).

Either way, it is worth waiting for a good, clear day to climb Mweelrea. With so much steep and dangerous ground, the consequences of a navigational error in poor visibility could be severe.

NATURAL HISTORY

Mweelrea differs from many of the mountains in County Mayo and Connemara in consisting mainly of gritstone and sandstone laid down in an ancient sea about 500 million years ago. Although later bent and squashed by convulsions in the earth's crust, these rocks are hard and resistant to erosion. Conglomerates, slate and some volcanic material are also present. However, Mweelrea is similar to most other mountains in the region in displaying the effects of the last Ice Age, especially in the spectacularly deep corries scooped out of its northern and eastern flanks (see the boxed text 'Signs of a Glacial Past', p24).

HISTORY

Beside the road along Doo Lough is a cairn erected 'for the poor and hungry who died here in 1847 (and in the third world today)'. The earlier remembrance is of people who walked from Louisburgh to Delphi Lodge in the dark years of the famine. Seeking admission to the poorhouse in Louisburgh, hundreds of starving people were told they would have to apply to the Board of Guardians, which was meeting the following day at Delphi Lodge. After spending the night in the open, the group walked to Delphi. When they arrived they were told the board was at lunch and could not be disturbed. Eventually they did meet but assistance was refused. That day it rained and snowed, and some died of cold and hunger in the lodge grounds, while others perished on the way back to Louisburgh. The road itself was built in 1896 as one of the projects of the Congested Districts Board to improve conditions for people in the poorest parts of the country.

PLANNING
Maps
The OSI 1:50,000 map No 37 covers the walk. Ben Lugmore on the eastern ridge is not named on this map.

GETTING TO/FROM THE WALK
The route starts and finishes from the northwestern end of Doo Lough, situated alongside the R335 around 15km northwest of Leenaun and 13km south of Louisburgh. A few parking spaces are on the verge here. The alternative finish is 4.5km south of the start along the R335. Walkers are requested not to use the car park at Delphi Adventure Centre, but limited parking spaces are available beside the road close to the centre.

THE WALK (see map p236)
Follow a rough vehicle track away from the road, passing parallel to the northwestern shore of Doo Lough. Cross a small stream on stepping stones at a ford, or by a footbridge about 100m upstream, and rejoin the track shortly before it dwindles and disappears. Continue generally south and, above a stock pen, cross the stream that drains Coum Dubh and follow it up into the corrie.

The ground underfoot is rough and occasionally marshy until, about 45 minutes from the start, you reach the foot of the only break in the lower line of cliffs around the head of the corrie. Climb a grassy spur between two streams and bear right, following the natural line of the slope with cliffs close to your left. After a few hundred metres, move further to the right and continue up on a grassy spur. Eventually you reach a narrow path across a scree slope, which leads to a grassy col on the edge of the plateau where there is a substantial cairn (one hour from the bottom of the corrie).

The next objective is **Ben Bury** (795m) on the northern rim. The views from either of the small cairns on the flattish summit extend far into north Mayo across Clew Bay. The driest route southwest and southwards to the col

below Mweelrea's summit is on the left, across flat, stony outcrops. From the col climb steeply, veering left for an aerial view of the wide and deep corrie embracing Lough Lugaloughan. The flattish **summit** (one hour from the large cairn) is badly eroded but an outstanding vantage point: Killary Harbour, the Maumturks and the Twelve Bens, Clare and Achill Islands, Croagh Patrick and the Nephin Begs are all laid out below. The contrasting flatlands far to the east graphically mark the limits of the mountainous area.

Return to the cairn southeast of Ben Bury by working your way across its slope just

Mweelrea, Killary Harbour & Doughruagh

below the most extensive drifts of scree. Continue steadily up the eroded slope and along the airy crest above Coum Dubh, across a small col and steeply up to the pinnacle of **Ben Lugmore** (803m).

From here you can continue to the Alternative Finish (below) at Delphi or return to Doo Lough by retracing your steps back along the ridge to the large cairn marking the descent into Coum Dubh. Descend with care into the corrie and back out to Doo Lough.

Alternative Finish: Delphi
1–1½ hours, 4km
From Ben Lugmore, drop down into a grassy gap and then climb a short distance to a broad, unnamed summit with a fine view back to Mweelrea. Turn to the northeast and enjoy some excellent, easy walking along a broad ridge with the rim of Coum Dubh on your left. Ahead the Sheefry Hills and Ben Creggan dominate the view.

At the end of this ridge turn slightly south of east and descend the shoulder running down towards the Delphi Adventure Centre. This deposits you on some boggy and rough ground in the Owennaglogh valley; follow an old boundary wall towards the adventure centre. Aim to the west of the buildings to reach the river close to a small bridge carrying a water pipe. Ford the river near here – a straightforward undertaking in normal water levels, but probably impossible in flood. The bridge can be used with care, although it does not seem to be designed with walkers in mind. Now follow the obvious track down to the centre and onto the R335.

Connemara

The very name of Connemara is enough to capture the imagination. Mist-veiled mountains, lonely glens, rugged crags, the restless sea; all are images evocative of the area. Situated in the northwest corner of County Galway, Connemara consists of a compact group of mountains, valleys and moorlands, with Killary Harbour bordering the region to the north, and a seemingly

endless maze of lakes and lower hills stretching away to the east and south. Dominated by the formidable peaks of the Twelve Bens and the Maumturks, but also including more accessible hills and glens, as well as the Connemara National Park, the area has a great deal to offer walkers.

Connemara is reasonably well served by public transport and has a good range of inexpensive accommodation options. Not surprisingly, it also experiences the worst of the notorious west coast weather, although on good days there are few finer places in which to be in the Irish hills.

HISTORY
In prehistoric times and until at least the 12th century, farming and fishing communities and monastic settlements shunned the inhospitable and infertile interior of Connemara and clung to the narrow, coastal fringe and nearby islands. They left behind a large number of burial tombs and intriguing arrangements of stones, believed to be linked with rituals surrounding the solstice.

During the 19th century, Connemara was more favourably regarded by landowners; roads were built, the town of Clifden was founded between 1810 and 1820, and piers were built at Leenaun and Roundstone. However, the people of Connemara, whose numbers had grown phenomenally during the 19th century, were decimated by the Great Famine of the late 1840s. Estates changed hands in the ensuing years and, in the case of Kylemore (near Letterfrack), for the good of the local community – see the boxed text 'Kylemore Abbey' (p242). From 1891 the Congested Districts Board, and later the Irish Land Commission, guided a huge improvement in the fortunes of the area, putting the fishing industry on a firmer foundation, and reorganising land holdings and parcelling them out among former tenant farmers.

Since independence and especially in recent years, Connemara's Gaeltacht parts have certainly held their own, if not prospered. Forestry and fish farming have come as mixed blessings, bringing environmental problems as well as new industries. Fishing and farming are still vital, although tourism has become another economic mainstay of the area.

NATURAL HISTORY

The principal building block of most of the mountains in Connemara is hard, white quartzite; rock that has been transformed by upheavals in the earth's crust from the sand and grit of an ancient ocean about 500 million years old. Beds of limestone also began transforming around this period to become the bands of marble that are a distinctive feature of Connemara today. Over subsequent aeons these rocks, and sedimentary rocks formed during a later period, were subjected to erosion; the quartzite was not worn down to the same extent as the less resistant schist, which now underlies extensive areas of the lowlands and the valleys between the mountain groups. Volcanic rocks are less common in the area, being mainly confined to the hard, black gabbro that makes up a few of the smaller hills in Connemara, including Doughruagh and Errisbeg.

During the last Ice Age most of Connemara was buried under ice; the advance and retreat of the glaciers carved out and deepened valleys, and gouged corries in the mountainsides. Killary Harbour, explored on one of the routes in this chapter, is one of the most spectacular examples of a glacial feature; more accurately described as a fjord, it was sculpted into a U-shape, then submerged when the climate warmed and the ice melted about 10,000 years ago (for more details, see the boxed text 'Signs of a Glacial Past', p24).

Centuries after the end of the Ice Age, extensive forests of oak, hazel and other species developed, only to be felled by Neolithic farmers around 3000 BC. Blanket bog – accumulations of decayed plant material – gradually spread across low-lying ground and still covers large, poorly drained areas of south Connemara. Today native woodlands are largely confined to sheltered sites, while unsightly and unprofitable commercial plantations of lodgepole pine and sitka spruce cover many of the area's glens and hillsides.

PLANNING
Maps & Books
The Mountains of Connemara – A Hill-Walker's Guide, by Joss Lynam, and the accompanying 1:50,000 map are almost indispensable. Connemara: Part 1, Introduction and Gazetteer and the accompanying 1:63,360 Connemara map, by Tim Robinson, are also beautifully written and designed, and are invaluable for historical and cultural background. Paddy Dillon's Connemara is also a comprehensive guide to walks in the region.

Information Sources
Cleggan-based **Connemara Tourism** (☎ 095-44955; W www.connemara-tourism.org) can provide information about accommodation, activities and the history of the area.

ACCESS TOWNS
Clifden
A lively town, Clifden (An Clochán) holds the title of capital of Connemara. It has adapted to a growing number of visitors over recent years, and now offers a wide range of tourist facilities.

The town's **TIC** (☎ 095-21163; Market St; open Apr-Sept) offers advice on local accommodation and activities. **Connemara Walking Centre** (☎ 095-21379; Island House, Market St; open year-round) arranges guided walks, and stocks a good selection of local maps and guidebooks.

There are also several bookshops, banks, an Internet café, numerous **pubs** and a large **supermarket** situated in the compact town centre.

Places to Stay Centrally located **Clifden Town Hostel** (☎ 095-21076; Market St; dorm beds/doubles from €12/32) is bright and friendly. **Brookside Hostel** (☎ 095-21812; Fairgreen; dorm beds/doubles €11.50/30; open Mar-Oct) is quieter and located beside the Owenglin River, off the bottom of Market St. There are also numerous B&Bs in and around the town. **Kingstown House** (☎ 095-21470; Bridge St; singles/doubles €35/50) is large, central and one of the cheapest B&Bs around.

Getting There & Away There are regular **Bus Éireann** (☎ 091-562 000) services between Clifden and Galway (€8.25, two hours 15 minutes, three to five daily Monday to Saturday and once or twice on Sunday). There is also a summer service (July and August only) to/from Westport (€9.75, one hour 35 minutes, once daily Monday to Saturday).

Leenaun

Generally spelled Leenane within the village, this is a compact settlement centred around a crossroads at the eastern end of Killary Harbour. It has been on the Connemara tourist circuit for many years, but manages to provide a large number of visitor facilities without sacrificing its small-village feel. It has a small **grocery shop** (which also sells local walking maps and guidebooks), a petrol pump, and several **pubs** and **cafés**. **Leenane Cultural Centre** (☎ 095-42323; open Apr–Sept), just over the bridge north of the main crossroads, provides basic tourist information, stocks local walking maps and has a reasonable range of local history books; it also has a café.

Places to Stay & Eat There are several B&Bs in and around the village. More central options include **Killary House** (☎ 095-42254; singles/doubles €35/60), located in a converted farmhouse, and **Portfinn Lodge** (☎ 095-42265; singles/doubles €30/60), with its celebrated seafood restaurant that is also open to nonresidents. The largest hotel in the village is **Leenane Hotel** (☎ 095-42249; singles/doubles from €35/70 Sept–June & €62/124 July & Aug); food is served in both the bar and the restaurant.

For meals, **The Village Grill** (☎ 095-42253) offers an array of burgers and fried stuffs, while **Blackberry Café** (☎ 095-42240) serves lunches; in the evenings more formal dishes are available from an appetising menu.

Getting There & Away There is a **Bus Éireann** (☎ 091-562 000) service connecting Leenaun to Galway (€9, one hour 50 minutes, twice daily Monday to Saturday July and August, and Tuesday and Saturday only

during the rest of the year). There are also connections to Clifden (€3.20, 50 minutes, once daily Monday to Saturday July and August, and Tuesday and Saturday only during the rest of the year) and summer services to Westport (€7.50, 45 minutes, once daily Monday to Saturday July and August).

Killary Harbour

Duration	3½–4 hours
Distance	10km
Difficulty	easy
Start/Finish	GR 814619
Nearest Towns	Rosroe (p240), Leenaun (p239)
Transport	private
Summary	A low-level circuit exploring the southern shores of Killary Harbour, including a deserted hamlet, a famine road and wonderful mountain scenery.

Killary Harbour is the 16km-long sea inlet that marks the northern boundary of Connemara. It is often described as Ireland's only true fjord, having been scoured by glaciers descending from the surrounding peaks during the last Ice Age. The surrounding backdrop is one of rugged mountain scenery, with steep, craggy peaks framing the harbour on each side. The slopes of Mweelrea, the highest mountain in Connaught, rise steeply from the northern shores of the harbour, while the summits to the east and south are no less impressive.

The natural splendour of the setting is only one of the attractions of this route, which, for the most part, follows good tracks along the southern shores of the harbour. There is also a poignant human history associated with the area. This part of the country was particularly badly affected by the Great Famine of 1845–49, and evidence of the hardship of that era is impossible to avoid. Ruined buildings of the now deserted settlement of Foher, which was depopulated around the time of the famine, are visited on this route. A famine relief road dating back to 1846 – constructed by

CENTRAL WEST

locals in return for food rations – is followed over another section.

The route also offers the opportunity to explore the tiny fishing community of Rosroe at the mouth of Killary Harbour. It is also possible to stay overnight here, and start and finish the walk from this point.

The terrain covered is a mixture of quiet tarmac lanes, grassy *boreens* and rugged paths. Salrock Pass marks the modest high-point of the circuit at 130m, making this route an ideal option if clouds are lying low over higher peaks in the area. The total ascent is 180m. Despite the route's low altitude, boots will be appreciated in wet conditions, when sections of the trail can become boggy or muddy.

PLANNING
Maps
OSI's 1:50,000 map No 37 and Harvey's Superwalker 1:30,000 map *Connemara* both cover this route.

NEAREST TOWNS
See Leenaun (p239).

Rosroe
This is a little-visited hamlet centred around a working harbour at the mouth of Killary. It has no facilities besides a hostel and tranquillity is guaranteed. The An Óige **Killary Harbour Youth Hostel** (☎ 095-43417; dorm beds €13) is generally pretty quiet and the spacious common room has an incomparable view of Mweelrea across the harbour.

To reach Rosroe follow signs for the 'Killary Harbour Youth Hostel', turning west from the N59, 700m south of the Bunowen River and 400m south of the turn-off described to the start of the Killary Harbour walk. Continue for 7.5km, veering right, to the end of the road.

GETTING TO/FROM THE WALK
The route starts and finishes at the end of a minor road (GR 814619) heading northwest from the N59 on the southern side of Killary Harbour. The turn-off from the N59 is marked by signs for the Sli na Chonamara, and is located 300m south of the Bunowen

River, around 7.5km west of Leenaun and 12km east of Letterfrack. Parking at the end of the road is limited to three cars – other small parking spots are available further back along the road.

Large groups would do better to start the circuit at Rosroe, where there is plenty of parking space by the pier (GR 769650).

There is no public transport to the start of the route, although the **Bus Éireann** (☎ 091-562 000) Clifden–Leenaun service passes by on the N59 and could be used if the timetable is convenient (see Getting There & Away, p239, for Leenaun).

THE WALK (see map p236)
Two gates and a sign, indicating that private vehicles may not proceed further, mark the start of the route. Pass through the right-hand gate and continue along the lane for a little over 1km. Lines of floats securing salmon pens bob in the harbour to the north and will be a constant presence for the first half of the route. The lane soon becomes a gravel track, and then, after passing through a couple of gates and crossing a bridge, which spans a waterfall, the track narrows again to become a grassy *boreen*.

Around 3km from the start you come to a semi-ruined cottage, the first of several ruinous stone buildings that once made up the village of Foher. Follow the *boreen* along the front of the ruins, and pass over a stone stile in the wall to the west. The *boreen* now dwindles to a single-file path and climbs up and around a rock outcrop. The retaining walls of the famine road are obvious at the side of the path.

The rugged landscape is now dotted with boulders and bands of rock, although the buildings and boats of Rosroe soon come into view ahead (1½ to two hours from the start). Pass along the south side of a large stone wall enclosing a field, and exit the *boreen* beside a cottage. Join the minor road leading to Rosroe harbour; the pier is a about 200m along the road to the right, and well worth the short detour.

From the pier, retrace your steps along the road, continuing past the point where you came down off the *boreen*. Killary Harbour

Little (or 'Little Killary') is the picturesque inlet to the south, its shape mimicking the larger-scale fjord further north. Follow the road for around 1km, climbing to a sharp right turn. Leave the lane here, continuing ahead (east) through a wooden gate. A short but steep ascent now leads to Salrock Pass, from where Killary Harbour and Little Killary are both visible.

The descent down the eastern side of the pass is even steeper, though it is not long before you come to a junction of a fence and stone wall on your right. Cross the low wire fence at the corner and then turn immediately left through a gate in the wall. You are now at the top of the ruined settlement of Foher that you passed on your outward journey. Turn right and trace the wall as it descends gradually through the ruins, rejoining the *boreen* at the eastern end of the hamlet. Retrace your initial steps back to the road and your starting point.

Doughruagh & Benchoona

Duration	3–3½ hours
Distance	7km
Difficulty	moderate
Start/Finish	Kylemore Abbey
Nearest Towns	Letterfrack (p241), Leenaun (p239)
Transport	bus

Summary A surprisingly straightforward ascent of a rugged mountain massif providing great views over the Twelve Bens.

The dark, craggy slopes of Doughruagh (Dúchruach or Black Stack) tower above Kylemore Abbey and appear almost impenetrable. In reality, the ascent to the summit is simple. A flight of steps climbs to the prominent white statue of the Sacred Heart, set high on the hillside above Pollacappul Lough. From here, an old track and then a stretch of open ground lead to the summit plateau. The top provides a vantage point that is unsurpassed in terms of views over the Twelve Bens. The total ascent is 520m.

Kylemore Abbey is one of the biggest tourist attractions in Connemara and is an impressive place to start and finish the walk. See the boxed text 'Kylemore Abbey' (p242) for details.

For those who can handle the transport logistics of a linear route, a recommended continuation of this walk leads north from Doughruagh, passes over the larger neighbouring summit of Benchoona, and makes a descent on the north side of the massif. This moderate-demanding option finishes at the northern outlet of Lough Muck. See the Alternative Finish: Lough Muck (p244) for details.

PLANNING
Maps

OSI 1:50,000 map No 37 covers this walk. It shows neither the path from Kylemore Abbey to the statue, nor the statue itself.

NEAREST TOWNS

See Leenaun (p239).

Letterfrack

This small village has just enough facilities to make it a convenient base for walks in north Connemara. The closest banking facilities are in Clifden (p238). **Connemara National Park visitor centre** (☎ 095-41054; N59; open mid-March–mid-Nov), 500m west of the village and just inside the entrance to the park, is a source of abundant information. The centre carries a range of walking maps and guides, and also offers snacks.

Places to Stay & Eat A spacious old building, **the Old Monastery Hostel** (☎ 095-41132; @ oldmon@indigo.ie; camping per

Kylemore Abbey

In an area where deciduous woodlands are relatively rare, it is well worth taking the opportunity to wander round the grounds of imposing Kylemore Abbey (☎ 095-41146; ⓦ www.kylemoreabbey .com; open 9.30am-6pm daily). Entry costs €5 to the abbey grounds or €10 if you also want to visit the Victorian walled garden. There is a visitor centre and restaurant on site.

Kylemore is the anglicised version of the Irish *coill mór*, meaning 'big wood'. Research carried out on pollen grains preserved in nearby peat boglands has shown that a mixed woodland of pine, hazel, elm and oak began to take hold in the area about 8000 years ago, after the end of the last Ice Age. However, by the mid-19th century only fragments of native woodland had survived wholesale felling for shipbuilding and iron smelting. Fortunately the Kylemore estate was bought by wealthy Englishman Mitchell Henry in 1862. Several years later he set about replanting the woodlands, and introducing native Irish and other trees and shrubs to the estate.

Foremost among the native trees is the stately Irish yew. The timber of the sessile oak, another native, is particularly well suited to shipbuilding. Other local species include silver birch, hazel, alder, ash, the white-flowering hawthorn and the handsome Scots pine, which was once native to Ireland.

Among the several introduced species in the woods are western red cedar, rowan, larch (the only deciduous conifer), beech and English oak, which often hybridises with the native sessile oak. Unfortunately, the most prominent and colourful import, rhododendron, has become a catastrophic pest (see the boxed text 'Scourge of the Rhododendron', p269).

The castle overlooking Pollacappul Lough was built for Mitchell Henry between 1864 and 1868, providing a much needed boost to the local economy. Henry developed the estate into a thriving, almost self-contained community with extensive gardens, glasshouses, stables and a hydro-electricity plant. The estate was eventually sold in 1903. It came into the possession of the Irish Benedictine nuns in 1920 after they had been forced to flee their 250-year-old abbey home in Ypres (Belgium) during WWI. The rights and privileges of the abbey were transferred from Ypres to Kylemore, now the monastic home of the nuns, who also operate an international girls school on the estate.

person/dorm beds/doubles €6/12/32), 500m up the rough road heading southeast from the crossroads in the centre of the village, is run in a relaxed manner. The kitchen is too small for such a popular hostel but a breakfast of porridge and home-made scones is included in the price. **The Bard's Den** (☎ 095-41042; *singles/doubles €25/50*), one of the three pubs by the crossroads, is the most central B&B. **Veldon's Restaurant & Bar**, adjacent to the well-stocked **shop**, serves food all day.

Getting There & Away There are **Bus Éireann** (☎ 091-562 000) services connecting Letterfrack to Galway (€9, two hours 10 minutes, once daily Monday to Saturday July and August, and Tuesday and Saturday only during the rest of the year). The Letterfrack to Clifden service operates on the same days (€3.20, 20 minutes). During

July and August only, there are also regular services via Leenaun to Westport (€9, one hour 10 minutes, once daily Monday to Saturday).

Michael Nee Coaches (☎ 095-51082) also operates bus services in the area between mid-June and early September. During this period there are regular connections between Letterfrack and Galway (€8, twice daily), and Clifden, Letterfrack and Kylemore Abbey (€4, three times daily).

GETTING TO/FROM THE WALK

The entrance to Kylemore Abbey is clearly signed from the N59, 4km east of Letterfrack and 15.5km west of Leenaun.

Michael Nee Coaches (☎ 095-51082) runs a regular bus service between Kylemore Abbey, Letterfrack and Clifden (€4, three times daily from mid-June to early-September). Bus times are convenient for a day walk if you are coming from either Letterfrack or Clifden. All **Bus Éireann** (☎ 091-562 000) services through Letterfrack also pass the entrance to Kylemore Abbey, 4km east of the village, and will drop you off if you ask the driver – see Getting There & Away (p242) for Letterfrack for details.

To locate Lough Muck (the alternative finish) follow a minor road (signed to Killary Harbour Youth Hostel) that branches west from the N59, 7.5km west of Leenaun and 12km east of Letterfrack. There is limited parking around 6km further on, 650m northwest of the church on the eastern shore of Lough Muck.

THE WALK (see map p236)

Walk towards the abbey from the visitor centre, but almost immediately bear left through the double gates to the school and

walk up the road to a car park. Here, a sign points the way to the statue. Climb the steps, gaining height steadily as you pass through dense thickets of rhododendron. About 25 minutes later you should arrive at the white **statue of the Sacred Heart**, commanding a marvellous view of Kylemore Lough and the northern peaks of the Twelve Bens.

Continue northeast along an old, grassy path that climbs gently across the steep slope. The path is generally well defined, although after only 200m it becomes a bit obscure as you round a tight bend. Look for the remnant stone bank on the downhill edge to keep on course. About 1km from the statue, the path dips slightly and crosses a spur, opening up wider views of Benchoona ahead. Some care is then needed to follow the path as it traverses a rocky slope towards a col; keep close to the foot of the

Connemara National Park & Diamond Hill

Connemara National Park was established in 1980, and comprises almost 20 sq km of blanket bog stretching from sea level to the summit of Benbaun (729m) in the Twelve Bens. With such a beautiful landscape it is little wonder that the park has proved popular. In the year of its opening some 9000 people visited the park; within 20 years this total had risen to around 75,000.

Diamond Hill (445m) dominates the western section of the park, and soon became established as one of the most popular walks in Connemara, with an estimated 10,000 people setting out to climb to the summit each year. Inevitably, the trampling of so many feet caused erosion problems and the fragile bogland was soon bearing obvious scars. In 2002, Dúchas, the government agency that manages the country's national parks, declared Diamond Hill and the surrounding area off limits to walkers. It outlined a plan to replace the eroded footpath with a boardwalk that would cost an estimated €1.27 million and take three years to complete.

While all parties agreed on the need to protect the environment and prevent further damage to the area, the decision to close the mountain entirely has proved a controversial one. The MCI (Mountaineering Council of Ireland) expressed concerns over the timescale, saying that three years seemed a long time to keep the mountain closed. The countryside access group Keep Ireland Open also came out against the three-year 'prohibition', claiming that the route was a public right of way. It proposed that an alternative path could be used for the duration of path construction.

The issue highlights many of the underlying problems associated with off-road walking, particularly those of access and damage limitation. At the time of writing, however, Diamond Hill remained out of bounds until 2005. If you are walking after this date, the three-hour, 5km walk to the summit is well recommended. It involves 420m of ascent but offers wonderful coast and mountain views, and is particularly suited as an introduction to mountain walking in Connemara.

In the meantime, visitors to the park can follow two nature trails (the longest of which, the Sruffaunboy Nature Trail, stretches for 1.5km), observe the herd of Connemara ponies, and visit the exhibitions in the visitor centre (see Letterfrack, p241). The entrance to the park is along the N59, 500m west of Letterfrack. The park is open year-round and entry costs adult/child €2.75/1.25.

steeper ground. A large cairn marks the col (about 45 minutes from the statue).

To climb Doughruagh, head southwest from the col, passing just left of the crest of the spur at first to avoid some crags. The summit plateau is an intriguing mosaic of tarns, grass patches and rock outcrops. Before you proceed too far onto the plateau, check your position to ensure that you will be able to recognise the descent route on your return. The **summit** can be difficult to locate among the crags, but is close to the northwestern edge and is distinguished by a rusted fence post near a cairn. It provides a particularly good vantage point for views southeast to the Twelve Bens, north to Clare Island and west across Tully Mountain to Inishbofin Island.

Retrace your steps to the large cairn on the col. Here you can continue north to Lough Muck (see Alternative Finish, below) or return to the abbey. If you are returning directly to the abbey, simply retrace your steps, this time enjoying the outlook across Kylemore Lough (1½ hours from the summit).

Alternative Finish: Lough Muck
2–2½ hours, 5km, 370m ascent
From the large cairn, cross wet ground to the northeast and climb the steep, grassy slope to a broad ridge. Keep to the western side of this as you head north, over a rounded bump, and down to a peaty gap. Cross this near its eastern edge and climb to the summit of Garraun (598m), which is topped with a small cairn (one hour from the col). The main bulk of Benchoona now lies across a steep-sided gap cradling a small tarn. **Benchoona's highest point** (581m), marked with a cairn, is just west of Lough Benchoona, near the western end of the knobbly plateau.

To reach Lough Muck head northwest from the summit of Benchoona, taking care to keep to the highest ground as you descend the extremely steep, rocky spur. When the angle of the slope eases, change course and head north. Pass over a rocky outcrop and a domed hill, then descend through turf cuttings to a rough bridge across the outlet stream from Lough Muck. It is then a short walk to the road.

Central Maumturks

Duration	5–5½ hours
Distance	12km
Difficulty	moderate–demanding
Start/Finish	Maumeen car park
Nearest Town	Clifden (p238)
Transport	private

Summary A high-level walk across an intricate, rocky ridge in the heart of the magnificent Maumturk Mountains.

Any walk in the Maumturk Mountains is a serious undertaking. The terrain is more rugged than it looks from below, accurate route finding is a challenge even in good weather, and maps don't show the intricate jumble of knolls, spurs and tarns along the main summit ridge. For fans of such high rocky ground, however, this should prove an immensely rewarding route.

The walk described here crosses the central section of the range, and takes in its highest peak, Binn Idir an Dá Log (Peak Between Two Hollows), at 702m. It begins by following part of the Western Way (p340) over an old pilgrimage route to a pass graced by a small chapel, an outdoor altar and a collection of small, stone-carved Celtic crosses, one for each station of the cross. St Patrick himself is said to have blessed the land of Connemara from this point, and he couldn't have picked a more scenic spot to do it from. Walkers may be inspired to do the same thing! The route finishes with a 4km section along a quiet minor road, although this could be avoided if two vehicles are available. There is a total ascent of 750m.

Unless you are confident in your navigation skills, tackle the Maumturks only in good weather – route finding in poor visibility is particularly tricky. It is worth noting that there is a mountain rescue post at **Ben Lettery Youth Hostel** (*☎ 096-34636*), situated along the N59 around 13km west of the start.

PLANNING
Maps
Harvey's Superwalker 1:30,000 map *Connemara* is best for this walk. OSI 1:50,000

maps Nos 37 and 44 also cover the walk; No 44 shows only about 2km of road and track near the start of the walk.

GETTING TO/FROM THE WALK

If you are approaching the route by car, turn northeast from the N59 along a minor road signed to 'Mamean', 12km west of Maam Cross and 2km east of Recess. The car park is 3.2km further on at GR 892495. To avoid the road walk back to the start, there are a few small parking spaces near the bridge at GR 873521.

Bus Éireann (☎ 091-562 000) services stop at Recess, which is about 4km southwest of the start of the walk. From here there are regular connections to Galway (€9, one hour five minutes, once or twice daily) and Clifden (€3.20, 15 minutes, at least twice Monday to Saturday and one on Sunday).

THE WALK

From the Maumeen car park go through the large gate and walk up the wide track that climbs steadily northeast towards the mountains. After about 30 minutes you reach the tiny, stone **chapel** in the col of Maumeen, which is near the highest point on the track. The outdoor altar is topped with a slab of green-seamed Connemara marble, and the cairns marking the stations of the cross are scattered nearby.

From here, set a northeasterly course towards a grassy spur at the foot of low bluffs, soon crossing the path to the holy well on the left. Cross a fence and climb steeply northwest towards the crest of the spur. Here you meet the fence once again – it provides an occasionally useful guide as you continue northwest, climbing to a bumpy plateau strewn with rock slabs and masses of shattered white quartzite. The summit, **Binn Chaonaigh** (633m), is about 100m northwest of a tiny lough (one hour from the chapel).

From this summit, descend steeply west for about 700m before veering north close to the edge of cliffs. Continue down along a narrow ridge to a col. Here and there are traces of a stony path underfoot, although it isn't continuous enough to provide reliable guidance. Climb to a small cairn on the first of a cluster of tops, the highest (659m) marking a change in direction at an eastern extremity of the ridge.

Then comes another descent, followed by a steady climb first west then north over a jumble of bumps and hollows, now following a clear path underfoot. Continue to

Maumturks Walk

Twenty-four kilometres of horizontal distance and 2336m of ascent probably aren't the criteria for most walkers' notion of a pleasant day's outing. Nevertheless, in May each year since 1975 a couple of hundred walkers have thought otherwise and taken part in the National University of Ireland Mountaineering Club's Maumturks Walk.

Traditionally, the walk starts about 3km south of Maam Bridge on the road to Maam Cross and finishes at Leenaun, where there are enough pubs to cater for all weary walkers. On average, participants cover the distance in about 10 hours, although some speedy souls have been known to do it in six.

The Maumturks make their own weather, within an area notorious – or famous – for its meteorological mayhem. In 1975 conditions were so bad for the Maumturks Walk that only a handful of the 70 starters saw out the distance. In 2002 the event was cancelled altogether.

The rugged terrain has also taken its toll – during the 1997 and 1998 events, a helicopter had to be summoned to lift injured walkers to safety.

For more information about the annual event, contact the university's mountaineering club c/ Mountaineering-Sports Centre, Aran na MacLeinn, National University of Ireland, Galway City, County Galway.

Central Maumturks

0 .... 1 .... 2km
0 .... 0.5 .... 1mi
1:100,000
Contour Interval 50m

Pine Plantation

To R344, N59,
Leenaun &
Letterfrack

Lough Maumahoge

Failmore

Maumgawnagh

River

Binn Idir
an Dá Log
(702m)

659m

Lehanaghbeg
Lough

Lehanagh
Lough

Binn
Chaonaigh
(633m)

Western Way

Western Way

Pine
Plantation

Holy Well
Maumeen

Pine
Plantation

START/
FINISH

Pine
Plantation

To N59, Recess & Clifden

Binn Idir an Dá Log (702m), the main summit of the range, which is marked by a cairn on a chunky crag (1½ hours from Binn Chaonaigh).

Sporadic cairns indicate the route onwards, north across a plateau to the descent route along a narrow ridge tending northwest. A squat cairn on the northwest edge of a sloping shelf marks the start of a very steep section down through broken crags, although there are alternative ways down to the left with more grass and less rock. At the base of the descent lies the delightful **Lough Maumahoge** (45 minutes from the summit).

Cross the rocky spur west of the lough to a small col, where a steep descent leads down a grassy passage to the wide valley below. The gradient of the descent soon eases and an easy wander beside a picturesque stream brings you to the road; the Maumeen car park is 4km along the lane to the left.

Glencoaghan Horseshoe

Duration	7–7½ hours
Distance	12km
Difficulty	demanding
Start	Glencoaghan
Finish	Ben Lettery Youth Hostel
Nearest Town	Clifden (p238)
Transport	bus

Summary A classic among Irish mountain walks, this exhilarating route demands fitness, surefootedness and confidence over steep and rocky ground.

A walk over some of the renowned Twelve Bens' peaks is akin to a rite of passage for walkers in Connemara, if not Ireland. This immensely rugged mountain range dominates the heart of Connemara and is arranged in a cluster of five interlocking horseshoes, with peaks ranging in height from Benbaun (729m) to Benlettery (577m). Intervening cols are typically extremely steep and bands of steep cliffs run around the central summits, making them look almost impregnable.

The Bens offer walkers a variety of routes, all of them strenuous. The six southern summits fit neatly into the Glencoaghan Horseshoe, probably the most popular walk in the range. This route is immensely rewarding, but demands a high degree of fitness and hillwalking experience. It involves some 1670m of ascent and the terrain can be rough; in several places steep slopes call for the use of hands, and rock steps demand minor scrambling manoeuvres. It is also only possible to escape the ridge in one or two (rather inconvenient) places, and navigation in poor visibility is far from straightforward. In many places along the ridge a rutted path has been worn by the passage of feet, but on many of the steeper slopes you are on your own. Other circuits in the Twelve Bens share many of the difficulties and rewards associated with this route. See Benbaun Circuit (p254) for a route around the northern summits.

Note that there is a mountain rescue post at **Ben Lettery Youth Hostel** (☎ 096-34636), at the end of the walk.

PLANNING
Maps

Harvey's Superwalker 1:30,000 map *Connemara* is the ideal map for this route. OSI 1:50,000 maps Nos 37 and 44 cover the walk, although most of the route is on No 37 (on this map, Bengower is misnamed Glengower).

NEAREST TOWN & FACILITIES

See Clifden (p238).

Glencoaghan Area

There are a couple of convenient accommodation options in the Glencoaghan area close to the walk. **Ben Lettery Youth Hostel** *(☎ 095-51136; dorm beds €13)* is on the N59 at the end of the walk. **Canal Stage House B&B** *(☎ 095-51064; singles/doubles €32/50)* is along the minor road leading to the start of the walk.

GETTING TO/FROM THE WALK

To reach the start of the walk, turn north off the N59 onto a minor road, around 7km west of Recess, 15km east of Clifden and 1.7km east of the Ben Lettery Youth Hostel. The start is about 2.5km along this road. Park at a small quarry just west of the bridge over the Glencoaghan River, around 1.5km from the N59; alternatively, there are individual spaces about 1km further on. At the end of the walk, parking is available on the old road close to the hostel entrance.

Bus Éireann *(☎ 091-562 000)* Clifden–Galway services ply the N59. You can be dropped off at the minor road near the start of the walk and Canal Stage House B&B, or at Ben Lettery Youth Hostel (check with the driver). There are services at least twice daily Monday to Saturday, and once on Sunday. See Getting There & Away (p239) for Clifden for further details.

THE WALK

Walk east from the road, across rising ground to the ridge crest; a worn path leads up the western side of the rocky ridge to the summit of **Derryclare** (673m, 1½ hours from the start). The views southwards across the Connemara lake lands to the low ridge of Errisbeg (p248) are particularly fine. An easy

descent, by Twelve Bens standards, takes you to a peaty col. Then, a steep, rocky ascent leads to the compact summit and sprawling cairn on **Bencorr** (Binn Chorr, 711m, about 45 minutes from Derryclare). The extra elevation here brings Mweelrea and the Benchoona massif into view. Continue northwest along the ridge over a couple of dips and bumps to a cairn at the top of the next, very steep, descent westwards. At first you have to negotiate some unstable scree, then massive rock slabs forming a downhill pavement lead to a narrow peaty col, Mam na bhFonsaí (30 minutes from Bencorr).

The next climb begins over rock slabs, then on to more broken rock and up to the small top of **Bencollaghduff** (Binn Dhubh, 696m, 30 minutes from the col). This peak is right in the midst of the Bens, at the apex of the horseshoe. Then comes another steep drop, but the gradient eases for the descent to a slender col. Here you make a major change in direction, turning generally southwards at

Glencoaghan Horseshoe

Gleninagh River

Muckanaght (654m)
Beufree (638m)
Benbaun (729m)
Bencollaghduff (696m)
Bencorrbeg (577m)

Connemara National Park

Mam na bhFonsaí
Bencorr (711m)

Pine Plantation

Benbreen (691m)

Derryclare (673m)

Bengower (664m)
Benglenisky (516m)

Benlettery (577m)

START

To Clifden

Ben Lettery Youth Hostel **FINISH**

Ballynahinch

N59

To Roundstone

Pine Plantation

Lake

R341

To Recess

0   0.5   1   2km
0   0.5   1mi
1:125,000
Contour Interval 50m

the head of the western arm of the horseshoe – with some interesting route-finding problems looming up ahead.

The next climb starts easily but, as the ridge steepens, the rocks are less dissected; keep to the left to surmount the bluff guarding the edge of the elongated and bumpy summit arc of **Benbreen** (Binn Bhraoin, 691m); the cairn on the highest point is at the southern edge (1¼ hours from the last col). Ribbons of scree lead down to the next gap, from which the most exciting ascent of the day rises southwards. At the first apparent barrier, a well-defined ramp provides a good way up; next, a narrow gully is climbed via its own, in-built 'steps'; the last obstacle is overcome by bearing right along a path around the bluff. Up on **Bengower** (Binn Gobhar, 30 minutes from Benbreen) you are rewarded with a very fine view of the Connemara lake lands to the south.

Continue south and down to a broad and grassy col, and on to **Benlettery** (Binn Leitir, 40 minutes from Bengower). Follow the badly eroded path from the summit, keeping west for the best route through the crags. On the way down aim for the ruinous stone building just north of the hostel. Go through a gap in the fence above the ruin, which you pass on your left, and continue towards the hostel, crossing its enclosing fence via a stile.

Errisbeg

Duration	2–3 hours
Distance	6km
Difficulty	easy–moderate
Start/Finish	Roundstone (p248)
Transport	bus

Summary An ascent of a rugged little hill; the modest effort is rewarded with far-reaching views across the loughs, bogs, coast and the mountains of Connemara.

If you are staying in or just passing through southern Connemara, don't miss doing this short walk. On a good day the views from the summit – at only 300m – embrace most of, if not all, the major peaks, the coast and the boglands in Connemara. Although the summit plateau and its approaches are littered with cairns of all shapes and sizes, there aren't any clearly defined paths. You will have to cross some minor boggy patches, but the going is mostly grass, heather and rocky ground. Roundstone itself is a popular weekend destination with a beautiful harbour view that has attracted the eye of many painters.

This route can be extended into a longer coastal circuit by descending steeply from the summit of Errisbeg to Dogs Bay and Gurteen Bay. Rough ground is covered on the descent and you'll need to avoid walking across land close to the many cottages along the R341. Good coastal walking leads from Gurteen Bay back to Roundstone. Allow an extra two hours for this route.

NATURAL HISTORY
The geology of Errisbeg is unusual in that it has formed from an isolated outcrop of the volcanic rock gabbro – a rock type not common in Ireland. The acclaimed Irish naturalist Robert Lloyd Praeger (1865–1953) talks at length in his book *The Way That I Went* about the botanical delights of the area around Errisbeg. He identified several interesting plant species including Mediterranean heath, pipewort, slender naiad and the close-flowered orchid.

PLANNING
Maps & Books
Use OSI 1:50,000 map No 44 for this walk. Tim Robinson's 1:63,360 *Connemara* map and the accompanying booklet *Introduction and Gazetteer* have a wealth of local information.

NEAREST TOWN
Roundstone
A small, compact and picturesque fishing village, Roundstone has great views of the Twelve Bens and is a popular spot with visitors during the summer months. There is a good choice of restaurants and cafés and several shops, including **Michael Ferron's**, which sells OSI maps and local walking guides. The nearest banking facilities are in Clifden (p238).

Places to Stay & Eat In a wonderful location at the back of a beach, 2km west of the village, is **Gurteen Beach Caravan & Camping Park** (☎ 095-35882; camping per person €7.50). Among the most central of the B&Bs is **St Joseph's B&B** (☎ 095-35865; singles/doubles €40/60). Also very central is **Eldon's Hotel** (☎ 095-35933; singles/doubles €50/70 Oct-Apr & €65/100 June-Aug), which serves a good selection of bar meals. **Beola Seafood Restaurant** (☎ 095-35871) offers something a bit more special.

Getting There & Away There are regular Bus Éireann (☎ 091-562 000) services from Roundstone to Galway (€9, one hour 30 minutes, twice daily July and August, and Wednesday, Friday and Sunday only the rest of the year) and Clifden (€5, 35 minutes, twice daily July and August, and Wednesday, Friday and Sunday only the rest of the year).

By car, Roundstone is well signed from the Galway–Clifden road (the N59). There is plenty of parking around the village centre.

THE WALK

From the main street in Roundstone, turn uphill at the corner of O'Dowd's pub onto a narrow road. Climb steeply for a short distance to gain more level ground above the village. Continue straight along this road for the next 1km, passing over a crossroads, before climbing steeply again to reach a house at the road end. To the left of the house is a wooden gate. Pass through this and follow the eroded path out onto the

open hillside. Aim for easier slopes slightly north of the east summit of Errisbeg. As you gain height the path becomes fainter and diverges into many separate, barely discernible trails, before disappearing altogether. Continue ahead, climbing towards the unnamed eastern summit at 252m, crossing wonderfully rugged terrain with tussock grass and heather filling the hollows between outcrops of rough gabbro.

Looking back to the east from this first top, views extend across the many inlets and islands of Galway Bay. To the north the vast mosaic of bog and lough extends right up to the slopes of the Twelve Bens. Head west across a few intervening little summits to reach the trig point on **Errisbeg** (300m). Expect to take around 1½ hours to reach this point from Roundstone. On a clear day the panorama of coastal views to the west opens out and it can be difficult to discern exactly where the mainland ends and the ocean begins, such is the chaotic complexity of the coastline. To the south the low profiles of the Aran Islands are conspicuous, and beyond these Black Head (p252) and the limestone pavements of the Burren show up white or grey depending on whether there is sun or cloud overhead.

Return to Roundstone by retracing your outward journey.

The Burren

The Burren landscape is one of Ireland's most famous natural attractions, and justly so. This is a unique area, characterised by expanses of pale grey limestone pavement and terraced hillsides (see the boxed text 'Karst Wonders of the Burren', p251) that stretch right down to the Atlantic. The name Burren comes from the Irish word *boireann*,

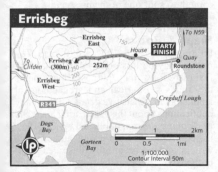

Errisbeg

meaning 'place of rocks'. In reality, however, only 20% of the Burren is bare rock, while the remainder of the terrain is composed of green fields and hills that boast the richest concentration of plant species in Ireland. The geological and botanical wonders of the area are offset by ancient human interest; the Burren also has a remarkable number of archaeological features, especially prehistoric burial tombs, forts and early Christian chapels.

Curiously, given the wealth of natural and historic interest concentrated in the area, the Burren is not as accessible for walkers as most other parts of the country, and there are comparatively few good, sustained walks. Access problems mean that the route along the top of the Cliffs of Moher – previously one of the most popular walks in the area – is no longer open. Nevertheless, one or two routes are possible, and are highly recommended as a way to properly appreciate the unusual beauty of the area. Accommodation is convenient and plentiful, and public transport is adequate, although a car and/or bike would enable you to explore the heart of the Burren well inland and off the beaten track.

HISTORY

Communities have been living in the Burren for about 5000 years. For the earliest peoples of the Neolithic and Bronze ages, the building of resting places for their dead was of great importance, as the remains of their graves (dolmens) suggest. Enormous upstanding slabs form wedge-shaped or rectangular tombs supporting a massive lid or capstone. From about 600 BC, Celtic people settled in the area and built round or oval enclosures known as raths, *dúns*, cashels or *lios* (see the boxed text 'Dolmens & *Dúns*', p19). The Burren has the best collection of these structures in Ireland – as many as 450 are still identifiable.

Forest clearance began to open up more land for grassland grazing in around AD 300, although extensive areas of woodland were still standing in the 15th century; the wholesale clearance came later as the population increased and the demand for timber grew. The popularity of the Burren as a tourist destination is a late-20th-century phenomenon, although there are more than a few residents who defend the area's lack of development and resist attempts to turn it into a theme park, rightly maintaining that it is best appreciated by first-hand exploration.

NATURAL HISTORY

The Burren is one of the finest 'botanical showplaces' in Europe, earning this distinction on two main counts: the wealth of species of flowering plants (especially rare ones) and the presence of species happily flourishing far from their normal habitats. Species of flower that usually grow high in the European Alps are abundant in the Burren, and many plants that are otherwise rare in Ireland also find a suitable habitat here; of the 27 species of orchid in Ireland, 23 are resident in the Burren.

Small herds of feral goats are quite common in the region, usually under the command of a fearsome billy with long horns and a wonderfully shaggy, dark coat. The goats, who feed enthusiastically on young trees, actually ensure the proliferation of wildflowers by keeping down the spread of hazel scrub. Other unusual, albeit domestic, native mammals that can be seen in the area are bog ponies – small, rotund horses about the same size as Shetland ponies, with wide, flowing manes. Traditionally used as working animals by farmers, these miniature wonders are now relatively rare. Several small herds are managed by enthusiasts in the Burren area, and you may be lucky enough to spot one of them.

PLANNING
Maps & Books

Folding Landscapes' 1:31,680 map *The Burren* may be less practical than standard OSI maps for walking purposes, but it marks the area's geological and archaeological landmarks in exhaustive detail. Of the many publications about this fascinating area, *The Book of the Burren*, published by Tír Eolas, has contributions from several authoritative writers, and is a beautifully illustrated, comprehensive guide and reference. For the

Karst Wonders of the Burren

Few landscapes anywhere in Ireland, except perhaps the Giant's Causeway in Antrim, have the surreal, other-worldly appearance of the limestone pavements and terraces of the Burren.

The limestone of which they are formed is about 340 million years old and began as vast quantities of lime-rich material, much of it from the shells and skeletons of marine creatures that dissolved in the warm, shallow sea under which 'Ireland' was then submerged. Long after the sea had retreated, these beds were then stripped of a relatively thin layer of overlying material during the last Ice Age. Subsequent erosion, accelerated by the clearing of trees by early farmers, left what looks like a rock desert, with precious few spaces where soil could develop. The Burren limestone is up to 780m thick, and the bare pavements and terraces cover an area of 250 sq km.

The limestone beds are imprinted with lines of weakness – cracks or joints. When rainwater works its way down into these spaces the limestone, being a water-soluble rock, dissolves a little along the lines of the cracks. In their widened form these are called grikes; the slabs in between are the clints. Intricate networks of hollows, channels and pinnacles are the result of this water erosion. When rainwater has penetrated as far as it can go into the limestone, it then turns sideways, still dissolving the rock, and eventually networks of underground caves are formed. The landform resulting from the process of disappearing water and underground cave formation is called karst, after an area in (former) Yugoslavia where it was first studied. The Burren is Ireland's best known karst area and has the longest known cave system in the country.

Typically for karst country, the Burren is virtually river-less. However, turloughs are a feature of the limestone country unique to Ireland. Derived from the Irish words *tur loch*, meaning 'dry lake', they are ephemeral lakes. They appear in shallow hollows only after heavy rain, when the water table (the level at which the ground is permanently saturated) rises and allows water to spill out and quickly fill the hollow, usually to a depth of about 2m. During a dry spell the water seeps away into the ground and the turlough recedes and may even disappear. Some turloughs materialise during autumn and fade away the following spring and summer

serious enthusiast there is also *The Natural History of the Burren*, by Gordon D'Arcy & John Hayward.

Information Sources

The nearest TIC to the Burren is at the Cliffs of Moher (☎ 065-708 1171; open year-round). It provides an accommodation booking service and sells walking maps and guidebooks. There is also a restaurant on site. **The Burren Centre** (☎ 065-708 8030; open Mar-Oct; €5/3 adults/children), in Kilfenora, also offers informative displays and audio-visual presentations about the area and its history, and runs guided tours. The shop has a good stock of books, maps and crafts.

ACCESS TOWN
Doolin

A spread-out but lively village, Doolin is a good base for walks in the Burren, having

the greatest choice of accommodation. The village is also renowned for traditional Irish music. Note, however, that there are no banking facilities in the village.

Places to Stay & Eat Of several camping grounds near Doolin, **Nagles Doolin Caravan and Camping Park** (☎ 065-707 4458; camping per tent/person €6/3), 100m from the pier for the Aran Islands ferry, has grassy pitches and good facilities, including a campers kitchen. There are also several hostels in Doolin that are spread out around the village. **Paddy's Doolin Hostel** (☎ 065-707 4006; dorm beds/doubles €11.50/33) is at the southern end of the village. **Aille River Hostel** (☎ 065-707 4260; camping per person/dorm beds/doubles €5.50/11/26) is in a 17th-century farmhouse beside the river. **Rainbow Hostel** (☎ 065-707 4415; dorm beds/doubles €11/26) is on the main road at the northern end of the village. Of numerous modern B&Bs, **Killilagh House** (☎ 065-707 4392; singles/doubles €50/64) is opposite the Doolin Café.

There is also a good choice of places for a meal. **McGann's Pub** and **Gus O'Connor's Pub** both offer hearty bar food, while the **Doolin Café** is a little quieter. There are also two small **grocery shops** in the village.

Getting There & Away There are **Bus Éireann** (☎ 091-562 000) services between Doolin and Galway (€10.70, one hour 35 minutes, three to five services Monday to Saturday, and two on Sunday). There is also a scheduled service from Doolin, through Limerick, to Dublin (€19, six hours 15 minutes, twice daily).

By car, Doolin is 7km west of Lisdoonvarna and the N67.

Black Head

Duration	5 hours
Distance	14.5km
Difficulty	moderate
Start/Finish	Fanore (p252)
Transport	bus
Summary	A wonderful circuit exploring the unique, shattered limestone landscape and ancient stone enclosures of the Burren.

On the northwestern tip of the Burren, Black Head (Ceann Boirne) and the ridge rising southeast from its rocky shores have some of the finest expanses of limestone pavement in the area. This route explores the terraces and pavements of the mountainous headland, which also offers far-reaching coastal views and provides a showcase for many of the plant species that make the region a botanist's delight. The circuit begins with a 3.5km section of paved road that traces the Caher River, the only surface river in the Burren. It then joins the route of the Burren Way for a short distance before heading across two rocky mountain summits. Ascents are not long or steep (the total ascent is 410m), but negotiating the shattered rock

terrain demands constant attention. Stepping into one of the numerous fissures in the rock is a sure way to break an ankle! The final attraction of the route is a visit to the Iron Age stone fort of Cathair Dhúin Irghuis, before one of the region's evocative old green roads is followed back to Fanore. The route can be followed in either direction, though sea views are better in the direction described.

PLANNING
When to Walk
May and June are the optimum months if you want to observe the region's profusion of wildflowers.

What to Bring
Bring all the water that you need for the trip with you as there is none available en route (water from the Caher River is not suitable for drinking).

Maps & Books
OSI 1:50,000 map No 51 covers the route. In *West of Ireland Walks*, Kevin Corcoran describes a route over Gleninagh Mountain, a continuation of this walk from the fort.

NEAREST TOWN
Fanore
This is a scattered village that boasts a long, sandy beach but has little in the way of amenities. There is a small **shop** and B&B is available at **Admiral's Rest Seafood Restaurant** (☎ 065-707 6105; singles/doubles €20/40), where good-quality evening meals are also on offer to guests and nonguests alike. Alternatively, **Rocky View Farmhouse** (☎ 065-707 6103; singles/doubles €25/30) also does B&B and is signed towards the coast from the northern end of the village; evening meals are also available here.

Bus Éireann (☎ 091-562 000) has a limited service between Fanore and Doolin (€3.10, 40 minutes, once daily Tuesday and Thursday). Buses leave Doolin at 8.45am and return from Fanore at 7.32pm, meaning journey times are convenient for a day trip. There is also a direct bus service between Fanore and Galway (€7.85, one hour 30 minutes, once daily Tuesday and Thursday).

By car, Fanore is located along the R477 ('the coast road'), around 11km west of Ballyvaughan and 16km north of Doolin.

THE WALK

From the entrance to St Patrick's church, turn east and begin walking along the Khyber Pass road. This narrow road climbs steadily for most of the 3.5km that you are on it, but traffic is light and the tumbling waters of the Caher River to your left offer distraction. Around an hour from the church another road joins from the right, and way-marking posts signal that you are now on the route of the Burren Way. Continue ahead for around 20m, then turn left to follow the Burren Way up a winding stone track.

Follow the track to the brow of a hill, passing a jumble of ruined farm buildings and the just-discernible fort of Cathair an Aird Rhois on the right. At the top of the rise, leave the track and cross a stone wall on the left, heading north across open mountain terrain. The green mound that marks the summit of Gleninagh Mountain (317m) is prominent to the north, and this is where you are heading. The route veers west and then east to reach the top, following a natural line along the top of the rounded ridge. Numerous stone walls will need to be negotiated at the start of this section, and the grassy terrain is interspersed with sections of limestone pavement.

From the concrete trig pillar at the summit of **Gleninagh** (2½ to three hours from the start), sweeping views allow full appreciation of the Burren landscape; grey, rock-terraced hills stretch away on three sides, while the waters of Galway Bay offset the scene to the north. The large cairn of Dobhach Brainin (possibly of Neolithic origin) dominates the skyline to the northwest, and marks the second (unnamed) summit of the route at 314m.

A ridge links Gleninagh and this next peak. The ridge takes you down into a col and several short cliffs will need to be negotiated on the descent – easier points can generally be found by skirting a short distance along their edge. Once in the col, keep close to a wall running along its northeastern

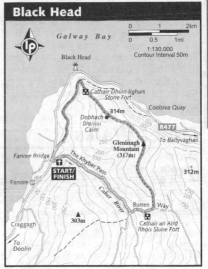

edge. The terrain now consists almost entirely of limestone pavement and this will continue for the remainder of the mountain crossing.

Veer to the east as you make the final climb to the **summit** (45 minutes from Gleninagh), a fine viewpoint for the coasts of Clare and Galway. The three Aran Islands are visible a few kilometres across the Atlantic to the east. Descend northwest from the summit, negotiating several more cliff-like terraces along the way. The round walls of **Cathair Dhúin Irghuis** soon come into view ahead; cross a couple of stone walls and pass alongside the ruins on your descent towards Black Head.

Shortly after the fort the coast road comes into view, and you soon reach the grassy line of an old green road, enclosed on both sides by stone walls. Join the green road and turn left (southwest) to follow it the remaining 2.5km back to Fanore. Several stone walls now span the breadth of the old road and will need to be crossed, but nothing takes away from the delightful experience of following this ancient route through wildflower meadows and sections of dramatic limestone pavement. The end of the green road is now obscured by a jumble of rocks; avoid this by passing along the edge of the field to the left. Cross a final wall to emerge on a small road just above Fanore. Follow the road downhill to a junction with the main road (the R477) and turn left. After 400m turn left again to rejoin the Khyber Pass road, where St Patrick's church is just a short distance ahead.

Other Walks

MAYO
Nephin Beg
Nephin Beg (617m) lies in a remote area of bog and forestry plantations, north of Clew Bay. The walk starts from the road head at Srahmore Lodge, close to where the Bangor Trail and Western Way split. The waymarked Bangor Trail is followed for the first 6km, from where the southwest ridge of Nephin Beg can be climbed. Summit views encompass most of Mayo. The steep eastern slopes are then descended to reach the Western Way, and a 7km walk along tracks leads back to the start. Allow six to seven hours for this moderate–demanding, 18km-long route. Use OSI 1:50,000 map No 23. Access to this route is by private transport only.

Maumtrasna & the Devil's Mother
A challenging mountain circuit that is best kept for a fine day, this walk starts and finishes from the N59 at Glennacally Bridge, 6km east of Leenaun. This demanding route traces a clockwise horseshoe around Glennacally River, beginning with a steep ascent to the wide summit plateau of Maumtrasna (673m). From here, the route veers southwest, passing over Knocklaur to a 3km-long section of ridge that sweeps around to the Devil's Mother (645m) before descending steeply back to the road. The route is 14km long and involves 1040m of ascent; allow at least seven to eight hours. OSI 1:50,000 maps Nos 37 and 38 cover the route. Bus Éireann's Leenaun–Westport service plies the N59 during July and August only, and will drop you at the start/finish of this route if you ask the driver; see Getting There & Away (p239) for Leenaun.

CONNEMARA
Benbaun Circuit
This strenuous but scenic route traverses some of the major northern summits of Connemara's famous Twelve Bens, including the highest peak, Benbaun (729m). It traces a clockwise horseshoe

around the Gleninagh River, also crossing Bencorr (711m) and Bencollaghduff (696m). The OSI 1:50,000 map No 37, and Harvey's Superwalker 1:30,000 map *Connemara* both cover the walk, which is also described in Paddy Dillon's *Connemara*. The walk starts and finishes along the R344, at the bridge over Tooreenacoona River. Allow seven hours for the 13km circuit, which involves 1190m of ascent. Access to this route is by private transport only.

Tully Mountain
Tully Mountain (356m) rises in splendid isolation well west of the higher peaks of Connemara. A surprisingly complex hill littered with crags, tarns and rocky summits, it is an ideal option for days when higher peaks are covered by cloud. Access the start along the minor road to Tully Cross from Letterfrack and the N59; turn off after 3km to the Ocean's Alive Visitor Centre. From here, walk northeast along the road above the harbour for about 3km to a parking bay, and then veer northeast and climb to the summit. Descend southeast down the long ridge and follow a rough vehicle track back to the road. This easy–moderate outing is 8km long, involves 450m of ascent, and takes around three hours. OSI 1:50,000 map No 37 covers the walk. Access to this route is by private transport only.

THE BURREN
Abbey Hills
Overlooking Aughinish Bay, an inlet on Galway Bay, Abbey Hill (240m) is a fairly isolated outlier of Slievecarran to the southeast. An old green road, skirting the hill's north and northwestern slopes, provides an easy stroll (6km return), taking in a good sample of limestone landscape and fine views over the stone-walled fields around the bay. OSI 1:50,000 map No 51 covers the walk, which is described in Kevin Corcoran's *West of Ireland Walks* and also in *Walk Guide: West of Ireland*, by Whilde & Simms. Bus Éireann's Galway–Doolin service plies the nearby N67, and will drop you near the start/finish of this route if you ask the driver; see Getting There & Away (p252) for Doolin.

Burren National Park
Burren is the smallest of Ireland's five national parks. Its 13 sq km protects a tiny sample of the Burren's natural features, and includes limestone pavement, turloughs, woodland, grassland and hazel scrub. The centrepiece is magnificent Mullaghmore (237m), a wonderful case study of limestone geology constructed of gently tilted terraces. A *boithrin an ghorta* (green road) in the

southwest corner of the park passes through a deep, dry valley and dense hazel woodland, as well as some fine outcrops of limestone pavement. Although it is only 3.5km in length, it is worth exploring on an easy stroll. The green road (with its eastern end at GR 304945) is joined at either end by two minor roads that branch northeast from the Kilfenora–Corofin road (the R476) in the vicinity of the hamlet of Killinaboy. OSI 1:50,000 map No 51 covers the area. Access to this route is by private transport only.

WAYMARKED WAYS

Waymarked Ways in the central west include: the Cavan Way, the Sligo Way, the Leitrim Way and the Miners & Historical Way in Counties Sligo and Leitrim; the Bangor Trail and the Foxford Way in County Mayo; the Suck Valley Way in Counties Roscommon and Galway; the Western Way traversing Counties Mayo and Galway; and the East Clare Way, the Mid Clare Way and the Burren Way in County Clare. See the Waymarked Ways chapter (p335) for more details of these routes.

Northwest

For many, County Donegal in Ireland's northwest corner is second to none among the country's generous collection of walking areas. Donegal is a favourite thanks to its sheer wealth of places to explore, including the amazingly indented coastline (with towering cliffs and secluded inlets), as well as remote and rugged mountains, glens and moors. Although Donegal's mountains are quite modest when set against Ireland's other peaks (there is only one rising above 700m), they lack nothing in scenic quality and variety: the clean lines of Errigal's white cone contrast sharply with the sprawling, flat-topped massif of nearby Muckish.

Donegal has large Gaeltacht areas, where Irish is the first language, and Irish culture is ardently promoted and nurtured. Overall, the northwest has a rather seductive and intriguing otherworldly feel, somewhat isolated from the rest of Ireland. It's often said that you can never leave Donegal for good; even after one visit, it's easy to agree.

HISTORY

There are many reminders of Donegal's ancient past in the countryside, including prehistoric burial cairns, Iron Age forts and carved Celtic crosses. In historic times Donegal (meaning 'fort of the foreigners', most likely a reference to Viking invaders) was part of the old Irish kingdom of Ulster.

The county has been the setting for some crucial events in Ireland's history. These include the work of early Christian missionaries (led by Columba who was born in Glenties, County Donegal) and the flight of the Earls (the last of Ulster's Celtic chiefs) from Rathmullan on the Fanad coast in 1607. The latter event was the prelude to the colonisation of County Donegal as part of Ulster by English and Scots settlers.

At the start of the 19th century, Napoleon's empire-building activities alarmed British authorities and, in response, watchtowers were built along the Irish coast, in sight of each other. Many of these survive,

Hiking the southeast ridge of Errigal with the Aghlas in the background

GARETH McCORMACK

Highlights

- Wandering the delightful forest and coastal paths of the Ards Peninsula (p267)
- Enjoying far-ranging views from the splendidly named peaks of Muckish (p272), the Aghlas (p274) and Errigal (p276)
- Exploring Glenveagh (p277), Ireland's largest national park, with its dramatic glacial landscapes and precious native woodlands
- Walking some of the finest sea cliffs in Europe between Slieve League and Slievetooey (p281)

to a greater or lesser extent, at prominent outposts in the region such as Horn Head. A few coastguard lookouts erected during WWI are also still standing.

Several places described in this chapter were caught up in the civil war of the early 1920s, notably the castle in Glenveagh

National Park. Although Ireland remained neutral during WWII, the strife could not be ignored, as is demonstrated by the prominent warnings to aircraft, in the form of the word 'Eire' written in stones, that can still be seen here and there along the coast.

NATURAL HISTORY

County Donegal is perhaps the most geologically complex part of Ireland. Many of its most prominent peaks are composed of quartzite, schist and marble, which were deposited about 600 million years ago and folded and compressed 200 million years later. This was one phase of the major earth-building event known as the Caledonian orogeny. In another phase, the mountains were pushed up and granite formed below the surface. Aeons later this rock underlayer was exposed, and is now visible as the rounded Derryveagh and Glendowan Mountains. Later again, during the last Ice Age, ice filled gaps and dykes in the surface rock and wore away the surrounding stone to form U-shaped valleys, notably at Glenveagh.

Today some alpine and arctic species survive in sheltered spots in the sparse soils of the mountain uplands. The glens and lower slopes support holly, rowan and juniper, and orchids and butterworts are quite common. Remnants of native woodland are few, one of the most extensive being in Glenveagh National Park

The most prominent feature of the Donegal landscape is peat bog, of which there are extensive tracts. While bogs are normally not places where walkers linger intentionally, they are relatively rich in wildlife, especially insectivorous plants and insects. The moorlands support a good range of birds, from the small and tuneful skylark and meadow pipit, to the larger and much less harmonious red grouse, crow and raven. The corncrake, one of Ireland's threatened species, is making a comeback in north Donegal thanks to the Corncrake Project, a

NORTHWEST

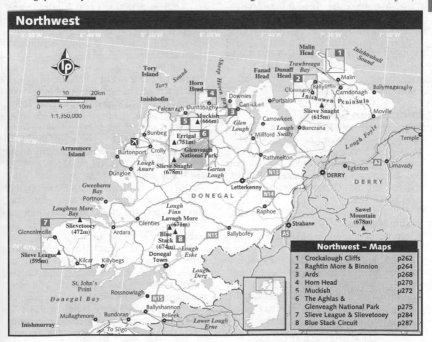

Northwest

	Northwest – Maps	
1	Crockalough Cliffs	p262
2	Raghtin More & Binnion	p264
3	Ards	p268
4	Horn Head	p270
5	Muckish	p272
6	The Aghlas & Glenveagh National Park	p275
7	Slieve League & Slievetooey	p284
8	Blue Stack Circuit	p287

voluntary cooperative conservation scheme between farmers and BirdWatch Ireland. Under the scheme, grants are paid to farmers who are happy to delay mowing for hay or silage until 1 August. By then, young corncrakes are usually sufficiently independent to survive the mowing. During spring and autumn you may see red deer in Glenveagh National Park, and golden eagles have also been reintroduced to Ireland in this area.

INFORMATION
Maps
The best map for overall planning is the OSNI 1:250,000 Holiday Map *North*.

Books
If you are planning an extended stay in Donegal and are looking for even more ideas for walks, two guidebooks can be recommended. *Hill Walker's Donegal*, by David Herman, describes 38 coast and mountain routes; the maps are adequate for orientation and the descriptions generally reliable. *Walk Guide West of Ireland*, by Tony Whilde & Patrick Simms, includes 20 walks around Donegal. This book has plenty of background information and is handy for its wide coverage, but is sometimes rather vague about parking places.

Information Sources
Sligo's **North West Tourism** (☎ 071-916 1201; ⓦ www.ireland-northwest.travel.ie; *Temple St, Sligo; open year-round*) has a great website, worth checking for transport and accommodation information. The site also has links to several guided-walk operators in the area.

Place Names
A significant proportion of Donegal – especially around the coast – is a designated Gaeltacht area, where Irish is the first language written and spoken. In these places, road signs and place names are often written in Irish only, without the usual English translation. To facilitate navigation through these areas, Irish names are given in the text. See also the Gazetteer (p358).

GATEWAYS
Derry
Just across the border in Northern Ireland, the city of Derry (p294) has a wealth of accommodation and transport connections, and makes a very convenient gateway for the northwest.

Donegal Town
Normally shown on maps and road signs simply as Donegal, this is the gateway to walks in southwest Donegal. Life in the town revolves around the Diamond – the compact and colourful square in the centre of this busy but relatively small settlement. On summer weekends the many beds in town can be booked out, so it is wise to phone ahead. The **TIC** (☎ 074-972 1148; *the Quay; open Mar-Nov*) is by the River Eske, 100m south of the Diamond. It sells a range of local guidebooks and maps, including OSI maps. **The Four Masters Bookshop** (☎ 074-972 1526; *the Diamond*) also stocks an excellent selection of Irish titles, maps and guides. Internet access is available at **Blueberry Café** (☎ 074-972 2933; *the Diamond*). There are no outdoor equipment suppliers in town.

Places to Stay & Eat There are two good hostels around Donegal Town. About 1.5km west of town at Doonan is **Donegal Town Independent Hostel** (☎ 074-972 2805; *Killybegs Rd; camping/dorm beds/doubles from €6/10.50/24*), which is signed off the N56. More remote, on a peninsula 5km from town, is **Ball Hill Hostel** (☎ 074-972 1174; *Ball Hill; dorm beds €12.50; open daily Apr-Sept, Sat & Sun only Oct-Mar*). However, the sea views from this former coastguard station are worth the effort; from the Donegal Town centre, take the Killybegs Rd (N56) and look for signs on the left.

Among the numerous B&Bs are **Drumcliffe House** (☎ 074-972 1200; *Killybegs Rd; singles/doubles from €25/50*) and **Castle View House** (☎ 074-972 2100; *Waterloo Place; singles/doubles €22/44*). The popular and very central **Abbey Hotel** (☎ 074-972 1014; *the Diamond; singles/doubles from €57/114*) has 85 rooms with bathroom and serves everything from bar meals to à la carte menus.

There are several good **supermarkets** close to the Diamond and there is no shortage of reasonably priced places for a meal. Pick of the crop is probably the **Blueberry Café** (☎ 074-972 2933; the Diamond), which serves good-value evening meals. Nearby **McGroarty's Bar** offers decent bar food.

Getting There & Away Frequent **Bus Éireann** (074-972 1101) services connect Donegal Town to Dublin (€13.30, four hours 15 minutes, five daily Monday to Saturday and four on Sunday) via Enniskillen. There are also regular services to Derry (€10.20, one hour 25 minutes, seven daily Monday to Saturday and three on Sunday) and Galway (€15.20, three hours 35 minutes, four daily Monday to Saturday and three on Sunday). There are connections to most other major Irish towns. All of these buses leave from outside the Abbey Hotel in the Diamond. **McGeehan Coaches** (☎ 074-954 6150) operates services between Donegal Town and Dublin (€16.50, four hours, twice daily Monday to Saturday and once on Sunday), while **Busanna Feda** (☎ 074-954 8114) operates services between Donegal Town and Galway (€13, three hours, twice daily).

Letterkenny

This is the gateway to north Donegal. It is a working town rather less geared to tourism than other Irish gateways; it has a relatively poor selection of accommodation, but has plenty of other amenities and services. The **Chamber of Commerce Visitor Information Centre** (☎ 074-912 4866; Port Rd; open Mon-Fri) has lots of free literature and advice. The **Bord Fáilte TIC** (☎ 074-912 1160; Derry Rd) is 1.5km out of town and can also provide accommodation booking and information services; maps and guidebooks are available. **Outdoor Pursuits** (☎ 074-912 7788; Rathmelton Rd) opposite the bus station stocks a range of outdoor equipment.

Places to Stay & Eat There are no camping areas within easy reach of Letterkenny

and only one hostel. **Port Hostel** (☎ 074-912 5315; 24 Port Rd; dorm beds/doubles €9.50/23) is centrally located just behind the An Grianan Theatre. Nearby the **Covehill House** (☎ 074-912 1038; Port Rd; singles/doubles €23/46) is a good B&B in a quiet but central location. Another option is **Gallagher's Hotel** (☎ 074-912 2066; 100 Upper Main St; singles/doubles €35/70).

There are several **supermarkets** in the shopping centre next to the bus station and at the south end of town. There is also a good choice of places to eat in Main St. **The Yellow Pepper Café** (☎ 074-912 4133; open daily until late) understands vegetarians. **Galfees**, at the top end of Main St, serves good breakfasts and lunches.

Getting There & Away Scenic **Donegal International Airport** (☎ 074-954 8284; Carrickfinn; W www.donegalairport.ie) is in a relatively remote location on a narrow peninsula, about 45 minutes drive from Letterkenny. It is well signed from the N56 at Crolly (between Gweedore and Dungloe), from where it is 10km west via the R259.

There are daily flights to Dublin (€39) operated by **Euroceltic Airways** (☎ 0818-300 100; W www.euroceltic.com). **Avis** (☎ 074-954 8469) has hire cars are available at the airport.

Letterkenny bus station is beside a large roundabout on the Derry Rd. **Bus Éireann** (☎ 074-912 1309) has frequent services to Dublin (€12.70, four hours five minutes, five daily), Galway (€15.20, five hours, four daily Monday to Saturday and three on Sunday), via Donegal Town and Sligo, and Derry (€5.80, 35 minutes, seven daily Monday to Saturday and three on Sunday).

Busanna Feda (☎ 074-954 8114) also has a service to Galway (€13, three hours 50 minutes, twice daily). While **John McGinley Coaches** (☎ 074-913 5201) runs a daily service between Dublin and Letterkenny (€13, 3¾ hours, twice daily) and through to the main villages in the north of Donegal. The same company also runs a shuttle to/from Belfast International Airport (€20, 3½ hours, once daily July and August, four times weekly September to June).

Inishowen

Inishowen Peninsula, culminating in Malin Head, is Ireland's northern most extremity and, with the broad reaches of Lough Foyle to the southeast, Lough Swilly to the west and the Atlantic Ocean to the north, the sea is never far away. Popularly described as 'Ireland in miniature', the landscape is varied: beaches, rugged coastal cliffs, wooded glens, rolling moorland and craggy hills are all crowned by Slieve Snaght (615m).

The diversity of landscape is reflected in the walks described in this section. While the routes are relatively short, they are not lacking in quality and the long-distance views of Scotland's southernmost Outer Hebrides add an international dimension to the experience. Overall, Inishowen's great variety, range of accommodation and relatively good access combine to make it an area worth more than a fleeting visit.

PLANNING
Information Sources
For help arranging accommodation within Inishowen, try **Inishowen Tourism Society** (☎ 074-937 4933; **W** www.inishowenonline .com; Chapel Street; open Mon-Fri) in Carndonagh. The website also has useful accommodation links for the area.

ACCESS TOWNS
Clonmany
This is a small and relatively compact village in the northwest of Inishowen. The nearest banking facilities are in Carndonagh, a larger village 10km to the east.

Places to Stay & Eat The closest camping is at **Tullagh Bay Camping & Caravan Park** (☎ 074-937 8997; camping per tent €12.60; open May-Sept), at the back of Tullagh Strand about 3.5km northwest of Clonmany. **Glen House B&B** (☎ 074-937 6745; Straid; singles/doubles €28/56) is in a Georgian manor house conveniently located beside Glenevin Waterfall, at the start of the Raghtin More route (see Getting to/from the Walk, p263).

There are several **pubs** and a good **supermarket** in the village. **The Village Diner**, in the centre of Clonmany, offers a selection of snacks and simple meals.

Getting There & Away There are **North West Busways** (☎ 074-938 2619) services between Clonmany and Letterkenny (€8.50, one hour five minutes, three daily Monday to Friday and twice on Saturday). **Lough Swilly Bus Co** (☎ 074-912 2863, 028-7126 2017) runs buses between Clonmany and Derry (€7.50, 1¼ hours, three daily Monday to Friday and two on Saturday).

Ballyliffin
The small holiday village of Ballyliffin is less than 2km northeast of Clonmany. Popular because of its beach and golf course, it has plenty of accommodation but only at the more expensive end of the scale. There are few other facilities, apart from a small **shop**.

Ard Donn House (☎ 074-937 6156; singles/ doubles €30/50) and **Rossaor House** (☎ 074-937 6498; singles/doubles €45/70) are two of the numerous B&Bs in the village. Hotels include **The Strand Hotel** (☎ 074-937 6107; singles/doubles €55/85) in the centre of the village. All of the hotels serve food.

Bus services to/from Clonmany also pass through Ballyliffin – see Getting There & Away for Clonmany, above.

Crockalough Cliffs

Duration	4–4½ hours
Distance	12km
Difficulty	easy–moderate
Start/Finish	Malin Well Beach
Nearest Town	Malin Head (p261)
Transport	private

Summary An undulating, cliff-top walk overlooking myriad offshore rock stacks and islets close to Malin Head.

The Crockalough Cliffs fringe the northeastern coastline of the Inishowen Peninsula, a few kilometres short of Malin Head, Ireland's northernmost point (see the boxed text 'Malin Head – Northern Exposure', below). While these cliffs may lack the awesome elevation of Slieve League in south Donegal, they yield nothing in their exhilarating scope of panoramic views. This out-and-back walk provides the chance to enjoy the best of the scenery from different angles; the vicinity of Black Hill is the recommended turnaround point (the southern section is less scenic and somewhat scarred by human activity).

The overall height gained on the route is not great (the total ascent is 420m), but feels significant as it's accumulated in several short, steep climbs rather than one long haul. Ground underfoot consists mainly of grass and heather. Boggy areas, especially around the extensive peat diggings, can usually be avoided by keeping as close as safely possible to the cliff edge. Keep an eye open for the numerous seabirds that live on the cliffs and offshore rocks along the route, notably cormorants, fulmars and guillemots.

PLANNING
Maps
The OSI 1:50,000 map No 3 covers the walk.

NEAREST TOWN
Malin Head
Ireland's northernmost community at Malin Head (Cionn Mhálanna) is a somewhat scattered settlement, but offers a reasonable choice of accommodation. The nearest banking facilities are in Carndonagh.

Places to Stay & Eat A friendly place, **Sandrock Holiday Hostel** (☎ 074-937 0289; Port Ronan pier; dorm beds €9), 1.2km northwest of the post office, has great facilities; sheet hire costs €1.25. **Malin Head Hostel** (☎ 074-937 0309; dorm beds/doubles €10/30), opposite the post office, is also clean and friendly. Both hostels hire bikes. **Harkin's B&B** (☎ 074-937 0183; singles/doubles €24/40), also near the post office, is the most central of several B&Bs.

NORTHWEST

Malin Head – Northern Exposure

There is a special fascination about the extremities of islands, and Malin Head is no exception. Although it is not directly on the route of any of the walks described in this chapter, it is a prominent feature in the views from all of the walks in Inishowen and – on a clear day – can also be seen from Horn Head, several peninsulas to the west. Despite its geographic significance, Malin Head is not a place of great scenic drama: it is a low, flat, grassy point fringed with modest cliffs. However, it has played a crucial role in the development of Irish communications and meteorological forecasting.

A watchtower was built at the head early in the 19th century to keep a lookout for, and to record the identity of, passing ships. This information was then passed on to Lloyds, the shipping insurers in London.

In the following century, Lloyds, at the forefront of the revolution in communication brought about by the invention of the wireless, installed a new-fangled contraption in the tower. This device could 'catch' Morse code signals sent over relatively short distances at the rate of five words per minute. It wasn't until 1950 that the Irish government took over what was by then Malin Head radio station.

Weather reports were first issued from Malin Head in 1870, a service that continues to this day. The buildings near the head are now the base for the meteorological station that broadcasts storm warnings and weather reports. The Irish Maritime Emergency Service also has a base here.

During WWII, Ireland's defence forces had a lookout post at the head, next to the old tower. The letters EIRE, formed from white stones set on the grass, were the simple but effective way of warning passing aircraft that they were entering the air space of a neutral nation.

Around 200m east from the head, **The Cottage** (☎ 074-937 0257), originally built in the mid-18th century, has a small display of early radio equipment and some historical photographs of the area. It's also a good place for soup, sandwiches, cakes and drinks.

Crossroads Inn, in the centre of the village, serves bar food all day. There are several small **shops** within walking distance of the village centre. The best of these is **Mullin's**, around 1km from the Crossroads Inn; head north from the pub and take the first right to arrive at the shop.

Getting There & Away To get to Malin Head from Clonmany, follow the R238 through Ballyliffin to Carndonagh. From here Malin Head is well signed to the north, first along the R238 and then on the R242. **Lough Swilly Bus Co** (☎ 074-912 2863, 028-7126 2017) has a scheduled service between Derry and Malin Head (€10.50, one hour 25 minutes, two daily Monday to Friday and three on Saturday). Between Letterkenny and Malin Head, take the **North West Busways** (☎ 074-938 2619) service to Carndonagh (€10, one hour 20 minutes, three daily Monday to Friday and two Saturday) and then link up with the Lough Swilly service.

GETTING TO/FROM THE WALK
From Mullin's shop in Malin Head, continue east along a minor road for a little over 1km. Turn left at a junction and descend

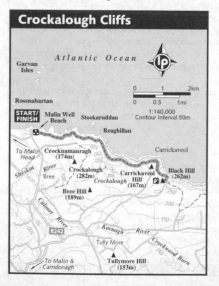

Crockalough Cliffs

Atlantic Ocean

Garvan Isles

Rossnabartan

0   1   2km
0   0.5   1mi
1:140,000
Contour Interval 50m

START/FINISH Malin Well Beach Stookaruddan

Reaghillan

To Malin Head   Crocknamanragh (174m)   Crockalough (282m)   Carrickaveol

Sheskin River   Bree   Crockalough   Carrickaveol Hill (167m)   Black Hill (262m)

Bree Hill (189m)

Culdaff River

R242   Keenagh River   Crockwood Burn

Tully More

To Malin & Carndonagh   Tullymore Hill (153m)

steeply for 400m to a shingle beach, where there is adequate parking for several cars.

THE WALK
Starting at the ruins of the stone church (which is believed to be of 16th-century origin), head east along the shingle of Malin Well Beach. At the headland at the end of the beach, pick up a faint path that climbs steeply up the left-hand gully to arrive at the **cliff top** above. In general throughout the walk it is best to keep as close to the cliff edge as is safely possible to avoid peat banks, boggy patches, and rough sections of heather and grass.

Straight away, great views open up to the north. On a fine day, the distinctive tapering peaks of the Paps of Jura (on the Isle of Jura in Scotland's Outer Hebrides) and the long profile of the Isle of Islay are clearly visible to the east.

The going is quite rough for a few kilometres, but improves once you draw level with the impressive bulk of the island of Stookaruddan. Climb steeply along the cliff edge north of Crockalough (282m); as you gain height more bumps appear on the northeast skyline – perhaps the island of Tiree. The Kintyre Peninsula comes into view to the east, as does the Antrim Coast, stretching away to the cliffs of Fair Head.

The scenery closer by is ever-changing too: scalloped shingle beaches lie at the foot of broken black cliffs and numerous miniature rock stacks are scattered just offshore.

A short stretch of track can be followed across the top of the ascent but then you must strike out across open ground towards Carrickaveol Hill (167m). Skirt around to the east of this small summit before climbing to the desolate summit cairn that marks **Black Hill** (262m; about two to 2½ hours from the start).

Much of the Inishowen Peninsula is now spread out before you, notably the Raghtin and Urris hills (see the Raghtin More walk, p263). The higher summits of north Donegal can also be picked out when conditions are favourable.

Retrace your outward route back to Malin Well Beach.

Raghtin More

Duration	3½–4 hours
Distance	7km
Difficulty	moderate
Start/Finish	Glenevin Waterfall car park
Nearest Towns	Clonmany (p260), Ballyliffin (p260)
Transport	private

Summary A visit to picturesque Glenevin Waterfall is followed by a steady climb to a wild quartzite summit with tremendous panoramas.

Raghtin More (502m), dominating the north-west corner of Inishowen, is the highest summit of a range of mid-level quartzite mountains that includes the Urris Hills to the southwest. Despite its rounded and relatively uniform profile, the rock-strewn summit of Raghtin More offers wonderful coastal views, encompassing Malin Head and the mountainous interior of north Donegal. The route described here – perhaps the easiest circuit over the mountain – begins by tracing woodland paths along a stream to the 10m-high Glenevin Waterfall. A track then leads up Butler's Glen, crossing alarmingly soft sphagnum moss sponges on its upper reaches. Once on the slopes of Raghtin More, heather and bilberry are widespread, and the ground is generally well drained. The total ascent is 500m.

Although Raghtin More is the highest peak in the area, Mamore Hill (423m) and the Urris Hills (with their high point at 417m) are a continuation of the range to the southwest. Without transport at both ends it is difficult to walk across all of the summits and avoid a lengthy return along roads. If you have two vehicles, however, one can be left at Clonmany and the other at Lenankeel, a tiny settlement to the north of the Urris Hills. A direct route can then be traced over the summits of Raghtin More, Mamore Hill and the peaks of the Urris Hills, with a descent along the western bank of the outlet stream of Crunlough. Terrain is generally rugged; crags and bluffs decorate the Urris Hills, although informal paths have been worn along the summit ridge. Allow

four hours for this 11km route. See Other Walks (p288) for details of another circuit in the Urris Hills.

PLANNING
Maps

OSI 1:50,000 map No 3 covers the walk. Note that the path to Glenevin Waterfall is not shown on this map.

GETTING TO/FROM THE WALK

Glenevin Waterfall car park is well signed; it's adjacent to Butler's Bridge on the minor road around the northeastern slopes of Raghtin More. From Clonmany, follow the road signed to Tullagh Bay, cross the river and bear right at an intersection. Butler's Bridge and the waterfall car park are about 1km further on.

THE WALK (see map p264)

The path to Glenevin Waterfall is well marked from Butler's Bridge; climb the stile beside the metal gate and follow signs directing you along Butler's Glen. A wide path leads upstream through pleasant birch and rowan woodland, crossing and recrossing the stream via wooden footbridges as the cliffs of a small gorge close in on either side. Benches and picnic tables are placed along the path, although you may feel that you don't deserve a rest just yet! The trail ends after 800m at **Glenevin Waterfall**.

From here there are two options. Either locate a faint path that climbs steeply out of the eastern side of the gorge, around 10m back from the waterfall. Clamber up the steep peaty slope and cross a 50m section of heather to join a track. Alternatively, if the slope seems too steep for your liking, retrace your route downstream and take the first right at a junction of paths. This path climbs more gently over a lower part of the gorge wall, and will lead you to the same track.

Wherever you join the track, turn right and follow it as it climbs gradually southwest. Firm ground soon gives way to marshy terrain, and at times the track is more like a corridor of reeds and spongy mosses. The western edge of the track generally offers the firmest ground. Continue past a fenced area and climb until you are roughly level with the summit of Raghtin More, to the west. Leave the track here and head west, descending slightly to cross a stream before commencing the climb up the heather-clad slopes beyond.

Arc around to the northwest as you climb, aiming for the col between Raghtin More and Crockmain. Views over Mamore Gap and the Urris Hills become more extensive as you gain height. Heather begins to give way to jumbles of sharp quartzite as you near the wide **summit plateau** (2½ hours

from the start). A high ring of rocks makes for a prominent summit cairn, although the views are better from the **trig point**, which is 50m to the west. From here, the sweeping panorama embraces Malin Head to the northeast, the Urris Hills to the southwest and beyond that a maze of coastal inlets backed by the fascinating profiles of north Donegal's mountains.

Descend relatively steep ground northeast from the summit to the col between Raghtin More and Raghtin Beg. The summit of **Raghtin Beg** (418m) is a short distance to the north and can be readily visited

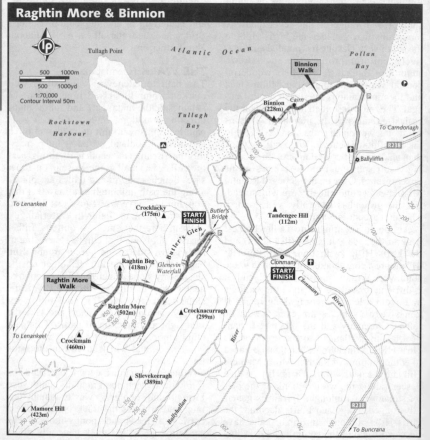

Raghtin More & Binnion

for more good views, especially across the sandy beach at Tullagh Bay. Return to the col and begin to descend through short heather, heading for the fenced area beside the track that you passed on the outward journey. Cross the stream in front of the enclosure, turn left at the track, and follow this back to the car park at the start of the walk.

Binnion

Duration	3–4 hours
Distance	9km
Difficulty	easy–moderate
Start/Finish	Clonmany (p260)
Transport	bus

Summary Golden beaches surround a short but rugged hill walk with some awkward ground underfoot. The effort is rewarded by magnificent coastal views.

From most points inland, Binnion (228m) seems like a nondescript hill, barely warranting attention. It's only when you reach the coast on either side of the mountain that its true character is revealed, with slopes rising in rugged folds of heather and quartzite.

The route across the summit is a wonderful mixture of a hill walk and a coastal walk; it includes visits to two golden-sand beaches, yet the mountain section is typical of Donegal's higher ground. The terrain here is firm and well drained, yet rugged; thick heather pulls at your feet and sharp quartzite boulders hidden beneath it test your ankles.

The modest distance of the route, and the fact that more than half of it is on paved roads, makes it a good option for walkers who prefer not to take on long mountain routes, yet want to experience the character that they evoke. The coastal views are of the highest quality and are surprisingly expansive given the modest elevation of Binnion's summit. The total ascent is 300m.

PLANNING
Maps
Use the OSI 1:50:000 map No 3.

THE WALK (see map p264)
From the wide central street in Clonmany, walk northeast up a steep hill to a junction with the R238. Turning left, Ballyliffin is just over 1km along this road. Turn left in Ballyliffin, following signs for Pollan Bay. Descend to a parking area at the southern end of a long, sweeping beach (45 minutes to one hour from the start). From the parking area walk onto the beach and head northwest. Pick a route though rock outcrops and cross a small stream. When the coast begins to swing around to the west, climb steeply onto grassy slopes and cross an old concrete stile. Now begin to climb the gentle slopes leading towards a prominent cairned summit to the southwest. Cross a fence; beyond this, walk across a broad, flat area. Descend into a boggy hollow where the remains of old shelters are scattered around, indicating that this was once a booley or summer settlement occupied by the minders of livestock brought up here to graze on the fresh shoots (see the boxed text 'Booleying – Summer in the Mountains', p224).

The slope now steepens significantly. Tackle this directly; you will need to use your hands for balance in places. If this angle of attack seems too demanding, contour around to the south for a short distance before cutting back west to join an obvious track – turn right onto this to rejoin the route.

The direct ascent is rewarded by a sudden arrival at a cairn. This is not the summit, however, which should now be visible a few hundred metres to the southwest. Descend slightly from the cairn and join the track mentioned above. This track leads almost as far as the top; from its end, a short climb across heather slopes brings you to the summit cairn of **Binnion** (228m; 1½ hours from the Pollan Bay beach). There are tremendous views west across Tullagh Bay and the cliffs of Dunaff Head, and to the northeast across Pollan Bay to Malin Head.

Descend steeply southwest towards Tullagh Bay. Begin by following a large, diagonal stone wall before climbing through a gap near an adjoining wall. Descend to a second wall, again running diagonally across

NORTHWEST

the steep slopes. Follow this for around 100m until you can walk through a second gap. Pick your way around a rock outcrop and descend onto a flat shelf, where bracken grows thickly in late summer. Follow the shelf south and then descend easier slopes to the small estuary where the Clonmany River reaches the sea. If the tide is out you can ford the river and enjoy a walk on the sands of Tullagh Bay before returning to the route (the coastline offers good walking all the way to Tullagh Point, 3km to the west).

Back at the Clonmany River follow a small path that leads along the east bank of the river to a footbridge; cross this and join a track on the opposite bank. Follow the track south to a small road. Turn left after 1km and a few minutes of walking will bring you back into Clonmany.

North Donegal

Mountainous north Donegal is dominated by rugged peaks. Its ranges include one of the most accessible and recognisable summits in the county, the distinctive cone of Errigal. In the heart of the mountains, Glenveagh National Park embraces a marvellous array of loughs, hills, glens, and expanses of wild and lonely moorland. The coast is ever present, and offers a fine backdrop to the views from many of the peaks; Horn Head in particular has some of the most dramatic and varied coastline in Donegal. Walkers are spoilt for choice here; the walks described in detail are but a distillation of the best from a generous range of possibilities.

This is also a remote and sparsely populated area, with a fringe of small towns and villages close to the coast and beaches. Nevertheless, a good range of reasonably priced accommodation is available, although dedicated users of public transport will need to be patient and flexible to make the most of their visit.

ACCESS TOWNS
Dunfanaghy

This is a compact village that receives plenty of visitors during the summer. **McAuliffe's**,

in the main street, stocks OSI maps and walking guidebooks, and also has a range of local and general Irish interest books. The village has a bank (opposite the Carrig Rua Hotel) but no ATM facilities.

Places to Stay & Eat A memorable place, **Corcreggan Mill Hostel** (☎ 074-913 6409; *camping per person/dorm beds/doubles €5/ 10/26*) is on the N56, 3km southwest of Dunfanaghy. Some beds are in an old railway carriage. **Carrig Rua Hotel** (☎ 074-913 6133; *singles/doubles €58/116*) is in Dunfanaghy's main street. **Carrigan House B&B** (☎ 074-913 6276; *singles/doubles €40/54*) is just a five minute walk along the main road to the east of the village. **Forest Lodge B&B** (☎ 074-913 6104; *singles/doubles €25.50/51*), 1km northwest of the village along Horn Head Drive, is beside Hornhead Bridge and is a good option for walkers on the Horn Head route.

In the square there is a small **supermarket**. For snacks and light lunches, **Muck and Muffins**, also in the square, is hard to beat. Most **bars** and **hotels** along the main street offer food; **Danny Collins Bar & Restaurant** (☎ 074-913 6205) is one of the best options.

Getting There & Away Regular **Lough Swilly Bus Co** (☎ 074-912 2863) services connect Dunfanaghy to Letterkenny (€5.70, one hour, four daily Monday to Saturday); most of these services also continue to Derry in Northern Ireland. There are also connections west, through Falcarragh (€1.10, 15 minutes, three or four daily Monday to Saturday) and Burtonport (€4.40, 1½ hours, one or two daily) to Dungloe (€4.40, one hour 55 minutes, two or three daily).

Busanna Feda (☎ 074-954 8114) provides two services daily between Dunfanaghy and Letterkenny (€4, 35 minutes), Donegal Town (€6, one hour 35 minutes), Sligo (€8, two hours 55 minutes) and Galway (€13, 5½ hours). **John McGinley** (☎ 074-913 5201) has a regular Dunfanaghy–Dublin bus service that goes through Letterkenny (€15, five hours, twice daily).

Dunfanaghy is on the N56, around 30km northwest of Letterkenny and 12km east of Falcarragh.

Dunlewy

A tiny settlement, Dunlewy (Dún Lúiche) is at the foot of Errigal, in the heart of the best hill-walking country of north Donegal. This makes the village a convenient base for walks in the area.

Places to Stay & Eat The An Óige **Errigal Hostel** (☎ 074-953 1180; dorm beds €13) is on the northeastern edge of the village. **Dunlewy Lakeside Hostel** (☎ 074-953 2133; camping per person/dorm beds/doubles €5/10/26; open Easter-Sept) is situated opposite McGeadys pub. **Radharc an Ghleanna B&B** (☎ 074-953 1835; doubles €48; open May-Sept) is 1.5km from the pub, east along the R251 and then south along the minor road signed to the Poisoned Glen. There is a small **shop** at the petrol station in the village, but nowhere serving evening meals.

Getting There & Away Dunlewy is on the R251, around 14km west of the Glenveagh National Park entrance (the park is well signed from the N56 to both the east and the west). There are no buses to Dunlewy, although buses on the Dunfanaghy–Dungloe route pass the junction of the N56 and the R251, 3km west of the village, and the driver will drop you off if you ask in advance (see Dunfanaghy Getting There & Away, p266, for details of these services).

Ards

Duration	2–2½ hours
Distance	7km
Difficulty	easy
Start/Finish	Ards Forest Park car park
Nearest Town	Dunfanaghy (p266)
Transport	private

Summary A pleasant and straightforward route offering a very scenic mix of coastal and forest walking.

Among the bold promontories of north Donegal, the Ards Peninsula is rather modest. Tucked away in a corner of Sheephaven Bay, Ards constantly loses and regains its promontory status with the procession of the tides. On each low tide, the flats of the Campion Sands are exposed and flocks of eager, long-billed waders follow the receding waters in search of invertebrates. The humble rivers of the estuaries are left naked as thin, meandering ribbons of water. Just a few hours later the ocean returns to surround the peninsula, stretching down for 3km or more on either side. The craggy backbone of hills that leads southwest along the peninsula towards Muckish Mountain gives rise to the name Ards, derived from the Irish *ardai*, meaning 'heights'.

Much of the peninsula is taken up by Ards Forest Park (Páirc Foraoise Na hArdaidh), except for a thin strip of arable land running along the eastern side, and a treeless area on the most exposed tip of the peninsula. Although the forest park has a network of way-marked trails, this far more interesting route steps out of the park's boundaries and explores the end of the peninsula. Using tracks and rough paths throughout, this route is perfect for an easy afternoon or on a day when the cloud is down on the hills. The total ascent of this route is 160m.

HISTORY

During the plantation of Ulster, Ards was granted by the English Crown to Turlough Og O'Boyle and was then removed from that family after their part in the 1641 rebellion. By 1700 the Wray family from Yorkshire had acquired the land and in 1708 they built Ards House (now the Capuchin Friary). In 1782 title passed to the Stewarts who held it until 1926, when the Irish Land Commission finally broke the estate up and gave the northern half over to forestation. Ards Forest Park is now managed by Coillte, the state-owned forestry body.

NATURAL HISTORY

Over the years the peninsula has been variously planted and cleared into patchwork stands of broad-leaved and coniferous trees. Most of the main broad-leaved species are present in a small but important growth of semi-natural native woodland: sessile oak, ash, birch, rowan, and some yew, hawthorn and elm can be found. Many mature beech (an introduced species) are also in evidence, while the range of conifers is at least more varied than in other Coillte forests: it includes the ubiquitous sitka spruce, as well as more interesting species such as western hemlock, silver fir, European larch, Scots pine and Corsican pine. Areas undergoing felling are to be replanted with native broad-leaved species, reflecting the fact that Ards is in essence a recreational rather than a commercial forest. However, the forest does have significant colonies of the invasive rhododendron, which will hinder the growth of new broad-leaved trees (see the boxed text 'Scourge of the Rhododendron', p269).

Wading birds are attracted to the estuarine areas that border the peninsula, and shoals of fish gather in the nutrient-rich deeper waters at the mouths of the estuaries. In spring and summer, seabirds such as gannets and arctic terns come here from the colonies on Horn Head (p269), and can often be seen dive-bombing just off Binnagorm Point. Low-lying ground near the Back Strand has been inundated with a mix of fresh and salt water to produce fens, salt marshes and freshwater lakes. The peninsula is also a haven for some of Ireland's rarer mammals such as the red squirrel and otter.

PLANNING

Entry to Ards Forest Park is free, except for a parking charge of €5 on weekends and busy summer weekdays. The gates close at sunset.

Maps

The walk is covered by OSI 1:50,000 map No 2, although this map has insufficient detail to identify the smaller tracks and paths.

GETTING TO/FROM THE WALK

Ards Forest Park entrance is 3km north of Creeslough and 5.5km southeast of Dunfanaghy on the N56, and is well signed. From the entrance, follow the access road for 3km to a large parking area where there are toilets, a play area and picnic tables.

Capuchin Friary is an alternative start/finish. To get there, turn right from the N56 just over 1km north of Creeslough.

The buses that service the Letterkenny–Dunfanaghy route use the N56, and pass by the entrance to Ards Forest Park; drivers will drop you at the entrance if you ask in advance (see Dunfanaghy Getting There & Away, p266, for details of these services).

THE WALK

From the car park it is a short stroll north to Back Strand. Here you can assess the state of the tide; if it is well out you can follow the sands right around to Clonmass Bay. If the tide is high then follow the obvious path running northeast parallel to the shore. Keep left at a junction, passing through thick woodland and several waterlogged areas where flag iris thrives in early summer. Once back in the open an optional side path on the left leads through marram grass to the edge of some high dunes overlooking Clonmass Bay. Return to the main path and follow it further east to reach the beautiful beach at **Clonmass Bay**, where the low-tide and high-tide routes are reunited (30 minutes from the start). There are fine views across Sheep Haven Bay to Rosguill Peninsula, while the hills of Fanad Head Peninsula can be seen in the distance to the east.

Follow the path as it loops back to the south, climbing to join a gravel track. Turn left and follow the track to a fine viewpoint across Clonmass Bay. Continue to a hairpin turn, where you should spot a small but well-defined path leading straight ahead from the apex into thickets of birch. Follow this delightful path (which can be muddy in places) as it winds through the trees and through a

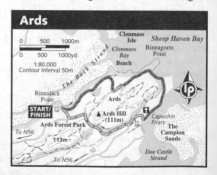

Scourge of the Rhododendron

In late spring and early summer the purple blooms of the rhododendron bring splashes of colour to the uniform greens, greys and browns of the countryside. However, far from being an adornment, *Rhododendron ponticum* is threatening to engulf both native and introduced woodlands. Nowhere is this alarming prospect more striking than in Ards Forest Park (p267) and Glenveagh National Park in County Donegal (p277), and Killarney National Park in southwestern Ireland.

A native of the eastern Balkans, Turkey and Lebanon, the plant was introduced to Ireland early in the 19th century to beautify the grounds of many large estates. Surprisingly, in Ireland the rhododendrons found all the elements that made life comfortable for them on the fringes of the Mediterranean: a damp climate, no great extremes of temperature, acidic soils, freedom from disease, and from the mouths of sheep and cattle (the leaves are poisonous). Add to this ideal environment the capacity to proliferate with alarming rapidity and you have an ecological disaster in the making.

Each bush can produce a million tiny, highly mobile seeds annually and, once established, the plants can spread rapidly – low level branches produce roots wherever they touch the soil. Rhododendrons develop a dense canopy of branches and thick leaves, shading out and choking less robust native species. The rhododendrons' fallen leaves also upset the normal chemistry of the soil, making it virtually impossible for native plants to regain a foothold until several years after the rhododendrons have been exterminated. However, getting rid of them is a long, slow process involving cutting down the tangled branches, then applying herbicides during successive growing seasons. In light of this, even one tree planted in innocence or ignorance in a private garden seems an avaricious monster.

wooden gate. The path leads out to **Binnagorm Point**; getting right out to the very tip of the point is complicated by a deep gully, which can be negotiated with a little scrambling. Meanwhile the path swings around to the east and descends to a small beach. Cross the beach and climb the steep slopes on the other side using a set of old concrete steps.

The path continues south across open ground. There is a boundary wall on the right and behind it grow stands of mature broadleaved trees. Pass through an old iron gate and beyond this a concrete path continues around a sandy bay. The path widens into a track, wooded on both sides, and after a few hundred metres brings you to **Capuchin Friary** (1½ hours from the start). There is a large car park and **café** at the friary.

Walk past the front of the house and follow the road uphill to the right of the car park. Take the second right from this road onto a forest track. Climb steadily to another junction where you should turn right and continue across the main spine of the peninsula. In spring this section is ablaze with the yellow blossom of gorse and the air is thick with the distinctive coconut fragrance.

Descend steeply through forest, keeping left at the first junction and right at the second, following signs for the car park, which is only another 10 to 15 minutes' walk downhill.

Horn Head

Duration	5½–6 hours
Distance	17km
Difficulty	moderate
Start/Finish	Hornhead Bridge
Nearest Town	Dunfanaghy (p266)
Transport	private
Summary	An exhilarating walk along dramatic and beautiful cliffs with deep inlets, rock arches and quiet, unspoiled beaches.

The sea cliffs around Horn Head (Corrán Binne or Curve of a Horn) boast the most impressive coastal scenery of north Donegal. Although these cliffs and their structures – including natural rock wonders such as Marble Arch – dominate the foreground, great coastal views extend further afield; Tory Island is prominent to the northwest.

This is a circular route that explores the entire peninsula of Horn Head. It can be walked in either direction, but on a warm day it is worth considering that there is a safe swimming beach (Pollaguill Bay) on the western side of the peninsula, near the end of the route as it is described. The total ascent of 450m is a good approximation; the route is sinuous and the climbs and descents numerous, although never prolonged. For most of the route, a well defined but informal path makes for relatively easy walking, although it often passes vertiginously close to the cliff edge. Elsewhere, the route crosses rough ground cloaked with heather or tussock grass. Extensive patches of bracken on the southeastern section of the route can also obscure the path in midsummer – be prepared for some bushwhacking here from July onwards. Fortunately the greater part of the walk along the west coast is over short grass that is heavily grazed by sheep, making for the easiest possible progress.

As always, care is needed when walking near the cliff edge.

NATURAL HISTORY

The southwest quarter of the Horn Head Peninsula is mostly a huge, grassed sand dune; the rest of the peninsula consists of a rugged ridge rising to 252m, from which cliffs plunge dramatically into the waters of Sheep Haven Bay and the Atlantic. Much of this area is covered by a shallow layer of peat, still being cut on a small scale south of the head. The dunes extend south to Tramore Strand, just inland from which is New Lake – a tidal marsh until a protective layer of marram grass on the fringing sand was stripped during WWI (for horse bedding) and sand accumulated from the west, isolating the marsh from the sea.

Horn Head also supports one of Ireland's most important seabird colonies, guillemots and gannets being the predominant residents. In spring and early summer the dunes

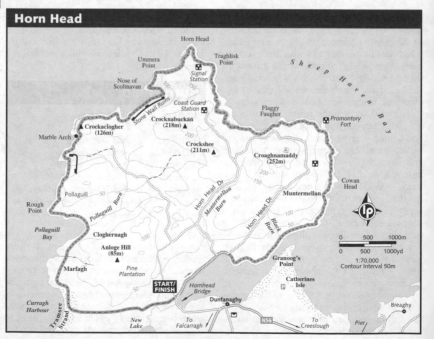

Horn Head

are carpeted with wildflowers, including masses of purple and pink thrift, small yellow seaside pansies and yellow bird's foot trefoil.

PLANNING
Maps & Books

The walk is covered by OSI 1:50,000 map No 2. This does not show any of the paths, the signal station ruins or some of the offshore rock features. David Herman's *Hill Walker's Donegal* describes an alternative circuit on Horn Head.

GETTING TO/FROM THE WALK

From the western end of Dunfanaghy, turn right along a minor road, signed 'Horn Head Drive'. You will arrive at Hornhead Bridge in around 1km. Cars can be parked in rough lay-bys on the right-hand side of the road just north of the bridge.

Horn Head Drive is a 10km scenic route around minor roads on the peninsula. It comes close to the route of this walk near Flaggy Faugher and at the old coastguard station, either of which could serve as starting points for a shorter walk.

THE WALK

Walk along the road northeast for 1km to the point where it turns inland. Pick a way down to the shore and continue around the low point ahead – this could be a little awkward at high tide. Cross a small beach and climb up to the dunes. From here an informal path leads through the thickets of bracken, across Black Burn and out onto heather-covered slopes.

Near Cowan Head look out for a natural bridge, where a wide band of rock crosses a gully in the cliff face. The path, occasionally vague, leads up to a low col. A little further on it comes as a surprise to see a couple of stunted oaks clinging to the edge of a deep cleft above the sea. Then, on the steep slopes of Croaghnamaddy (252m), the highest point on the peninsula, comes another surprise: the ruins of a **small settlement** – two groups of stone buildings overlooking an extensive, elaborate pattern of fields bounded by stone walls.

Further on, as you climb around sheer cliffs above a substantial promontory (which is mapped as a promontory fort), the towering cliffs of Traghlisk Point and Horn Head come into view. The path fades somewhat for the next few hundred metres; descend slightly to cross a small stream, contour below a small patch of scree, climb steeply for about 30m, then veer right and the path reappears. Now the ruins of the **signal station** near Horn Head become visible ahead. Around the curiously named Flaggy Faugher the terrain varies between heather and peat, keep close to the cliff edge and aim for the signal station. From the ruins of this once handsome building, a wide path leads up to **Horn Head** itself (3½ to four hours from the start) – a breathtaking eyrie, surrounded by cliffs crowded with nesting seabirds. On a clear day the wide views take in Tory and Inishbofin Islands to the west, and Malin Head to the east.

Descend to the southwest, looking back for spectacular views of the rocky crown of Horn Head. From the narrow inlet east of Nose of Scoltnavan, follow a ruinous stone wall southwest over low crags, then over Crockaclogher (126m). On the other side of this hill, **Marble Arch**, a magnificent natural rock formation, can be seen, but only if you look back! Continue along firm grass, soon coming to a fine example of the stone-wall-builder's art. Cross this at a junction with another wall. The path then leads around Pollaguill, a vast sand dune, and down to the beach at Pollaguill Bay.

From the far side of the bay the path crosses another shallow valley and ridge. It then heads directly for Tramore Strand, crossing a fence separating the pasture from the dunes at the corner on the right. Descend a rock outcrop to the beach and walk south along the sand. After around 300m, a jumble of pebbles at the top of the beach marks the access path. Follow this away from the strand, passing through a metal gate and crossing through the marram-grassed dunes to the east. The path eventually arrives at a forestry plantation, where it crosses a stream and turns right. Cross a stile and continue across machair (sandy plain) to Hornhead Bridge.

Muckish

Duration	3–3½ hours
Distance	8km
Difficulty	moderate
Start/Finish	GR 009309
Nearest Towns	Dunfanaghy (p266), Dunlewy (p267)
Transport	private

Summary A steep climb leads to the flat-topped summit of a northern landmark. Views open up to provide marvellous panoramas of coastline and mountains.

A walk up Muckish (An Mhucais or Pig's Back, 666m) looks to be a formidable proposition from any direction. In reality, however, ascents from either the north or south are steep but relatively straightforward. The northern approach is longer but more adventurous, passing through the remains of a sand quarry and following the old Miners' Path up through towering crags and pinnacles. Much of this path is eroded (you will need to use your hands for balance in a few places), although sporadic arrows indicate the line to follow. The total ascent for this route is 500m. From Muckish Gap to the south, you have the advantage of a higher starting point and a more direct, less rocky route (see Alternative Route: From the South, p273). While most arrive at the summit via an out-and-back route from one end or the other, a through walk is ideal if transport can be arranged. This is actually the first stage of the Glover Highlander Walk (see the boxed text, p273).

In good weather, it is worth allowing plenty of time to survey the marvellous views from the broad summit plateau. In poor visibility, however, the plateau can be a confusing place; it is almost 1km long, virtually flat and has few distinguishing features to break the uniformity of the rock-strewn terrain. Locating the narrow descent path is a serious proposition in bad weather, and steep surrounding cliff faces mean finding the right route is vital. In such conditions, consider turning back at the top of your ascent path rather than wandering too far onto the plateau.

PLANNING
Maps
OSI 1:50,000 map No 2 covers the walk. On the northern approach, the Miners' Path is not marked above the quarry nor is the survey pillar shown (GR 005287). On the southern side, Muckish Gap is labelled only as 'Gleennaneor'.

GETTING TO/FROM THE WALK
For the northern approach, turn off the N56 7.5km south of Dunfanaghy or 2km north of Creeslough, almost opposite a large cemetery. Follow this minor road for 5km; park on the left in the bypassed hairpin bend of an older road.

For the south, turn north off the R251, 14km east of Dunlewy and 3km west of the Glenveagh National Park entrance. Follow this minor road (signed to Falcarragh) for 3km to Muckish Gap, where there is a small shrine on the north side of the road. Park here or beside the bend northwest of the shrine.

THE WALK
Set out along the road and the rough pavement will peter out after 500m; continue around to the left. The track climbs steadily

south and southwest up to the large concrete loading bays of the former quarry (40 minutes from the start). The hard, fine-grained grey and white quartzite of Muckish yields almost pure silica sand, which was once used to make high quality optical glass. The quarries on this side of the mountain were operational until 1955. Cross the stream on the right (west) and climb the spur between two small streams, following the rough steps of the well-graded Miners' Path. You soon come to a maze of fallen rocks and disturbed ground; keep to the left and continue up a rock-strewn gully, picking your way up the stony path to the left of a steep, heathery spur.

With the guidance of a series of painted arrows, stone cairns, rusty metal poles and wooden posts, follow the path as it weaves through the near-vertical cliffs. Cross a gully choked with fine sand and small rocks and climb beneath impressive bluffs to the site of the main **quarry**, reduced to several pieces of old machinery and the remains of various concrete structures (40 minutes from the loading bays). It is hard to imagine how this heavy, bulky machinery was brought up to this remote location.

From here, the path is on your left as you face the mountain; now much narrower, it squeezes past a crag and twists and turns up to the broad, rock-strewn **summit plateau** (another 20 minutes). The official summit, marked by a survey pillar, is about 400m to the east-northeast and is dwarfed by two enormous cairns. One cairn is on the northeast edge of the plateau and the other to the southwest. The cairn close to the eastern rim is the best place for coastal views. To the northeast the Urris Hills and Malin Head are prominent, while extensive sand dunes flank Horn Head nearer to hand. Inland, the steep outlines of the Aghlas, overlooked by Errigal, contrast with the more rounded Derryveagh Mountains southeast.

Retrace your steps to the start.

Alternative Route: From the South

2½–3 hours, 6km, 410m ascent

From the bend in the road, about 75m northeast of the shrine, a rather indistinct path

The Glover Highlander

Organised marathons, or long walks, are established annual features of the walking scene in Ireland. Generally organised by local clubs, they follow challenging routes through the best known walking areas in the country. The Maumturks Walk is the toughest (see the boxed text, p245); it is closely followed by the Glover event.

This route was initiated in memory of Joey Glover, a leading member of the North West Mountaineering Club, who was killed by the IRA on 23 November 1976. The walk crosses the best known peaks in Donegal, including Muckish, the Aghlas and Errigal (all covered in this chapter). It takes place each September and involves 19.5km and 2020m of ascent. The walk starts by crossing Muckish after an ascent via the Miners' Path, then descends to Muckish Gap. The route to the Aghlas passes Crocknalaragagh and crosses the stream from Lough Aluirg. Then it's down to Altan Lough and on across Beaghy, Mackoght and finally Errigal before descending to the finish in Dunlewy.

To prevent erosion, numbers are restricted. Any surplus from the registration fee goes to repair environmental damage on the slopes of Errigal. For further information, see Ⓦ www.simonstewart.ie/longwalk/long.htm.

leads north across soggy grassland towards the mountain. Aim for a steep gully (GR 001273) with a low, black crag on the northern side and ascend it to a col. Here, you are faced with a very steep ascent over short heather, grass and some bare ground. There is no real path, although as you approach the plateau rim (45 minutes from the gap) a trail does begin to form in the peat. On the rock-strewn **summit plateau**, small cairns mark the line of approach to an enormous cairn. The official summit, marked by a survey pillar, is 500m to the northeast. The **cairn** close to the eastern rim is the best place for coastal views (about 25 minutes from the plateau rim).

Return to Muckish Gap by retracing the outward route.

The Aghlas

Duration	4 hours
Distance	10km
Difficulty	moderate–demanding
Start/Finish	Procklis Lough fish farm
Nearest Town	Falcarragh (p274)
Transport	private

Summary A fine circuit of three attractive peaks affording superb coastal views.

Standing between the higher peaks of Muckish and Errigal, the three hills known as the Aghlas (from *eachla*, which means 'stable') receive relatively little walker traffic and are adorned by only modest summit cairns. Aghla More (584m) is not the highest of the trio of peaks: the nameless central summit claims this distinction at 603m.

Apart from the boggy approach to Aghla More and the boggy lower reaches of the descent from Aghla Beg, the route crosses relatively firm, heathery ground. However, these mountains are essentially built of white and grey quartzite, and large drifts of scree cover many of the upper slopes. In clear conditions route finding is straightforward, but in poor visibility care is needed to avoid steep slopes on the northern and southern faces of Aghla More and during the descent from the highest peak towards Lough Nabrackbaddy. The total ascent is 700m.

While the route described here offers the satisfaction of a natural horseshoe, the Aghlas can also be climbed from the south. This approach is recommended if you want to visit these peaks in conjunction with Errigal (p276). The Aghlas form the central section of the Glover Highlander Walk (see the boxed text, p273).

PLANNING
Maps
OSI 1:50,000 maps Nos 1 and 2 are needed.

NEAREST TOWN
Falcarragh
A compact village, Falcarragh (An Fál Carrach) has several pubs. There is a bank (with ATM) at the eastern end of the main street.

Most of the accommodation is B&Bs. **Ferndale** (☎ 074-916 5506; singles/doubles €36/46) is 200m west of the village centre. **Cuan-na-Mara** (☎ 074-913 5327; Ballyness; singles/doubles €25/50), 1km north of the village, has wonderful sea views. There is a good **supermarket** at the bottom of the road signed to Muckish Gap, at the east end of the village. **Fulacht Fiadh** on the main street serves lunches, light meals and coffee, while the nearby **Gweedore Bar** offers more expensive fare.

Almost all bus services to/from Dunfanaghy also pass through Falcarragh. See Dunfanaghy Getting There & Away (p266).

GETTING TO/FROM THE WALK
From Falcarragh head southeast along the minor road signed to Glenveagh National Park. Turn right after 2km onto an unmarked road (just past a stand of conifers). At a fork, 4km further on, bear left and continue for a little over 1km to Procklis Lough fish farm. Park beside the road slightly uphill from the farm entrance.

THE WALK (see map p275)
Walk north along the road and, about 100m beyond the bridge over the Tullaghobegly River, turn right along a farm track, stepping over a fence to do so. Bear left past the house and around to the right past the farm buildings. Go through a gate and you are out on the open, trackless moor, which is relatively well drained for the most part. Head east over rising ground to the crest of a spur, then descend slightly to cross a stream: the upper reaches of the Owenbeg River. Continue up the heathery slope, bearing southeast and encountering patches of scree as you gain height. The large summit cairn of **Aghla Beg** (564m; 1½ hours from the start) is just beyond an old fence and is a fine viewpoint for Muckish to the northeast.

From the summit descend southeast to a col, following the line of the fence to the point where it veers right. Continue south along the shoulder, climbing to the rocky, rounded **summit** of the unnamed peak (20 minutes from Aghla Beg), marked by three cairns. You can see the interlocking ridges of the Derryveaghs extending to the south-west and Tory Island appears just a stone's throw from the mainland to the northwest.

Descend southwest over stony ground above Lough Nabrackbaddy, then make your way past some large peat hags (areas where erosion or turf cutting has left peat exposed) near Lough Feeane. A final, steep climb then brings you to the small summit of **Aghla More** (584m; an hour from the unnamed peak). From this vantage point it is the con-cave, scree-streaked flank of Errigal that de-mands attention, rising from the opposite shore of Altan Lough to the southwest.

Take care to ensure that you leave the top via the northwest spur to avoid steep ground to the north and southwest. Descend steeply over grass and heather, heading towards Altan Lough and crossing the stream issu-ing from Lough Feeane on the way. The lower slopes are rather soggy, but not as wet as in many other areas. Walk along the lough shore and cross the mouth of the out-let stream on stepping stones. Bear right to a gravel road, climb a stile beside a gate and continue to the road. The fish farm entrance where you started is 500m to the right (one hour from Aghla More).

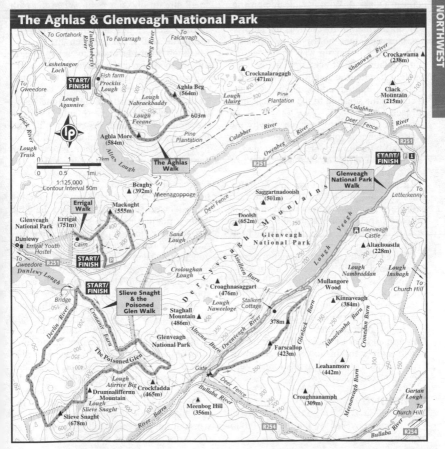

NORTHWEST

Errigal

Duration	3½ hours
Distance	8km
Difficulty	moderate
Start/Finish	Errigal car park
Nearest Town	Dunlewy (p267)
Transport	private

Summary A classic of the northwest: climb the most easily recognisable mountain in Donegal for superb, panoramic views.

At 751m, the Errigal summit is the highest point in Donegal. With its volcanic profile, the mountain has also become something of an icon for the northwest. It is not surprising, therefore, that the trip to the top is the most popular mountain walk in the region. Unfortunately the effects of so many passing feet have caused quite serious erosion problems, although a programme designed to combat the scarring of the hillside is now in place.

It is not difficult to understand why the walk is such a favourite: although it takes only half a day to complete, this route has few rivals in terms of dramatic terrain or scenic splendour.

The trip begins with a traverse of soggy grassland, but you soon come face to face with steep scree and crag-covered slopes. A well-worn path then climbs the quartzite rock of the southeast spur to the summit ridge.

Conventionally, the return route retraces the outward climb. However, a variation that includes the trip over the neighbouring summit of Mackoght (555m), adding up to a total ascent of 650m, is described here. For the straightforward out-and-back route up Errigal, deduct around 150m of ascent, 2km and an hour of walking time from the statistics given for this route. The summit of Errigal is part of Glenveagh National Park (see the boxed text, p278).

PLANNING
Maps
The walk is covered by the OSI 1:50,000 map No 1.

GETTING TO/FROM THE WALK
Errigal car park is situated on the northern side of the R251, around 3km east of Dunlewy and 14km west of the entrance to Glenveagh National Park. There is adequate parking for around 20 vehicles.

THE WALK (see map p275)
Take the obvious path that leads north from the car park. Signs ask that you stick to the approach route marked by a series of poles; please do so to avoid exacerbating the existing erosion problems. Follow the path straight up the grassy slope ahead; keep the small stream on your right. When the path peters out continue climbing north-northwest across steep slopes and small hollows to reach the rocky col between Errigal and Mackoght. Turn left (southwest) and begin the climb of Errigal's magnificent eastern ridge, sweeping in a graceful arc to the conspicuous twin summits.

The dissected cliffs of the Poisoned Glen and the dome of Slieve Snaght dominate the views to the south. As you gain height, the views in other directions steadily unfold: Arranmore Island just offshore to the west and the Aghlas and Muckish to the northeast.

Soon you reach the summit ridge and a line of large cairns (1¼ hours from the start). The squarish **cairn** close to the edge bears a plaque in memory of Joey Glover (see the boxed text 'The Glover Highlander', p273). A short amble along the ridge takes you to the twin summits of **Errigal**. The prospect now embraces a huge sweep of coast, from Malin Head in the north as far south as Slieve League.

To return to the start via Mackoght, head northeast from the col. The spur to the right of a wide gully gives a good start to the relatively short climb to the cairn on the summit of **Mackoght** (555m). You are rewarded with a fine view of the Aghlas and Altan Lough nearby, Inishfree Bay and Errigal's spectacular cliffs.

Descend steeply southeast down the broad spur. On flatter ground, to avoid the worst of the peat hags, follow the line of an old fence for a few hundred metres, then head south to meet a wide path about 250m from the road. It's about 12 minutes' walk down the road to the car park.

Glenveagh National Park

Duration	6½–7 hours
Distance	24km
Difficulty	moderate–demanding
Start/Finish	Glenveagh National Park Visitor Centre
Nearest Town	Dunlewy (p267)
Transport	private

Summary In Ireland's largest national park, an easy walk beside beautiful Lough Veagh leads to a scenic and rugged high-level return route.

By simply following the road along the southeastern shore of Lough Veagh to the watershed of the Owenveagh River, you will gain a good overall impression of the landscape, flora and fauna of Glenveagh National Park. The road is paved as far as Glenveagh Castle (3km from the visitor centre) and then turns into a gravel track. If your visit coincides with a spell of dry weather and you are used to walking over trackless country, the variation described here for the return from the watershed is well worthwhile. This takes you over the hill with the intriguing name Farscallop (on the OSI map) or Scollops (on the national park map), which rises above the upper reaches of the Owenveagh River. From the northeastern end of this hill, the views across Lough Veagh and to the northeast are outstanding, while the outlook across bleak and empty moorland to the south conveys a profound sense of isolation. The only drawbacks are that a maze of peat hags pits parts of the hill and that tussocks of moor grass are widespread.

NATURAL HISTORY
The U-shaped valley of Glenveagh was gouged out of the granite rock of the Derryveagh Mountains by glaciers in the last Ice Age. Today the area's bare, rocky uplands support sparse and unusual vegetation:

arctic-alpine species that have adapted to short, cool summers and to the buffeting of wind by growing close to the ground and seeking the shelter of rock clefts.

The woodlands along the shores of Lough Veagh stand in luxuriant contrast to the surrounding boglands. This is one of the few stands of native trees surviving in County Donegal. Fenced enclosures protect new seedlings of oak, holly, rowan, birch and hazel, which will eventually replenish the natural oak wood. With a daunting battle being waged against the rhododendron (see the boxed text 'Scourge of the Rhododendron', p269), the regeneration programme has a fighting chance.

Golden eagles were successfully reintroduced to the park in 2001.

PLANNING
Deer are culled (selectively shot) in the park between August and February each year. If you are walking over Farscallop during these months, contact the **park office** (☎ 074-913 7090) beforehand to find out when and where culling will be taking place.

Maps & Books
The walk is covered by the OSI 1:50,000 map No 6.

A variety of publications giving more information about the park are available at the visitor centre. These include *The History of Glenveagh*, *Glenveagh Gardens* and the beautifully illustrated *Glenveagh National Park – A Visitors' Guide*.

GETTING TO/FROM THE WALK
The entrance to Glenveagh National Park is on the southern side of the R251, around 17km east of Dunlewy. The route to the park is well signed from the N56 to both the east and the west, and there is a large car park in front of the visitor centre.

A regular shuttle bus service (€2) operates during the national park visitor centre opening hours, transporting people from the entrance to Glenveagh Castle, 3km inside the park boundary. Using this service will cut 6km (1¼ hours) from the length of the walk.

THE WALK (see map p275)

From near the visitor centre (see the boxed text 'Glenveagh National Park', below, for details), the park road leads southeast across the **Owencarrow River**, the outlet from Lough Veagh. Here there is a fine view down the lough in the centre of this U-shaped, glacial valley. The buildings on the left just before the bridge were once part of a dairy farm run by the former owners of the estate. The house next to the bridge was built by John Adair as a police barracks. A little further on, the modern buildings on the right are the park offices and research centre.

About 2km from the start, you pass the Lough Inshagh road, which heads southeast across the moors to the village of Church Hill. This is the way to the old, narrow-gauge Letterkenny to Burtonport railway (see Lough Agher, p289).

Walk through the grounds of **Glenveagh Castle** (see the boxed text 'Glenveagh National Park', below) and past the old sawmill on the left. After about 2km the road enters **Mullangore Wood**, the best of the natural oakwoods in Glenveagh; sessile oak, birch and hazel are the main species. On the lough shore are some Scots pines, survivors

Glenveagh National Park

Glenveagh National Park (Páirc Náisiúnta Ghleann Bheatha) consists of 140 sq km of some of the wildest, most rugged and spectacular terrain in County Donegal. The park comprises four separate blocks: the largest is centred on the valley of Glenveagh and the surrounding Derryveagh Mountains. To the southeast is a tract of peat bogland around Lough Muck, in the northwest are the quartzite hills topped by Crocknafarragh, while the smallest block includes the conical summit of Errigal and the village of Dunlewy.

It is a neat historical irony that John George Adair, one of the more notorious characters in Donegal's history, was also indirectly responsible for the establishment of the park. By 1859 Adair had become landlord of a large area embracing Derryveagh and Glendowan. A series of disputes soon led him to evict his tenants amid scenes of appalling misery and heartlessness. Some resettled locally, others had to retreat to the Letterkenny poorhouse, and about 150 people emigrated to Australia and succeeded in making new lives in New South Wales.

Adair married a wealthy American widow and in the late 1860s built Glenveagh Castle, an incongruous pile on the shore of Lough Veagh. After he died in 1885, Cornelia Adair devoted much of her time and money to improving the estate. Red deer were reintroduced to provide sport for the estate's guests and for lessees of the shooting rights. The first animals were a stag and five hinds from England and then, in 1910, 170 more deer were introduced from elsewhere in Ireland, England and Scotland. Today the herd numbers about 650 animals. The 45km-long, 1.8m-high fence that contains the deer was originally built in the 1890s and remains a quite remarkable construction, running in straight lines across the area's rugged hills, almost oblivious of steep crags and marshy boglands.

After several subsequent owners (including the IRA and the Irish Free State Army, who occupied the castle during the upheavals of the early 1920s), the estate was finally sold to the Office of Public Works in 1975. Glenveagh National Park was opened to visitors in 1984 and the castle two years later.

Glenveagh National Park Visitor Centre (☎ 074-913 7090; open 10am-6pm daily mid-Apr–Oct) is at the entrance to the park. The centre provides information, exhibits and audiovisual displays about the area and its natural history. It also has a cafeteria that serves hot and cold snacks. It is still possible to enter the park when the visitor centre is closed.

Glenveagh Castle is open to the public by guided tour only. The cost is €2.50/1.20 per adult/child and tours can be booked through the visitor centre. The castle tearooms are open during Easter and from late-May to September.

of a former plantation. About 45 minutes' walk from the castle brings you level with the beach at the end of Lough Veagh. Ahead, Astelleen Burn plunges 215m down the rocky hillside in three impressive cascades into the Owenveagh River.

Beyond the small, white-painted **stalkers' cottage** (15 minutes from the beach) the enormity of the rhododendron problem becomes abundantly obvious; the steep hillside ahead on the left is liberally blanketed with it and in early summer the rhododendron's relentless spread is betrayed by patches of mauve on the northwest hillside as well. The walled enclosure nearby once protected a vegetable garden, cultivated by estate staff who lived here in the early 1920s; it also housed imported red deer before they were released.

The road becomes more like a path as it gains height, leaving the protection of the woodlands. A 45-minute walk from the cottage brings you to a gate in the deer fence. From here, you can either retrace your steps back to the visitor centre or continue ahead towards the mountain of Farscallop. For the latter route, climb fairly steeply northeast from the gate. The northwest edge of the slope provides the easiest ground. After about 1km the spur flattens out; continue in a northeasterly direction. The unmistakable peak of Errigal is dramatically framed above a dip in the Derryveagh Mountains to the northwest; the moorland to the south has a compelling fascination in its bleakness and apparent emptiness. An hour's effort should bring you to the summit of **Farscallop** (423m). The views are best to the west and north, taking in wide stretches of the coast.

Continue along the ridge, now rather less bog-ridden, across a dip and up to a lesser **summit** (378m). This modest top affords the walk's best views, spanning the full length of Lough Veagh with the Derryveagh Mountains rising steeply from the far shores. Continue down over damp and grassy ground to the woodland below and pick up an old bridle path, which leads generally west down through trees to the lakeside road. From here it is about 1½ hours' walk back to the visitor centre.

Slieve Snaght & the Poisoned Glen

Duration	6½–7 hours
Distance	14km
Difficulty	demanding
Start/Finish	Cronaniv Burn bridge
Nearest Town	Dunlewy (p267)
Transport	private

Summary A challenging valley and ridge walk high above the spectacular Poisoned Glen, with some of the finest views from any of Donegal's peaks.

The walk into the Poisoned Glen makes an easy and scenic half-day outing. It also leads to the start of the superb ridge walk that culminates in the ascent of Slieve Snaght (Sliabh Sneachta or 'Mountain of the Snows', 678m), the second highest peak in County Donegal. Apart from the initial rough path, there are no clearly defined paths for the walk. Although sheep and deer have cut a network of short paths in several places, these have a tendency to end abruptly on the edge of vertical cliffs.

The route described from the Poisoned Glen to the Slieve Snaght ridge is different from descriptions given in other walking guides for the area, which suggest climbing an extremely steep gully that could easily be hazardous if the grass is wet (which it often is). It would be impossible to break a fall in the gully, which is at least 50m high.

This longer alternative (which includes a total ascent of 800m) entails negotiating the deer fence (see the boxed text 'Glenveagh National Park', p278) around part of the national park boundary in two places, but it is possible to squeeze between the wires without impairing their tension.

Along the final section of the walk beside the Devlin River (Abhainn Dhuibhlinne), it's impossible to avoid patches of soggy swamp, made treacherous by extremely slippery mats of decaying moor grass. Fortunately, a path of sorts gradually becomes clear as you pass above the river gorge, but take care as the going remains rough and uneven.

NORTHWEST

NATURAL HISTORY

Slieve Snaght is the crowning feature of the Derryveagh Mountains, a sprawling granite massif that is largely located within the boundaries of Glenveagh National Park. The rounded summits are interspersed by numerous small tarns. The Poisoned Glen, on the northwest flank of the mountains and on the edge of the national park, has been described as 'the most perfect example of a glaciated feature within the park'. During the last Ice Age, a northwest-flowing glacier filled the glen. Today's valley floor is the remnant of a lake, held back by moraine left by the retreating ice. The towering rock buttresses on the sides of the glen were exposed and scraped smooth as the glacier melted.

The thin soil of the Derryveagh uplands supports a sparse cover of mosses and low shrubs, including the evergreen juniper. Boglands are confined to the approaches, where heathers and butterworts are the main plant species. The name Poisoned Glen may refer to the one-time presence of Irish spurge; a milky juice from this plant was once used by salmon and trout poachers to poison water.

PLANNING

Slieve Snaght is on the northwest boundary of Glenveagh National Park. If you are planning to do the walk between August and February, the deer culling season in the park, it would be prudent to check with the **park office** (☎ 074-913 7090) about the location and time of the cull.

Maps

OSI 1:50,000 map No 1 covers the walk.

GETTING TO/FROM THE WALK

From Dunlewy, follow the R251 east for 1km and turn right along a minor road, signposted to the Poisoned Glen. There are parking spaces about 1km along this road, either near the hairpin bend at GR 930189 or beside a large, roofless church nearby.

THE WALK (see map p275)

A rough path leads southeast from the bend in the road, soon crossing a stream via an old stone, humpback bridge. Rocky in places

and boggy in others, the path traces the northeastern bank of the Cronaniv Burn and leads into the dramatic amphitheatre of the **Poisoned Glen**.

Cross a broad spur where the stream makes a right-angle bend and continue east. Ford the stream below a cascade and follow a tributary northeast, heading into a wide glen framed by broken cliffs. Negotiate the deer fence and continue through the glen to its head, ascending a rocky gully on the right (GR 956165). About two hours from the start you will emerge on the broad, dissected, rocky ridge.

Make your way generally southwest, keeping as close as safely possible to the rim of the steep crags on the right. The sections of bog become more sporadic and broad sheets of granite offer firmer terrain. After about 15 minutes, cross the deer fence again; the next major feature is the narrow **Lough Atirrive Big**, which you keep on your left. Climb the steep flank beyond and continue over the sprawling bump of Drumnaliffernn Mountain. From here, impassable cliffs bar the route southwest; veer south instead and descend to Lough Slieve Snaght (about 1½ hours after arriving on the ridge).

The final, steep climb to the spacious summit plateau of **Slieve Snaght** (678m; about 30 minutes from the lough) is straightforward. The large **cairn** marks a superlative vantage point; it is in the middle of the mountains but set back from the impressive trio of Errigal, the Aghlas and Muckish. The Donegal coast, at least as far south as Slieve League, is included in the backdrop.

Start the descent on a south-southwesterly course, aiming to reach the valley just south of the col (GR 919146) via a steep, grassy gully between the crags. Then head generally north, but keep well to the east of a small stream, and drop down into the wide valley of the Devlin River. Follow the southern bank of this downstream past many small loughs; the going is rough and unavoidably wet in places. After about 1.5km the river straightens out and dives into a steep-sided **gorge**, which provides shelter for a luxuriant woodland of oak, birch, hazel, rowan and, unfortunately, rhododendron. Where the river turns north, continue northeast; cross Cronaniv Burn via the stone bridge and return to the start of the walk (about two hours from the summit).

South Donegal

In a country generously endowed with magnificent coastline, it is County Donegal's southwestern reaches that stand supreme, offering some of the finest coastal walking in Europe. The cliffs of Slieve League in particular display a spectacular variety of rock formations. Standing on the narrow ridge of One Man's Pass, just beneath the summit of Slieve League, and facing the seemingly limitless Atlantic Ocean, there is a keen sense of being on the edge of the world. Yet this is an area that has been settled for 5000 years, and has a special place in Irish history as the heartland of Christianity as established by St Columba. The rugged interior north of Donegal Town is dominated by the Blue Stack Mountains, one of the parts least visited on foot.

Slieve League & Slievetooey

Duration	2 days
Distance	46km
Difficulty	moderate–demanding
Start	Bunglass
Finish	Maghera
Nearest Towns	Kilcar (p282), Ardara (p282)
Transport	private

Summary A truly exhilarating traverse of some of Europe's highest and most extensive sea cliffs. The beautiful cliff-ringed beach at Trabane, the antiquities of Glencolmcille and the deserted village of Port add extra flavour.

This route combines two of Ireland's most outstanding coastal cliff walks. The first day over Slieve League climbs to almost 600m above what are arguably the highest sea cliffs in Europe. These cliffs are second to none in their diversity of form and colour,

and this section of the route is deservedly popular with walkers and day-trippers alike. The day includes a traverse of One Man's Pass, a narrow ridge between the two highest points on the Slieve League massif, which is actually less intimidating than it sounds. The pass is an arête about 1.5m wide, with steep but not vertiginous drops on either side. There is also a rocky knife edge on the way to the first summit from Bunglass, which could be described as a one man's pass, but which is easily bypassed on the left.

Local communities market Slieve League as the highest sea cliffs in Europe, but the slopes falling into the ocean from Croaghaun on Achill Island are almost 100m higher. Slieve League devotees would argue that the cliffs on Slieve League are steeper and more continuous, but there is no denying that both are tremendously impressive.

The second day of the route, over Slievetooey, is a longer and more strenuous walk, although the coastal scenery is no less spectacular. The knife-edge ridge of the Sturrall promontory is the centrepiece of this section. While it makes a wonderful through route, the two days described here can also be walked as separate one-day walks. You can climb to the summit of Slieve League and back in a single day, starting from Malin Beg or Bunglass (a slightly easier route), or from Carrick via the Pilgrims' Path (see Alternative Start, p284). If you are willing to carry a tent, it is also possible to take three days and camp either at Port or by the Glenlough River on the second night.

Underfoot, the route crosses a variety of terrain: heather moor, peat boglands and jumbles of rock predominate, while the cliffs are often fringed by short grass. Fine days without much wind offer ideal walking conditions, both to make the most of the long views and to minimise the hazards of walking near the cliff edge. Even on calm days, however, care is needed along the cliff sections of the route.

PLANNING
Maps
OSI 1:50,000 map No 10 covers the walk.

Place Names

Spellings for the village of Glencolmcille are numerous, including variations such as Glencolumbkille (on the OSI map) and Glencolumbcille. You'll also see the Irish spelling – Gleann Cholm Cille – on road signs.

NEAREST TOWNS
Kilcar

A small village, Kilcar (Cill Chártha) has a good choice of pubs but no banking facilities. The **community centre** (☎ *074-973 8376*) can provide tourist information.

Places to Stay & Eat Camping is available at **Dun Ulun House** (*074-973 8137; camping per person €5, singles/doubles with breakfast €23.50/47*), at the western end of the village; the camping ground is opposite the house. Alternatively, **Derrylahan Hostel** (☎ *074-973 8079; camping per person/dorm beds/doubles €6/10/28*) is on a farm 3km west of the village, halfway between Kilcar and Carrick. Guests arriving by bus should ask for 'The Rock' bus stop near the hostel. **Kilcar Lodge B&B** (☎ *074-973 8156; singles/ doubles €34/56*) is in the village centre.

There is a good-sized **grocery shop** on the main street. Several **pubs** in the village offer cheaper bar food than **Restaurant Teach Barnai** (☎ *074-973 8160*) on the main street, which serves rather expensive but high quality meals.

Getting There & Away A regular **Bus Éireann** (☎ *074-972 1101*) service links Kilcar to Glencolmcille (€3.75, 25 minutes) to the west and Donegal Town (€7.35, 1¼ hours) to the east. There are between one and three buses daily.

> ### Warning
>
> This walk can be extremely hazardous in poor visibility and/or strong winds, both of which are common. More than one fatality has occurred on the mountain as the result of a fall on a very windy day. There are secure landward alternatives to most of the more exposed sections of the walk.

During summer, **McGeehan's Coaches** (☎ *074-954 6150*) also links Kilcar to Glencolmcille (€2.60, 20 minutes), Ardara (€4, 50 minutes), Donegal Town (€5, one hour 20 minutes) and Dublin (€19, five hours 10 minutes). These services operate twice daily from June to mid-September.

To reach Kilcar turn west off the N56 onto the R263, 12km south of Ardara and 30km west of Donegal Town. Continue through Killybegs to Kilcar.

Ardara

A small town, Ardara (Árd an Rátha) has plenty of facilities, including a bank with an ATM. **Ardara Heritage Centre** (☎ *074-954 1262; the Diamond; open Easter-Sept*) houses historical displays covering the area, offers tourist information and sells OSI maps. **McGills** (☎ *074-954 1262; Main St*) also sells OSI maps.

Places to Stay & Eat Very central is **Drumbarron Hostel** (☎ *074-954 1200; the Diamond; dorm beds/doubles €10/23*). Opposite the hostel, **Drumbarron House B&B** (☎ *074-954 1200; singles/doubles €30/46*) provides great breakfasts. For something a bit different try **Green Gate B&B** (☎ *074-954 1546; singles/doubles €30/60*), 1.5km from Ardara along the road to Donegal Town. The rustic-style accommodation is in traditional cottages and comes highly recommended.

There is a good **supermarket** in the town. **Charlies West End Café**, at the western end of Main St, serves meals from breakfast to dinner, and many of the pubs in the village also offer bar food.

Getting There & Away There is a **Bus Éireann** (☎ *074-972 1101*) service to Donegal Town (€6.70, one hour 10 minutes, at least once daily). During summer only, **McGeehan's Coaches** (☎ *074-954 6150*) also links Ardara to Donegal Town (€4, 35 minutes) and Dublin (€16.50, four hours five minutes). The same company also connects Ardara to Glencolmcille (€4.50, one hour 10 minutes) and Kilcar (€4, 50 minutes). These services operate twice daily from June to mid-September.

Ardara is 42km northwest from Donegal Town along the N56.

GETTING TO/FROM THE WALK

To reach Bunglass car park at the start of the walk, turn off the N56 onto the R263, 12km south of Ardara and 30km west of Donegal Town. At Carrick (An Charraig), turn left (south) down a minor road signed to Bunglass. Pass through the village of Teelin 2km further on, and turn right up a signed road to Bunglass. The car park is 5km from Teelin, along a very narrow road.

If you're travelling by public transport, the easiest option is to start the walk in Carrick (see Alternative Start, p284). All the bus services to Kilcar also pass through Carrick, about 10 minutes away. See Getting There & Away (p282) for details.

To reach Maghera at the end of the walk, turn west off the N56 1km south of Ardara, and follow a minor road 8km along the shore of Loughros Beg Bay to Maghera Strand. There is a car park at the back of the beach, beside a signpost for the beach and caves. Adjacent to the car park are toilet facilities and a kiosk selling snacks, but there is a €3 charge for parking. Alternately, limited free parking can be found about 100m further on, near an old quarry on the right.

THE WALK
Day 1: Bunglass to Glencolmcille

6–7 hours, 22km, 640m ascent

Bunglass car park, perched 120m above the sea near the cliff edge, is a great start to the day, and provides the classic view of Slieve League's massive cliffs. A well-used path (paved for a short distance) leads northeast from the car park, close to the cliff edge, towards the summit of **Scregeighter** (308m). From here the path turns northwest, following the line of the cliffs. Views open up of the green valley of the Glen River, a mosaic of inlets and Rathlin O'Birne Island close to Malin Beg.

Continue up and over the aptly named **Eagles Nest** (323m), perched above vertical cliffs. The path divides to traverse the heathery slopes of Crockrawer – the higher option

is preferable – and the trails merge again higher up. Soon you are confronted with a steep, rocky ridge rising to a narrow crest. The landward slope is cobwebbed with paths detouring away from the ridge. The crest narrows at one point to a fin of rock perhaps 1m wide (the real One Man's Pass?), with dangerous drops on either side. With care and balance this can be negotiated and enjoyed by the adventurous walker. The easier option around the side is preferable in wet or windy weather. Either path brings you to a large cairn and onto open moorland (1½ hours from Bunglass). The Pilgrims' Path (see Alternative Start, p284) joins the main Slieve League route at this point, and walkers with plenty of energy might want to have a look at the **ruined chapel** along the pilgrims' route to the north.

Suddenly the ridge narrows to **One Man's Pass**, a 250m-long arête with steep slopes on either side. The path along the top is wide and there is little danger – it is certainly not as difficult as the rocky crest encountered previously. Once across the pass, a final climb takes you up to the broad summit of **Slieve League** (595m) with its survey pillar and assorted cairns. On a really good day, the unmistakable profiles of Errigal to the north and flat-topped Benbulbin to the south can be seen.

To continue to Malin Beg, follow a rough path that descends steeply west, mostly over grass. Keep close to the cliff edge to locate the firmest terrain, crossing an unnamed stream just below a line of low crags. Then climb steeply over two spurs that extend seaward from the moorland dome of Leahan to the north. From here there are fine views back to Slieve League's cliffs, rock pillars and almost vertical drifts of scree. There is no clear path as you continue west around some small streams. Soon, the gentle arc of Trabane (White Beach) comes into view; walk along the low cliff top to the car park above the beach (two hours from the summit of Slieve League).

At the car park join a minor road and follow it northwest through Malin Beg. You will soon pass **Malinbeg Hostel** (☎ 074-973 0006; dorm beds/doubles €10/14) on the

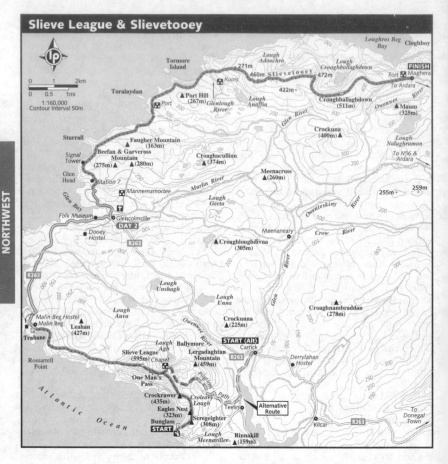

Slieve League & Slievetooey

left, an option for an early finish. To continue to Glencolmcille, take the first right and climb a hill, descending to join the R263 on the other side (1km from Malin Beg). Turn right and follow the road for another 6km to Glencolmcille.

Alternative Start: Carrick
3–3½ hours, 7km, 560m ascent

For those without private transport, starting in Carrick and following the Pilgrims' Path is the easiest way to the summit of Slieve League. The Pilgrims' Path is also a good option for vertigo sufferers and those who

don't like the sound of One Man's Pass, although it misses out on the magnificent side view of Slieve League from Bunglass. The path is a straightforward route that ascends an obvious track for its duration.

To reach the start of the path, head south from the village of Carrick for 2km and then turn right along a minor road signed to Slieve League. Continue for 1.5km, following signposts, to the informal car park near the end of the road.

Continue along the road, which turns into a stony track heading up to a shallow col above Lough Agh. Here there is a ruined stone **chapel** (marked on the OSI map as 'Ch') that is associated with a disciple of St Columba can be seen alongside the path. It is set into the slope, just to the right of a cairn topped by a large, slender rock. Also nearby is a **holy well**, the water from which is believed to cure arthritis, once inducing hopeful sufferers to make what was no doubt a painful pilgrimage to the site.

Glencolmcille

A scattered village, Glencolmcille (Gleann Cholm Cille) has a remote feel. The nearest banking facilities are in Ardara. **Teach an Lása** (☎ 074-913 7306), in the village centre, sells local-interest guidebooks. **Glencolmcille Folk Museum** (☎ 074-973 0017; open Easter-Oct), 1km west of the village centre along the Malin Beg road, has a craft shop that also sells local guides and OSI maps.

Places to Stay & Eat Near the end of a minor road about 2km southwest of the village, **Dooey Hostel** (☎ 074-973 0130; camping per person/dorm beds/doubles €5.50/ 10/21) overlooks scenic Glen Bay. Ireland's first independent hostel, the main house is rather intriguingly built into the hillside. **Corner House** (☎ 074-973 0021; singles/ doubles €33/50), centrally located, is one of the village's cosy B&Bs.

There is a reasonable-sized **shop** in the village and a **teahouse** at the Folk Museum. **Lace House Restaurant** (☎ 074-973 0444) offers inexpensive snacks and meals.

Getting There & Away A regular **Bus Éireann** (☎ 074-972 1101) service links Glencolmcille to Kilcar (€3.75, 25 minutes) and Donegal Town (€9, 1¼ hours). There are between one and three buses daily.

During summer, **McGeehan's Coaches** (☎ 074-954 6150) also links Glencolmcille to Kilcar (€2.60, 20 minutes), Ardara (€4.50, one hour 10 minutes), Donegal Town (€5, one hour 40 minutes) and Dublin (€19, 5½ hours). These services operate twice daily from June to mid-September.

Glencolmcille is well signed 12km northwest of Kilcar along the R263. From Ardara, follow the N56 south; after 2km turn right onto a minor road (signposted for Glencolmcille) and continue over the scenic Glengesh Pass and through Meenaneary to Glencolmcille.

Day 2: Glencolmcille to Maghera

7–7½ hours, 24km, 1000m ascent

From Glencolmcille, walk along minor roads across the Murlin River, following signs for Columba's Chapel and Well. Keep left and pass around the back of the beach. Cross a bridge and where the signs indicate to go left at a junction, turn right instead, following a narrow road. After a few hundred metres, turn right onto a track and then almost immediately follow a fence to the

> ### Barefoot Pilgrimage
>
> It would be easy to spend a day walking around the ancient tombs, pillars and churches of Glencolmcille. The village's name comes from St Columba (St Colmcille) who brought Christianity to the area in the 6th century. There are many visible remains of his time, including standing pillars decorated with crosses and geometric designs. The annual *turas* (pilgrimage), which begins at midnight on 9 June and must be completed by sunrise, visits 15 'stations' including pillars and monuments of early-Christian and pre-Christian origin. Pilgrims traditionally walk the 5km route barefoot. It is not difficult to follow the route and the excellent guide *Gleann Cholm Cille*, available locally, marks the stations on a small-scale map of the village. *Turas* (like the annual *turas* on Croagh Patrick, p231) are common in other parts of western Ireland and are believed to be of pre-Christian origin. During the 19th century they were actively discouraged by the Catholic church.
>
> There are also several megalithic tombs scattered around Glencolmcille. One of the easiest to visit is Mannernamortee, dated to around 3500 BC and the largest of its kind in Ireland. The tomb is signed on the left of the minor road leading towards Beefan and Garveross Mountain just north of the village.

right off this track, climbing grassy slopes for 100m to reach **station six** of the Turas Cholm Cille (see the boxed text 'Barefoot Pilgrimage', p285). This station is marked by a simple silver crucifix set on a rock where a spring emerges.

Climb 50m past station six to reach the large **cairn** marking station seven. This site is particularly impressive, comprising a small shrine within a massive mound of cobbles, a statue holding strings of rosary beads, an old stone Celtic cross, three carved slabs and a well. Climb up to the left behind the cairn and follow a path through the bracken to rejoin the track at a hairpin bend. Follow this steeply uphill and where the gradient eases and the track begins to peter out, head northwest to Glen Head. The **signal tower** on Glen Head is one of three in the region, built by the British during the Napoleonic Wars to provide early warning of French invasion.

Immediately after the tower the bold promontory of Sturrall comes into view. This is a shattered ridge of rock, 150m high, that pushes 500m into the Atlantic. With care you can scramble a little way along it, although the outer sections require a rope to be reached safely. In 1870 the *Sydney*, a 1118-ton freighter, was wrecked on the northern side of Sturrall. Local belief has it that the captain was drunk and mistook lights further along the coast for the mouth of the River Clyde in Scotland. However, the *Sydney* is not the only vessel to have foundered on these shores; this is the same stretch of coast that wrecked several ships of the Spanish Armada in 1588.

Awkward walking across bog and eroded gullies brings you to a track leading down to Port (2½ to three hours from Glencolmcille). This is a magical place to spend an hour or two. The village was deserted in the 1940s and the ruined cottages and stone walls, lying amid such wild scenery, are evocative of the harshness of life in remote parts of western Ireland. There are plenty of flat areas for **camping**.

Climb along the cliffs towards the top of Port Hill, where 250m of space draws the eye down to a jumble of stacks and islands below. Tormore Island is particularly prominent. From here, descend to sea level and a stream crossing at **Glenlough** (1½ hours from Port). There are a few small flat areas around the stream for **camping**. Glenlough has a distinctly lonely atmosphere (see the boxed text 'Art & Literature in Glenlough', this page) but it must once have been more lively: not far upstream are the ruins of two stone cottages, low field walls, enclosures and the ribbed pattern of once-cultivated ground.

Climb steeply east-northeast to cross a spur, then veer east-southeast to the top of a **rise** (460m). This point offers the best views yet of the rugged coast. Keep to the north of two loughans on the ridge and continue to a flattish rocky summit (472m) that forms the eastern end of Slievetooey. Descend a broad spur to a col and then climb steeply east to the survey pillar on **Croaghballaghdown** (511m; 1½ hours from the top of the rise), passing an eagle's-eye view down to Lough Croaghballaghdown on the way.

From the trig point descend gently across peat hags and rocky ground to the northeastern outlier of the main summit. Beyond this a steeper descent to the southeast brings you to a broad shelf above some substantial bluffs. Heather-filled gullies provide a

Art & Literature in Glenlough

It is difficult to imagine when you visit Glenlough today that this remote elemental landscape, accessible only on foot, has attracted more than its fair share of artistic talent. The acclaimed American landscape painter Rockwell Kent (1882–1971), a winner of the Lenin Prize, spent several years here creating notable works which include *Annie McGinley*, *Dan Ward's Stack* and *Shipwreck Coast of Ireland*. The welsh poet Dylan Thomas also spent a few weeks in the house that Kent had used. He will be less than fondly remembered here for describing the area to a friend as '...a wild unlettered and un-French-lettered country, too far from Ardara, a village you can't be too far from...'.

straightforward descent onto more gentle slopes below. At the top of a line of low crags, descend steeply to the right to a fence. Cross this and descend to a second fence, which you should follow through a boggy hollow to a rocky knoll. Here there are the remains of a prehistoric **fort** that dates possibly from the Iron Age (about 1500 BC–AD 200). The roughly circular tumble of stones has sections of wall that still stand up to 2m high despite their mortar-free construction. Views north from here to the mountainous interior of north Donegal are tremendous. Keep the fence on your left and descend increasingly steep slopes to a gate just above the minor road and old quarry at Maghera.

Blue Stack Circuit

Duration	6–7 hours
Distance	18km
Difficulty	moderate–demanding
Start/Finish	Edergole
Nearest Town	Donegal Town (p258)
Transport	private
Summary A beautiful, rugged walk over rough and often boggy ground.	

The Croaghgorm or Blue Stack Mountains, as they are more commonly known, rise above Lough Eske, a few miles north of Donegal Town and Donegal Bay. They are a wild, rough and very beautiful range of granite summits, which give good views of central and southern Donegal. This route, which includes 780m of ascent, takes in most of the main summits on a circuit that has Lough Belshade (Loch Bel Sead or Lake with the Jewel) at its centre.

The Blue Stacks drain poorly and the going can be exceptionally boggy after heavy rain. On the plus side, wet weather brings the best out of the 30m-high Eas Doonan waterfall and the many other small cascades along the Corabber River. Once up on the highest sections of the route, the rough terrain and lack of distinct summits and ridges makes navigation tricky in poor visibility.

PLANNING
Maps
Use the OSI 1:50,000 map No 11.

GETTING TO/FROM THE WALK
To reach the start, take any one of three different turns that are signed for Lough Eske from the N15, between 4km and 7km northeast of Donegal Town. These will lead you onto the Lough Eske Drive, which runs anti-clockwise around the lake. At the northern end the road climbs steeply above the lake and there are two hairpins. The second of these has a small road running off its apex. Follow this road to its end at Edergole, where you'll find some outhouses, an old walker signpost and room to park several cars. Be careful not to block any of the nearby lanes or gates.

THE WALK
The walker post is an old marker from the Donegal section of the Ulster Way. Most of this route was never waymarked and it has now been abandoned. Go through the farm gate and follow a wide track along a small forestry plantation to a ford, then continue steeply to the splendid **Eas Doonan** waterfall.

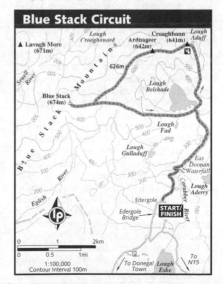

Pass a small boulder dam and head up along the banks of the Corabber River; a fairly distinct path leads across the boggy ground. After 1km you reach the point where the Corabber doglegs on its way down from Lough Belshade. Follow along its bank on informal paths – if there's been rain you'll pass several powerful little waterfalls – to reach **Lough Belshade** (about 1½ hours from the start) and a sudden view of its encircling cliffs with the main Blue Stack summits behind.

Cross the Corabber at a boulder dam and head across the eastern shores of the lake aiming for a grassy notch in the spur that descends right to the lake in front of you. Pass through this and pick up a sheep track that leads into a wide gully. Climb north out of the gully when the stream peters out and continue across increasingly rocky, but drier, ground. A couple of outcrops are easily negotiated before reaching the summit of **Croaghbann** (641m) from where there are tremendous views across Lough Belshade and Lough Eske.

Turn west along a ridge and scramble down over slabs and rocky ground before climbing up to **Ardnageer** (642m), with its views across the rocky shelf above Lough Belshade. It's now a couple of kilometres over a number of rises to the main top of **Blue Stack** (674m), which is reached after a long, gradual ascent over grassy slopes. On the way to the summit you'll pass a conspicuous, brilliant-white outcrop of quartz, which from a distance looks like a patch of snow. The Irish for quartz, *grianchloch*, translates aptly as 'sunstone'.

The view from Blue Stack (four to five hours from the start) is vast, in particular to the north where the pyramid of Errigal is prominent beyond the more prosaic outlines of the Derryveagh Mountains. To the south are Donegal Bay and the mountains of Yeats Country. About 600m to the northeast of the summit is the site where a WWII bomber crashed. A plaque marks the site, which is difficult to locate.

Retrace your steps from Blue Stack for 1km and descend to the east back to Lough Belshade, moving down through a vague gully. The route is intricate, zigzagging down through outcrops and crossing delightfully rough granite slabs in a very wild situation.

When you reach the southeast corner of Lough Belshade, simply reverse the approach route back along the Corabber River to Edergole.

Other Walks

INISHOWEN
Urris Hills Circuit

The Urris Hills are the southwest extension of Raghtin More (p263) and form a rugged ridge of low, knobbly hills that give amazing views considering their modest height. From a start at Lenankeel (GR 307436, OSI 1:50,000 map No 3) you can climb southwest past Lough Fad to the main summit at 417m. The ridge can then be followed northeast across several small dips to the Gap of Mamore. Follow the minor road down to a crossroads and turn left for Lenankeel. The total distance is 8km with 560m of ascent. Expect this moderate route to take around four hours. There is no public transport in the area.

Slieve Snaght

A northeast-to-southwest ridge of mountains stretches down the middle of the Inishowen Peninsula, with the summit of Slieve Snaght (the highest point on the headland at 615m and not to be confused with Slieve Snaght on the boundary of Glenveagh National Park) dominating the range. A moderate 10km walk exploring the area starts from a minor road between Buncrana and Carndonagh, at GR 438364. The route ascends Damph and Slieve Main (475m) to reach Slieve Snaght, crossing fields and rough, often boggy ground. The views from the summit are impressive. Allow four hours and use OSI 1:50,000 map No 3. The nearest bus route is the Lough Swilly Bus Co service from Derry, along the R240 between Carndonagh and Quigley's Point, 5km to the northeast.

NORTH DONEGAL
Melmore Head

At the tip of the Rosguill Peninsula, undulating Melmore Head has grasslands rich in wildflowers in early summer and fine coastal views from the low, steep-sided hills. An easy–moderate three hour walk of about 10km (with 220m of ascent) makes a circuit of the headland. The best walking is on the western shore, where a series of secluded sandy beaches are separated by rocky

Benbulbin, a Yeats Country landmark between Glencar and Glenade

Kylemore Abbey in County Mayo, at the foot of Doughruagh

RICHARD MILLS

EOIN CLARKE

Pilgrims' Path to Croagh Patrick, County Mayo | A megalithic tomb (dolmen) in the Burren

GARETH McCORMACK

Looking across to Mweelrea from Ben Lugmore at sunset

headlands. The clusters of caravans monopolising the eastern side can be largely avoided by keeping close to the shore or by returning over the higher ground of the central ridge. Use OSI 1:50,000 map No 2. To reach the start of the route, from the N56, 1km south of Creeslough, follow the R245 to Carrickart. Continue towards Downies for 2.2km to a fork, then follow the signs for the youth hostel. After 5km along minor roads, turn left to 'Tra' (the beach) and a car park.

Dooish

For a rugged and challenging hill walk in Glenveagh National Park, try a circuit taking in Dooish Mountain (652m). Start from Glenveagh Castle (use the shuttle bus from the visitor centre) and follow tracks to the southwestern end of Lough Veagh. Ford the Owenveagh River and climb the steep slopes beside the Astelleen Waterfall. Now head north across rough ground in a very wild situation to the summit of Dooish. The descent runs northeast for 5km to reach the northeast end of Lough Veagh and the car park and visitor centre. The total distance of 13km includes 600m of ascent. Expect to take at least six hours for this route, which merits a grade of moderate–demanding for its rugged terrain alone. Use OSI 1:50,000 map No 6. See the Glenveagh National Park walk description (p277) for details of the park and public transport.

Lough Agher

This is an easy walk of 7km with only 50m ascent, in the shadow of the towering cliffs of Muckish. The route partly follows the track of a former narrow gauge railway between Letterkenny and Burtonport. Start in the same place as the northern approach to Muckish (p272). Follow the hill tracks generally southwest and west, then the old railway formation and the road on the northwest side of Lough Agher. Return via another section of the railway. Allow 1½ to two hours, and use OSI 1:50,000 map No 2.

SOUTH DONEGAL
Lavagh More

From a starting point in the Sruell Valley (GR 913881, OSI 1:50,000 map No 11), a wonderfully scenic and rugged circuit taking in the summits of Lavagh More (671m) and Lavagh Beg (650m) can be completed via Sruell Gap and the Grey Mare's Tail Waterfall. You'll need the OSI map to navigate the 12km of minor roads leading north from Donegal Town to the start. An old track leads up into Sruell Gap; from the end of this bear northwest and then northeast across Binnasruell, passing several loughs before reaching the summit of Lavagh Beg. Head southeast to Lavagh More and then descend steeply along the Sruell River back to the start. Expect to take 4½ to five hours for the 11km route, which has a total of 720m ascent and a grading of moderate–demanding.

WAYMARKED WAYS

Waymarked Ways in the northwest include The Bluestack Way. See the Waymarked Ways chapter (p335) for more details.

Northern Ireland

For walkers the real Northern Ireland is to be found in the beauty of its varied landscapes. Nothing could feel further from sectarian strife than gazing over the Mourne Mountains from a high peak or braving the winds to walk a cliff-top path as squalls buffet the unique north Antrim coast. The slow consolidation of Northern Ireland's chaotic politics and the widespread evidence of prosperity and optimism among its welcoming people should help to consign the North's notorious reputation to the history books.

The walks described in this chapter are the elite of Northern Ireland's walks. Beginning in Belfast the gentle North Down Coast Path follows the varied shores of Belfast Lough. The highlight of the northeast is the world-famous Causeway Coast, matched by walks around beautiful Glenariff. There are some rugged outings in the Mournes, balanced by the historic Newry Canal Way. In the west are the relatively gentle Sperrin Mountains, south of which is Cuilcagh's lakeland summit and the remarkable karst landscape nearby.

HISTORY

The northeast of what is now Northern Ireland was home to some of Ireland's earliest human inhabitants. Evidence suggests that Middle Stone Age people arrived on the Antrim coast from Scotland 9000 years ago. The north was quickly settled and the countryside is littered with stone-built monuments from the Neolithic period. St Patrick used the area as a base from which to spread Christianity throughout Ireland; much later the north was the last stronghold of the Irish chiefs. The defeat of Hugh O'Neill, Earl of Tyrone, and his departure from Ireland in 1607 left the north of Ireland leaderless.

Soon after, Elizabeth I and then James I set out the 'plantation' of Ulster, removing Catholic landowners and replacing them with Scottish and English Protestants. This wholesale removal of people from their land, coupled with religious antagonism, initiated the conflict which still has two significant

Highlights

The Mourne Wall leads all the way to the top of Slieve Donard, Mourne Mountains

- Exploring the spectacular cliffs and fascinating geology of the Giant's Causeway on the Causeway Coast Way (p303)
- Wandering along the historic Newry Canal, a little-known but fascinating part of the North's industrial heritage (p312)
- Delighting in the airy views across the rugged Mourne Mountains from the summit of Slieve Donard (p322)
- Revelling in the wildness and remoteness of County Fermanagh's dramatic Cuilcagh Mountain (p330)

sections of the North's population at odds. It is also the source of the population pattern that led to partition. In 1921, while the rest of Ireland was winning independence, the Anglo Irish Treaty provided for the six predominantly Protestant counties of Ulster to remain within the United Kingdom, creating the province of Northern Ireland.

Times were tough in the North during the Depression of the 1930s and WWII, but the country rumbled along until the late 1960s. Civil rights protests by Catholics in Derry and the unfortunate intervention of the police and British army ignited the Troubles, pitting Loyalists against Republicans for more than 25 years of violence, killings and civil unrest. Attempts to bring peace began in the early 1990s and were marked by endless talks in which the British and Irish governments played key roles. Under the historic Good Friday Agreement of 1998, Northern Ireland elected its own Assembly and gained control over some of its own affairs. Early in the new millennium sectarian strife has waxed rather than waned, but progress towards real peace is being made, if at times almost imperceptibly.

NATURAL HISTORY

Northern Ireland packs a great variety of topography and geology into its small area, measuring only 150km east to west and 130km north to south. Lough Neagh, the largest lake in Ireland (383 sq km), is the centrepiece of the province, surrounded by the flat, low-lying valleys of the River Bann

Northern Ireland

0   20   40km
0   10   20mi
1:1,800,000

Malin Head
Inishtrahull
Inishtrahull Sound
Malin
Slieve Snaght (615m)
Inishowen Head
Portballintrae
Rathlin Island
Giant's Causeway
Ballintoy
Ballycastle
Portstewart
Coleraine
Armoy
Cushendun
Red Bay
Glenariff
Lough Foyle
Limavady
Carnlough

Slieve Snaght (683m)
Letterkenny
DERRY
DONEGAL
DERRY
Lavagh More (672m)
Glenties
Ballybofey
Strabane
Plumbridge
Sawel Mountain (678m)
Maghera
TYRONE
Gortin
Magherafelt
Ballymena
ANTRIM
Larne
Larne Lough
Donegal
Donegal Bay
Ballyshannon
Bundoran
Lower Lough Erne
Omagh
Cookstown
Antrim
Lough Beg
Lough Neagh
Carrickfergus
Belfast Lough
BELFAST
Bangor Groomsport
Holywood
Newtownards
Lough Melvin
Killadeas
Clogher
Dungannon
Crumlin
Lisburn
Comber
Strangford Lough
Belcoo
Enniskillen
Portadown
Dromore
Ballynahinch
Carryduff
LEITRIM
Blacklion
Cuilcagh (666m)
FERMANAGH
Upper Lough Erne
Clones
Armagh
Banbridge
Scarva
DOWN
Killyleagh
Portaferry
Strangford
Downpatrick
Lough Allen
Drumshanbo
MONAGHAN
Monaghan
Keady
ARMAGH
Ardglass
Lough Key
Leitrim
Castleblayney
Slieve Gullion (573m)
Newry
Rostrevor
Newcastle
Slieve Donard (850m)
Dundrum Bay
Ardglass
REPUBLIC OF IRELAND
Cavan
CAVAN
Carrickmacross
Omeath
Carlingford
Annalong
Strokestown
Rinn Lough
Dromod
Lough Sheelin
DUNDALK
LOUTH
Dundalk Bay
Ardee

NORTHERN IRELAND

Calling Northern Ireland

If calling Northern Ireland from within the North, you only have to dial the eight-digit number supplied in this chapter.

If calling Northern Ireland from outside the province, you have to use the area code of ☎ 028, followed by the eight-digit number.

However, if calling Northern Ireland from the Republic, there is a cheaper option; you can use the special area code of ☎ 048, followed by the eight-digit number.

and its tributaries. Rolling hills of glacial origin, technically known as drumlins, and moorland between 300m and 500m typify much of the rest of the North. In the southeast, the granite Mourne Mountains with their sharply angled peaks stand out in this gently rounded landscape. Slieve Donard (850m), the North's highest peak, dominates the Mournes. Volcanic rock (predominantly basalt) typifies the north and northeast; in the west, the Sperrins are made up of schists and quartzite. Limestone is the main rock type of the southwestern lakelands, giving way to sandstone on the upper reaches of Cuilcagh Mountain.

Ireland's flora and fauna know no political boundaries and are dealt with in Watching Wildlife (p27). Many of the province's woodland and wetland ecosystems are managed by the National Trust, and large numbers have been designated as reserves of one kind or another.

CLIMATE
Northern Ireland is subject to the same wet, westerly airflow which brings rain in abundance to most of Ireland. The mountains of Donegal, Sligo and Leitrim do, however, bear the brunt of the Atlantic frontal systems so these have discharged some of their load by the time they hit the North. Indeed, weak fronts which dampen Donegal may only be able to manage broken cloud in eastern counties. The Mourne Mountains normally enjoy better weather than other areas of high ground in the North, especially when northwesterly winds prevail. However, it is these northwesterly winds to which Northern Ireland is most exposed and which normally bring frequent, heavy showers.

INFORMATION

Maps
The OSI 1:250,000 map *North*, in the Holiday series, gives a good overview of the areas covered in this chapter.

Information Sources
For all visitor inquiries, including accommodation reservations, the Northern Ireland Tourist Board (NITB) can be contacted at the Belfast Welcome Centre (see Information, below). The NITB has an extensive network of TICs throughout Northern Ireland, details of which are given in the walk sections later.

The daily forecast for Northern Ireland is available from the **Meteorological Office** (☎ 09003-444 900, fax 09060-100 419; phone/fax per minute £0.60/1).

GATEWAYS
Belfast
The North's capital is a world apart from the rest of the province, a city of bewildering contrasts with new office blocks and hotels, almost side by side with boarded-up, fire-blackened buildings and evidence of passionately held sectarian beliefs. But it is remarkably cosmopolitan and full of pleasant surprises, and the logical place to start a visit to Northern Ireland.

Information Staff at the **Belfast Welcome Centre** (☎ 9024 6609; ⓦ www.gotobelfast.com; 47 Donegall Place) can arrange accommodation, and provide all the usual TIC services. You can leave luggage there during the day for £2 per bag up to four hours, or £4 for longer, but definitely not overnight (this service is not available at train or bus stations). An on-site Internet café is open daily; £2.50 will buy you 30 minutes and for £3.50 you'll get coffee too.

Revelations Internet Café (☎ 9032 0337; ⓦ www.revelations.co.uk; 27 Shaftesbury Sq; open daily) charges £1 per 15 minutes.

Supplies & Equipment A good stock of maps and guides is available at **Tiso** (☎ 9023 1230; 12-14 Cornmarket), which also carries the full range of stove fuels. There's also **Millets** (☎ 9024 2264; 1 Cornmarket). **Eason's bookshop** (16 Ann St) stocks loads of maps and guides (and general titles about the life and times of Belfast).

Spar, Mace and **Centra** supermarkets are dotted about the city and there's a **Tesco Metro** (cnr Royal Ave & Bank St; open daily) supermarket in the city centre. On Fridays go to **St Georges Market** (cnr Oxford & May Sts) for fresh fruit, vegetables and fish.

Places to Stay & Eat There are no camping grounds in the Belfast area.

The **Ark** (☎ 9032 9626, fax 9032 9647; W www.harth.co.uk; 18 University St; dorm beds from £8.50) is a lively place with decent dorms, a kitchen and laundry. An annexe at 27 Cromwell St has three rooms for singles or couples (from £20), a well set-up kitchen and a bit more peace. **Belfast International HINI** (☎ 9031 5435, fax 9043 9699; W www .hini.org.uk; 22-32 Donegal Rd; dorm beds/ singles £8/16) is a large hostel with loads of facilities, including laundry and coffee shop.

The contemporary decor inside **Greenwood Guesthouse** (☎ 9020 2525, fax 9020 2530; e info@greenwoodguesthouse.com; 25 Park Rd; singles/doubles £37.50/55) contrasts superbly with the exterior of this fine two-storey Victorian house; the breakfast is second to none. **Maranatha Guesthouse** (☎ 9026 0200; 254 Ravenhill Rd; singles/doubles £26/ 46) has tastefully furnished rooms, most with bathroom en suite, and a friendly host who cooks up good breakfasts.

Belfast has a wide range of restaurants, coffee shops and cafés, generally offering good value for money.

Moghul Restaurant (☎ 9032 6677; 62a Botanic Ave; mains to £12; open daily) is a superior Indian establishment where it's difficult to choose between curries, Balti, Handi, Karahi and vegetarian dishes. An Indian beer or three (Kingfisher and Cobra are available) goes down well with the generous serves. **Thai Village** (☎ 9024 9269; 50 Dublin Rd; mains to £12.50; open daily) is absolutely authentic and offers a varied menu including delicious vegetarian dishes; the set dinners (per person £19 or £21) are good value. **Villa Italia** (☎ 9032 8356; University Rd; mains £4.60-12.95; open daily) is a very popular

---

Is the Ulster Way History?

The idea of a route passing through all Northern Ireland's varied landscapes was proposed by Wilfred Capper 50 years ago, but it was not until 1983 that an access order enabled his dream to become a reality. The Ulster Way, 900km in length, was Ireland's most ambitious waymarked way, but when Capper died in 1998 he left a legacy with an uncertain future.

Despite its scope, legal status and strong popular image, the actual route never matched the original vision – long stretches of tedious walking, often on roads and unrelieved by even basic facilities, linked the more attractive off-road sections. What's more, few walkers were prepared to spend five weeks walking the full distance, so large parts of the route were a commercial failure.

A 1994 review proposed several shorter Ways, based on the original route. Promotion of the Way continued, but by the millennium scarcely a quarter of it was adequately waymarked, and chunks had just disappeared or weren't covered by access agreements. It was generally agreed that the North needed more and better waymarked routes, rather than one often unattractive monster. By 2002, eight new Ways had been opened (see Causeway Coast, p303, Moyle, p306, and Newry Canal, p312, walks and the Waymarked Ways chapter, p335) and six more were slated for development across Northern Ireland.

At the same time a consultation project was launched to sort out what to do about the surviving, recognisable sections of the original Ulster Way. For more information contact the **Environment & Heritage Service** (☎ 9025 1477; W www.ehsni.gov.uk; 35 Castle St, Belfast BT1 1GU).

Italian restaurant. There's pizza and the usual range of pastas, plus meat and seafood dishes. You can order Italian wines and beer and finish with a properly bitter espresso.

Getting There & Away For information about international services see Getting There & Away (p348) in the Travel Facts chapter. The omnibus website W www.translink.co.uk covers transport services in Northern Ireland. **Belfast International Airport** (☎ 9448 4848; W www.belfastairport.com) is 30km north of the city. There's a half-hourly Ulsterbus service (No 300 – Airbus) to Belfast's Europa bus centre (£5, 35 minutes, Monday to Saturday). **Belfast City Airport** (☎ 9093 9093; W www.belfastcityairport.com) is 6km northeast of the city centre. Citybus No 21 provides a link to Donegall Square (£1, every 20 minutes); across the road from the bus terminal is Sydenham station on the Bangor train line. Hourly trains go to Botanic and Belfast stations (£1.05, eight minutes, Monday to Friday). There's also a bus from the city airport terminal to Belfast's Europa bus station (£2.50, 40 minutes).

Ulsterbus (☎ 9066 6630) and **Bus Éireann** (☎ 01-836 6111) operate service No 200 between Belfast's Europa bus centre (☎ 9033 7011) and Dublin's Busáras (£10.31, two hours 55 minutes, seven daily Monday to Saturday, six on Sunday). Ulsterbus's service No 212 links Belfast's Europa and Derry bus station (£7.50, one hour 40 minutes, 14 daily Monday to Saturday, six on Sunday).

Northern Ireland Railways (NIR; ☎ 9066 6630) and **Iarnród Éireann** (☎ 01-836 6222) operate the cross-border Enterprise service between Belfast Central (☎ 9089 9400) and Dublin Connolly (£35, two hours five minutes, eight daily Monday to Saturday, five on Sunday). It's not fast compared with trains in other countries, but much less stressful and subject to delays than driving. NIR also has a service from Belfast Central to Derry (£7.80, two hours 10 minutes, 11 daily Monday to Saturday, four on Sunday).

Belfast is 167km (103 miles) from Dublin; gaps in the M1 between the border and Dublin are slowly being filled but progress continues to be plagued with hold-ups. The linking major roads in the North are generally better.

Derry

Northern Ireland's second city combines the old walled town with residential and commercial suburbs spilling far out into the countryside and is full of historical and contemporary political interest. Flights from Britain make it an attractive place from which to start exploring Ireland, especially the west. Letterkenny (p259) and Donegal Town (p258), just over the border, have good transport connections to major centres in the Republic and serve as alternative gateways to the North.

Information The TIC (☎ 7126 7284; W www.derryvisitor.com; 44 Foyle St; open daily June-Sept, Mon-Sat rest of year) has desks for the NITB and the Republic's **Bord Fáilte** (☎ 7136 9501; W www.ireland.travel.ie). It's an excellent source of information, maps, and books about Derry, and provides the usual accommodation and exchange services.

Internet access is available at the **Central Library** (☎ 7127 2300; 35 Foyle St; open Mon-Sat); the service is free for up to an hour once you've produced proof of identity. The Internet café **Bean-there.com** (☎ 7128 1303; W www.bean-there.com; 20 the Diamond; open daily) charges £2.50 for 30 minutes, and offers a good selection of sandwiches and coffee.

Supplies & Equipment There's a large **Tesco** (Quayside shopping centre, Strand Rd; open daily) supermarket. The place to go for maps, walking guides, stove fuels and walking gear is **Tiso** (☎ 7137 0056; 2-4 Carlisle Rd).

Places to Stay & Eat There are no camping grounds in or even vaguely near Derry. **Derry International Hostel** (☎ 7128 0280; fax 7128 0281; W www.hini.org.uk; 4-6 Magazine St; dorm beds £10-12.50, en suite doubles £17.50) is within the town walls and has plenty of useful features, including a kitchen and Internet access (50p for 10 minutes); single rooms are also available. **Merchant's**

House (☎ 7126 9691, fax 7126 6913; W www .thesaddlershouse.com; 16 Queen St; singles/ doubles £25/45) is a superbly stylish Georgian terrace with friendly, helpful hosts. The **Saddler's House** (☎ 7126 9691, fax 7126 6913; W www.thesaddlershouse.com; 36 Great James St; singles/doubles £27.50/45) is a restored Victorian townhouse where all the homely rooms have en suite bathrooms; it is several minutes' walk from the old town centre. The **Sunbeam House** (☎ 7126 3606; 147 Sunheam Tçe; singles/doubles £22/40) is in a very convenient, small brick terrace only five minutes west of the town wall.

Apart from the numerous pubs that offer decent bar meals, there are a few restaurants worth hunting down.

Fitzroys (☎ 7126 6211; 2-4 Bridge St; mains £6.50-11.95) is an informal place with quite an ambitious menu, such as lamb with red onion *confit* (preserve) and champ potatoes (mashed with spring onions) and vegetarian dishes (£6 to £7) including curry. **La Sosta** (☎ 7137 4817; 45a Carlisle Rd; mains £7.80-15.50), a truly Italian restaurant with linen tablecloths, serves plenty of pasta temptations; fish is treated with Italian flair.

Getting There & Away Basic details of international flights to Derry are given under Getting There & Away (p348). **Derry airport** (☎ 7181 0784; W www.cityofderryairport.com) is 11.3km northeast of the town centre on the A2 Derry–Coleraine road. Ulsterbus service No 234 (Derry–Coleraine) calls at the airport on its way to Derry (£2.20, 20 minutes, once daily Monday to Friday).

British Airways (UK ☎ 0845 773 3377, Ireland ☎ 1800 626 747; W www.britishairways .com) flies between Derry and Dublin (one way/return £44.40/28, 50 minutes, twice daily).

For information about bus and train services between Belfast and Derry, see Getting There & Away (p294) under Belfast.

Ulsterbus (☎ 9066 6630) and **Bus Éireann** (☎ 01-836 6111) operate a cross-border service (No 274) between Derry (☎ 7126 2261) and Dublin Busáras (£10.31, four hours 20 minutes, at least four daily). The No 64 cross-border service (at least three daily),

links Derry with Letterkenny (€13.90, 35 minutes) and Donegal Town (€15.50, one hour 25 minutes).

By road, Derry is 117km (73 miles) from Belfast, 30km (19 miles) from Letterkenny and 69km (43 miles) from Donegal.

Around Belfast

Few would describe Belfast itself as beautiful but there are some surprisingly scenic and interesting walks lurking nearby.

This section features two easy walks: the North Down Coast Path along the southern shore of Belfast Lough, and the River Lagan, following the historic navigation route along the river from the city centre to Lisburn. Both are well served by public transport.

PLANNING
Maps & Books
A street atlas is a good investment and the Collins *Belfast Streetfinder Colour Atlas* with 1:15,000 maps is recommended.

Paddy Dillon's *25 Walks In and Around Belfast* is worth a look if you'll be spending some time in the city.

North Down Coastal Path

Duration	4½–5 hours
Distance	20km (12.4 miles)
Difficulty	easy–moderate
Start	Holywood
Finish	Groomsport
Nearest Towns	Holywood (p297), Bangor (p297)
Transport	train, bus

Summary A varied coastal path passing harbours, beaches, secluded woodlands and sites of historical interest with fine views across Belfast Lough.

During this walk you can learn something of the upside of Belfast's history and spend a surprising amount of time in relatively natural surroundings. The shoreline is home to seals and many bird species: oyster-catchers, cormorants, lapwings, eider ducks and curlews are all quite common. During spring and summer wildflowers are common, especially thrift, bird's foot trefoil and ragged robin.

Apart from the very occasional Ulster Way sign (see the boxed text 'Is the Ulster Way History?', p293) there's no waymarking, nor any need for it. Much of the walk is along paved paths, with rough rocky stretches for variety and scope for beach walking at low tide.

HISTORY

The name Holywood is apparently pre-Christian in origin, but Bangor developed from a monastic settlement dated to around 558 AD. During the 12th century the lough took on a strategic significance when the Normans built shoreline castles. That significance endured, so it wasn't surprising that Grey Point was chosen as the site for the lough's war defences. Built in 1907, the Grey Point fort saw service during both world wars and was closed in 1957. It had two six-inch artillery guns on a commanding site above the lough. Together with a

similar emplacement across the lough at Kilroot, it provided a formidable barrier for unwelcome vessels approaching Belfast. During WWII, British and US warships gathered in Bangor Bay en route to Normandy and the D-day invasions. These days, the south side of the lough has become the place for Belfast's affluent citizens to live; you can't miss the several golf and yacht clubs nearby.

PLANNING

Some parts of the path could be awash at high tide or in rough weather; tide times are published daily in the *Irish Times*.

There is a convenient watering hole in Crawfordsburn Country Park, roughly midway along the walk, and easily accessible shops and cafés in Holywood, Bangor and Groomsport.

Maps & Books

The OSNI 1:50,000 map No 9 *Larne* covers the walk. A free set of 23 cards, *Your Guides to Walks: Walking in the Kingdoms of Down*, is available from the TIC in Bangor, which you'll pass on the walk. The cards cover the entire county.

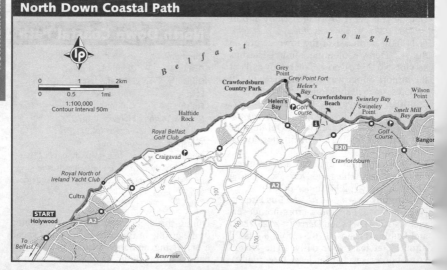

North Down Coastal Path

NEAREST TOWNS
Holywood

As an alternative to Belfast, consider staying in or near this small seaside suburb; it lacks the range of amenities but accommodation is slightly cheaper. There's one ATM in High Street. The nearest TICs are in Belfast (p292) and Bangor (this page).

Places to Stay & Eat There are no camping grounds in the area; the nearest hostels are in Belfast.

Braeside Country House (☎/fax 9042 6665; ⓦ www.braesidecountryhouse.com; 10 Brown's Brae, Croft Rd; singles/doubles £40/60) is a restored 19th-century cottage with beautifully furnished rooms, close to the town centre. The **Rayanne Country House** (☎/fax 9042 5859; ⓦ www.coastofdown.com /rayannecountryhouse; 60 Demesne Rd; singles/doubles £50/70) is a highly commended Victorian manor house with homely rooms and en suite bathrooms.

If you need to buy snacks for the day, there are two supermarkets, **Tesco** and **Centra**, in High Street, and a bakery. Apart from pubs, opportunities for eating out are limited. **Fontana** (☎ 9080 9908; 61a High St;

mains to £12; open Tues-Sat) near the Shore Rd corner is a cut above your average eclectic restaurant, as turbot with lemon aioli and parsley pesto suggests. **Jiggery** (☎ 9042 1769; 30 High St; mains to £14; open daily) offers more prosaic bistro fare.

Getting There & Away There's an **NIR** (☎ 9066 6630) service from Belfast Central to Holywood (£1.60, 11 minutes, frequent); on weekends the **Ulsterbus** (☎ 9066 6630) B1 service replaces the train, departing from outside Central station.

Bangor

This spread-out town has long outgrown its origins as a seaside resort but is still popular on summer weekends. It's convenient to Belfast and a less expensive, alternative place to stay. The **TIC** (☎ 9127 0069; ⓔ bangor@ nitc.net; 34 Quay St; open daily June-Sept, Mon-Sat rest of year) provides all the normal services and has a good range of maps and guides.

Places to Stay & Eat There are no camping grounds nearby; the nearest hostels are in Belfast.

Hebron House (☎ 9146 3126, fax 9127 4178; ⓦ www.hebron-house.com; 59 Queens Rd; singles/doubles £30.45/60.90) is the first B&B you hit on reaching Bangor and you could do worse. It's an award-winning establishment with beautifully furnished rooms, one with a sea view. **Pierview** (☎ 9146 3381; 28 Seacliff Rd; singles/doubles £22/44) is on the Groomsport side of the seafront so its rooms, most with shared facilities, have marvellous sea views. **Snug Harbour** (☎ 9145 4238; 144 Seacliff Rd; singles/doubles £18/36) is a brightly painted place in a traditional seaside terrace; one of the rooms has an en suite bathroom.

Genoa's Restaurant (☎ 9146 9253; Quay St; three courses £21; open Tues-Sat) occupies the mid–19th-century Harbour Master's office on the seafront and naturally concentrates on fish and other seafood. **Jenny Watts** (☎ 9127 0401; 41 High St; mains £5-6) dishes up better-than-average bar suppers in Bangor's oldest pub.

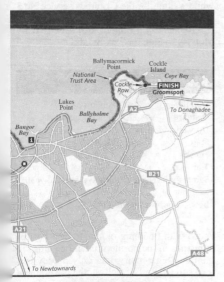

NORTHERN IRELAND

Getting There & Away There's an NIR (☎ 9066 6630) service to **Bangor station** (☎ 9127 1143) from Belfast Central (£3, 34 minutes, at least 16 daily Monday to Friday). On weekends the Ulsterbus (☎ 9066 6630) B1 service takes over (£2.50, 45 minutes, at least eight daily); the first Sunday bus from outside Belfast Central departs at 10.18am.

THE WALK

If you arrive in Holywood by bus, walk along Main Street to Shore Rd where Ireland's only maypole stands at the junction, and down to the beachside promenade. From the train station turn left and take the first left under the railway to the promenade.

On the promenade follow the concrete path northeast, at first between the railway and the shore. From the start there's plenty of water-borne activity: yachts, cargo boats, catamaran and ferries to and from Scotland. About 20 minutes brings you to the **Royal North of Ireland Yacht Club** at Cultra, a lively scene at weekends. Another 2km on and you pass the sweeping fairways of Royal Belfast Golf Club at Craigavad. Between here and Grey Point you may see oystercatchers and curlews on the shoreline rock shelves.

An hour or so's walking brings you to dense woodland on the western boundary of **Crawfordsburn Country Park**. It's another 20 minutes to a path leading to **Grey Point fort** (open 2-5pm Wed-Mon). Around Grey Point and along Helen's Bay beach and you come to the wide expanse of Crawfordsburn Beach. Here signs point you to the country park's visitor centre and café, a few hundred metres inland. The **visitor centre** (☎ 9185 3621; open 10am-5pm daily) has excellent displays about the park's wildlife, mainly aimed at young folk, and information about short walks. The park, established in 1971, stretches along the coast for 3.5km, and embraces the timbered glen around Crawfordsburn and flower-filled fields. The park's name perpetuates the Crawfords, a local post-plantation family, who planted native and exotic trees in the glen. The adjacent **Woodlands Café** keeps slightly shorter hours than the centre and serves enormous lunches, including fish and chips (to £4), snacks and drinks.

Back on the coast, if it's very clear, you can make out Scotland's southwest coast on the northeast horizon. Another 5km of varied walking takes you along Swineley Bay, around Swineley Point, Smelt Mill Bay and Wilson Point. The feeling of seclusion here is scarcely diluted by the proximity of Bangor, so that Bangor Bay's noisy fun park and crowded marina comes as something of a shock. Follow the seaside promenade around Lukes Point to quieter Ballyholme Bay. From the eastern end of the bay, pick up a path beside the sea wall; continue along a field-edge path through the National Trust's **Ballymacormick Point** property. For 2km you're back in relatively wild surroundings where seabirds gather on the rocky shore.

Just beyond the point is the sleepy outlier of Bangor, Groomsport, with its pleasant harbour. Continue to the main road (two hours from Crawfordsburn beach), passing **Cockle Row** (admission free; open daily during the afternoon mid-June–mid-Sept), two restored 17th-century thatched cottages. Groomsport has few facilities. There's a **Spar** minimarket in Main St, next to **Cunningham's Coffee Shop**, both more or less opposite the **Lock & Quay** pub, where you could slake your thirst while waiting for the Ulsterbus service No 3 to take you to Bangor bus and train station (£1.10 one way, 13 minutes, at least 15 daily Monday to Saturday, six Sunday).

River Lagan

Duration	4¼–4¾ hours
Distance	17.7km (11 miles)
Difficulty	easy
Start	Belfast (p292)
Finish	Lisburn (p300)
Transport	train

Summary Riverside paths and a canal towpath lead out of Belfast into peaceful countryside beside a historic waterway.

Faced with booming output from a host of industries in the northern inland counties in the mid-18th century, and only muddy cart tracks to the Port of Belfast, the government and entrepreneurs turned to the resource Ireland has in plenty – waterways. Using long stretches of quiet rivers and bypassing relatively sharp drops by 'cuts' or canals, 'navigations' – different from canals, which were entirely artificial and not associated with rivers – were the answer. To link Lough Neagh and its tributaries with the Port of Belfast, the Lagan Navigation was built between 1756 and 1796. A channel was dug from Lough Neagh to Lisburn, where the five Union Locks overcame the 8m difference in level down to the River Lagan; there were 12 locks between there and Stranmillis. Like the

Newry Canal (p312), the Lagan boomed during the 19th century but its fortunes plummeted during the 20th and it was closed to traffic in stages between 1947 and 1958.

Lagan Valley Regional Park was created in 1967; its 16 sq km protect a winding green corridor, 17.6km long, on either side of the old Lagan Navigation, linking the southwestern fringe of Belfast and the large town of Lisburn.

This walk starts right in Belfast and perhaps relives the journey of a 19th-century horse-drawn barge upstream to Lisburn. Although the canal is now largely filled in,

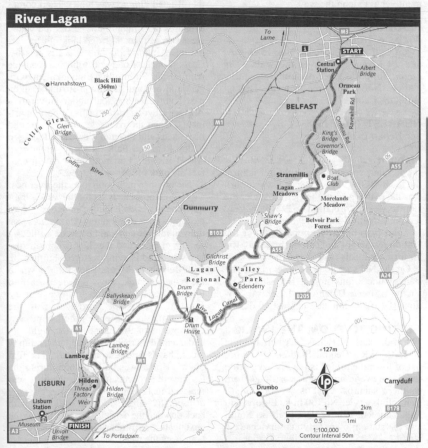

many locks and old bridges are intact so the journey is not entirely a feat of the imagination. The full distance is on hard-surfaced paths and the route is well waymarked and signposted. You could continue upstream from Union Bridge to Union Locks, but the path is very suburban and noisy – the spell has been broken when you reach the tumultuous traffic on Union Bridge.

You could join the walk at several places along the route described, especially if you can organise car transport; Albert Bridge merely serves as a very convenient starting point. There are no easy-to-reach refreshment venues along the way.

PLANNING
Maps & Books
Two OSNI 1:50,000 maps, Nos 15 *Belfast* and 20 *Craigavon*, cover the walk. *The Lagan Towpath*, a set of four descriptive leaflets, is available free from the Belfast Welcome Centre.

NEAREST TOWNS
See Belfast (p292).

Lisburn
If you fancy spending the night in Lisburn, the local TIC (☎ 9266 0038; W *www.lisburn .gov.uk; Marking St)* or the Belfast Welcome Centre (see Information, p292) can help with information and reservations.

Apart from numerous pubs, head for the **Station restaurant and coffee shop** *(Railway St)* for light meals (to £5).

On the NIR's (☎ 9066 6630) Portadown–Bangor line; trains stop at Belfast's Great Victoria Street, Botanic and Central Stations (£2.10, 32 minutes, at least 10 daily).

GETTING TO/FROM THE WALK
The walk starts at Belfast's Albert Bridge, close to NIR's Central Station; if staying out of town the bridge is readily accessible from Holywood and points east, and from southern suburbs. **Citybus** *(☎ 9066 6630)* Centrelink service No 100 links Europa and Laganside bus centres, Donegall Sq South and the station; other Citybus services (eg, Nos 17, 23, 25, 34) cross Albert Bridge.

To reach **Lisburn station** *(☎ 9266 2294)* from Union Bridge, the end of the walk, cross the dual carriageway, turn left and walk uphill to the centre of town and Market Square. Beyond this, follow Railway St to the station.

THE WALK
From Albert Bridge a paved path, signposted to Stranmillis, leads off beside the river, past apartments and shortly across a lifting bridge beside a small boat harbour. Across the river are restored warehouses and a gantry at the famous **Harland & Wolff shipyards** (where the ill-fated *Titanic* was built). Then comes Central station on your right and the green expanses of Ormeau Park across the water. Near Ormeau Road bridge look out for Republican murals on house walls nearby. Cross Ormeau Road and follow a roadside path beside Stranmillis Embankment with parkland beyond. Continue in this fashion past King's Bridge, and under Governor's Bridge. Beyond Stranmillis Wharf apartments, leave the riverside to divert around boat sheds and through a car park to **Lagan Valley Regional Park** (about an hour from Albert Bridge). For more information contact the **park office** *(☎ 9049 1922)*.

The bitumen path soon joins the river near a **weir** and the scene is set for the walk – tranquil river, wooded banks, and occasional pastoral views. After about 15 minutes you draw alongside an island between a filled-in section of canal and the river, where the native woodland is being restored. Further on, with **Belvoir Park Forest** reaching down to the opposite bank, cross the river via **Red Bridge**, then follow another bridge over the canal at what is the third lock with the boarded-up lock keeper's house nearby. Continue with the canal on the right; go under a modern road bridge and up a ramp to cross **Shaw's Bridge** to a car park. The first Shaw's Bridge was built in 1655 during the Cromwellian occupation of Ireland; it was replaced in 1709 by the surviving, but now disused, five-arch structure. Follow a path back down to the densely tree-lined river; the next feature is timber **Gilchrist Bridge** (an hour from the weir). The bridge gives access to nearby Edenderry village, which thrived during the heyday of the local linen industry.

The river soon heads off independently and you continue beside a relatively long section of canal, past two locks. As tall, 19th-century **Drum House** comes into view, rejoin the river and pass under the Drum road bridge. Next, cross a footbridge and go on, back beside the river. You're now passing through more open country, although the muted roar of traffic on the motorway intrudes slightly. Shortly before you pass beneath it via a subway, the canal again takes up as the river meanders away northwards. Along here the path is spanned by elegant double-arched **Ballyskeagh Bridge**, built of red sandstone and dating from around 1760.

Reuniting with the river, you soon pass the faintly incongruous Coca-Cola bottling plant – less so when you realise it needs a reliable water supply. After passing the ninth lock, cross Tullynacross Rd beside Lambeg Bridge. Still tree-lined, the river spills over a weir and another section of canal takes off with the houses of Hilden not too far away. Cross a road near Hilden Bridge and further on across the river is a decrepit factory producing thread for a well-known brand of outdoor wear. Go under a pedestrian bridge and soon, with suburbia pressing in, meet Canal St and pass through a portal of two metal arcs, the entry to impressive **Island Site**, formerly Vitriol Island, the site of a spinning mill. Here the 12th lock has been superbly restored; the modern building is Lisburn council headquarters. Back beside the river, follow a suburban street to Union Bridge (2¼ hours from Gilchrist Bridge).

The Northeast

The northeast of Northern Ireland is blessed with some of the finest scenery in the province. In this section, the best of the Causeway Coast Way takes in the famous Giant's Causeway, the Moyle Way leads through moorland to beautiful Glenariff, excellent paths explore highly scenic Glenariff Forest Park and a traverse of the wild Garron plateau is described. An exploration

of nearby Rathlin (p188) is included in the Atlantic Islands chapter.

NATURAL HISTORY

A succession of valleys separated by moorland plateaus extends north from Belfast, ending abruptly at the precipitous Fair Head between Cushendun and Ballycastle. The main rock type is basalt, deposited by volcanic activity 60 million years ago. Below the basalt, and exposed in many places along the coast, is a layer of limestone, making for dramatic black-and-white cliffs. The moorland plateaus and their slopes are rich in flora, notably saxifrages, roseroot and butterwort. The glens shelter pockets of woodland, carpeted with bluebells, primroses and wild garlic in spring and early summer. The moors are home to curlews and golden plovers and you may see buzzards, unknown in Northern Ireland outside Glenariff.

PLANNING
Books

Antrim Coast & Glens Industrial Heritage, by Fred Hamond, is comprehensive and well illustrated. *The Nine Glens*, by Maureen Donnelly, concentrates on folklore and cultural heritage.

ACCESS TOWNS
Ballycastle

The largest town in the area, Ballycastle nonetheless still looks and feels like a traditional market town; it has the widest range of facilities close to the Causeway Coast.

Information The **TIC** (☎ 2076 2024; w *www .causewaycoastandglens.com; 7 Mary St; open daily July & Aug, Mon-Fri rest of year*) provides accommodation information, and also stocks local maps (but not the OSNI series) and books.

There's an ATM in Ann St, the main shopping street.

Places to Stay & Eat There are grassy pitches and very good facilities with fine views towards the sea cliffs at **Glenmore Caravanning & Camping Park** (☎ 2076 3584, fax 2076 2378; 94 Whitepark Rd; camping per person £6), 4km west of Ballycastle. **Silver-cliffs Holiday Village** (☎ 2076 2550, fax 2076 2259; 21 Clare Rd; camping per person £12) on the western edge of town is largely self-contained for the denizens of scores of mobile homes; space for tents is limited.

Ballycastle Backpackers (☎ 2076 3612; 4 North St; dorm beds/doubles £7.50/20) near the beach has some en suite doubles (£5 extra). It's very popular, so book ahead. **Castle Hostel** (☎ 2076 2337; w www.castlehostel .com; 62 Quay Rd; dorm beds/doubles £7/34) is closer to the centre of town; you won't be cramped for space in this Victorian terrace where the facilities include kitchens and a laundry.

Fragrens (☎ 2076 2168; e jgreen@aol.com; 34 Quay Rd; singles/doubles £19/36) is a friendly B&B, conveniently located, with light and airy rooms and a pleasant outlook over playing fields. **Glenmore House** (☎ 2076 3584, fax 2076 2378; 94 Whitepark Rd; singles/ doubles £30/40) is a welcoming B&B with en suite rooms with sea views in a rural setting. The attached **restaurant** (mains £8, three courses £12) offers excellent-value, genuinely home-cooked meals; snacks are available during the day.

The **Coop** supermarket adjacent to the Diamond is open daily. Nearby on the Diamond is an excellent **fruit and vegetable shop**. In Ann St you'll find **butchers** and a **bakery**, and in Quay St, the extension of Ann St, the alluring **Park Deli** (☎ 2076 8563; 5 Quay Rd; four courses £13; open for dinner Fri & Sat), especially good for Irish cheeses. The Park Deli also puts on international themed gourmet nights, when getting through all that's on offer is a challenge. It's also good for coffee and snacks. The **Strand Restaurant** (☎ 2076 2349; 9 North St; mains to £10.60), overlooking the beach, is an informal place with an extensive menu, including a better than average range of vegetarian dishes.

Getting There & Away The **Ulsterbus** (☎ 9066 6630) service No 217 links Belfast's Laganside bus centre and Ballycastle (£6.70, one hour 50 minutes, two daily Monday to Friday). While the Antrim Coaster service No 252 departs Belfast's Europa bus centre for Coleraine, via Larne and Ballycastle (£7.40, three hours 20 minutes, one daily Monday to Saturday from June to mid-September, one on Sunday from July to late September). Throughout the year No 256 leaves Belfast Laganside (one daily Monday to Saturday) for Larne bus station, where you join the Antrim Coaster. Service No 172 links Ballycastle and Portrush via Portballintrae (£3.30, 45 minutes, Sunday only) at the end of the Causeway Coast Way walk.

By road, Ballycastle is 87km (54 miles) from Belfast.

Waterfoot & Glenariff

Waterfoot is a small village at the seaward end of Glenariff; it has one shop and there's a reasonable choice of accommodation in the area. The nearest TIC is in Ballycastle (p301); the nearest ATM is in Cushendall 3km (1.8mi) north along the coast.

Places to Stay & Eat The facilities are excellent at spacious, grassy **Glenariff Caravan Park** (☎ 2175 8232; 98 Glenariff Rd; camping per person £10); beware of soft ground after heavy rain. The tariff includes entry to the nearby forest park (see Glenariff Forest Park walk, p308). The **Ballyeamon Camping Barn** (☎ 2175 8451; w www.taleteam.demon.co.uk; Glenariff Rd; dorm beds £9) is close to the end of the Moyle Way and offers dorm accommodation and self-catering facilities in a converted farm building.

Dieskirt Farm (☎ 2177 1308, fax 2177 1185; w www.dieskirt.8k.com; 104 Glen Rd; singles/doubles £20/33) provides B&B on a secluded working farm close to the forest park; bunkhouse accommodation (£9) is available or you can camp for free. **Sanda B&B** (☎ 2177 1785; e sanda-antrim@ukf.net; 29 Kilmore Rd; singles/doubles £25/36) has two comfortable en suite rooms; extras include a drying room and a pick-up service from the end of a walk.

In the village is small **Kearney's Costcutter** supermarket.

Angela's Restaurant (☎ 2177 1700; Garron Rd; mains to £12.95), a homely place in the centre of the village, offers generous plate-fuls from an uncomplicated menu. To take advantage of Angela's BYO licence, drop into nearby **Saffron Bar**. The **Glenariff Tea House** (☎ 2175 8769; meals £7-10; open 10am-5pm) is well placed for walks in the surrounding forest park. Full-scale meals include steak and fish and chips; snacks are available during the day. The tea house isn't licensed. The Lodge, which houses **Manor Lodge Restaurant** (☎ 2175 8221; 120 Glen Rd; mains to £15), dates back to the 1890s. The varied menu includes fish and steaks; you won't go hungry here. Go for a table in the extension teetering over Glenariff River. Bar meals are slightly cheaper.

Getting There & Away The **Ulsterbus** (☎ 9066 6630) Antrim Coaster service No 252 (see Ballycastle, p301) goes through Waterfoot but you'd need to arrange lifts to and from your accommodation.

Ulsterbus service No 150 from Ballymena to Cushendun passes the entrance to Glenariff Forest Park (see Getting to/from the Walk, p307) and goes through Waterfoot (£4.30, 50 minutes, at least three daily Monday to Saturday). Rail and bus connections are available at Ballymena.

By road, Waterfoot is 72km (44.7 miles) from Belfast.

Causeway Coast Way Highlight

Duration	5–5½ hours
Distance	24km (14.9 miles)
Difficulty	moderate
Start	Larrybane car park
Finish	Portballintrae
Nearest Towns	Ballintoy (p304), Portballintrae (p304)
Transport	bus
Summary	A superb coastal walk past rock stacks, around tiny coves and along a beach to cliff-top paths and the spectacular Giant's Causeway.

This is a walk along the best of the Causeway Coast Way, a 52km-long Waymarked Way linking Ballycastle and Portstewart,

the highlight (among many outstanding features) being the Giant's Causeway (see the boxed text 'A Mythical Bridge to Scotland', p304). The route is adequately waymarked and follows good firm paths, with beach walking and some rock hopping.

The National Trust acquired the Giant's Causeway in 1962 and has since purchased other coastal lands and negotiated access agreements with landowners between the Causeway and Carrick-a-rede with its thrilling rope bridge. The rest of the Way (not described here) involves a 9.5km road walk east to Ballycastle, and attractive though dramatic coast west from Portballintrae to Portstewart.

Many seabird species frequent the cliffs, including razorbills, guillemots and puffins. The lovely blue harebell, thrift and yellow tormentil are quite common among the wildflowers along the path.

The walk can be shortened by finishing at White Park Bay, Dunseverick Castle or the Causeway Visitor Centre (see Getting to/from the Walk, p305).

PLANNING
Maps & Books
The path is marked on OSNI 1:50,000 map No 5 *Ballycastle*.

The very lavish official brochure for the Causeway Coast Way is of greatest use for background information; it's available at the Causeway Visitor Centre (£0.60); see below. *The Giant's Causeway & the North Antrim Coast*, by Philip Watson, is an affordable introduction to the area.

Information Sources
If you have a car, it's worth calling at the Causeway Visitor Centre first to learn something about what you'll be seeing along the way (although it costs an outrageous £5 to park). The centre's **TIC** (☎ 2073 1855; 44 Causeway Rd; open daily) stocks maps and local guidebooks and provides the usual services. The **National Trust** (☎ 2073 1159) runs a gift shop, a tea room for soup, sandwiches and cakes (to £2.60) and the visitor centre (all open daily), where you can watch an informative audiovisual (£1.50).

A Mythical Bridge to Scotland

The Giant's Causeway is Ireland's first World Heritage site. Along the shore stand almost 40,000 hexagonal stone columns which, legend has it, were built by the Irish giant Finn MacCool to make a causeway across to Scotland. Prosaic geologists, however, have spoiled a good story with their scientific explanation.

The rocks are a product of the volcanic activity which blanketed the northeast with lava 60 million years ago. As successive lava flows slowly cooled, the rock fractured along lines of tension and force, much as the surface of drying mud often cracks in a roughly hexagonal pattern.

The process wasn't uniform throughout and you can find columns with four, five, seven and even eight sides. In fact, from the cliff path you can make out three distinct layers in a cross-section of basalt in the cliffs. The lowest has the best columns, the middle layer is column-free and the top layer has quite irregular columns. Another product of the cooling process was ball-and-socket jointing within the columns. The sockets survive as bowl-like depressions on the top of the columns, in which local people evaporated sea water to make salt in the 19th century.

NEAREST TOWNS
Ballintoy

This small village is on the coast road, close to the National Trust's Larrybane car park, the starting point of the walk. There's a small post office and **shop** next to the hostel.

Places to Stay & Eat The very well set-up **Sheep Island View Hostel** (☎ 2076 9391; fax 2076 9994; W sheepisland.hypermart.net; 42a Main St; dorm beds £9) is in the centre of the village, with en suite dorms and family rooms. **Fullerton Arms Guest House & Restaurant** (☎ 2076 9613; e info@fullertonarms .co.uk; 22 Main St; singles/doubles £33/50) has lovely rooms with en suites. In the stylish **restaurant** (mains £6.95-10.95) you can choose from a menu strong on steak and lamb, with some standard vegetarian dishes. **Knocksaughey House** (☎/fax 2076 2967; 122 Whitepark Rd; singles/doubles £22.50/35) is a modern bungalow, nearest to Larrybane among the local B&Bs, with brightly furnished, comfortable en suite rooms. **Portcampley B&B** (☎/fax 2076 8200; W www .portcampley.8k.com; 8 Harbour Rd; singles/ doubles £17.50/35) is a renovated traditional Irish cottage with en suite rooms close to the coastal path.

Getting There & Away The **Ulsterbus** (☎ 9066 6630) service No 172 from Bally-castle (£1.80, 15 minutes, on Sunday only)

stops at Ballintoy en route to the Giant's Causeway (£1.90, 20 minutes).

Ballintoy is 9km (5.5 miles) by road from Ballycastle.

Portballintrae

Though obviously prosperous, this small town is lacking in facilities. The nearest TIC is in the Causeway Visitor Centre. There are plenty of **shops** and ATMs in the town of Bushmills on the A2, 2km to the south.

Places to Stay & Eat Serried ranks of caravans dominate **Portballintrae Caravan Park** (☎ 2073 1478; Ballaghmore Ave; camping per person £7), which has only a handful of tent sites.

Bushfoot (☎ 2073 2501; 1a Bushfoot Dr; singles/doubles £27/36) is a B&B in a quiet residential street about 15 minutes' walk from the coast; all rooms have en suite bathroom. **Manor House** (☎ 2073 2002, fax 2073 0042; 51 Beach Rd; singles/doubles £35/48) B&B is on the seafront so most of the en suite rooms in this traditional terrace gaze seawards. **Bayview Hotel** (☎ 2073 4100, fax 2073 4330; W www.bayviewhotelni.com; 2 Bay-head Rd; singles/doubles from £75/150) is a large establishment by the beach with luxurious rooms furnished to international hotel standard. The hotel's **Porthole restaurant & bar** offers meals to the standard you'd expect of such a place.

Anne's Coffee Shop, next to Manor House, is open for snacks and light meals, but only until 5.30pm Wednesday to Sunday.

Getting There & Away Antrim Coaster service No 252, run by **Ulsterbus** (☎ 9066 6630), has one late-afternoon departure from Portballintrae (hotel corner) for Ballycastle (£3.30, 43 minutes) via Ballintoy (£2.50, 23 minutes). On Sunday No 172 departs in the early evening for Ballycastle via Ballintoy.

By road, Portballintrae is 23km (14.3 miles) from Ballycastle.

GETTING TO/FROM THE WALK

Ulsterbus' (☎ 9066 6630) Antrim Coaster bus stops near the junction of the A2 road and the minor road to the National Trust's Larrybane car park. From mid-June to mid-September, Ulsterbus's Causeway Rambler No 376 runs from Ballintoy to the Larrybane car park (Carrick-a-rede on the timetable; 95p, two minutes, seven daily Monday to Saturday) and, in the other direction, the Causeway Visitor Centre (£1.90, 18 minutes). This service plies between Larrybane and the visitor centre via White Park Bay and Dunseverick Castle.

If you do bring your car, note that it costs £3 to park at Larrybane; this fee includes access to the rope bridge.

THE WALK

Before setting out on the main walk, it's worth taking time to have a look at, or even walk, the famous **Carrick-a-rede rope bridge** (*open at least 10am-6pm daily mid-Mar–Sept*); it's 2km there and back from the car park along a good path. The **Rope Bridge Tea Room** (*open noon-6pm daily June-Aug,*

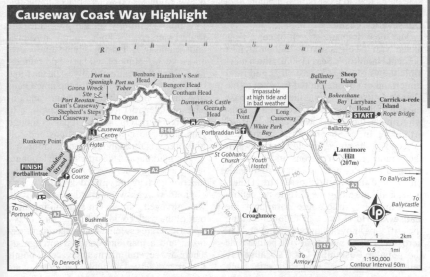

Causeway Coast Way Highlight

NORTHERN IRELAND

Sat & Sun May) beside the car park serves snacks, light meals and drinks.

Then set out westwards along the cliff-top path above Boheeshane Bay to a minor road and follow it down to Ballintoy harbour. Small rocky islands and crumbling stacks are scattered offshore along the next stretch where you cross fields and walk around a low headland to **White Park Bay**. Partway along is the **Whitepark Bay Youth Hostel** (☎ 2073 1745, fax 2073 2034; Ⓦ www.hini .org.uk; 157 Whitepark Rd; dorm beds £9), a modern, purpose-built place with en suite rooms and an exceptional view. It's close to the bus stop for the Causeway Rambler service No 376 (see Getting to/from the Walk, p305). This fine sandy beach, more than 1km long, ends at high limestone cliffs and a jumble of boulders – which may be impassable at high tide or when heavy seas are running; retreat to the B14 road if you need to bypass this section. Hop across the boulders to secluded Portbraddan harbour; beside the second house sits **St Gobhan's**, the smallest church in Ireland. Continue through a natural arch, along a shingly cove and the indented, rocky shore to Dunseverick Harbour. From here a minor road and shoreside paths lead to a car park and picnic area opposite the skeletal remains of 16th-century **Dunseverick Castle**.

The most dramatic stretch of coast rises ahead with the cliffs soaring to their highest point at **Hamilton's Seat** (100m); the panoramic views of rugged coast cliffs and rural hinterland are uninterrupted for 4km to the **Giant's Causeway**. Along the way you pass the site of the last known wreck of the Spanish Armada, the *Girona*, which sank in 1588. At the top of the **Shepherd's Steps** you can descend to the shore for close-up views of the famous rock formations and the cliffs north to Port Reostan; a bitumen road leads on to the **Causeway Visitor Centre**. Otherwise, continue along the cliffs to the centre.

From there follow the path past the **Causeway Hotel** (☎ 2073 1226) and along the cliff tops above Runskerry Point and on, across a bridged burn to a wide path beside the popular **Bushmills–Giant's Causeway railway**. After about 250m, if the tide is out, drop down to Bushfoot Strand. At its western end, a large footbridge crosses the River Bush; here you rejoin the path beside the railway. Continue along it to the large car park on the edge of Portballintrae.

Moyle Way

Duration	9–9½ hours
Distance	30km (18.6 miles)
Difficulty	moderate–demanding
Start	Ballycastle
Finish	Glenariff Forest Park
Nearest Towns	Ballycastle (p301), Waterfoot & Glenariff (p302)
Transport	bus

Summary A scenic and varied Waymarked Way through forests and across rough, wild moorland with fine views from several vantage points.

Unusually among official Ways in the North, the Moyle Way isn't made up of long stretches of road walking joined by bits of paths and tracks – the reverse, in fact. The walk was surveyed during Ireland's wettest summer ever, which should explain the heavy emphasis on watery places in the following description – but it can't always be like this! Definitely on the plus side, the route twice crosses high ground, at Slieveanorra and near Trostan, giving fine views and a keen feeling of wildness and remoteness. From the centre of Ballycastle the route traverses two of the finest of the nine Glens of Antrim – Glenhesk and Glendun – and finishes in Glenariff, opposite the entrance to the forest park. On the way it passes though woodland and conifer plantations and follows streams through moorland and forest.

Waymarking and the official map brochure leave a lot to guesswork – several crucial junctions, where the onward direction wasn't obvious, weren't waymarked when the walk was surveyed. Stream crossings in the latter part of the walk could be difficult after heavy rain. Boots are essential for the moorland sections, and a map and compass throughout. There are several intermediate access points that are not served by public transport but are useful if you can juggle car transport. There's nowhere to stop for a bite and a drink along the way. The route ascends a total of 980m.

PLANNING
Maps & Books
The OSNI 1:50,000 maps No 5 *Ballycastle* and No 9 *Larne* show the route. The official illustrated guide *Moyle Way* is informative but its depiction of the route is unreliable, especially around Orra Beg. *The Moyle Way*, a set of eight route cards with 1:100,000 maps, is published by Moyle District Council and the Environment Service. Both guides are available from the Ballycastle TIC.

GETTING TO/FROM THE WALK
The end of the walk, Glenariff Forest Park, is 7.5km (4.7 miles) south of Waterfoot via the A43 road. **Ulsterbus** (☎ *9066 6630*) service No 150 between Cushendun and Ballymena, via Waterfoot, stops near the park entrance (Waterfoot to Glenariff Forest Park £1.60, 11 minutes, at least three services each way daily Monday to Saturday). Convenient services heading to Waterfoot/Cushendun pass the park entrance at around 4.20 and 6.20pm.

THE WALK
Walk down Fairhill St from the Diamond in Ballycastle; just beyond the end of the bitumen turn right along the formation of the old Ballymena railway. A few hundred metres along join a forest road which soon starts to gain height. At a T-junction turn right; soon, looking back, there are views of Ballycastle and Rathlin Island. Near its highest point, the track becomes a bitumen road. Turn left at a junction; as you descend to a T-junction fine views of Glenhesk open up; turn right then left at another junction to Ballyveely car park and picnic area (1½ hours from Ballycastle).

The next section, along Glenhesk road, is a road walk true enough, but an extremely scenic one with hedgerow-separated fields, farms and moorland beyond. The road takes you to a minor road and Breen bridge car park (an hour from the picnic area). Cross and continue on a vehicle track. This passes briefly through **Breen Oakwood National Nature Reserve**; turn right to gain height.

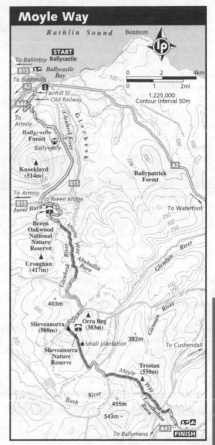

After a slight dip go left along a path and soon descend into upper Glenhesk through a plantation. Cross a bridge over Glenhesk River and head upstream. It's pretty rough and rather wet going through the valley to Altahullin Burn. Cross it and go up to a path leading south through the plantation. If you reach a forest track with dry feet you'll be doing well; turn right and continue to a bitumen road. Turn left and walk along the road for 1km to a forest road on the right near Orra Beg (2½ hours from Breen bridge car park).

This road takes you up into moorland and the **Slieveanorra** summit (508m) and a small

NORTHERN IRELAND

nature reserve; the wide view takes in Rathlin Island to the north and fertile plains westwards. Walk down the road (south) for about 50m then head southeast across moorland following waymarker posts, soon along a wide boggy path. This skirts a small, isolated plantation; the going then gets wetter through another plantation. Turn left at a dry forest road, then the first right and soon you reach a road (two hours from Orra Beg).

Turn right; a short stretch of road leads to a path down to the Glendun River bridge. Waymarkers show the route over rough moorland, east and east-southeast across the upper slopes of **Trostan**. On the crest of a broad spur descend southeastwards to a plantation boundary and follow it for several hundred metres. At a left bend (GR181227) dive into the trees and look for a rough path, mainly through conifers, soon reaching Essathohan Burn. A path generally follows it down, with a few crossings; after a while you emerge into the open. Cross the end of a forest track and continue ahead, past a fine **waterfall** on the right and down to the B14 road. Cross it to a forest track; go right at a T-junction and in the same direction at the next junction and soon you reach the A43 road opposite the Glenariff Forest Park entrance (two hours from Glendun River road).

Glenariff Forest Park

Duration	2¼–2½ hours
Distance	9km (5.6 miles)
Difficulty	easy–moderate
Start/Finish	Glenariff Forest Park
Nearest Towns	Waterfoot & Glenariff (p302)
Transport	bus

Summary A rare opportunity to enjoy bog-free walking on firm paths through this magnificently scenic forest park with towering trees, thundering waterfalls and wide views.

Often referred to as 'the Queen of the Glens' and once glorified as 'Switzerland in miniature', Glenariff, a classic U-shaped glaciated valley, certainly has the most dramatic natural features of any of the nine Glens of Antrim. This walk explores the waterfalls, gorges and woodland of Glenariff Forest Park. Keep in mind that the walk is described in the opposite direction to that presumed by the waymarkers, which have arrows on one side only; the route is nevertheless easy to follow. It ascends a total of 250m.

Iron ore deposits were discovered in the glen in the late 19th century. A narrow-gauge railway (the first in Ireland) was built in 1873 from the Cloghcor mines to the coast at Red Bay. The mines were short-lived but the rail links built to serve them gave birth to tourism in the glen.

The 11.85-sq-km park is bisected by the Glenariff and Inver Rivers cutting steeply down through basalt in a series of waterfalls and narrow gorges. The damp humid microclimate around a 1km stretch of gorge on the Glenariff River supports a wide range of mosses, liverworts and ferns, protected in a National Nature Reserve (the path through here may be closed). Elsewhere relatively rich soil supports various oaks and beeches and commercial conifers. In spring wood sorrel, bluebells and aromatic wild garlic carpet the forest floor, giving way in summer to herb robert and purple loosestrife.

The park is home to badgers, red squirrels and foxes; buzzards have returned to the glen's escarpments.

PLANNING
Maps
The OSNI 1:50,000 map No 9 *Larne* puts the walk in its wider geographical setting, but the forest park's brochure shows the waymarked trails much more clearly; it's available at the park entrance or from the tea house. Contact the **North District Forest Office** (☎ 7776 8075) for more information.

GETTING TO/FROM THE WALK
See Getting to/from the Walk (p307) for Moyle Way.

THE WALK
From the car park's northeast corner follow white waymarked paths to pass below the tea house; at a three-way junction go straight, now with red waymarkers. Descend steadily,

soon northeastwards, close to the tumbling Inver River; the wild garlic around here is particularly pungent in spring. At a track junction immediately before a bridge over the river, you could break for refreshments at nearby Manor Lodge Restaurant – just continue downstream to a bridge spanning Glenariff River, right beside the hotel.

Back on the route, cross the bridge and tackle the steep rise to the line of the old narrow-gauge railway. This makes for easy walking so you're scarcely aware of the gain in height, but it doesn't last! A couple of sharp bends and some steps take you well up the side of the glen, with fine wide views. Soon the track leaves the forest and descends to cross the Inver River and two tributaries. From the third bridge go up to a track and turn right; if it's wet don't miss the nearby shelter shed (1¾ hours from the start).

Next, turn right at a T-junction and almost immediately left at a fork. The track soon swings around the end of a spur and into the valley of Glenariff River. Having lost more height, cross first the forest park access road, then shortly the access road. Turn right along a path with the Glenariff River below, to return along a scenic path to the car park.

Garron Plateau

Duration	3¾–4¼ hours
Distance	15km (9.3 miles)
Difficulty	moderate
Start	Carnlough (p310)
Finish	Waterfoot (p302)
Transport	bus

Summary Across one of the largest blanket bogs in Northern Ireland, with panoramic views of Carnlough Bay and a spectacular descent into Glenariff.

If the crowds on part of the coast and the cultivated landscapes of the glens leave you with the feeling that something is missing from your experience of the northeast, then head for the Garron Plateau. In the midst of this wild and lonely upland, between the coast and Glenariff, it's not difficult to imagine you're on another planet, with only skylarks and curlews for company. The gentle undulations of the bogs and moors are enlivened with a scattering of lakes, some mere puddles, others large enough for a bit of boating. By way of contrast, the first part of the walk follows the line of an old mineral railway, built to bring limestone from a quarry on the escarpment northwest of the town to a whiting mill beside Carnlough harbour where it was crushed to a fine powder. The Ulster Way still traverses the plateau (see the boxed text 'Is the Ulster Way History?', p293); its weather-beaten waymarkers should still provide a fairly reliable guide from the farm above Cranny Falls down into Glenariff. It's worth remembering that the Glenariff River, which you follow into Waterfoot, can burst its low reedy banks after a few days' rain. The route climbs 360m in total.

PLANNING
More so than usual, map and compass are essential for this walk, as are boots and gaiters. It would *not* be a good idea to set out in bad weather.

Maps
The OSNI 1:50,000 map No 9 *Larne* shows the route accurately enough.

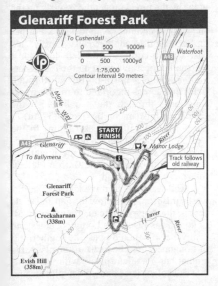

Glenariff Forest Park

To Cushendall
To Waterfoot
A43
0   500   1000m
0   500   1000yd
1:75,000
Contour Interval 50 metres

Moyle Way
START/FINISH
A43   Glenariff
To Ballymena
Manor Lodge
Track follows old railway
Glenariff Forest Park
Crockaharnan (338m)
Inver River
Evish Hill (358m)

NEAREST TOWNS
See Waterfoot & Glenariff (p302).

Carnlough
This is a small coastal town steadily expanding along the main road with an interesting history based on limestone quarrying nearby.

There's an ATM in Bay Rd. The nearest TIC is in Ballycastle (p301).

Places to Stay & Eat There are no camping grounds or hostels nearby.

Bethany Guest House (☎ 2888 5667; 5 Bay Rd; singles/doubles £19/38) is a plain establishment in the centre of town; some rooms have shared facilities. **7 Shingle Cove B&B** (☎ 2888 5638; 7 Shingle Cove; singles/ doubles £25/40) is a modern bungalow with nicely set-up rooms just back from the main road at the southern end of the town.

There's a **Mace** supermarket in High St parallel to Bay Rd, and a **Spar** supermarket in Bay Rd.

Harbour Lights Café & Bar (☎ 2888 5950; Bay Rd; mains to £12; open Wed-Sun) offers steaks, vegetarian dishes, snacks and harbour views. **Waterfall Bar** (☎ 2888 5606; High St; mains to £7.50) does good bar suppers.

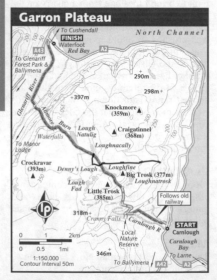

Getting There & Away The Ulsterbus (☎ 9066 6630) service No 162 from Larne to Cushendun passes through Carnlough (£5.40, 41 minutes, at least five daily Monday to Saturday, one Sunday), as does the Antrim Coaster (see Getting There & Away, p302, for Ballycastle). Carnlough is 67km (41.6 miles) from Belfast.

THE WALK
Walk up the steps from the main road in Carnlough, on the harbour side of Harbour Lights café, to an open grassed area, the site of the one-time **whiting mill**. Follow a path along the formation of the old railway northwestwards to the base of the limestone cliffs, where there was once a quarry. Veer left and shortly turn right along a minor road. Here you could take time here to visit Cranny Falls, the focus of a **Local Nature Reserve** noted for its limestone flora.

Walk up the road for about 300m, then turn sharp right up a concrete road and follow it past a farmhouse on the right, through a gate, about 100m beyond which the way onwards is via a rough track on the right. Some old Ulster Way signs and stiles around here were very precarious so may not be obvious by the time you get there. Walk up the track and turn right after about five minutes and, still ascending, go up to a gate. Further on bend right to another gate. Shortly, just past a fence corner on the left, look for a waymarker post in a field on the left. It sets you on course north-northwest through fields and across moorland to meet a track. This leads through the gap between the seemingly misnamed Big Trosk (377m) to the north and Little Trosk (385m) to the west. At the gap (about 1½ hours from Carnlough) the wild, empty – some might say desolate – moorland of the **Garron Plateau** rolls away gently ahead.

A well-waymarked route takes off northwestwards from just below the gap and leads across the boggy plateau, between small Loughfine and Denny's Lough, over a stone wall via a stile, and on past the southern tip of Loughnacally. The heart of the plateau is a quiet but not silent place, with the plaintive calls of curlews and golden plovers and the soughing of the wind. Then it's across a low ridge, and beyond tranquil Lough Natulig, Glenariff comes into view; on a good day you can see Scotland's Mull of Kintyre. As you start the steep descent, the going underfoot improves wonderfully to firm, cropped grassland. Drop down, generally on the southwestern side of Altmore Burn, to a rough farm track, which takes you comfortably to the minor road on the eastern side of Glenariff (1½ hours from the Trosks gap).

Turn right for no more than 100m, then left along a waymarked path beside a small stream and on to the path beside the Glenariff River. This grassy, possibly overgrown path carries you all the way downstream to a side street in Waterfoot, a short step from The Mariners Bar on the main road (45 minutes from the Glenariff road).

The Southeast

The southeast presents a striking contrast to the soft and rounded uplands, and dramatic coastline of the northeast. The Mournes are the highest, steepest and most rugged mountains in Northern Ireland. Their compactness and the more adventurous nature of walks there, and proximity to Belfast and even Dublin, have made them one of the most visited walking (and climbing) areas in Ireland. What's more, they're ess likely to turn boggy, even during and after wet weather, than areas in the northeast and west. The four walks in the Mournes described here take in the best scenery and most outstanding features of the range; the Newry Canal Way to the northwest of the mountains – and from where they're often in view – is completely different: flat, and focused on human endeavours rather than natural landscapes.

NATURAL HISTORY

The Mourne Mountains dominate the southeast and their granite rock is the intruder in an area of Silurian slates and grits. The range, formed 50 million years ago, is probably the youngest mountain group in Ireland. Their steep slopes and poor acidic soils don't support a great variety of flora and fauna but they are well endowed with evidence of relatively recent glaciation. Distinctive features on several summits are huge craggy tors (rock towers). It's most likely they were formed during the last Ice Age when the very tops of these mountains just poked out of the ice sheet and so were not scoured by glaciers; technically they're called nunataks. Frost shattered the weaker rock, leaving behind towers and pinnacles of harder rock.

PLANNING

Maps & Books

The OSI 1:250,000 *North* map in the Holiday series gives an overall view of the area.

Your Guide to Walks: Walking in the Kingdoms of Down is a free set of 21 route cards describing mostly easy to moderate walks throughout the county; each has a small extract from the relevant OSNI 1:50,000 map. They're available from local TICs and the regional website (see Information, below).

In the Geological Survey's *Landscapes from Stone* series, *Mourne, Gullion & Cooley* comprises descriptions of 10 circular walks with 1:50,000 maps. *25 Walks in Down District*, by Leonard Lawson, con centrates on the area around and to the north and northeast of Newcastle. *Bernard Davey's Mourne: 10 Walks with the Weatherman* has lots of illustrated background and a set of route cards; a second volume in the series describes 10 more walks by Ireland's best-known weather forecaster.

ACCESS TOWN

Newcastle

This sizable coast town, with lingering stalwarts of old-time seaside resort attractions alongside trendy coffee shops, is an ideal base for exploring the Mournes.

Information The TIC (*☎ 4372 2222; 10-14 Central Promenade; open daily June-Aug*) has maps and walking guides, and provides the usual currency-exchange and accommodation reservationservices; the TIC's town map is useful. The regional website **W** www.kingdomsofdown.com has loads of information and good accommodation links.

Mourne Heritage Trust (☎ 4372 4059; e mht@mourne.co.uk; 87 Central Promenade; open Mon-Fri) provides comprehensive information about the mountains' natural and cultural heritage. Pick up a copy of the magazine Mourne Matters. During summer, guided walks are run fortnightly on weekends. The fee is £5 per person and booking is essential.

Newcastle Library (☎ 4372 2710; Main St) is the place to go (beside the Shimna River bridge) for Internet access. The fee is £2 for 30 minutes; it may be necessary to book ahead and you must produce proof of a permanent address. It's open Monday to Friday, Saturday morning and Sunday afternoon.

There are three ATMs in Main St and at Tesco in Castlewellan Rd just north of town.

Supplies & Equipment There's a **Tesco** (Castlewellan Rd; open daily) supermarket about 1km from the town centre. There's also a **Lidl** (Railway St; open daily) supermarket. There **bakeries** in Main St and on Central Promenade, and **greengrocers** in Main St.

For maps, liquid fuel and canned gas drop in to **Hill Trekker** (☎ 4372 3842; 115 Central Promenade).

Places to Stay & Eat There are grassy pitches and good facilities at spacious **Tollymore Caravanning & Camping Site** (☎ 4372 2428; Bryansford Village; camping per person £12), 6km from Newcastle via the A50 (Castlewellan) road.. The tariff includes entry to the surrounding forest park. There's a tea house here, open to 6pm in summer and on weekends, for snacks and light meals.

Newcastle IYH (☎/fax 4372 2133; 30 Downs Rd; dorm beds £9; closed 11am-5pm) is close to the sea front; the dorms (with four to seven beds) and the kitchen have plenty of space to spread out and a friendly atmosphere prevails. A self-contained family annexe is available.

Beach House (☎/fax 4372 2345; 22 Downs Rd; singles/doubles £35/60) has uncompromised sea views from a traditional terrace house; the high-ceilinged rooms have en suites. The **Golf Links House** (☎ 4372 2054, fax 4372 5955; e golflinkshouse@hotmail.com;

109 Dundrum Rd; singles/doubles £18/30) is a slightly old-fashioned place on the northern edge of town by the A2 road; it is quiet and welcoming and represents good value. The **restaurant** (mains to £9.00) offers a fairly standard, homely and inexpensive menu in a relaxed atmosphere, and quantities are generous.

Rooneys (☎ 4372 6239; 36 Downs Rd; mains £6.50-14) is close to the beach and tempts you with some unusual items including shark and kangaroo; vegetarian dishes are on the spicy side. **Sesalt** (☎ 4372 5027; 51 Central Promenade; set menu Fri & Sat £19.50) is a small, informal place with the prized sea view; the choice for the set-price menu is wide among steaks, local fish and vegetarian dishes.

Getting There & Away The Ulsterbus (☎ 9066 6630) service No 237 links Belfast's Europa bus centre and Newcastle (£5, one hour 10 minutes, at least four daily Monday to Saturday, two on Sunday). From Newry, on the Belfast–Dublin train line, you can catch bus No 240 to Newcastle (£4.20, 37 minutes, four daily Monday to Saturday, two on Sunday). **Newcastle bus station** (☎ 4372 2296) is in Railway St at the eastern end of Main St.

By road, Newcastle is 46km (28.6 miles) from Belfast.

Newry Canal Way

Duration	6½–7 hours
Distance	30.4km (18.9 miles)
Difficulty	moderate
Start	Portadown (p314)
Finish	Newry (p314)
Transport	train, bus

Summary A long, flat leg-stretcher beside one of Ireland's oldest canals through beautiful, tranquil, ever-changing countryside.

Some say that canal walks are boring, but this one surely disproves such a claim. The walk is rather like turning the pages of a book, as the scene changes constantly and subtly. Linking the town of Portadown and the busy city of Newry at the head of Carlingford Lough, its northern section goes through flat country, whereas the southern half winds through hillier farmlands. Although it's more than 50 years since the canal closed, you'll pass many of its original working features in varying states of repair. Bird life, in woodlands and on the water, is plentiful and the woodlands and hedgerows are endowed with rich and varied flora. This is one of Northern Ireland's official Waymarked Ways – and part of the National Cycle Route (NCR) 9; there are plenty of information boards and mileposts along the way. The greater proportion of the distance is along gravel or earth tracks separating not unduly long stretches of bitumen road.

The walk starts and finishes in the centres of the respective towns. It is possible to do a shorter version of the walk by using one of two **Ulsterbus** (☎ 9066 6630) services. Bus No 63, from Portadown to Newry, passes through Scarva (£1.90, 30 minutes) and Poyntz Pass (£2.30, 38 minutes) twice every afternoon from Monday to Saturday. Bus No 66 from Scarva to Banbridge is more frequent (£1.60, 15 minutes, eight daily Monday to Friday, three Saturday); there are connections at Banbridge to Belfast and Newry (Nos 200 and 238). Trains stop at Scarva and Poyntz Pass but the limited timetable for commuters is inconvenient for walkers.

HISTORY

Linking Lough Neagh and Carlingford Lough, the Newry Canal was the first summit level canal in Britain. Such canals are fed at their highest level, water flowing down from there in both directions. Consequently locks have to be built on either side of the summit to raise and lower the canal's level so that barges can travel through. This may not sound difficult, but the engineering involved was ground-breaking at the time; 14 locks levelled the 24m difference between the highest and lowest points.

Impelled by the discovery of coal within reach of Lough Neagh, the canal was built between about 1730 and 1741 and began carrying traffic a year later. It was a resounding success, carrying enormous quantities of raw materials and goods to and from foreign ports. Canalside towns and villages mushroomed and industries thrived for 150 years – brewing, grain milling and linen manufacture, to highlight but three. Trade declined early in the 20th century as rail and road traffic exerted their superiority and by 1947 revenue had fallen so far short of upkeep costs that the canal was closed to navigation. There are still many reminders of this prosperous past in bridges and locks, a few lock-keepers' houses and merchants' warehouses beside Newry's four quays. The

Canal People

Although a few famous men were associated with the origins, building and life of the canal, including the Cromwellian General George Monck, who first thought of it, and John Wesley, the father of Methodism, who sang its praises – the heroes of the canal were legions of anonymous, 'ordinary' folk.

Navvies flocked to the construction site from all corners of Ireland, bringing their own shovel or pick, to be paid the equivalent of today's £0.03 per day for the backbreaking work of digging through boggy ground and clearing dense thickets of trees.

Lightermen piloted the timber-built, 21m-long barges, often named after their wives, children or girlfriends, and endured long absences from home and the vagaries of the weather. Teenage boat boys had to be just as hardy; often barefoot and ill-clad, they led the barge-pulling ponies along the towpath, and were paid a pittance. This could be fun in summer but in winter the icy path must have been torture. Toll collectors lived beside each lock and received the dues; dredge operators ensured that the canal remained navigable – shifting silt, clearing debris and repairing collapsed banks. In winter they piloted iceboats, the ancestors of the modern icebreakers that navigate polar regions.

canal's Waymarked Way was opened in March 2002.

PLANNING
Maps

The OSI 1:50,000 maps No 20 *Craigavon* and No 29 *The Mournes* show the route of the Way. The official colour brochure for the Way is long on background information (some of peripheral relevance) and short on useful maps. For practical purposes, the free NCR leaflet *Newry Canal* (available from TICs) is a better bet, with a 1:100,000 map and detailed maps of Portadown and Newry. The **Banbridge TIC** (☎ *4062 3322;* Ⓦ *www .banbridge.com/tourism; 200 Newry Rd; open year-round*) is the best source of information about the Way.

NEAREST TOWNS
Portadown

Notorious for sectarian conflict at certain times of the year, Portadown with its barred streets is a disquieting place, especially in the evening. Alternatively, you could arrive from Belfast by train or bus early enough to complete the walk to Newry.

There are several ATMs in High St. The nearest TICs are in Banbridge (see Maps, above) and Newry (this page).

Places to Stay & Eat There are no camping grounds or hostels in or near Portadown. The **Cherryville House** (☎ *3885 2323, fax 3885 2526; 180 Dungannon Rd; singles/ doubles £30/46*), about 10km northwest of town, is a beautifully decorated contemporary mansion where breakfast served in the conservatory is a great way to start the day. Transport into town is available if need be. From High St (outside the Bank of Ireland) or the train station catch the No 75 **Ulsterbus** (☎ *9066 6630*) Dungannon service (£0.60, 10 minutes, at least six daily Monday to Saturday). Closer to town, the **Bleu Apple** (☎ *3885 2188, fax 3885 2430; 12 Cannagola Rd; singles/doubles £29/46*) is a spacious home in a secluded rural setting with its own orchard. **Redbrick Country House** (☎ *3833 5268; Corbrackey Lane; singles/doubles £20/ 36*) is a modern bungalow. Redbrick is also

a friendly place where most rooms have en suite bathrooms.

For supplies before you set out, there's a **Super Valu** supermarket, a **greengrocer** and **bakeries** in High St.

The choice of places to eat in the evening is rather limited. **Pizza Palazzo** (☎ *3835 0012; High St; mains £5-7; open daily until late*) is reason enough to stay in Portadown, but it's really only a takeaway place – so hurry back to wherever you are spending the night. **Town House** (☎ *3833 2555; 21 Church St; mains to £12; open Tues-Sat*) brings an almost incongruous touch of elegance to eating out in Portadown.

Getting There & Away The cross-border **NIR** (☎ *9066 6630*) Enterprise service from Belfast to Dublin stops at Portadown (£4.70, 27 minutes, at least nine daily Monday to Saturday, five on Sunday).

Ulsterbus (☎ *9066 6630*) service No 251 from Belfast's Europa bus centre to Armagh goes through Portadown (£4.50, 45 minutes, at least nine daily Monday to Saturday, four on Sunday).

By road, Portadown is 43km (27 miles) from Belfast.

Newry

A busy city, Newry has transformed itself from a wealthy early 20th-century trading town to a commercial and shopping centre for the southern corner of the North.

Information The **TIC** (☎ *3026 8877; Town Hall; open Mon-Fri*) is a useful source of local information including a town map.

There are ATMs in Hill St (just west of the TIC) and along Trevor Hill (opposite Sugar Island). Internet access is available at **Coffee Net** (☎ *3083 3383*), which is in the bus station on the Mall; it'll cost you £1.50 for 15 minutes.

Places to Stay & Eat There are no hostels or camping grounds in or near Newry. **Clanrye House** (☎ *3026 2381; 24 Belfast Rd; singles/doubles £27/46*) is a large modern home just 10-minutes' walk from the city centre. At **Millvale House** (☎ *3026 3789;*

8 Millvale Rd; singles/doubles £25/50) you'll be very comfortable, and can be assured of a friendly welcome and generous breakfast. The hosts provide a pick-up service from the town centre, and an evening meal by arrangement.

Friar Tuck's *(☎ 3026 9119; Sugar Island; mains £3-6)* is a brightly decorated restaurant, more attractive than the gloomy pubs in town, with a standard fast-food-style menu of burgers, fish and chips and pizzas. The chef at **Riverside** *(☎ 3026 7773; 3 Kildare St; mains £7-8.50, 6-course dinner for 2 £28)* is strong on prawns, duck and chicken and produces generous enough, flavoursome dishes with remarkable speed.

Getting There & Away A free bus service, No 341, from Newry bus station *(☎ 3026 3531)* meets **NIR** Dublin–Belfast Enterprise trains (£6, 49 minutes, at least nine daily Monday to Saturday, five on Sunday). The return trip to Portadown takes around 25 minutes (£1.70).

Ulsterbus *(☎ 9066 6630)* service No 238 links Newry and Belfast's Europa bus centre (£5.60, 1¼ hours, up to 16 daily). Service No 240 goes to Newcastle (£4.20, 37 minutes, four daily Monday to Saturday, two on Sunday).

By road, Newry is 61km (38 miles) from Belfast.

THE WALK

From Portadown train station, go through the underpass then keep left across a car park towards the High St Mall building; go through it to reach High St. Turn left to the start of the walk at a bridge spanning the River Bann where there are signs for the Bann Boulevard and the Ulster Way, and less obviously, a Newry Canal Way information board. The introduction to the canal is quite low-key, along a bitumen path through the residential fringes of Portadown and out into flat, open countryside. Barely 1km along you reach the **Point of Whitecoat**, the merging of the Rivers Bann and Cusher. Cross the canal to a gravel path, so that you have the canal on the left and the Cusher River on the right. Further on, at

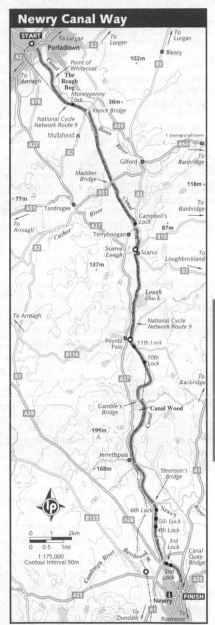

Moneypenny Lock (the northernmost lock, No 14) are stables and a cottage, but in mid-2002 a museum in the lock-keeper's house here was firmly closed. Pass under Knock Bridge, then, from a point south of Mullahead, the Mourne Mountains come into view and reappear from time to time, providing a gauge of your progress. Cross the A51 road at Madden bridge. Water birds frequent the quiet waters – mute swans jealously guarding small flotillas of downy grey cygnets in early summer, lanky grey herons looking for lunch.

About 1½ hours along, and just south of a short section of road walking, is 'Campbell's Lock' or, according to the official brochure, Terryhoogan Lock. The chamber is more or less intact though the gates are fragmentary. Beside the lock is **Terryhoogan House**, where John Wesley stayed several times in the mid-18th century. Just 20 more minutes' walking lands you at the village of **Scarva** in good time to enjoy refreshments at the **Visitor Centre** (☎ 3883 2163; open noon-5pm Tues-Fri, from 2pm Sat & Sun). The café does excellent, home-made soup with thick bread (£3.20), light meals (to £4), sandwiches, cakes and drinks. On the walls are several fascinating panels describing the canal and the village of Scarva. If the centre isn't open, there's a small **shop** and the **Park Inn** nearby.

Leave Scarva on a bitumen-surfaced path; shortly you pass Acton Lake Visitor Centre, then comes pretty **Lough Shark** – a sluice linked it to the canal to maintain water levels – the summit-level factor. Soon you reach the halfway mark, as a National Cycle Route milepost reassures you, and in so doing cross the Bann-Newry watershed. About an hour from Scarva you reach a road crossing; the village of Poyntz Pass, beside the A27 road, is around 200m up to the right. In Poyntz Pass you'll find a **Spar** supermarket.

Back on the canal and now a bitumen path, the lock chamber nearby is intact, as is the 10th lock a bit further on. Mercifully the bitumen ends about an hour from Poyntz Pass at **Gamble's Bridge**, known as Crack Bridge, both for its fragile condition

and because locals would gather there for crack – a chat. Continue on a kinder gravel-and-earth track. The valley is closing in now and the countryside is hillier with the ever-present hedgerows, the fertile grazing fields and the dense woodlands; the occasional passing train scarcely mars the sylvan peace. You soon pass **Canal Wood**, one of Northern Ireland's Millennium woodlands, where native woodlands are being restored by the Woodland Trust. Then there's more bitumen underfoot, but the Mourne Mountains encouragingly reappear, now very prominent. About 1¾ hours from Poyntz Pass you come close to the tiny village of **Jerrettspass**, where a slightly forlorn **shop** sells ice creams.

As you pass under **Steenson's Bridge** Newry is only 5km further on. The next feature is **Forsythe's Lock**. As No 6 out of 14 it's another marker of your progress, with the countdown starting in the north. The lock chamber and a mooring post are intact but the keeper's house much less so. Although the busy A27 road is now close, it rarely intrudes – a thick screen of trees absorbs most of the noise, and largely hides an industrial estate on the opposite bank. It's back to the bitumen surface from a minor road crossing as you enter suburbia. Pass under the cacophonous A1 road to the peace and quiet of the final stretch into Newry. Three potentially operational locks here have, sadly, been vandalised. Shortly the canal path ends at a suburban street; the eider ducks are more numerous here than anywhere else – no doubt for the ready sources of food. Continue beside the canal to Canal Quay Bridge, where there is a car park (1¾ hours from Jerrettspass). Although the canal was built through to Carlingford Lough, it's squeezed between buildings for most of the rest of the way, robbing it of any feeling of being a waterway – so the journey has ended. To reach Newry bus station from Canal Quay bridge, stay on the north side of the river, past Sugar Island and along Merchants Quay to the intersection with Monaghan St. Turn left, then right along the Mall for a short distance to the station.

Mournes Trail

Duration	9–10 hours
Distance	35km (21.7 miles)
Difficulty	demanding
Start	Rostrevor (p317)
Finish	Newcastle (p311)
Transport	bus

Summary A scenically varied, rewarding introduction to the Mournes, involving a mix of path and quiet road walking and some challenging cross-country going, deep in the mountains.

There's something very satisfying about completing a long through walk that probably comes from the experience of moving through the countryside, marking off your progress as you approach, pass and look back to particular landmarks.

The Mournes Trail offers just this experience. Part of the Ulster Way, and still very intermittently marked as such, the trail traverses the full length of the mountains and their foothills. It comprises a bit of almost everything, from rough moorland to bitumen roads, a mountain summit and a beach. This walk provides a fine introduction to the glens, passes and peaks of the Mourne Mountains and should fire enthusiasm for many more. The climbing along the walk amounts to 960m.

If you can organise your own transport, it is possible to break the trip into two sections; there is an informal parking area beside the B27 Kilkeel–Hilltown road, close to Spelga Dam.

PLANNING
What to Bring

You need a fine, dry summer day to safely reach Newcastle. Alternatively, you could consider camping; there's an informal site near where you meet the Trassey Track, evidently much used although rather exposed. There's also the problem of fresh water – this is sheep country, so you'd need to thoroughly purify any water drawn from the Trassey River. Whatever, you need to be completely self-contained for the walk – there are no cafés along the way.

Maps

OSNI 1:25,000 *Mourne Country* is ideal for cross-country route finding. The OSNI 1:50,000 map No 29 *The Mournes* also covers the route.

NEAREST TOWNS

See Newcastle (p311).

Rostrevor

This smallish coastal town at the southwestern foot of the Mournes has relatively limited but adequate facilities.

The nearest TICs are in Newry and Newcastle. There's an ATM in Warrenpoint, 4km west along the A2 from Rostrevor.

Places to Stay & Eat The well-run **Kilbroney Caravan Park** (☎/fax 4173 8134; Shore Rd; camping per person £6.20) has vast areas of grass, scattered trees and excellent facilities. **Fir Trees** (☎ 4173 8602, fax 4173 8563; 16 Killowen Rd; singles/doubles £25/40) is perched on the hillside towards Kilkeel, so the sea views are unbeatable. Also with good views, **Glenbeigh** (☎ 4173 8025; 18 Victoria

The Great Wall of Mourne

If you've never been to the Mournes before, you may wonder, 'What on earth is an imitation of the Great Wall of China doing here?' Running for 35km over 15 summits in the range, it's generally about 2m high and a good metre wide, a magnificent feat of drystone wall construction, being completely cement-free. It was built between 1904 and 1922 to mark the boundary of the catchments of the Silent Valley and Ben Crom reservoirs. Apart from this, the only explanation for its construction, during a turbulent period in Irish history, would seem to be 'we built it because we could'.

Until the mid-1990s the wall was the focus of the biggest organised walk in Ireland, with thousands following the course of the wall across the Mournes in June each year. The event was scrapped in response to concerns about the extent of erosion around the wall.

NORTHERN IRELAND

Square; singles/doubles £30/50), off the A2 bypass, is a 19th-century terrace house with large rooms looking over Carlingford Lough.

Both the **Spar** and **Costcutter** supermarkets in Bridge St are open daily; there is also a good butcher and a bakery nearby. The **Grapevine**, also in Bridge St, carries a slightly wider range of drinks than do the supermarkets.

At **Celtic Fjord** (☎ 4173 8005; *6 Mary St; 2 courses £17; 3 courses £21; open Wed-Sun)* the name reflects the area's dual cultural heritage, which may inspire such intriguing combinations on the menu as cod with coconut and pepper risotto. The **Kilbroney** (☎ 4173 8390; *31 Church St; mains £7-14)* is a popular place which specialises in steaks on its bar supper menu, and also offers curries and pasta dishes. **Kilbroney Park Café** (☎ 4173 8134; *Kilbroney Park; mains £4.50-9; open to 8.30pm in summer)* is convenient for campers, an informal, friendly place for standards such as fish and chips and excellent quiches and pies; it's also open for snacks during the day. It is not licensed.

Getting There & Away The **Ulsterbus** (☎ 9066 6630) service No 39 between Newry

and Rostrevor (£6.50, 1¾ hours, 14 daily Monday to Friday, nine Saturday, two Sunday), which stops in Bridge St, connects with the Belfast service No 238 (see Getting There & Away, p315, for Newry).

By road, Rostrevor is 76km (47 miles) from Belfast.

THE WALK

From the northern end of Kilbroney caravan park, 500m southeast of Rostrevor on the A2 road, follow the road (the bitumen surface lasts for only a short distance); waymarkers direct you to a forest track, which you follow for nearly 7km through Rostrevor Forest and up through the Kilbroney River valley. There are good views of the valley between breaks in the forest. Climb a stile over stone-built **Batts Wall** (about 1½ hours from the start) and leave the forest behind to follow a rougher path across bouldery slopes. Scots Pines are scattered about, in greatest numbers on the hillside above you. The fine view northwards extends across the broad, flat valley of the River Bann. Ford a wide stream and turn right to follow a track into the western outliers of the Mourne Mountains. About 1km from

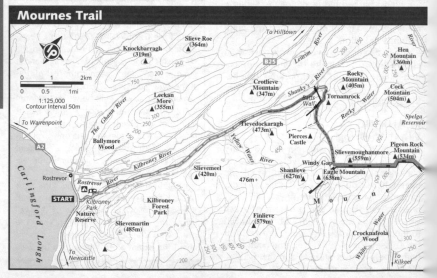

Mournes Trail

the ford leave the relative comfort of the track and head east across a gap between Tornamrock and Pierces Castle; there are neither a clear path nor any waymarkers across the heathery moorland, though you may find a lonely weather-beaten waymarker at the confluence of Rocky Water and a tributary cascading down from Windy Gap. Deep in the mountains here, you can see some fine examples of classic Mournes tors on Hen Mountain to the north. There's an intermittent, faint path on the south side of this tributary, across wettish ground and up to **Windy Gap**, between Eagle Mountain and Slievemoughanmore (two hours from Batts Wall).

Cross stiles over a minor wall and a more substantial one. The latter serves as a hand-rail as you tackle the steep slope of Slieve-moughanmore, although the route bypasses the peat hag–ridden summit to the south. Then it's down and up again, over Pigeon Rock Mountain, from where you descend to the minor road (B27) near **Spelga Dam** (about 1¼ hours from Windy Gap). Follow this road northeast, very soon crossing the youthful River Bann just below its source across rather bleak moorland, through the

northern slopes of the Mournes, past a road junction on the left and down into the upper valley of the Shimna River. After about 45 minutes, Ulster Way signs point to the escape from the road via a stile over a wall to a path; this descends to cross a stream feeding the nearby Fofanny Dam. Turn left and walk along a track between the dam and a channel; cross a footbridge at the northern end of the dam, then a stile, and shortly pick up a rough track. Follow this across the lower slopes of Slieve Meelbeg and Slieve Meelmore to the Trassey River. Normally, fording the river should be easy; then join the **Trassey Track** (see the boxed text 'Smuggling in the Mournes', p324) about an hour from the B27.

Walk down the track, go through a large gate near some sheep pens, and continue descending, through a conifer plantation on Clonachullion Hill, to a minor road; turn right here, just above a large car park. Follow the waymarked track through woodland and into Tollymore Forest. Turn right just beyond signposted Maria's Bridge, following red waymarkers which take you quite steeply up to the southern edge of the forest. Along here there are good views of

NORTHERN IRELAND

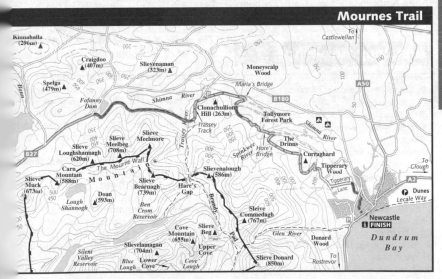

Mournes Trail

the high, spiky-topped peaks of the Mourne Mountains. Then a steeply winding track descends to **Hore's Bridge** over Spinkwee River. A short distance further on leave the forest track and ascend again (there is no mercy on this route!) to the forest edge for more Mournes views. As the track swings around **Curraghard** the outlook changes to take in Slieve Donard, Newcastle and Dundrum Bay. A switchbacking descent takes you to the eastern boundary of Tollymore Forest Park.

Ignore a yellow waymarker pointing left and walk down the minor road for a few hundred metres. Turn left along a gravel road with a Public Footpath sign – this is Tipperary Lane; about 700m along you enter Tipperary Wood, a dense deciduous grove with the track running beside the Shimna River. Turn left at a suburban street, cross a bridge and enter parkland on the right. Follow paths close to the river, across the first footbridge you meet, then left, across another bridge and left to a road. Cross diagonally to a path through what is Castle Park and go on to Central Promenade; cross this to reach the beach about 100m further on – a much more fitting end to this walk than a busy road (2½ hours from Trassey River).

Annalong Horseshoe

Duration	7–7½ hours
Distance	20km (12.4 miles)
Difficulty	demanding
Start/Finish	Carrick Little car park
Nearest Town	Annalong (p320)
Transport	bus

Summary One of the finest traverses in the Mournes – a challenging circuit over peaks guarding the upper Annalong valley with spectacular, far-ranging views.

This outstanding walk takes you deep into the Mournes and features a traverse of the deeply undulating ridge on the western side of the Annalong valley. Most of the summits are crowned with clusters of rounded, purple-grey granite, reminders of the mountains' glacial past. The principal peak is Slieve Binnian, at 747m the third-highest in Northern Ireland. It is a popular route, so paths are well-trodden and, of course, a bit squishy here and there. The day's ascent amounts to 1240m. You'll need to be entirely self-contained for this walk, as it's far from any refreshment stops.

The walk can be shortened by about 2km and the amount of upping and downing considerably reduced (about 500m less ascent) by giving Slieve Binnian a miss and ascending directly to the col between that peak and Slievelamagan to the north.

PLANNING
Maps
The OSNI 1:25,000 map *Mourne Country* and the 1:50,000 map No 29 *The Mournes* cover this walk.

NEAREST TOWN
Annalong
For such a hard day as this, it's worth staying in this small town, scattered about both sides of the A2 road, although the walk could be done, using a private car, from a base in Newcastle. The nearest TICs are in Newcastle (p311) and **Kilkeel** (☎ 4176 2525; 28 Bridge St), a larger town 5km southwest. The same holds for ATMs; in Kilkeel you'll find one in Greencastle St.

Places to Stay & Eat The nearest camping ground and hostel are in Newcastle.

Fair Haven (☎ 4376 8153; 16 Moneydarragh Rd; singles/doubles £25/36) is a smallish bungalow and the closest of the local B&Bs to the main road, but furthest from the start of the walk; two of the three comfortable rooms are en suite. The **Heathdene** (☎ 4376 8822; 76 Mill Rd; singles/doubles £17.50/35), about 2km north of the main road, is a spacious B&B with fine sea views. Where else but **Sycamores** (☎ 4376 8279; 52 Majors Hill Rd; singles/doubles £25/40) can you lie in bed and contemplate the route of the day's walk? The rooms are beautifully furnished in this very friendly place and breakfast is superb.

Bridge into Poisoned Glen, Derryveagh Mountains, County Donegal

Sunset over the cliffs and ridges of Slievetooey, County Donegal

Summit tor on Slieve Binnian, Mourne Mountains

Carrick-a-rede rope bridge, County Antrim

Giant's Causeway on the Causeway Coast Way

There's a **Centra** supermarket on the A2 road, and a **Spar** in Main St between the A2 and the harbour.

Harbour Inn (*☎ 4376 8678; 6 Harbour Dr; mains £5-13; open daily from 7pm*) has a spacious 1st-floor restaurant overlooking the harbour and miles of coastline. The menu highlights seafood and vegetarians are not all at sea. The **Top Nosh Restaurant** (*☎ 4376 8600; 32 Kilkeel Rd; mains £6-11*) is a busy, homely place on the A2. Top Nosh serves steaks, chicken and fish in the usual pub-fare mode, but neglects vegetarians; it is not licensed.

Getting There & Away The **Ulsterbus** (*☎ 9066 663*) service No 37 linking Newcastle and Kilkeel passes through Annalong (£1.90, 23 minutes, at least 11 daily Monday to Saturday, six on Sunday). Good connections are available in Newcastle (p311); the fare from Annalong to Belfast is £5.60.

By road, Annalong is 12km (7.6 miles) from Newcastle and 58km (36 miles) from Belfast.

GETTING TO/FROM THE WALK

Turn off the A2 in the centre of Annalong at a crossroads with a large church on the

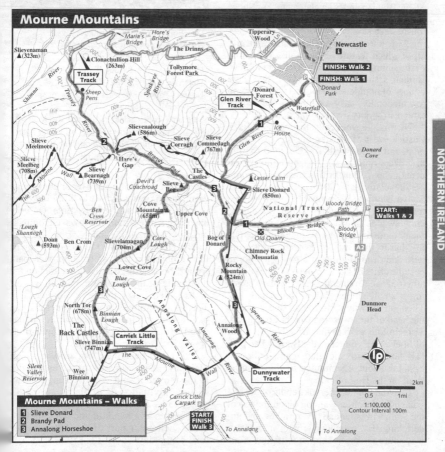

Mourne Mountains

Mourne Mountains – Walks
1. Slieve Donard
2. Brandy Pad
3. Annalong Horseshoe

NORTHERN IRELAND

southwest corner; this is Majors Hill Rd. Follow it for about 1km to an intersection and turn right up Oldtown Rd. About 2km further on you come to a T-junction; Carrick Little car park, surrounded by a stone wall, is in front of you.

THE WALK (see map p321)

Walk up the Carrick Little Track for about 1km to a gate where the track meets the Mourne Wall. Cross a stile over the wall; if you're bypassing Slieve Binnian, continue generally northwestwards along the track, ignoring right turns, to reach the col between Slieve Binnian and Slievelamagan. For Slieve Binnian, simply follow the wall up the seriously steep slope, soon passing a sign showing 23 features in the panoramic view, nearly all of which feature in this walk. At the foot of the summit tors, swing right to gain Slieve Binnian's summit ridge between two large clumps of boulders; the highest will succumb to a moderately easy scramble on the far side (about 1½ hours from the start).

Then make your way through the Back Castles, west of the first cluster, east of the next, and on to North Tor. Descend sharply to a deep, muddy col. A steep bouldery ascent of about 300m brings you to the summit of **Slievelamagan** (704m), 1½ hours from Slieve Binnian. It's probably the most central peak in the Mournes so the 360-degree view sweeps right around the range and to many more distant places, including the Isle of Man to the east. Walk northwards from here and drop slightly to a gap, then go up past the cliffs of Upper Cove to Cove Mountain (655m). Another descent involves crossing a small stream below the actual gap. Then, on the way up to Slieve Beg you pass the head of the awesome **Devils Coachroad**, a precipitous gash in the cliffs. Not far north of Slieve Beg you reach the Brandy Pad path (1¼ hours from Slievelamagan). Follow it east for about 45 minutes to the **Mourne Wall** on the Bog of Donard.

To avoid the treacherous depths of the bog you could consider walking along the top of the Wall, a popular and dry, if rather airy, undertaking. By whichever route, make your way south for about 1km; at a shallow angle in the wall diverge a few metres up to the right to join a fairly good path. This parallels the wall along the eastern flank of Rocky Mountain for about 750m. What is now a track lopes off southwards and descends (the route being rough in places and grassy in others) around to the southwest and down to meet Dunnywater Track in a forest (about 1¼ hours from the Bog of Donard). Turn left and follow the track down to a bitumen road; Carrick Little car park is about 1.5km westwards (another 45 minutes).

Slieve Donard

Duration	4½–5 hours
Distance	9km (5.6 miles)
Difficulty	moderate
Start	Bloody Bridge
Finish	Newcastle
Nearest Town	Newcastle (p311)
Transport	bus

Summary Follow clear paths and the Mourne Wall along an extremely scenic route over Northern Ireland's highest mountain, with great views from the summit on the right day.

Slieve Donard (850m) is a real magnet – its dominating presence overlooking the town of Newcastle makes it irresistible. On very clear days the summit views encompass most of Northern Ireland.

The **National Trust** (☎ 9751 0721) owns land embracing part of the approach path from Bloody Bridge and a large tract on the north side of the mountain, extending west across Glen River to Slieve Commedagh. The trust continues to invest generously in path repair and maintenance work, and has installed information boards on the various approaches to Slieve Donard.

The route described, not truly circular, offers the chance to see two different sides of the mountain and is convenient to Newcastle. Navigational problems are negligible; paths are well used, and the Mourne Wall serves as a handrail and possibly welcome shelter for part of the distance. The total of the day's ascent is 850m.

HISTORY
The mountain once went by the name Slieve Slanga, after Slainge, the son of Partholan, who was buried under a cairn on the summit. The peak and the summit cairns later became associated with St Domangard, a 5th-century follower of St Patrick, and his name (anglicised to Donard) has stuck. Of the cairns, the authentic one is now buried under heaps of stone, while a second can be seen 250m to the northeast.

Bloody Bridge derives its name from an incident in 1641 when Protestants were massacred there. In more light-hearted vein, the mountain's eastern sweep to the sea inspired Percy French to write the famous song *The Mountains of Mourne*.

PLANNING
What to Bring
Slieve Donard is susceptible to the vagaries of Irish mountain weather so make sure you take adequate warm and protective clothing, and all the food and drink you'll need for the walk.

Maps
Both the OSNI 1:25,000 map *Mourne Country* and the 1:50,000 map No 29 *The Mournes* cover this walk.

GETTING TO/FROM THE WALK
The walk begins at the Bloody Bridge parking area, 3km south of Newcastle on the A2 road. **Ulsterbus** (☎ 9066 6630) service No 37 stops here (£1.20, 10 minutes, 12 daily Monday to Saturday, six Sunday).

THE WALK (see map 321)
From the car park and bus stop, cross the road to a gate giving access to the National Trust's ground at Bloody Bridge. The original bridge is set just behind the adjacent road bridge. The clear path climbs steadily beside the river; in spring and early summer the vivid yellow-flowering, aromatic gorse is quite spectacular here. After about 1km, immediately above some cascades, you can cross to a wide vehicle track or stay on the north bank of the river, following a well-defined walkers path. A couple of kilometres

deep into the valley you pass an old quarry on the left, the source of large quantities of granite, some of which finished up in the foundations of the Stormont parliament building near Belfast. Here you join a wide, rough path coming from the quarry, which takes you up to the **Mourne Wall** on the Bog of Donard (1½ hours from Bloody Bridge).

Follow the wall northwards, up the steep slope to the **Slieve Donard** summit (850m), with a massive Belfast Water Works pillar and a sprawling cairn nearby (40 minutes from the Bog of Donard). With luck you'll be able to pick out the features of the unrivalled vista. To the north, the drumlin-dotted landscape merges with Strangford Lough and the Belfast Hills, topped with communications towers. To the west is the vast expanse of Lough Neagh and beyond, the rounded Sperrin Mountains. On a clear day you can see Scotland's Mull of Kintyre to the north, the Isle of Man to the east and even Howth Hill near Dublin in the south.

Descend the steep path beside the wall northwestwards to the col between Slieve Donard and Slieve Commedagh (about 25 minutes from the top); here in summer 2002 National Trust workers began tackling the massive task of repairing the path. Then, leaving the Wall behind, take to the Glen River path, leading northeast down the deep valley. For about three-quarters of the distance to the edge of a conifer plantation you can enjoy the relative ease of walking on a pitched path rather than picking you way through boulders, as you eventually have to do beside Donard Wood. The views ahead of long beaches and jumbled dunes are superb. A curious beehive structure across the river on the right, close to the forest edge, is a restored ice house (built in the mid-19th century for the local estate). A short distance further on, beside a forest road, is a large sign explaining the history of the estate and these ingeniously built structures.

From the road a rough path descends beside the Glen River for 1km through **Donard Forest**, its magnificent mature Scots pines, oaks, larch and beeches making it a wonderful place to finish the walk. You cross the river on solid old bridges twice on the way down to the lawns of Donard Park. Stay on the right side of this open area until you reach a car park; Newcastle's Central Promenade is a short distance further on (about 1½ hours from the col).

Brandy Pad

Duration	5½–6 hours
Distance	20km (12.4 miles)
Difficulty	moderate
Start	Bloody Bridge
Finish	Newcastle
Nearest Town	Newcastle (p311)
Transport	bus

Summary Imagine you've joined a smuggling party with a load of brandy, marching through the Mournes without the need to scale peaks or use route-finding skills.

This walk (see the boxed text 'Smuggling in the Mournes', below) follows the route of the Slieve Donard walk to the first encounter with the Mourne Wall, then much further on, across the heads of the Annalong and Silent valleys and over Hare's Gap, you join the Mournes Trail route at Clonachullion car park. You'll be on walkers paths and forest tracks but no bitumen roads at all, finishing towards the southern end of Newcastle. You'll ascend a total of 720m.

PLANNING
Maps

You should carry either the OSNI 1:25,000 *Mourne Country* map or the 1:50,000 map No 29 *The Mournes*.

GETTING TO/FROM THE WALK

See Getting to/from the Walk (p323) for Slieve Donard.

THE WALK (see map p321)

The first part of this walk follows the route of the Slieve Donard (p322) excursion, from Bloody Bridge up to the **Mourne Wall** on the Bog of Donard (about 1½ hours from Bloody Bridge). From here a wide path leads west, then north, across the lower slopes of Slieve Donard. Soon you descend slightly into the catchment of the Annalong River and set out on the very scenic traverse below the Castles, a huddle of purple-grey weathered granite blocks. Beyond crossings of some eroded streams, the path leaves the Annalong valley and descends, partly on well-made steps, into the valley of the Kilkeel River (or Silent Valley), harbouring Ben Crom reservoir, and on to Hare's Gap and a reunion with the **Mourne Wall** (one to 1¼ hours from the Bog of Donard). The fine view north and northwestwards takes in fertile plains merging seamlessly with the sea.

A path of sorts leads away to the left (west) below cliffs and across a steep slope through

Smuggling in the Mournes

Paths through the Mournes now carry legions of walkers and climbers clad in Gore-Tex, but they were originally created by the boots of smugglers and the hooves of their heavily laden ponies. Smuggling in the Mournes probably came about because of the mountains' proximity to a stretch of coast which, during the 18th and 19th centuries, was lonely and hazardous.

Cargoes of tobacco, wine, spirits, leather, silk and spices arrived at night on small, manoeuvrable, schooner-rigged craft called wherries. After a signal from smugglers in mountain lookouts the contraband was landed on an isolated beach and then spirited off into the wilderness or carried along the Brandy Pad and down the Trassey Track for distribution inland. The village of Hilltown was a favourite destination and in 1835 almost half the houses there were pubs. Many other smuggling tracks branched from the Brandy Pad at the head of the Annalong Valley to other accessible bays or beaches.

The tracks are now used for entirely innocent pursuits, though smuggling still goes on between the North and the Republic. Nowadays the cargoes of cattle or diesel fuel are carried by fishing boat or road transport.

a maze of boulders and heather. After about 15 minutes of this, look for a path dropping down to the right to a vehicle track; this path saves you from being stranded on top of some precipitous boulders. Walk down the track – the **Trassey Track** – splashing (perhaps) through a couple of stream crossings. About 30 minutes from the gap take a short cut to the left – if you've had enough of the stony track – down to a large gate by a knot of old sheep pens and the Trassey River (40 minutes from Hare's Gap). From here follow the route of the Mournes Trail (p317) down to the car park below Clonachullion Hill, and on to Tollymore Forest Park, through the park via Maria's and Hore's Bridges and Curraghard. Then follow Tipperary Lane, a track through Tipperary Wood and suburban parkland paths to Newcastle's Central Promenade (2¼ hours from Trassey River).

The West

West of Lough Neagh are the Sperrin Mountains, the largest upland area in Northern Ireland, with rolling, boggy hills separated by very beautiful, quiet rural valleys. The main range sprawls east-west with 10 summits above 500m. From the Glenelly valley at the foot of the southern slopes it's possible to reach several of these peaks; one walk described here strides across the two highest, Sawel and Dart. Nearby Gortin Glen Forest Park is the scene of a variable walk through the forest to a commanding vantage point.

Further southwest in County Fermanagh is a very different landscape of lakes, dominated by Cuilcagh, a mountain of great natural history interest and the focus of the other two walks in this section.

PLANNING
Maps
The OSI 1:250,000 *North* Holiday map is useful for finding your way about.

ACCESS TOWNS
Belcoo
With a very scenic setting on the western shore of Lough Macnean Lower, this village is a pleasant base for the Cuilcagh Mountain walks. Its name is not a dreadful pun about bovines, but an infelicitous anglicisation of the Irish Béal Cú, meaning 'mouth of the hound'.

The nearest TIC is in Enniskillen. There is an ATM in the **Vivo** supermarket; failing that, the nearest is in Enniskillen.

Places to Stay & Eat Overlooking the lake is **Bella Vista** (☎ 6638 6469; Cottage Dr; singles/doubles £25/40), a welcoming, two-storey family home with comfortable en suite rooms. **Bush Cottage** (☎ 6638 6242; Cottage Dr; singles/doubles £20/34) dates from the 1840s and has an unusual rectangular floor plan; the homely rooms are not en suite to preserve the cottage's architecture. **Customs House Country Inn** (☎ 6638 6285, fax 6638 6936; e info@customs-house .co.uk; 25-27 Main St; singles/doubles £30/60) is a restored old building with sizable, well-appointed en suite rooms, most with lake views. Timber-furnished **Fiddlesticks** (mains £7.50-11.25; open daily) restaurant is part of the Customs House. It specialises in chicken (Thai, Creole, Mexican) and offers a couple of competent if unexciting vegetarian dishes.

The **Spar** supermarket in Main St is open daily, as is the **Vivo** supermarket beside the B52 just up from Main St. There's a **Costcutter** supermarket a little further out along the B52 next to a service station; the **post office** hides in here.

Cassie Quinn's (☎ 6638 6629; Main St; mains £8-16; open daily) is a classy but informal restaurant; the menu offers a good choice across steaks, chicken and fish. The vegetarian choices include delicious Thai spiced vegetables in coconut cream sauce.

Getting There & Away The **Ulsterbus** (☎ 9066 6630) service No 64 from Enniskillen passes through Belcoo (£2.50, 25 minutes, at least two daily). However, public transport is only practical for the Cuilcagh walks if you can arrange a lift to and from the village.

By road, Belcoo is 18km (11 miles) west of Enniskillen via the A4.

NORTHERN IRELAND

Enniskillen

An attractively sited, prosperous town around the banks of the River Erne, Enniskillen is almost unavoidable en route to the Cuilcagh Mountain walks and has more of everything, except peace and quiet, than Belcoo.

Fermanagh TIC (☎ 6632 3110; ⓦ www .fermanagh-online.com; Wellington Rd) is open daily during summer for all manner of information about the county, OSNI and OSI maps and walks guides. **Easons** in High St also stocks maps and local guides.

At the town's **library** (☎ 6632 2886; Halls Lane) you can check email (£1.50 for 30 minutes); it's open Monday to Saturday, including Tuesday and Thursday evenings.

The most central ATMs are in East Bridge St and Town Hall St.

Places to Stay & Eat There are no official camping grounds near Enniskillen, although you can pitch a tent on Castle Island at the **Lakeland Canoe Centre** (☎ 6632 4250; camping per person £8).

The **Bridges Youth Hostel** (☎ 6634 0110, fax 6634 6873; Belmore; dorm beds £11), opened in mid-2002, has en suite four-bed dorms, a small gleaming kitchen, and dining and living rooms with huge windows overlooking the river. **Ashwood House** (☎ 6632 3019; Sligo Rd; singles/doubles £26/38) is a vast modern home in extensive landscaped grounds on the western edge of town; most of the comfortable rooms are en suite. **Bellevue Lodge** (☎ 6632 3373; 58 Sligo Rd; singles/doubles £25/44) is a comfortable modern bungalow just 2km from the town centre; the rooms have shared facilities.

For self-caterers there are two big supermarkets: **Safeway** in the Erneside shopping centre (where you can get hold of Ireland's very own Carlow Brewery beers), and **Dunne's** at Fairgreen on the eastern side of the town centre. In High St are a couple of **bakeries**, a **butcher** and a **greengrocer**. You will find the **Health Store** at 30 East Bridge St and, to balance things, **Mulligans Wine Cellars** in Darling St.

Franco's (☎ 6632 4424; Queen Elizabeth St; mains £9.75-20) has an imaginative carnivorous menu including the challenging New Age pizza with lots of smoky ingredients; the wine list is quite varied. **Oscar's** (☎ 6632 7037; 29 Belmore St; mains £8-17.50) has a menu as florid and outrageous as its namesake (Oscar Wilde, educated in Enniskillen) was in his day, but does acknowledge vegetarians with a spicy African stir-fry.

Getting There & Away The **Ulsterbus** (☎ 9066 6630) service No 261 (£7.80, two hours 20 minutes, nine daily Monday to Saturday, four Sunday) runs from Belfast's Europa bus centre to **Enniskillen bus station** (☎ 6632 2633; Shore Rd).

By road, Enniskillen is 138km (86 miles) west of Belfast and 98km (61 miles) south of Derry.

Gortin

A fairly large, rather dour village, Gortin is centrally located for the Sperrins and Gortin Glen walks.

The bank in Main St has an ATM. The nearest official visitor centre is the **Omagh TIC** (☎ 8224 7831; ⓦ www.omagh.gov.uk /tourism.htm; 1 Market St, Omagh), the town being 15.4km to the south. The Sperrin Heritage Centre (see Sawel & Dart, p327) can also help with accommodation information, but not with reservations.

Places to Stay & Eat You'll find secluded **Gortin Glen Caravan Park** (☎ 8163 8108; Lisnaharney Rd, Lislap; camping per person £4.50-9) 4.8km south of Gortin with plenty of grassed space for tents, and decent facilities. The **Gortin Accommodation Suite** (☎ 8164 8346; ⓦ www.gortin.net; 62 Main St; dorm beds £7.50, self-contained family rooms £26, cottages for 4/6 people per day £40/48) is modern and very well equipped.

In Main St you'll find a **Costcutters** supermarket, a **nearbuy** minimarket and a **butcher**. **Badoney Tavern** (☎ 8164 8157; 16 Main St; mains £4.25-7; open daily) offers a small menu, including Irish stew, but nothing specific for vegetarians. **Pedlars Rest** (☎ 8164 7942; 66 Main St; mains £3.50-7; open to 7pm Fri-Sun) presents standard pub fare, including one vegetarian special.

Getting There & Away The Ulsterbus
(☎ 9066 6630) Sperrin Rambler service No
182 operates twice daily from Monday to
Saturday between Omagh and Castledawson
via Gortin (£2.20, 25 minutes), Plumbridge
(£2.70, 32 minutes) and the Sperrin Heritage
Centre (£3.20, one hour). Bus connections
to Belfast are available at Omagh (Nos 273,
274) and Castledawson (Nos 212, 278).

By road, Gortin is 36km (22.4 miles)
south of Derry via the A5 and B48 roads.

Plumbridge

This village is closer than Gortin to the
Sperrins walk but has few facilities. There's
an ATM inside the **nearbuy** (open Mon-Sat)
on the Dunnamanagh road. You'll find a **VG**
grocery (open daily) on the Gortin road.

Slievemore B&B (☎ 8164 8512; 21 Landa-
hussy Rd; singles/doubles £23/46) is a large,
modern bungalow with fine views of the
Sperrins, beside a minor road 1.5km east of
the B48 Plumbridge–Gortin road; all rooms
are en suite.

The only hope for a meal locally is at
Leo's (☎ 8164 8417; 4 Dergborough Rd), next
to the prominent Pete's of the Plum pub,
where you might get a bar supper.

See Getting There & Away (above) under
Gortin for details of the Sperrin Rambler bus
service which passes through Plumbridge.
By road, the village is 30km (18.6 miles)
south of Derry via the A5 and B48 roads.

Sperrins Out of Bounds

Some landowners in the Sperrins are happy
for responsible walkers to cross their land;
others aren't so keen. If you encounter a
landowner who asks you to turn back (and
they are within their rights to make such a request), then do so. However, it's fairly unlikely
that you will have any problems on the walk
described.

There is, however, no access west of the
summit of Dart Mountain.

Beware of old fencing wire lurking in the
heather just waiting to trip you up into the
nearest bog.

Sawel & Dart

Duration	5–5½ hours
Distance	14km (8.7 miles)
Difficulty	moderate
Start/Finish	B47 road at GR 654946
Nearest Towns	Plumbridge (p327), Gortin (p326)
Transport	bus

Summary An ascent of the highest peaks in the
Sperrin mountains with wonderfully wide views
and a remote feeling.

The Irish name for the Sperrin Mountains –
Cnoc Speirín, meaning 'pointed hills' – is
something of a misnomer. They're a gently
rounded, unassuming range, composed of
glaciated schist and quartzite, with few rocky
outcrops poking through the deep blanket
bog. Their special, discreet charm derives
more from their setting – the mosaics of
green fields, hedgerows and woodlands in the
surrounding valleys – than the hills them
selves. This circular walk, over Sawel Mountain (678m) and Dart (619m) covers some
rough ground, but the route is straightforward
so you don't have to cope with navigation
problems, especially as there are convenient,
long fences to follow – very helpful in poor
visibility. The route ascends 650m in total.

It's definitely best to do this walk after a
dry interlude – after a few days' rain the
boggy ground can be very heavy.

The duration given for the walk is from
the point where you leave the B47 road and
back, so you'll need to make allowances for
your own transport arrangements.

The discovery of gold was the most exciting event in the Sperrins' recent history.
The **Sperrin Heritage Centre** (☎ 8164 8142;
W www.strabanedc.com; 274 Glenelly Rd;
open daily Apr-Oct; admission £2.20), 4.5km
from the start of the walk, houses exhibits
explaining the area's ecology and history. It
also has a small shop that sells OSNI and
Geological Survey maps. At the attached
Glenelly Kitchen you can tuck into sandwiches or toasties (£1.30 to £2) or excellent
scones and cakes with hot and cold drinks.
In summer the heritage centre organises a

NORTHERN IRELAND

programme of hill walks, mostly of around six hours duration. The fee is £6 per person; booking is essential.

PLANNING
Maps
Use the OSNI 1:50,000 map No 13 *The Sperrins*. A set of cards in the Geological Survey's 'Landscapes from Stone' series, also called *The Sperrins* and featuring 1:50,000 maps and descriptions of 10 circular walks, helps to unravel the area's geological mysteries.

GETTING TO/FROM THE WALK
The walk starts from the B47 road, 1.6km east of the Mount Hamilton (Sperrin) crossroads. Approaching from the west, pass a small conifer plantation, then an adjacent farm. About 200m further on, there's a rickety gate set at an angle to the road. The walk starts here.

The nearest possibilities for safe car parking are 1km west of the start, on the south side of the B47 at GR 638944, or 1.6km west on the southeast side of the intersection of the B47 and Corramore Rd (GR 634941). There's also the large parking area at the Sperrin Heritage Centre, 4.5km

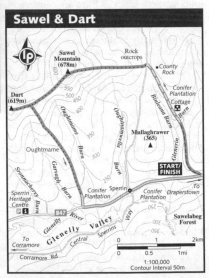

west of the start but only 1.5km west of the point where you reach the B47 after descending from Dart at the end of the walk.

The Sperrin Rambler bus service (see Getting There & Away, p327, for Gortin) stops at the Heritage Centre; alternatively, the driver may be prepared to drop you right at the start of the walk.

THE WALK
Negotiate the makeshift gate and follow the track as it curves around into lonely Glenerin. About 1.5km from the start the well-graded track crosses an unnamed tributary of Glenerin Burn, which could be difficult after heavy rain. A few metres further on, join a firm vehicle track which gains height northwestwards above Binleana Burn, passing a **deserted cottage** in a small conifer plantation. On the horizon you may spot the profile of **County Rock**, a conspicuous boulder which stands, as does most of the Sperrin range, on the border between Counties Tyrone and Derry. Follow the track up to a tarmac road near the rock (an hour from the start). Cross the road and, with a fence on your right, ascend a cluster of rock outcrops, then the occasionally soggy, unremittingly steep slope; fortunately, the ground becomes firmer the higher you go. At the point where another fence comes up on the left, cross the fence on your right and continue uphill. Where the fence bends away southwards continue west for about 150m to the summit of **Sawel Mountain** (678m), marked by a trig cairn and a mound of stones (an hour from the road).

Cross a stile over a nearby fence and descend southwest to the col between Sawel and Dart Mountains; the peat hags and mosses here and those on the slopes of Dart aren't too malevolent. You'll soon meet a fence which runs generally southwest towards Dart Mountain. Dart, dotted with rocks, is a hill of greater character though less elevation than Sawel. Follow the fence up to the summit of **Dart** (619m), 45 minutes from Sawel. The view is better than from its taller neighbour as you're closer to beautiful Glenelly and the huge corrie on the southeast face of Mullaghclogha to the west; the towers on Mullaghcarn to the south-southeast stand out clearly.

The descent is simply a matter of following a fence, first back down Dart's eastern spur, then south from a rocky knoll down the broad, tussocky spur of Oughtmame. At a fence across your line of travel go through a gate on the left beside a small pine plantation (not shown on the OSNI map); no more than 250m further south a green lane materialises. This makes for an easy final stage down through three more gates to the B47 (an hour from Dart). Turn left; the start of the walk is 3km along the road.

Gortin Glen

Duration	5½–6 hours
Distance	13km (8.1 miles)
Difficulty	moderate
Start/Finish	Gortin (p326)
Transport	bus
Summary	Plenty of variety here; secluded streamside paths, tall forests and a windswept moorland hilltop with far-ranging panoramic views.

Riverside paths from Gortin, then forest tracks, lead south through dramatic Gortin Gap to Gortin Glen Forest Park, where a waymarked route follows good paths up to Ladies View lookout. For far better views, a not-too-rough, intermittently boggy track rises from there to the ridge on the park's eastern boundary.

Gortin Gap is a glacial breach created during the last Ice Age when meltwater from retreating ice sheets spilled over high ground. The small hummocks just north of the gap are classic drumlins – moraine deposits covered with peat and heather.

Most of the trees in Gortin Glen Forest Park are the commercial conifers Sitka spruce and lodgepole pine, though in recent years broad-leaved species have been planted in cleared areas.

You don't have to go the full distance of this walk to explore the park or enjoy good views. Go direct to the forest park, 3km south from Gortin along the B48 Omagh road and follow the walk from there. Alternatively, you could ignore the moorland section up to the ridge and just take in the sights from Ladies View. If you drive to the park, you may have to pay the £2.50 entry fee. The gates close at 9pm in summer.

PLANNING
Maps

The OSNI 1:50,000 map No 13 *The Sperrins* covers the walk, though it doesn't show the intricate path network clearly. A leaflet depicting the marked paths in the forest park exists but isn't easy to come by unless there's someone on duty at the park entrance.

THE WALK

From the bridge beside Mossey's Bar in Gortin's Main St, walk up a lane on the eastern side of Gortin Burn. Cross a stile and join the path which winds up the lightly wooded glen beside the stream, crossing and recrossing on small timber bridges. Emerging into the open, cross a field and climb a stile to a minor road which leads to the B48 road. Walk up it for about 150m and turn right along a forest road, following waymarkers for the Ulster Way (and National Cycle Route 92). Gain some height to a T-junction and turn left, then left again at the next two junctions. About 150m from the second junction, break off to the left down a discreetly marked path through conifers and on to the B48, right in dramatic **Gortin Gap**. Cross a stile on the far side of the road and follow the wide track into Gortin Glen, descending steadily for several hundred metres; cross a bitumen road to a path through conifers. Not much further on cross the road again and go down beside Doherty's Burn to a path T-junction near the forest park car park (1½ hours from Gortin).

From the car park follow Ladies View Trail, waymarked with red arrows. It gains height beside Pollan Burn, crossing several timber bridges as the stream slices through a small gorge. After about 1.6km the route goes steeply up through the forest to a bitumen road at **Ladies View** (40 minutes from the car park).

Cross the road to a picnic table from where a narrow path leads to a nearby **direction finder**, pointing out, among many other features, Mullaghclogha (635m) towards the western end of the Sperrins range. Continue up along this narrow path, southeastwards through the heather. Several minutes further on you come to a wider, though not clearly defined track; turn left here and keep ascending. Soon Mullaghcarn, crowned with buildings and towers, comes into view. At the next track intersection turn left to follow another wide track which briefly drops off the broad spur

you've been following, then swings round to make a beeline for the high ground on the skyline. The flimsy remains of what was once a forestry fire-lookout tower sit just below the highest point on a domed hilltop at **Watch Tower** (so named on the OSNI map), an hour from Ladies View. The wide views to the west and southwest take in pastoral, settled countryside; to the north the Sperrins roll gracefully across the skyline.

Retrace your steps to Ladies View. Cross the road and follow the red waymarkers just to the left along a path and down through the plantation to open ground, and on to rejoin the outward route at the first bridge over Pollan Burn. From here the rest is easy – mostly downhill, either to the forest park car park or all the way back to Gortin.

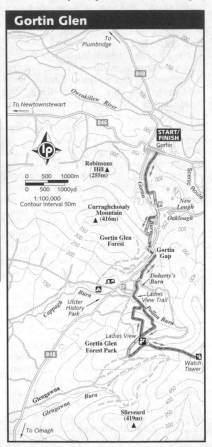

Gortin Glen

Florence Court & Cuilcagh

Duration	7¼–7¾ hours
Distance	20km (12 miles)
Difficulty	moderate–demanding
Start/Finish	Florence Court Forest Park car park
Nearest Towns	Belcoo (p325), Enniskillen (p326)
Transport	private

Summary The ordered gardens of historic Florence Court estate contrast with beautiful views of lakes, hills and fertile farmland from the lakeland counties' highest peak.

Cuilcagh (666m) is the highest peak in the lakeland region of Counties Fermanagh, Cavan and Leitrim. The summit of the big, reverse L-shaped massif straddles the border between Northern Ireland and the Republic and on a clear day it's possible to see both the Irish Sea off County Louth and the Atlantic Ocean near Sligo. This walk, involving 650m of ascent, explores the woodlands and forests of the Florence Court estate and the diverse limestone and moorland landscapes on the wild, remote northern side of the mountain.

In 1954 the **National Trust** (☎ 6634 8249) took over the stately 18th-century Florence Court House and its grounds from the son of the 5th Earl of Enniskillen. Between 1997 and 2002 the trust acquired many historic items belonging to the Enniskillen family; these items are now preserved in the house. The grounds (admission £2.50) are open daily and the house (admission £3.50) from noon to 6pm daily during summer and less frequently at other times. The parking fee is refunded if you visit the house. Beside the house are a shop and a tearoom for lunches and snacks; they keep the same hours as the house.

The forest park was acquired by the **Forest Service** (☎ 6634 8497) from the Enniskillen family in 1975.

NATURAL HISTORY

Florence Court Forest, surrounding the National Trust's estate, protects magnificent stands of oak, beyond which are commercial conifer species.

During the Carboniferous era, 320 to 330 million years ago, the region lay on the boundary of a warm, tropical sea to the south and uplands to the north. Here masses of sand and silt were deposited in river deltas; the deposits on the sea bed became mudstone (shale) and those in the deltas were transformed into sandstone. Wherever the sea was shallow, coral thrived and the resulting lime-rich mud turned into limestone, the area's predominant rock type.

The steep-sided Cuilcagh massif comprises layers of shale and hard sandstone; the latter erodes more slowly, and survives as cliffs and precipitous slopes. On Cuilcagh's lower slopes you will find typical features of limestone topography (see the boxed text 'Karst Wonders of the Burren', p251), including sinkholes and patches of limestone pavement.

The limy soils support many species of wildflowers including wild thyme, blue harebell and bird's foot trefoil. Moorland species are largely confined to heathers, bog cotton, swamp orchids, and grasses, sedges and mosses. While skylarks and golden plovers fill the air with their song.

PLANNING
When to Walk

The mountain is prone to disappearing into thick swirling mist so a fine, settled day is preferable.

What to Bring

Given the extent of bog-trotting on this walk, gaiters and waterproof boots are essential for comfort and safety.

Maps & Books

The OSNI 1:50,000 *Lough Allen* map is the one to carry. There is lots of background information in *25 Walks in Fermanagh*, by Noel Parker & Eamonn Keaveney, available from Fermanagh TIC in Enniskillen (p326). *Walk Cuilcagh*, in the Geological Survey's 'Landscapes from Stone' series, is a set of illustrated plastic cards describing 10 walks and outlining geological and archaeological features.

GETTING TO/FROM THE WALK

To reach Florence Court Forest Park from Enniskillen, drive south along the A32 for 9.4km to a crossroads and turn right; 900m further on, turn left. The entrance to the park and the National Trust's Florence Court estate is 500m along. The gates are open daily from 10am to sunset. From Belcoo the most direct route is via Blacklion, across the bridge in the Republic; turn left there and drive 11.8km southeast to a signposted junction on the right and follow signs to Florence Court.

THE WALK (see map p332)

From the eastern side of the southern forest park car park follow the Glenwood Trail (red waymarkers). Keep your eye on these as the trail marches in tandem with other forest trails for a while, around the northern and eastern sides of the grounds of **Florence Court House**, of which there are some good views. Shortly before a bridge over the Finglass River, the Glen Trail goes solo and follows the river up a dank, mossy glen with magnificent beeches and oaks, past **Glen Wood Forest Nature Reserve**, then through conifer plantations. At a sharp bend a good hour from the start the signposted Hikers Trail heads south (the Glen Trail leads northwest here). Continue along the Hikers Trail for about 25 minutes to a stile over a fence and into open ground.

From here you follow yellow-topped posts for several kilometres. Keep in mind the warning sign by the stile: if you stray from the path you could find yourself closely inspecting the depths of one of the many sinkholes in the karst limestone landscape. The marked route generally pursues a southwesterly course through limestone country, across tributaries of the Finglass River, then moorland around the upper reaches of the Owenbrean River. Beyond that lies a couple of kilometres of relatively featureless, wet moorland, splendidly relieved by the prospect of Cuilcagh ahead. The last waymarker post stands on a broad knoll at the foot of a steep slope (about two hours from the forest edge). From here, make your way southeast to a steep grassy spur and clamber up to the **summit**, marked by a large cairn and trig pillar (40 to 50 minutes from the last waymarker).

Retrace steps to the junction of the Hikers and Glen Trails, and turn left to complete a clockwise circuit of the latter trail

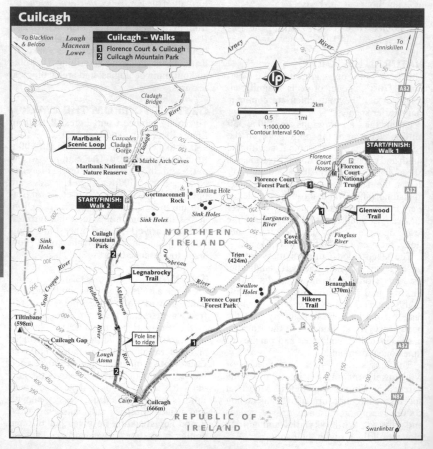

through plantations to the lawns and flower beds around Florence Court House. Go past the house itself – with luck the adjacent tearoom will still be open – then back to the forest park car park (three to 3¼ hours from the summit).

Cuilcagh Mountain Park

Duration	5–5½ hours
Distance	13km (8 miles)
Difficulty	moderate
Start/Finish	Marlbank Scenic Loop car park
Nearest Town	Belcoo (p325)
Transport	private

Summary A low reading on the bogginess scale for this route to the Cuilcagh plateau, through a unique reserve protecting a now rare area of blanket bog.

This is a less strenuous, more direct and drier approach to Cuilcagh Mountain than via the Hikers Trail from Florence Court Forest Park. About two-thirds of the distance is along the meandering Legnabrocky Trail, floating on the surrounding blanket bog. A waymarked route leads up to Cuilcagh's summit plateau, from where you have to make your own way to the summit. It's a climb of 480m in total.

You can find out much more about the park at **Marble Arch Caves Visitor Centre** (☎ 6634 8855; *Marlbank Scenic Loop; open 10am-4pm daily Mar-Sept*). There is also a shop here which stocks local references and maps, and a cafeteria serving soup, sandwiches, cakes and drinks. Guided tours of the caves leave the visitor centre regularly.

A return walk of about an hour (3km or 1.9 miles) through Cladagh Gorge from the visitor centre is highly recommended. From the centre a well-built path with steps and bridges leads down through Marlbank National Nature Reserve surrounding the spectacular Cladagh Gorge. You pass Marble Arch, a bridge of limestone through which the Cladagh River surges from the caves system, the beautiful Cascades and fine deciduous woodland. Retrace your steps to the visitor centre.

NATURAL HISTORY

Between the Cuilcagh massif and the limestone grasslands to the north is one of the most extensive areas of blanket bog in Ireland. Responding to the drastic impact on river levels wrought by draining of the bogs for mechanised, large-scale peat extraction, Fermanagh District Council set up Cuilcagh Mountain Park in 1998. The aims were to protect undisturbed bogland, restore damaged areas and raise awareness of the crucial environmental importance of bogs. Early in 2002 the park and nearby Marble Arch Caves, described as 'one of Europe's finest show caves', became a European Geopark. They joined a select but growing network of 12 such parks in seven countries. Check w www.europeangeoparks.org to learn more about Geoparks.

PLANNING
When to Walk

Good weather is essential for this walk as the Cuilcagh plateau falls away steeply on all sides and is riven with crevices and fissures.

Maps

The OSNI 1:50,000 map No 26 *Lough Allen* covers the walk; it's available from the Marble Arch Caves Visitor Centre.

GETTING TO/FROM THE WALK

The walk starts and finishes at a car park on the Marlbank Scenic Loop (GR 120336). This well-signposted, narrow road arcs around the southern side of a road between the A32 (at a junction 9.5km south of Enniskillen) and the village of Blacklion, immediately south across the bridge from Belcoo. Coming from Blacklion, the turn-off is 2.4km to the southeast.

THE WALK (see map p332)

Climb the stile beside the gate at the car park and set out along the wide Legnabrocky Trail, initially through rich green limestone grassland. You soon leave this behind and pass through bogland where there's evidence of continuing restoration works in the shape of dams and drains, with boardwalks if you want a closer look. Next, it's the real thing – what's called active blanket bog, where natural ecosystems are more or less undisturbed. The trail comes to an end just beyond a gate and stile, in an area of wet heath (an hour from the start). The easily followed waymarked route, with posts in line of sight bearing the park's eye-catching logo, crosses the heath and ascends Cuilcagh's less wet, steep slopes. The pole line ends on the summit plateau, so you're on your own as you head southeast across the broken, rocky surface for about a kilometre to the summit (about 1½ hours from the trail end).

The return is simply back the way you came; the outlook north towards Lough Erne over beautiful pastoral landscape is very different indeed.

Other Walks

AROUND BELFAST
Belfast Hills
The hills north of Belfast give excellent wide views, and can be traversed in a day's walk (five to six hours, 18km/11 miles) from Colin Glen Forest Park, via Black Hill, Black Mountain, Divis, Squires Hill and Cavehill in Cave Hill Country Park. The route is part of the original Ulster Way and is still very intermittently waymarked as such and shown on the OSNI 1:50,000 map No 15 *Belfast*. It involves forest paths, minor roads, rough moorland and vehicle tracks. **Citybus** (☎ *9066 6630*) service No 540 from Castle St, Belfast, stops near the forest park entrance; several Citybus services pass the entrance to Belfast Zoo at the end of the walk. In 2003 the National Trust purchased 600 hectares of the Belfast Hills, including Black Mountain and

Divis. Walkers can look forward to greatly improved facilities under the trust's management.

THE SOUTHEAST
Waymarked Ways
The Ring of Gullion Way, southwest of Newry, and the Lecale Way, from Strangford to Newcastle, are outlined in the Waymarked Ways chapter (p335).

Tollymore Forest Park
On the very edge of the Mourne Mountains, this park features in two walks described earlier in this chapter – Mournes Trail (p317) and Brandy Pad (p324). These routes follow part of the Long Haul Trail, one of four waymarked trails in the park, which range from the short Arboretum and Forest Plots Trail (1.75km/1 mile) to the full length of the Long Haul (13km/8 miles). Passing through conifer and deciduous forests, and – for nostalgic Aussies – a stand of eucalypts, plus historic and archaeological sites, the trails are ideal for days when the hills are mist-shrouded. The park is 6km (3.7 miles) west of Newcastle, from where access roads are clearly signposted. A brochure outlining the trails and including a map is available at the park entrance; the gate is open daily from 10am to sunset. Contact the **Forest Service** (☎ *4372 2428;* Ⓦ *www.forestserviceni .gov.uk*) for more information. There are a café and camping ground on site (see Places to Stay & Eat, p312, for Newcastle). The OSNI 1:25,000 *Mourne Country* map or 1:50,000 map No 29 *The Mournes* cover the area.

THE WEST
Waymarked Ways
The Central Sperrins Way, the Carleton Trail, a circular route from Clogher in County Tyrone, and the Sliabh Beagh Way, in Counties Tyrone and Fermanagh and County Monaghan in the Republic, are covered in the Waymarked Ways chapter (p335).

NORTHERN IRELAND

Waymarked Ways

There are more than three thousand kilometres of official Waymarked Ways across the length and breadth of Ireland. They range from the 214km-long Kerry Way in the rugged southwest to the 26km Cavan Way in the upper Shannon valley, and can take walkers to some of the least known and most beautiful parts of both countries.

In the South the Ways originated in the late 1970s when walking groups set their sights on an Ireland Way right around the country, similar to the Ulster Way then being developed in the North. The project was launched with the Wicklow Way (p84), which was completed in 1982. A handful of Ways followed during the 1980s, while the original Ireland Way idea was supplanted by numerous individual routes that could also provide shorter local walks.

Plentiful EU funding during the 1990s enabled the opening of new Ways and the upgrading of existing ones; by 2002 the total number had reached 31. Six Ways: Wicklow, South Leinster, East Munster, Blackwater, Kerry (part) and Beara have been designated as the western end of the 'E8', one of the vast network of **European Ramblers** (W *www.era-ewv-ferp.org*) routes. The E8 currently starts in Central Europe and finishes on the Irish southwest coast – a distance of about 4400km, although there's nothing to mark this 'milestone'.

In the meantime, the ambitious Ulster Way had run into difficulties; shorter routes were planned, mostly using sections of the original Way; eight had been opened by late 2002 and several more were in the pipeline (see the boxed text 'Is the Ulster Way History?', p293).

All routes are waymarked with posts bearing a yellow arrowhead and walking person logo, and most also have sign posts at crucial junctions. Experience shows that maintenance is inadequate – paths become overgrown and waymarkers hidden by vegetation.

Before dashing out and buying guide books, think about these points. With a few

exceptions, much of the distance of each way is along forest tracks and/or minor and not so minor public roads. Those with substantial off-road sections include the Kerry, Sheep's Head, Dingle and Suck Valley Ways, and the canal towpaths. Finding accommodation each night can necessitate time-consuming detours or very long days between places to stay. Nevertheless, the Ways offer a rich resource from which to pick and choose, and to discover Ireland off the beaten track.

This chapter comprises summary information about those Ways not described in full or in part in the earlier walks chapters. The Ways covered in those chapters are the Causeway Coast, Moyle and Newry Canal Ways in Northern Ireland; the Wicklow and Barrow Ways in the South & Southeast; and Kerry, Beara, Sheep's Head and Dingle Ways in the Southwest.

For general information about the Ways contact the following organisations:

National Waymarked Ways Advisory Committee (☎ 01-240 7727, W www.walkireland.ie) 21 Fitzwilliam Sq, Dublin 2. This committee publishes a booklet giving basic details of the Ways, but it is not always up to date.

Countryside Access & Activities Network (☎ 028-9038 3848, W www.countrysiderecreation.com) Upper Malone Rd, Belfast BT9 5LA. This network distributes its lavishly illustrated guides to the North's Ways.

Dublin & Beyond

TÁIN WAY

This is a circular route of 40km around the Carlingford Mountain massif in County Louth, right on the border. Much of the western half is along bitumen and forest roads; the northern section is more scenic and the road fairly quiet. However, all this is scarcely worth bothering about with Carlingford Mountain (Slieve Foye, 589m) looming invitingly above. Although not on the Way, the mountain provides a fine walk in its own right. OSNI 1:50,000 map No 29 *The Mournes* shows almost all of the Way; the missing bit is on OSI 1:50,000 map No 36. *The Táin Way* map guide published by EastWest Mapping is invaluable. Bus Éireann services link Carlingford with Dundalk and Newry.

OFFALY WAY

Only the northern section of this 29km route between the Grand Canal Way near Ferbane and Cadamstown in the Slieve Bloom foothills is really worth walking. This takes you through the Turraun Nature Reserve, a restored former cutaway peatland. The southern section, via the village of Kilcormac, is along mostly straight and rather monotonous bitumen roads. You'll need OSI 1:50,000 map No 54; a basic leaflet published by Offaly County Council describes features en route. The Way connects with the Grand Canal Way near Ferbane, which is linked by a Bus Éireann

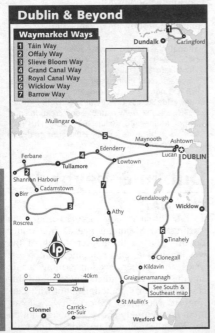

Dublin & Beyond

Waymarked Ways
1 Táin Way
2 Offaly Way
3 Slieve Bloom Way
4 Grand Canal Way
5 Royal Canal Way
6 Wicklow Way
7 Barrow Way

service with Tullamore, itself easily accessible from Dublin by bus and train.

SLIEVE BLOOM WAY

In the heart of Ireland, this 70km-long Way makes a middle-level circuit of the Slieve Bloom Mountains, crossing deep valleys on all sides. It follows forest roads, paths and, mainly in the west, bitumen roads. Conifer plantations feature prominently, but there are also many fine, wide views. It's a pleasantly varied, remote-feeling route, which takes in the wooded River Barrow valley and breezy moorland, but it doesn't pass through any towns or villages so you need to diverge for varying distances to find accommodation. You'll need OSI 1:50,000 map No 54 or EastWest Mapping's *The Slieve Bloom Way* guide. The Way is not directly served by public transport; Bus Éireann services pass through Birr and Kilcormac (No 19, Dublin to Birr), Mountrath and Roscrea (No 12, Dublin to Limerick) and Mountmellick (No 73, Waterford to Athlone) on the Way's periphery. The route of the Way was under review at the time of writing.

GRAND CANAL WAY

For around 120km the Grand Canal meanders west from Dublin through the central plains to the River Shannon. The Way follows the still largely intact towpath and provides easy walking. West from Tullamore there are two days' good walking to the Shannon, with plenty of canal features and varied wildlife. You'll need five OSI 1:50,000 maps, Nos 47, 48, 49, 50 and 53, for the full distance. The useful *Guide to the Grand Canal of Ireland*, published by Dúchas, is available from the **Waterways Visitor Centre** (☎ *01-677 7510; Grand Canal Quay, Dublin*). Dublin Bus services go to Lucan and Milltown; trains link Dublin Heuston, Sallins and Tullamore. Bus Éireann operates services (Nos 71, 72 and 120) from Dublin to Edenderry, Daingean, Tullamore, Ferbane and Banagher.

ROYAL CANAL WAY

You can follow this canal from Dublin for 70km to Mullingar; the Royal continues for another 70km to the River Shannon, but this section isn't yet open for walkers. The section between Ashtown and Maynooth once provided a pleasant day's walk, but in 2002 it was sadly neglected – the water stagnant, algae-encrusted and littered with rubbish – although efforts were being made to clean it. It's then another 50km from Maynooth to Mullingar, mostly along the towpath. You'll need four OSI 1:50,000 maps, Nos 41, 48, 49 and 50. The informative Dúchas publication *Guide to the Royal Canal of Ireland* is available from **Waterways Visitor Centre** (*☎ 01-677 7510; Grand Canal Quay, Dublin*). Bus Éireann services (Nos 19, 20, 22, 111, 115 and 118) go through Ashtown, Maynooth, Enfield, Killucan and Mullingar. Trains from Dublin Connolly to Mullingar go via Ashtown, Clonsilla, Maynooth and Enfield.

South & Southeast

SOUTH LEINSTER WAY

The northeastern end of this 102km-long Way at Kildavin is 4km beyond Clonegall, the southern extremity of the Wicklow Way; its most southwestern point at Carrick-on-Suir links directly with the East Munster Way. The attractive-sounding route crosses groups of hills separating the valleys of the Slaney, Barrow, Nore and Suir Rivers. However, much of it is along bitumen roads and through conifer plantations, notably from Kildavin to the River Barrow and from Mullinavat to Carrick. The best bits are along the River Barrow (coinciding with the Barrow Way) and over the slopes of Brandon Hill en route to Inistioge. Carry three OSI 1:50,000 maps, Nos 68, 75 and 76, and EastWest Mapping's *South Leinster Way* map guide. Bus Éireann service No 5 from Dublin to Waterford goes through Kildavin; service No 7, Dublin to Cork, passes through Carrick-on-Suir; Mullinavat is on service No 4, Dublin to Waterford; Piltown is served by No 55, Galway to Rosslare.

EAST MUNSTER WAY

There's some good walking to be had along this 70km Way from Carrick-on-Suir to Clogheen. From Carrick to Kilsheelan village the route is beside the River Suir; the Way then crosses the northern extremity of the Comeragh Mountains to the historic town of Clonmel. Much of the western end, across the forested lowermost slopes of the Knockmealdown Mountains, is scenic out of the conifers. Unfortunately, into Clogheen the route (about 5km) is down a fairly busy road. Carry two OSI 1:50,000 maps, Nos 74 and 75, and EastWest Mapping's *East Munster Way Guide*. Bus Éireann service No 7 linking Dublin and Cork goes via Carrick-on-Suir, Clonmel and Clogheen. By train from Dublin Heuston, catch either the service to Waterford or one to Limerick Junction, and change for Carrick-on-Suir and Clonmel.

TIPPERARY HERITAGE WAY

Extending for 55km between the Vee (southeast of Clogheen) and the historic town of Cashel, this Way descends from the Knockmealdowns and follows minor roads and tracks generally close to the River Suir, passing through Ardfinnan and Caher en route. The longest off-road stretches are just south and north of the village of Golden (between Caher and Cashel). 'Heritage' encompasses a great variety of historic and

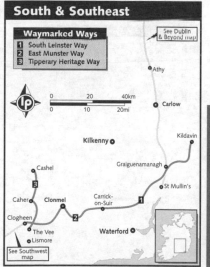

South & Southeast

Waymarked Ways
1 South Leinster Way
2 East Munster Way
3 Tipperary Heritage Way

See Dublin & Beyond map

0   20   40km
0 10 20mi

Athy

Carlow

Kilkenny

Kildavin

Cashel

Graiguenamanagh

Caher   Clonmel   Carrick-on-Suir   St Mullin's

Clogheen

The Vee   Waterford
Lismore

See Southwest map

WAYMARKED WAYS

natural features, including castles and abbeys, native woodland and riverside wildlife. You'll need two OSI 1:50,000 maps, Nos 66 and 74, and EastWest Mapping's *Tipperary Heritage Way* map guide. Bus Éireann service No 7 linking Dublin and Cork goes via Ardfinnan and Clogheen, which is around 5km northwest of the Vee. Bus service No 8 linking Dublin and Cork stops in Cashel; service No 71, Cork to Athlone, passes through Cashel.

Southwest

BLACKWATER WAY

Stitched together to link the East Munster and Kerry Ways, this 188km-long Way has some good walking at or near each end. From Clogheen the Way crosses the western Knockmealdown Mountains with minimal road walking and follows country lanes to the picturesque town of Fermoy on the River Blackwater (47km). The Millstreet to Shrone section is largely off-road and very scenic (21km). Take four OSI 1:50,000 maps, Nos 74, 79, 80 and 81, and EastWest Mapping's *Blackwater Way* map guide. Bus Eireann

service No 7 linking Dublin and Cork goes via Clogheen; No 14 links Dublin and Killarney via Limerick; No 40 (Tralee to Cork) goes through Millstreet and Rathmore (near Shrone). Trains run from Dublin Heuston to Millstreet and Killarney.

BALLYHOURA WAY

Following a historic route dating back to the 17th century, this 90km-long Way has its eastern end, inexplicably, at Limerick Junction on a busy road about 4.5km north of Tipperary. South of there, it passes through pleasant countryside, traverses the Ballyhoura hills and finishes rather tamely in the lowlands at St John's Bridge. The best parts of the Way are between Ballyorgan and Ballyhea, and along the northern side of the Glen of Aherlow. Take four OSI 1:50,000 maps, Nos 66, 72, 73 and 74, and the Ballyhoura Fáilte Society's *Ballyhoura Way* map guide, available locally. Bus Éireann service No 55, from Limerick to Waterford, passes through Tipperary. The closest place to the western end of the walk served by public transport is Kanturk, about 6km south of St John's Bridge, on Bus Éireann service No 242 linking Cork and Newmarket.

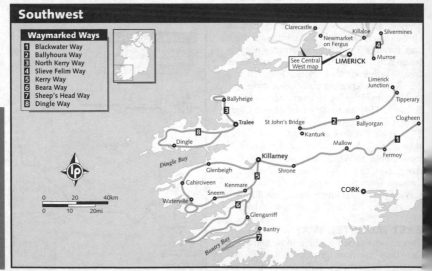

NORTH KERRY WAY

Rarely far from the sea, this low-level 48km Way heads west from Tralee, then north, close to the coast overlooking Tralee Bay and Banna Strand. From the village of Ballyheige the Way does an extremely scenic loop over Maulin Mountain above Kerry Head. It follows *boreens* (country lanes) and quiet country roads. Carry two OSI 1:50,000 maps, Nos 63 and 71, and *North Kerry Way – Sli Chiarrai Thuaidh*, published by North Kerry Walks Co, which is available locally. Bus Éireann service No 13 links Dublin and Tralee via Limerick. Trains run from Dublin Heuston to Tralee. Bus Éireann service No 274 links Tralee and Ballyheige via Banna Cross.

SLIEVE FELIM WAY

This 30km-long Way between Murroe in the south and Silvermines in the north meanders through clusters of hills east of Limerick separated by varied valleys, from the broad Clare River to the secluded upper reaches of the Doonane River. Unfortunately, the route keeps well below the highest ground and more than half the distance is through conifer plantations; elsewhere you're on bitumen roads. You'll need three OSI 1:50,000 maps, Nos 59, 65 and 66, and the *Slieve Felim Way Walking Trail* map guide, published by **Shannon Development** (☎ *061-361 555;* **w** *www .shannon-dev.ie/tourism/holidays)* and available locally. You can reach Murroe by Bus Éireann service No 332 from Limerick; a limited service links Newport (Tipperary) and Nenagh via Silvermines.

Central West

LOUGH DERG WAY

From Limerick this 64km route follows the old City Canal, the River Shannon, minor roads and another canal to the village of O'Briensbridge; then it's road walking to Killaloe beside Lough Derg (also on the East Clare Way). From there the 40km to Dromineer, at the northern end of the Way, is mostly along minor roads and tracks. The views of the lough and surrounding hills are, however, excellent. You will need three OSI 1:50,000 maps, Nos 58, 59 and 65, and *Lough Derg Way* map guide, available from Shannon Development (see Slieve Felim Way, this page). Bus Éireann services (Nos 13, 14 and 15) link Dublin and Limerick. Iarnród Éireann operates a service from Dublin Heuston to Limerick. There is no public transport from Dromineer; Bus Éireann's No 323 links Limerick and Killaloe.

EAST CLARE WAY

From Killaloe (also on the Lough Derg Way) beside Lough Derg, this 172km Way wanders around in a huge loop through relatively

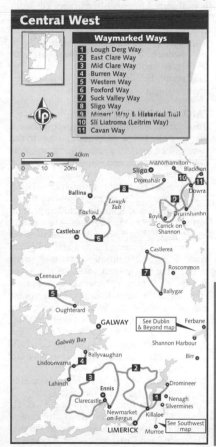

Central West

Waymarked Ways
1. Lough Derg Way
2. East Clare Way
3. Mid Clare Way
4. Burren Way
5. Western Way
6. Foxford Way
7. Suck Valley Way
8. Sligo Way
9. Miner's Way & Historical Trail
10. Slí Liatroma (Leitrim Way)
11. Cavan Way

See Dublin & Beyond map

See Southwest map

little-known hills and valleys. Just on half the distance is along quiet bitumen roads – narrow, hedge-bound and less than ideal for walkers. The best part, between Tulla, Feakle and Mountshannon, offers three days of quite scenic and varied walking, mainly following forest and hill tracks, and paths across moorland. Take four OSI 1:50,000 maps, Nos 52, 53, 58 and 59, the *East Clare Way* map guide and *The East Clare Way*, an illustrated guidebook published by **East Clare Way Ltd** (☎ *065-683 5912;* e *walks.ennis@ eircom.net; Tulla Business Centre, Tulla*) and available from EastWest Mapping. Limerick is well served by Bus Éireann services from Dublin and major towns, and by trains from Dublin Heuston. From Limerick, Bus Éireann service No 323 goes through Killaloe and Scariff; No 346 to Mountshannon, Whitegate and Broadford; and No 348 to Flagmount, Feakle and Tulla. Most services are infrequent.

MID CLARE WAY

This varied, 130km-long Way describes a big, wavy loop that starts and finishes in the town of Ennis near the Shannon estuary. Following rural roads and forest tracks, it leads south then west through farmland; north over low, forested Ben Dash; through undulating countryside with scattered plantations; and via the villages of Kilmaley and Kilnomona to the Dysert O'Dea Museum – one of the way's highlights. The museum focuses on the local castle, round tower and religious sites. The route continues east and south through the lake-dotted valley of the River Fergus, via Crusheen, Newmarket on Fergus and Clarecastle, back to Ennis. From a point east of Crusheen, the Way links to the East Clare Way north of Tulla. Two OSI 1:50,000 maps, Nos 57 and 58, cover the route; the *Mid Clare Way* map guide should be available from the publisher, **Mid Clare Way Ltd** (☎ *065-6835912;* e *walks.ennis@eircom.net; Tulla Business Centre, Tulla*). Ennis is on Bus Éireann routes Nos 12 (Dublin to Ennis), 17 (Shannon Airport to Galway) and 51 (Galway to Cork), the last of which also passes through the towns of Newmarket on Fergus, Clarecastle and Crusheen on the Way.

BURREN WAY

This 45km route links Lahinch and Ballyvaughan in western County Clare. You have to follow roads for around 24km, past the village of Doolin, before escaping from the bitumen to tracks across the Slieve Elva uplands and the Caher Valley. Roads and tracks skirt Cappanawalla and the route finishes along nearly 3km of fairly busy road. Along the Way there are magnificent views of the Aran Islands, many archaeological and historic features, and the unique Burren karst landscape and flora to see. Unfortunately, a dispute has closed off access to the wonderful Cliffs of Moher, along which the Way once passed. Carry two OSI 1:50,000 maps, Nos 51 and 57, and Shannon Development's *The Burren Way* map guide. Bus Éireann services (Nos 15 and 333) from Limerick pass through Lahinch and Doolin; the Galway to Cork service No 50 stops at both places and at Ballyvaughan, though infrequently from mid-September to early June. Limerick, Galway and Cork are well served by buses and trains.

WESTERN WAY

This 50km route from the village of Oughterard, on the western shore of Lough Corrib, to Leenaun beside Killary Harbour takes you through some truly wild country. It leads north beside the lough, over Mám Éan (a low pass in the Maumturk Mountains), through the Inagh Valley and over to Leenaun. Not quite half the distance is along minor roads – the rest is forest and hill tracks, and even a path or two. The scenery is magnificent and there's much of historical interest en route. Use four OSI 1:50,000 maps, Nos 37, 38, 44 and 45, and either OSI's *Western Way* map guide or *The Western Way in Connemara*, published by Folding Landscapes. From late June to late August Bus Éireann service No 61 goes from Galway to Westport via Oughterard, Maam, and Leenaun; it goes only to Oughterard infrequently at other times. Service No 419 from Galway also goes to Oughterard, Maam and Leenaun. Galway is well served by buses from Dublin, Cork and major towns, and by trains from Dublin.

FOXFORD WAY

In northern County Mayo, this 74km Way explores the southern end of the Slieve Gamp or Ox Mountains, and the complex of lakes and streams west and southwest of Foxford. A 12km extension crosses the mountains northeastwards and virtually links with the Sligo Way at Lough Talt. The Way is rich in historical and archaeological interest, and provides fine and varied views. It follows quiet rural roads, tracks and some shortish cross-country stretches, but also has a handful of kilometres along major roads. You'll need three OSI 1:50,000 maps, Nos 24, 31 and 32, and *The Foxford Way, Bealach Béal Easa* guide, available from **Foxford Visitor Information Centre** (☎ *094-925 6488;* Ⓦ *www .visitmayo.com)*. Foxford is on Bus Éireann's services No 22 linking Dublin and Ballina, and No 66, linking Belfast to Westport via Enniskillen and Sligo. Foxford is also on the Dublin to Sligo train line.

SUCK VALLEY WAY

This 100km-long Way is an elongated loop through lowland farm country in the valley of the River Suck. The Way follows farm and forest tracks, and some minor roads, through several villages, including Castlerea, Ballymoe, Ballygar, Athleague and many sites with interesting historical connections. Although the highest point is only 157m, there are plenty of good views. Carry two OSI 1:50,000 maps, Nos 39 and 40, and the *Suck Valley Way* map guide, by Joss Lynam, available locally. Bus Éireann service No 21, Dublin to Westport, stops in Castlerea and Ballymoe; the Galway to Cavan service No 65 (with connections to Belfast) stops in Ballygar and Athleague. Castlerea is on the Dublin to Wesport train line.

SLIGO WAY

A 73km route between Lough Talt in the Ox Mountains and Dromahair (about 10km southeast of Sligo), this Way follows roads and forest tracks along the lower slopes of the Ox Mountains and into the wide valley of the Owenmore River. The best part is from Collooney to Dromahair, with minimal road walking and some excellent views. The Way

virtually links with the Foxford Way near Lough Talt. Use two OSI 1:50,000 maps, Nos 24 and 25, and EastWest Mapping's *The Sligo Way* map guide. There is no public transport to the southern end of the Way at Lough Talt. Bus Éireann services Nos 23 (Dublin to Sligo) and 64 (Derry to Galway via Sligo) pass through Collooney (50km from Lough Talt); Nos 462 and 469 link Sligo and Dromahair at the north end. Collooney is also on the Dublin to Sligo train line.

MINERS' WAY & HISTORICAL TRAIL

These two Ways form an ingenious figure eight route, with a northern tail. Covering 118km, they pass though several villages (Dowra, Arigna, Boyle and Castlebaldwin) in Counties Leitrim, Roscommon and Sligo, and links with the Leitrim and Cavan Ways at Dowra. Miners' Way follows centuries-old routes used by coal miners working at Arigna; the Historical Trail passes a variety of features including an abbey, a battle site and prehistoric passage graves. Both Ways comprise a mix of shortish stretches of minor roads, tracks and paths, and together involve around 2100m ascent – almost guaranteeing good views. You'll need two OSI 1:50,000 maps, Nos 25 and 33, OSNI 1:50,000 map No 26 and *Miners' Way & Historical Trail* map guide, which is available from EastWest Mapping. Bus Éireann service No 23 links Dublin and Sligo via Boyle, Ballinafad and Castlebaldwin; Nos 462 and 469 (both limited) from Sligo pass through Dowra and Drumshanbo.

SLÍ LIATROMA

This 48km route through isolated countryside from Drumshanbo to Manorhamilton offers a very varied and interesting two-day walk. It follows quiet roads and *boreens* through woodland, across limestone pavements and past historical and archaeological features. You can stop overnight in Dowra, which is on the Miners' Way and at the southern end of the Cavan Way. Take OSNI 1:50,000 map No 26 and *Leitrim Way* map guide, published by Leitrim County Council and available locally. Bus Éireann service

No 66 (Belfast to Westport) goes through Manorhamilton; Nos 462 and 469 (both limited) from Sligo pass through Dowra and Drumshanbo.

CAVAN WAY

This scenic Way makes a very pleasant day walk of 26km from Dowra to Blacklion, especially in the northern half around Burren Forest. The route also passes Shannon Pot, official source of Ireland's longest river. The off-road sections can be boggy, but the Way passes interesting archaeological and historical sites. Dowra is also on Slí Liatroma (above) and the Miners' Way. You'll need OSNI 1:50,000 map No 26 and the *Cavan Way* map guide, available locally or from EastWest Mapping. Bus Éireann services Nos 462 and 469 (both limited) from Sligo pass through Dowra; service No 66 links Enniskillen (in the North) and Sligo via Blacklion.

Northwest

BLUESTACK WAY

This 48km route explores some of the more remote parts of County Donegal between Donegal Town, Glenties and Ardara; the highlights are beautiful Lough Eske, a rugged spur of the Blue Stack Mountains and fine views from Luaghnabrogue (411m). The greater part of the distance is along paths and tracks, although the route often crosses boggy ground. Alternative loop routes have been set up, including a circuit of Lough Eske. There is also an unmarked link to the village of Pettigo, southeast of Donegal Town.

Carry two OSI 1:50,000 maps, Nos 10 and 11. The *Bluestack Way* map guide, with 1:50,000 maps, is published by the **Bluestack Environmental Group** (**W** *www.bluestack.org*) and is available locally or online. There are Bus Éireann services to Donegal Town and from there to Glenties and Ardara.

SLÍ DHÚN NA NGALL

Four circular routes in the Gaeltacht heartland of Donegal make up a total distance of 290km. **Slí an Earagail** (80km) features good coast walking between Derrybeg and Bloody Foreland, and routes on Tory Island (8km) and Gola Island (4km); **Slí na Rosann** (64km) passes through Dungloe and Burtonport on a road-dominated route through the lake-studded scenery of the Rosses, and includes a 20km loop on nearby Aran Island; **Slí na Finne** (24km) loops around the River Finn valley from Fintown and combines minor roads, tracks and paths across wild moorland; **Slí Cholmcille** (70km), an inland route, passes through Ardara, Kilcar, Carrick and Glencolmcille with the section south of Slievetooey as the dramatic highlight. There is also a mostly off-road 20km link between Slí na Rosann and Slí na Finne. Four OSI 1:50,000 maps, Nos 1, 6, 10 and 11, cover the Way. *Slí Dhún na nGall*, an excellent set of leaflets, is available from **Gaelsaoire** (**☎** *1800 621 600 Ireland, 0800 783 5708 UK;* **W** *www .gaelsaoire.ie*). There are Bus Éireann services to Donegal, and from there to Kilcar, Ardara and Glencolmcille. **John McGinley** (**☎** *074-913 5201*) operates a service from Dublin through Falcarragh, Gortahork, and Annagry; **Feda O'Donnell** (**☎** *074-954 8114*) buses link Galway and Letterkenny via Falcarragh, Gortahork and Gweedore.

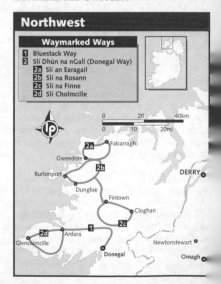

Northwest

Waymarked Ways
1 Bluestack Way
2 Slí Dhún na nGall (Donegal Way)
  2a Slí an Earagail
  2b Slí na Rosann
  2c Slí na Finne
  2d Slí Cholmcille

Northern Ireland

RING OF GULLION WAY

You don't normally associate volcanoes with the Irish landscape, but the Ring of Gullion in South Armagh is all that's left of one that exploded eons ago. The 57.5km-long Way, between Newry and Derrymore near Camlough (4km west of Newry) skirts the summit of Slieve Gullion (and several other hills near its route) and passes several interesting archaeological and historic features. There is an unofficial marked route to the wonderfully scenic lookout of Slieve's summit. The Way follows forest tracks and paths, and minor roads for considerable distances. Carry the OSNI 1:50,000 map No 29 *The Mournes* and the official illustrated guide. See Newry (p314) for transport details.

LECALE WAY

Easily the best part of this 65km Way, from the village of Raholp near Strangford Lough to the town of Newcastle, is through Murlough Nature Reserve and along Dundrum Bay beach to Newcastle. There's also a good off-road stretch between the villages of Ballyhornan and Ardglass south of Strangford. The Way features a variety of coastal wildlife and excellent views of the Mourne Mountains. About two-thirds of the distance is along bitumen roads; elsewhere you're on tracks and paths. Carry two OSNI 1:50,000 maps, Nos 21 *Strangford Lough* and 29 *The Mournes*, and the official illustrated guide. Ulsterbus service No 16E links Downpatrick and Strangford via Raholp; service No 215 goes to Downpatrick from Belfast. See Newcastle (p311) for transport details.

CENTRAL SPERRINS WAY

The lovely Glenelly River valley separates the high moorland summits of the Sperrin Mountains to the north from a lower, more pastoral range of hills to the south. This 48km Way consists of a big, all-road eastern loop and a shorter, very scenic western loop along tracks and paths. Both routes dip across the southern hills to explore the Owenkillew River valley; the waymarking near Slievemore on the western loop may be somewhat sparse. Both loops start and finish at Barnes car park between Plumbridge and Sperrin Heritage Centre. Carry OSNI 1:50,000 map No 13 *The Sperrins* and the official illustrated guide. Public transport is sparse in Glenelly; for details see Gortin (p326).

CARLETON TRAIL

This circular route, based on the village of Clogher in County Tyrone, commemorates the 19th-century writer William Carleton, who was born near Clogher. Archaeological and historic sites, woodlands and lovely views of the River Blackwater valley are the highlights of this 48km Way. Around three-quarters of the route is along quiet rural roads; elsewhere it follows forest tracks. Carry OSNI 1:50,000 maps Nos 18 *Enniskillen* and 19 *Armagh*, and the official illustrated guide. Ulsterbus service No 85

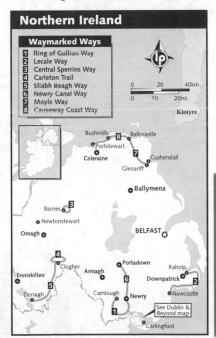

Northern Ireland

Waymarked Ways
1 Ring of Gullion Way
2 Lecale Way
3 Central Sperrins Way
4 Carleton Trail
5 Sliabh Beagh Way
6 Newry Canal Way
7 Moyle Way
8 Causeway Coast Way

0   20   40km
0   10   20mi

Kintyre

Bushmills · 8 · Ballycastle
Portstewart · 7
Coleraine · Cushendall
Glenariff

Ballymena

Barnes · 3
Newtonstewart
Omagh · BELFAST

4
Clogher · Portadown · Raholp
Enniskillen · Armagh · 6 · Downpatrick
Donagh · 5 · Camlough · Newry · Newcastle
1
See Dublin & Beyond map
Carlingford

links Omagh and Clogher; there are good connections at Omagh for Belfast and other large towns in the North.

SLIABH BEAGH WAY

Wandering through a little-known part of the North, this Way takes a 46km route from Altadaven Wood, east of the small town of Clogher, to the village of Donagh, southeast of Enniskillen. An exercise in contrasts, it passes through drumlin-dotted countryside, valleys, woodlands, plantations and past many small picturesque lakes.

There are plenty of good views and wildlife is abundant. The proportion of walking along roads is lower than on other Northern Ways; otherwise you follow forest tracks and paths. You'll need three OSNI 1:50,000 maps, Nos 18 *Enniskillen*, 19 *Armagh* and 27 *Upper Lough Erne*. Ulsterbus service No 85 links Omagh and Clogher, about 8km west of the northern end of the Way. There are good connections in Omagh for Belfast and other towns in the North. Donagh village is close to the route of service No 95, Enniskillen to Clones.

Travel Facts

TOURIST OFFICES
Local Tourist Offices

Representing tourism interests in the Republic and Northern Ireland respectively are **Bord Fáilte** *(Irish Tourist Board; ☎ 01-602 4000, fax 602 4100;* **W** *www.ireland.travel.ie; Baggot St Bridge, Baggot St, Dublin 2)* and **Northern Ireland Tourist Board** *(NITB; ☎ 028-9024 6609;* **W** *www.discovernorthernireland .com; Belfast Welcome Centre, 47 Donegall Place, Belfast BT1 5AU).*

As well as operating separate networks of tourist information centres (TICs) throughout Ireland, Bord Fáilte and the NITB produce some joint publications and operate **Gulliver** *(☎ 1800 668 668;* **W** *www.gulliver .ie)*, a computerised information and accommodation reservation service.

Although not likely to affect the services provided at local TICs, it is worth noting that the responsibilities, composition and name of Bord Fáilte are currently being reviewed, and a new authority is expected to be operational by June 2003.

Dublin and Belfast also have their own tourism agencies: **Dublin Tourism** *(☎ 01-605 7700;* **W** *www.visitdublin.ie; 2 Suffolk St)* and **Belfast Visitor & Convention Bureau** *(☎ 028-9024 6609;* **W** *www.gotobelfast.com; 47 Donegall Place)*.

Throughout the Republic and the North, there's a TIC in almost every town big enough to have a few pubs. Services include approved accommodation bookings for a fee; souvenirs, maps and books are their stock in trade.

TICs in regional centres open all year, usually Monday to Friday from 9am to 5pm, and Saturday 9am to 1pm; during summer they're open daily and for longer hours. Offices in smaller towns open only seasonally, generally from late April or early May to the end of September.

Tourist Offices Abroad

The Republic and the North are represented internationally by **Tourism Ireland** *(* **W** *www*

.tourismireland.com), which promotes tourism to the island of Ireland. Tourism Ireland offices include:

Australia *(☎ 02 9299 6177)* 5th Level, 36 Carrington St, Sydney, NSW 2000
Canada *(☎ 0800 223 6470)* 2 Bloor St West, Suite 1501, Toronto, Ontario M4W 3E2
France *(☎ 01 70 20 00 20)* 33 rue de Miromesnil, 75008 Paris
Germany *(☎ 069-6680 0950)* Untermainanlage 7, D-60329 Frankfurt-am-Main
Netherlands *(☎ 020-504 0689)* Spuistraat 104, 1012 VA Amsterdam
UK *(☎ 0800 0397 000)* 1 Regent St, London SW1Y 4XT
USA *(☎ 800 223 6470)* 345 Park Ave, New York, NY 10154

VISAS & DOCUMENTS
Passports

Make sure your passport is valid for six months after your arrival date. British citizens born in the UK, when travelling from Britain or Northern Ireland, don't require a passport to visit the Republic, but should carry some form of identification to use when cashing travellers cheques or hiring a car. EU nationals can enter Ireland with either a passport or national ID card.

Visas

Citizens of Australia, Canada, New Zealand, South Africa and the USA, do not need a visa to enter the Republic or Northern Ireland. EU nationals can stay indefinitely, other visitors for three to six months.

Travel Insurance

Buy a policy that generously covers you for medical expenses, theft or loss of luggage and tickets, and for cancellation of and delays in your travel arrangements. It may be worth taking out cover specifically for walking activities and the cost of rescue. Check your policy doesn't exclude walking as a dangerous activity.

Buy travel insurance as early as possible to ensure you'll be compensated for any

Copies

All important documents (passport, credit cards, travel insurance policy, driving licence etc) should be photocopied before you leave home. Leave one copy at home and keep another with you, separate from the originals.

Another way of storing your travel documents is with Lonely Planet's free online Travel Vault. Create your own vault at W www .ekno.lonelyplanet.com.

unforseen accidents or delays. If items are lost or stolen get a police report immediately – otherwise your insurer might not pay up.

Driving Licence

EU, US and Canadian drivers can use their normal licence; it will be valid for 12 months from the date you enter Ireland, provided you've held it for two years. If you don't hold one of these, you should obtain an International Driving Permit from your home automobile association.

Travel Discounts

Membership of Hostelling International (HI) opens the doors of An Óige hostels in the South and those of Hostelling International Northern Ireland (HINI) in the North (see Youth Hostels, p42); you can take out temporary membership when you arrive at your first youth hostel.

The International Student Identity Card (ISIC) gives discounts on public transport. You can get this card from usitNOW offices (see Youth Organisation, p49) in Ireland, or from a wide range of student organisations elsewhere. If you're under 26 and not a student, you can obtain an International Youth Card or a European Youth Card, which offer similar discounts to an ISIC.

EMBASSIES & CONSULATES
Irish Embassies & Consulates
Irish diplomatic offices overseas include:

Australia (☎ 02-6273 3022, e irishemb@ cyberone.com.au) 20 Arkana St, Yarralumla, Canberra, ACT 2600

Canada (☎ 613-233 6281, e embassyofireland@ rogers.com) 130 Albert St, STE 1105, Ottawa, Ontario KIP5 G4
France (☎ 01 44 17 67 00, e irembparis@ wanadoo.fr) 4 rue Rude, 75116 Paris
Germany (☎ 030-220 720) Friedrichstrasse 200, 10117 Berlin
Netherlands (☎ 70-363 0993, e info@ irish-embassy.demon.nl) de Kuyperstraat 9, 2514 BA The Hague
New Zealand (☎ 09-977 2252, e consul@ ireland.co.nz) 18 Shortland St, Auckland 1001
Scotland (☎ 0131-226 7711) 16 Randolph Cr, Edinburgh EH3 7TT
Wales (☎ 0207-225 7700) 2 Fitzalan Rd, Cardiff CF24 0EB
UK (☎ 020-7235 2171) 17 Grosvenor Place, London SW1X 7HR
USA (☎ 202-462 3939, e embirlus@aol.com) 2234 Massachusetts Ave NW, Washington, DC 20008-2849

For diplomatic information on Northern Ireland, contact your local UK embassy or consulate.

Embassies in Ireland
Countries with diplomatic offices in Dublin include:

Australia (☎ 01-676 1517, e austemb .dublin@dfat.gov.au) 2nd floor, Fitzwilton House, Wilton Terrace, Dublin 2
Canada (☎ 01-478 1988) 4th floor, 65 St Stephen's Green, Dublin 2
France (☎ 01-260 1666) 36 Ailesbury Rd, Dublin 4
Germany (☎ 01-269 3011) 31 Trimleston Ave, Booterstown, Dublin 4
Netherlands (☎ 01-269 3444, e nethemb@ indigo.ie) 160 Merrion Rd, Ballsbridge, Dublin 4
New Zealand (☎ 01-660 4233, e nzconsul@ indigo.ie) 37 Leeson Park, Dublin 6
UK (☎ 01-205 3700, e passport.dubli@ fco.gov.uk) 29 Merrion Rd, Dublin 4
USA (☎ 01-668 8777) 42 Elgin Rd, Ballsbridge, Dublin 4

Countries with consular representation in Belfast include:

Netherlands (☎ 028-9077 9088) c/o All-Route Shipping (NI) Ltd, 14–16 West Bank Rd
USA (☎ 028-9032 8239) Queen's House, 14 Queen St

CUSTOMS

You may only bring limited amounts of duty-free goods into Ireland: 200 cigarettes, 1L of spirits or 2L of wine and other dutiable goods to the value of €175. However, EU rules stipulate that goods purchased in any one of the 20 EU member countries, in which duties and taxes have been paid, may be imported in unlimited quantities, provided they are for personal consumption (alcohol and tobacco are generally cheaper outside Ireland).

MONEY
Currency

In the Republic, the euro (€) is divided into 100 cents. The notes come in denominations of €5, €10, €20, €50, €100, €200 and €500. The coins are one, two, five, 10, 20 and 50 cents, plus €1 and €2.

The pound sterling (£) is used in Northern Ireland. Notes are printed in denominations of £5, £10, £20 and £50; they are not generally accepted outside the North. Coins come in denominations of 1p ('p' for 'penny'), 2p, 5p, 10p, 20p, 50p, £1 and £2.

Exchange Rates

A good currency converter is W www.oanda .com. At the time of going to print exchange rates were:

country	unit	euro	pound
Australia	A$1	€0.55	£0.36
Canada	C$1	€0.61	£0.45
UK	£1	€1.51	£1
USA	US$1	€0.93	£0.62

Exchanging Money

The best exchange rates are obtained at banks. Many building societies, post offices and TICs in larger towns also handle foreign exchange. Exchange bureaus operate longer hours, but the rate and/or commission will be less favourable. You can also use unofficial moneychangers, usually petrol stations, near the border between the North and South.

Travellers Cheques & Eurocheques

In Ireland, most major currencies and brands of travellers cheques are readily accepted by banks, but not elsewhere. Eurocheques can also be cashed at banks.

Credit Cards & ATMs Visa, MasterCard and Access credit cards are widely accepted, although many hostels, camping grounds, B&Bs and small petrol stations are still geared to cash only. American Express and Diners Club might not be accepted in small establishments or in remote areas.

Pass cards and credit cards can be used to withdraw cash from selected banks and automatic teller machines (ATMs). Check with your bank which ATMs will accept your card before leaving home.

On the Walk

Walking in Ireland doesn't take you into very remote areas for days on end, so maintaining a cash supply isn't a major problem. Nevertheless, if your funds are running low, seize the chance to stock up as soon as it arises.

Costs

A typical daily budget might include:

item	€	£
youth hostel	12	9
camping ground	10	6
B&B	25	22
pint of milk	0.45	0.31
loaf of bread	0.95	0.70
pint of beer	3.20	2.10
litre unleaded petrol	0.85	0.75
newspaper	1.30	0.75

Tipping

Fancy hotels and restaurants usually add a 10% or 15% service charge and no additional tip is required. Simpler places don't add a service charge; if you decide to tip, round up the bill or add no more than 10%.

Taxes & Refunds

Value-added tax (VAT) is a sales tax applied to most goods in Ireland (except books and children's clothing or footwear), at the rate of 20% in the Republic and 17.5% in the North. Visitors who are not EU residents and who intend to export goods outside the EU can claim the VAT, minus an administration fee. There is no restriction on the amount that can be claimed – but remember airline baggage allowances. Most shops displaying the 'Tax Free Shopping' sign carry leaflets explaining how to claim your refund at your port of departure or by post. Visit ⓦ www.globalrefund.ie for further information.

POST & COMMUNICATIONS
Post
From the Republic, postcards and airmail letters cost €0.41 to Britain, €0.44 to continental Europe and €0.57 to the rest of the world. A packet of five aerogrammes costs €2.80.

From North Ireland, postcards cost 28p to Britain, 38p to continental Europe and 46p to the rest of the world. The basic rate for 1st-/2nd-class letters to Britain is 20/28p; for airmail letters to Europe it's 38p and to the rest of the world it's 69p. A pack of six aerogrammes costs £2.20.

Nearly all letters within the country are delivered the next working day. They take three to five days to Britain and the rest of Europe, a week to 10 days to Australia and about 10 days to North America.

Mail to the North and the Republic can be addressed to poste restante at post offices but is officially held for two weeks only. The words 'hold for collection' may have some effect.

Telephone
When calling the Republic from abroad, dial your international access code, followed by ☎ 353 and then the domestic number minus the initial '0'. When calling Northern Ireland from abroad, dial your international access code, then ☎ 44 28 and the local number.

If you are calling Northern Ireland from the Republic, the local number should be prefixed by the special ☎ 048 area code rather than ☎ 028, which also works but is more expensive.

From within Ireland, international calls can be dialled directly from payphones.

For emergency telephone numbers, see Emergency Communications (p66).

Phonecards Known as callcards in the South, phonecards are convenient but, in isolated areas, a coin-only phone may be the sole option.

Callcards issued by Eircom come in three denominations: €4, €7 and €15. The cost of a call per minute is different for each of the three cards and several charge bands also apply. Eircom's global card, for international calls, costs €12.70. International calls (across nine bands) average around €0.70 per minute.

In the North, the post office's phonecard also comes in three denominations: £5, £10 and £20. They can be used throughout Ireland; calls to the UK, the South (from the North), North America, Australia and some European countries cost 5p per minute from a payphone; calls to mobile phones incur a hefty surcharge.

Phones operated by credit cards can be found in the cities and large towns.

Lonely Planet's eKno Communication Card, specifically aimed at travellers, provides competitive international calls (avoid using for local calls), messaging services and free email. Visit ⓦ www.ekno.lonelyplanet .com for information about joining and using the service.

Mobile Phones Ireland uses GSM 900/1800, which is compatible with the rest of Europe and Australia, but not with North American GSM 1900 or the totally different system in Japan. There are three service providers in Ireland, Eircell (087), ESAT Digifone (086) and Meteor (085). All three are linked with most international GSM providers, which will allow you to 'roam' onto a local service, but you will be charged at the highest possible rate.

However, mobile phone coverage in mountain areas is poor. The Mountaineering Council of Ireland's website (ⓦ www .mountaineering.ie) has a page on the subject, worth checking if you're keen to use a mobile in Ireland.

Email & Internet Access
Internet cafés are fairly plentiful in the two capital cities and you should find at least

one in the larger towns, where you can usually relax with a coffee and a snack while you are checking your emails; expect to pay around €3/£2.50 for 30 minutes. Some youth and independent hostels also offer Internet access.

TIME

The Republic and Northern Ireland are on Greenwich Mean Time (GMT), the same as London. Without allowing for daylight saving time changes, when it is noon in Dublin, Belfast and London, it is 1pm in Paris, 10pm in Sydney, 3am in Los Angeles or Vancouver, and 7am in New York.

Clocks are put forward by one hour at 1am on the last Sunday in March and put back on the last Sunday in October.

ELECTRICITY

In both Northern Ireland and the Republic, electricity is 220V, 50Hz and plugs are usually the three flat pin type.

WEIGHTS & MEASURES

Metrication is coming slowly and somewhat haphazardly to Ireland. Distances on road signs in the Republic are in kilometres but you may still see signs with distances in miles. All distances in the North are still in miles. Vehicle speed is measured in miles per hour everywhere. In keeping with EU directives, food is generally weighed in metric measurements, although you may find both imperial and metric for fruit and vegetables. Beer is served in pints (568mL), but you'll buy it in metric cans. Car fuel is priced by the litre throughout. Totally confused?! – a conversion table is at the back of this book.

BUSINESS HOURS

Business hours vary between the Republic and Northern Ireland, and in remote areas opening times may be more limited, but some general guidelines are:

Banks
Republic: Open 10am to 4pm weekdays; most stay open till 5pm on Thursday or Friday.
Northern Ireland: Open 9.30am to 4.30pm weekdays and most open until 5pm Thursday.

Post Offices
Republic: Open from 8.30am (9.30am on Wednesday) to 5.30pm or 6pm Monday to Friday, 9am to noon or 1pm Saturday; small offices may close for lunch.
Northern Ireland: Open from 9am to 5.30pm Monday to Friday and 9am to 1pm Saturday.

Pubs
Republic: Open from 10.30am to 11.30pm Monday to Wednesday, 10.30am to 12.30am on Tuesday and Saturday and from 12.30pm to 11pm on Sunday. However noon opening is still quite common.
Northern Ireland: Pubs can only sell alcohol between 11.30am and 11pm Monday to Saturday and 12.30pm and 10pm on Sunday.

Shops Open from 9am to 5.30pm or 6pm Monday to Saturday; supermarkets may keep slightly longer hours. On Thursday and/or Friday shops stay open later; many open on Sunday, typically from noon to 6pm. Outside cities, shops often close for one afternoon per week. In small towns most close for an hour at lunchtime.

PUBLIC HOLIDAYS

Public (bank) holidays in the North and South don't always coincide, so if you're in the border area, you should be aware of both. In the North most shops open on Good Friday but close on the Tuesday after Easter Monday.

Public holidays in the Republic (IR), Northern Ireland (NI) or both are:

holiday	date
New Year's Day	1 January
St Patrick's Day (IR)	17 March
Good Friday	March/April
Easter Monday	March/April
May Holiday (IR)	1 May
Spring Bank Holiday (NI)	first & last Monday in May
June Holiday (IR)	first Monday in June
Orangeman's Day (NI)	12 July
August Holiday (IR)	first Monday in August
August Holiday (NI)	last Monday in August
October Holiday (IR)	last Monday in October
Christmas Day	25 December
St Stephen's Day (Boxing Day)	26 December

Getting There & Away

It's easy to get to Ireland – take your pick from numerous airlines, and high-speed and not so fast ferries from several British and a couple of French ports; these ports can be reached by train and/or bus.

AIR

Dublin is the Republic's major international airport; international flights also use Cork and Shannon. Some smaller airports, including Waterford and Knock handle direct flights to the UK.

Most international flights to Northern Ireland land at Belfast airport, which is 30km (19 miles) northwest of the city; the more central Belfast City airport handles flights from some British regional airports. City of Derry airport takes flights from Britain and Dublin.

Departure Tax

A travel tax is built into the price of an air ticket for the Republic and Northern Ireland, and is also paid as part of the ticket if you leave the Republic by ferry.

The UK

Direct flights leave London, Birmingham, Manchester and Glasgow for Dublin, Cork, Shannon, Kerry, Knock and Waterford in the Republic and Belfast in the North; there

---

Warning

The information in this chapter is particularly vulnerable to change: prices for international travel are volatile, routes are introduced and cancelled, schedules change, special deals come and go, and rules and visa requirements are amended. You should check directly with the airline or a travel agent to make sure you understand how a fare (and ticket you may buy) works and be aware of the security requirements for international travel.

The upshot of this is that you should get opinions, quotes and advice from as many airlines and travel agents as possible before you part with your hard-earned cash. The details given in this chapter should be regarded as pointers and are not a substitute for your own careful, up-to-date research.

---

are also flights between London and Derry and Edinburgh and Belfast.

The main carriers are:

Aer Lingus (☎ 0845 084 4444, W www .aerlingus.com)
British Airways (☎ 0845 773 3377, W www .britishairways.com)
British Midland (☎ 0870 607 0555, W www .flybmi.com)
easyJet (☎ 0870 600 0000, W www .easyjet.com)
Ryanair (☎ 0870 156 9569, W www .ryanair.com)

Continental Europe

Direct flights leave Amsterdam, Paris, Frankfurt, Munich, Milan and Rome to Dublin, from Amsterdam, Frankfurt and Paris to Shannon and Cork and from Amsterdam to Belfast.

In addition to Aer Lingus, easyJet and Ryanair (see the UK), the main carriers are:

Air France (☎ 0820 820 820, W www.airfrance .com) 119 ave des Champs-Élysées, 75008 Paris, France
Alitalia (☎ 06-656 34951, W www.alitalia.it) Leonardo da Vinci Airport, Rome
Lufthansa (☎ 01803 803 803, W www .lufthansa.com) Von Gablenz Strasse 2-6, 50679 Köln, Germany

---

Baggage Restrictions

Airlines impose tight restrictions on carry-on baggage. No sharp implements of any kind are allowed onto the plane, so pack items such as pocket knives, camping cutlery and first-aid kits into your checked luggage.

If you're carrying a camping stove you should remember that airlines also ban liquid fuels and gas cartridges from all baggage, both check-through and carry-on. Empty all fuel bottles and buy what you need at your destination.

The USA & Canada

Direct flights leave New York, Boston, Baltimore, Chicago and Los Angeles for Shannon, Dublin and Belfast. There are no nonstop scheduled services from Canada to Ireland; the best plan is to connect to a transatlantic flight in the USA or fly to London and connect for Ireland there.

As well as Aer Lingus (see the UK), the main carriers are:

American Airlines (☎ 800 433 7300, W www .aa.com)
Continental (☎ 800 231 0856, W www .continental.com)
Delta (☎ 800 241 4141, W www.delta.com)

Australia & New Zealand

There are no direct scheduled flights from Australia or New Zealand to Ireland; generally it's cheapest to fly to London or Amsterdam for a connecting flight to Ireland. Round-the-World (RTW) tickets can be real bargains.

In addition to British Airways (see the UK), the main carrier is:

Qantas (☎ 02-9691 3636, W www.qantas.com) Qantas Centre, 203 Coward St, Mascot NSW 2020, Australia

Best-Value Air Tickets

For short-term travel, it's usually cheaper to travel midweek and to take advantage of short-lived promotional offers. Return tickets usually work out cheaper than two one-ways.

Booking through a travel agent or via airlines' websites are generally the cheapest ways to get tickets. However, while online ticket sales are fine for a simple one-way or return trip on specified dates, they're no substitute for a travel agent who is familiar with special deals and can offer all kinds of advice.

Buying tickets with a credit card should mean you get a refund if you don't get what you paid for. Go through a licensed travel agent, who should be covered by an industry guarantee scheme.

Either way, make sure you take out travel insurance (see Visas & Documents, p345).

SEA

Ferries and catamarans provide a variety of services between Britain, France and Ireland. Special discounts and return fares compare favourably with cheaper air fares. If you're planning to drive around Ireland, it could be cheaper to put your vehicle on the ferry than to hire a car when you get there.

The UK

Numerous services link ports in England, Scotland, Wales and the Isle of Man to the Republic and the North. It's worth planning ahead because fares vary widely according to season, day of the week, time of day and length of stay. Return fares are usually good value and discounts may be available for ISIC cardholders, HI/YHA members and senior citizens.

The shipping lines are:

Irish Ferries (☎ 0870 517 1717, W www.irishferries .com) Corn Exchange Building, Brunswick St, Liverpool L2 7TP. This company has ferry and fast boat services from Holyhead to Dublin, and ferry services from Pembroke to Rosslare.
Isle of Man Steam Packet Company (☎ 01624-661661, W www.steam-packet.com) Imperial Buildings, Douglas IM1 2BY. This company operates ferry and fast boat services from Liverpool to Dublin and Heysham to Belfast.
Norse Merchant Ferries (☎ 0870 600 4321, W www.norsemerchant.com) Canada Dock, Liverpool L20 1DQ. Norse has ferry services from Liverpool to Dublin and Belfast.
P&O Irish Sea (☎ 0870 242 4777, W www .poirishsea.com) Cairnryan DG9 8RF. P&O operates ferry and fast boat services from Cairnryan to Larne, and ferry services from Troon to Larne, Fleetwood to Larne, and Liverpool and Mostyn to Dublin.
SeaCat (☎ 0870 552 3523, W www.seacat.co.uk) SeaCat Terminal, Donegall Quay, Belfast BT1 3AL. SeaCat has fast boat services from Heysham or Troon to Belfast and Liverpool to Dublin.
Stena Line (☎ 0870 570 7070, W www.stenaline .com) Charter House, Park St, Ashford TN24 8EX. Stena has ferry services from Holyhead to Dun Laoghaire and Stranraer to Belfast, also fast boat services from Holyhead to Dublin, from Fishguard to Rosslare, and from Stranraer to Belfast.
Swansea Cork Ferries (☎ 01792 456116, W www .swansea-cork.ie) Harbour Office, Kings Dock, Swansea SA1 1SF. This company has ferry services from Swansea to Cork.

France

Shipping lines operating between France and Ireland are:

Brittany Ferries (☎ 021-427 7801 in Ireland, 02 98 29 28 00 in France, **W** www.brittany-ferries .co.uk) Brittany operates a seasonal service between Roscoff and Cork.

Irish Ferries (☎ 01-661 0743 in Dublin, 053-33158 in Rosslare, 02 33 23 44 44 in Cherbourg, 02 98 61 17 17 in Roscoff, **W** www.irishferries.com) Irish Ferries operates services to Rosslare from Cherbourg and Roscoff. Eurail cardholders and Inter-Rail pass holders may be entitled to a substantial fare reduction; advance reservation is compulsory during July and August.

LAND & SEA

Both **Bus Éireann** (☎ 01-836 6111; **W** www .buseireann.ie) and Britain's **National Express** (☎ 0870 808080; **W** www.gobycoach.com) operate **Eurolines** (**W** www.eurolines.ie) services direct from London and other British cities to Dublin and Belfast, with connections to regional towns and cities.

Ulsterbus (☎ 028-9066 6630; **W** www .translink.co.uk), with National Express and **Scottish Citylink** (**W** www.citylink.co.uk), has express services between Belfast and major cities in Britain.

Both Bus Éireann and Ulsterbus offer combined rail and ferry tickets.

Getting Around

Despite an extensive network of roads and relatively short distances between towns, travelling around Ireland can be a complicated business. Direct road routes between even major centres are rare, and minor roads are devious and not designed for fast travel. Public transport, especially trains, can be expensive and/or infrequent, and is nonexistent in some walking areas. Having your own transport is essential if you have a fairly tight timetable.

AIR

Despite Ireland's small size there are several internal flights, which would be a quick although expensive way of getting around.

Flights connect Dublin with Carrickfinn (County Donegal), Charlestown (County Mayo), and the cities of Cork, Galway, Kerry, Shannon, Sligo and Derry.

Aer Rianta (☎ 01-844 4900; **W** www .aer-rianta.com), the Republic's national airport authority, provides information about airport services and flight schedules, as well as arrivals and departures from Dublin, Cork and Shannon.

The main domestic airlines are:

Aer Lingus (☎ 0818 365 000, **W** www.aerlingus.com)
Ryanair (☎ 01-609 7800, **W** www.ryanair.com)
Aer Arann (☎ 1890-462 726 from within Ireland, 0800 587 2324 from the UK, **W** www.aerarann.ie)

BUS

The two main bus companies operating in Ireland are:

Bus Éireann (☎ 01-836 6111, **W** www.buseireann .ie) This company operates services throughout the South and to the North. Many services almost vanish outside the peak season (late June to the end of August). The Expressway Timetable (€2) includes details of discount fares and all provincial bus stations. It's available from major bus stations, larger bookshops and on the company's website, which also has an online booking service. In this book, details of bus services are given for individual walks, quoting the relevant timetable number.

Ulsterbus (☎ 028-9066 6630, **W** www.translink .co.uk) Ulsterbus serves the North, and publishes four free regional timetables, available in Belfast at the Europa Buscentre in Glengall St and the Laganside Centre in Oxford St, and at larger regional bus stations. This information is also available online.

Also operating in the South are private bus companies that compete with Bus Éireann on some routes, and provide services in areas not covered by the national company.

Another bus alternative is **Stray Travel Network** (☎ 01-605 7702 in Dublin, ☎ 0207-373 7737 in London; **W** www.straytravel.com), which offers Stray Travel Passes (valid for up to four months) allowing you to jump on and off its mini coaches at several pick-up points around Ireland.

TRAIN

The operators of Ireland's rail networks are:

Iarnród Éireann (Irish Rail; ☎ 01-836 6222, [W] www .irishrail.ie) This company operates trains in the Republic on routes generally radiating from Dublin. Train travel to the main centres (Waterford, Cork, Limerick, Galway, Belfast) is faster but more expensive than by bus but the rail network is much less extensive.

Northern Ireland Railways (NIR; ☎ 028-9066 6630, [W] www.translink.co.uk) NIR operates four routes from Belfast. One links with the system in the South via Newry to Dublin; the other three go east to Bangor, northeast to Larne and northwest to Derry via Coleraine. Printed timetables are available free from most stations.

Reservations

Reservations for Irish Rail can be made online, at most train stations or at **Iarnród Éireann Travel Centres** (*35 Lower Abbey St, Dublin 1 • 65 Patrick St, Cork*). Tickets can also be booked by phone (☎ 01-703 4070, 021-504 888).

Reservations for NIR services can be made by phone (☎ 028-9066 6630).

CAR & MOTORCYCLE

There is a good network of motorways in the North but in the Republic the comparatively few motorways are confined to the east and the Dublin ring road. Main roads (designated 'A' in the North, 'N' in the South) are generally good quality, although you'll find some alarming lapses in the west of the Republic. Most of the more recent 'N' roads have a left side lane, marked with an orange dotted line, used by people walking, jogging, riding or hitching, and by slow vehicles. Minor roads ('B' in the North, 'R' in the South, and others without a designation) are generally narrow and often lined with high hedges; many in the Republic are in poor repair and have dangerous bends. Traffic can be chaotic in the towns, especially in the Republic, but is rarely busy elsewhere.

Road Rules

Safety belts must be worn by the driver and all passengers. Children under 12 years may not sit on the front seat. Motorcyclists and pillion passengers must wear helmets.

Speed limits are the same in the North and South: 70mph (112km/h) on motorways, 60mph (96km/h) on other roads and 30mph (48km/h) or as signposted in towns.

Metric and imperial measurements still appear in confusing coexistence. In the Republic, speed limits are in miles per hour (though in kilometres in some eastern areas). Green distance signs and new white ones are in kilometres, but older white signs, with raised black letters, show miles and the old route numbering system ('R' and 'T' roads). In the North, imperial measurements are still the norm. Printed copies of the road rules do exist; major post offices and perhaps TICs are the most likely sources.

Parking in cities and towns can be a problem; it's best to find designated, off-street parking areas for which you may have to pay. Roadside parking is fraught with regulations, and usually just deepens the confusion.

Rental

Car rental in Ireland is expensive, so much so that it may be cheaper to hire a vehicle in Britain and take it across on a ferry. It's wise to book ahead in the high season (June to August). Off-season rates are considerably lower. Make sure that the price you are quoted includes insurance, Collision Damage Waiver (CDW) and VAT. If you plan to travel into the North from the Republic, check that your insurance covers this. There may be an additional charge for extra drivers, as well as an extra daily charge if you cross the border in either direction.

You must be at least 21 years old to hire a car; the majority of rental companies require drivers to be at least 23 and to have had a valid driving licence for no less than 12 months or even two years. Some companies will not rent to people over 70. In most cases you only need your own licence to arrange hire for up to three months.

The international rental companies Avis, Budget, Hertz, Europcar and Thrifty, and the major local operators Murray's, Dan Dooley and Malone have offices all over Ireland. There are many smaller and local operators. Motorcycles are not available for hire.

Road Distances (km)

	Athlone	Belfast	Cork	Derry	Donegal	Dublin	Galway	Kilkenny	Killarney	Limerick	Rosslare Harbour	Shannon Airport	Sligo	Waterford	Wexford
Athlone	---														
Belfast	227	---													
Cork	219	424	---												
Derry	209	117	428	---											
Donegal	183	180	402	69	---										
Dublin	127	167	256	237	233	---									
Galway	93	306	209	272	204	212	---								
Kilkenny	116	284	148	335	309	114	172	---							
Killarney	232	436	87	441	407	304	193	198	---						
Limerick	121	323	105	328	296	193	104	113	111	---					
Rosslare Harbour	201	330	208	397	391	153	274	98	275	211	---				
Shannon Airport	133	346	128	351	282	218	93	135	135	25	234	---			
Sligo	117	206	336	135	66	214	138	245	343	232	325	218	---		
Waterford	164	333	126	383	357	163	220	48	193	129	82	152	293	---	
Wexford	184	309	187	378	372	135	253	80	254	190	19	213	307	61	---

Automobile Clubs

The **Automobile Association** (AA; ☎ 028-9032 8924 Belfast; W www.theaa.com • ☎ 01-617 9540 Dublin; W www.aaireland.ie) is active across Ireland. The AA free call breakdown number in the Republic is ☎ 1800 667 788 and in the North the number to call is ☎ 0800 887 766.

In the North, members of the **Royal Automobile Club** (RAC; ☎ 0800 029 029; W www .rac.co.uk) can phone ☎ 0800 828 282 for breakdown service.

BICYCLE

Cycling is very popular in Ireland, and it seems that Irish motorists are generally courteous towards cyclists. Many hostels have bicycles for hire to their guests, and bicycle hire shops are fairly common in larger towns. Look out for Lonely Planet's *Cycling Ireland*, packed with cyclist-friendly information, Ireland's best cycling tours and the description of a challenging, 42-day ride around the Emerald Isle.

HITCHING

Hitching is never safe in any country and we don't recommend it. Women travelling alone should be extremely cautious.

BOAT

Ferries provide the main means of reaching the islands featured in the Atlantic Islands chapter (p186), which has details of services.

LOCAL TRANSPORT

There are comprehensive local bus services in Dublin (Dublin Bus), Belfast (Citybus) and some other larger towns.

Dublin is served by four suburban railway lines, the Dublin Area Rapid Transport (DART) line and a light rail system (Lucas). In the North, NIR operates all rail services within the province.

Glossary

Here you'll find some of the more commonly encountered Irish organisations and words, including those used in place names on maps; some are followed by an anglicised version in brackets. Also included are English terms that may not be familiar.

abhainn (ow, owen) – river, stream
achadh (agha, augh) – field
alt – height, high place
An Óige – Irish youth hostel association, literally 'The Youth'
arête – narrow ridge, particularly between glacial valleys

baile (bally) – village, settlement, town
bán (baun) – white
barr – top
beag (beg) – small
bealach (ballagh) – pass, *col*
beann (ben) – peak
bearna (barna) – *gap*
bia – food
binn – peak
bó – cow
bog – wet, spongy ground consisting of decomposing plant matter, see also *peat, peatland*
booleying – traditional practice of moving herds to upland pastures in summer
boreen – old country lane or narrow road
bóthar (boher) – road
breac (brack) – speckled
Bronze Age – the earliest metal-using period, about 2000 to 500 BC in Ireland, after the Stone Age and before the Iron Age
brook – stream
buaille (booley) – summer cattle pasture
buí – yellow
bullaun stone – stone with a depression, probably used as mortar for grinding medicine or food and found on monastic sites
bun – river mouth
burn – stream (Northern Ireland)

cashel – prehistoric stone fort, *rath, dún, caher, lios*
calladh (callows) – lakeside or riverside grasslands prone to regular flooding

carn (cairn) – pile of stones
carraig (carrick) – rock
caher – prehistoric stone fort, city, *rath, dún, cashel, lios*
ceann (kin) – headland
Celts – people who arrived in Ireland about 300 BC
ceol – music
cill (kil) – church, chapel
cillín (killeen) – children's graveyard
clachan – beehive-shaped, *dry-stone* hut; *clochain*
clint – a natural cobblestone, the slabs between the cracks *(grikes)* found in a natural limestone pavement
cloch – stone
clochain – beehive-shaped, *dry-stone* hut; *clachan*
cluain – meadow
cnoc (knock, crock) – rocky hill
coill (kil) – woodland
coire – *corrie*
col – low point or pass between two peaks
cor – rounded hill
corrán (carraun) – serrated or crescent-shaped mountain
corrie – small, high, cup-shaped valley, often of glacial origin; cirque, *coire, coum*
coum – small, high, cup-shaped valley, often of glacial origin; cirque, *coire, corrie*
crag – steep cliff
crannog – an ancient lake dwelling on a natural or artificial island
cruach, cruachan – steep hill
cuan – bay
cúm (coum) – small, high, cup-shaped valley, often of glacial origin; cirque, *coire, corrie*
curragh – rowing boat with a wooden frame and outer skin of tarred canvas
cutaway peatland – an area where *peat* harvesting has finished

Dáil Éireann – Irish Assembly
dearg – red
dheas – south
doire (derry) – oak wood

doline – a bowl-shaped depression down which water percolates in limestone country, *sink hole*

dolmen – chamber of prehistoric tomb comprising huge supporting stones and one or two large capstones

druim (drum) – ridge

drumlin – a rounded or teardrop-shaped hill formed from *moraine*

dry stone – a technique of building in stone without using mortar or cement

dubh (duff, doo) – black, dark

Dúchas – government agency responsible for parks, monuments and gardens in the Republic

dún – prehistoric stone fort, *rath*, *cashel*, *caher*, *lios*

eaglais – church

eas – waterfall

Éire – Irish name for the Republic of Ireland

escarpment – steep slope or cliff

fen – flat *bog*

fionn (fin) – white, clear

fraoch (freagh) – heather

fulachta fiadh – Bronze Age cooking place

gabher (gower) – goat

Gaelige – Irish language

Gaeltacht – Irish-speaking area

gaoith (gwee) – wind

gap – mountain pass, *col*

garbh – rough

garda – Irish Republic police, plural gardaí

glas – green

gleann (glen) – valley

gorm – blue

gort – tilled field

green road – an old country route or unsealed road, usually with a grassed surface

grid reference – quoted in the text as GR followed by six figures, the accurate method of giving the location of a place, explained in the margin of Irish Ordnance Survey maps

grike – one of a network of semi-regular cracks between natural cobblestones *(clints)* found in limestone pavement

Iarnród Éireann – Irish Railways

inbhear (inver) – river mouth

inis – island

Iron Age – in Ireland the Iron Age lasted from around the end of the Bronze Age in about 500 BC to the arrival of Christianity in the 5th century

jaunting car – pony and trap

kil – church, chapel, woodland

killeen – children's graveyard

kin – headland

knock – rocky hill

lágh (law) – hill

leac – flat rock, flagstone

leataobh – lay-by, small roadside parking place

leithreas – toilets

leitir (letter) – rough hillside

liath (lea) – grey

lios – fort, defended settlement, *rath*, *dún*, *caher*, *cashel*

lough (loch) – lake, inlet

loughan – small lake, *tarn*

lug, lag, log – hollow

machair (maghera) – sandy plain or flat area near the sea

mám (maum) – pass

marriage stones – a pair of stones, often with a hole through which people made marriage vows

mass path – walking path created by Catholics going to hidden places of worship during times of religious persecution

meall, maol (mweel) – bare hill

móin – turf

móna – turf

mór (more) – big

moraine – ridge or mound of debris deposited by retreating glacier

motte – a substantial, flat-topped earth mound on which a timber tower was built

mullach – summit

Neolithic – era characterised by the use of stone implements, about 4000 to 2000 BC

North, the – the six counties constituting the political entity of Northern Ireland

nunatak – a mountain peak that poked above an ice sheet and escaped the scouring action of glaciers

Ogham stones – marker stones engraved with primitive writing, known as Ogham
oifig an phoist – post office
oileán – island
ow, owen – river, stream

pairc – field
passage grave – Stone Age megalithic tomb in a large, domed cairn with a narrow passage leading to the burial chamber
peat – partly decomposed vegetable matter found in *bogs* and traditionally used as fuel
peat hags – area of *bog* where erosion or turf cutting has left small clumps of *peat* exposed
peatland – an area consisting of *peat bogs*
pitch – camp or tent site
pitched path – path laid with flat stones
plantation – the settlement of Protestants in Ireland in the 16th and 17th centuries
pobal – public
poll – hole, pond, small bay

radharc – view, scenery
raised bogs – areas of *peat* covered with heather and moss
rath – fort, defended settlement, *cashel*, *caher*, *dún*, *lios*
reeks – ridge, crest
Republic, the – the 26 counties of the Republic of Ireland *(the South)*
riabhach – grey
ride – forest clearing or track for horse riding
ring fort – a term covering *rath*, *lios*, *dún* and *cashel* – all roughly circular structures of stones and earth that probably date from around 800 to 700 BC, some were still used into the Middle Ages
rinn – headland
roisin – small promontory
ros – promontory
round tower – tall, tapering circular tower possibly used as a lookout or refuge
route – a cross-country course where there isn't any path or track
rua, ruadh – red
rundale – system of land tenure based on the communal use of unenclosed grazing land

scellig (skellig) – small rocky islands
sceir (sker, skerry) – rock visible at sea, reef
sea stack – rock pinnacle close to the coast

sean – old
sidh (shee) – fairy, hill inhabited by fairies
sink hole – bowl-shaped depression down which water percolates in limestone country, *doline*
slí – path
sliabh (slieve) – mountain
slidhe (slee) – road, track
slí geill – yield right of way (road sign)
souterrain – underground chamber, possibly of prehistoric origin
South, the – *the Republic* of Ireland
spate – flood
spinc (spink) – pinnacle
sráid – street
srón – nose-like mountain feature
sruth, sruthán – stream
stuaic (stook) – pinnacle
suí, suidhe (see) – seat

talus – scree
Taoiseach – Irish prime minister
tarn – small mountain lake or pool
teampall – church
teach – house
theas – south
thiar – west
thoir – east
thuaidh – north
tir (teer) – land, territory
tobar – well
togher – ancient wooden trackway across *peatland*
tombolo – narrow sand or shingle bar, which links an island to the mainland or to another island
tor – tower-like rock formed by frost shattering a *nunatak*
townland – a traditional rural area, which may be near a town of the same name
trá – sandy beach
trig point or pillar – summit survey marker
tulach – small hill
turas – journey, pilgrimage
turlach – seasonal lakes or ponds in limestone country, *turlough*
turlough – seasonal lakes or ponds in limestone country, *turlach*

way – a (marked) long-distance trail
waymarker – directional pointer on walking routes, usually a 'walking person' symbol

Gazetteer

abbreviations – counties

An – Antrim	Dow – Down	Leit – Leitrim	Sl – Sligo
Ar – Armagh	Du – Dublin	Lo – Louth	Ti – Tipperary
Car – Carlow	Fe – Fermanagh	Li – Limerick	Ty – Tyrone
Cav – Cavan	Ga – Galway	Ma – Mayo	Wa – Waterford
Cl – Clare	Ke – Kerry	Me – Meath	Wes – Westmeath
Cor – Cork	Kild – Kildare	Mo – Monaghan	Wex – Wexford
De – Derry	Kilk – Kilkenny	Of – Offaly	Wi – Wicklow
Don – Donegal	La – Laois	Ro – Roscommon	

abbreviations – provinces

Co – Connaught	Le – Leinster	Mu – Munster	Ul – Ulster

place	Irish name	co	prv	place	Irish name	co	prv
Achill	An Caol	Ma	Co	Black Head	Ceann Boirne	Cl	Mu
Achill Sound	Ghob a'Choire	Ma	Co	Blacklion	An Blaic	Cav	Ul
Adrigole	Eadargóil	Cor	Mu	Blasket Islands	Na Blascaodaí	Ke	Mu
Allihies	Na hAilichí	Cor	Mu	Borris	An Bhuiríos	Car	Le
Annalong	Áth na Long	Don	Ul	Brandon	Cé Bhréannain	Ke	Mu
Antrim	Aontroim	An	Ul	Bray	Bré	Wi	Le
Aran Islands	Oileáin Árainn	Ga	Co	Bunbeg	An Bun Beag	Don	Ul
Ardara	Árd na Rátha	Don	Ul	Bunclody	Bun Cloídí	Wex	Le
Ards	Ardai	Don	Ul	Buncrana	Bun Cranncha	Don	Ul
Arklow	An tInbhear Mór	Wi	Le	Bundoran	Bun Dobhráin	Don	Ul
Armagh	Ard Mhacha	Ar	Ul	Burren, the	Boireann	Cl	Mu
Arranmore	Árainn Mhór	Don	Ul	Burtonport	Ailt an Chórrain	Don	Ul
Aughrim	Eachroim	Wi	Le	Bushmills	Muileann na Buaise	An	Ul
Ballina	Béal an Átha	Ma	Co	Cahir	An Cathair	Ti	Mu
Ballintoy	Baile an Tuaighe	An	Ul	Carlingford	Cairlinn	Lo	Le
Ballycastle	Baile an Chaisil	An	Ma, Ul Co	Carlow	Ceatharlach	Car	Le
Ballyferriter	Baile an Fheirtearaigh	Ke	Mu	Carndonagh	Cardomhnach	Don	Ul
Ballyliffin	Baile Lifin	Don	Ul	Carnlough	Carnlach	An	Ul
Ballymacarbry	Baile Mhac Cairbre	Wa	Mu	Carrick-on-Suir	Carraig na Siúire	Ti	Mu
Ballymena	An Baile Meánach	An	Ul	Carrowteige	Ceathrú Thaidhg	Ma	Co
Ballyvaughan	Baile Uí Bheacháin	Cl	Mu	Cashel	Caiseal Mumhan	Ti	Mu
Banbridge	Droíchead na Banna	Don	Ul	Castlebar	Caisleán an Bharraigh	Ma	Co
Bangor	Beannchar	Don	Ul	Castletownbere	Baile Chais Bhéara	Cor	Mu
Bantry	Beanntraí	Cor	Mu	Cavan	An Cabhán	Cav	Ul
Belcoo	Béal Cú	Fe	Ul	Clare	An Clár	Cla	Mu
Belfast	Béal Feirste	Don	Ul	Clear Island	Oileán Cléire	Cor	Mu
Belmullet	Béal an Mhuirthead	Ma	Co	Clifden	An Clochán	Ga	Co
Birr	Biorra	Of	Le	Cloghane	An Clochán	Ke	Mu
				Clogheen	An Chloichin	Ti	Mu

place	Irish name	co	prv
Clonegal	Cluain na nGall	Car	Le
Clonmacnoise	Cluain Mhic Nóis	Of	Le
Clonmel	Cluain Meala	Ti	Mu
Cobh	An Cobh	Cor	Mu
Coleraine	Cúil Raithin	De	Ul
Connemara	Conamara	Ga	Co
Cookstown	An Chorr Chríochach	Ty	Ul
Cork	Corcaigh	Cor	Mu
Creeslough	An Craoslach	Don	Ul
Culdaff	Cúil Dabhcha	Don	Ul
Dalkey	Deilginis	Du	Le
Derry/Londonderry	Doire	De	Ul
Dingle	An Daingean	Ke	Mu
Donegal	Dún na nGall	Don	Ul
Dowra	An Damhshraith	Leit	Co
Drogheda	Droichead Átha	Lo	Le
Drumshanbo	Droim Seanbhó	Leit	Co
Dublin	Baile Átha Cliath	Du	Le
Dunfanaghy	Dún Fionnachaidh	Don	Ul
Dungannon	Dún Geanainn	Ty	Ul
Dungloe	An Clochán Liath	Don	Ul
Dunlewy	Dún Lúiche	Don	Ul
Dunquin	Dún Chaoin	Ker	Mu
East Town	Baile Thoir	Don	Ul
Ennis	Inis	Cl	Mu
Enniscorthy	Inis Coirthaidh	Wex	Le
Ennis	Áth an Sceire	Wi	Le
Enniskillen	Inis Ceithleann	Fe	Ul
Falcarragh	An Fál Carrach	Don	Ul
Fanore	Fánóir	Cl	Mu
Florence Court	Mullach na Seangán	Fe	Ul
Galway	Gaillimh	Ga	Mu
Giant's			
Causeway, the	Clochán an Aifir	An	Ul
Glenade	Gleann Éada	Leit	Co
Glenariff	Gleann Aireamh	An	Ul
Glenarm	Gleann Arma	An	Ul
Glencar	Ghleann an Chairthe	Sl	Co
Glencolmcille	Gleann Cholm Cille	Don	Ul
Glendalough	Gleann dá Loch	Wi	Le
Glengarriff	An Gleann Garbh	Cor	Mu
Glenties	Na Gleannta	Don	Ul
Glenveagh	Gleann Beatha	Don	Ul
Goresbridge	An Droichead Nua	Ki	Le
Gortahork	Gort an Choirce	Don	Ul
Gortin	An Goirtín	Ty	Ul
Graiguenamanagh	Gráig na Manach	Ki	Le
Great Blasket			
Island	An Blascaod Mór	Ke	Mu

place	Irish name	co	prv
Greystones	Na Chloch Liath	Dow	Ul
Groomsport	Port an Ghialla		
	Chruama	Dow	Ul
Gweedore	Gaoth Dobhair	Don	Ul
Hollywood	Cillín Chaoimhín	Wi	Le
Holywood	An Mhic Nasca	Dow	Ul
Howth	Binn Éadair	Du	Le
Inisheer	Inis Oírr	Ga	Co
Inishmaan	Inis Meáin	Ga	Co
Inishmore	Inis Mór	Ga	Co
Inishowen	Inis Eoghain	Don	Ul
Keel	An Caol	Ma	Co
Kilcar	Cill Chártha	Don	Ul
Kildare	Cill Dara	Kild	Le
Kildavin	Cill Damhain	Car	Le
Kilkeel	Cill Chaoil	Dow	Ul
Kilkenny	Cill Chainnigh	Ki	Le
Killaloe	Cill Dalua	Cl	Mu
Killarney	Cill Airne/Cill Ála	Ke	Mu
Killybegs	Ceala Beaga	Don	Ul
Kilmacanoge	Cill Mocheanóg	Wi	Le
Kilmainham	Cill Mhaigneann	Du	Le
Knock	Cnoc Mhuire	Ma	Co
Laragh	Láithreach	Wi	Le
Lauragh	Láith Reach	Ke	Mu
Larne	Lutharna	An	Ul
Leenaun	An Líonán	Ga	Co
Leitrim	Liatroim	Leit	Co
Letterfrack	Leitir Fraic	Ga	Co
Letterkenny	Leitir Ceanainn	Don	Ul
Limerick	Luimneach	Li	Mu
Lisburn	Lios na gCearrbhach	An	Ul
Liscannor	Lios Ceannúir	Cl	Mu
Lisdoonvarna	Lios Dún Bhearna	Cl	Mu
Lismore	Lios Mór	Wa	Mu
Lough Neagh	Loch nEathach	An	Ul
Louisburgh	Cluain Cearbán	Ma	Co
Maam Cross	Crois Mám	Ga	Co
Magheraroarty	Machaire Uí		
	Rabhartaigh	Don	Ul
Malin	Málainn	Don	Ul
Malin Head	Cionn Mhálanna	Don	Ul
Manorhamilton	Cluainín	Leit	Co
Maynooth	Maigh Nuad	Kild	Le
Mayo	Maigh Eo	Ma	Co
Mitchelstown	Baile Mhistéala	Ti	Mu
Monaghan	Muineachán	Mo	Ul

GAZETTEER

place	Irish name	co	prv
Mt Brandon	Cnoc Bhréannain	Ke	Mu
Mountshannon	Baile Uí Bheoláin	Cl	Mu
Mullaghmore	An Mullach Mór	Sl	Co
Mullingar	An Muileann gCearr	Wes	Le
Mulrany	An Mhala Raithní	Ma	Co
Naas	An Nás	Kild	Le
Newcastle	An Caisleán Nua	Dow	Ul
Newry	An tIúr	Dow	Ul
Newtownards	Baile Nua na hArda	Dow	Ul
Newtown-stewart	An Baile Nua	Ty	Ul
O'Briensbridge	Droichead Uí Bhriain	Cl	Mu
Omagh	An Omaigh	Ty	Ul
Oughterard	Uachtar Árd	Ga	Co
Pettigo	Paiteagó	Don	Ul
Plumbridge	Droichead an Phlum	Ty	Ul
Pollatomish	Poll an Tómais	Ma	Co
Porta	Port an Dúnáin	Ar	Ul
Portballintrae	Port Bhaile an Trá	An	Ul
Portlaoise	Port Laoise	La	Le
Portrush	Port Rois	An	Le
Portstewart	Port Stíobhaird	De	Ul
Poyntz Pass	Pas an Phointe	Ar	Ul
Rathlin Island	Reachlainn	An	Ul
Recess	Straith Salach	Ga	Co
Roscommon	Ros Comáin	Ro	Co
Roscrea	Ros Cré	Ti	Mu
Rosslare	Ros Láir	Wex	Le

place	Irish name	co	prv
Rostrevor	Caislean Ruairi	Dow	Ul
Roundstone	Cloch na Rón	Ga	Co
Scariff	An Scairbh	Cl	Mu
Shillelagh	Siol Ealaigh	Wi	Le
Skellig Islands	Oileáin na Scealaga	Ke	Mu
Skibbereen	Sciobairín	Cor	Mu
Sligo	Sligeach	Sl	Co
Strabane	An Srath Bán	Ty	Ul
Strangford	Baile Loch Cuan	Dow	Ul
Strangford Lough	Loch Cuan	Dow	Ul
Swords	Sord	Du	Le
Tara	Teamhair	Me	Le
Tinahely	Tigh na hÉile	Wi	Le
Tipperary	Tiobraid Árann	Ti	Mu
Tory Island	Oileán Thóraigh	Don	Ul
Tralee	Trá Lí	Ke	Mu
Tullamore	Tulach Mór	Of	Le
Valentia Island	Oileán Dairbhru	Ke	Mu
Ventry	Ceann Trá	Ke	Mu
Warrenpoint	An Pointe	Dow	Ul
Waterford	Port Láirge	Wa	Mu
Westport	Cathair na Mairt	Ma	Co
West Town	Baile Thiar	Don	Ul
Wexford	Loch Garman	Wex	Le
Wicklow	Cill Mhantáin	Wi	Le
Youghal	Eochaill	Cor	Mu

Index

Bold indicates maps.
For a full list of maps, see the
    map index (p8).
For a full list of walks, see the
    walks table (pp4-7).

Bold indicates maps.
For a full list of maps, see the map index (p8).
For a full list of walks, see the walks table (pp4-7).

Bold indicates maps.
For a full list of maps, see the
    map index (p8).
For a full list of walks, see the
    walks table (pp4-7).

N

O

P

Q

R

LONELY PLANET OFFICES

Australia
Locked Bag 1, Footscray, Victoria 3011
☎ 03 8379 8000 fax 03 8379 8111
email: talk2us@lonelyplanet.com.au

USA
150 Linden St, Oakland, CA 94607
☎ 510 893 8555 TOLL FREE: 800 275 8555
fax 510 893 8572
email: info@lonelyplanet.com

UK
10a Spring Place, London NW5 3BH
☎ 020 7428 4800 fax 020 7428 4828
email: go@lonelyplanet.co.uk

France
1 rue du Dahomey, 75011 Paris
☎ 01 55 25 33 00 fax 01 55 25 33 01
email: bip@lonelyplanet.fr
www.lonelyplanet.fr

World Wide Web: www.lonelyplanet.com *or* AOL keyword: lp
Lonely Planet Images: www.lonelyplanetimages.com